# Lecture Notes in Artificial Intelligence 7506

Subseries of Lecture Notes in Computer Science

LNAI Series Editors

Randy Goebel
  *University of Alberta, Edmonton, Canada*
Yuzuru Tanaka
  *Hokkaido University, Sapporo, Japan*
Wolfgang Wahlster
  *DFKI and Saarland University, Saarbrücken, Germany*

LNAI Founding Series Editor

Joerg Siekmann
  *DFKI and Saarland University, Saarbrücken, Germany*

T0224130

Chun-Yi Su  Subhash Rakheja
Honghai Liu (Eds.)

# Intelligent Robotics and Applications

5th International Conference, ICIRA 2012
Montreal, QC, Canada, October 3-5, 2012
Proceedings, Part I

 Springer

Series Editors

Randy Goebel, University of Alberta, Edmonton, Canada
Jörg Siekmann, University of Saarland, Saarbrücken, Germany
Wolfgang Wahlster, DFKI and University of Saarland, Saarbrücken, Germany

Volume Editors

Chun-Yi Su
Concordia University
Department of Mechanical and Industrial Engineering
Montreal, QC H3G 1M8, Canada
E-mail: cysu@alcor.concordia.ca

Subhash Rakheja
Concordia University
Department of Mechanical and Industrial Engineering
Montreal, QC H3G 1M8, Canada
E-mail: rakheja@alcor.concordia.ca

Honghai Liu
The University of Portsmouth
School of Creative Technologies
Portsmouth, PO1 2DJ, UK
E-mail: honghai.liu@port.ac.uk

ISSN 0302-9743                          e-ISSN 1611-3349
ISBN 978-3-642-33508-2                  e-ISBN 978-3-642-33509-9
DOI 10.1007/978-3-642-33509-9
Springer Heidelberg Dordrecht London New York

Library of Congress Control Number: 2012946931

CR Subject Classification (1998): I.2.8-11, I.5.3-4, I.4.8-9, K.4.2, J.2, J.3, C.3, C.2, G.1.10

LNCS Sublibrary: SL 7 – Artificial Intelligence

*Typesetting:* Camera-ready by author, data conversion by Scientific Publishing Services, Chennai, India

Printed on acid-free paper

Springer is part of Springer Science+Business Media (www.springer.com)

# Preface

The Organizing Committee of the 5<sup>th</sup> International Conference on Intelligent Robotics and Applications aimed to facilitate interaction among participants in the field of intelligent robotics, automation, and mechatronics. Through this conference, the committee intended to enhance the sharing of individual experiences and expertise in intelligent robotics with particular emphasis on technical challenges associated with varied applications such as biomedical applications, industrial automations, surveillance, and sustainable mobility.

The 5<sup>th</sup> International Conference on Intelligent Robotics and Applications was most successful in attracting 271 submissions addressing state-of-the-art developments in robotics, automation, and mechatronics. Owing to the large number of submissions, the committee was faced with the difficult challenge of selecting the most deserving papers for inclusion in these lecture notes and for presentation at the conference, held in Montreal, Canada, October 3–5, 2012. For this purpose, the committee undertook a rigorous review process. Despite the high quality of most of the submissions, a total of 197 papers were selected for publication in 3 volumes of Springer's Lecture Notes in Artificial Intelligence, a subseries of Lecture Notes in Computer Science.

The selected articles were submitted by scientists from 25 different countries. The contribution of the Technical Program Committee and the referees is deeply appreciated. Most of all, we would like to express our sincere thanks to the authors for submitting their most recent work and the Organizing Committee for their enormous efforts to turn this event into a smoothly running meeting. Special thanks go to Concordia University for their generosity and direct support. Our particular thanks are due to Mr. Alfred Hofmann and the editorial staff of Springer-Verlag for enthusiastically supporting the project.

We sincerely hope that these volumes will prove to be an important resource for the scientific community.

July 2012

Chun-Yi Su
Subhash Rakheja
Honghai Liu

# Conference Organization

## International Advisory Committee

| | |
|---|---|
| Jorge Angeles | McGill University, Canada |
| Suguru Arimoto | Ritsumeikan University, Japan |
| Hegao Cai | Harbin Institute of Technology, China |
| Tianyou Chai | Northeastern University, China |
| Clarence De Silva | University of British Columbia, Canada |
| Han Ding | Huazhong University of Science and Technology, China |
| Sabina Jeschke | RWTH Aachen University, Germany |
| Ming Li | National Natural Science Foundation of China, China |
| Zhongqin Lin | Shanghai Jiao Tong University, China |
| Ding Liu | Xi'an University of Technology, China |
| Jinping Qu | South China University of Technology, China |
| Bruno Siciliano | University of Naples, Italy |
| Mohammad Siddique | Fayetteville State University, USA |
| Mark W. Spong | University of Texas at Dallas, USA |
| Kevin Warwick | University of Reading, UK |
| Ming Xie | Nanyang Technological University, Singapore |
| Youlun Xiong | Huazhong University of Science and Technology, China |

## General Chairs

| | |
|---|---|
| Chun-Yi Su | Concordia University, Canada |
| Rama B. Bhat | Concordia University, Canada |
| Xiangyang Zhu | Shanghai Jiao Tong University, China |

## Program Chairs

| | |
|---|---|
| Subhash Rakheja | Concordia University, Canada |
| Jangmyung Lee | Pusan National University, South Korea |
| Camille Alain Rabbath | DRDC, Canada |

## Publicity Chairs

| | |
|---|---|
| Tongwen Chen | University of Alberta, Canada |
| Li-Chen Fu | National Taiwan University, Taiwan |
| Shuzhi Sam Ge | National University of Singapore, Singapore |

| | |
|---|---|
| Naoyuki Kubota | Tokyo Metropolitan University, Japan |
| Kok-Meng Lee | Georgia Institute of Technology, USA |
| Ning Xi | City University of Hong Kong, Hong Kong |
| Xiaohua Xia | University of Pretoria, South Africa |
| Peter Xu | University of Auckland, New Zealand |
| Huayong Yang | Zhejiang University, China |
| Bin Yao | Purdue University, USA |
| Xinghuo Yu | Royal Melbourne Institute of Technology, Australia |
| Chaohai Zhang | Harbin Institute of Technology, China |

## Organized Session Chairs

| | |
|---|---|
| Mirco Alpen | Helmut Schmidt University, Germany |
| Shengyong Chen | Zhejiang University of Technology, China |
| Weidong Chen | Shanghai Jiao Tong University, China |
| Xiang Chen | University of Windsor, Canada |
| Xinkai Chen | Shibaura Institute of Technology, Japan |
| Mingcong Deng | Tokyo University of Agriculture and Technology, Japan |
| Jun Fu | Massachusetts Institute of Technology, USA |
| Xin Fu | Zhejiang University, China |
| Haibo Gao | Harbin Institute of Technology, China |
| Yueming Hu | South China University of Technology, China |
| Yangmin Li | University of Macau, Macau, SAR China |
| Zhijun Li | South China University of Technology, China |
| Guangjun Liu | Ryerson University, Canada |
| Xinjun Liu | Tsinghua University, China |
| Daniel Schilberg | RWTH Aachen University, Germany |
| Yandong Tang | Shengyang Institute of Automation, CAS, China |
| Danwei Wang | Nanyang Technological University, Singapore |
| Enrong Wang | Nanjing Normal University, China |
| Caihua Xiong | Huazhong University of Science and Technology, China |
| Simon Yang | University of Guelph, Canada |
| Hongnian Yu | Staffordshire University, UK |
| Jianhua Zhang | Shanghai University, China |
| Youmin Zhang | Concordia University, Canada |
| Limin Zhu | Shanghai Jiao Tong University, China |

## Publication Chairs

| | |
|---|---|
| Honghai Liu | University of Portsmouth, UK |
| Xinjun Sheng | Shanghai Jiao Tong University, China |

# Award Chair

Farhad Aghili                      Canadian Space Agency, Canada

# Registration Chairs

Zhi Li                             Concordia University, Canada
Sining Liu                         Concordia University, Canada

# Finance Chair

Ying Feng                          South China University of Technology, China

# Local Arrangement Chairs

Wen-Fang Xie                       Concordia University, Canada
Chevy Chen                         Concordia University, Canada

# International Program Committee

Amir Aghdam                        Concordia University, Canada
DongPu Cao                         Lancaster University, UK
Qixin Cao                          Shanghai Jiao Tong University, China
Jie Chen                           Beijing Institute of Technology, China
Mingyuan Chen                      Concordia University, Canada
Zuomin Dong                        University of Victoria, Canada
Guangren Duan                      Harbin Institute of Technology, China
Shumin Fei                         Southeast University, China
Gang Feng                          City University of Hong Kong, China
Huijun Gao                         Harbin Institute of Technology, China
Luis E. Garza C.                   Tecnológico de Monterrey, México
Andrew A. Goldenberg               University of Toronto, Canada
Guoying Gu                         Shanghai Jiao Tong University, China
Jason J. Gu                        Dalhousie University, Canada
Peihua Gu                          University of Calgary, Canada
Zhi-Hong Guan                      Huazhong University of Science & Technology,
                                     China
Shuxiang Guo                       Kagawa University, Japan
Lina Hao                           Northeastern University, China
Henry Hong                         Concordia University, Canada
Liu Hsu                            Federal University of Rio de Janeiro, Brazil

| | |
|---|---|
| Huosheng Hu | University of Essex, UK |
| Qinglei Hu | Harbin Institute of Technology, China |
| Chunqing Huang | Xiamen University, China |
| Wei Lin | Case Western Reserve University, USA |
| Derong Liu | University of Illinois at Chicago, USA |
| Min Liu | Tsinghua University, China |
| Peter X. Liu | Carleton University, Canada |
| Jun Luo | Shanghai University, China |
| Tao Mao | Dartmouth College, USA |
| Daniel Miller | University of Waterloo, Canada |
| Yuichiro Oya | University of Miyazak, Japan |
| Hailong Pei | South China University of Technology, China |
| Juntong Qi | Chinese Academy of Sciences, China |
| Joe Qin | University of Southern California, USA |
| Yaohong Qu | Northwestern Polytechnical University, China |
| Lbrir Salim | The University of Trinidad and Tobago, Trinidad and Tobago |
| Inna Sharf | McGill University, Canada |
| Yang Shi | Victoria University, Canada |
| Gangbing Song | University of Houston, USA |
| Jing Sun | University of Michigan, USA |
| XiaoBo Tan | Michigan State University, USA |
| Yonghong Tan | Shanghai Normal University, China |
| Yong Tang | South China University of Technology, China |
| Gang Tao | University of Virginia, USA |
| Didier Theilliol | University of Lorraine, France |
| Hong Wang | University of Manchester, UK |
| Xingsong Wang | Southeast University, China |
| Pak Kin Wong | University of Macau, Macau, SAR China |
| Shaorong Xie | Shanghai University, China |
| Xin Xin | Okayama Prefectural University, Japan |
| Zhenhua Xiong | Shanghai Jiao Tong University, China |
| Bugong Xu | South China University of Technology, China |
| Jianxin Xu | National University of Singapore, Singapore |
| Deyi Xue | University of Calgary, Canada |
| Zijiang Yang | Ibaraki University, Japan |
| Dingguo Zhang | Shanghai Jiao Tong University, China |
| Guangming Zhang | Nanjing University of Technology, China |
| Yanzheng Zhao | Shanghai Jiao Tong University, China |
| Wenhong Zhu | Canadian Space Agency, Canada |

# List of Reviewers

We would like to acknowledge the support of the following people, who peer reviewed articles from ICIRA 2012.

Achint Aggarwal
Farhad Aghili
Jose Alarcon Herrera
Mirco Alpen
Nicolas Alt
Philippe Archambault
Ramprasad Balasubramanian
Mark Becke
Andrey Belkin
Francisco Beltran-Carbajal
Stanley Birchfield
Swetha Sampath Bobba
Hans-Joachim Böhme
Itziar Cabanes
Yifan Cai
Yang Cao
Zhiqiang Cao
Alberto Cavallo
Abbas Chamseddine
Mingyuan Chen
Xiang Chen
Wei Chen
Diansheng Chen
Xinkai Chen
Shengyong Chen
Yixiong Chen
Xiang Chen
Weidong Chen
Chaobin Chen
Shengyong Chen
Chevy Chen
Zhao Cheng
Yushing Cheung
Dong-Il Cho
Yunfei Dai
David D'Ambrosio
Krispin Davies
Hua Deng
Mingcong Deng
Wenhua Ding
Xuejun Ding
John Dolan

Mitchell Donald
Xiao-Gang Duan
Su-Hong Eom
Ole Falkenberg
Yuanjie Fan
Yongchun Fang
Wei Feng
Simon Fojtu
Gustavo Freitas
Klaus Frick
Zhuang Fu
Jun Fu
Xin Fu
Luis Garza
Shuzhi Sam Ge
Jason Geder
Hernan Gonzalez Acuña
Guo-Ying Gu
Tianyu Gu
Yongxin Guo
Zhao Guo
Roger Halkyard
Jianda Han
Lina Hao
Mohamed Hasan
Syed Hassan
Michal Havlena
Jiayuan He
Sven Hellbach
Abdelfetah Hentout
Katharina Hertkorn
Trent Hilliard
Johannes Höcherl
Joachim Horn
Mir Amin Hosseini
Qinglei Hu
Yonghui Hu
Jin Hu
Chunqing Huang
Jidong Huang
Aitore Ibarguren
Satoshi Iwaki

Markus Janssen
Qiuling Jia
Ying Jin
Balajee Kannan
Jun Kanno
Bijan Karimi
Mohammad Keshmiri
Sungshin Kim
Alexandr Klimchik
Yukinori Kobayashi
Tim Köhler
Naoyuki Kubota
Xu-Zhi Lai
Lin Lan
Marco Langerwisch
Jangmyung Lee
Sang-Hoon Lee
Min Lei
Yan Li
Shunchong Li
Jing Li
Zhijun Li
Hengyu Li
Nanjun Li
Yinxiao Li
Qingguo Li
Yangming Li
Zhi Li
Binbin Lian
Junli Liang
Guanhao Liang
Miguel Lima
Xinjun Liu
Han Liu
Chengliang Liu
Peter Liu
Chao Liu
Jia Liu
Sining Liu
Jun Luo
Xiaomin Ma
Yumin Ma
António Machado
Werner Maier
Jörn Malzahn

Mohamed Mamdouh
Ida Bagus Manuaba
Tao Mao
Farhat Mariem
Luis Mateos
Iñaki Maurtua
Aaron Mavrinac
Deqing Mei
Yi Min
Lei Mo
Abolfazl Mohebbi
Vidya Murali
Mahmoud Mustafa
Keitaro Naruse
Ashutosh Natraj
Myagmarbayar Nergui
Bin Niu
Scott Nokleby
Farzad Norouzi fard
Farzan Nowruzi
Ernesto Olguín-Díaz
Godfrey Onwubolu
Tomas Pajdla
Chang-Zhong Pan
Lizheng Pan
Ricardo Pérez-Alcocer
Andreas Pichler
Charles Pinto
Erion Plaku
Peter Poschmann
Radius Prasetiyo
Marius Pruessner
Juntong Qi
Xiaoming Qian
Guo Qiwei
Yaohong Qu
Mohammad Rahman
Ahmed Ramadan
Christian Rauch
Laura Ray
Hamd ul Moqeet Riaz
Martijn Rooker
Miti Ruchanurucks
Kunjin Ryu
Iman Sadeghzadeh

Thomas Schlegl
Christian Schlette
Sven Severin
Inna Sharf
Karam Shaya
Huiping Shen
Huimin Shen
Xinjun Sheng
Thierry Simon
Olivier Simonin
Dalei Song
Zhenguo Sun
Tadeusz Szkodny
XiaoBo Tan
Wenbin Tang
Yandong Tang
Alberto Tellaeche
Didier Theilliol
Christopher Tomaszewski
Abhinav Valada
Prasanna Velagapudi
Tianmiao Wang
Xiaoyan Wang
Xinmin Wang
Jingchuan Wang
Yancheng Wang
Xin Wang
Enrong Wang
Ralf Waspe
Zhixuan Wei
Graeme Wilson
Jonas Witt
Christian Wögerer
Pak Kin Wong
Olarn Wongwirat
Chong Wu
Yier Wu
Jianhua Wu
Min Wu
Xiaojun Wu
Baihua Xiao
Fugui Xie
Rong Xie
Shaorong Xie
Pu Xie
Wen-Fang Xie

Le Xie
Xin Xin
Jing Xin
Zhenhua Xiong
Rong Xiong
Caihua xiong
Bugong Xu
Bin Xu
Xiong Xu
You-Nan Xu
Deyi Xue
Zijiang Yang
Jie Yang
Chenguang Yang
Wenyu Yang
Jing Yang
Chang-En Yang
Lin Yao
Gen'ichi Yasuda
Michael Yeh
Zhouping Yin
Yong-Ho Yoo
Haoyong Yu
Xinghuo Yu
Mimoun Zelmat
Shasha Zeng
Jie Zhang
Zhengchen Zhang
Gang Zhang
Xiaoping Zhang
Jianjun Zhang
He Zhang
Dingguo Zhang
Yifeng Zhang
Xuebo Zhang
Yequn Zhang
Jinsong Zhang
Wenzeng Zhang
Chaohai Zhang
Yanzheng Zhao
Pengbing Zhao
Zhaowei Zhong
Hangfei Zhou
Li-Min Zhu
Asier Zubizarreta

# Table of Contents – Part I

## Estimation and Identification

## Intelligent Visual Systems

## Application of Differential Geometry in Robotic Mechanisms

## Unmanned Systems Technologies and Applications

# New Development on Health Management, Fault Diagnosis, and Fault-Tolerant Control

# Biomechatronics

## Intelligent Control of Mechanical and Mechatronic Systems

## Integrative Production Technologies

# Table of Contents – Part II

## Robotics for Rehabilitation and Assistance

# Mechatronics and Integration Technology in Electronics and Information Devices Fabrication

# Man-Machine Interactions

# Manufacturing

# Micro and Nano Systems

## Mobile Robots and Intelligent Autonomous Systems

## Motion Control

## Multi-agent Systems and Distributed Control

## Multi-sensor Data Fusion Algorithms

# Table of Contents – Part III

## Robot Actuators and sensors

## Robot Design, Development and Control

## Robot Intelligence, Learning and Linguistics

## Robot Mechanism and Design

## Robot Motion Analysis and Planning

# Robotic Vision, Recognition and Reconstruction

## Planning and Navigation

# Control Strategies of a Mobile Robot Inspector in Inaccessible Areas

Farrokh Faramarzi[1], Mohammadreza Motamedi[2],
Amir A. Javid[3], and Ameneh Vatani[4]

[1] Mechanical and Automotive Department, Kingston University, London, United Kingdom
farrokh.faramarzi@akersolutions.com
[2] GPA Department, École de technologie supérieure (ETS), Montréal, Québec, Canada
mohammadreza.motamedi.1@ens.etsmtl.ca
[3] Computer Science Department, Kingston University, London, United Kingdom
a.javid@dynamicboost.com
[4] Electrical and Computer Engineering Department, Concordia University, Montreal, Canada
a_vatani@encs.concordia.ca

**Abstract.** The current research is devoted to the field of sensor data processing and communication system. The purpose of this research is to develop an autonomous mobile robot to organize automatic inspection platform for inspection tasks in areas which are not easily accessible by humans such as small range pipelines. This paper investigates a new sensing approach for inspection of inaccessible tubular structures that is able to exceed the restrictions of available inspection systems. A well-organized platform using various sensors and actuators has been proposed. The purpose of this paper is to develop a mobile robot which acts as a pipe inspector, along with presenting a control system to design the navigation system of such platform.

**Keywords:** Pipeline inspection, Mobile robot, Controlling mobile inspector.

## 1 Introduction

All over the world, there are millions' miles of pipelines carrying different types of liquid from water to crude oil, these sources are necessary for our everyday life and our everyday growing industries to survive.. Any chemically stable substance could be conveyed all the way through a pipeline. One of the main problems of these pipelines is that they are prone to damage by internal and external corrosion, third party damages, cracking and manufacturing flaws, and many other different factors that may lead to form different types of defects in pipelines. Thus, distinctive industries spend huge amount of money for their pipelines to be inspected and also to be repaired to avoid causing dangerous failures [1]. Despite these pipelines inspections there are many types of pipes that have narrow width and hence are inaccessible for inspectors to get inside them and perform required inspection. The only solution remains here is to use some sort of automatic machines to do the job for us. The massive development in robotic systems makes robots a good option for such a purpose [2, 3]. More specifically, automatic mobile robots can be the best intelligent

C.-Y. Su, S. Rakheja, H. Liu (Eds.): ICIRA 2012, Part I, LNAI 7506, pp. 1–10, 2012.
© Springer-Verlag Berlin Heidelberg 2012

agents invented by human kinds that can be used to do the inspections we want. For centuries, people have been involved in constructing machinery that duplicates the behaviors and capabilities of living beings. Perception and action are tightly coupled in living beings, animals execute particular head and eye activities to see around them, to act reciprocally with the environment, they foresee the result of their actions and forecast the performance of other substance [4].Consequently, considering the problems in pipelines, we can say that using robots for inspection is the only way to diagnose defects in inaccessible pipelines particularly. In inspection of pipeline in service, an automatic system is inevitable due to the big range of inspection manuals making it hard to be performed accurately and perfectly by humans. Beside inaccessibility of such areas, the other problem in some conditions is that these areas are very dangerous for human due to different kind of hazardous gases or lack of oxygen which may danger the human life [5]. Moreover, apart from inspection, in most cases analyzing the data by means of automation systems is faster than interpreting by technician. For instance, in financial field, accountants use computer as an autonomous system to execute their task. Using such a system in industrial field will save time and increases the accuracy of the task. Nowadays, many robotic systems for pipeline inspection and monitoring have been developed. Such systems range from small to large-sized in different functionality [6-9]. Suzumori [10] designed a small-sized (12 mm diameter) mobile robot inspector. A pneumatic power was used for activating a camera and the micro arm, but the inspection method was not satisfactory enough in sharply curved pipelines. In [11] the authors proposed several types of inspector robots ranging from 25, 50, up to 150 mm diameter pipe.The presented mechanism not only overcomes the existing limitations, but also enables the robot to detect any fine or coarse obstacles such as any contaminations in the pipeline. A comprehensive model based on reflectance theory used in an ultrasonic transducer, analysis of the output signals of such a sensor, and path analysis by controlling DC motors has been developed precisely.

## 2    State of the Art of Robotic Platform for Pipe Inspection

Study for pipe inspection robots have been done for a long time, and so far many original motion concepts have been suggested to solve the enormous difficulties related to the altering in pipe diameter, elbows, curves and energy supply. Below some of these robots have been noted as a review.

### 2.1   Heli-Pipe

Heli-pipe family comprise of four diverse types of robots for in-pipe inspection. The robots have two divisions expressed with a worldwide joint. One part, which is called stator, is directed along the pipe by a set of wheels stirring parallel to the axis of the pipe. A single motor (With gear reducer built-in) is located between the two bodies to construct the movement. All the wheels are established on a deferment to house for varying curves in the pipe and tube diameter. The robots carry their own radio links and batteries, so they are autonomous [12]. The schematic of Heli-pipe robots is depicted in Fig. 1.

**Fig. 1.** Heli-Pipe inspector [12]

## 2.2    Multifunctional Robotic Crawler for In-Pipe Inspection

This robot has six slider-crank mechanisms, which are organized at 120° one from the other one, each of these bands have a specific driving wheel. The wheels are activated by belt transmission and DC motors. The robot is deliberated as the springs (see Fig. 2) to activate the mechanisms with the same power. This arrangement enables the robot to shift within pipes with vertical, horizontal, and elbow-typed parts. But the progress of the robot within T junctions is not doable [13].

**Fig. 2.** Multifunctional robotic crawler for in-pipe inspection [13]

## 3    Kinematics of the Robot DaNI

Kinematics is the fundamental sympathetic of how a mechanism moves. It does not regard the forces implicated, only the motion. Kinematics is significant to recognizing where a robot can go and how to obtain that position. In this case, motion means driving from point A to point B given the position and orientation in a reference coordinate system such as one shown in Fig. 3 [14]. Global coordinates depict the area where the robot works, and local coordinates explain the position and orientation of the robot. The entire dimensionality of the DaNI differential drive robot chassis on the plane is three, two for position in the plane and one for orientation along the vertical axis.

Using the orientation of the local coordinate system in Fig. 3 what is the equation that describes the distance moved in straight forward driving in connection with linear robot velocity

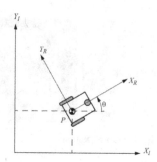

**Fig. 3.** Local and global coordinate frames

What is the equation that states the affiliation between motor rotating velocity and wheel distance travelled? The answer to all of these questions is in the equation below.

$$Lw = \frac{\pi d}{revolution} \times \dot{\varphi}_w \times t \qquad (1)$$

Where Lw is wheel distance travelled, d shows wheel diameter which is 4 inches for DaNI, and $\dot{\varphi}_w$ is wheel rotational velocity (radians/s).

If both wheels are driving forward at the same speed with no sliding, the equation which explicates the relationship between the wheel distances travelled and the robot linear speed $\dot{x}_r$ is:

$$\dot{x}_r = \frac{Lw}{t} \qquad (2)$$

Which considers turning as well as driving straight forward? The equation that describes the angle $\boldsymbol{\theta}$ rotated about the left wheel and the robot rotational velocity $\dot{\boldsymbol{\theta}}_r$ in connection with the linear velocity of the right wheel, $\dot{x}_{r1}$ (for wheel 1) is:

$$\theta = 360°/2\pi l \times \text{wheel distance travelled} \qquad (3)$$

Where L = distance between each wheel and
P = 6.5 inch for DaNI
Circle perimeter distance = $2\pi l$

$$WDT = \pi d/\text{rotation} \times \dot{\varphi}_w \times t\pi d/\text{rotation} \times \dot{\varphi}_w \times t \qquad (4)$$

And finally the equation that relates wheel rotational speed $\dot{\theta}_w$ (Rad/s) to robot rotation speed $\omega_0$ when turning about one wheel is:

$$\omega = (\dot{\varphi}_w \text{ rad/s})(1/2\pi \text{ rev/rad})(4\pi \text{ in/rev})(\frac{360}{2} \times 13\pi °/\text{in})$$

To budge from point A to point B (the goal position) in Fig. 4, one might first direct the robot at point B by rotating in place. Thus, only the orientation is changed and not the coordinates of the robot.

The equation relating wheel rotational velocity $\dot{\varphi}_w$ (rad/s) to robot rotation velocity $\omega$ when turning the robot in place is:

$$\omega = (\dot{\varphi}_w \text{ rad/s})(1/2\pi \text{ rev/rad})(4\pi \text{ in/rev})(360/2 \times 13\pi \text{ °}/in) \qquad (5)$$

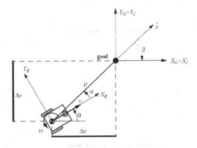

**Fig. 4.** Frames to move from start to goal

## 4    Ultrasonic Transducer

DaNI which has been used as a prototype robot in this study is equipped with an ultrasonic transducer. The range of the ultrasonic transducer in DaNI is between 0.2 and 3 meter, but for real experiment we should test the tolerance of the sensor, since DaNI's sensor like other transducers can detect noises as well (Fig. 5). Taking the noise into consideration, DaNI's sensor does not give good values when the sensor is perpendicular to the detected surface. On the contrary, if this angle is increased, the results from the sensor would be more acceptable. To find the suitable sensor angle, different angles have been tested for DaNI which were between 0° and 90°, 30° is the best one for this robot (Fig. 6).

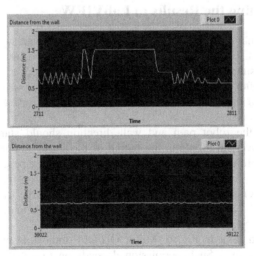

**Fig. 5.** Graph of sensor distance with noise (top) and without noise (bottom)

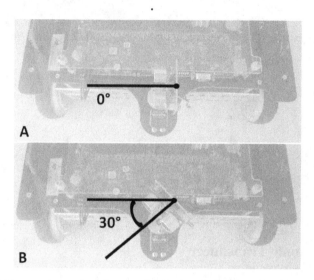

**Fig. 6.** The best sensor angle value to reduce noises during detecting the pipe wall

For this task, DaNI should be moved toward an obstacle with diverse distances and then data have to be compared. According to the results, the minimum and maximum differences are between 0 and 0.07 meters. The differences are due to the noise in the environment, thus we can ignore them, since the exact distance is not very important in this study and we can fix a desired distance and find the suitable one by trial and error method.

## 5    Programing the Results in LabVIEW

In this part, the main written program in LabVIEW software will be demonstrated. Using Open and Close FPGA VI is the first step. The positive point in presented program is that a simple and complete program has been used.

The first step after calling FPGA is specifying the value of sensor angle. According to the algorithm of the system, the robot should check its front to detect any possible obstacles.

The angle of the robot path and wall direction should start from zero at the beginning. Moreover, in this loop the output of the sensor should be filtered due to noises as was mentioned earlier. In Fig. 7 the first loop of the program is depicted.

The next part is to adjust the velocity of motors based on the output that sensor provides. But depending on the distance from the robot to the wall, the velocities of the motors should be altered. In fact, the velocity of each motor will be added or subtracted to a specific value.

There is an indicator in Fig. 9 (Motor ON/OFF indicator) which shows that the robot can move or not. Such permission depends on two factors: 1) is the Motor On/Off Switch on and 2) is there any obstacle in front of the robot. In Fig. 9, the combination of the two above mentioned conditions has been shown to be applied in the program. One technique that has been used in this program is using "Local

Variable" in LabVIEW. According to this technique instead of using many wires in the program, Local Variables of any command have been employed such as "Motor ON/OFF indicator".

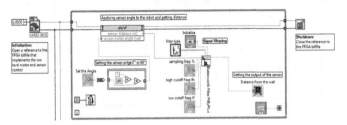

**Fig. 7.** First loop: calling FPGA, set the sensor angle, get sensor distance and then filtering

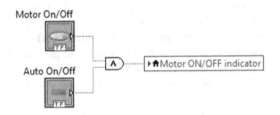

**Fig. 8.** Adjusting the velocities of the motors

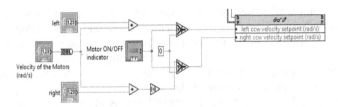

**Fig. 9.** Running motors permission

Next step is adjusting the sensor angle. The sensor should stay at its front for 1 second and locate to the wall for 3 second. This task has been done by means of while loop, wait until and shift register as shown in Fig. 10.

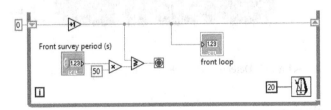

**Fig. 10.** Setting the time period for sensor by means of while loop, wait until and shift register

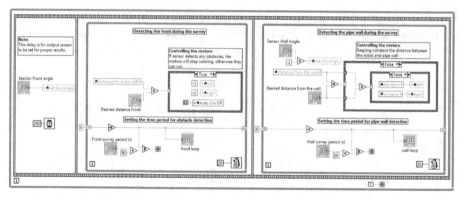

**Fig. 11.** Adjusting the velocities of the motors

Another point which needs to be pointed out is that applying time periods should be in order, so using "Flat Sequence Structure" command is inevitable. The reason of using "Wait" command in the first sequence is that when the sensor turns back to the 0°, it takes time to give a proper distance to the program, and this problem leads to run the motors for a short distance. Although this movement is small, it is not negligible since experiences showed that after 5 to 7 seconds the robot will get to the obstacle which is fault. The experimental results of the sensor output during the survey are shown in Fig. 12. The top signals are the distance from the obstacle and the bottom signals are the distances from the pipe wall. Due to the noises which have been noted by red ellipse in Fig. 12 it seems that the sensor detects a spurious obstacle. However it is not obstacle. Experimental results showed that the best time period in "Wait" command for this purpose is 250 milliseconds.

In order to get the above presented results, extensive programming and work has been done and the authors have come up with some new empirical rules (such as proper angle of DaNI for noise rejection) through trial and error.

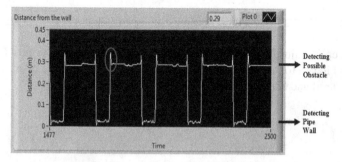

**Fig. 12.** Detecting obstacle and pipe wall by the sensor

# 6    Conclusion

The performed research proved that a sensing approach of exploiting a mobile controllable platform to attain smooth movement develops the inspection during the survey. In the framework of this approach, the growth of a comprehensive model came up with a perception into the behavior of the ultrasonic transducer in the pipe environment and promoted precise sensor detection.

The system algorithm has been initiated to match the sensor and actuators of the platform and the programming of such algorithm has been done in one of the high-level programming languages. The system has been evaluated for pipes through experiments in simulated environments, and developments in both sensing quality and automation aspects are achieved.

To sum up, the results of the ultrasonic transducer outputs were analyzed and developed. Following that, the importance of sensor orientation was presented to get more accurate results. In addition the system algorithm to control sensor and DC motors was designed and the hierarchy of that was explained. And finally, to run the robot, the programming of the system in LabVIEW software was done.

# References

1. Hideyuki, T., Hiroyuki, C., Ato, K.: Gel-type sticky mobile inspector to traverse on the rugged wall and ceiling. In: IEEE International Conference on Robotics and Automation, ICRA 2009, pp. 1591–1592 (2009)
2. Lim, R.S., Hung Manh, L., Zeyong, S., Weihua, S.: Developing a crack inspection robot for bridge maintenance. In: 2011 IEEE International Conference on Robotics and Automation (ICRA), pp. 6288–6293 (2011)
3. Wilson, J.C., Berardo, P.A.: Automatic inspection of hazardous materials by mobile robot. In: IEEE International Conference on Systems, Man and Cybernetics, Intelligent Systems for the 21st Century, vol. 4, pp. 3280–3285 (1995)
4. SunSin, H., JangMyung, L.: Path-selection control of a power line inspection robot using sensor fusion. In: IEEE International Conference on Multisensor Fusion and Integration for Intelligent Systems, MFI 2008, pp. 8–13 (2008)
5. Eich, M., Vogele, T.: Design and control of a lightweight magnetic climbing robot for vessel inspection. In: 2011 19th Mediterranean Conference on Control & Automation (MED), pp. 1200–1205 (2011)
6. Hoon, L., Jae Yeon, C., Byung-Ju, Y., Byoung Kyu, K.: Development of Semi-Automatic Inspection System for Indoor Pipeline. In: International Conference on Mechatronics and Automation, ICMA 2007, pp. 3640–3645 (2007)
7. Muramatsu, M., Namiki, N., Koyama, R., Suga, Y.: Autonomous mobile robot in pipe for piping operations. In: Proceedings. 2000 IEEE/RSJ International Conference on Intelligent Robots and Systems (IROS 2000), vol. 3, pp. 2166–2171 (2000)
8. Roh, S.G., Ryew, S.M., Yang, J.H., Choi, H.R.: Actively steerable in-pipe inspection robots for underground urban gas pipelines. In: Proceedings of IEEE International Conference on Robotics and Automation, ICRA 2001, vol. 1, pp. 761–766 (2001)
9. Se-gon, R., Hyouk Ryeol, C.: Differential-drive in-pipe robot for moving inside urban gas pipelines. IEEE Transactions on Robotics 21, 1–17 (2005)
10. Suzumori, K., Hori, K., Miyagawa, T.: A direct-drive pneumatic stepping motor for robots: designs for pipe-inspection microrobots and for human-care robots. In: Proceedings of IEEE International Conference on Robotics and Automation, vol. 4, pp. 3047–3052 (1998)

11. Hirose, S., Ohno, H., Mitsui, T., Suyama, K.: Design of in-pipe inspection vehicles for 150 pipes. In: Proceeding of IEEE International Conference on Robotics and Automation, vol. 3, pp. 2309–2314 (1999)
12. Pierre. Pipe inspection robot 1, HELI-PIPE, http://www.ulb.ac.be/scmero/robotics.html
13. Tatar, O., Mandru, D., Ardelean, I., Zia, T.: Development of mobile minirobots in pipe inspection tasks. Mechanika, 60–64 (2007)
14. King, R.: Mobile Robotics Experiments with DaNI. N. Instruments, Ed., ed. NI (2011)

# Advanced High Precision Control for XY-Table

Xinkai Chen

Department of Electronic Information Systems, Shibaura Institute of Technology,
307 Fukasaku, Minuma-ku, Saitama-shi, Saitama 337-8570, Japan
chen@shibaura-it.ac.jp

**Abstract.** The XY-table is composed of two piezo electric actuators (PEA) and a positioning mechanism (PM). Due to existence of hysteretic nonlinearity in the PEA and the friction in the PM, the high precision control for the XY-table is a challenging task. This paper discusses the high precision adaptive control for the XY-table, where the hysteresis is described by Prandtl-Ishlinskii model. The proposed control law ensures the global stability of the controlled stage, and the position error can be controlled to approach to zero asymptotically. Experimental results show the effectiveness of the proposed method.

**Keywords:** XY-table, piezo electric actuators, hysteresis, adaptive control.

## 1 Introduction

Recently, piezo-actuated stage has many effective applications in ultra-high precision positioning systems [2]-[6]. The piezo electric actuator (PEA) is used to meet the requirement of nanometer resolution in displacement, high stiffness and rapid response. However, the main disadvantage of PEA is the hysteresis phenomenon between the applied electric voltage and the displacement. Due to the undifferentiable and nonmemoryless character of the hysteresis, it causes position errors which limit the operating speed and precision of the PEA. The development of control techniques to mitigate the effects of hysteresis has been studied for decades and has recently re-attracted significant attention. Interest in studying dynamic systems with actuator hysteresis is motivated by the fact that they are nonlinear system with nonsmooth nonlinearities for which traditional control methods are insufficient and thus require development of alternate effective approaches. Development of a control frame for the piezo-actuated stage is quite a challenging task.

About the challenge of controlling the piezo-actuated stage, the thorough characterization of the hysteresis forms the foremost task [1] [10]. Appropriate hysteresis models may then be applied to describe the nonsmooth nonlinearities for their potential usage in formulating the control algorithms. It is reported in the author's previous work [2] that the Prandtl-Ishlinskii (PI) model can describe the hysteretic nonlinear relation between the applied electric voltage and the displacement in the piezo electric actuator. The basic idea of PI hysteresis model consists of the weighted aggregate effect of all possible so-called elementary hysteresis operators. Elementary hysteresis operators are noncomplex hysteretic nonlinearities with a

C.-Y. Su, S. Rakheja, H. Liu (Eds.): ICIRA 2012, Part I, LNAI 7506, pp. 11–21, 2012.

simple mathematical structure, where the stop operator which is parameterized by a single threshold variable is employed [1] [10].

In order to effectively drive the piezo-actuated stage, it is by nature to seek means to fuse the PI hysteresis models with the available control techniques to mitigate the effects of hysteresis, especially when the hysteresis is unknown, which is a typical case in many practical applications. However, the results on the fusion of the available hysteresis models with the available control techniques is surprisingly spare in the literature[2], [7]-[9]. The most common approach in coping with hysteresis in the literature is to construct an inverse operator, which is pioneered by Tao and Kokotovic [12], and the reader may refer to, for instance, [5] [6] [9] and the references therein. Essentially, the inversion problem depends on the modeling methods of the hysteresis. Due to multi-valued and non-smooth features of hysteresis, the inversion always generates certain errors and possesses strong sensitivity to the model parameters. These errors directly make the stability analysis of the closed-loop system very difficult except for certain special cases.

This paper tries to fuse of the adaptive control techniques with the Prandtl-Ishlinskii hysteresis model for the XY-table, which is composed of two PEAs and a positioning mechanism. The advantage is that only the parameters in the formulation of the controller need to be adaptively estimated, and the real values of the parameters of the stage need to be neither identified nor measured. The proposed control law ensures the global stability of the adaptive system, and the position error of the XY-table can be controlled to approach to zero asymptotically. Experimental results confirm the effectiveness of the proposed method.

## 2    Problem Statement

### 2.1    System Description

In this paper, the nano-positioner is composed of two peizo-actuators and a positioning mechanism (PM). The scheme of the positioner is shown in Figure 1. First, let us consider one direction of the table, say y-axis. The positioning mechanism can be modeled as a mass-spring-damper mechanic system. The PEA can be regarded as a force generator which generates force due to the applied voltage. The dynamic equation of the piezo-actuated stage in y-axis can be formulated as follows

$$m_y \ddot{y}(t) + \xi_{y1} \dot{y}(t) + \xi_{y2} y(t) = u_y(t) , \tag{1}$$

where $y(t)$ represents the y-axis displacement of the table, $u_y(t)$ is the force generated by the PEA in y-axis; $m_y$ is the mass of the y-axis mover, $\xi_{y1}$ is the viscous friction coefficient (which is very small) of the PM in y-axis and $\xi_{y2}$ is stiffness factor satisfying $\xi_{y2} \gg \xi_{y1}$.

Now, express (1) as

$$\frac{d}{dt}\begin{bmatrix} y(t) \\ \dot{y}(t) \end{bmatrix} = \begin{bmatrix} 0 & 1 \\ -\dfrac{\xi_{y2}}{m_y} & -\dfrac{\xi_{y1}}{m_y} \end{bmatrix}\begin{bmatrix} y(t) \\ \dot{y}(t) \end{bmatrix} + \begin{bmatrix} 0 \\ \dfrac{1}{m_y} \end{bmatrix} u_y(t). \tag{2}$$

Let $T$ be the sampling period and suppose $u_y(t)$ is constant during the sampling instants. By discretizing system (2) based on ZOH input, the input-output discrete time expression of system (1) can be given by

$$a(q^{-1})y(k) = q^{-1}b(q^{-1})u_y(k), \tag{3}$$

where $q^{-1}$ is the delay operator, $a(q^{-1})$ and $b(q^{-1})$ are polynomials defined by

$$a(q^{-1}) = 1 + a_1 q^{-1} + a_2 q^{-2}, \tag{4}$$

$$b(q^{-1}) = b_0 + b_1 q^{-1}. \tag{5}$$

The parameters $a_1$, $a_2$, $b_0$ and $b_1$ are unknown.

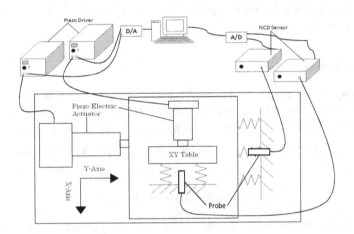

**Fig. 1.** The experimental setup

**Lemma 1.** If $T \ll 0.1$, then $a(q^{-1})$ and $b(q^{-1})$ are coprime, $b(q^{-1})$ is a Hurwitz polynomial, and $b_0 > 0$.

Now, consider the discrete time model of the Positioner. By referring (3) and considering the interference between the two axes, the model of the Positioner can be expressed by the following relation

$$A(q^{-1})z(k) = q^{-1}B(q^{-1})u(k), \tag{6}$$

$$z(k) = [x(k), y(k)]^T, \quad u(k) = [u_x(k), u_y(k)]^T \tag{7}$$

with

$$A(q^{-1}) = 1 + A_1 q^{-1} + A_2 q^{-2}, \quad B(q^{-1}) = B_0 + B_1 q^{-1} \tag{9}$$

$$A_i = \begin{bmatrix} a_{11}^{(i)} & a_{12}^{(i)} \\ a_{21}^{(i)} & a_{22}^{(i)} \end{bmatrix} \text{ (for } i = 1,2 \text{)}, \quad B_0 = \begin{bmatrix} b_{11}^{(0)} & 0 \\ 0 & b_{22}^{(0)} \end{bmatrix}, \quad B_1 = \begin{bmatrix} b_{11}^{(1)} & b_{12}^{(1)} \\ b_{21}^{(1)} & b_{22}^{(1)} \end{bmatrix} \tag{10}$$

where $x(k)$ represents the x-axis displacement of the table, $u_x(k)$ is the force generated by the PEA in x-axis. Let $v_x(k)$ and $v_y(k)$ be the voltages applied to the actuators, and express the relation between $v_x(k)$ and $u_x(k)$ and the relation between $v_y(k)$ and $u_y(k)$ as

$$u_x(k) = H_x[v_x](k), \quad u_y(k) = H_y[v_y](k), \tag{11}$$

where $H_x[\cdot]$ and $H_y[\cdot]$ are the hysteresis operators which will be given later.

The control purpose is to drive the position $z(k) = [x(k), y(k)]^T$ of the Positioner to track a uniformly bounded signal $z_d(k) = [x_d(k), y_d(k)]^T$ for the system (6) together with (11).

## 2.2    Hysteresis Model

In this paper, we adopt the Prandtl-Ishlinskii (PI) model in discrete time. The hysteresis is denoted by the operator $w(k) = H[v](k)$, where $v(k)$ is the input (voltage), $w(k)$ is the output (generated force) of the PEA. The basic element of the PI operator is the so-called stop operator $\omega(k) = E_r[v; w_{-1}](k)$ with threshold $r$. For arbitrary piece-wise monotone function $v(k)$, define $e_r : R \to R$ as

$$e_r(v) = \min(r, \max(-r, v)). \tag{12}$$

For any initial value $w_{-1} \in R$ and $r \geq 0$, the stop operator $E_r[\cdot \; ; w_{-1}](k)$ is defined as

$$E_r[v; w_{-1}](0) = e_r(v(0) - w_{-1}), \tag{13}$$

$$E_r[v; w_{-1}](k) = e_r(v(k) - v(k_i) + E_r[v; w_{-1}](k_i)), \tag{14}$$

for $k_i < k \leq k_{i+1}$, where the function $v(k)$ is monotone for $k_i \leq k \leq k_{i+1}$. The stop operator is mainly characterized by the threshold parameter $r \geq 0$ which determines the height of the hysteresis region in the $(v, w)$ plane. For simplicity, denote $E_r[v; w_{-1}](k)$ by $E_r[v](k)$ in the following of this paper. It should be noted that the stop operator $E_r[v](k)$ is rate-independent. The PI hysteresis model is defined by

$$w(k) = \int_0^R p(r)E_r[v](k)dr,$$     (15)

where $p(r)$ is the density function which is usually unknown, satisfying $p(r) \geq 0$ with $\int_0^\infty rp(r)dr < \infty$, $R$ is a positive constant which is sufficient large.

For the piezo electric actuator, the constant $R$ depends on the saturation input voltage.

## 3     Adaptive Control Design

### 3.1     Some Preliminaries

To begin with, define the variable

$$s(k) = C(q^{-1})(z(k) - z_d(k)),$$     (16)

where $C(q^{-1})$ is in the form

$$C(q^{-1}) = \begin{bmatrix} C_1(q^{-1}) & 0 \\ 0 & C_2(q^{-1}) \end{bmatrix} = I + C_1 q^{-1} + C_2 q^{-2},$$     (17)

$C_1(q^{-1})$ and $C_2(q^{-1})$ are Schur polynomials, and $C_i = \begin{bmatrix} c_{11}^{(i)} & 0 \\ 0 & c_{22}^{(i)} \end{bmatrix}$ for $i = 1, 2$.

Clearly, $\lim_{k \to \infty} s(k) = 0$ implies $\lim_{k \to \infty} (z(k) - z_d(k)) = 0$.

Now, consider the polynomial matrix equation

$$C(q^{-1}) = A(q^{-1}) + q^{-1}F(q^{-1}),$$     (18)

where $F(q^{-1})$ is in the following form

$$F(q^{-1}) = F_0 + F_1 q^{-1},$$     (19)

$F_0$ and $F_1$ are $2 \times 2$ matrices. Thus, if the parameters $A_1$ and $A_2$ are known, then the parameters in $F(q^{-1})$ can be determined uniquely.

Multiplying (18) with $z(k)$ and employing (6) gives

$$C(q^{-1})z(k+1) = B(q^{-1})u(k) + F(q^{-1})z(k),$$     (20)

where $u(k)$ is the force generated by the PEAs defined as

$$u(k) = [u_x(k), u_y(k)]^T = \left[ \int_0^R p_x(r)E_r[v_x](k)dr, \int_0^R p_y(r)E_r[v_y](k)dr \right]^T,$$     (21)

$p_x(r)$ and $p_y(r)$ are respectively the density functions of of PEAs in x and y axes. Substituting (21) into (20) yields

$$C(q^{-1})z(k+1) = \theta^T \phi(k) + \int_0^R B_0 \begin{bmatrix} p_x(r)E_r[v_x](k) \\ p_y(r)E_r[v_y](k) \end{bmatrix} dr + \int_0^R B_1 \begin{bmatrix} p_x(r)E_r[v_x](k-1) \\ p_y(r)E_r[v_y](k-1) \end{bmatrix} dr \quad (22)$$

with

$$\phi(k) = [z^T(k), z^T(k-1)]^T, \quad \theta = [F_0, F_1]^T. \quad (23)$$

Relation (22) will be used to formulate the adaptive control.

## 3.2    Parameter Estimation

Since the parameters $A_1$ and $A_2$ are unknown in practice, the parameters in $F(q^{-1})$ can not be obtained. Furthermore, the density functions $p_x(r)$ and $p_y(r)$ are also unknown in practice. In the following, we will try to estimate the unknown parameters. Let

$$\hat{\theta}(k) = [\hat{F}_0(k), \hat{F}_1(k)]^T \quad (24)$$

denote the estimate of the unknown parameter $\theta$ at the $k$-th step and let

$$\hat{B}_i(r,k) = \begin{bmatrix} \hat{b}_{11}^{(i)}(r,k) & \hat{b}_{12}^{(i)}(r,k) \\ \hat{b}_{21}^{(i)}(r,k) & \hat{b}_{22}^{(i)}(r,k) \end{bmatrix} \quad (25)$$

with $\hat{b}_{12}^{(0)}(r,k) = \hat{b}_{21}^{(0)}(r,k) = 0$ be the estimate of $B_i P(r)$ for a fixed $r$ at the $k$-th step, where $P(r)$ is defined as $P(r) = \begin{bmatrix} p_x(r) & 0 \\ 0 & p_y(r) \end{bmatrix}$.

By observing (22) and replacing the parameters $\theta$ and $B_i P(r)$ in the right hand side with their corresponding estimates, the estimation error can be defined as

$$e(k) = [e_1(k), e_2(k)]^T$$
$$= C(q^{-1})z(k) - \hat{\theta}^T(k-1)\phi(k-1) - \sum_{i=0}^{1} \int_0^R \hat{B}_i(r, k-1)E_r[v](k-1-i)dr \quad (26)$$

Define

$$E_r[v](k) = [E_r[v_x](k), E_r[v_y](k)]^T \quad (27)$$

$$\chi(k-1) = \phi^T(k-1)\phi(k-1) - \sum_{i=0}^{1} \int_0^R E_r^T[v](k-1-i)E_r[v](k-1-i)dr. \quad (28)$$

$\hat{B}_i(r,k)$ and $\hat{\theta}(k)$ are updated by the following adaptation laws with constraints

$$\hat{\theta}(k) = \hat{\theta}(k-1) + \gamma \frac{\phi(k-1) \cdot e^T(k)}{1 + \chi(k-1)} \tag{29}$$

$$\hat{B}_1(r,k) = \hat{B}_1(r,k-1) + \gamma \frac{E_r[v](k-2) \cdot e^T(k)}{1 + \chi(k-1)} \tag{30}$$

$$\hat{b}_{11}^{(0)}(r,k) = \left| \hat{b}_{11}^{(0)}(r,k-1) + \gamma \frac{E_r[v_x](k-1) \cdot e_1(k)}{1 + \chi(k-1)} \right| \tag{31}$$

$$\hat{b}_{22}^{(0)}(r,k) = \left| \hat{b}_{22}^{(0)}(r,k-1) + \gamma \frac{E_r[v_y](k-1) \cdot e_2(k)}{1 + \chi(k-1)} \right|. \tag{32}$$

The initial conditions should be chosen such that $\hat{b}_{ii}^{(0)}(r,0) > 0$ and $\int_0^\infty r \hat{b}_{ii}^{(0)}(r, 0) dr < \infty$. The adaptation gain $\gamma$ should be chosen as $0 < \gamma < 2$.

**Lemma 2.** For the adaptation algorithm in (29)-(32), the following properties hold.

(P1). $\hat{\theta}(k)$ and $\int_0^R \left\| \hat{B}_i(r,k) \right\|_2 dr$ are bounded for all $k > 0$.

(P2). $\lim_{k \to \infty} \dfrac{\left\| e(k+1) \right\|_2^2}{1 + \chi(k)} = 0$

(P3). For any positive finite integer $v$,

$$\lim_{k \to \infty} \left( \hat{\theta}(k) - \hat{\theta}(k-v) \right) = 0, \quad \lim_{k \to \infty} \int_0^R \left( \hat{B}_i(r,k) - \hat{B}_i(r,k-v) \right) dr = 0$$

## 3.3   Control Input Design and Stability Analysis

The control input is determined so that $\lim_{k \to \infty} s(k) = 0$.

Define

$$W(k) = \begin{bmatrix} w_1(k) \\ w_2(k) \end{bmatrix}$$

$$= -\hat{\theta}^T(k)\phi(k) - \int_0^R \hat{B}_1(r,k)E_r[v](k-1)dr + C(q^{-1})z_d(k+1) + \delta \cdot s(k), \tag{33}$$

where $\delta$ is defined as $\delta = \begin{bmatrix} \delta_1 & 0 \\ 0 & \delta_2 \end{bmatrix}$ with $0 < \delta_i < 1$ for $i = 1, 2$. It is obvious that $W(k)$ is an available signal at instant $k$.

In the following, we try to derive a signal $V_i^*(k)$ such that

$$\int_0^R \hat{b}_{ii}^{(0)}(r,k)E_r[V_i^*](k)dr = W_i(k). \tag{34}$$

Let $\lfloor v_{1,\min}, \ v_{1,\max} \rfloor$ and $\lfloor v_{2,\min}, \ v_{2,\max} \rfloor$ be the corresponding practical input ranges to the PEAs in x-axis and y-axis, and define

$$\overline{W}_{i,sat}(k) = \int_0^R \hat{b}_{ii}^{(0)}(r,k)E_r[v_{i,\max}](k)dr, \tag{35}$$

$$\underline{W}_{i,sat}(k) = \int_0^R \hat{b}_{ii}^{(0)}(r,k)E_r[v_{i,\min}](k)dr. \tag{36}$$

Thus, it yields $\underline{W}_{i,sat}(k) \le \int_0^R \hat{b}_{ii}^{(0)}(r,k)E_r[\alpha](k)dr \le \overline{W}_{i,sat}(k)$ for any $v_{i,\min} \le \alpha(k) \le v_{i,\max}$.

For simplicity, we give the algorithm of deriving $V_i^*(k)$ for the case $i=1$. Without loss of generality, suppose $W_1(k)$ is monotonically increasing on $k_i < k \le k_{i+1}$.

For each $k_i < k \le k_{i+1}$, define new variables $\overline{V}_\mu(k)$ and $W_\mu(k)$, where $\mu$ is a parameter varying in the range $\mu \in \lfloor 0, \ v_{1,\max} - v_{1,\min})$

$$\overline{V}_\mu(k) = V_1^*(k-1)+\mu, \tag{37}$$

$$W_\mu(k) = \int_0^R \hat{b}_{11}^{(0)}(r,k)E_r[\overline{V}_\mu](k)dr. \tag{38}$$

If $W_1(k) > \overline{W}_{1,sat}(k)$, let $V_1^*(k) = v_{1,\max}$;

If $W_1(k) < \underline{W}_{1,sat}(k)$, let $V_1^*(k) = v_{1,\min}$;

If $\underline{W}_{1,sat}(k) \le W_1(k) \le \overline{W}_{1,sat}(k)$, the value of $V_1^*(k)$ is derived from the following algorithm.

Step 1: Let $\mu$ increase from 0.

Step 2: Calculate $\overline{V}_\mu(k)$ and $W_\mu(k)$. If $W_\mu(k) < W_1(k)$, then let $\mu$ increase continuously and go to Step 2; Otherwise, go to Step 3.

Step 3: Stop the increasing of $\mu$, memorize it as $\mu_0$ and define $V_1^*(k) = \overline{V}_{\mu_0}(k)$.

Similarly, $V_2^*(k)$ can be derived. In this paper, the adaptive control input is considered as

$$v_x(k) = V_1^*(k), \ v_y(k) = V_2^*(k). \tag{39}$$

**Theorem 1.** Consider the system (6) together with (21) controlled by the derived input (39). If $\underline{W}_{i,sat}(k) \le W_i(k) \le \overline{W}_{i,sat}(k)$ for $i=1,2$, then all the signals in the closed-loop remain bounded and $\lim_{k\to\infty} e(k) = 0$. Furthermore,

$$\lim_{k\to\infty}(z(k) - z_d(k)) = 0. \tag{40}$$

## 4    Experimental Results

For the experiment setup shown in Figure 1, the piezo electric actuators used in the experiment are PFT-1110 (Nihon Ceratec Corp.). The generated maximum force is not less than 80kgf. The maximum displacement is not smaller than $83\mu m$. The applied voltage range is -10V~150V. The non-contact capacitive displacement (NCCD) sensors (PS-1A, Nanotex Corp.) with 2nm resolution are used to measure the displacement of the stage. The real values of the parameters $A_1$, $A_2$, $B_0$, $B_1$ and the density functions in $P(r)$ are needed neither to be measured nor to be identified. The experiments are conducted for the following desired signal.

$$x_d = 5\sin(2\pi(k \times 10^{-3})) \ \mu m \ ,$$

$$y_d = 5\cos(2\pi(k \times 10^{-3})) \ \mu m \ .$$

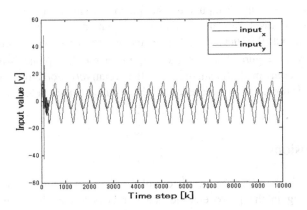

**Fig. 2.** Control inputs

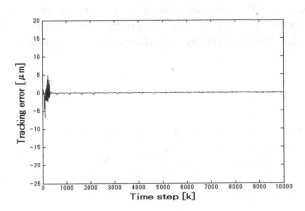

**Fig. 3.** Output tracking error in x-axis

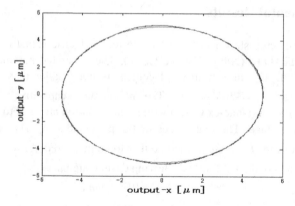

**Fig. 4.** Outputs in XY plane

Figure 2 shows the control inputs to the piezo actuators in x-axis and y-axis. Figure 3 shows the displacement error in x-axis, where the maximum error in the steady state is about $0.02\mu m$. The displacement error in y-axis is similar to that shown in Figure 3. Figure 4 shows the outputs in the XY plane, where a circle tracking can be confirmed. It can be seen that relatively good results have been obtained. Furthermore, the convergence of the estimated parameters has also been confirmed.

## 5    Conclusions

This paper has discussed the adaptive control for the piezo-actuated Positioner. The hysteresis existing in the piezo electric actuator is described by Prandtl-Ishlinskii model. Only the parameters directly needed in the formulation of the controller are adaptively estimated online, where the parameters of the table need not to be identified or measured. The proposed control law ensures the global stability of the controlled piezo-actuated positioner, and the position error can be controlled to be relatively small. Experimental results have shown the effectiveness of the proposed method.

## References

1. Brokate, M., Sprekels, J.: Hysteresis and Phase Transitions. Springer, New York (1996)
2. Chen, X., Hisayama, T.: Adaptive sliding mode position control for piezo-actuated stage. IEEE Transactions on Industrial Electronics 55, 3927–3934 (2008)
3. Fleming, A.J., Moheimani, S.O.R.: Sensorless vibration suppression and scan compensation for piezoelectric tube nanopositioners. IEEE Trans. on Control Systems Technology 14, 33–44 (2007)

4. Iyer, R.V., Tan, X., Krishnaprasad, P.S.: Approximate Inversion of the Preisach Hysteresis Operator with Application to Control of Smart Actuators. IEEE Transactions on Automatic Control 50, 798–810 (2005)

5. Krejci, P., Kuhnen, K.: Inverse control of systems with hysteresis and creap. Proc. Inst. Elect. Eng. Control Theory Applications 148, 185–192 (2001)

6. Kuhnen, K., Krejci, P.: Compensation of complex hysteresis and creep effects in piezoelectrically actuated systems – A new Preisach modeling approach. IEEE Transactions on Automatic Control 54, 537–550 (2009)

7. Su, C.-Y., Wang, Q., Chen, X., Rakheja, S.: Adaptive variable structure control of a class of nonlinear systems with unknown Prandtl-Ishlinskii hysteresis. IEEE Transactions on Automatic Control 50, 2069–2074 (2005)

8. Tao, G., Kokotovic, P.V.: Adaptive control of plants with unknown hysteresis. IEEE Trans. on Automatic Control 40, 200–212 (1995)

9. Tan, X., Baras, J.S.: Modeling and control of hysteresis in magnetostrictive actuators. Automatica 40, 1469–1480 (2004)

10. Visintin, A.: Differential Models of Hysteresis. Springer, New York (1994)

# Application of Fixed-Structure Genetic Programming for Classification

Xiaojun Wu[1,2,*] and Yue Ma[2]

[1] Key Laboratory of Modern Teaching Technology(Shaanxi Normal University), Ministry of Education, Xi'an Shaanxi 710062, China
[2] School of Computer Science, Shaanxi Normal University, Shaanxi Xi'an 710062, China
wythe@snnu.edu.cn

**Abstract.** There are three improvements based on GP algorithm in this paper and a fixed-structure GP algorithm for classification was proposed. Traditional GP algorithm relies on non-fixed-length tree structure to describe the classification problems. This algorithm uses a fixed-length linear structure instead of the traditional structure and optimizes the leaf nodes' coefficients based on the hill-climbing algorithm. Meanwhile, aiming at the samples on the classification boundaries, an optimization method of classification boundaries is proposed which makes the classification boundaries continuously tend to the optimal solutions in the program evolution process. At the end, an experiment is made by using this improved algorithm and a two- categories sample set with classification boundary is correctly classified (This sample set is an accurate data set from UCI database) Then it shows the analysis of classification results and the classification model produced by this algorithm. The experimental results indicates that the GP classification algorithm with fixed structure could improve the classification accuracy rate and accelerate the solutions' convergence speed, which is of great significance in the practical application of classification systems based on GP algorithm.

**Keywords:** GP algorithm, Classifier systems, Data mining, Classification boundary.

## 1 Introduction

Classification is an important part of data mining, its goal is to extract models which can describe the basic characteristics of classes from the data set and use these models to classify each sample in the data set into one of the known categories [1]. In machine learning field, the commonly used methods for classification in theory and application including Bayesian method, decision tree method, neural network, support vector machine (SVM) method, K-the nearest (KNN) method and so on. However, the applications of these methods have some limitations because of the complexity of classification problems. For example, Bayesian method requires the data have accurate distribution probability and does not support classifications based on features

---

* Corresponding author.

C.-Y. Su, S. Rakheja, H. Liu (Eds.): ICIRA 2012, Part I, LNAI 7506, pp. 22–33, 2012.

combination [2]; Decision tree method may cause the tree's structure very complicated so that the classification efficiency is low when the class space is huge; The Neural network has high requirements on weights, local convergence or divergence may occur if the weights chose improperly [3]; SVM method has some difficulties on solving multiple classification problems and is hard to carry out on a large scale of training samples [4]; KNN method needs to compare in all the sample spaces which makes the classification efficiency very low. Study on the limitations of these methods is one of the hot topics in this field.

Genetic Algorithm (Genetic Algorithm, GA) is a random method which uses the law of evolution (the survival of the fittest) for reference [5]. It is a general optimization algorithm, which does not need the certain rules and adaptively adjust the search direction in the search space. On the basis of it, American scholar Koza put forward the Genetic Programming Algorithm (Genetic Programming, GP) which uses the hierarchical computer program to describe a problem in the 1990s [6,7]. Compared with the traditional genetic algorithm using the long linear string to express problems, genetic programming uses a tree structure to describe the hierarchical problem and evolves by the thought of genetic algorithm. The most important feature of genetic programming algorithm is achieving the concurrent optimization of the structure and parameters. In recent years, it has been widely used in fields such as prediction and classification, image and signal processing, data mining, information retrieval and robot path planning [8].

## 2      GP Algorithm and Classification Problems

### 2.1      GP Algorithm

GP has the same frame with GA. At first, it creates a random population, then evaluates the fitness function of each individual, after that, applies evolution genetic operators Reproduction /Crossover/ Mutation) probabilistically to obtain a new computer program and evaluates the fitness function of new population after the new computer program is inserted into it. Repeat the last 3 steps until it finds the optimal solution.

We should notice that: 1. the GP individuals have tree structures, nodes of the trees are divided into two categories, branch nodes and leaf nodes. We must choose the proper candidate solutions for these two types of nodes before initialization. The branch nodes' candidate solution set is called functions set while that of the leaf nodes' is called terminals set. Individuals of original population are combined with n functions in functions set F: F= $\{f_1, f_2, \cdots, f_n\}$ and n terminals in terminals set T: T = $\{a_1, a_2, \cdots, a_n\}$. The functions in F can be mathematical operators, logical operators, trigonometric functions, logarithmic functions and exponential functions, conditional expressions, and iterated functions, etc. T includes constant and variable elements [9].

2. The genetic operation process of GP is much different from GA because the tree structures of GP can produce solutions of arbitrary size and complexity, as opposed to the fixed-length genetic algorithms. For example, in crossover operation, it randomly picks crossover points in both parents and swaps the sub trees. If the parents are same,

the offspring will often be different. The mutation is to pick a mutation point in one parent and replace its sub-tree with a randomly generated tree. The new tree's size may be different from the old one. Thus, the tree structure allows the GP algorithm to search the solution space more freely and makes the algorithm not easily fall into the local optimal solution.

3. Different from selection, crossover and mutation are operated in cycles in the groups, the genetic operations of GP is separately carried out in cycles. The next generation of groups includes some individuals after selection operation, some individuals after crossover operation and a small part if ones after mutation operation, which makes the better individuals retain in a higher rate.

4. In solving practical problems, GP algorithm constantly evolves and stops immediately when meeting the termination conditions. According to actual situations, usually there are two terminate standards: 1). reaching the maximum evolution generation; 2). Meeting the pre-set problem-solving conditions (such as the fitness of some individuals in groups reaches 0). For some problems, we couldn't determine their solving conditions, so the evolution is usually terminated according to the approximate successful conditions; we could also decide whether to terminate the evolution or not by analyzing the results when the evolution generation reaches a certain value if the problem-solving conditions could hardly be established.

## 2.2    GP Classification Algorithm

Appling the GP algorithm to solve classification problems is to find the link between data and mathematical expressions quickly by its own learning and do not need to reserve a lot of priori knowledge. Its algorithm structure is easy to combine with other algorithms, thus the classifier system based on GP algorithm has greater optimization spaces in all aspects. Its flexibility and powerful evolutionary search capability also show a strong advantage during the process of solving classification problems. Therefore, the GP algorithm's applying research has great advantages and significance in the classification areas.

The difficulty of GP classification algorithm lies in the classification boundaries determination and the fitness function design. How to determine the class boundaries has a direct impact on the classification accuracy. The common boundary determining methods are static class boundary method and based on center dynamic class boundary method.

The static class boundary method pre-sets class boundary values according to priori knowledge. The regions between the boundaries map different categories linearly and these boundary values and categories orders keep constant during the evolutionary process. That means for n-categories classification problems, we must pre-set n-1 boundaries and judge the sample's category according to which region the algorithm's output falls in[10,11], as shown in the following equation:

$$Class(X_i) = \begin{cases} class1 & if \ T(X_i) \le b_1 \\ class2 & if \ b_1 \le T(X_i) \le b_2 \\ \cdots\cdots \\ classn-1 & if \ b_{n-3} \le T(X_i) \le b_{n-2} \\ classn & if \ b_{n-2} \le T(X_i) \le b_{n-1} \end{cases} \tag{1}$$

The advantages of this method are fixed boundaries and the classification model in the evolutionary process does not need to be repeated calculation boundary, fast operation. However, in the iterative process of the program, the best boundary is a dynamic variable, the pre-set boundaries may not be the best and the demand for a priori knowledge of the method has some limitations.

The method based on the center of the dynamic boundary is a improvement method on the basis of static boundary method. Class boundary with a genetic program evolution process adjusts gradually, and the class order is nonlinear distribution with changing boundaries. The dynamic choosing boundary processes are as follows [12]:

**Step1:** Some fixed real number is given in advance as the initial boundary.

**Step2:** Every generation of evolution population genetic program has obtained the program output value. Repeat execution Step3 and Step4 in the evolutionary process.

**Step3:** According to the mean of the categories dynamically adjust the classification boundary. New boundaries and type of order are calculated by equation (2) and (3).

$$center_i = \frac{\sum_p \sum_{u_i} f(fitness_p) \times result_{pui}}{\sum_p \sum_{u_i} f(fitness_p)} \tag{2}$$

$$f(fitness) = \frac{2 \times (fitness \times (weight - 1) + 1)}{weight + 1} \tag{3}$$

p is the population scale. $u_i$ represents the sum of individuals which belong to class $i$. $center_i$ is the mean value of class $i$. $fitness_p$ is the fitness value of program p. $result_{pui}$ is the output value of the p-th genetic program of the k-th training sample in class $i$. f is a function which determines the weighting factor of procedures. The weight is the user-defined weighting factor.

**Step4:** Calculate the value of classification boundary according to the area and the mean of the adjacent categories.

**Step5:** Calculate the category that map the output vector of genetic program through the new boundary values and the fitness of a genetic program.

The dynamic boundary method does not need to rely on people's feeling and priori knowledge to set fixed class boundaries like static boundary method, which makes use of the system ability of self-study to dynamically determine the boundary range. This method strengthens the practicability of the classification system and expands its application domain. But the calculating formula of classification produced by dynamic boundary method is relatively complex, increased the amount of calculation program and cause the speed reduced. In this paper we made some improvements to the method of the dynamic boundary, the new method dynamically adjusts the classification boundary according to the errors of classification output model in the evolutionary process. The improvement algorithm avoids that using trivial mathematical formula repeatedly calculates the result, and reduces the calculation of program and complexity of the algorithm, improve the computational speed.

The implementing steps of GP classification algorithm is shown in figure 1. Initialization is to determine the training parameters, such as the crossover probability and mutation probability, population size, iteration number etc.

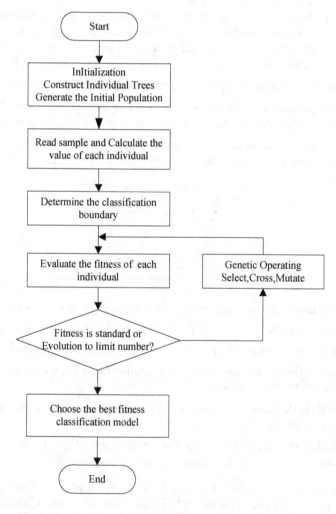

**Fig. 1.** The implementing steps of GP classification algorithm

## 3    Fixed-Structured GP for Solving Classification Problems

### 3.1    Fixed Structured Genetic Programming

In the evolution process of GP, the bloat, defined as an excess of tree growth without a corresponding improvement in fitness, may happen. This leads to the creation of a huge tree [13], which is useless and can also slow down the speed of evolution.

This paper firstly changes the description of classification problems to control the bloat. Instead of tree-structured traditional GP, we use a fixed-length linear table to describe the results of problems. A fixed structured Genetic Programming, which effectively controls the bloat problem, is proposed. Meanwhile, traditional description of hierarchical problem is changed into a fixed-length linear structure, thus, many improved algorithms of GA can be used to optimize the classification problems. For example, complete binary tree as shown in figure 2 describes the formula (4). # represents the terminator or function which has been neglected.

$$y = a * \ln(x_1) + b * \exp(x_1 * x_2) \tag{4}$$

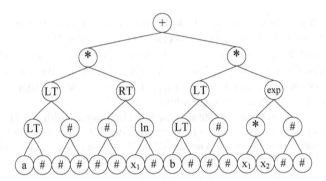

**Fig. 2.** The expressions of complete binary tree of formula (4)

Assume that the expression tree's depth is d, a fixed-length linear table with $2^d - 1$ nodes is used to store this binary tree and the tree could be got by preorder traversing this linear table. Makes $D = 2^d - 1$, then all expressions represented by a depth d binary tree can be described by a D-dimensional vector. The tree's structure is determined by traversal order. If it is preorder traversal, figure 2 can be expressed as string S shown in table 1.

**Table 1.** The ordinal expression of formula (4)

| Position | 1 | 2 | 3 | 4 | 5 | 6 | 7 | 8 | 9 | 10 | 11 | 12 | 13 | 14 | 15 | 16 |
|----------|---|---|---|---|---|---|---|---|---|----|----|----|----|----|----|----|
| Symbol | + | * | LT | LT | a | # | # | # | # | RT | # | # | # | ln | $x_1$ | # |
| Position | 17 | 18 | 19 | 20 | 21 | 22 | 23 | 24 | 25 | 26 | 27 | 28 | 29 | 30 | 31 | |
| Symbol | * | LT | LT | b | # | # | # | # | exp | * | $x_1$ | $x_2$ | # | # | # | |

The expression of fixed structured GP is made up of functions and terminals which are the same as traditional GP. Moreover, two additional functions, LT and RT, are added in the function set. LT means to get the left child of the node, while RT means to get the right one. Thus, the function set F={LT, RT, $f_1$, $f_2$, ..., $f_n$}. The terminal set is the same as before. By changing the function set, the result of hierarchical problem can be described by a complete binary tree. And the leaf node we defined in this paper includes two parts, a variable which represents the corresponding input of a specific system and a coefficient by which the variable is multiplied [14].

A complete binary tree with the depth d can be expressed by a linear table with the length $2^d - 1$. The order of nodes in the linear table is decided by the traversal sequence of the tree. In fixed structured GP, all trees have the same depth while the details of nodes vary from each other. Therefore, before the evolution, the positions of nodes in the linear table are fixed and would not change during the process, so the detail of a node, whether it's a leaf node or not and which function or terminal it represents, can be told by its position.

## 3.2    Hill-Climbing Algorithm

In the fixed structured GP for classification problems we proposed in this paper, every individual in the population represents a classification model. We have mentioned that the individual in this paper is a fixed-length linear table, and every leaf node is made up of a variable and a coefficient. Experiments have proved that the coefficients have a great influence on the precision of the model. Therefore, it is necessary to optimize the coefficients individually during the evolution.

In this paper, we used the thought that the hill-climbing algorithm [15] could find the local best to optimize the coefficients. Firstly, a specific climb time and the changing scope of coefficients are defined. The scope should not be too large, here we use -0.5 to 0.5. The processes of hill-climbing in this paper are as follows:

1) Calculate the fitness of the individual before its hill-climbing, named f(1)
2) Make a little change of coefficient in every leaf node, and every change is to plus a random number in [-0.5, 0.5]
3) Calculate the fitness of the individual after 2, named f(2)
4) Compare f(1) and f(2). If f(1)>f(2), representing that the changing individual is better than the original one, then the original individual is substituted by the changing one. Else if f(1)<f(2), representing the changing individual is not better, then the original individual stays.
5) Climb time add 1.
6) Repeat step 2~5 until climb time reaches the specified value

In this paper, every time when new individual is created, hill-climbing is used to optimize its coefficients. For example, after the population is initialized, every individual is optimized by hill-climbing. Also after crossover or mutation, new individual is optimized.

Hill-climbing of the coefficients can improve the precision of one individual, and finally we can get better classification model.

### 3.3   The Optimization of Classification Boundary and the Design of Fitness Function

Two-class classification is the foundation of multi-class classification. For two-class classification problems with classification boundary, the classification result can be signed as 1, -1, and 0, which 0 means the sample is on the boundary. However, the classification problems in our daily life usually don't have a boundary. Experiments have shown that fixed structured GP is effective to solve these problems, and the success ratio to classify the samples could reach 100% easily. Samples with values on the boundary, however, are hard to classify. Therefore, how to find the correct function of the boundary is the most essential problem to solve in the fixed structured GP. Classification boundary is shown in figure 3.

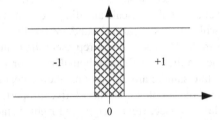

**Fig. 3.** Classification boundary

To classify the samples with values on the boundary, we proposed a method to find the boundary's function. First of all, a specific scope of classification error is given, and set a rule that the error value couldn't exceed the scope. This way is to prevent the circumstance that the fitness doesn't converge or the convergence speed is too slow. During the iteration of the algorithm, the classification error decreases constantly, and finally we could get a classification boundary model with the minimum error, which is the best boundary function of the samples. The detailed process is as follows:

1) The initial error value, e0, is given, 0.5, for example
2) The scope of classification error is given, (-0.5, 0.5), for example
3) Judge the current input sample, if the real classification of the sample is 0, then the sample is on the boundary
4) Calculate the output value, v, of the sample, if v is in the error scope, then e0= v, else e0 is still equals to 0.5

The classification error for samples not on the boundary is defined as follows:
If the real classification of the sample is 1 and the output value calculated is a positive number, then the classification error is 0, which means the classification for this sample is correct.

Else if the real classification of the sample is -1 and the output value calculated is a negative number, then the classification error is also 0.

Else, which represent the classification is wrong, and then the classification error is set to be a given number.

The method to calculate the fitness of an individual in the fixed structured GP is to calculate the quadratic sum of all samples' classification error. The experiment shows that the proposed optimization method of classification boundary could make the fitness converge to 0 quickly and efficiently, and finally we can get a better classification model.

# 4     The Classification of Balance Scale Sample

## 4.1     Sample Introduction

The classification of samples used for standard data sets in the UCI database. The sample name as follows: Balance Scale Data Set [16], contains the contents of the weight of left and right ends of balance scale and distance data. The samples are the two types of classification with the classification boundary, 0 is the classification boundary. There are 625 samples in the Data Set, which represent the equilibrium sample are 49 groups and these samples in the classification boundary, their value is 0. On behalf of the left state and right state sample are 288 groups, their category value is -1 and 1 in respectively. Each group of samples consists of five properties, from left to right: category, left weight, left distance, right weight and right distance. For example, the sample: [-1 1 4 3 1], which mean this sample's category value is -1and its left weight, left distance, right weight, right distance are 1,4,3and1 in respectively. All attribute values are integers, the attribute value intervals are [1 5] except class attribute value. There are no missing attribute values in the sample set.

Attribute Information:

1) Class Name: 3 (-1, 0, 1)
2) Left-Weight: 5 (1, 2, 3, 4, 5)
3) Left-Distance: 5 (1, 2, 3, 4, 5)
4) Right-Weight: 5 (1, 2, 3, 4, 5)
5) Right-Distance: 5 (1, 2, 3, 4, 5)

We used the $X_0$, $X_1$, $X_2$ and $X_3$ to represent the left weight, left distance, right weight and right distance. The correct way to find the class is $Y = (X_2 X_3 - X_0 X_1)$, and $Y$ is the result. If the result is 0, then the sample is on the classification boundary and its value is 0. If the result is negative, then the sample category to the left and its value is -1. If the result is positive, the sample category to the right and its value is 1.

In this algorithm, we used four properties as the input value except the category of sample to get an actual output value, and compared this value with the category value to obtain the classification error and fitness function value.

## 4.2    Analyze the Classification Model of the Fixed Structure

This paper used a fixed structured GP classification algorithm to generate classification model expressions, from which we selected several ones with different forms shown in Table 2 together with their corresponding simplified expressions.

**Table 2.** Classification Model Expression

| Classification Model Expression | Simplified Expression |
|---|---|
| $Y = 1.162763 X_2 \times 0.788191 X_3 - 0.980876 X_1 \times 0.934356 X_0$ | $Y = 0.916 \left( X_2 X_3 - X_0 X_1 \right)$ |
| $Y = 1.295937 X_2 \times 0.981643 X_3 - 1.037292 X_1 \times 1.226415 X_0$ | $Y = 1.272 \left( X_2 X_3 - X_0 X_1 \right)$ |
| $Y = 0.977162 X_3 \times 0.831456 X_2 - 0.546259 X_0 \times 1.487345 X_1$ | $Y = 0.813 \left( X_2 X_3 - X_0 X_1 \right)$ |
| $Y = 0.387432 X_3 \times (-0.293868 X_2) - 2.281428 X_1 \times 0.874852 X_0$ $+ 1.605700 X_2 \times 1.313906 X_3$ | $Y = 1.996 \left( X_2 X_3 - X_0 X_1 \right)$ |

Coefficients in the table above do not affect the classification results. From the table above, we can see that the classification models generated by the fixed structured GP classification algorithm are all equivalent, almost consistent with the accurate classification formula mentioned in section 4.1, proved that the classification models are able to classify the samples correctly. In this paper, the samples with classification boundary are divided into three types: 1, 0 and -1 according to the output. If the output $Y<0$, the sample category is -1; If $Y=0$, the sample is on the boundary; If $Y>0$, the sample category is 1.That is:

$$Y \begin{cases} >0 & \in CLASS\ 1 \\ =0 & \in CLASS\ 0 \\ <0 & \in CLASS-1 \end{cases}$$

The type of variable $X_0$, $X_1$, $X_2$ and $X_3$ is the characteristic parameters of a single sample. For example, to sample[1.0,1.0,1.0,1.0,2.0],the first value represents the sample of category -1,and the other values represents the characteristic parameters of sample, in the above model corresponding $X_0$, $X_1$, $X_2$ and $X_3$ four variables.

## 4.3    Model Validation

We randomly selected 15 groups samples from a given samples, each category contains five groups. Choose the first model from Table 2 to class the samples, the calculation results are shown in table 3.

**Table 3.** The Result of classification

| Category | Characteristic Parameter | | | | Result |
|---|---|---|---|---|---|
| | $X_0$ | $X_1$ | $X_2$ | $X_3$ | $Y$ |
| -1 | 1 | 2 | 1 | 1 | -0.916 |
| | 2 | 2 | 1 | 1 | -2.748 |
| | 3 | 2 | 1 | 3 | -2.748 |
| | 4 | 2 | 1 | 1 | -6.412 |
| | 5 | 3 | 2 | 4 | -6.412 |
| 0 | 1 | 1 | 1 | 1 | 0 |
| | 2 | 2 | 1 | 4 | 0 |
| | 3 | 2 | 2 | 3 | 0 |
| | 4 | 5 | 4 | 5 | 0 |
| | 5 | 4 | 5 | 4 | 0 |
| 1 | 1 | 2 | 3 | 4 | 9.165 |
| | 2 | 1 | 3 | 4 | 9.165 |
| | 3 | 1 | 4 | 1 | 0.916 |
| | 4 | 2 | 3 | 3 | 0.916 |
| | 5 | 3 | 5 | 4 | 4.582 |

From table 2, the optimal classification model that was trained out by the GP fixed structure classification algorithm can correctly class the given sample.

## 5    Conclusion

As a branch of GA, GP algorithm is widely used nowadays. This paper deeply researched the basic principle of GP algorithm and described the steps for solving classification problems by GP algorithm. Furthermore, some improvements are made on GP classification algorithm. The new algorithm is proved to be feasible by making experiments with real samples. In this paper, the classification models that generated by the fixed structured GP classification algorithm made the expression form of problems more simple and avoided the scale explosion phenomenon of traditional GP. It is convenient for us to use all kinds of GA improved methods on this algorithm to get better results. At the same time, the fixed structured GP classification algorithm obviously improved the classification accuracy rate and accelerated the solutions' convergence speed which makes it quite important for the practical application of classification systems based on GP algorithm.

**Acknowledgments.** This work reported in this paper was supported by the NSF of China (Grant no. 11172342), NSF of Shaanxi Province, China (Grant no. 2012JM8043) and Program for New Century Excellent Talents in University of Ministry of Education , China (Grant no. NCET-11-0674). The authors thank the referees for their valuable suggestions and comments.

# References

1. Zhang, Y., Gao, X.: Quantitative Evaluation of Classification Algorithms Used in Data Mining. J. Journal of Northwestern Polytechnical University 26(6), 718–722 (2008)
2. Luo, K., Lin, M., Xi, D.: Review of Classification Algorithms in Data Mining. J. Computer Engineering 31(1), 3–5 (2005)
3. Tong, X., Zhang, X., Liu, M.: Neural Network Classification with Optimization by Genetic Algorithms for Remote Sensing Imagery. J. Journal of Tong Ji University (Natural Science) 36(7), 985–989 (2008)
4. Cui, J., Li, Q., Liu, Y., Zong, D.: Fast SVM classification method based on the decision tree. J. Systems Engineering and Electronics 33(11), 2558–2563 (2011)
5. Holland, J.H.: Genetic Algorithms, pp. 66–72. Scientific American (July 1992)
6. Koza, J.R.: Genetic Programming: On the Programming of Computers by Means of Natural Selection. MIT Press, Cambridge (1992, 1994)
7. Koza, J.R.: Genetic Programming II: Automatic Discovery of Reusable Programs. MIT Press (1994)
8. Niu, A.: Study on Improvement and Application of Genetic Programming (2006)
9. Yun, Q., Huang, G., Wang, Z.: Genetic Algorithm and Genetic Programming. Metallurgical Industry Press, Beijing (1997)
10. Faraoun, K.M., Boukelif, A.: Genetic Programming Approach for Multi-Category Pattern Classification Applied to Network Intrusions Detection. International Journal of Computational Intelligence 3(1) (2006)
11. Winkler, S.M., Affenzeller, M.: Using enhanced genetic programming techniques for evolving classifiers in the context of medical diagnosis. Genetic Program Evolvable Mach., 111–140 (2009)
12. Ma, X.: The Research on Genetic Programming Techniques for Multi-classificatio. (2007)
13. Levenick, J.: Inserting introns improves genetic algorithm success rate: taking a cue from biology. In: Proceedings of the Fourth International Conference on Genetic Algorithm, pp. 120–131 (1991)
14. Wu, X., Xue, H., Li, M., Lan, Z.: A new programming of mixed genetic algorithm with particle swarm optimization. J. Journal of Northwest University (Natural Science Edition) 35(1), 39–43 (2005)
15. Hoffmann, J.: A Heuristic for Domain Independent Planning and Its Use in an Enforced Hill-Climbing Algorithm. In: Raś, Z.W., Ohsuga, S. (eds.) ISMIS 2000. LNCS (LNAI), vol. 1932, pp. 216–227. Springer, Heidelberg (2000)
16. Generated to model psychological experiments reported by Siegler, R. S. Three Aspects of Cognitive Development. Cognitive Psychology 8, 481–520 (1976)

# Variable Universe Fuzzy PID Control Strategy of Permanent Magnet Biased Axial Magnetic Bearing Used in Magnetic Suspension Wind Power Generator

Guangming Zhang, Lei Mei, and Yuhao Yuan

College of Automation and Electrical Engineering, Nanjing University of Technology
211816, Nanjing, China
zgmchina@163.com

**Abstract.** Improvements of wind power generator in energy utilization rate, electric generation efficiency and reliability can be achieved when maglev technology is applied. This paper presents a maglev horizontal axis wind power generator with two radial permanent magnet bearings and one permanent magnet biased axial magnetic bearing. The structure and working principle of the maglev wind power generator and axial magnetic bearing are presented. The finite element simulations of electromagnetic field in the axial magnetic bearing are performed by ANSYS, and the current stiffness and displacement stiffness are obtained. In order to fit the rapidity and randomness of wind load, the axial displacement of the rotor is controlled based on the variable universe fuzzy PID control strategy. The simulation of the control system is performed in MATLAB.

**Keywords:** wind power, magnetic bearing, variable universe, fuzzy PID control.

## 1    Introduction

Magnetic bearing is a new bearing part. It attracts great attention for its advantages of no mechanical contact, no wearing and no lubrication [1]. Applying the maglev technology to wind power generator can greatly improve the energy utilization rate, electric generation efficiency and reliability of the generator [2, 3].

Magnetic bearing can be classified into two types - passive magnetic bearing and active magnetic bearing, according to their controllability. Passive magnetic bearing can be further classified into normal permanent magnet bearing [4] and superconducting magnetic bearing [5]. For normal permanent magnet bearing, the natural repulsion or attraction force between magnetic materials is used to bear the rotor. For superconducting magnetic bearing, the diamagnetism of superconductor is used to provide suspension force.

On the other hand, active magnetic bearing can actively control the magnetic force between stator and rotor and realize stable suspensions of rotor. An active magnetic bearing system consists of electromagnet, displacement sensor, controller and power

C.-Y. Su, S. Rakheja, H. Liu (Eds.): ICIRA 2012, Part I, LNAI 7506, pp. 34–43, 2012.
© Springer-Verlag Berlin Heidelberg 2012

amplifier. According to the difference in the bias magnetic field establishment, the active magnetic bearing can be categorized into electromagnetic biased type and permanent magnet biased type. Conventional pure electromagnetic bearings have large power consumption because their bias magnetic fields and control magnetic fields are both created by electromagnets. In comparison, permanent magnet biased magnetic bearings have lower power consumption, smaller volume and lighter weight [6].

This paper presents a 5-DOF magnetic levitation wind power generator which consists one generator, two radial permanent magnet bearings and one permanent magnet biased axial magnetic bearing. The rotor is passively suspended by permanent magnet bearings in radial axis and actively controlled by permanent magnet biased magnetic bearing in axial axis. Such magnetic levitation system has low cost and energy consumption, and it has high application value in fields which with high demand on cost and power consumption such as electric power generation and energy storage systems[7, 8].

However, active magnetic bearing system is highly nonlinear and hard to develop a practical mathematical model base on. Hence, traditional PID control strategy is difficult to obtain the best control parameters, and the control parameters also cannot realize real-time online adjustment. the parameters tuning is more difficult especially when wind force which changes rapidly and randomly is the the load of magnetic bearing Many experts and engineers have been dedicated to the research of self-adjusting parameters. They combined fuzzy-control of intelligent control with traditional PID control and called it fuzzy-PID control [9]. In order to get better dynamic and static performance indicators of the system, this paper introduces the thought of variable universe [10] and suggests gives a brand-new PID control method variable universe fuzzy-PID control. It can improve the control precision of fuzzy-PID control system.

# 2     Structure of the Prototype

## 2.1    5-DOF Magnetic Levitation Wind Power Generator

The structure of a 5-DOF magnetic levitation wind power generator is shown in Fig. 1.

Two radial permanent magnet bearings are made of NdFeB rare earth material and magnetized in radial direction. The force between the stator and rotor is repulsive. The main load of these two radial permanent magnet bearings is the weight of the whole rotor. The two auxiliary bearings - are normal ball bearings and they support the rotor in radial and axial direction when the load goes beyond the capacity of the magnetic bearings or the active magnetic bearing losses its stability. The axial magnetic bearing is an active magnetic bearing and its bias magnetic field is established by permanent magnets to reduce energy consumption. The main load of the axial magnetic bearing is the axial components of the wind force imposed on the rotor though the impeller.

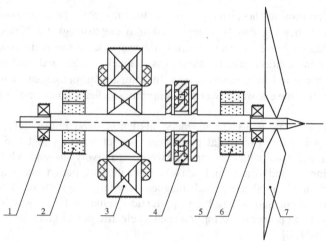

1. auxiliary bearing Ⅰ 2. radial permanent magnet bearing Ⅰ 3. generator
4. permanent magnet biased axial magnetic bearing 5. radial permanent magnet bearing Ⅱ 6.
auxiliary bearing Ⅱ 7. impeller

**Fig. 1.** Structure of 5-DOF magnetic levitation wind power generator

## 2.2    Permanent Magnet Biased Axial Magnetic Bearing

The structure of the permanent magnet biased axial magnetic bearing is given in Fig.
2. The axial stator and rotor core are made with solid soft magnetic material. The
axial control coils are made with enameled wires. The permanent magnet ring is made
from NdFeB rare earth material and magnetized in radial direction.

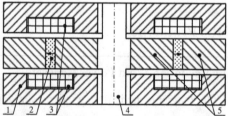

1. axial stator 2. permanent magnet ring 3. axial control coils 4. rotor 5. Rotor Core

**Fig. 2.** Structure of permanent magnet biased axial magnetic bearing

The body parameters of the permanent magnet biased axial magnetic bearing are
given in Table 1.

**Table 1.** Body parameters of the permanent magnet biased axial magnetic bearing

| Name | Value |
| --- | --- |
| Length of air gap | 0.5 mm |
| Total length | 43 mm |
| Total diameter | 68 mm |
| Rated bearing force | 800 N |

# 3    Mathematical Modeling of Magnetic Bearing Control System

## 3.1    Magnetic Bearing Closed-Loop Control System

Accordjng to the working principle of the active magnetic bearing system, the structure of single-degree-of-freedom magnetic bearing closed-loop control system is shown in Fig. 3.

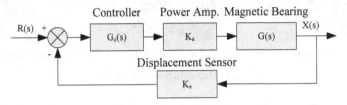

**Fig. 3.** Magnetic bearing closed-loop control system

The power amplifier and displacement sensor are both expressed as a proportional constant: $K_a$ and $K_s$, and $K_a=1$, $K_s=2000$.

In general, the linearized motion equation of magnetic bearing is expressed as Equation (1).

$$G(s) = \frac{X(s)}{I(s)} = \frac{-K_i}{ms^2 - K_x} \tag{1}$$

$m$: the weight of rotor.
$K_x$: the displacement stiffness.
$K_i$: the current stiffness.

The proportional constant $K_a$ and $K_s$ should be obtained before establishing the mathematical modeling of magnetic bearing.

## 3.2    Displacement Stiffness and Current Stiffness

In order to get the displacement stiffness and current stiffness of the axial magnetic bearing we establish a 3D finite element model in ANSYS, a software for finite element simulation. The meshed 3D finite element model is shown in Fig. 4.

**Fig. 4.** Meshed 3D finite element model of axial magnetic bearing

The simulation results of bias magnetic field, control magnetic field and superimposed magnetic field are shown in Fig. 5.

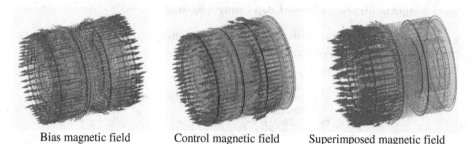

Bias magnetic field          Control magnetic field        Superimposed magnetic field

**Fig. 5.** Magnetic field simulation

After adjusting the rotor displacement from 0 to 0.25mm and obtaining from ANSY the bearing force in different displacements, we can get the displacement stiffness of the magnetic bearing, as shown in the left picture in Fig. 6. When the rotor is in the central place, adjust the control current from 0 to 3A and get from ANSY the bearing force in different current, then we can get the current stiffness of the magnetic bearing, as shown in the right picture in Fig. 6. From the curves we can get that the displacement stiffness is about 2800N/mm and the current stiffness is about 270N/A.

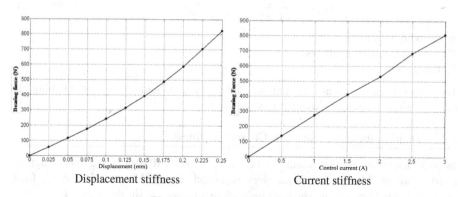

Displacement stiffness                  Current stiffness

**Fig. 6.** Magnetic field simulation

# 4      Variable Universe Fuzzy PID Control Strategy

## 4.1      Theory of the Variable Universe Fuzzy PID Control Strategy

The theory of variable universe says that under the premise of the same universe's fuzzy division, the universe contracts with decreasing error decreasing, and expands with increasing error. Universe contraction makes local refinement of rules, equivalent to increasing the number of rules. With that, the precision of the system control improves.

Assume that the fuzzy domain of input variable $x_i$ is $X_i=[-E, E]$, and the fuzzy domain output variable $y_j$ is $Y_j=[-U, U]$. Variable domain refers to the domain $X_i$ and $Y_j$ with changes in variables $x_i$ and $y_j$. Hence, we get:

$$X_i(x_i)=[-\alpha_i(x_i)\cdot E, \ \alpha_i(x_i)\cdot E] \tag{2}$$

$$Y_j(y_j)=[-\beta_j(y_j)\cdot U, \ \beta_j(y_j)\cdot U] \tag{3}$$

$\alpha_i(x_i)$: the expansion factor of input domain.
$\beta_j(y_j)$: the expansion factor output domain.
$i$: the number of input variables.
$j$: the number of output variables.

The key problem of variable universe fuzzy-PID controller is how to determine a reasonable mechanism of domain expansion. In other words, the key is to determine the appropriate expansion factor to guarantee ultimate control to meet requirements. Expansion factor commonly used is based on the function model.

So far, expansion factor of variable universe fuzzy control algorithm has not been in uniform forms, This article adopts the more commonly used function model of the universe expansion factor. Equation (4) and (5) present this function model used.

$$\alpha(x) = 1 - \lambda \exp(-kx^2) \tag{4}$$

where $\lambda \in (0, 1)$, $k>0$.

$$\beta(t) = K_i \sum_{i=1}^{n} p_i \int e_i(\tau)d\tau + \beta(0) \tag{5}$$

The structure of variable universe fuzzy-PID controller is given in Fig. 7. The control system primarily includes a conventional PID controller and a variable universe fuzzy controller.

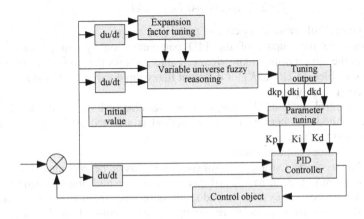

**Fig. 7.** Variable universe fuzzy PID control system

## 4.2    Design and Simulation of the Variable Universe Fuzzy PID Control Strategy

1) Selection and fuzzification of quantitative factors

According to the results of simulations, the basic domain of the input variables' displacement deviation $e$ and the deviation rate $ec$ are [-0.3, 0.3] and [-12, 12] Respectively, as for the output variables $\Delta k_p$ $\Delta k_i$ $\Delta k_d$, the basic domain are [-3, 3], [-0.6, 0.6], [-3, 3]. The fuzzy domain of all the variables is {-6, -5, -4, -3, -2, -1, 0, 1, 2, 3, 4, 5, 6}.

Quantization factor of the input variable e: qe=6/0.3=20;

Quantization factor of the input variable ec: qec=6/12=0.5;

Scaling factor of the output variable Δkp: qp=3/6=0.5;

Scaling factor of the output variable Δki: qi=0.6/6=0.1;

Scaling factor of the output variable Δkd: qd=3/6=0.5.

For these two input variables $e$ and $ec$ and output variables $\Delta k_p$ $\Delta k_i$ $\Delta k_d$ above, we take seven fuzzy subsets- NL (Negative Large), NM (Negative Medium), NS (Negative Small), ZE (Zero), PS (Positive Small), PM (Positive Medium), and PL (Positive Large) respectively.The shape of the membership function has an effect on the control performance. Taking into account the convenience of programming calculation in practice, we select the symmetric triangular function as the membership for all the variables.

2) Selection of expansion factors

According to the function model of expansion factor in Equation (4), we select $\lambda = 0.6$, $k = 0.5$.Then the expansion factors of the input domain are $\alpha(e)=1-0.6\exp(-0.5e^2)$, $\alpha(ec)=1-0.6\exp(-0.5ec^{2)}$ respectively.

Adopt the following principles for the expansion factor of output domain: the expansion factor of output variable $\Delta k_p$, $\Delta k_d$ should be monotonous consistent with error, while the expansion factor of output variable $\Delta k_i$ should be monotonous opposite to error. Therefore, the expansion factor of the output domain should make $\Delta k_p$, $\Delta k_d$ sufficiently large, and $\Delta k_i$ appropriately small. To do this, select the expansion factor of $\Delta k_p$, $\Delta k_d$ using the Equation (6) listed below:

$$\beta_p=2|e|; \; \beta_i=1/(|e|+0.7); \; \beta_d=2|e| \tag{6}$$

3) Fuzzy control rules and fuzzy control table

According to the impact of the PID parameters on system performance and referring to the expert domain knowledge, Table 2 shows the fuzzy control rule table of output variables $\Delta K_p, \Delta K_i, \Delta K_d$ for different fuzzy input variables $E$ and $EC$.

4) Fuzzy control algorithm

In this control system, the fuzzy rules are obtained according to 'Mamdani' reasoning method, the center of gravity method is selected as fuzzy inference and defuzzification method.

5) The initial values of parameters

According to chart of structure of magnetic suspension bearing closed-loop control system shown in Fig. 3, in MATLAB environment, we built the simulation diagram of the magnetic bearing system that adopted the conventional PID control based on SIMULINK. PID parameters were debugged and adjusted, and ultimately we obtained a suitable set of PID parameters $k_{p0}=5$, $k_{i0}=0.02$, $k_{d0}=0.01$, which are also the initial values of the variable domain PID control system.

**Table 2.** $\Delta Kp$, $\Delta Ki$, $\Delta Kd$ fuzzy control table

| E | EC | | | | | | |
|---|---|---|---|---|---|---|---|
| | NL | NM | NS | ZE | PS | PM | PL |
| NL | PB/PB/PB | PB/PB/PM | PM/PB/PB | PM/NM/PB | PS/NM/PB | ZE/NS/ZE | ZE/ZE/PS |
| NM | PB/PB/PM | PB/PB/PS | PM/PM/PB | PS/NS/PM | PS/NS/ZE | ZE/ZE/NM | NS/ZE/PS |
| NS | PB/PB/PS | PM/PB/ZE | PS/PS/PS | ZE/ZE/PS | NS/ZE/PS | NS/PS/PS | NM/PS/PS |
| ZE | PM/PB/PS | PS/PS/NB | PS/PS/PM | ZE/ZE/NS | NS/PS/SZ | NS/PM/NS | NM/PM/PS |
| PS | PS/PM/NS | PS/PS/NS | ZE/ZE/PS | NS/ZE/NS | NS/PS/SZ | NM/PB/ZE | NM/PB/PS |
| PM | PS/PS/NB | ZE/ZE/PS | NS/ZE/PS | NM/NS/ZE | NM/PS/NS | NM/PB/NS | NB/PB/PS |
| PL | ZE/ZE/NB | ZE/ZE/PS | NM/ZE/NS | NM/NM/ZE | NM/PB/PS | NB/PB/NM | NB/PB/PS |

According to equation (1) and stiffness parameters from finite element simulation, we established the simulation model in MATLAB. The variable universe fuzzy self-adaptive subsystem is given in Fig. 8, and the PID control subsystem is given in Fig. 9.

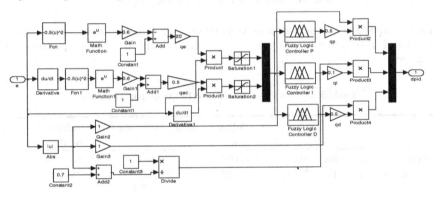

**Fig. 8.** Variable universe fuzzy self-adaptive subsystem

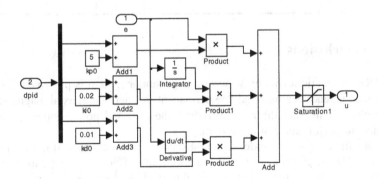

**Fig. 9.** PID control subsystem

Imposing a step-input with amplitude of 0.2 (The amplitude express the given input value which was set when thrust plate displacement the equilibrium position of 1 mm), we got the simulation curve shown in Fig. 10. The curve (3), (2), (1) represent the different controllers of magnetic bearing control system in Fig. 3, which are conventional PID control, conventional fuzzy PID control and variable universe fuzzy PID control.

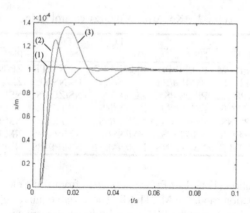

**Fig. 10.** Compare of different control strategy

Table 3 shows the comparison of conventional PID control, conventional fuzzy PID control and variable universe fuzzy PID control in control performance parameters.

**Table 3.** Comparison in control performance parameters

|  | Overshoot | Adjusting time (s) | Peak time (s) | Adaptive ability |
|---|---|---|---|---|
| Conventional PID control | 38% | 0.052 | 0.017 | No |
| Conventional fuzzy PID control | 21% | 0.025 | 0.013 | Good |
| Variable universe fuzzy PID control | 8% | 0.013 | 0.008 | Very good |

## 5    Conclusions

A 5-DOF magnetic levitation wind power generator system is presented. Two radial permanent magnet bearings and one permanent magnet biased axial magnetic bearing are applied to suspend the rotor to reduce the cost and power consumption and to advance the performance of the system.

A 3D finite element model is established in finite element simulation software ANSYS. The displacement stiffness and current stiffness of the permanent magnet biased axial magnetic bearing are obtained through magnetic field simulation.

In order to improve the control performance of the axial magnetic bearing, a variable universe fuzzy PID control strategy is investigated. The simulation results in MATLAB show that the variable universe fuzzy-PID control strategy is superior to conventional PID control strategy and conventional fuzzy PID control strategy in static performance and dynamic performance.

# References

1. Schweitzer, G.: Active Magnetic Bearings-Chances and Limitations. In: Sixth International Conference on Rotor Dynamic, pp. 1–14. Elsevier Ltd., Australia (2002)
2. Shrestha, G., Polinder, H., Bang, D.J., Ferreira, J.A.: Structural Flexibility: A Solution for Weight Reduction of Large Direct-Drive Wind-Turbine Generators. IEEE Transactions on Energy Conversion 25(3), 732–740 (2010)
3. Kumbernuss, J., Jian, C., Wang, J., Yang, H.X., Fu, W.N.: A Novel Magnetic Levitated Bearing System for Vertical Axis Wind Turbines. Applied Energy 90(1), 148–153 (2012)
4. Younet, J.P.: Passive Magnetic Bearings with Permanent Magnets. IEEE Transactions on Magnetics 14(5), 803–805 (1978)
5. Hull, J.R.: Superconducting bearings. Supercond. Sci. Technol. 13, 1–15 (2000)
6. Ehmanm, C., Sielaff, T., Nordmann, R.: Comparison of Active Magnetic Bearings with and without Permanent Magnet Bias. In: Ninth International Symposium on Magnetic Bearings, pp. 105–110. University of Kentucky, USA (2004)
7. Wu, H., Wang, Z., Hu, Y.: Study on Magnetic Levitation Wind Turbine for Vertical Type and Low Wind Speed. In: Asia-Pacific Power and Energy Engineering Conference, pp. 1–4 (2010)
8. Nguyen, T.D., Tseng, K.J., Zhang, S., Nguyen, H.T.: A Novel Axial Flux Permanent-Magnet Machine for Flywheel Energy Storage System Design and Analysis. IEEE Transactions on Industrial Electronics 58(9), 3784–3794 (2011)
9. Chen, K.-Y., Tung, P.-C., Tsai, M.-T., Fan, Y.-H.: A Self-Tuning Fuzzy PID-Type Controller Design for Unbalance Compensation in an Active Magnetic Bearing. Expert Systems with Applications 36(4), 8560–8570 (2009)
10. Shan, W., Ma, Y., Newcomb, R.W., Jin, D.: Analog Circuit Implementation of a Variable Universe Adaptive Fuzzy Logic Controller. IEEE Transactions on Circuits and Systems 55(10), 976–980 (2008)

# Adaptive Dynamic Surface Control
## of a Class of Nonlinear Systems
## with Unknown Duhem Hysteresis

Yong-Hua Liu[1], Ying Feng[1,*], Juan Du[1], and Chun-Yi Su[1,2]

[1] College of Automation Science and Engineering,
South China University of Technology, Guangzhou, Guangdong, 510641, China
[2] Department of Mechanical and Industrial Engineering,
Concordia University, Montreal, Quebec, H3G 1M8, Canada
{scutliux,chunyi.su}@gmail.com, {yfeng,dujuan}@scut.edu.cn

**Abstract.** In this paper, the tracking problem for a class of uncertain perturbed strict-feedback nonlinear systems with unknown Duhem hysteresis input is investigated. Different with the conventional nonlinear systems, the existence of the unknown preceded hysteresis will affect the system performance and bring a challenge for the controller design. To overcome the difficulties caused by the unknown hysteresis, the Duhem model is used to describe the hysteresis in this paper. The properties of the Duhem model are utilized to get the explicit expression of the hysteresis output, which makes it possible to deal with the unknown hysteresis input. Following the conventional backstepping design procedure, a dynamic surface control method in each step is used to avoid "the explosion complexity" in the backstepping design, and the Nussbaum function method is used to solve the time-varying coefficient problem in the explicit expression of the Duhem model. Under the proposed control approach, the semiglobal uniform ultimate boundedness of all the signals in the close-loop system is guaranteed. The effectiveness of the proposed design scheme is validated through a simulation example.

**Keywords:** Nonlinear systems, hysteresis, dynamic surface control.

## 1 Introduction

As a class of strongly nonlinear phenomena, hysteresis nonlinearities occur in numerous physical systems and industrial elements, such as electromagnetic fields, mechanical systems, and smart materials-based actuators [1–3]. Compared with the conventional nonlinearities, non-smooth and multi-values properties of hysteresis limit the system performance, and the available traditional control approaches may not be effective for these systems. Therefore, the modeling and control problems for the controlled systems with hysteresis have attracted more attention, and the unknown hysteresis as the systems input becomes a new challenge for the control system design.

---

* Corresponding author.

C.-Y. Su, S. Rakheja, H. Liu (Eds.): ICIRA 2012, Part I, LNAI 7506, pp. 44–55, 2012.

Addressing this challenge, the hysteresis modeling methods become the primary step for the control design. So far, hysteresis models can be simple classified as operator-based hysteresis models, such as Preisach model, Krasnosel'skii-Pokrovskii (KP) model, and Prandtl-Ishlinskii (PI) model etc. [4–6], and differential equation-based hysteresis models, such as backlash-like model, Bouc-Wen model and Duhem model etc. [7–9].

Recently, lots of new control strategies based on the above various hysteresis model are developed to suppress the detrimental effects caused by hysteresis non-linearities [10–12]. These control approaches can also be classified as constructing the hysteresis inverse and without constructing the hysteresis inverse. Constructing the hysteresis inverse approach is pioneered by Tao and Kokotovic [13]. The main advantage of this approach is to cancel the negative effects caused by hysteresis directly, when the inverse model matches the hysteresis exactly. However, this method is very sensitive to the model parameters and may cause a new difficulty for the stability analysis. To avoid these difficulties, another alternative control approach without constructing the hysteresis inverse is developed in [7]. As an illustration, a robust adaptive control law was investigated for a class of nonlinear systems with unknown backlash-like hysteresis [7]. Adaptive variable structure control was proposed for a class of nonlinear systems preceded by PI hysteresis in [14]. The common feature of this scheme is the hysteresis model can be decomposed as linear component and nonlinear bounded component[15–17], and this property can be utilized in the control design.

In this paper, the Duhem model is used to represent the hysteresis nonlinearities. The Duhem model can describe a class of general hysteresis shapes by choosing different input functions. However, due to the existence of the nonlinear input functions, it generates the difficulty for the controller design, which needs a special new treatment. By exploring the characteristics of the Duhem model, the explicit expression of the Duhem model can be transferred as a linear input with time-varying coefficient, which facilitates the control design. Different with the classical backstepping method, the dynamic surface control (DSC) method without the inverse of the Duhem hysteresis is discussed in this paper. This method can mitigate the effects caused by the Duhem hysteresis effectively and avoid "the explosion complexity" coming from the backstepping by applying the low-pass filters in the design of dynamic control laws [18]. Under the proposed control approach, semiglobal uniform ultimate boundedness of all the signals in the close-loop system is guaranteed. Finally, the effectiveness of the proposed design scheme is validated through a simulation.

## 2   Problem Statement

Consider a class of perturbed strict-feedback nonlinear systems with unknown hysteresis nonlinearities described as

$$
\begin{cases}
\dot{x}_i = \theta_i f_i(\bar{x}_i(t)) + g_i x_{i+1}(t) + d_i(x(t), t) \\
\dot{x}_n = \theta_n f_n(x(t)) + g_n w(t) + d_n(x(t), t) \\
y = x_1
\end{cases}
\tag{1}
$$

where $\bar{x}_i(t) = [x_i(t), ..., x_i(t)]^T \in R^i, i = 1, ..., n$ are the system states, $x(t) := \bar{x}_n(t) = [x_1(t), ..., x_n(t)]^T \in R^n$. $y \in R$ is the system output. $g_i, \theta_i, i = 1, ..., n$ are unknown system parameters. $d_i(x(t), t), i = 1, ..., n$ denote the unknown uncertain disturbances. $f_i(\cdot), i = 1, ..., n$ are known smooth functions. $w(t) \in R$ is the system input, which is also the output of the preceded hysteresis. In this paper, the hysteresis is represented by the Duhem model in [9] as follows:

$$\frac{dw}{dt} = \alpha \left| \frac{du}{dt} \right| (\lambda(u) - w) + \frac{du}{dt} \psi(u) \tag{2}$$

where $u$ is the input of the hysteresis, $\alpha$ is a constant, and the Duhem hysteresis model discussed in this paper satisfies three conditions[6].

*Condition 1.* $\lambda(u)$ is piecewise smooth, monotone increasing, odd, with $\lim_{u \to \infty} \dot{\lambda}(u)$ finite.

*Condition 2.* $\psi(u)$ is piecewise continuous, even, with

$$\lim_{u \to \infty} \psi(u) = \lim_{u \to \infty} \dot{\lambda}(u) \tag{3}$$

*Condition 3.* $\dot{\lambda}(u) > \psi(u) > \alpha e^{\alpha u} \int_u^\infty |\dot{\lambda}(\zeta) - \psi(\zeta)| e^{-\alpha \zeta} d\zeta$ for all $u > 0$.

Satisfying the above conditions, the Duhem model defined in (2) can be solved explicitly as [6]

$$w = \lambda(u) + \varphi(u) \tag{4}$$

where

$$\varphi(u) = [w_0 - \lambda(u_0)] e^{-\alpha(u - u_0) sgn(\dot{u})}$$
$$+ e^{-\alpha u sgn(\dot{u})} \int_{u_0}^u [\psi(\zeta) - \dot{\lambda}(\zeta)] e^{\alpha \zeta sgn(\dot{u})} d\zeta$$

In [6], it has been proven that $\varphi(u)$ is bounded.

Since $\lambda(u)$ in Duhem model satisfies Condition 1, it is obvious that the mean value theorem can be used for $\lambda(u)$. By choosing $\lambda(\theta) = 0$, $\lambda(u)$ in (4) can be expressed as follows

$$\lambda(u) = \lambda(u) - \lambda(\theta) = \dot{\lambda}(\vartheta(u))(u - \theta) \tag{5}$$

where $\vartheta(u) = \varsigma u + (1 - \varsigma)\theta$ with $0 \le \varsigma \le 1$.

Utilizing this transform based on mean value theorem, the Duhem hysteresis output $w$ can re-presented as

$$w(t) = \dot{\lambda}(\vartheta(u))u - \dot{\lambda}(\vartheta(u))\theta + \varphi(u(t)) \tag{6}$$

For the convenience of expression, we define the function $L(t)$ as

$$L(t) = \dot{\lambda}(\vartheta(u(t))) \tag{7}$$

then $w$ can be expressed as

$$w(t) = L(t)u(t) + S(t) \qquad (8)$$

where $S(t) = -L(t)\theta + \varphi(u(t))$.

Substituting (8) into the controlled systems defined in (1), it has

$$\begin{cases} \dot{x}_i = \theta_i f_i(\bar{x}_i(t)) + g_i x_{i+1}(t) + d_i(x(t), t) \\ \dot{x}_n = \theta_n f_n(x(t)) + g_n[L(t)u(t) + S(t)] + d_n(x(t), t) \\ y = x_1 \end{cases} \qquad (9)$$

## 3   Adaptive DSC Design and Stability Analysis

In this section, the adaptive dynamic surface control design method and the stability of the closed-loop system are presented.

In order to present the developed control laws, the following assumptions regarding the systems (9) and a lemma are required.

*Assumption 1.* The desired trajectory vectors are continuous and available, and $[y_d, \dot{y}_d, \ddot{y}_d]^T \in \Omega_d$ with known compact set $\Omega_d = \{[y_d, \dot{y}_d, \ddot{y}_d]^T : y_d^2 + \dot{y}_d^2 + \ddot{y}_d^2 \le B_0\}$ $\subset R^3$, whose size $B_0$ is a known positive constant.

*Assumption 2.* The signs of $g_i$ are known, and there exist unknown positive constants $g_{i0}$ and $g_{i1}$ such that $0 < g_{i0} \le |g_i| \le g_{i1} < \infty$. Without loss of generality, it is assumed that $0 < g_{i0} \le g_i, i = 1, ..., n$.

*Assumption 3.* The disturbances terms $d_i(x(t), t), i = 1, \dots, n$ satisfy

$$|d_i(x(t), t)| \le b_i \rho_i(\bar{x}_i(t)) \qquad (10)$$

where $\rho_i(\bar{x}_i(t))$ are known positive smooth functions and $b_i$ are unknown positive constants.

*Assumption 4.* There exist unknown positive constants $h_0$ and $h_1$, such that

$$0 < h_0 \le \dot{\lambda}(u) \le h_1 \qquad (11)$$

*Remark 1.* Assumption 1 is a basic requirement of dynamic surface control method. For Assumptions 2, it is reasonable to assume the bound of the disturbances terms $d_i(x(t), t), i = 1, \dots, n$. Assumption 3 is a basic condition for control system (9) to avoid the controller singularity. It should be noted that the values of $g_{i0}$ and $g_{i1}$ are not needed to be known. Assumption 4 implies that $L(t)$ and $\varphi(u(t))$ are bounded, and further means the term $S(t)$ is bounded, we denote it as $D$, where $D$ is an unknown positive constant.

*Lemma 1.* Let $V(.), \zeta(.)$ be the smooth functions defined on $[0, t_f]$ with $V(t) \geq 0, \forall t \in [0, t_f]$, and let $N(.)$ be an ever smooth Nussbaum-type function [19]. If the following inequalities holds:

$$V(t) \leq c_0 + e^{-c_1 t} \int_0^t [G(.)N(\zeta) + 1]\dot{\zeta}e^{c_1 \tau} d\tau \qquad (12)$$

where $c_0$ represents some suitable constant, $c_1$ is a positive constant, and $G(.)$ is a time-varying parameter which takes values in the unknown closed intervals $I = [l^-, l^+]$, with $0 \notin I$, and then $V(t), \zeta(t)$, and $\int_0^t G(.)N(\zeta)\dot{\zeta}d\tau$ must be bounded on $[0, t_f]$.

## 3.1   Adaptive DSC Design

Due to the strong nonsmooth and multi-values properties of the hysteresis, the conventional control approaches may not be effective for the systems preceded by hysteresis. Besides, the system input is not obtained since the output of the hysteresis is unknown, which brings a new challenge for the controller design. In this section, one adaptive dynamic surface controller is investigated for a class of nonlinear systems to explore the way handling the unknown hysteresis input.

Firstly, the following coordinate transformation are used: $z_1 = x_1 - y_d$ and $z_i = x_i - s_{i-1}, i = 2, ..., n$, where $s_{i-1}$ are the output of a first order filters with the input $\alpha_{i-1}$ as

$$\mu_i \dot{s}_i + s_i = \alpha_i, \quad s_i(0) = \alpha_i(0), \quad i = 1, ..., n - 1. \qquad (13)$$

where $\mu_i$ are the filter parameters, $\alpha_i$ are the intermediate control for the $i$th subsystems and their definitions will be given thereinafter.

For the dynamic surface control design, the boundary filter errors $e_i$ are defined as

$$e_i = s_i - \alpha_i, \quad i = 1, ..., n - 1. \qquad (14)$$

*Step i* $(1 \leq i \leq n - 1)$. For convenience, we denote $\frac{e_0}{\mu_0} = -\dot{y}_d, g_0 = 0$. Utilizing $z_i = x_i - s_{i-1}$ and the definitions for $s_i$ and $e_i$ in (13) and (14), it has

$$s_i = e_i + \alpha_i, \dot{s}_i = -\frac{e_i}{\tau_i}, i = 1, ..., n - 2. \qquad (15)$$

$$\begin{aligned}
\dot{z}_i &= \theta_i f_i(\bar{x}_i(t)) + g_i x_{i+1}(t) + d_i(x(t), t) + \frac{e_{i-1}}{\tau_{i-1}} \\
&= \theta_i f_i(\bar{x}_i(t)) + g_i[z_{i+1} + \alpha_i + e_i] + d_i(x(t), t) + \frac{e_{i-1}}{\tau_{i-1}}
\end{aligned} \qquad (16)$$

Choose the following Lyapunov functions as

$$V_i = V_{i-1} + \frac{1}{2}\left(\frac{1}{g_i}z_i^2 + \frac{1}{\gamma_{\theta_i}}\tilde{\theta}_{g_i}^2 + \frac{1}{\gamma_{b_i}}\tilde{b}_{g_i}^2 + \frac{1}{\gamma_{\bar{g}_i}}\tilde{\bar{g}}_{g_i}^2\right) \qquad (17)$$

where $\tilde{\theta}_{g_i} = \theta_{g_i} - \hat{\theta}_{g_i}, \tilde{b}_{g_i} = b_{g_i} - \hat{b}_{g_i}$ and $\tilde{\bar{g}}_{g_i} = \bar{g}_{g_i} - \hat{\bar{g}}_{g_i}$ with $\hat{\theta}_{g_i}, \hat{b}_{g_i}$ and $\hat{\bar{g}}_{g_i}$ as the estimation of $\theta_{g_i} = \theta_i/g_i, b_{g_i} = b_i/g_i$ and $\bar{g}_{g_i} = 1/g_i$, respectively. $\gamma_{\theta_i}, \gamma_{b_i}$ and $\gamma_{\bar{g}_i}$ are positive design parameters. Then we have

$$\dot{V}_i = \dot{V}_{i-1} + \frac{z_i}{g_i}(\theta_i f_i(\bar{x}_i(t)) + g_i[z_{i+1} + \alpha_i + e_i] + d_i(x(t), t) + \frac{e_{i-1}}{\tau_{i-1}})$$

$$+ \frac{1}{\gamma_{\theta_i}}\tilde{\theta}_{g_i}\dot{\hat{\theta}}_{g_i} + \frac{1}{\gamma_{b_i}}\tilde{b}_{g_i}\dot{\hat{b}}_{g_i} + \frac{1}{\gamma_{\bar{g}_i}}\tilde{\bar{g}}_{g_i}\dot{\hat{\bar{g}}}_{g_i}$$

$$\leq \dot{V}_{i-1} + z_i(z_{i-1} + \theta_{g_i}f_i(\bar{x}_i(t)) + \alpha_i + b_{g_i}\rho_i(\bar{x}_i(t))\tanh(\frac{z_i\rho_i(\bar{x}_i(t))}{\omega}) + \bar{g}_{g_i}\frac{e_{i-1}}{\tau_{i-1}})$$

$$+ z_i z_{i+1} - z_i z_{i-1} + z_i e_i + 0.2785\omega b_{g_i} + \frac{1}{\gamma_{\theta_i}}\tilde{\theta}_{g_i}\dot{\hat{\theta}}_{g_i} + \frac{1}{\gamma_{b_i}}\tilde{b}_{g_i}\dot{\hat{b}}_{g_i} + \frac{1}{\gamma_{\bar{g}_i}}\tilde{\bar{g}}_{g_i}\dot{\hat{\bar{g}}}_{g_i}$$

$$= \dot{V}_{i-1} + z_i(z_{i-1} + \hat{\theta}_{g_i}f_i(\bar{x}_i(t)) + \alpha_i + \hat{b}_{g_i}\rho_i(\bar{x}_i(t))\tanh(\frac{z_i\rho_i(\bar{x}_i(t))}{\omega}) + \hat{\bar{g}}_{g_i}\frac{e_{i-1}}{\tau_{i-1}})$$

$$+ z_i z_{i+1} - z_i z_{i-1} + z_i e_i + 0.2785\omega b_{g_i} + \tilde{\theta}_{g_i}(z_i f_i(\bar{x}_i(t)) - \frac{1}{\gamma_{\theta_i}}\dot{\hat{\theta}}_{g_i})$$

$$+ \tilde{b}_{g_i}(z_i\rho_i(\bar{x}_i(t))\tanh(\frac{z_i\rho_i(\bar{x}_i(t))}{\omega}) - \frac{1}{\gamma_{b_i}}\dot{\hat{b}}_{g_i}) + \tilde{\bar{g}}_{g_i}(z_i\frac{e_{i-1}}{\tau_{i-1}} - \frac{1}{\gamma_{\bar{g}_i}}\dot{\hat{\bar{g}}}_{g_i}) \quad (18)$$

By choosing the adaptive virtual control $\alpha_i$ and adaptive laws for $\hat{\theta}_{g_i}, \hat{b}_{g_i}$ and $\hat{\bar{g}}_{g_i}$ for the $i$th subsystem as

$$\alpha_i = -k_i z_i - z_{i-1} - \hat{\theta}_{g_i}f_i(\bar{x}_i(t))$$
$$- \hat{b}_{g_i}\rho_i(\bar{x}_i(t))\tanh(\frac{z_i\rho_i(\bar{x}_i(t))}{\omega}) - \hat{\bar{g}}_{g_i}\frac{e_{i-1}}{\tau_{i-1}} \quad (19)$$

$$\dot{\hat{\theta}}_{g_i} = \gamma_{\theta_i}(z_i f_i(\bar{x}_i(t)) - \varpi_i\hat{\theta}_{g_i}) \quad (20)$$

$$\dot{\hat{b}}_{g_i} = \gamma_{b_i}(z_i\rho_i(\bar{x}_i(t))\tanh(\frac{z_i\rho_i(\bar{x}_i(t))}{\omega}) - \mu_i\hat{b}_{g_i}) \quad (21)$$

$$\dot{\hat{\bar{g}}}_{g_i} = \gamma_{\bar{g}_i}(z_i\frac{e_{i-1}}{\tau_{i-1}} - \nu_i\hat{\bar{g}}_{g_i}) \quad (22)$$

where $k_i, \varpi_i, \mu_i, \nu_i$ are positive design parameters, and using the following inequalities

$$\varpi_i\tilde{\theta}_{g_i}\hat{\theta}_{g_i} \leq \frac{\varpi_i}{2}(-\tilde{\theta}_{g_i}^2 + \theta_{g_i}^2) \quad (23)$$

$$\mu_i\tilde{b}_{g_i}\hat{b}_{g_i} \leq \frac{\mu_i}{2}(-\tilde{b}_{g_i}^2 + b_{g_i}^2) \quad (24)$$

$$\nu_i\tilde{\bar{g}}_{g_i}\hat{\bar{g}}_{g_i} \leq \frac{\nu_i}{2}(-\tilde{\bar{g}}_{g_i}^2 + \bar{g}_{g_i}^2) \quad (25)$$

it can be obtained

$$\dot{V}_i \leq -\sum_{j=1}^{i} k_j z_j^2 - \sum_{j=1}^{i}\left(\frac{\varpi_1}{2}\tilde{\theta}_{g_1}^2 + \frac{\mu_1}{2}\tilde{b}_{g_1}^2 + \frac{\nu_i}{2}\tilde{\bar{g}}_{g_1}^2\right)$$

$$+z_i z_{i+1} + \sum_{j=1}^{i}\left(z_j e_j + 0.2785\omega b_{g_j} + \frac{\varpi_j}{2}\tilde{\theta}_{g_j}^2 + \frac{\mu_i}{2}\tilde{b}_{g_j}^2 + \frac{\nu_i}{2}\tilde{\bar{g}}_{g_j}^2\right) \quad (26)$$

*Step n.* In the last step, the control law $u(t)$ will be designed to ensure the performance of the closed-loop system. Similarly, Considering $z_n = x_n - s_{n-1}$ and $\dot{s}_{n-1} = -e_{n-1}/\mu_{n-1}$, it has

$$\dot{z}_n = \theta_n f_n(x(t)) + g_n[L(t)u(t) + S(t)] + d_n(x(t), t) + \frac{e_{n-1}}{\tau_{n-1}} \quad (27)$$

and the Lyapunov-Krasovskii function for the system can be chosen as

$$V_n = V_{n-1} + \frac{1}{2}\left(z_n^2 + \frac{1}{\gamma_{\theta_n}}\tilde{\theta}_{g_n}^2 + \frac{1}{\gamma_{b_n}}\tilde{b}_{g_n}^2 + \frac{1}{\gamma_{\bar{g}_n}}\tilde{\bar{g}}_{g_n}^2\right) \quad (28)$$

where $\tilde{\theta}_{g_n} = \theta_{g_n} - \hat{\theta}_{g_n}, \tilde{b}_{g_n} = b_{g_n} - \hat{b}_{g_n}$ and $\tilde{\bar{g}}_{g_n} = \bar{g}_{g_n} - \hat{\bar{g}}_{g_n}$ with $\hat{\theta}_{g_n}, \hat{b}_{g_n}$ and $\hat{\bar{g}}_{g_n}$ as the estimation of $\theta_{g_n} = \theta_n, b_{g_n} = b_n, \bar{g}_{g_n} = g_n D$, respectively. $\gamma_{\theta_n}, \gamma_{b_n}$ and $\gamma_{\bar{g}_n}$ are positive design parameters.

Based on the expression for $z_n$ in (27), we have

$$\dot{V}_n = \dot{V}_{n-1} + z_n\left(\theta_n f_n(x(t)) + g_n[L(t)u(t) + S(t)] + d_n(x(t), t) + \frac{e_{n-1}}{\tau_{n-1}}\right)$$

$$+\frac{1}{\gamma_{\theta_i}}\tilde{\theta}_{g_n}\dot{\tilde{\theta}}_{g_n} + \frac{1}{\gamma_{b_n}}\tilde{b}_{g_n}\dot{\tilde{b}}_{g_n} + \frac{1}{\gamma_{\bar{g}_n}}\tilde{\bar{g}}_{g_n}\dot{\tilde{\bar{g}}}_{g_n}$$

$$= \dot{V}_{n-1} + z_n\theta_n f_n(x(t)) + z_n g_n L(t)u(t) + z_n g_n S(t) + z_n d_n(x(t), t)$$

$$+z_n\frac{e_{n-1}}{\tau_{n-1}} + \frac{1}{\gamma_{\theta_n}}\tilde{\theta}_{g_n}\dot{\tilde{\theta}}_{g_n} + \frac{1}{\gamma_{b_n}}\tilde{b}_{g_n}\dot{\tilde{b}}_{g_n} + \frac{1}{\gamma_{\bar{g}_n}}\tilde{\bar{g}}_{g_n}\dot{\tilde{\bar{g}}}_{g_n} \quad (29)$$

By using the following inequalities in [20]

$$z_n g_n S(t) \leq \bar{g}_{g_n}|z_n| \leq \bar{g}_{g_n} z_n \tanh\left(\frac{z_n}{\omega}\right) + 0.2785\omega\bar{g}_{g_n}$$

$$z_n d_n(x(t), t) \leq b_n|z_n|\rho_n(x(t))$$

$$\leq b_n z_n\rho_n(x(t))\tanh\left(\frac{z_n\rho_n(x(t))}{\omega}\right) + 0.2785\omega b_n \quad (30)$$

we have

$$\dot{V}_n \leq \dot{V}_{n-1} + z_n\theta_n f_n(x(t)) + z_n g_n L(t)u(t) + \bar{g}_{g_n} z_n \tanh\left(\frac{z_n}{\omega}\right)$$

$$+0.2785\omega\bar{g}_{g_n} + 0.2785\omega b_n + b_n z_n\rho_n(x(t))\tanh\left(\frac{z_n\rho_n(x(t))}{\omega}\right)$$

$$+z_n\frac{e_{n-1}}{\tau_{n-1}} + \frac{1}{\gamma_{\theta_n}}\tilde{\theta}_{g_n}\dot{\tilde{\theta}}_{g_n} + \frac{1}{\gamma_{b_n}}\tilde{b}_{g_n}\dot{\tilde{b}}_{g_n} + \frac{1}{\gamma_{\bar{g}_n}}\tilde{\bar{g}}_{g_n}\dot{\tilde{\bar{g}}}_{g_n}$$

$$\leq \dot{V}_{n-1} + z_n z_{n-1} + z_n \hat{\theta}_n f_n(x(t)) + z_n g_n L(t) u(t) + \hat{\bar{g}} z_n \tanh(\frac{z_n}{\omega})$$

$$+ 0.2785 \omega \bar{g}_{g_n} + 0.2785 \omega b_n + \hat{b}_n z_n \rho_n(x(t)) \tanh(\frac{z_n \rho_n(x(t))}{\omega}) + z_n \frac{e_{n-1}}{\tau_{n-1}}$$

$$+ \tilde{\theta}_{g_n}(z_n f_n(x(t)) - \frac{1}{\gamma_{\theta_n}} \dot{\hat{\theta}}_{g_n}) + \tilde{b}_{g_n}(z_n \rho_n(x(t)) \tanh(\frac{z_n \rho_n(x(t))}{\omega}) - \frac{1}{\gamma_{b_n}} \dot{\hat{b}}_{g_n})$$

$$+ \tilde{\bar{g}}_{g_n}(z_n \tanh(\frac{z_n}{\omega}) - \frac{1}{\gamma_{\bar{g}_n}} \dot{\hat{\bar{g}}}_{g_n}) - z_n z_{n-1} \tag{31}$$

In the last step, the adaptive virtual control $u$ and adaptive laws for $\zeta, \hat{\theta}_{g_n}, \hat{b}_{g_n}$ and $\hat{\bar{g}}_{g_n}$ for the $n$th subsystem can be chosen as

$$u = N(\zeta)[k_n z_n + z_{n-1} + \hat{\theta}_{g_n} f_n(x(t)) + \hat{\bar{g}}_{g_n} \tanh(\frac{z_n}{\omega})$$

$$+ \hat{b}_{g_n} \rho_n(x(t)) \tanh(\frac{z_n \rho_n(x(t))}{\omega}) + \frac{e_{n-1}}{\tau_{n-1}}] \tag{32}$$

$$\dot{\zeta} = k_n z_n^2 + z_n z_{n-1} + z_n \hat{\theta}_{g_n} f_n(x(t)) + \hat{\bar{g}}_{g_n} z_n \tanh(\frac{z_n}{\omega})$$

$$+ z_n \hat{b}_{g_n} \rho_n(x(t)) \tanh(\frac{z_n \rho_n(x(t))}{\omega}) + z_n \frac{e_{n-1}}{\tau_{n-1}} \tag{33}$$

$$\dot{\hat{\theta}}_{g_n} = \gamma_{\theta_n}(z_n f_n(x(t)) - \varpi_n \hat{\theta}_{g_n}) \tag{34}$$

$$\dot{\hat{b}}_{g_n} = \gamma_{b_n}(z_n \rho_n(x(t)) \tanh(\frac{z_n \rho_n(x(t))}{\omega}) - \mu_n \hat{b}_{g_n}) \tag{35}$$

$$\dot{\hat{\bar{g}}}_{g_n} = \gamma_{\bar{g}_n}(z_n \tanh(\frac{z_n}{\omega}) - \nu_i \hat{\bar{g}}_{g_i}) \tag{36}$$

where $k_i, \varpi_i, \mu_i, \nu_i$ are positive design parameters.

By using the following inequalities

$$\varpi_n \tilde{\theta}_{g_n} \hat{\theta}_{g_n} \leq \frac{\varpi_n}{2}(-\tilde{\theta}_{g_n}^2 + \theta_{g_n}^2) \tag{37}$$

$$\mu_n \tilde{b}_{g_n} \hat{b}_{g_n} \leq \frac{\mu_n}{2}(-\tilde{b}_{g_n}^2 + b_{g_n}^2) \tag{38}$$

$$\nu_n \tilde{\bar{g}}_{g_n} \hat{\bar{g}}_{g_n} \leq \frac{\nu_n}{2}(-\tilde{\bar{g}}_{g_n}^2 + \bar{g}_{g_n}^2) \tag{39}$$

it can be obtained

$$\dot{V}_n \leq -\sum_{j=1}^{n} k_j z_j^2 - \sum_{j=1}^{n} (\frac{\varpi_j}{2} \tilde{\theta}_{g_j}^2 + \frac{\mu_j}{2} \tilde{b}_{g_j}^2 + \frac{\nu_j}{2} \tilde{\bar{g}}_{g_j}^2)$$

$$+[g_n L(t) N(\zeta) + 1]\dot{\zeta} + 0.2785\omega \bar{g}_{g_n} + \sum_{j=1}^{n-1} (z_j e_j)$$

$$+ \sum_{j=1}^{n} (0.2785\omega b_{g_j} + \frac{\varpi_j}{2}\theta_{g_j}^2 + \frac{\mu_i}{2}b_{g_j}^2 + \frac{\nu_i}{2}\bar{g}_{g_j}^2) \qquad (40)$$

## 3.2   Stability Analysis

The semiglobal boundedness of all of the signals in the closed-loop system will be given.

Based on (15) and (19), it can be obtained that

$$\dot{e}_i = \dot{s}_i - \dot{\alpha}_i$$

$$= -\frac{e_i}{\tau_i} + (\frac{\partial \alpha_i}{\partial z_i}\dot{z}_i + \frac{\partial \alpha_i}{\partial \hat{\theta}_{g_i}}\dot{\hat{\theta}}_{g_i} + \frac{\partial \alpha_i}{\partial \hat{b}_{g_i}}\dot{\hat{b}}_{g_i} + \frac{\partial \alpha_i}{\partial \hat{\bar{g}}_{g_i}}\dot{\hat{\bar{g}}}_{g_i})$$

$$= -\frac{e_i}{\tau_i} + B_i(z_1, ..., z_i, \hat{\theta}_{g_1}, ..., \hat{\theta}_{g_i}, \hat{b}_{g_1}, ..., \hat{b}_{g_i}, \hat{\bar{g}}_{g_1}, ..., \hat{\bar{g}}_{g_i}, y_d, \dot{y}_d, \ddot{y}_d) \quad (41)$$

where $B_i(z_1, ..., z_i, \hat{\theta}_{g_1}, ..., \hat{\theta}_{g_i}, \hat{b}_{g_1}, ..., \hat{b}_{g_i}, \hat{\bar{g}}_{g_1}, ..., \hat{\bar{g}}_{g_i}, y_d, \dot{y}_d, \ddot{y}_d) = \frac{\partial \alpha_i}{\partial z_i}\dot{z}_i + \frac{\partial \alpha_i}{\partial \hat{\theta}_{g_i}}\dot{\hat{\theta}}_{g_i} + \frac{\partial \alpha_i}{\partial \hat{b}_{g_i}}\dot{\hat{b}}_{g_i} + \frac{\partial \alpha_i}{\partial \hat{\bar{g}}_{g_i}}\dot{\hat{\bar{g}}}_{g_i}$, which are continuous functions, $i = 1, ..., n-1$.

Thus, it follows

$$e_i \dot{e} \le -\frac{e_i^2}{\tau_i} + \left| e_i B_i(z_1, ..., z_i, \hat{\theta}_{g_1}, ..., \hat{\theta}_{g_i}, \hat{b}_{g_1}, ..., \hat{b}_{g_i}, \hat{\bar{g}}_{g_1}, ..., \hat{\bar{g}}_{g_i}, y_d, \dot{y}_d, \ddot{y}_d) \right| (42)$$

Denote $\Omega_i := \{[z_1, ..., z_i, \hat{\theta}_{g_1}, ..., \hat{\theta}_{g_i}, \hat{b}_{g_1}, ..., \hat{b}_{g_i}, \hat{\bar{g}}_{g_1}, ..., \hat{\bar{g}}_{g_i}] : V_n + \sum_{i=1}^{n-1} e_i^2 \le 2P_0\} \subset R^{4i}$ as the compact set of the initial conditions with $P_0$ a positive constant. Combining Assumption 1, for any $B_0 > 0, P_0 > 0$, the set $\Omega_d$ and $\Omega_i$ are compact in $R^4$ and $R^{4i}$. Thus, $B_i(z_1, ..., z_i, \hat{\theta}_{g_1}, ..., \hat{\theta}_{g_i}, \hat{b}_{g_1}, ..., \hat{b}_{g_i}, \hat{\bar{g}}_{g_1}, ..., \hat{\bar{g}}_{g_i}, y_d, \dot{y}_d, \ddot{y}_d)$ has a maximum value $M_i, i = 1, ..., n-1$ on $\Omega_d \times \Omega_i$.

*Theorem 1.* Under Assumptions 1-4, considering the closed-loop system (1) with unknown Duhem hysteresis (2), the designed controller and adaptive control laws are given in (32)-(36), then for any initial conditions $\Omega_i$, there exist control feedback gains $k_i$ and filter parameters $\mu_i$, such that the closed-loop control system is semiglobally stable in the sense that all signals in the closed-loop remain ultimately bounded.

The proof is omitted due to the space limit.

## 4   Simulation Studies

In this section, a nonlinear system (43) with Duhem hysteresis is used to illustrate the effectiveness of the proposed scheme in Section III.

$$\begin{cases} \dot{x} = \theta f(x(t)) + gw(t) + d(x(t), t) \\ y = x \end{cases} \qquad (43)$$

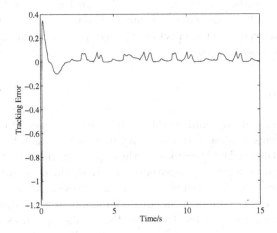

**Fig. 1.** Tracking error of the closed-loop system

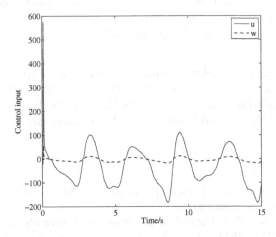

**Fig. 2.** Control signal $u$ and the Duhem hysteresis output $w$

where $\theta = 1, g = 1, f(x(t)) = \frac{1-e^{-x}}{1+e^{-x}}, d(x(t), t) = e^{-0.5x}$. Correspondingly, $b = 1, \rho(x) = e^{-0.5x}$. For the Duhem model, $\lambda(u) = \tanh(u) + 0.1u$ and $\psi(u) = \dot{\lambda}(u)(1 - 0.58e^{-|u|})$. The objective is make the output $y$ of system (43) to track the desired trajectory $x_d(t) = 5\sin(2t) + \cos(3.2t)$.

In this simulation, the Nussbaum function is chosen as $N(\zeta) = e^{\zeta^2}\cos(\frac{\pi\zeta}{2}), \omega = 0.01$. The initial parameters for update laws are chosen as $\hat{\theta}_{g_1}(0) = 0, \hat{b}_{g_1}(0) = 0, \hat{\tilde{g}}_{g_1}(0) = 0, \zeta(0) = 0$, and the initial condition of system is chosen as $x(0) = 0.5$. The control parameters are chosen as $k = 15, \gamma_{\theta_1} = 5, \gamma_{b_1} = 8, \gamma_{\tilde{g}_1} = 10$. The filter parameter and $\sigma$-modification parameters is defined as $\tau_1 = 0.01$ and $\varpi_1 = \mu_1 = \nu_1 = 0.1$ respectively.

The simulation results are shown in Figs. 1-2. In Fig. 1, the tracking error is shown and Fig. 2 shows the control input $u$. From the results, the proposed control scheme can overcome the effects of the hysteresis and ensure the boundedness of the closed-loop system.

## 5   Conclusion

In this paper, an adaptive dynamic surface controller for a class of uncertain perturbed strict-feedback nonlinear systems with unknown Duhem hysteresis input is developed. By utilizing DSC technique, "the explosion complexity" in the classical backstepping design method is avoided. To avoid the difficulties of the last recursive step caused by the unknown Duhem hysteresis, the unknown Duhem model is decomposed as nonlinear smooth component and nonlinear bounded component. By using mean value theorem, the nonlinear smooth component can be transformed as an unknown time-varying coefficient form, which makes it possible to solve the control design difficulty. Semiglobal uniform ultimate boundedness of all the signals in the close-loop system is guaranteed under the proposed control approach. Finally, simulation studies are given to demonstrate the effectiveness of the proposed design scheme.

**Acknowledgment.** This work was supported by the National Natural Science Foundation of China under grants (61020106003, 61074097, 61105081), the National 973 Project of China under Grant 2009CB320600 and by the Fundamental Research Funds for the Central Universities, SCUT under Grant 2011ZZ0019.

## References

1. Mayergoyz, I.: Mathematical Models of Hysteresis and Their Applications. Elsevier Series in Electromagnetism (2003)
2. Nordin, M., Gutman, P.O.: Controlling mechanical systems with backlashA survey. Automatica 38, 1633–1649 (2002)
3. Webb, G.V., Lagoudas, D.C., Kurdila, A.J.: Hysteresis modeling of SMA actuators for control applications. J. Intell. Mater. Syst. Struct. 9(6), 432–448 (1998)
4. Preisach, F.: ber die magnetische Nachwirkung. Zeitschrift fr Physik 94, 277–302 (1935)
5. Krasnoskl'skii, M.A., Pokrovskii, A.V.: Systems with Hysteresis. Springer, New York (1989)
6. Macki, J.W., Nistri, P., Zecca, P.: Mathematical models for hysteresis. SIAM Review 35, 94–123 (1993)
7. Su, C.-Y., Stepanenko, Y., Svoboda, J., Leung, T.P.: Robust adaptive control of a class of nonlinear systems with unknown backlash-like hysteresis. IEEE Trans. Autom. Control 45, 2427–2432 (2000)
8. Wen, Y.K.: Method for random vibration of hysteretic systems. Journal of Engineering Mechanics 102(2), 249–263 (1976)
9. Duhem, P.: Die dauernden Aenderungen und die Thermodynamik. I, Z. Phys. Chem. 22, 543–589 (1897)

10. Krejci, P., Kuhnen, K.: Inverse control of systems with hysteresis and creep. IEE Proc. Control Theory Appl. 148(3), 185–192 (2001)
11. Belbas, S.A., Mayergoyz, I.D.: Optimalcontrol of dynamical systems with Preisach hysteresis. International Journal of Non-Linear Mechanics 37(8), 1351–1361 (2002)
12. Goudovich, A., Quincampoix, M.: Optimal Control with Hysteresis Nonlinearity and Multidimensional Play Operator. SIAM Journal on Control and Optimization 49, 788–807 (2011)
13. Tao, G., Kokotovic, P.V.: Adaptive control of plants with unknown hysteresis. IEEE Trans. Autom. Control. 40, 200–212 (1995)
14. Su, C.-Y., Wang, Q., Chen, X., Rakheja, S.: Adaptive variable structure control of a class of nonlinear systems with unknown Prandtl-Ishlinskii hysteresis. IEEE Trans. Autom. Control 50, 2069–2074 (2005)
15. Zhou, J., Wen, C.-Y., Zhang, Y.: Adaptive backstepping control of a class of uncertain nonlinear systems with unknown backlash-like hysteresis. IEEE Trans. Automat. Contr. 49(10), 1751–1757 (2004)
16. Ikhouane, F., Manosa, V., Rodellar, J.: Adaptive control of a hysteretic structural systems. Automatica 41, 225–231 (2005)
17. Wang, Q., Su, C.-Y.: Robust adaptive control of a class of nonlinear systems including actuator hysteresis with Prandtl-Ishlinskii presentations. Automatica 42, 859–867 (2006)
18. Swaroop, D., Hedrick, J.K., Yip, P.P., Gerdes, J.C.: Dynamic surface control for a class of nonlinear systems. IEEE Trans. Autom. Control 45, 1893–1899 (2000)
19. Ge, S.S., Hong, F., Lee, T.H.: Adaptive neural control of nonlinear time-delay systems with unknown virtual control coefficients. IEEE Trans. Syst., Man, Cybern. B, Cybern. 34, 499–516 (2004)
20. Polycarpou, M.M., Ioannou, P.A.: A robust adaptive nonlinear control design. Automatica 32, 423–427 (1996)
21. Ryan, E.P.: A universal adaptive stabilizer for a class of nonlinear systems. Syst. Control Lett. 16(3), 209–218 (1991)

# Balancing and Posture Controls
# for Biped Robots with Unmodelled Dynamics*

Zhijun Li[1] and Shuzhi Sam Ge[2,3]

[1] Department of Automation, Shanghai Jiao Tong University, Shanghai 200240
[2] Robotics Institute, and School of Computer Science and Engineering
University of Electronic Science and Technology of China, Chengdu, China, 610054
[3] Department of Electrical and Computer Engineering
The National University of Singapore, Singapore 117576

**Abstract.** This paper presents a structure of robust adaptive control for biped robots which includes balancing and posture control for regulating the center of mass position and trunk orientation of bipedal robots in a compliant way. First, the biped robot is decoupled into the dynamics of center of mass (COM) and the trunks. Then, the adaptive robust controls are constructed in the presence of parametric and functional dynamics uncertainties. The control computes a desired ground reaction force required to stabilize the posture with unknown dynamics of COM and then transforms these forces into full-body joint torques even if the external disturbances exist. The verification of the proposed control is conducted using the extensive simulations.

## 1 Introduction

Recently, advances in both mechanical and software systems have promoted development of biped robots around the world [1], [2]. Although, many works on dynamics and control of biped robot had been investigated in [2], [3], the realization of reliable autonomous biped robots is still limited by the current level of motion control strategies. For example, some control algorithms were proposed by introducing passive dynamics, linearized model, and reduced-order nonlinear dynamic model for biped robots in the past two decades [7], [8].

Most biped robots founded in the real world are composed of a lot of inter-connected joints, and the dynamic balance and posture need to be considered simultaneously. As such, nonlinear biped systems are one of the most difficult control problems in the category. Owing to the complexity of the multi-degrees-of-freedom (multi-DOF) mechanism of humanoid robots, an intuitive and efficient method for whole-body control is required. However, how to improve the

* This work is supported by the Natural Science Foundation of China under Grants 60804003, 61174045, 61111130208, the International Science and Technology Cooperation Program of China under 0102011DFA10950, and the Fundamental Research Funds for the Central Universities (No. 2011ZZ0104), National Basic Research Program of China (973 Program) under Grant No. 2011CB707005, National High Technology Research and Development Program of China(863, 2011AA040701).

C.-Y. Su, S. Rakheja, H. Liu (Eds.): ICIRA 2012, Part I, LNAI 7506, pp. 56–65, 2012.

tracking performance of biped robots through designed controls is still an challenging research topic that attracts great attention from robotic community. In this paper, considering both the dynamic balance and the posture position to be guaranteed, we decouple the dynamics of biped into the dynamics of center of mass (COM) and the trunks, and then implement decoupled control structure due to the biped's specific physical nature.

Due to the finite foot support area, pure position control is insufficient for executing bipedal locomotion trajectories. Therefore, some approaches utilized force sensors in the feet for implementing an inner force or ZMP (Zero Moment Point) control loop [9], [10], and [11]. However, in this paper, we propose an approach which gives a desired applied force from the robot to the ground to stabilize the posture position and ensures the desired contact state between the robot and the ground, then distributes that force among predefined contact points and transforms it to the joint torques directly. The approach does not require contact force measurement or inverse kinematics or dynamics.

Since, along the walk, toe and heel are independently characterized by non penetration and no-slip constraint with the ground, in this paper, we consider the holonomic and nonholonomic constraints [5] into the biped dynamics. The biped robot is firstly decoupled into the dynamics of center of mass (COM) and the trunks. Then, the adaptive robust control is constructed in the presence of parametric and functional dynamics uncertainties. The control computes a desired ground reaction force required to stabilize the posture with unknown dynamics of COM and then transforms these forces into full-body joint torques even if the external disturbances exist. Finally, simulation results are presented to verify the effectiveness of the proposed control.

## 2 Dynamics of Biped Robots

Consider a multi-DoF biped robot contacting with the ground, as shown in Fig. 1. Let $r \in \mathbb{R}^3$ be translational position coordinate (e.g., base position) and $q \in \mathbb{R}^n$ be the joint angles and attitude of the base. Using the generalized coordinates $x = [r^T, q^T]^T \in \mathbb{R}^{3+n}$, the exact nonlinear dynamics of the biped with the holonomic constraints and nonholomic constraints (generated by the respective situations of one or both feet grounded with no-slip) can be derived using a standard Lagrangian formulation

$$\mathbf{M}(x)\ddot{x} + \mathbf{C}(x,\dot{x})\dot{x} + \mathbf{G} + \mathbf{D} = u + J^T \lambda_G \tag{1}$$

where $\mathbf{M}(x) = \begin{bmatrix} M_r & M_{rq} \\ M_{qr} & M_q \end{bmatrix} \in \mathbb{R}^{(n+3)\times(n+3)}$ is the inertia matrix; $\mathbf{C}(x,\dot{x}) = \begin{bmatrix} C_r & C_{rq} \\ C_{qr} & C_q \end{bmatrix} \in \mathbb{R}^{(n+3)\times(n+3)}$ is the centrifugal and Coriolis force term; $\mathbf{G} \in \mathbb{R}^{(n+3)}$ is the gravitational torque vector; $\mathbf{D} \in \mathbb{R}^{(n+3)}$ is the external disturbance vector; $u = [0_{3\times1}, \tau_{n\times1}^T]^T \in \mathbb{R}^{(n+3)}$ is the control input vector; $J = [J_n^T, J_h^T]^T$ and $\lambda_G = [\lambda_n^T, \lambda_h^T]^T$ are Jacobian matrix and Lagrangian multiplier corresponding to the nonholonomic and holonomic constraints.

Let $r_c = [x_c, y_c, z_c]^T \in \mathbb{R}^3$ be the position vector of the center of mass (COM) coordinate, and $r_p = [x_p, y_p, z_p]^T \in \mathbb{R}^3$ be the position vector from COM to the contact point. The contact point does not move on the ground surface. The constraint forces $\lambda_G = [\lambda_n^T, \lambda_h^T]^T$ and a ground reaction force $f_R$ satisfy $\lambda_G + f_R = 0$.

If we replace $r$ by $r_c$, we can rewrite the dynamics (1) as the decoupled dynamics [12]

$$\begin{bmatrix} M_{rc} & 0 \\ 0 & M \end{bmatrix} \begin{bmatrix} \ddot{r}_c \\ \ddot{q} \end{bmatrix} + \begin{bmatrix} 0 \\ C(q, \dot{q})\dot{q} \end{bmatrix} + \begin{bmatrix} G \\ 0 \end{bmatrix} + \begin{bmatrix} D_r \\ D_q \end{bmatrix} = \begin{bmatrix} 0 \\ \tau \end{bmatrix} + \begin{bmatrix} I \\ J^T \end{bmatrix} \lambda_G \qquad (2)$$

where $M_{rc} \in \mathbb{R}^{3 \times 3}$ is the diagonal mass matrix for the center of mass (COM) of the biped, $M \in \mathbb{R}^{n \times n}$ is the inertia matrix, $C(q, \dot{q})\dot{q} \in \mathbb{R}^n$ is the centrifugal and Coriolis term, and $I \in R^{3 \times 3}$ denotes the identity matrix.

The first part of equation(2) corresponding to the dynamics of the COM is the simple linear dynamics

$$M_{rc}\ddot{r}_c + G + D_r = \lambda_G \qquad (3)$$

which can be used to produce the desired forces from the ground for dynamic balancing of the biped.

There are some useful properties for the dynamics of COM listed as follows.

*Property 1.* Matrix $M_{rc}$ is symmetric and positive definite.

*Property 2.* There exist some finite unknown positive constants $\vartheta_2$, $\vartheta_2$, $\vartheta_2$ such that $\forall q, \dot{q} \in \mathbb{R}^n$, $\|M_{rc}\| \leq \vartheta_1$, $\|G\| \leq \vartheta_2$, and $\sup\|D_r\| \leq \vartheta_3$.

The second part of equation (2) corresponding to the dynamics of trunks is the nonlinear dynamics

$$M(q)\ddot{q} + C(q, \dot{q})\dot{q} + D_q = \tau + J^T \lambda_G \qquad (4)$$

## 3    Ground Constraints

### 3.1    Nonholonomic Constraints

Consider no-slip between each foot and the ground. The biped is subjected to nonholonomic constraint with matrix $J_n$. Assume that the $l$ nonintegrable and independent velocity constraints can be $J_n(q)\dot{q} = 0$, where $J_n(q) \in \mathbb{R}^{l \times n}$. Since $J_n(q) \in \mathbb{R}^{l \times n}$, there exists define an auxiliary time function $\dot{z}(t) = [\dot{z}_1(t), \cdots, \dot{z}_{n-l}(t)]^T \in \mathbb{R}^{n-l}$ such that

$$\dot{q} = S(q)\dot{z}(t) = s_1(q)\dot{z}_1(t) + \cdots + s_{n-l}(q)\dot{z}_{n-l}(t) \qquad (5)$$

It is easy to have

$$\ddot{q} = \dot{S}(q)\dot{z} + S(q)\ddot{z} \qquad (6)$$

Considering (5) and (6), we can rewrite (1) as

$$M(q)S(q)\ddot{z} + [M(q)\dot{S}(q) + C(q,\dot{q})S(q)]\dot{z} + D_q = \tau + J_n^T(q)\lambda_n + J_h^T(q)\lambda_h \quad (7)$$

Multiplying (7) by $S^T(q)$, we have

$$M_1\ddot{z} + C_1\dot{z} + D_1 = S^T\tau + S^T J_h^T\lambda_h \quad\quad (8)$$

where $M_1 = S^T(q)M(q)S(q)$, $C_1 = S^T(q)[M(q)\dot{S}(q) + C(q,\dot{q})S(q)]$, and $D_1 = S^T(q)D_q$.

The force multiplier $\lambda_n$ can be obtained by (7)

$$\lambda_n = Z_1\left((M(q)\dot{S}(q) + C(q,\dot{q})S(q))\dot{z} + D_q - \tau - J_h^T\lambda_h\right) \quad (9)$$

where $Z_1 = (J_n(q)M^{-1}(q)J_n^T(q))^{-1}J_n(q)M^{-1}(q)$. Consider the control input $\tau$ decoupled into the locomotion control $\tau_a$ and the interactive force control $\tau_b$ as $\tau = \tau_a - J_n^T\tau_b$. Then, (8) and (9) can be changed to

$$M_1\ddot{z} + C_1\dot{z} + D_1 = S^T\tau_a + S^T J_h^T\lambda_h \quad\quad (10)$$

$$\lambda_n = Z_1\left([M(q)\dot{S}(q) + C(q,\dot{q})S(q)]\dot{z} + D_q - \tau_a - J_h^T\lambda_h\right) + \tau_b \quad (11)$$

## 3.2  Holonomic Constraints

Assume that both feet are in contact with a certain constrained surface $\Phi(z)$ that is represented as $\Phi(\chi(z)) = 0$, where $\Phi(\chi(z))$ is a given scalar function, $\chi(z) \in \mathbb{R}^m$ denotes the position vector of the end-effector in contact with the environment.

It is easy to have matrix $\mathbf{J}(z) = J_h S = \partial\Omega/\partial z$, which can be partitioned as $\mathbf{J}(z) = [\mathbf{J}_1, \mathbf{J}_2]$ with $\mathbf{J}_1 = \partial\Omega/\partial z_h$ and $\mathbf{J}_2 = \partial\Omega/\partial z_c$, and the Jacobian matrix $\mathbf{J}_2 \in \mathbb{R}^{m\times m}$ never degenerates in the set $\Omega$. It is easy to have $\dot{z} = H\dot{z}_h$ with $H = \left[I_{n-l-m} \;\; -\mathbf{J}_1\mathbf{J}_2^{-1}\right]^T$, where $H(q)$ is full column rank if and only if $\mathbf{J}_2^{-1}$ exists. There exists a matrix $\mathbf{J}^T$ such that $H^T\mathbf{J}^T = 0$. Consider the control input $S^T(q)\tau_a$ decoupled into $\tau_{a1}$ and the force control $\tau_{a2}$ as $S^T(q)\tau_a = \tau_{a1} - \mathbf{J}^T\tau_{a2}$, and $\dot{z} = H\dot{z}_h$, a reduced-order model is obtained by taking the above constraints into consideration, one obtains

$$M_2\ddot{z}_h + C_2\dot{z}_h + D_2 = U \quad\quad (12)$$

$$\lambda_h = Z_2[C_1\dot{z} + D_1 - \tau_{a1}] + \tau_{a2} \quad\quad (13)$$

where $M_2 = H^T M_1 H$, $Z_2 = (\mathbf{J}M_1^1\mathbf{J}^T)^{-1}\mathbf{J}M_1^{-1}$, $C_2 = H^T[M_1\dot{H} + C_1 H]$, $D_2 = H^T D_1$, $U = H^T\tau_{a1}$.

From (11) and (13), it is easy to have

$$\lambda_h = Z_2(q)H^{+T}(q)M_2(q)\ddot{z}_h + \tau_{a2} \quad\quad (14)$$

$$\lambda_n = Z_1(q)S^{+T}(q)M_1(q)\ddot{z} + \tau_b \quad\quad (15)$$

where $H^+(q) = H(q)(H^T(q)H(q))^{-1}$ is the pseudo-inverse of $H(q)$ and $S^+(q) = S(q)(S^T(q)S(q))^{-1}$ is the pseudo-inverse of $S(q)$.

*Remark 1.* [5] Matrices $H^+(q)$ and $S^+(q)$ exist and are bounded for all $q$.

*Property 3.* Matrix $M_2$ is symmetric and positive definite and matrix $\dot{M}_2 - 2C_2$ is skew-symmetric.

*Property 4.* There exists a unknown finite positive vector $\mathbb{C} = [c_1, c_2, c_3, c_4]^T$ with $c_i > 0$, such that $\forall q, \dot{q} \in \mathbb{R}^n$, $\|M_2\| \le c_1$, $\|C_2\| \le c_2 + c_3\|\dot{q}\|$, $\sup_{t \ge 0}\|D_2\| \le c_4$.

*Property 5.* All Jacobian matrices are uniformly bounded and uniformly continuous if $q$ is uniformly bounded and continuous.

According to the definition of (12), $z_{hj}$ is denoted as the $j$th element of $z_h \in \mathbb{R}^{(n-l-m)}$, and $z_h = [z_{h1}, z_{h2}, \dots, z_{h(n-l-m)}]^T$, $M_2 = [m_{ji}]_{(n-l-m) \times (n-l-m)}$, $C_2 = [c_{ji}]_{(n-l-m) \times (n-l-m)}$, $D_2 = [d_j]_{(n-l-m) \times 1}$, then we can obtain the $j$th local dynamics as

$$m_{jj}\ddot{z}_{hj} + c_{jj}(q,\dot{q})\dot{z}_{hj} + d_j + \sum_{i=1, i \neq j}^{n-l-m} m_{ji}\ddot{z}_{hi} + \sum_{i=1, i \neq j}^{n-l-m} c_{ji}(q,\dot{q})\dot{z}_{hi} = U_j \quad (16)$$

## 4   Control Objective

In order to balance the biped, we should give the desired position $r_c^d$ and velocity $\dot{r}_c^d$ for the COM. Therefore, the first control objective is to design a balancing control such that the tracking error of $r_c$ and $\dot{r}_c$ from their respective desired trajectories $r_c^d$ and $\dot{r}_c^d$ to be within a small neighborhood of zero, i. e. $\|r_c - r_c^d\| \le \varepsilon_1$, and $\|\dot{r}_c - \dot{r}_c^d\| \le \varepsilon_2$. The desired reference trajectory $z_h^d$ is assumed to be bounded and uniformly continuous, and has bounded and uniformly continuous derivatives up to the second order.

The second control objective can be specified as designing a controller that ensures the tracking error of $z_h$ from their respective desired trajectories $z_h^d$ to be within a small neighborhood of zero, i.e., $\|z_h(t) - z_h^d\| \le \epsilon_1$, $\|\dot{z}_h(t) - \dot{z}_h^d\| \le \epsilon_2$ where $\epsilon_1 > 0$ and $\epsilon_2 > 0$. Ideally, $\epsilon_1$ and $\epsilon_2$ should be the threshold of measurable noise.

In order to avoid the slipping or slippage and tip-over, from (3), $r_c \to r_c^d$ brings the ground applied constraints force to a desired value $\lambda_G^d = [\lambda_n^{dT}, \lambda_h^{dT}]^T$, therefore, the constraint force errors and $(\lambda_G - \lambda_G^d)$ should be to be within a small neighborhood of zero, i.e., $\|\lambda_G - \lambda_G^d\| \le \varsigma$, where $\varsigma > 0$ is the threshold of measurable noise. For the impact phase, we should guarantee the system stability during the transition phase.

The controller design will consist of two stages: (i) a virtual control input $\lambda_G^d$ is designed so that the subsystems (3) converge to the desired trajectory, and (ii) the actual control input $\tau$ is designed in such a way that $z_h \to z_h^d$ and $\lambda_G - \lambda_G^d$ to be stabilized to the origin.

**Lemma 1.** *For $x > 0$ and $\delta \geq 1$, we have $\ln(\cosh(x)) + \delta \geq x$ [5].*

**Assumption 41.** *Time varying positive function $f(t)$ converges to zero as $t \to \infty$ and satisfies*

$$\lim_{t \to \infty} \int_0^t f(\omega) d\omega = \varrho < \infty$$

*with a finite constant $\varrho$.*

## 5  Adaptive Robust Control

### 5.1  Balancing Control

For the subsystem (3), we can define $e_c = r_c - r_c^d$, $\dot{r}_c^r = \dot{r}_c^d - \Lambda e_c$, $s = \dot{e}_c + \Lambda e_c$ with $\Lambda$ being diagonal constant matrix. Considering the above definition , we can rewrite (3) as

$$M_r \dot{s} = \lambda_G - \Delta \tag{17}$$
$$\Delta = M_r \ddot{r}_c^r + G + D_r \tag{18}$$

where $M_r$ is diagonal and $\lambda_G \in \mathbb{R}^3$.

**Lemma 2.** *Consider Property 2, the upper bound of $k$th sub-vector $\Delta_k$ of $\Delta$ satisfies*

$$\|\Delta_k\| \leq \ln(\cosh(\|\Psi_k\|)) + \delta \tag{19}$$

*where $\delta \geq 1$ is a small function, $\Psi_k = \gamma_k^T \varphi_k$ with $\varphi_k = [1, \sup \|s_k\|]^T$ , and $\gamma_k = [\gamma_{k1}, \gamma_{k2}]^T$ is a vector of positive constants defined below.*

For the $k$th vector $\lambda_{Gk}$, we can design the desired producing constrain force $\lambda_{Gk}$ as

$$\lambda_{Gk} = -\Upsilon_k s_k - \ln(\cosh(\hat{\Psi}_k))\mathrm{sgn}(s_k) - \delta\mathrm{sgn}(s_k) \tag{20}$$
$$\hat{\Psi}_k = \hat{\gamma}_k^T \varphi_k$$
$$\dot{\hat{\gamma}}_k = -\eta\hat{\gamma}_k + \kappa\varphi_k\|s_k\| \tag{21}$$

where the designed constant $\Upsilon_k > 0$, $\kappa > 0$, if $s_k \geq 0$, $\mathrm{sgn}(s_k) = 1$, else $\mathrm{sgn}(s_k) = -1$; $\delta \geq 1$ and in the simulation, we choose $\delta = 1 + \frac{1}{(1+t)^2}$; and $\eta$ satisfies Assumption 41, i.e., $\lim_{t\to\infty} \eta(t) = 0$ and $\lim_{t\to\infty} \int_0^t \eta(\omega)d\omega = \varrho_\eta < \infty$ with the finite constant $\varrho_\eta$, i.e. $\eta$ can be chosen as $\frac{1}{(1+t)^2}$.

**Theorem 1.** *Consider the dynamics of COM described by (3), using the control law (20) and the adaptive law (21), the following hold for any $(r_c(0), \dot{r}_c(0))$:*

*(i) $r_c = [r_{c1}, r_{c2}, r_{c3}]^T$ converges to the desired trajectory $r_c^d = [r_{c1}^d, r_{c2}^d, r_{c3}^d]^T$ as $t \to \infty$;*

*(ii) $e_{ck}$ and $\dot{e}_{ck}$ converge to 0 as $t \to \infty$, and $\lambda_G$ is bounded for $t \geq 0$.*

## 5.2   Posture Control

Let $e = z_h - z_h^d$, $\dot{z}_h^r = \dot{z}_h^d - \Lambda e$, $r = \dot{e} + \Lambda e$ with $\Lambda$ being diagonal positive definite constant matrix. Considering the above equations, we can rewrite (12) as

$$M_2 \dot{r} + C_2 r = U - \Xi \tag{22}$$
$$\Xi = M_2 \ddot{z}_h^r + C_2 \dot{z}_h^r + D_2 \tag{23}$$

According to the definition of $\Xi \in \mathbb{R}^{(n-l-m)}$, we denote $\Xi_k$, $k = 1, 2, \ldots, (n - l - m)$ as the $k$th elements of $\Xi$, which corresponds to the $k$th equation in the dynamics of the $j$th sub-system. Similarly, we denote $r_k$ as the $k$th element of $r \in \mathbb{R}^{(n-l-m)}$, and in addition, denote $r = [r_1, r_2, \ldots, r_{n-l-m}]^T$.

We define the $k$th component of trunk dynamics in (22) as

$$\sum_{j=1}^{n-l-m} m_{kj} \dot{r}_j + \sum_{j=1}^{n-l-m} c_{kj}(q, \dot{q}) r_j = \mathcal{U}_k - \Xi_k \tag{24}$$

**Lemma 3.** *Consider Property 4, the upper bound of $\Xi$ satisfies*

$$\|\Xi_k\| \le \ln(\cosh(\|\Phi_k\|)) + \delta \tag{25}$$

*where $\delta$ is a small function, $\Phi_j = \alpha_k^T \varphi$ with $\varphi = [1, \sup \|r\|, \sup \|r\|^2]^T$, and $\alpha_k = [\alpha_{k1}, \alpha_{k2}, \alpha_{k3}]^T$ is a vector of positive constants defined below.*

We propose the following control for the biped

$$U_k = -k_k r_k - \ln(\cosh(\hat{\Phi}_k)) \operatorname{sgn}(r_k) - \delta \operatorname{sgn}(r_k) \tag{26}$$
$$\tau_{a2} = \lambda_h^d - K_h(\lambda_h - \lambda_h^d) \tag{27}$$
$$\tau_b = \lambda_n^d - K_n(\lambda_n - \lambda_n^d) \tag{28}$$
$$\hat{\Phi}_k = \hat{\alpha}_k^T \varphi_k$$
$$\dot{\hat{\alpha}}_k = -\Sigma \hat{\alpha}_k + \Gamma \varphi_k \|r_k\| \tag{29}$$

where $k_k > 0$, $\delta > 1$, if $r_k \ge 0$, $\operatorname{sgn}(r_k) = 1$, else $\operatorname{sgn}(r_k) = -1$, and $\Gamma > 0$, $\Sigma$ satisfies Assumption 41, such as, $\lim_{t \to \infty} \Sigma = 0$, and $\lim_{t \to \infty} \int_0^t \Sigma(\omega) d\omega = \rho_\Sigma < \infty$ with the finite constant $\rho_\Sigma$, i.e. $\Sigma = \frac{1}{(1+t)^2}$. It is observed that the controller (26) only adopt the local feedback information.

**Theorem 2.** *Consider the mechanical system described by (12) and its dynamics model (24), using the control law (26) and (29), the following hold for any $(z_h(0), \dot{z}_h(0))$:*

*(i)   $r_k$ converges to a set containing the origin as $t \to \infty$;*
*(ii)  $e_k$ and $\dot{e}_k$ converge to 0 as $t \to \infty$; and $\tau$ are bounded for all $t \ge 0$; and*
*(iii) $\lambda_G - \lambda_G^d = [e_h^T, e_n^T]^T = [(\lambda_h - \lambda_h^d)^T, (\lambda_n - \lambda_n^d)^T]^T$ is bounded and can be made arbitrarily small.*

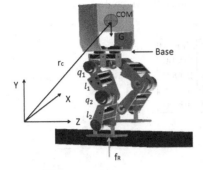

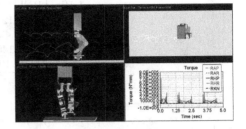

**Fig. 1.** The biped robot      **Fig. 2.** The video snapshots of walking

## 6   Simulations

Consider a 12-DOF biped robot shown in Fig. 1 modeling using ADAMS, which consists of a torso, and a pair of legs composed of six links. The left and right legs are numbered Legs 1 and 2, respectively. The height of the biped is 1.2m, the lower limbs are 460mm, and the height of foot is 90mm, the weight is 22kg.

In this study, a cycloidal profile is used for the trajectories of the hip and ankle joints of the swinging leg, which can be found in [4]. This profile is used because it shows a similar pattern to a human's ankle trajectory in normal walking and it describes a simple function which can be easily changed for different walking patterns. The equations are given as follows: $x_a(i) = \frac{a}{\pi}[\frac{2\pi}{\kappa}i - \sin(\frac{2\pi}{\kappa}i)]$, $z_a(i) = \frac{d}{2}[1 - \cos(\frac{2\pi}{\kappa}i)]$, $x_h(i) = \frac{1}{2}x_a(i) + \frac{a}{2}$, $z_h(i) = \frac{1}{2}z_a(i) + l_1 + l_2 - \frac{d}{2}$, where $x_h$ and $z_h$ denote the positions of the hip, and $x_a$ and $z_a$ denote the positions of the swinging angle, $a$ is the step length, $d$ is the height of the swinging ankle, $\kappa$ is the total sampling number of a step, and $i$ is the sampling index, and $l_i$ is the length of link $i$. In order to avoid the tumbling, we design the lateral trajectory as $y_h(i) = 102.5\sin(\frac{\pi}{\kappa}i)$, where $y_h$ is the projection of COM on the ground such that the position of COM is in the foot support area, $n$ is the total sampling number of a step, and $i$ is the sampling index, and 102.5mm is the distance between the COM and support leg. In the simulation, we choose the parameters as $a = 200mm$, $d = 120mm$, and $l_1 = 235.5mm$, $l_2 = 233.5mm$, $n = 200$. Therefore, we can obtain the every joint in the working space. For the support leg, $q_1$ and $q_2$, the constraint equation is given by $l_1\cos(q_1) + l_2\cos(q_2) = z_h$, therefore, $q_1$ is independent coordinate, and $q_2 = \Phi(q_1) = \cos^{-1}\frac{z_h - l_1\cos(q_1)}{l_2}$ we design the $H = [1,0,0,0;\frac{\partial\Phi}{\partial q_1},0,0,0;0,1,0,0;0,0,1,0;0,0,0,1]$, $J_n = [1, 0_{1\times 5}]$. The parameters in the adaptive control are set as $\hat{\vartheta} = [0.0, 0.0, 0.0]^T$, $\hat{\alpha} = [0.0, \ldots, 0.0]^T$, and $\kappa = \Gamma = \text{diag}[1.0]$, $\eta = \Sigma = \text{diag}[\frac{1}{(1+t)^2}]$, $\delta = 1 + \frac{1}{(1+t)^2}$, the balance control gain are choose as $\Lambda = 10$ and $\Upsilon = [20000, 20000, 20000]^T$. The posture control gain is listed in Table 1.

**Table 1.** The parameters in the adaptive control

| Joints | DOF | $\Lambda$ | k |
|--------|-------|-----|--------|
| Hip | Roll | 20 | 250000 |
| Hip | Pitch | 125 | 20000 |
| Knee | Pitch | 45 | 20000 |
| Angle | Roll | 140 | 3500 |
| Angle | Pitch | 10 | 40000 |

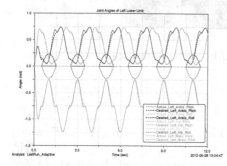

**Fig. 3.** The trajectories of left leg (rad)

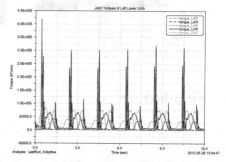

**Fig. 4.** The torques of left leg (Nmm)

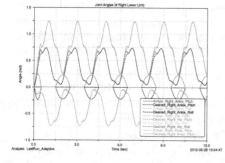

**Fig. 5.** The trajectories of right leg (rad)

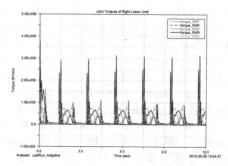

**Fig. 6.** The torques of right leg (Nmm)

The video snapshots are shown in Fig. 2. The positions tracking for each joint profiles of the left and right leg are shown in Figs. 3 and 5. Similarly, the input torques for the joints of the left and right leg are shown in Figs. 4 and 6.

## 7    Conclusions

In this paper, a structure of adaptive robust control has been presented for a biped robot which includes balancing control and posture control for regulating the center of mass position and trunk orientation of bipedal robots in a compliant way. The controller computes a desired ground reaction force required to stabilize the posture with unknown dynamics of COM and then transforms these forces into full-body joint torques even if the external disturbances exist. The verification of the proposed control has been conducted by using the extensive simulations.

# References

1. Ferreira, J.P., Crisostomo, M.M., Coimbra, A.P., Ribeiro, B.: Control of a biped robot with support vector regression in sagittal plane. IEEE Trans. Instrumentation and Measurement 58(9), 3167–3176 (2009)
2. Braun, D.J., Goldfarb, M.: A control approach for actuated dynamic walking in biped robots. IEEE Trans. Robotics 25(6), 1292–1303 (2009)
3. Morimoto, J., Atkeson, C.G.: Learning biped locomotion. IEEE Robotics & Automation Magazine, 41–51 (June 2007)
4. Juang, J.: Fuzzy neural network approaches for robotic gait synthesis. IEEE Trans. Syst., Man., Cybern., Part B: Cybernetics 30(4), 594–601 (2000)
5. Li, Z., Ge, S.S., Ming, A.: Adaptive robust motion/force control of holonomic constrained nonholonomic mobile manipulators. IEEE Trans. System, Man, and Cybernetics, Part B 37(3), 607–617 (2007)
6. Panteley, E., Stotsky, A.: Adaptive trajectory/force control scheme for constrained robot manipulators. Int. J. Adapt. Control Signal Processing 7(6), 489–496 (1993)
7. Shih, C., Gruver, W.A.: Control of a biped robot in the double-support phase. IEEE Trans. System, Man, and Cybernetics 22(4), 729–735 (1992)
8. Freidovich, L.B., Mettin, U., Shiriaev, A.S., Spong, M.W.: A passive 2-DOF walker: hunting for gaits using virtual holonomic constraints. IEEE Trans. Robotics 25(5), 1202–1208 (2009)
9. Vukobratovic, M., Borovac, B.: Zero-moment point thirty five years of its life. Int. J. Humanoid Robot 1(1), 157–173 (2004)
10. Harada, K., Kajita, S., Kaneko, K., Hirukawa, H.: ZMP analysis for arm/leg coordination. In: Proc. IEEE/RSJ Int. Conf. Intell. Robots Syst., Las Vegas, NV, pp. 75–81 (October 2003)
11. Hirai, K., Hirose, M., Haikawa, Y., Takenaka, T.: The development of Honda humanoid robot. In: Proc. IEEE Int. Conf. Robot. Autom., Leuven, Belgium, vol. 2, pp. 1321–1326 (1998)
12. Hyon, S., Hale, J.G., Cheng, G.: Full-body compliant human–humanoid interaction: balancing in the presence of unknown external forces. IEEE Trans. Robotics 23(5), 884–898 (2007)

# Adaptive Learning Prediction on Rolling Force in the Process of Reversible Cold Rolling Mill

Gang Zheng[*], Zhe Yang, Rui Cao, Wenhua Zhang, and Haowen Li

Faculty of Automation and Information Engineering,
Xi'an University of Technology, Xi'an, 710048, China
zhenggang@xuat.edu.cn

**Abstract.** Rolling force model is a basic model of cold rolling process control system, and the main influential factors on forecasting accuracy of rolling force are the material deformation resistance and friction coefficient. Bland-Ford-Hill model which is the classic rolling force model of cold rolling process is selected to calculate rolling force. Five methods of calculating friction coefficient are explained. Deformation resistance is calculated by the deformation resistance formula derived through Bland-Ford-Hill formula, and its model parameters are acquired through the least squares method. Then the friction coefficient and the deformation resistance are substituted into the rolling force model to calculate rolling force. By comparing with the actual rolling force, the method 4 can make the average error smaller. therefore, method 4 is selected to establish the model library of friction coefficient and deformation resistance of different kinds of steels. Finally, the model parameters adaptive learning method is proposed to improve the prediction precision of rolling force in this paper.

**Keywords:** rolling force, deformation resistance, friction coefficient, model parameters adaptive learning.

## 1    Introduction

Precise prediction of the rolling force plays an important role in the presetting of cold rolling production control and the key of improving rolling force prediction precision is to select two appropriate sub-models which are the material deformation resistance $K$ model and the friction coefficient $\mu$ model. Therefore, high-precision sub-models must be established to guarantee the accuracy of rolling force prediction [1], then the model parameters adaptive method should be applied to improve the prediction accuracy of rolling force. In the solution of $K$ and $\mu$, many scholars have made outstanding contributions, such as inverse Stone equation, calculation of forward slip[2], the establishment of $K$ model and $\mu$ model[3]. However, most models are very complex, and the model parameters are not readily available. As a result, the $K$ and $\mu$

---

[*] He received B. S. degree from Hunan University in 1982 and M. S. degree from Xi'an Jiao tong University in 1989. He is now the vice dean of School of Automation and Information Engineering, Xi'an University of Technology.

C.-Y. Su, S. Rakheja, H. Liu (Eds.): ICIRA 2012, Part I, LNAI 7506, pp. 66–75, 2012.
© Springer-Verlag Berlin Heidelberg 2012

are not easy to determine. In this paper, a method which establishes the deformation resistance $K$ model and the friction coefficient $\mu$ model is presented, and a library of $K$ and $\mu$ model of different steels can be created by this method. By using the model parameters adaptive method, the $K$ and $\mu$ of the next coil about the same steel can be predicted. In the rolling process of the site, the rolling force can be predicted by using the model parameters in model library and the measured process parameters.

## 2    Establishment of Model Library by Measured Data

### 2.1    Rolling Force Model

The Bland-Ford-Hill cold rolling force model, which is strict in theory and takes full account of the external friction, tension, roll elastic flattening and other factors, is the classic theoretical model of cold rolling force. So this model is applied as the rolling force model to calculate the rolling force, the Bland-Ford-Hill rolling force model[4] is as follows:

$$\begin{cases} P = BLQ_p K_T K (\text{KN}) \\ L = \sqrt{R'\Delta h}\,(mm) \\ R' = R(1+2.11\times10^{-5}\dfrac{P}{B\Delta h})(mm) \\ Q_p = 1.08+1.79\mu\varepsilon\sqrt{1-\varepsilon}\sqrt{R'/h_1}-1.02\varepsilon \\ K_T = 1-\dfrac{\tau_b+\tau_f}{2K} \end{cases} \qquad (1)$$

,where $P$ is the rolling force (KN); $B$ is the strip width (mm); $L$ is the contact arc length of the flattening deformation zone (mm); $R$ is the roll radius (mm); $R'$ is the flatten roll radius (mm); $Q_p$ is the influence coefficient of friction; $K_T$ is the influence coefficient of tension; $K$ is the strip deformation resistance(MPa), and $K = 1.15 * \sigma_s$, $\sigma_s$ the principal stress (mm); $\varepsilon$ is the reduction rate at each pass, $\varepsilon = (h_0 - h_1)/h_0$, in which $h_0$ and $h_1$ are the strip thickness of entry and exit respectively at every pass (mm); $\tau_f$ and $\tau_b$ are the front and back tensile stress respectively (MPa).

In this equation, only the $\mu$ and $K$ can not be measured directly.

### 2.2    Calculation of the Friction Coefficient

Friction coefficient varies in the production process, and almost all the process and device parameters can affect the friction conditions of deformation zone which causes changes in $\mu$, and it makes the determination of $\mu$ very complicated. The $\mu$ is usually a function relation of the forward slip which can be measured by the test, so we can get it through the inverse computation of forward slip[5].

According to the characteristics of cold rolling process, the status characteristics of rolling process is greatly reflected by the strip thickness of exit $h_1$ and reduction rate $\varepsilon$ at each pass; therefore, an initial model form of friction coefficient[6] is obtained.

$$\mu = b_0 + b_1 h_1 + b_2 \varepsilon \tag{2}$$

,where $b_0$, $b_1$ and $b_2$ are the coefficients to be estimated. Lots of data indicate that whether it is high-speed broadband steel or low narrow strip, this form can well fit the experimental results, and is a better model form.

In this way, five kinds of methods can be used to calculate the $\mu$ at each pass with measured data.

Method 1: Based on the measured forward slip and rolling force[7], the $\mu$ can be calculated by the Stone equation, which is:

$$\mu = \frac{\dfrac{1}{2}\sqrt{\dfrac{\Delta h}{R'}}}{1 - 2\sqrt{(1-\varepsilon)\dfrac{f}{\varepsilon}}} \tag{3}$$

Method 2: Equation (2) should be applied to linear fit the $\mu$ of each pass calculated by method 1, and then the $\mu$ of each pass can be calculated with the fitted model parameters.

Method 3: Computation of the $\mu$ can be inversed by using the forward slip equation based on the measured forward slip and rolling force, in which $\gamma$ is neutral angle, which is :

$$\begin{cases} f = \dfrac{R}{h_1} r^2 \\ r = \dfrac{1}{2}\sqrt{\dfrac{\Delta h}{R'}}[1 - \dfrac{1}{2\mu}(\sqrt{\dfrac{\Delta h}{R'}} - \dfrac{B(h_1\tau_f - h_0\tau_b)}{P})] \end{cases} \Rightarrow \mu = \frac{\sqrt{\dfrac{\Delta h}{R'}} - \dfrac{B(h_1\tau_f - h_0\tau_b)}{P}}{2(1 - 2\sqrt{\dfrac{fh_1}{h_0 - h_1}})} \tag{4}$$

Method 4: Equation (2) should be applied to linear fit the $\mu$ of each pass calculated by method 3, and then the $\mu$ of each pass can be calculated with the fitted model parameters.

Method 5: The $\mu$ is selected by the experience, and it is different in different rolled piece and rolling conditions. In this paper, the $\mu$ is 0.03.

## 2.3    Calculation of Deformation Resistance

Only the $\mu$ and $K$ in equation (1) can not be measured directly, and the $\mu$ can be obtained by the five kinds of methods in 2.2, so the calculation equation of $K$ can be reversely derived according to equation (1) as follows:

$$K = \frac{P}{B\sqrt{R'\Delta h}Q_p} + \frac{1}{2}(\tau_b + \tau_f) \tag{5}$$

Since the $\mu$ of each pass by the five methods is obtained, the $K$ of each pass can be calculated when the measured process parameters are substituted into the equation (5). According to the characteristics of the cold rolling process, the $K$ primarily relates to the corresponding $\varepsilon_\Sigma$, so the regression model of the $K$ is chosen as follows:

$$\sigma_s = \sigma_0 + \beta \varepsilon_\Sigma^n \tag{6}$$

,where $\sigma_s$ is principal stress that has the relationship with the $K$ that $K = 1.15 * \sigma_s$ ;$\sigma_0$ is the initial principal stress, and $\sigma_0$, $\beta$ and $n$ are the coefficients which need to be fitted; $\varepsilon_\Sigma$ is the cumulative reduction rate, and $\varepsilon_\Sigma = \dfrac{1}{3}\dfrac{H - h_0}{H} + \dfrac{2}{3}\dfrac{H - h_1}{H}$, in which $H$ is the original strip thickness that is the entry thickness of the first pass.

Select a set of measured process parameters as the calculating data.

**Table 1.** Measured process parameters

| Pass number | Entry thickness (um) | Exit thickness (um) | Measured rolling force(KN) | Forward slip (%) | Back tension $T_b$ (KN) | Front tension $T_f$ (KN) |
|---|---|---|---|---|---|---|
| 1 | 2405 | 1580 | 6961 | 0.248 | 9 | 132 |
| 2 | 1580 | 1000 | 6378 | 0 | 118 | 104 |
| 3 | 1000 | 630 | 6124 | 0.032 | 84 | 65 |
| 4 | 630 | 400 | 5927 | 0.359 | 64 | 44 |
| 5 | 400 | 282 | 5964 | 4.608 | 47 | 30 |

Where $R$ is the roll radius, $R = 194$ (mm); $B$ is the strip width, $B = 1219$ (mm); $T_b$ and $T_f$ are the back and front tension respectively, the relationship between the back, front tension and the back, front tensile stress is as follows:

$$\begin{cases} \tau_f = \dfrac{T_f}{Bh_1} \\ \tau_b = \dfrac{T_b}{Bh_0} \end{cases} \tag{7}$$

The calculated principal stress by five methods is as follows:

**Table 2.** Relationship between the calculated principal stress and the cumulative reduction rate by five methods.

| Pass num | Cumulative reduction rate $\varepsilon_\Sigma$ | Method 1 principal stress (MPa) | Method 2 principal stress (MPa) | Method3 principal stress (MPa) | Method 4 principal stress (MPa) | Method 5 principal stress (MPa) |
|---|---|---|---|---|---|---|
| 1 | 0.24 | 494.52 | 495.05 | 527.23 | 522.18 | 512.11 |
| 2 | 0.51 | 593.73 | 591.27 | 588.70 | 601.83 | 569.59 |
| 3 | 0.69 | 667.34 | 670.68 | 656.30 | 659.25 | 603.36 |
| 4 | 0.81 | 743.02 | 741.86 | 723.72 | 704.73 | 630.76 |
| 5 | 0.87 | 712.95 | 712.89 | 678.41 | 680.90 | 674.35 |

These data are drawn into a curve which can be more intuitive to study the relationship of change, as shows below:

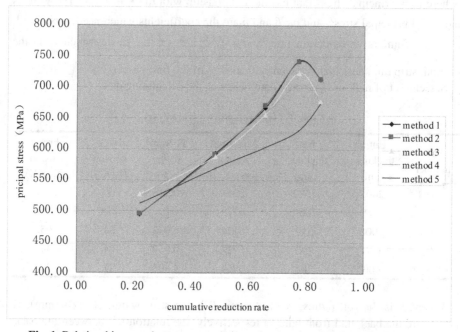

**Fig. 1.** Relationship curve between cumulative reduction rate $\varepsilon_\Sigma$ and principal stress $\sigma_s$

It can be seen from Figure 1 that no matter which method is used to calculate the principal stress, $\varepsilon_\Sigma$ and $\sigma_s$ is almost in a linear relationship when the $\varepsilon_\Sigma$ is small, that is $n=1$, and $\sigma_s = \sigma_0 + \beta * \varepsilon_\Sigma$ ; therefore, the $\sigma_0$ can be obtained by linear fitting the $\varepsilon_\Sigma$ and $\sigma_s$ of the first four passes .

After the $\sigma_s$ is obtained, the original model can be transformed, transposing into $\sigma_s - \sigma_0 = \beta * \varepsilon_\Sigma^n$ .Taking logarithmic of both sides $\ln(\sigma_s - \sigma_0) = \ln\beta + n\ln\varepsilon_\Sigma$ , the nonlinear model can be changed into the linear model $y=a+bx$ by ordering $y = \ln(\sigma_s - \sigma_0)$, $x = \ln\varepsilon_\Sigma$, $a = \ln\beta$ , and $b = n$ .As the coefficient $a$ and $b$ can be got using the least squares regression, and $\beta = e^a, n = b$ can be obtained, then all the coefficients can be calculated in $\sigma_s = \sigma_0 + \beta\varepsilon_\Sigma^n$ ,and then the new $K$ can be calculated.

## 2.4　Calculation of Rolling Force

The rolling force can be calculated by substituting the $\mu$ and $K$ calculated by the above methods into the equation (1). First, calculate the rolling force $P_0$ according to the $R$. Second, inverse compute the $R'$ according to $P_0$.Third, re-calculate the rolling pressure $P_1$ according to $R'$ . Then compare $P_0$ and $P_1$. If the error is less than the preset error, it is done. If it is larger than the preset, iteration should be continued. The flow chart of calculation is as follows:

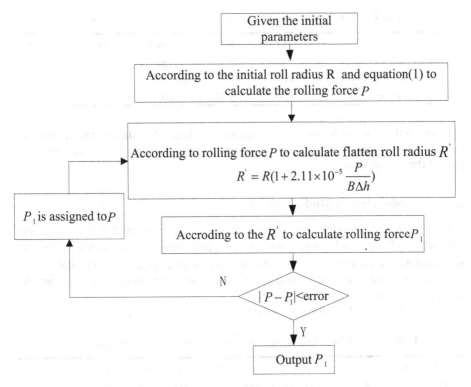

**Fig. 2.** Bland-Ford-Hill iterative equation flow chart

Computed rolling force by five methods is as follows:

**Table 3.** Comparison of computed rolling force and measured rolling force by five methods

| Pass num | Measured P(KN) | Compu P1(KN) | Error1 (%) | Compute dP2(KN) | Error2 (%) | Compute d P3(KN) | Error3 (%) | Compute d P4(KN) | Error4 (%) | Compute dP5(KN) | Error5 (%) |
|---|---|---|---|---|---|---|---|---|---|---|---|
| 1 | 6961 | 6940.9 | 0.29 | 6935.1 | 0.37 | 6916.3 | 0.64 | 6966.6 | -0.08 | 6943.9 | 0.25 |
| 2 | 6378 | 6941.7 | -1.78 | 6528.8 | -2.37 | 6616.7 | -3.74 | 6401.2 | -0.36 | 6410.5 | -0.51 |
| 3 | 6124 | 6146.8 | -0.37 | 6105.0 | 0.31 | 6097.7 | 0.43 | 6057.7 | 1.08 | 6254.1 | -2.12 |
| 4 | 5927 | 5551.4 | 6.34 | 5562.6 | 6.15 | 5450.1 | 8.05 | 5682.6 | 4.12 | 6039.5 | -1.90 |
| 5 | 5964 | 6281.0 | -5.32 | 6279.0 | -5.28 | 6323.7 | -6.03 | 6318.7 | -5.95 | 5623.3 | 5.71 |
| Average absolute error (%) | | | 2.82 | | 2.90 | | 3.78 | | 2.32 | | 2.10 |

P1, P2, P3, P4, and P5 in the above table are rolling force computed by five methods respectively. This is just a set of test data, so it may not be a good description of which method is better. In order to ensure the accuracy of the results, 1000 sets of data are selected for testing, and the test results are as follows.

**Table 4.** Rolling force errors using five methods by 1000 sets of test data

|  | Error 1 (%) | Error 2 (%) | Error 3 (%) | Error 4 (%) | Error 5 (%) |
|---|---|---|---|---|---|
| Average absolute error (%) | 1.45 | 1.87 | 1.40 | 1.24 | 1.27 |
| Mean square error | 1.43 | 1.71 | 1.45 | 1.22 | 1.22 |

From Table 4, it can be intuitively seen that method 4 has the minimum error, so method 4 is chosen to calculate the coefficient friction and deformation resistance to predict the rolling force.

## 2.5   Establishment of Model Library

Since the model parameters of $\mu$ and $K$ are not known in the beginning, the parameters of $\mu = b_0 + b_1 h_1 + b_2 \varepsilon$ and $\sigma_s = \sigma_0 + \beta \varepsilon_\Sigma^n$ need to be calculated by the measured data of method 4, and then they will be stored to establish the model library. This makes it easy to apply model parameters adaptive method to improve the calculation accuracy of rolling force.

Model library is as the following format

**Table 5.** Model library of the deformation resistance and friction coefficient

| Steel types | $\sigma_{0\_}$ old | $\beta_\_$ old | $n_\_$ old | $\sigma_{0\_}$ next | $\beta_\_$ next | $n_\_$ next | $b_{0\_}$ old | $b_{1\_}$ old | $b_{2\_}$ old | $b_{0\_}$ next | $b_{1\_}$ next | $b_{2\_}$ next |
|---|---|---|---|---|---|---|---|---|---|---|---|---|
| Type 1 | 402.9 | 333.4 | 1.12 | 402.9 | 333.4 | 1.12 | 0.021 | 0.006 | 0.024 | 0.021 | 0.006 | 0.024 |
| Type 2 | 347.1 | 503.8 | 0.85 | 347.1 | 503.8 | 0.85 | 0.043 | 0.006 | -0.089 | 0.043 | 0.006 | -0.089 |
| Type 3 | 403.9 | 422.4 | 0.96 | 403.9 | 422.4 | 0.96 | 0.006 | 0.001 | 0.103 | 0.006 | 0.001 | 0.103 |
| Type 4 | 401.6 | 442.9 | 1.09 | 401.6 | 442.9 | 1.09 | 0.012 | 0.007 | 0.032 | 0.012 | 0.007 | 0.032 |
| Type 5 | 460.7 | 411.9 | 1.04 | 460.7 | 411.9 | 1.04 | 0.041 | 0.005 | -0.086 | 0.041 | 0.005 | -0.086 |

$\sigma_{0\_}$old, $\beta\_$old and $n\_$old are the $K$ model parameters of preceding rolled steel coil; $\sigma_0\_$next, $\beta\_$next and $n\_$next are the predicted $K$ model parameters of next rolling steel coil. Similarly, $b_0\_$old, $b_1\_$old and $b_2\_$old are the $\mu$ parameters of preceding rolled steel coil; $b_0\_$next, $b_1\_$next and $b_2\_$next are the predicted $\mu$ model parameters of next rolling steel coil. The model parameters of next rolling steel are the same as the preceding in the initialization of the model library.

# 3    Online Adaptation of Model Parameters

## 3.1    Prediction on the Model Parameters of Next Rolling Steel Coil by Exponential Smoothing

By establishing the model library through the above method, the model parameters of $\mu = b_0 \_ next + b_1 \_ next * h_1 + b_2 \_ next * \varepsilon$ and $\sigma_s = \sigma_0 \_ next + \beta \_ next * \varepsilon_\Sigma^{n\_next}$ stored in the model library of corresponding steel can be directly called to predict the $\mu$ and $K$ of next rolling steel coil, and then the rolling force can be calculated. Using this rolling force to roll, real-time measured data can be got, and then new model parameters by measured data can be obtained by reusing method 4, expressing as $\sigma_0$_new, $\beta$_new, $n$_new, $b_0$_new, $b_1$_new, and $b_2$_new, and the model parameters of next rolling steel roil can be predicted by using exponential smoothing method.

Equations are as follows:

$$\begin{cases} \sigma_0\_next = (1-\alpha)*\sigma_0\_new + \alpha*\sigma_0\_old \\ \beta\_next = (1-\alpha)*\beta\_new + \alpha*\beta\_old \\ n\_next = (1-\alpha)*n\_new + \alpha*n\_old \\ b_0\_next = (1-\alpha)*b_0\_new + \alpha*b_0\_old \\ b_1\_next = (1-\alpha)*b_1\_new + \alpha*b_1\_old \\ b_2\_next = (1-\alpha)*b_2\_new + \alpha*b_2\_old \end{cases} \qquad (8)$$

,where $\alpha$ is the smoothing factor, which has a range of 0-1. After the rolling parameters of next coil are predicted according to the smoothing method, they will be deposited into the model library, and parameters should be updated with $\sigma_0$_next, $\beta$_next, $n$_next and $b_0$_next, $b_1$_next, $b_2$_next. Then $\sigma_0$_old, $\beta$_old, $n$_old, $b_0$_old, $b_1$_old, $b_2$_old are replaced by $\sigma_0$_new, $\beta$_new, $n$_new, $b_0$_new, $b_1$_new, $b_2$_new, and finally the model library gets updated. And then the roll parameters of the next rolling steel coil can be continued to predict by the above steps.

## 3.2    Selection of the Smoothing Factor $\alpha$

Smoothing factor $\alpha$ is equivalent to the scale factor. The smaller $\alpha$ is, the more greatly predicted model parameters are affected by the preceding rolled steel coil, so select $\alpha$=0.1, 0.2, 0.3, 0.4, 0.5 , comparison results of the predicted rolling force error are as follows:

**Table 6.** Error of predicted rolling force by different smoothing factor

|  | $\alpha$=0.1 | $\alpha$=0.2 | $\alpha$=0.3 | $\alpha$=0.4 | $\alpha$=0.5 |
|---|---|---|---|---|---|
| Average absolute error | 4.12 | 4.08 | 4.10 | 4.08 | 4.13 |
| Mean square error | 6.40 | 6.28 | 6.30 | 6.19 | 6.22 |

Table 6 provides the errors of predicted rolling force with 1000 sets of data, which intuitively reflects that there is the minimum rolling force error of adaptive prediction when $\alpha$=0.4 , so select the smoothing factor as 0.4.

Since the errors in table 6 are calculated by the predicted model parameters, they are all larger than errors in the table 4 which calculated by the measured data.

## 3.3 Summary of Adaptive Steps

To facilitate understanding, the adaptive process of section 2 is simplified as the following steps, as shows below:

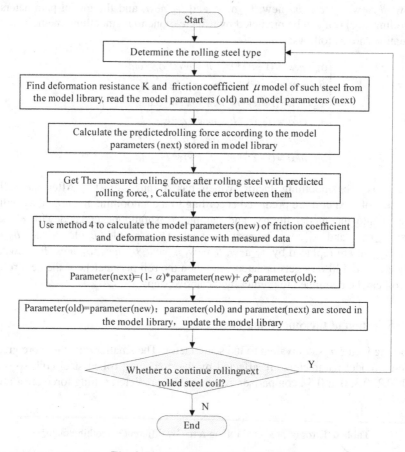

**Fig. 3.** Flow chart of adaptive process

# 4 Conclusion

The calculation results of 1000 sets of data show that the minimum error of rolling force appears when is fitted through the model $\mu = b_0 + b_1 h_1 + b_2 \varepsilon$, in which the $\mu$ is inversely computed by the forward slip equation based on the measured forward slip and rolling force. Hence, method 4 is selected to establish model library of $\mu$ and $K$. By the model parameters adaptive method, select $\alpha=0.4$, the adaptive predicted result is the most accurate, and errors are all less than 5%. As a result, the highly precise model parameters adaptive method can be applied in the actual production mill to meet the need for accurate prediction of rolling force in the industrial field.

**Acknowledgement.** This work was supported by the National Science Foundation of China under Grant 61075044。

# References

1. Liu, X.H., Hu, X.L., Du, L.X.: Computing Model and Application of the Rolling Parameters. Chemical Industry Press, Beijing (2007)
2. Sun, Y.K.: Computer Control of Strip Cold Rolling. Metallurgical Industry Press, Beijing (2002)
3. Wang, J.S., Jiang, Z.Y., Tieu, A.K., Liu, X.H., Wang, G.D.: A Method to Improve Model Calculation Accuracy of Process Control in Tandem Cold Mills. In: IEEE Conference on Industrial Electronics and Applications, pp. 2787–2790. IEEE Inst. of Elec., New York (2007)
4. Jiang, Z.Y., Xiong, S.W., Tieu, A.K., Jane, Q.: Modelling of the Effect of Friction on Cold Strip Rolling. J. Journal of Materials Processing Technology, 85–90 (2008)
5. Yang, J.M., Yang, Z.F., Che, H.J., Zhang, Q., Hao, R.F.: A New Method Based on Least 2 Squares of Regressing Deformation Resistance Model of St14 Steel. J. Iron and Steel 45(6), 44–48 (2010)
6. Guo, L.W., Yang, Q., Guo, L.: Comprehensive Parameters Self-adapting for a Rolling Force Model of Tandem Cold Rolling Process Control. J. Journal of University of Science and Technology 29(4), 413–416 (2007)
7. Li, X.Y., Song, H.P., Wu, C.H.: Rolling Theory Formula in the Cold Rolling Lubrication Experiments, p. 317. Metallurgical Industry Press, Beijing (1982)
8. Cao, H.D.: Mechanical Basis of Plastic Deformation and Rolling Principle. Mechanical Industry Press, Beijing (1979)

# Modeling and Simulation of Air-Boots for a Novel Soft-Terrain Walking Concept Vehicle

Cong Ma, Yang Cao, Fan Yu, and Zhe Luo

School of Mechanical Engineering, Shanghai Jiao Tong University, Shanghai, 200240, China
{mcmacong,fanyu,luozhe}@sjtu.edu.cn, caoyang0929@126.com

**Abstract.** It has been a difficult but hot subject to improve the vehicle trafficability in some complex soft-terrain environments in the research area for off-road vehicle dynamics and control. Based on previous study for a semi-tracked air-cushion vehicle, a novel soft-terrain concept vehicle with a walking mechanism by using six air-cushion boots is proposed. The vehicle motion is realized by driving-gears while the boots vertical motion is realized by air charging or discharging. Therefore the modeling of a single boot is the first important task for vehicle motion modeling and control. In this paper, the structure and working principle of the vehicle are described firstly. Then a parameterized steady-state model of air-boots considering the rubber elastic deformation is established, which is verified by comparing with finite element simulation results. The model can still be used while the size and material of boots changing. Finally, a numerical method to simulate boot air-charging process by using the established model is discussed, and a typical process is taken as an example. The research results provide useful references for future work on vehicle modeling and control algorithm design.

**Keywords:** Soft-terrain vehicle, Air-cushion boot, Finite element analysis, numerical simulation.

## 1    Introduction

It has been a difficult but hot subject to improve the vehicle trafficability in some complex soft-terrain environments in the research area for off-road vehicle dynamics and control [1]. Based on previous study for a semi-tracked air-cushion vehicle [2-4], a novel soft-terrain concept vehicle with a walking mechanism by using six air-cushion boots is proposed.

The new vehicle structure has potential advantages as follows,

- Air-cushion provides low ground pressure on soft terrain and good adaptive ability on uneven terrain.
- Non-conventional walking mechanism further improves vehicle's crossing-terrain ability.

Therefore, the novel vehicle may have a good performance on soft and uneven terrain conditions and also bring new inspiration.

C.-Y. Su, S. Rakheja, H. Liu (Eds.): ICIRA 2012, Part I, LNAI 7506, pp. 76–86, 2012.

Before taking some related actual experiments, it is necessary to make preliminary dynamics analysis for economy consideration. The modeling of a single boot would become the first important task for vehicle dynamics analysis.

In this paper, the structure and working principle of the vehicle are described firstly. Then a parameterized steady-state model of air-boots considering the rubber elastic deformation is established, which is verified by comparing with finite element simulation results. The model can still be used while the size and material of boots changing. Finally, a numerical method to simulate boot air-charging process by using the established model is discussed, and a typical process is taken as an example. The research results provide useful references for future work on vehicle modeling and control algorithm design.

## 2    Structure and Working Principle of the Vehicle

The structure of the novel soft-terrain vehicle is shown in fig. 1. In the design, the walking mechanism consists of six air-cushion boots (7 and 8) distributed in right and left sides symmetrically under the vehicle body. Each boot is similar to a diaphragm air spring and its capacity is variable. There is a high-pressure air chamber (2) inside the vehicle body. The pressure is maintained in an appropriate range by an air compressor (1) with driving motor under the control of designed algorithm. Each boot is connected with three-phase electromagnetic valve (3) through an airway (4). The volume of inner air is changed by switching phases. When the valve is switched to phase one, boot is connected with air chamber, the high-pressure air will flow into boot, then the boot is released on the ground. When the valve is switched to phase three, boot is connected with atmosphere, the air in the boot will be pushed out by an extension spring (6), then the boot is raised from the ground. The phase two is closed

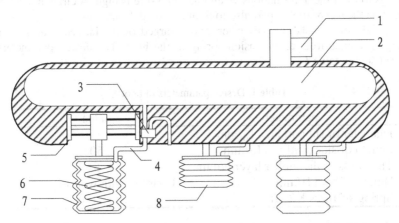

**Fig. 1.** Sketch map of the novel soft-terrain vehicle   (1-air compressor with driving motor 2-high-pressure air chamber 3-electromagnetic valve 4-airway    5-air-cushion boots longitudinal driving mechanism 6-spring(stretched) 7-air-cushion boot(charged) 8-air-cushion boot (discharged))

state, which will be switched to after a predetermined action finished to keep boot's current states. Furthermore, a low-pressure air chamber and one more phase could be added in case the rise up power is not enough. The longitudinal motion is realized by a longitudinal driving mechanism (5), whose structure detail will not be discussed in this paper.

# 3    Parameterized Steady-State Model of Air-Boots

## 3.1    Structure Detail of Air-Boots

A single air cushion boot is a hollow rotationally symmetric object, whose cross-section through symmetry axis is shown in fig. 2.

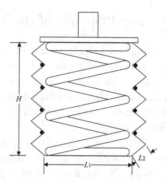

**Fig. 2.** Sketch map of air-boots

The air-cushion part of boots is made of rubber. In fig. 2, the black dots represent steel rings to limit the deformations when inner pressure is high. A circular steel plate is placed on the top of rubber part also to limit the top deformation.

The height of boot H changes when boot charged or discharged. The power of discharging comes from an extension spring in the boot. The design parameters of boot are listed in table 1.

**Table 1.** Design parameters of boot

| parameter | value |
| --- | --- |
| Diameter of support area $L_1$/mm | 300 |
| Length of side plotlines $L_2$/mm | 50 |
| Thickness of the rubber layer h/mm | 5 |
| Height of boot H/mm | Changes with working status |
| Spring stiffness K/(N/m) | 1000 |

## 3.2    Description of the Modeling Problem

Based on the structure of air-cushion boots, in the steady state, the height of boot H is only decided by inner pressure P and the volume of inner air V. The relationship can be expressed using the function,

$$H = f(P,V) \qquad (1)$$

(1) is what we are interested in actually. But it is hard to get the mapping from P V to H directly. On the other hand, if we know the mapping from H P to V, that is,

$$V = g(H,P) \qquad (2)$$

(2) can be treated as

$$V = h_p(H) \qquad (3)$$

Where $h_p(x) = g(x, y)|_{y=P}$ , then

$$H = h_p^{-1}(V) \qquad (4)$$

(4) is equivalent to (1).

So in this section, different displacement constraint and pressure load are applied on boot to observe the variation law of the volume of inner air, after getting the mapping relationship from H P to V, the specific form of (1) can be obtained by mathematical transformation.

### 3.3    Conventions and Assumptions

The conventions, simplifications and assumptions are as follows,

1. The thickness of ruber is treated as zero in geometric analysis.
2. Shown in fig. 3, the intersection polyline $DA_1B_1A_2B_2A_3B_3A_4B_4A_5B_5A_6E$ of a plane through the symmetry axis and the boot is used as object to study the deformation of boot.

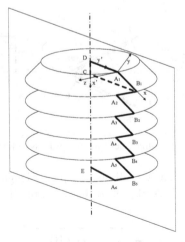

**Fig. 3.** Air-cushion boot ployline element

3. A coordinate system of Oxyz is established, whose origin is point $A_1$, x-direction is from $A_1$ to $B_1$, z-direction is perpendicular to the plane, y-direction is defined by right-hand rule.
4. Another coordinate system of Ox'y' is established, whose origin is point D, x'-direction is from D to C, y'-direction is from D to $A_1$.
5. Non-spring model is discussed in this session, the spring force will be treated as external force in the following research.
6. All lines in set { $A_iB_i$, $B_iA_{i+1}$ (i=1,2,3,4,5) }deformate symmetrically.

There are also some inferences.

1. The volume of air can be calculated as $V_{A_1B_1CD} \times 10$, where $V_{A_1B_1CD}$ represent the volume of body made by rotating the polygon $A_1B_1CD$ around the boot axis. The following part will focus on $V_{A_1B_1CD}$.
2. The shape of boots, the applied displacement constraint H and the pressure load P are all axisymmetric, so the total force applied on the ployline element in the z direction is 0.

## 3.4 Theoretical Derivation of the Model

$V_{A_1B_1CD}$ is defined by the location and sharp of line $A_1B_1$. In coordinate system of Ox'y', the coordinates of point $A_1$ never change, the coordinates of point $B_1$ are determined by displacement constraint and pressure load, the sharp of line $A_1B_1$ is determined only by pressure load. For steady-states analysis, it is feasible to assume that the coordinates of point $B_1$ determined by displacement constraint firstly(shown in fig. 4(a)), then the coordinates of point $B_1$ change caused by pressure load (shown in fig. 4(b)) and finally line $A_1B_1$ deformates caused by pressure load (shown in fig. 4(c)) .

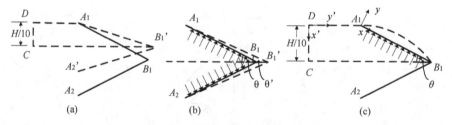

**Fig. 4.** The assumed deformation process of line $A_1B_1$

In condition of fig. 4(a), assume that all lines keep their length.
So $A_1B_1'=B_1'A_2'=A_1B_1=B_1A_2=L_2$, the distance R from $B_1'$ to C can be obtained by (5).

$$R = L_1/2 + \sqrt{L_2^2 - (H/10)^2} \qquad (5)$$

In condition of fig. 4(b), the pressure applied on line $A_1B_1$ is perpendicularity to line $A_1B_1$, so it does not affect the coordinates of point $B_1$. The pressure applied on line $A_2B_1$ makes line $A_1B_1$ stretched. The stretched length can be obtained by (6).

$$\Delta L = L_2 \times \frac{0.5 \times P \times L_2 \times b \times \sin 2\theta'}{E \times b \times h} = L_2 \frac{PL_2 \sin \theta' \cos \theta'}{Eh} \tag{6}$$

Where $E$ is rubber tensile elastic modulus, b is the breadth of the element which can be eliminate, $\theta'$ is shown in figure. In this condition, $\theta$ and $\theta'$ are treated as equal, so (6) can be translated to,

$$\Delta L = L_2 \frac{PL_2 \sin \theta \cos \theta}{Eh} \tag{7}$$

Where $\theta$ is defined by $\theta = \arcsin \frac{H/10}{L_2} = \arcsin \frac{H}{10L_2}$.

Condition of fig. 4(c) is similar to a typical condition in mechanics of materials, uniform load supply on simply supported beam. Reference to existing results, the deformation of line $A_1B_1$ can be expressed as (8) in coordinate system of Oxyz,

$$y = \frac{qx}{24EI}(L_2'^3 - 2L_2'x^2 + x^3) \qquad 0 \le x \le L_2' \tag{8}$$

Where $q$ is uniform load defined by $q = P \times b$, $I$ is moment of inertia defined by $I = bh^3/3$, $L_2'$ is the length of line $A_1B_1$ considering tensile deformation defined by $L_2' = L_2 + \Delta L$.

Rewrite (8) in coordinate system of Ox'y' in implicit function form,

$$\begin{cases} x' = x \sin \theta' - y \cos \theta' \\ y' = x \cos \theta' + y \sin \theta' + L_1/2 \end{cases} \tag{9}$$

Where $\theta' = \arcsin \frac{H/10}{L_2'} = \arcsin \frac{H}{10L_2'}$.

By calculus,

$$V_{A_1B_1CD} = \int_{x'=0}^{H/10} \pi y'^2 \, dx' = \int_{x=0}^{L_2} \pi (x \cos \theta' + y \sin \theta' + L_1/2)^2 \, d(x \sin \theta' - y \cos \theta') \tag{10}$$

And,

$$V = 10V_{A_1B_1CD} \tag{11}$$

(11) is the specific form of (2).

It is hard and not necessary to write the analytic form of (11) out. In the following discussion, the numerical solution of  (11) is used.

## 3.5    Finite Element Simulations

In order to examine the correctness of the model, take a kind of rubber and the design size (see in table 1) as example, the finite element simulations are carried. ANSYS is used as the software platform, whose effectiveness is recognized.

An actual experiment may be more persuasive. But actually, the change of boot volume is not significant, so it is hard to design a method to measure the volume of inner air precisely under the influence of measurement error. On the other hand, this paper is focus on preliminary analysis for economy consideration. So the actual experiment is postponed.

Choose SHELL208 as element type, and mooney-rivlin hyperelastic material 9-parameter model[5] as the Material model. The parameters of the mooney-rivlin hyperelastic model are listed in table 2.

**Table 2.** Mooney-rivlin hyperelastic model parameters

| C10 | C01 | C20 | C11 | C02 |
|---|---|---|---|---|
| 1.6MPa | $-0.858$MPa | 0.888Mpa | $-2.758$Mpa | 1.993Mpa |
| C30 | C21 | C12 | C03 | |
| 0.219Mpa | $-1.460$Mpa | 2.967Mpa | $-1.727$ Mpa | |

The rubber tensile elastic modulus is 10.52Mpa corresponding to the mooney-rivlin hyperelastic material model. Poisson ratio is set to 0.5.

Fig. 5 shows the simulation results and the error between theoretical model and simulation results.

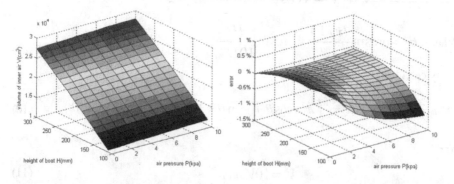

**Fig. 5.** Finite element simulation results (left) and the errors between theoretical model and simulation results (right)

The errors between theoretical model and simulation results are very small. So the assumptions made in this section are acceptable. The error may be caused by the difference of model detail.

Furthermore, specific form of (1) is got by numerical method using (11).

# 4    Air-Charging Process Simulation

## 4.1    Numerical Method

In order to design control algorithm, the air-charging transient dynamics process should be studied clearly. (The discharging process can be studied by the same way.) A numerical way to simulate the air-charging process is proposed in fig. 6.

(12) is used to calculate flow capacity [6]

$$Q_i = c_q A \sqrt{2 \frac{P_{in} - P_i}{\rho}} \tag{12}$$

Where $c_q$ is volumetric efficiency, A is cross-sectional area of airway, $\rho$ is air density.

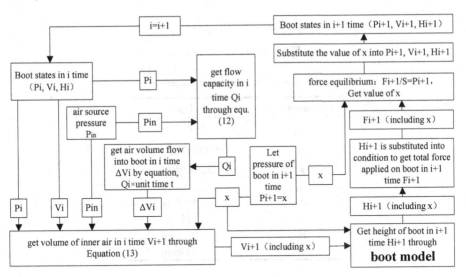

**Fig. 6.** The simulation flow diagram

Poisson's formula of the ideal gas is used to calculate the volume of inner air,

$$\begin{cases} P_i V_i^n = P_{i+1} V_i'^n \\ P_{in} \Delta V_i^n = P_{i+1} \Delta V_i'^n \\ V_{i+1} = V_i' + \Delta V_i' \end{cases} \tag{13}$$

Where n is polytropic exponent, the letters with apostrophe represent the volume of "air mass" of the i +1 time. It is worth mentioning that all P's appeared in (13) represent absolute air pressure, which is different from other equations.

The enlarged and bold "boot model" is the model discussed in section 3.

## 4.2    Simulation Condition

The condition is shown in fig. 7. An object placed on a fixed platform, with an air cushion boot connected to below the bottom. Air charging start until the height of boot is 300mm.

The simulation parameters are listed in table 3.

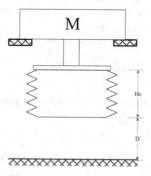

**Fig. 7.** Simulation condition

**Table 3.** Simulation parameters

| parameters | value |
|------------|-------|
| $c_q$ | 0.82 |
| A | $0.0007\text{m}^2$ |
| $\rho$ | $1.324\text{kg/m}^3$ |
| n | 1.4 |
| Pin | 10Kpa |
| M | 45kg |
| $H_0$ | 150mm |
| D | 100mm |

## 4.3    Simulation Results

Fig. 8 shows the changes of height of boot, flow capacity, volume of inner air and pressure of inner air over time.

The results show that after charging started 0.13s, the boot reaches the ground, then the object is lifted in about 0.01s, and the height of boot becomes 300mm finally.

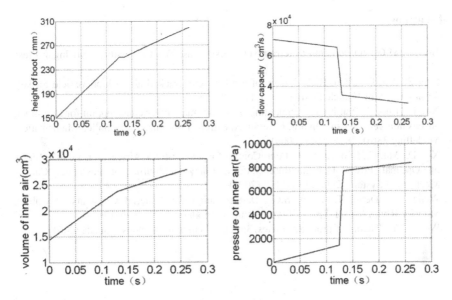

**Fig. 8.** Simulation results

## 5    Conclusions

This paper gets a parameterized steady-state model of air-boots considering the rubber elastic deformation, which is verified by comparing with finite element simulation results. This will benefits parameter design optimization. But the relationship between the model and the boot's size and material cannot be expressed in a concise form. An approximate analytical formula composed by boot's size and material constants could be studied in the further work.

A numerical method to simulate boot air-charging process is also discussed in this paper. The discharging process can be simulated in the same way. This will benefits the whole vehicle modeling and control algorithm design. The complete model including the soft-ground will be studied in the further work.

The novel soft-terrain concept vehicle may provide potential applications for the transportation and operation in some special requirements e.g. military and scientific exploration etc. Its feasibility will be further discussed and related control algorithm will be designed in the future.

**Acknowledgement.** The research is sponsored by the Specialized Research Fund for the Doctoral Program of Higher Education of China under Grant No. 20100073110063.

The authors would like to deeply thank the support from the fund.

# References

1. Bekker, M.G.: Introduction to terrain-vehicle systems. The University of Michigan Press (1969)
2. Luo, Z., Yu, F., Chen, B.C.: Design of a novel semi tracked air-cushion vehicle for soft terrain. Int. J. of Vehicle Design 31(1), 112–123 (2003)
3. Xie, D., Luo, Z., Yu, F.: The computing of the optimal power consumption for semi-track air-cushion vehicle using hybrid generalized extremal optimization. Applied Mathematical Modelling 33(6), 2831–2844 (2009)
4. Xie, D., Ma, C., Luo, Z., et al.: Pitch Control for a Semi-track Air-cushion Vehicle Based on Optimal Power Consumption. SAE International Journal of Passenger Cars - Mechanical Systems 2(1), 1136–1142 (2009)
5. Wang, W., Deng, T., Zhao, S.G.: Determination for Material Constants of Rubber Mooney-Rivlin Model. Special Purpose Rubber Products 25(4), 8–10 (2004)
6. Wong, J.Y.: Theory of ground vehicles, 3rd edn. John wiley & Sons, Canada (2001)

# Concept of Actuation and Control for the EO Smart Connecting Car (EO scc)

Michael Jahn, Martin Schröer, Yong-Ho Yoo,
Mehmed Yüksel, and Frank Kirchner

German Research Center for Artificial Intelligence,
DFKI Bremen - Robotics Innovation Center
Robert-Hooke-Str. 5, 28359 Bremen, Germany
(michael.jahn,martin.schroeer,yong-ho.yoo,
mehmed.yueksel,frank.kirchner)@dfki.de
http://robotik.dfki-bremen.de

**Abstract.** This paper describes the mechanical structure, electrical layout and control concept of the four-wheeled electric vehicle EO smart connecting car (EO scc). This car is able to change its shape, a feature provided by a foldable chassis, which also allows the coupling with suitable vehicle modules to thereby reconfigurable automobile unions. A concept for modular vehicle unions and extended maneuverability is provided by an innovative suspension. This suspension features 5 degrees of freedom for each wheel that can be controlled individually, being implemented as a parallel hybrid structure. The software control and the mechanical and electronic components, as well as simulation-based design of construction and mobility concepts of the EO scc are described.

**Keywords:** modular electric car, extended maneuverability, wheel hub motor, drive by-wire, morphology, car docking, road train.

**Fig. 1.** The EO Smart Connecting Car (EO scc)

C.-Y. Su, S. Rakheja, H. Liu (Eds.): ICIRA 2012, Part I, LNAI 7506, pp. 87–98, 2012.

# 1   Introduction

A constantly increasing number of road users leads to increasing occurrences of traffic jams and overcrowded roads, this poses a problem to be solved by new transport concepts utilizing new approaches. Examples of such concepts are the straddling bus concept (3D Express Coach) from Shenzhen Huashi Future Parking Equipment [1], the person cabs at high rails of SkyTran [1], the aerial cableway concept [2] or the autonomous cab transport system of the company Ultra [3]. The European Union project SARTRE [4] studied the coupling of road vehicles to road trains by communicating via radio link. In this paper, the software control and the mechanical and electronic components, as well as simulation-based design of construction and mobility concepts of the EO smart connecting car (EO scc) are described. The EO scc was developed and tested as real prototype (Figure 1) at DFKI RIC in Bremen[2].

# 2   Coupling Concept and Mechanical Structure

A coupleable chassis offers a possibility for a united vehicle entity to adapt to the desired space, transport capacity or age-appropriate accessibility of each individual demand. Aerodynamics or driving dynamics can be adjusted to the individual user behavior and environmental conditions. Smaller modular units are expandable to Multi Purpose Vehicles (MPVs) on demand.

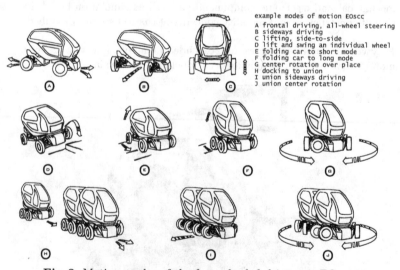

example modes of motion EOscc
A frontal driving, all-wheel steering
B sideways driving
C lifting, side-to-side
D lift and swing an individual wheel
E folding car to short mode
F folding car to long mode
G center rotation over place
H docking to union
I union sideways driving
J union center rotation

**Fig. 2.** Motion modes of the four-wheeled drive unit EO scc

---

[1] Shenzhen Huashi Future Parking Equipment http://www.hsfuture.com/
[2] DFKI EO scc,
   http://robotik.dfki-bremen.de/de/forschung/robotersysteme/
   eo-smart-connecting-car.html

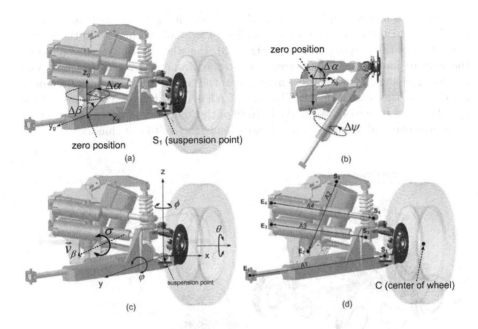

**Fig. 3.** Definition of EO scc suspension dynamics

Figure 2 illustrates the versatility of such a modular system, presenting some basic examples. Also, by attaching and detaching functional segments the vehicle configurations can be adapted to the individual task of transportation.

The central element of the EO scc for achieving this flexibility is the active suspension mechanism (Figure 3). The chassis configuration of the EO scc provides the possibility of a modular concatenation of multiple chassis elements by electromechanical clutches, analogous to reconfigurable robotic systems like Swarm-Bot [5]. In a basic setup resembling a usual car, two chassis axles with a folding mechanism provide a similar effect to space saving and shape changing, as also shown by the City Car concept of MIT [6].

Figure 2 illustrates the main maneuverability features of EO scc, both for a single vehicle and for a multi-vehicle unioned setup. The basic structure of the electric vehicle EO scc is characterized by a movable connection of the passenger cabin implemented by a pivoted front axle, inclinable and tiltable rear axle, and by the four individually adjustable suspensions with wheel hub motors. Small flexible electric vehicles with distributed drives for urban use were already presented, e.g. the Nissan Pivo [7]; active suspensions are already tested e.g. with the F 300 Life Jet [9] or used in series by BMW [8]. The EO scc integrates those technologies, altogether offering 23 individually adjustable degrees of freedom. Three independently controllable axes implement the folding mechanism, five adjustable axles hold each of the four wheel suspensions of the unit. The active suspensions provide the maneuverability necessary for positioning the coupling points and also offer the characteristics needed for different driving conditions onroad, offroad, stable driving along curves and entry-exit situations.

These suspensions implemented in the EO scc enable the vehicle to variably change it's geometry, based on the principle of a double wishbone. In the implementation of the suspension units (Figure 3), the wheel hub motor is bolted to the steering knuckle, which is directly controlled from the 2250N steering cylinder A3. The knuckle is rotatably mounted in the swivel-fork with a 2500N-linear actuator by the setting of A1. The axis of A1 is met at the pivot point, which links the lifting boom swivel at the bottom of the knuckle and provides the wheel to perform an additional horizontal movement relative to the chassis.

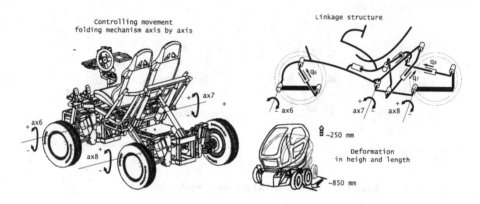

**Fig. 4.** Control and linkage of the folding mechanism

The height adjustment of the Eo scc suspensions (Figure 3(c)) is implemented by a 4-membered linkage between the knuckle and chassis carrier. This lifting boom is controlled by the 6800N-linear actuator A2 by a lever to the shock absorber. An additional 1100N linear actuator A4 is mounted for adjustment of the angular position of the fork by changing the regulating distance (wheel camber).

The folding mechanism (length and height adjustment) of the EO scc depicted in Figure 4 is based on a linkage of three variable transmission elements and offers one degree of freedom at the

**Table 1.** Characteristics of the EO scc, min and max values depend on the folding state of the vehicle, weight includes main battery (LiFePO$_4$)

| EO scc characteristics | | |
|---|---|---|
| | min. | max. |
| lenght | 1480mm | 2250mm |
| width | 1400mm | 1600mm |
| height | 1650mm | 2090mm |
| weight | approx. 755kg (unloaded) | |
| payload | approx. 200kg | |

front axle carrier and 2 DOF on the rear carrier. by use of the actuator q7, the inclination of the front and rear axle carrier can be adjusted relative to a horizontal plane by changing the length of q6 and q8. The console and seat module is also connected to the folding swing arm (q8), thereby an upright position of the driver is retained.

The variable wheelbase allows EO scc to adapt to all kinds of transportation needs, e.g. on space-saving parking, small ways, easy entry, united group driving or frontal wind resistance (Cf. table 1).

## 3   Simulation-Based Design

The EO scc morphology has been geometrically modeled in Solidworks [3] and the CAD data designed in Solidworks has been exported to the multi-body dynamic simulator ADAMS [4] to simulate and test its physical properties. In the ADAMS simulator, several physical properties, such as mass, spring, actuator dynamics, wheel-road contact dynamics with the pac2002 tire model [10], etc., have been modeled additionally. The low-level control properties such as kinematic algorithms and behavior patterns have been modeled and tested in the ADAMS/MATLAB co-simulation framework. Figure 3(a)-(d) show the wheel suspension with four cylinders. Algorithm 1 shows the inverse kinematic algorithm. The coordinates $S(x, y, z)$ and $E(x, y, z)$ of the cylinder-lengths A1, A2, A3 and A4 (Figure 3(d)) are rotated by the angles $\alpha$, $\beta$, $\phi$ and $\varphi$. Displacements $y$ and $z$ of the suspension point $S_1$ and rotation angles $\phi$ and $\varphi$ are the inputs to the inverse kinematic algorithm, are the outputs from them.

Given T (translation matrix), R (rotation matrix) on an arbitrary axis ($\vec{v}$), and U (input matrix), rotation about the axis is described by the Euler angle as follows,

$$Y = T^{-1} R_x^{-1} R_y^{-1} R_z R_y R_x T U \tag{1}$$

---

**Algorithm 1.** Inverse Kinematic Algorithm of Wheel Suspension

---

1: **Initialization:** $S_1, S_2, S_3, S_4, E_1, E_2, E_3, E_4, \alpha, \beta, \phi, \varphi, C$
2: **Input:** $\Delta y, \Delta z, \Delta \phi, \Delta \varphi$
3: calculate $\vec{v_\beta}$ from $\Delta \alpha, \Delta \sigma$ according to inputs $\Delta y, \Delta z$ (see Figure 3(c))
4: rotate points $S_1, S_2, S_3, S_4, E_3, E_4, C$ by $\Delta \sigma$ on the axis $\vec{v_\beta}$ using the Euler angle
5: rotate points $S_1, S_2, S_3, S_4, E_3, E_4, C$ by $\Delta \alpha$ on the z-axis of the zero position using the Euler angle
6: calculate $\vec{v_1}$ through $\overline{S_1 E_1}$
7: calculate $\Delta \psi$ of rotation on $\vec{v_1}$ in order to rotate $S_3, S_4, C$ by $\Delta \varphi$
8: rotate points $S_1, S_2, S_3, S_4, E_3, E_4, C$ by $\Delta \psi$ on the axis $\vec{v_1}$ using the Euler angle
9: calculate the flat vector of wheel $\vec{v_w}$
10: $\vec{v_2} \leftarrow$ cross product $\vec{v_1} \times \vec{v_w}$
11: rotate points $S_1, S_2, S_3, S_4, E_3, E_4, C$ by $\Delta \phi$ on the axis $\vec{v_2}$ using the Euler angle
12: calculate $S_2, E_2$ according to $S_1$ using the cosine rule.
13: $A1 \leftarrow \overline{S_1 E_1}$, $A2 \leftarrow \overline{S_2 E_2}$, $A3 \leftarrow \overline{S_3 E_3}$ and $A4 \leftarrow \overline{S_4 E_4}$
14: **Return** $A1, A2, A3, A4$

---

[3] Solidworks, http://www.solidworks.com
[4] ADAMS, http://www.mscsoftware.com

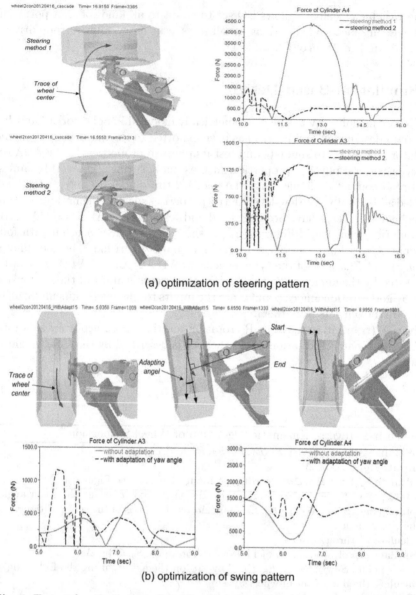

(a) optimization of steering pattern

(b) optimization of swing pattern

**Fig. 5.** Test and optimization of steering and swing behavior pattern in simulation

The driving modes proposed in Figure 2 have been achieved using the inverse kinematic algorithm and the motion-patterns have been developed and optimized. Figure 5(a) shows the motions for the mode-change from the frontal driving mode to the sideways driving mode (see Figure 2): The method 1 consists of two steps in which the first step is a swing and the second is a rotation, whereas the method 2 has the swing and rotation together in one step and it definitely reduces the force of cylinder A4. When the wheel has a swing motion without any changing of wheel angle, cylinder A4 has a big force like shown in Figure 5(b). An adaptation of yaw angle of the wheel belong to the motion of the wheel center can reduce the maximum force of cylinder 4: Figure 5(b) shows a comparison of the swing motions with the adaptation and without one.

## 4  Electrical Topology and Components

A 48V main power supply circuit of EO scc is used for the locomotion of the vehicle with 4 wheel hub motors, for adapting the morphology and changing

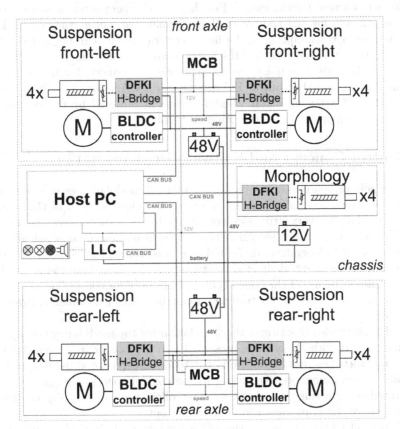

(M): 48V 4kW BLCD motor, ⊗⊗●◁: lighting system, BLDC controller: 4kW BLCD analogue motor controller, MCB: Motor contoller board interfacing BLDC controller, ⊏▭◖: electric linear actuator, DFKI H-Bridge: DFKI developed H-Bridge, LLC: low level controller for safety and peripherals, 48V: 48 V main battery and 12V 12V secondary battery

**Fig. 6.** EO scc electrical topology

the driving behavior through changing the suspensions run-time properties. A secondary power supply circuit based on 12V is used for the main control systems of the vehicle, peripheral devices and lighting system (Figure 6). Monitoring and control of the circuits is handled by a industrial PC and a low level controller implementing a basic battery and power management system.

The most power consuming elements in the main power circuit while driving are the brushless hub motors with related power of 2,5kW and a maximum power of 4kW. They can reach a maximum torque of 140Nm, a related rotational speed of 650rpm, a maximum speed of ca. 70km/h and up to 84,5 percent efficiency. Each motor is controlled by a 4kW analogue motor controller, which creates 3-phase pwm current for the motor. Per chassis axle there is one motor control board responsible for the control of these 2 analogue motor controllers. The maximum power consumption of the linear electric motors can be up to 800W by 48V. The control task of each of the linear motors was implemented by DFKI-developed H-Bridges. The H-Bridges of each axle are connected with the motor controller board and the control PC directly on a CAN-bus. The PC used is based on the PC/104 industrial standard [5] and is powered by the secondary power circuit independently of the primary circuit.

## 5    Control Concept and Software Implementation

As the vehicle presented here is highly modular, a modular approach has also been choosen for the control concept, even on the physical level of the implementation. That is, every drive element, consisting of a suspension unit and a wheel hub motor, is controlled exclusively. This is implemented physically by the utiziation of independent, dedicated electrical controllers, logically by the utiziation of independent, dedicated software tasks for each drive element. This approach allows the use of the control concept not only for controlling a certain, single vehicle, but rather for controlling a union of functional elements, together forming a vehicle.

This flexibility also constitutes the foundation for the modularity concept to be demonstrated with the vehicle presented here: If two or more vehicles are coupled together, the united vehicle is not to be understood consisting of two (or more) vehicles anymore. According to the control concept designed, it can be operated being a singe vehicle entity. The following sections will present the main aspects of the implementation of this concept.

With respect to the modular setup of the vehicle, each drive element is connected independently to the vehicle's central control unit. Within each single drive element, every active unit is controlled by a dedicated controller board. This is a controller for each of the four linear actor elements handling the wheel's position and orientation, plus one controller driving the wheel motor. These controllers use the CAN bus protocol for communication, all controllers of a single drive element form a CAN device using a certain address space. In the vehicle presented in this paper, two of these logical devices - corresponding to two drive elements - form one

---

[5] The PC/104 Consortium, http://www.pc104.org

**Table 2.** Technical data of the EO scc electrical topology

| Power supplies | | | |
|---|---|---|---|
| | battery type | voltage | capacity |
| main power circuit | option a: silicone lead-acid | 48V | 2x36Ah |
| | option b: lithium iron phosphate (LiFePO$_4$) | 52V | 70Ah |
| secondary power circuit | lead-acid | 12V | 36Ah |

| Actuators | | |
|---|---|---|
| type of actuators | usage area | max. force |
| linear electric actuators | 4 in each suspension | 1100-6800N |
| | 4 for morphology | 1100-6800N |
| wheel hub motor | 1 in each suspension | 140Nm |

| Control devices | | |
|---|---|---|
| device | quantity | purpose of use |
| Host PC (PC104) | 1 | main computer for the control of EO scc |
| DFKI H-Bridge | 20 | controller for electic linear actuator |
| motor controller board (mcb) | 2x1 (on each axle) | interface for BLDC motor controller |
| low level controller (llc) | 1 | battery management and switching of lighting system |

of the vehicle's axes and are connected to the central control unit using a single, dedicated CAN bus line (Figure 6). The complete vehicle is then constituted by using a number of such axes (e.g. two for the vehicle presented in this paper), each being connected to the central control unit. This "ordinary car" configuration of the vehicle has to be understood to be just one of many possible configurations (e.g. 2-wheeled, 3-wheeled, ..., $n$-wheeled) using the same control concept. For any given configuration, the software implementation maps the configuration of the vehicle to a corresponding object model.

At the highest level of the object model, all vehicle objects are contained in an abstract global vehicle object, which is also containing addiditonal objects for input controls and the folding mechanism. Controlling the whole vehicle is done by issuing commands to the global vehicle object, e.g. by using the input controls (Figure 7). When a command is issued to the vehicle, e.g. by a driver turning the steering wheel, this input is given to the top level vehicle object. The vehicle object is then computing the target values for it's direct child objects (e.g. axis objects) contained in the vehicle's current configuration, which are then refining the target values for their child objects. This process is continued until the target values for the actuator objects (e.g. drive element object) on the lowest level of the model have been computed and are then issued to the hardware.

This approach allows great flexibility in the control of each of the vehicle's axes, drive elements and wheel motors, and also constitutes the foundation needed for the vehicle's modularity concept. If, for example, two or more vehicles start a combined coupling maneouver, the control concept remains the same, even for this rather complex vehicle configurations. The addiditonal vehicle elements are just added to the control mechanism being additional logical objects using a corresponding set of parametrical inputs. The mechanism of calculation of the target position and orientation for each element can remain the same, it is then just serving a higher number of objects, calculating the corresponding target values for each object involved. For the actual implementation of the control software, Rock: the Robot Construction Kit [6,7], also developed at DFKI RIC, was used.

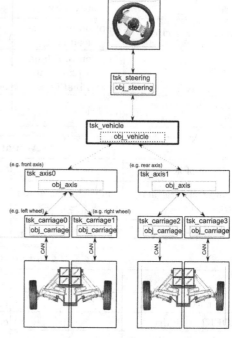

**Fig. 7.** Layout of the control concept

The user interface was designed and developed to offer a simple, intuitive way to control even such a complex device as the vehicle presented here. To achieve this, the vehicle is mainly controlled using controls that can be assumed to be well known: a steering wheel, two pedals and a 6-gears gear shift. Additionally, a touch screen element displays information about the vehicle's state (current mode of operation, battery state, motor current, etc.). In the initial mode of operation (1st gear), these elements can be used just like in a ordinary car, selecting the 2nd gear reverses the drive direction. But beyond that, by using the gear shift element, the user is able to switch to other, rather complex modes of operation, which will also change the way the input controls will drive the vehicle (Figure 8). If, e.g. the user sets the gear shift mechanism to 5th gear, the vehicle changes it's mode of operation to the "turn-in-place" mode, thus bringing each wheel into a 45 degrees position, that allows the vehicle to turn on the spot. To operate the vehicle in this mode of operation, the steering wheel is used. If it is turned in this mode, the vehicle will turn accordingly; the degree of turning determining the turn speed. Thus, the motion applied by the user to the wheel is reproduced by the whole vehicle - a very intuitive way of controlling this rather complex device.

---

[6] ROCK: the Robot Construction Kit http://www.rock-robotics.org
[7] ROCK is based on Orocos RTT http://www.orocos.org

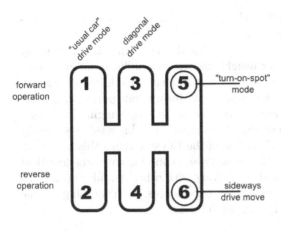

**Fig. 8.** Mapping of operation modes

Other modes of operation available are a diagonal movement mode, that allows the car to move diagonally forth (3th gear) and back (4th gear) and the sideways drive mode (6th gear), that allows the car to move sideways by bringing the wheels into a 90 degrees orientation (Cf. figure 2). If the user turns the steering wheel while in this operation mode, the car will move to the side the steering wheel was turned to, the degree of turn again determining the movement speed.

As the whole control mechanism is implemented being pure "drive-by-wire", thus every action command in the vehicle is issued electrically, the whole input controls setup and mapping presented here have to be understood to be just one demonstration of how the vehicle can be controlled - from the technical point of view there is virtually no limit for changing the whole input controls setup to another layout by just adjusting the corresponding parts of the control software.

# 6   Conclusions and Outlook

With the basic structure of the EO scc a new approach is offered, proving the advantages of adjustable wheel suspensions and a variable vehicle morphology for the coupling of vehicle segments. Energy management, easy navigation,

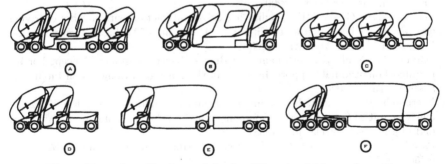

**Fig. 9.** Examples of basic modules for different vehicle configurations

enhanced maneuverability, contactless charging and unlimited range can be developed further using this concept.

While developing and implementing the vehicle described in this paper, many new experiences and a overall better insight into the possibilites and also problems of new approaches to electric mobility was gained. This knowledge is another step essential to the further development of future transport concepts for handling of a constantly growing number of road users and changing individual end environmental transportation needs. Furthermore, this knowledge is already used in the development of a second version of the EO scc. When this second iteration of the EO scc is completed, the mobility and coupling concepts described in this paper will be evaluated practically, along with other modular options as depicted in figure 9, which will give further experiences, then focusing on the features and characteristics of such unioned vehicles.

**Acknowledgement.** The development of the EO scc was funded by the BMVBS (German Federal Ministry of Transport, Building and Urban Development) and conducted within the Electric Mobility Pilot Regions project. Special appreciation goes to all members of the DFKI RIC Bremen supporting the accomplishment of this project, especially Roman Szczuka, David Grünwald, Philipp Kloss, Sujeef Shanmugalingam, Robert Thiel, Jens Mey and Andreas Scholz.

# References

1. Malewicki, D.J.: 2052: a retrospective of solid-state transportation systems. Proceedings of the IEEE 87(4), 680–687 (1999)
2. Seeber, A.: The Renaissance of the Cableway. Prokopp & Hechensteiner (2011)
3. Lowson, M.V.: PRT for Airport Applications, Paper 05-0432 TRB 84th Annual Meeting (2005)
4. Robinson, T., Chan, E., Coelingh, E.: Operating Platoons On Public Motorways: An Introduction To The SARTRE Platooning Programme. In: Proceedings of the 17th ITS World Congress, Busan (2010)
5. Gross, R., Bonani, M., Mondada, F., Dorigo, M.: Autonomous Self-assembly in a Swarm-bot. In: Proc. of the 3rd Int. Symp. on Autonomous Minirobots for Research and Edutainment, AMiRE 2005, pp. 314–322. Springer, Berlin (2006)
6. Mitchell, W.J., Chin, R.C.C., Sevtsuk, A.: The Media Laboratory City Car: A New Approach to Sustainable Urban Mobility. In: Droege, P. (ed.) Urban Energy Transition. Elsevier Science (2008)
7. Perchonok, J., Green, P.E.: Facilitating driver interaction with a robotic driving assistant: some insights from the literature. University of Michigan Transportation Research Institute, Ann Arbor (2009)
8. Schraut, M., Naab, K., Bachmann, T.: Bmw's Driver Assistance Concept For Integrated Longitudinal Support. In: Proc. of the 7th World Congress on Intelligent Systems, Turin (2000)
9. Neerpasch, U., Klander, P., Braun, D., Köhn, P., Holdmann, P.: Ein Konzeptfahrzeug mit aktiven Fahrwerkskomponenten. 7.Aachener Kolloquium Fahrzeug- und Motorentechnik,443–465 (1998)
10. Pacejka, H.B.: Tyre and Vehicle Dynamics. Butterworth-Heinemann (2002) ISBN 0 7506 5141 5

# Wavelet-Based Linearization
# for Single-Degree-Of-Freedom Nonlinear Systems

Xiao-Meng Ma, Wen-Fang Xie, Mohammad Keshmiri, and Abolfazl Mohebbi

Concordia University, Department of Mechanical and Industrial Engineering
Montreal, Quebec
wfxie@encs.concordia.ca

**Abstract.** This paper introduces a wavelet-based linearization method to estimate the single-degree-of-freedom (SDOF) nonlinear system response based on the traditional equivalent linearization technique. The mechanism by which the signal is decomposed and reconstructed using the wavelet transform is investigated. Since the wavelet analysis can capture temporal variations in the time and frequency content, a nonlinear system can be approximated as a time dependent linear system by combining the wavelet analysis technique with well-known traditional equivalent linearization method. Two nonlinear systems, bilinear hysteretic system and Duffing oscillator system, are used as examples to verify the effectiveness of the proposed wavelet-based linearization method.

**Keywords:** Wavelet Transform, Linearization, Bilinear hysteretic system, Duffing oscillator.

## 1    Introduction

Nonlinearity is an inherent phenomenon that inevitably occurs in physical systems. In mechanical and structural systems nonlinearities can arise in various forms and usually becomes progressively more significant as the motion amplitude increases and excites the nonlinear behavior [1]. Nonlinear systems may show complex effects, such as limit cycles, bifurcations and even chaos which are difficult to anticipate. Due to the inherent nonlinearities of almost all physical systems, the subject of nonlinear control is one of the important topics in control community. Among many methods dealing with a nonlinear system, the most commonly used one is to linearize it which allows taking advantage of mature linear system control techniques to control the nonlinear systems approximately. Powerful linearization techniques are required to analyze and predict nonlinear system's behaviour in order to design an accurate and desirable controller. Some popular linearization methods are reviewed in the following. The Lyapunov linearization technique [2] aims to approximate a nonlinear system by a linear one around the equilibrium point, and it is expected the behaviour of the linear system will be the same as that of nonlinear one.

Furthermore, feedback linearization is also a well-known approach [3] used in nonlinear system control. The basic concept of feedback linearization is to cancel the

C.-Y. Su, S. Rakheja, H. Liu (Eds.): ICIRA 2012, Part I, LNAI 7506, pp. 99–110, 2012.
© Springer-Verlag Berlin Heidelberg 2012

nonlinearities in a nonlinear system so that the closed-loop dynamics is linear [4]. Describing Function is another method for system linearization which is a statistical extension of linearization technique [5] and is an approximation procedure for analyzing certain nonlinear control problems that were originally developed by [6] and used as a tool in control engineering.

Moreover, statistical method or equivalent linearization method has proven to be a very useful approximate technique in structure dynamics and earthquake engineering [7]. The main idea of this method is that non-linear system is replaced by an equivalent linear equation through minimizing the difference between the two systems in some appropriate sense [8]. However, this kind of linearization is based on the time-dependent behavior of the nonlinear system. When the spectral characteristic of a nonlinear system is changing with time which is common in many processes, only the time domain analysis is not sufficient to describe the process accurately. It is necessary to consider both time and frequency contents of the nonlinear system for the linearization.

In the time-frequency analysis of signal processing,  wavelet transform as the popular tool for time-frequency analysis can be viewed as a synthesis of various ideas originating from different disciplines including [9], [10] mathematic, physics and engineering [11]. Pioneer research works on wavelet transformation topic can be found in [12]. The main reason for using wavelets in signal processing and time-frequency signal analysis is its localization in time and frequency domains and flexible resolution to a certain extent. Meanwhile, wavelet allows the signal to be decomposed into elementary forms at different positions and scales that are generated from a single function called "mother wavelet" by translation and dilation operations. This information is subsequently reconstructed with higher precision. Therefore, the wavelet transform can be used to capture both time and frequency behaviors of a nonlinear systems and thus to linearize the systems.

This paper presents a wavelet-based linearization method for linearizing SDOF nonlinear systems and finding their equivalent linear systems described by the corresponding wavelet coefficients.  The input - output relationships for a linearized system and nonlinear system are obtained by decomposing and reconstructing the input and output signals using the wavelet transform. Following the basic procedure of the traditional equivalent linearization approach, one can find the least mean square error between the linearized and nonlinear equations.  Since the wavelet analysis can capture temporal variations in the time and frequency content, the nonlinear system can be approximated as a time dependent linear system. The effectiveness of the proposed wavelet-based linearization method is validated on two nonlinear systems, i.e. bilinear hysteretic system and Duffing oscillator system.

The paper is organized as follows. Section 2 briefly introduces wavelet transform. The wavelet-based linearization method is proposed in Section 3. The simulation has been carried out to compare with the traditional equivalent linearization method in Section 4 and the paper concludes in Section 5.

## 2     Wavelet Transform

Grossmann and Morlet [12] first introduced the idea of wavelet as a family of function constructed from translation and dilation of a single function called "mother wavelet" $\varphi(t)$ defined by:

$$\varphi_{a,b}(t) = \frac{1}{\sqrt{|a|}}\varphi\left[\frac{(t-b)}{a}\right]; \ a, b \in R, a \neq 0 \tag{1}$$

where $a$ is called a scaling parameter and measures the degree of compression or scale, and $b$ is a translation parameter which determines the time location of the wavelet. Wavelet corresponds to high and low frequencies by choosing $|a|<1$ or $|a|>1$ respectively by compressing and decompressing the time width $\varphi(t)$. This is the main reason for wavelet success in signal processing and time-frequency signal analysis.

A more extensive study has been carried out by Grossman et al., [13] and the wavelet transform of function $f(t)$ is defined by:

$$W_\varphi[f](a,b) = (f, \varphi_{a,b}) = \int_{-\infty}^{\infty} f(t)\overline{\varphi}_{a,b}(t)dt \tag{2}$$

where $\varphi_{a,b}(t)$ plays the same role as the kernel $exp(iwt)$ in the Fourier transform. However, unlike the Fourier transform, the continuous wavelet transform is not a single transform, but any transform that can be obtained in this way. The inverse wavelet transform can be defined so that $f(t)$ could be reconstructed by means of the following formula:

$$f(t) = \frac{1}{C_\varphi}\int_{-\infty}^{\infty}\int_{-\infty}^{\infty}\frac{1}{a^2}W_\varphi[f](a,b)\varphi\left(\frac{t-b}{a}\right)dadb \tag{3}$$

where parameter $C_\varphi$ satisfies the so-called admissibility condition;

$$C_\varphi = 2\pi\int_{-\infty}^{\infty}\frac{|\hat{\varphi}(\omega)|^2}{\omega}d\omega< \infty \tag{4}$$

where parameter $\hat{\varphi}(\omega)$ is the Fourier Transform of the mother wavelet $\varphi(t)$. In practical applications involving fast numerical algorithms, the continuous wavelet can be computed at discrete grid points. To do this, a general function $\varphi_{a,b}(t)$ can be defined by replacing $a$ with $a_0^m$ $(a_0 \neq 0, 1)$, $b$ with $nb_0 a_0^m$ $(b_0 \neq 0)$, where $(m, n)$ are integers and making

$$\varphi_{m,n}(t) = a_0^{-m/2}\varphi(a_0^{-m}t - nb_0) \tag{5}$$

The discrete wavelet transform of $f(t)$ is defined as the

$$W_\varphi[f](m,n) = (f, \varphi_{m,n}) = \int_{-\infty}^{\infty} f(t)\varphi_{m,n}(t)dt \tag{6}$$

If the wavelets form an orthogonal and complete basis, $f(t)$ can be reconstructed from its discrete wavelet transform $\{f(m,n)=(f,\varphi_{m,n})\}$ by means of the formula $W_\varphi[f](m,n)$

$$f(t)=\sum(f,\varphi_{m,n})\varphi_{m,n}(t)$$

For some very special choices of $\varphi$ and $a_0, b_0$, the $\varphi_{m,n}$ constitute an orthogonal basis. In fact, if $a_0 = 2$ and $b_0 = 1$, there exists a function $\varphi$ with good time-frequency localization properties:

$$\varphi_{m,n}(t)=2^{-m/2}\varphi(2^{-m}t-n) \tag{6}$$

And it forms an orthogonal basis. These different orthogonal basis functions have been found to be very useful in application to speech processing [14], image processing, computer vision and so on [15].

# 3    Wavelet Linearization

## 3.1    Input - Output Relationship for a Nonlinear System

Consider a SDOF nonlinear system subject to external signal $f(t)$ with the equation motion:

$$\ddot{x}(t)+h(x,\dot{x}) = f(t) \tag{7}$$

where $h(x,\dot{x})$ is the nonlinear function. Performing the wavelet transform both sides of (7) yields [7]:

$$W_\varphi\ddot{x}(a,b)+W_\varphi h(a,b)=W_\varphi f(a,b) \tag{8}$$

where $W_\varphi\ddot{x}, W_\varphi h, W_\varphi f$ denote the wavelet transform of $\ddot{x}, h, f$ respectively. Performing the integration by part on $W_\varphi\ddot{x}(a,b)$ according to the characteristic of fast decaying for wavelet basis, the following expression can be obtained:

$$W_\varphi\ddot{x}(a,b)=\frac{1}{a^2}W_{\ddot{\varphi}}x(a,b) \tag{9}$$

where the term on the right hand side is the wavelet transform with the wavelet basis $\ddot{\varphi}$. The second order partial differential equation of $W_\varphi x(a,b)$ with respect $b$ can be expressed as:

$$\frac{\partial^2}{\partial b^2}W_\varphi x(a,b)=\frac{\partial^2}{\partial b^2}\int_{-\infty}^{\infty} x(t)\varphi\left(\frac{t-b}{a}\right)dt \tag{10}$$

Exchanging the differential operator with the integral operator on the right hand side, Equation (10) can be written as

$$\frac{\partial^2}{\partial b^2}W_\varphi x(a,b)=\frac{1}{a^2}W_{\ddot{\varphi}}x(a,b) \tag{11}$$

Thus, one has

$$\frac{\partial^2}{\partial b^2} W_\varphi x(a,b) = W_\varphi \ddot{x}(a,b) \tag{13}$$

The equation (8) can be expressed by:

$$\frac{\partial^2}{\partial b^2} W_\varphi x(a,b) + W_\varphi h(a,b) = W_\varphi f(a,b) \tag{14}$$

From this equation, the wavelet coefficient of the output can be obtained from the wavelet coefficient of the input. Because the parameter $b$ contains time information, the information for output response in time domain is achieved as well. Since the wavelet transform is a convolution operation in time, where the signal is decomposed in the distinct scales and translation values, the wavelet coefficients calculation is precisely similar to the calculation of the response of linear system that the convolution operation is implemented using impulse response function in the Linear Time Invariant (LTI) system. In the LTI system, the response calculation in the wavelet basis is obtained to replace the impulse function with the wavelet function. Thus, we can have the response information about time-frequency combination. Considering the nonlinear system (9), one can find the linearization system as follows:

$$\ddot{x} + \beta_{eq}\dot{x} + \omega_{eq}^2 x = f(t) \tag{15}$$

By using the input-output relationship introduced previously and performing the wavelet transform on both sides of the equation (15), the following form can be obtained: [19]

$$\frac{\partial^2}{\partial b^2} W_\varphi x(a,b) + \beta_{eq}\frac{\partial}{\partial b} W_\varphi x(a,b) + \omega_{eq}^2 W_\varphi x(a,b) = W_\varphi f(a,b) \tag{16}$$

The equivalent linearization method is based on replacing the original nonlinear system by a linear one, which is equivalent to the original system in some probabilistic sense. Following the basic procedure of the traditional equivalent linearization approach, one can first find the mean square least error between the equation (16) and (14)

$$\varepsilon^2 = (\beta_{eq}\frac{\partial}{\partial b} W_\varphi x(a,b) + \omega_{eq}^2 W_\varphi x(a,b) - W_\varphi h(a,b))^2 \tag{17}$$

The coefficients $\beta_{eq}$ and $\omega_{eq}^2$ are determined by the following equations:

$$\frac{\partial E(\varepsilon^2)}{\partial \beta_{eq}} = 0 \qquad \text{and} \qquad \frac{\partial E(\varepsilon^2)}{\partial \omega_{eq}^2} = 0 \tag{18}$$

Noting $E(x\dot{x}) = 0$, the two above equations lead to the following equations, respectively;

$$\beta_{eq} = \frac{E\left(W_\varphi h(a,b)\frac{\partial}{\partial b} W_\varphi x(a,b)\right)}{E\left(\frac{\partial}{\partial b} W_\varphi x(a,b)^2\right)} = 0 \tag{19}$$

$$\omega_{eq}^2 = \frac{E\left(W_\varphi h(a,b)W_\varphi x(a,b)\right)}{E\left(W_\varphi x(a,b)^2\right)} = 0 \tag{20}$$

In fact, the wavelet coefficients are calculated numerically. The parameters are to be discretized over all the time steps.

## 3.2    Discrete Wavelet-Based Linearization

The output $x(t)$ and $y(t)$ can be decomposed by using the harmonic wavelet:

$$x(t) = \sum_{j=0}^{n-2} x_j(t) \approx \sum_{j=0}^{n-2}\left( 2\operatorname{Re}\left( \sum_{k=0}^{2^j-1} a_{j,k} w(2^j t - k)\right)\right) \tag{21}$$

where Re() represents the real part of a complex number. The harmonic wavelet coefficients are defined as [20],

$$a_{j,k} = \int_{-\infty}^{\infty} x(t) w^*(2^j t - k) dt \tag{22}$$

Similarly, one has

$$y(t) = \sum_{j=0}^{n-2} y_j(t) \approx \sum_{j=0}^{n-2}\left( 2\operatorname{Re}\left( \sum_{k=0}^{2^j-1} a'_{j,k} w(2^j t - k)\right)\right) \tag{23}$$

$$a'_{j,k} = \int_{-\infty}^{\infty} y(t) w^*(2^j t - k) dt \tag{24}$$

where $w(2^j t - k)$ is the harmonic wavelet transform function represented by the level (scale) $j$ and time position of $k$. $a_{j,k}$ and $a'_{j,k}$ are the wavelet coefficients of $x(t)$ and $y(t)$ respectively, also giving the assumption that $x(t)$ and $y(t)$ are both real functions. In order to obtain the equivalent linear damping and stiffness parameters in the discrete domain, we use the method discussed previously i.e. wavelet-based linearization method. Performing the wavelet transform on both sides of the equations (9) and (16), the following equations can be obtained:

$$\frac{\partial^2}{\partial k^2} W_\omega x(2^j t - k) + W_\omega h(2^j t - k) = W_\omega f(2^j t - k) \tag{25}$$

$$\frac{\partial^2}{\partial k^2} W_\omega x(2^j t - k) + \beta_{eq}\frac{\partial}{\partial k} W_\omega x(2^j t - k) + \omega_{eq}^2 W_\omega x(2^j t - k)$$
$$= W_\omega f(2^j t - k) \tag{26}$$

The square of error between the nonlinear and linearized formulation at each scale $j$ and time position $k$ of the wavelet transform is:

$$\varepsilon_{j,k}^2 = \left\{ \beta_{eq}\frac{\partial}{\partial k} W_\omega x(2^j t - k) + \omega_{eq}^2 W_\omega x(2^j t - k) - W_\omega h(2^j t - k)\right\}^2 \tag{27}$$

The above error, when multiplied with reciprocal of the scale $1/2^j$ and summed over all scale values, represents the error in the instantaneous energy of the response at the time $t=k$. By minimizing this error of the instantaneous energy with respect to the equivalent damping parameter $\beta_{eq}$ and stiffness parameter $\omega_{eq}^2$, the instantaneous equivalent damping and stiffness parameters of the linearization can be obtained. Hence, a time variant linear system model is derived. The minimization conditions are:

$$\frac{\partial}{\partial \beta_{eq,k}} \sum_{allj} \frac{1}{2^j} E(\varepsilon_{j,k}^2) = 0 \tag{28}$$

$$\frac{\partial}{\partial \omega_{eq,k}^2} \sum_{allj} \frac{1}{2^j} E(\varepsilon_{j,k}^2) = 0 \tag{29}$$

Substituting equation (27) to (28) and (29) respectively yields:

$$\beta_{eq,k} = \frac{\sum_{allj} \frac{\partial}{\partial k} W_w x(j,k) W_w h(j,k)}{\sum_{allj} \left(\frac{\partial}{\partial k} W_w x(j,k)\right)^2} \tag{30}$$

$$\omega_{eq,k}^2 = \frac{\sum_{allj} W_w x(j,k) W_w h(j,k)}{\sum_{allj} (W_w x(j,k))^2} \tag{31}$$

Similarly, when summing the error for all the time positions, the error represents the energy of the process at each frequency band corresponding to a wavelet scale. Thus, the equivalent damping and stiffness parameters of this linearized system are determined as shown:

$$\frac{\partial}{\partial \beta_{eq,j}} \sum_{allk} \frac{1}{2^j} E(\varepsilon_{j,k}^2) = 0 \tag{32}$$

$$\frac{\partial}{\partial \omega_{eq,j}^2} \sum_{allk} \frac{1}{2^j} E(\varepsilon_{j,k}^2) = 0 \tag{33}$$

Thus, one has

$$\beta_{eq,j} = \frac{\sum_{allk} \frac{\partial}{\partial k} W_w x(j,k) W_w h(j,k)}{\sum_{allk} \left(\frac{\partial}{\partial k} W_w x(j,k)\right)^2} \qquad \omega_{eq,j}^2 = \frac{\sum_{allk} W_w x(j,k) W_w h(j,k)}{\sum_{allk} (W_w x(j,k))^2}$$

Thus, the wavelet method can examine the error between the nonlinear and linearized system either at each time interval or each frequency band corresponding to wavelet scale. This flexible feature is very important to solve the nonlinear response of systems.

## 4    Linearization Results

### 4.1    Bilinear Hysteretic System

Hysteresis phenomenon occurs in diverse disciplines ranging from physics to biology, from material science to mechanics, and from electronics to economics [16], [17] and [18]. The development of some new linearization strategies for hysteretic system for control utilization is a quite challenging task in control communities. In this section, a bilinear hysteretic system modeling is introduced. For a SDOF system with bilinear hysteresis, the system model is [17]:

$$\ddot{x} + \beta\dot{x} + h(\dot{x}, x, t) = f(t)$$
$$x(0) = \dot{x}(0) = 0 \tag{34}$$

where the hysteretic force is expressed as;

$$h(x, \dot{x}, t) = \alpha x + (1-\alpha)h_0(\dot{x}, y, x_y) \tag{35}$$

$$\dot{y} = h_1(\dot{x}, y, x_y) \tag{36}$$

and $h_0$ and $h_1$ is defined as follows;

$$h_0 = y\left\{u\left(y + x_y\right) - u\left(y - x_y\right)\right\}$$
$$+ x_y\left\{u\left(y - x_y\right)u\left(\dot{x}\right) - u\left(-y - x_y\right)u\left(-\dot{x}\right)\right\} \tag{37}$$
$$h_1 = \dot{x}\left\{\begin{matrix}u\left(y + x_y\right) - u\left(y - x_y\right)\\ + u\left(y - x_y\right)u\left(-\dot{x}\right) + u\left(-y - x_y\right)u\left(\dot{x}\right)\end{matrix}\right\}$$

where $y$ is the relative displacement of the purely elasto-plastic component $h_0$, $\alpha = 0.5$ and $x_y = 1$ are respectively the second slope ratio and the yield displacement, and $u(\bullet)$ is a unit step function.

The linearized model equivalent to the system is given by the following formula:

$$\ddot{x} + \beta\dot{x} + \alpha x + (1-\alpha)(c_1\dot{x} + c_2 x) = f(t) \tag{38}$$

Equation (38) can be written as:

$$\ddot{x} + (\beta + c_1(1-\alpha))\dot{x} + (\alpha + (1-\alpha)c_2)x = f(t) \quad \dot{y} = c_3\dot{x} + c_4 y \tag{39}$$

The above equation could be written as:

$$\ddot{x} + \beta_{eq}\dot{x} + \omega_{eq}^2 x = f(t) \tag{40}$$

$$\beta_{eq} = (\beta + c_1(1-\alpha)) \tag{41}$$

$$\omega_{eq}^2 = (\alpha + (1-\alpha)c_2) \tag{42}$$

where $\beta_{eq}$ and $\omega_{eq}^2$ are the equivalent parameters. In the case of a stochastic system, the equivalent parameters are obtained by minimizing the expected value of the square of the error between the nonlinear system and the linearized system. For $\beta_{eq}$ and $\omega_{eq}^2$, one has

$$\frac{\partial}{\partial \beta_{eq,j}} \sum_{allk} E\left[\varepsilon_{j,k,x}^2\right] = 0 \tag{43}$$

$$\frac{\partial}{\partial \omega_{eq,j}^2} \sum_{allk} E\left[\varepsilon_{j,k,x}^2\right] = 0 \tag{44}$$

The system is excited by the signal

$$f(t) = 15\sin(4t) + 10\sin(8t) + 5\sin(12t) + 5\sin(16t)$$

And the initial conditions are $\beta_{eq} = 0, \omega_{eq}^2 = 0$. Assume that the system is a linear one to obtain the responses at the different frequencies. By using the procedure demonstrated above and substituting the response to the expressions of equivalent parameters $\beta_{eq}$ and $\omega_{eq}^2$ in equations (30) and (31), the parameters converged after 4 times of iteration. Therefore, the time varying linear system is obtained and the similar procedure can be applied to the equivalent parameters $c_3$ and $c_4$ as well. Thus, the bilinear hysteretic system can be linearized as this time varying linear system and these results are compared with those responses which are obtained by the statistical method and numerical method. The linearization results are shown in Figure 1 (a) and (b).

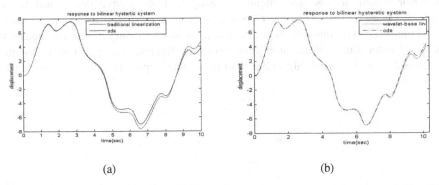

(a)　　　　　　　　　　　　　(b)

**Fig. 1.** (a) Equivalent linearization of bilinear hysteretic system to stationary excitation (b) Wavelet-based linearization method comparing with numerical solution

## 4.2　Duffing Oscillator System

Consider another single-degree-of-freedom nonlinear system i.e. an oscillator with non-linear stiffness [21]:

$$m\ddot{x}(t) + c\dot{x}(t) + g(x) = F(t) \tag{45}$$

where $m$ is the mass, $c$ is the viscous damping coefficient, $F(t)$ is the external excitation, and $x(t)$ is the displacement response of system. Dividing the equation by $m$, the equation becomes:

$$\ddot{x}(t) + \beta\dot{x}(t) + h(x) = f(t) \tag{46}$$

where $\beta$ is the damping parameter, $h(x)$ is the nonlinear restoring force that could depend on displacement, and $f(t)$ is a zero mean stationary random excitation. We can always find a way to decompose the non-linear restoring force to one linear component plus a non-linear component, that is:

$$h(x) = \omega_n^2 [x + \lambda H(x)]$$ (47)

where $\lambda$ is the non-linear factor that presents the type and degree of non-linearity in the system, and $\omega_n$ is the un-damped natural frequency for linear system. The idea of linearization is replacing the equation (46) by the following linear system:

$$\ddot{x}(t) + \beta_{eq}\dot{x}(t) + \omega_{eq}^2 x(t) = f(t)$$ (48)

where $\beta_{eq}$ is the equivalent linear damping coefficient per unit mass, $\omega_{eq}^2$ is the equivalent linear stiffness coefficient per unit mass. The example is given to display this procedure. The system is: $\ddot{x}(t) + \beta\dot{x}(t) + kx + \lambda kx^3 = f(t)$ ; $x(0) = \dot{x}(0) = 0$

where $\beta = 0.5, k = 16\pi^2, \lambda = 1, H(x) = kx^3$ and input signal is

$$f(t) = 15\sin(4t) + 10\sin(8t) + 5\sin(12t) + 5\sin(16t)$$

In order to obtain the linearized system, the wavelet-based linearization method is applied to the system defined in (48). Figure 2. (a) shows the response of Duffing oscillator system to stationary input by using traditional equivalent linearization method. Figure 2. (b) shows the response of non-linear system using the wavelet-based method comparing with the numerical solution of ordinary differential equation using 4th order Runge-Kutta algorithm. From the figures, one may notice that the developed wavelet-based algorithm yields a good approximation of the exact response.

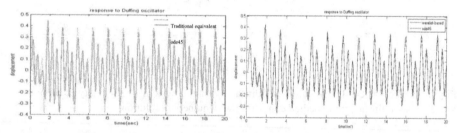

**Fig. 2.** (a) Equivalent linearization of Duffing oscillator system for stationary input, (b) Wavelet-based linearization methods comparing with numerical solution

The simulation results on two SDOF nonlinear systems demonstrate that the wavelet-based linearization method is a promising tool in linearizing nonlinear systems to their approximate linear ones.

# 5    Conclusion

In this paper, a wavelet-based linearization method for approximating the SDOF nonlinear system behavior to its equivalent linearized system is presented. The procedure of discrete wavelet-based linearization has been developed. The linearization approach has been tested by using the bilinear hysteretic system and

Duffing oscillator system as examples to verify the feasibility of this method. The simulation results exhibit the accuracy of the proposed linearization method, and a more accurate equivalent linear system can be obtained compared with traditional linearization methods.

# References

1. Mason, A.B.J.: Some Observations on the Random Response of Linear and Nonlinear Dynamical Systems. Ph. D. Dissertation, Calif. Inst. of Tech. Pasadena (1997)
2. Isidori, A.: Nonlinear Control Systems- An Introduction. Springer, New York (1989)
3. Grizzle, J.W., Kokotovic, P.V.: Feedback linearization of Sampled Data Systems. IEEE Trans. Auto. Control 33, 857–859 (1988)
4. Hedrick, J.K., Girard, A.: Feedback Linearization Theory and Application. Springer, New York (2005)
5. Kryov, N.N., Bogoliubov, N.N.: Introduction to Nonlinear Mechanics. Princeton University, Princeton (1947)
6. Booton Jr., R.C.: Nonlinear Control Systems with Random Inputs. IRE Trans. Circuit Theory CT-I (1), 9–17 (1954)
7. Agrawal, O.D.: Application of Wavelets in Modeling Stochastic Dynamic Systems. Journal of Vibration and Acoustics 120, 763–769 (1998)
8. Iwan, W.D., Mason Jr., A.B.: Equivalent Linearization for Systems Subjected to Non-stationary Random Excitation. International Journal of Nonlinear Mechanics 15, 71–82 (1980)
9. Chui, C.K.: Wavelet Analysis and Its Applications. An Introduction to Wavelets, vol. 1. Academic Press, Inc., New York (1992)
10. Chui, C.K.: Wavelet: A Tutorial in Theory and Applications. Academic Press, New York (1992)
11. Grochenig, K.: Foundations of Time-Frequency Analysis. Birkhäuser (2001)
12. Grossmann, A., Morlet, J.: Decomposition of Hardy Functions into Square Integral Wavelets of Constant Shape. SIAM Journal of Mathematical Analysis 15, 723–736 (1984)
13. Grossmann, A., Kronland-Martinet, R., Morlet, J.: Reading and Understanding Continuous Wavelet Transform. In: Combes, J.M., Grossmann, A., Tchamitchian, P. (eds.) Wavelet Time-Frequency Methods and Phase Space, pp. 2–20. Springer, Berlin (1989)
14. Kobayash, M.: Wavelets and their applications. SIAM, Philadelphia (1998)
15. Walker, J.: A Primer on Wavelets and their Scientific Applications. Chapman & Hall CRC, New York (1999)
16. Dobson, S., Noori, M., Hou, Z., Dimentberg, M.: Direct Implementation of Stochastic Linearization for SDOF Systems with General Hysteresis. Structure Engineering and Mechanics 6(5), 473–484 (1998)
17. Asano, K., Iwan, W.D.: An Alternative Approach to the Random Response of Bilinear Hysteretic Systems. Earthquake Engineering and Structural Dynamics 12, 229–236 (1998)
18. Xie, W.F., Fu, J., Yao, H., Su, C.-Y.: Neural Network Based Adaptive Control of Piezoelectric Actuator with Unknown Hysteresis. International Journal of Adaptive Control and Signal Processing 23, 30–54 (2009)
19. Basu, B., Gupta, V.K.: Seismic Response of SDOF Systems by Wavelet Modeling of Non-stationary Processes. Journal of Engineering Mechanics (ASCE) 124(10), 1142–1150 (1998)

20. Newland, D.E.: An Introduction to Random Vibrations, Spectral & Wavelet Analysis. Longman Scientific & Technical, New York (1993)
21. Roberts, J.B., Spanos, P.D.: Random Vibration and Statistical Linearization, Mineola, New York (1990)

# An Application of DCS Device
# to a Heat Exchange Process

Junya Okazaki[1], Shengjun Wen[1], Mingcong Deng[1], and Dongyun Wang[2]

[1] The Graduate School of Electrical and Electronic Engineering,
Tokyo University of Agriculture and Technology,
2-24-16 Nakacho, Koganei, Tokyo 184-8588, Japan
[2] School of Electronic Information, Zhongyuan University of Technology,
41 Zhongyuan Road, Zhengzhou, 45007, China

**Abstract.** In this paper, an application of distributed control system (DCS) device to a heat exchange process is shown. In details, first, nonlinear model and feedback tracking control scheme of a spiral heat exchange process are obtained. Second, the designed nonlinear feedback tracking control system is realized by using a DCS device. Then, the tracking performance of the proposed scheme is confirmed by a experimental result. Moreover, for the problem in realizing control system by using the DCS device, a robust evaluation is given. In addition, the effectiveness of the proposed evaluation method is investigated.

**Keywords:** DCS, Nonlinear Model, Nonlinear Control, Right Coprime Factorization, Robust Stability.

## 1 Introduction

Processes in large-scale industries have nonlinear properties. Nonlinear properties often make it difficult to design feedback control systems, nonlinear control system design is needed to control processes. In many situations, to deal with this control problem, approximate methods or linearization techniques are used. On the other hand, in order to control nonlinear processes, the operator approach has been attracting more and more attention and interest. In fact, some researchers reported the effectiveness of the approach for various processes [1]-[8]. In addition, many processes have uncertainties. Uncertainties affect tracking performances. As a result, to maintain robust stabilities of control systems may be difficult. Meanwhile, the operator approach makes it more easily to design nonlinear control systems considering robust stabilities. Moreover, distributed control system (DCS) device is used to control various plants in large-scale industries. DCS device performs proportional integral and derivative (PID) control or advanced control. However, there are few researches of applying the operator approach for nonlinear control using DCS devices [4]. Therefore, this paper is mainly concerned with the method of nonlinear control using the operator approach with DCS device for a spiral heat exchange system. Heat exchange occurs between two fluids that are at different temperatures and separated by a solid wall, it is one of nonlinear processes [9]. It

C.-Y. Su, S. Rakheja, H. Liu (Eds.): ICIRA 2012, Part I, LNAI 7506, pp. 111–120, 2012.

has also uncertainties resulting from the heat loss and the error of the heat exchange rate. In this paper, an application of DCS device to this nonlinear process with uncertainties is investigated. In detail, the designed nonlinear feedback tracking control system with the robust right coprime factorization is realized by using the DCS device. Previously, for the nonlinear process of water level and temperature, operator based the nonlinear feedback control system design with the DCS device was proposed [4]. Recently, a simulation study on a spiral heat exchange process was given in [5].

The outline of the paper is as follows. In Section 2, the experimental system and problem statement are introduced. In Section 3, the nonlinear feedback control system is realized by using the DCS device. The experimental result is given to show the effectiveness of the proposed method in Section 4. In Section 5, the conclusion of this research is shown.

## 2    System Description and Problem Statement

In the section, the experimental system of a spiral heat exchange process and DCS device are described.

### 2.1    Heat Exchange Process

The heat exchange process of this research is introduced in Fig. 1(a) and the equivalent diagram is shown in Fig. 1(b). This process has two tanks (Tank 1 and Tank 2) and pomps, a spiral heat exchanger (KUROSE KMSA-03). There is water in two tanks. In addition, Tank 1 has a heater in it , therefore, it can make hot water. Each tank's water is sent to the heat exchanger by a pomp and each flow rate of water is controlled by a actuator which opens or closes a valve. Resistance temperature detectors (SHIMADEN RD-11S: $\pm$ 0.3-0.8°C) are used to measure the water temperatures. Flow rates are measured by flow rate sensors (KEYENCE FD-81: $\pm$1.6-5.0 % of 10 L/min).

### 2.2    DCS Device

Fig.2 shows the DCS device (YOKOGAWA CENTUM CS 3000). The DCS device consists of human interface station (HIS) and field control station (FCS). HIS is a monitoring device, containing functions of engineering station, work station and remote monitor. FCS is a device that performs process control and composed of field compose unit, input/output (I/O) modules and communication interfaces. Several types of FCS are available for different applications and sizes. Communications between field control units and field devices are based on various types of I/O interfaces, such as extended serial backboard and field bus input output. FCS to HIS communications use Vnet/IP (Vnet/internet protocol) communication network. That is, processes are controlled via FCS by operating HIS.

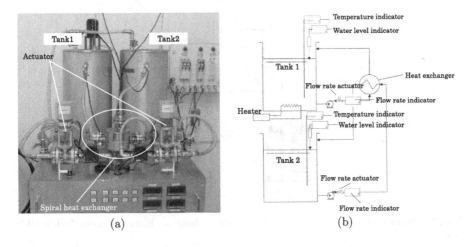

**Fig. 1.** (a) Heat exchange process with a spiral heat exchanger; (b) Equivalent diagram of a heat exchange process

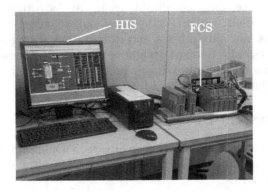

**Fig. 2.** DCS device (YOKOGAWA CENTUM CS 3000)

## 2.3 Experimental System

In Fig. 3, the experimental system is shown. This system is composed of a heat exchange process and DCS device. HIS and FCS communicate with each other and FCS controls the heat exchange process. Setting parameters with HIS, mass flow rates or a consume power of heater are controlled. Additionally, a monitor of HIS shows situations of the process. In this way, the experiment is performed.

## 2.4 Problem Statement

In large-scale industries, DCS devices are used to control processes. That is, to use these devices in large-scale industry, we have to validate the availability of the designed control system with the case of using DCS devises. However, some

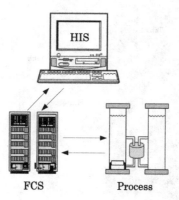

**Fig. 3.** Experimental system containing a spiral heat exchange process and a DCS device

mathematical calculations cannot be performed by using DCS devices accurately. It is because there are some unrealizable terms like logarithm function or differentiation. As a result, various methods of approximation are used in many situations. That is, not only process uncertainties but also these approximate approaches may also affect robust stabilities of control systems. So, the effectiveness of operator-based heat exchange process control using the DCS devise for the robust stability is discussed in this paper.

## 3    Control System Design

In this section, for the spiral heat exchange process, a nonlinear feedback tracking control system is considered. In addition, the obtained control system is realized by using the DCS device.

### 3.1    Process Modeling

The mechanism of the spiral heat exchanger is shown Fig. 4. $\dot{m}$ refers to the mass flow rate and $T$ is the water temperature. The subscripts h and c are the hot and cold water, whereas the subscripts i and o refer to the water inlet and outlet conditions. $c$ is the specific heat. The hot water enters at the center and flows in the outside direction, leaves at the outside. On the other hand, the cold water enters at the outside, flows in the inside direction and leaves at the center. For this spiral heat exchanger, the mathematical model was obtained in [5]. It is

$$y(t) = T_{c,i} + \frac{(T_{h,i} - T_{c,i})\left[\exp\left\{k\left(\vec{C_c} - \frac{1}{c_h u(t)}\right)\right\} - 1\right]}{\exp\left\{k\left(C_c - \frac{1}{c_h u(t)}\right)\right\} - \frac{1}{C_c c_h u(t)}} \, , \qquad (1)$$

where $u(t)$ is the process input and $y(t)$ is the process output. $u(t)$ and $y$ are defined as $T_{c,o}$ and $\dot{m}_h$, respectively. $C_c$ refers to $1/(\dot{m}_c c_c)$. $k$ is the product of the overall heat transfer coefficient $U$ and the transfer area $A$.

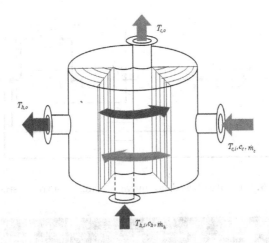

**Fig. 4.** Mechanism of the spiral heat exchanger

## 3.2   Nonlinear Feedback Tracking Control System

The nonlinear feedback tracking control system for the heat exchange process is also considered in [5]. It is shown in Fig. 5.
Each operator value is

$$S(y)(t) = (1 - K_{\mathrm{p}})\frac{C_{\mathrm{c}}(T_{\mathrm{h,i}} - T_{\mathrm{c,i}})\{\dot{y} + k(T_{\mathrm{h,i}} - y)\} - (y - T_{\mathrm{c,i}})(T_{\mathrm{h,i}} - y)}{\dot{y}(T_{\mathrm{h,i}} - y) + \{\dot{y} + k(T_{\mathrm{h,i}} - y)\}(y - T_{\mathrm{c,i}})} \quad , \quad (2)$$

$$R(u)(t) = \frac{K_{\mathrm{p}}}{c_{\mathrm{h}}}u(t) \quad , \quad (3)$$

$$N(\omega)(t) = T_{\mathrm{c,i}} + \frac{(T_{\mathrm{h,i}} - T_{\mathrm{c,i}})\left\{e^{k(C_{\mathrm{c}} - \omega(t))} - 1\right\}}{e^{k(C_{\mathrm{c}} - \omega(t))} - \omega(t)/C_{\mathrm{c}}} \quad , \quad (4)$$

$$D(\omega)(t) = \frac{1}{c_{\mathrm{h}}\omega(t)} \quad , \quad (5)$$

$$C(\tilde{e})(t) = k_{\mathrm{I}}\int_{0}^{t} \tilde{e}(\tau)d\tau + k_{\mathrm{P}}\tilde{e}(t) \quad , \quad (6)$$

where $\omega$ is the output of the operator $D$. $S$, $R$, $N$, $D$ are derived from operator-based robust the right coprime factorization [1]-[8]. The nominal process operator is given as $P = ND^{-1}$. However, the real process has uncertainties. There, considering the operator $\Delta N$ of uncertainties, we define the real process operator as $P + \Delta P = (N + \Delta N)D^{-1}$. $C$ refers to the PI controller to improve the tracking performance. $K_{\mathrm{p}}$ and $k_{\mathrm{P}}$, $k_{\mathrm{I}}$ are designed controller parameters.

## 3.3   Control System Realization Using DCS

The control systems by the DCS device are realized using function blocks. Fig. 6 shows the realized control system by using function blocks. Function blocks

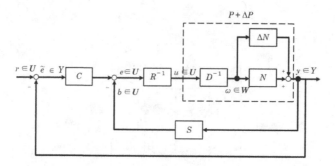

**Fig. 5.** Operator based nonlinear tracking control system

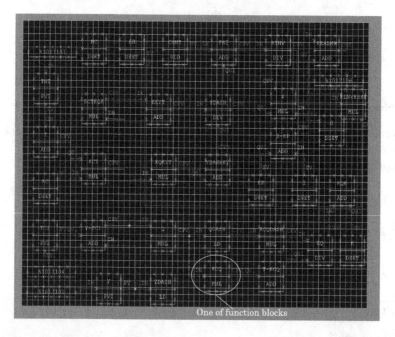

One of function blocks

**Fig. 6.** Nonlinear feedback control system realized by combination of function blocks

perform input processing, calculation processing, output processing, alarm processing. Input processing changes an input signal read from the connection destination of the input terminal of the function block into data that is suitable for calculation processing. Calculation processing reads data obtained by input processing, performs calculation processing and outputs the processing result. Output processing outputs data obtained by calculation processing to the connection destination of the output terminal as an output signal. Alarm processing performs various types of alarm check during input processing, calculation processing and output processing in order to detect a process error. Additionally, to perform data input/output with the process control input/output and other function blocks, a function block has input/output terminals. There are various types of function blocks. Especially, using function blocks called calculation blocks, we can perform various calculations. For example, ADD calculation block performs an addition, MUL functioin block performs a multiplication. Control systems can be realized by combinations of these calculation blocks.

## 4   Experimental Result

In this section, using the DCS device, the heat exchange process experiment is performed. The inlet hot fluid temperature and cold fluid temperature are 40 °C and 24 °C, respectively. The mass flow rate of cold temperature $\dot{m}_c$ is 2.0 L min$^{-1}$. The two specific heats $c_c$ and $c_h$ are 1.0 cal g$^{-1}$ K$^{-1}$. The overall heat transfer coefficient is 1500 kcal m$^{-2}$ hr$^{-1}$ K$^{-1}$, the heat transfer area is 0.3 m$^2$. In Fig. 7, the experimental result is shown. Designed parameters $K_p = 0.7$ and $k_P = 0.8$, $k_I = 0.01$. The reference input of the cold flow outlet temperature is set at 30 °C. From Fig. 7, we can find that the process output tracks to the reference input. Therefore, the effectiveness of the designed controllers using the DCS device is confirmed.

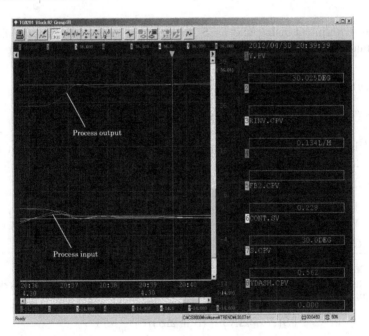

**Fig. 7.** Experimental result for the heat exchange process

## 5   Robust Stability Analysis

Previously, robust stabilities of nonlinear feedback control systems were measured by the condition [1], [2], [8]

$$\|S(N + \Delta N) - SN\|_{Lip} < 1 \ . \tag{7}$$

However, in general, we cannot use logarithm function or differential function directly. Therefore, approximate techniques are often use. As a result, robust stabilities may be affected. Here, the nonlinear feedback system considering the unrealizable term $\Delta S$ of the controller $S$ is shown in Fig. 8.

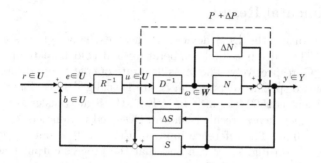

**Fig. 8.** Nonlinear feedback control system with a realizable controller

In the experiment using the DCS device, $\dot{y}$ is realized by using difference approximation. Here, the controller using difference approximation is redefined as $S$.

$$S(y)(t)$$
$$= (1 - K_p)\frac{C_c(T_{h,i} - T_{c,i})\{y' + k(T_{h,i} - y)\} - (y - T_{c,i})(T_{h,i} - y)}{y'(T_{h,i} - y) + \{y' + k(T_{h,i} - y)\}(y - T_{c,i})} \quad , \qquad (8)$$

where $y'$ is the difference approximation of $\dot{y}$. Moreover, $\Delta S$ is given as the following form.

$$\Delta S(y)(t)$$
$$= (1 - K_p)\left[\frac{C_c(T_{h,i} - T_{c,i})\{\dot{y} + k(T_{h,i} - y)\} - (y - T_{c,i})(T_{h,i} - y)}{\dot{y}(T_{h,i} - y) + \{\dot{y} + k(T_{h,i} - y)\}(y - T_{c,i})}\right.$$
$$\left. - \frac{C_c(T_{h,i} - T_{c,i})\{y' + k(T_{h,i} - y)\} - (y - T_{c,i})(T_{h,i} - y)}{y'(T_{h,i} - y) + \{y' + k(T_{h,i} - y)\}(y - T_{c,i})}\right] . \qquad (9)$$

That is, the ideal controller is $S + \Delta S$. There, the new robust condition is defined as the following form.

$$\|S(N + \Delta N) - (S + \Delta S)N\|_{Lip} < 1 . \qquad (10)$$

In Fig.9, the result of the robust stability analysis is shown. It meets the robust condition of $\|S(N + \Delta N) - (S + \Delta S)N\|_{Lip} < 1$. Therefore, the designed nonlinear tracking control system is stable. If the controllers satisfy the condition of (10), the robust stability of the spiral heat exchange process is given as the following Bezout identity

$$S(N + \Delta N) + RD = I , \qquad (11)$$

where $I$ is the identity operator.

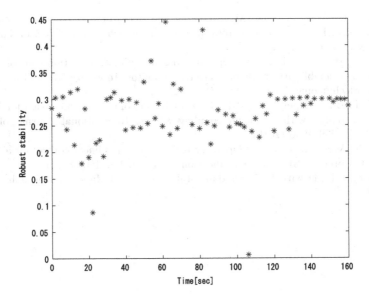

**Fig. 9.** Robust stability analysis

## 6   Conclusion

In this paper, an application of DCS device to a heat exchange process is considered. First, the mathematical model and nonlinear feedback tracking control system of the spiral heat exchage process is obtained. Second, the control system are designed by using the DCS device. Finally, the experimental result shows the effectiveness of the proposed method. In details, the heat exchange process has nonlinear properties concerning about temperatures or mass flow rates. For this process, we design the controller by using obtained model and operator based robust right coprime factorization approach. In addition, there are unrealizeable terms of the controller. Concerning this problem, the availability of the proposed system using the DCS device for the nonlinear process is proved.

## References

1. Wen, S., Deng, M.: Operator-based robust nonlinear control and fault detection for a Peltier actuated thermal process. Mathematical and Computer Modelling (accepted, 2012)
2. Bi, S., Deng, M.: Operator based robust control design for nonlinear plants with perturbation. International Journal of Control 84(6), 815–821 (2011)
3. Bu, N., Deng, M.: System design for nonlinear plants using operator-based robust right coprime factorization and isomorphism. IEEE Transactions on Automatic Control 56(4), 952–957 (2011)
4. Wen, S., Deng, M., Bi, S., Wang, D.: Operator-based robust nonlinear control and its realization for a multi-tank process by using DCS. Transactions of the Institute of Measurement and Control (accepted, 2012)

5. Okazaki, J., Wen, S., Deng, M.: Modeling and operator based nonlinear tracking control using DCS device of a spiral heat exchange process. In: Proc. of The 2012 ICAMechS, Japan (2012)
6. Deng, M., Inoue, A., Baba, Y.: Operator based nonlinear vibration control system design of a flexible arm with piezoelectric actuator. International Journal of Advanced Mechatronic Systems 1(6), 71–76 (2008)
7. Deng, M., Bi, S.: Operator-based robust nonlinear control system design for MIMO nonlinear plants with unknown coupling effects. International Journal of Control 83(6), 1939–1946 (2010)
8. Deng, M., Wen, S., Inoue, A.: Operator-based robust nonlinear control for a Peltier acutuated process. Measurement and Control 44(4), 116–120 (2011)
9. Incripera, F.P., Dewitt, D.P.: Fundamentals of heat and Mass Transfer. John Wiley (2001)

# Application of Driver-in-the-Loop Real-Time Simulations to the Design of SUV Differential Braking Controllers

Xuejun Ding and Yuping He

Faculty of Engineering and Applied Science, University of Ontario Institute of Technology,
2000 Simcoe Street North, Oshawa, Ontario, Canada L1H 7K4

**Abstract.** This paper presents the design and validation of a differential braking controller for sport utility vehicles (SUVs) using driver-in-the-loop real-time simulations. The yaw moment generated through the differential braking control system is applied to improve the lateral stability of SUVs. A linear vehicle model is generated to construct the controller. To validate the controller design, driver-in-the-loop real-time simulations are conducted on the UOIT vehicle simulator. Two test scenarios are simulated to validate the controller design on the vehicle simulator. The driver-in-the-loop real-time simulation results demonstrate the effectiveness of the proposed differential braking controller in the lateral stability and maneuverability improvement of the SUV.

**Keywords:** differential braking, stability control, driver-in-the-loop, real-time simulations.

## 1    Introduction

The past two decades has witnessed the advancement of vehicle active safety systems (ASSs) that prevent vehicles from dangerous accidents [1]. Previous studies indicate that ASSs are able to improve the lateral stability of vehicles and reduce highway accident rate. It is reported that rollover accidents account for almost 80% of non-collision fatal crashes, among which 70% are related to light trucks such as sport utility vehicle (SUV) and pickup [2]. SUVs have been rapidly increasing since 1990s. Compared with passenger cars, SUVs have higher center of gravities (CG) that may be the main reason for the higher rollover accident rate of these vehicles. SUV stability control has attracted the attention of researchers around the world [3,4].

SUV stability control by applying corrective yaw moment can reduce the deviation of vehicle behaviors. The control of yaw moment can be achieved by a variety of approaches, including torque distribution systems, active suspensions, and differential braking control systems. To date, differential braking control systems have been applied to road vehicles due to their cost-effective implementations based on the existing advanced braking techniques, such as anti-lock braking systems [5,6]. With the differential braking control technique, the required yaw moment can be achieved through manipulating the braking effects at the four wheels, differentiating braking pressures in the left/right and front/rear wheel cylinders [7].

To validate and improve the design of differential braking control systems, the field and road testing of the corresponding real physical prototypes is not dispensable

C.-Y. Su, S. Rakheja, H. Liu (Eds.): ICIRA 2012, Part I, LNAI 7506, pp. 121–131, 2012.

[8]. However, at the initial development stage, the field and road testing can be difficult, time-consuming, dangerous, and costly to accomplish. To date, real-time simulations have been used to evaluate the controller performance prior to in-vehicle field and road testing [9]. These real-time simulations are often based on conventional open-loop test methods, investigating the controller performance under the given driving inputs, such as a steering scheme. Stability of road vehicles has long been studied in the open-loop dynamic simulations without considering the driver, which may be a destabilizing part of the vehicle system. The overall performance of a road vehicle depends not only on how well the controller works, but also on its interaction with the human driver operations [10]. Thus, the open-loop real-time simulation method may not adequately address the driver-controller interactions and the overall performance of the vehicle system.

This paper presents a design and validation method for differential braking controllers of SUVs using driver-in-the-loop real-time simulations. A linear yaw plane vehicle model with 3 degrees of freedom (DOF) is generated to derive the differential braking controller. To validate and improve the controller design, the real-time version of the controller and the SUV model are reconstructed in LabView and CarSim software packages, respectively; with the integration of the controller and SUV model through the interface between the two software packages, the driver-in-the-loop real-time simulations are implemented on the vehicle simulator at the University of Ontario Institute of Technology (UOIT).

The rest of the paper is organized as follows. Section 2 introduces the 3 DOF linear yaw plane model for representing the SUV. In Section 3, the design and optimization of the differential braking controller is briefly described. Section 4 presents the configuration of the UOIT simulator and the integration of the real-time versions of the controller and the SUV model. Section 5 discusses and analyzes the results derived from the driver-in-the-loop real-time simulations. Finally, conclusions are given in Section 6.

## 2     Vehicle System Model

Fig 1 shows the schematic diagram of the yaw plane model to represent a SUV. Using Newton's second law, the equations of motion for the 3 DOF linear model are derived as

$$m\,(\dot{U} - V\,\gamma) = F_{xrl} + F_{xrr} + F_{xfl} + F_{xfr} \tag{1}$$

$$m\,(\dot{V} + U\,\gamma) = (F_{xfl} + F_{xfr} - c_f)\delta_f + c_f \cdot \frac{V + l_f\gamma}{U} + c_r \cdot \frac{V - l_r\gamma}{U} \tag{2}$$

$$I_z\dot{\gamma} = l_f(F_{xfl} + F_{xfr})\delta_f + c_f l_f(\frac{V + l_f\gamma}{U} - \delta_f) - c_r l_r\frac{V - l_r\gamma}{U} + d/2(F_{xfr} - F_{xfl} + F_{xrr} - F_{xrl}) \tag{3}$$

Note that the symbols used in the paper are defined in the offered nomenclature.

As shown in Fig 1, the difference of the four tire forces in longitudinal direction may produce a large yaw moment. The lateral tire forces in a small steering angle scenario are relatively small and lead to an insignificant yaw moment compared to that of the longitudinal tire forces. For simplicity, in the differential braking controller design, only the yaw moment due to the longitudinal tire forces is considered.

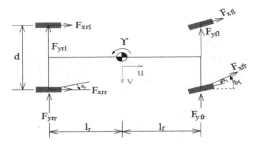

**Fig. 1.** Top view of the SUV handling model

The yaw moment control system is designed to adjust the longitudinal force on individual tires governed by the equations above. The moment $M_y$ is expressed as

$$M_y = \frac{d}{2}(F_{xfr} - F_{xfl} + F_{xrr} - F_{xrl})\tag{4}$$

To study the relationship between the brake pressures and the consequent forces, a brake system model is established. The brake force is simply approximated as a linear function of the corresponding brake pressure [12], including the saturation effect and the hydraulic lag that act as the nature of a hydraulic braking system.

It is assumed that the SUV is front-wheel driving with brake proportioning, which indicates the braking pressure of the rear tire on either side can be obtained by multiplying a constant gain from that of the front tire. The torque transferred from the transmission system is equally distributed to the left and right side of the front tires. The radius of the front and rear tires is the same and assumed remains a constant in the control process. Thus the longitudinal forces of the four tires can be assessed as

$$F_{xfl} = \frac{0.5T_t - K_{bf}P_{bfl}}{R_e}\tag{5}$$

$$F_{xfr} = \frac{0.5T_t - K_{bf}P_{bfr}}{R_e}\tag{6}$$

$$F_{xrl} = \frac{-K_{br}P_{brl}}{R_e} = -k_c\frac{K_{bf}}{R_e}P_{bfl}\tag{7}$$

$$F_{xrr} = \frac{-K_{br}P_{brr}}{R_e} = -k_c\frac{K_{bf}}{R_e}P_{bfr}\tag{8}$$

Fig 2 shows the schematic diagram of the SUV braking system model that is applied to estimate the longitudinal braking force and the resulting yaw moment from the front left and right tire braking pressures.

According to above assumptions, the control of the differential longitudinal forces of the entire four wheels can be reduced to only two wheels mounted on the front axle. This arrangement can greatly reduce the control computation cost and largely improve the simulation efficiency.

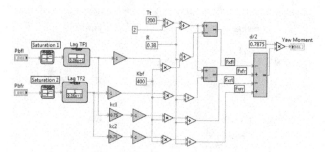

**Fig. 2.** Differential braking system model

# 3     Differential Braking Controller Design

The objective of the controller design is to improve the handling and stability of the SUV. With the yaw moment generated from the different braking forces of the left and right tires, two vehicle state variables, e.g., vehicle yaw rate and sideslip angle, are effectively controlled to remain the proper vehicle responses.

Equation (4) describes the relationship among the yaw moment, the studied tire forces and the track width. By including the braking pressure directly related to the yaw moment $M_y$, equation (4) can be re-arranged as

$$M_y = \frac{(1 + k_c) K_{bf} (P_{bfl} - P_{bfr}) d}{2 R_e} \tag{9}$$

The controller design is to manipulate the yaw moment by adjusting the control variables of left and right braking pressures of the four wheels. Fig 3 shows a schematic diagram of the controller design.

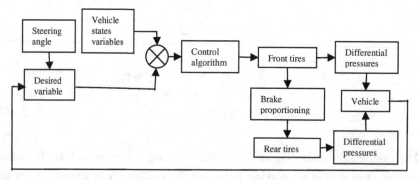

**Fig. 3.** Control scheme for differential braking controller design

As shown in Fig 3, the interrelated driver, controller and the vehicle (represented by the vehicle state variables) form a closed-loop control system. The input to the controller consists of the vehicle state variables and the driver input. The vehicle states, obtained from the embedded sensor system, are compared with those derived from the following desired vehicle model which is manipulated by the driver, perceiving the current vehicle states and operating condition. Their differences are forwarded to the controller, which optimally calculates the required braking pressures for the four wheels to generate the necessary yaw moment. These brake pressures are distributed to the four wheel cylinders to generate the corrective yaw moment for improving the SUV stability and handling characteristics.

The controller is derived using the linear yaw plane vehicle model discussed in section 2. The vehicle sideslip and yaw rate, which extensively affect the vehicle stability and handling, are controlled by the front steering angle and the required yaw moment. The resulting equations governing the lateral and yaw motions of the SUV are expressed as follows:

$$mU(\dot{\beta}+\gamma) = (\frac{0.5T_t - K_{bf}P_{bfl}}{R_e} + \frac{0.5T_t - K_{bf}P_{bfr}}{R_e} - c_f)\delta_f + c_f(\beta + \frac{l_f\gamma}{U} - \delta_f) + c_f(\beta + \frac{l_f\gamma}{U} - \delta_f) + c_r(\beta - \frac{l_r\gamma}{U}) \quad (10)$$

$$I_z\dot{\gamma} = l_f(\frac{0.5T_t - K_{bf}P_{bfl}}{R_e} + \frac{0.5T_t - K_{bf}P_{bfr}}{R_e})\delta_f + c_fl_f(\beta + \frac{l_f\gamma}{U} - \delta_f) - c_rl_r(\beta - \frac{l_r\gamma}{U}) + \frac{(1+k_c)k_{bf}(P_{bfl}-P_{bfr})d}{2R_e} \quad (11)$$

where the vehicle sideslip angle $\beta$ and the yaw rate $\gamma$ are defined as state variables, the brake pressure $P_{bfl}$ and $P_{bfr}$ are used as control variables, with which the yaw moment $M_y$ will be generated. The vehicle steering angle $\delta_f$ is the driver input that will drive the SUV to follow a designated path. Equations (10) and (11) can be rearranged in a state space form as

$$M\dot{x} = Ax + Bu + E\delta_f \quad (12)$$

where $x = \begin{bmatrix} \beta \\ \gamma \end{bmatrix}$, $u = \begin{bmatrix} P_{bfl} \\ P_{bfr} \end{bmatrix}$, $M = \begin{bmatrix} mU & 0 \\ 0 & I_z \end{bmatrix}$,

$$A = \begin{bmatrix} c_f + c_r & -mU + \frac{c_fl_f - c_rl_r}{U} \\ c_fl_f - c_rl_r & \frac{c_fl_f^2 + c_rl_r^2}{U} \end{bmatrix} \quad \text{and} \quad B = \begin{bmatrix} 0 & 0 \\ \frac{K_{bf}(k_c+1)d}{2R_e} & -\frac{K_{bf}(k_c+1)d}{2R_e} \end{bmatrix}$$

The controller is designed to minimize the difference between the measured state variables and their desired counterparts. It is necessary to determine the desired state variables for the controller to follow. The desired variables are defined to enable the vehicle to follow the designated path and to avoid inappropriate understeer and oversteer handling characteristics when negotiating a curved path. To incorporate the tire force into the control of the vehicle dynamics, the desired variables will be determined. The desired variables are changeable with the variation of vehicle-road operational condition. Previous studies have suggested that both the sideslip angle and yaw rate should be considered together to achieve a satisfactory vehicle stability control [3]. Thus, the desired state variables can be determined as follows

$$\beta_{des} = \frac{2c_fc_rl_r(l_f + l_r) - c_fl_fmV^2}{2c_fc_r(l_f + l_r)^2 - (c_fl_f - c_rl_r)mV^2}\delta_f \quad (13)$$

$$\gamma_{des} = \frac{2c_fc_rl_r(l_f + l_r)}{2c_fc_r(l_f + l_r)^2 - (c_fl_f - c_rl_r)mV^2}\delta_f \quad (14)$$

The output errors between the vehicle state variables and those from the desired model need to be suppressed. The function of differential braking will be implemented to form a feedback compensator using the Linear Quadratic Regulator (LQR) technology. The LQR algorithm is used to obtain optimal feedback control gain $K_{bk}$ by minimizing the following cost function

$$J = \int_{0}^{+\infty} (e^T Q e + u R u^T) dt \qquad (15)$$

where

$$e = x - x_{des} = \begin{bmatrix} \beta \\ \gamma \end{bmatrix} - \begin{bmatrix} \beta_{des} \\ \gamma_{des} \end{bmatrix} \qquad (16)$$

$e$ is the difference between the measured and the desired values of the state variables. Q and R are the weighting factors of state and control variables, respectively. The solution of the optimization is the feedback controller in the following form

$$u = -k \cdot x \qquad (17)$$

with optimal gain matrix k

$$k = R^{-1} B^T P \qquad (18)$$

where P is a symmetric, positive semi-definite symmetric matrix which satisfies the Riccati Equation

$$A^T P + P A - P B R^{-1} B P + Q = 0 \qquad (19)$$

The selection of the appropriate weighting factors Q and R is critical to achieve an acceptable and steady state solution of the above Riccati equation. The values of weighting factors are carefully tuned with acceptable performance measure under a range of vehicle maneuvers.

# 4    Real-Time Simulations and the Vehicle Simulator

The controller design is examined with real-time simulations on the vehicle simulator. The vehicle simulator provides an easy-to-use virtual testing environment that integrates the driver, vehicle dynamic model, controller and visual display in a real-time working mode. The configuration of the vehicle simulator is shown in Fig 4.

The vehicle simulator consists of a host computer, an animator computer, a target PC, and three monitors, the real-time operation system by National Instruments, communication link and I/O boards. The simulator allows the interactions between the driver and the controller such that the virtual vehicle is driven under the specified testing maneuvers.

One of the key points in setting up the virtual testing environment is to construct the real-time version of the controller and the vehicle model. The real-time controller based on the previous design is constructed in LabView package and the real-time SUV model is developed in CarSim software. The integration of the controller constructed in LabView and the vehicle model developed in CarSim is implemented on the vehicle simulator.

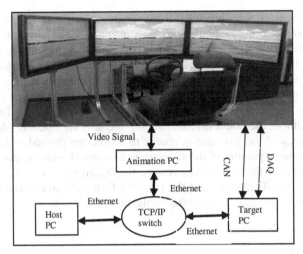

**Fig. 4.** System architecture of vehicle simulator at UOIT

Fig 5 shows the integration of the real-time SUV model and the controller. The nonlinear SUV model with a high fidelity is developed in CarSim. In the differential braking control, all the measured vehicle states are obtained from the CarSim vehicle model in real-time. The LQR controller designed in section 3 is reconstructed in LabView. With the integration and synchronization of the vehicle model and the controller in real-time on the vehicle simulator, the interactions among the human driver, the controller, the virtual vehicle and road can be fully investigated for the design and validation of the differential braking controller.

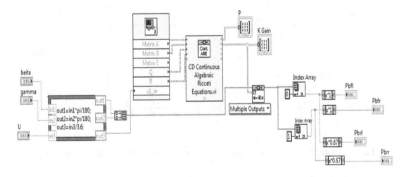

**Fig. 5.** Differential braking controller design in the LabVIEW RT system

## 5    Simulation Results

The driver-in-the-loop real-time simulations have been conducted in two different cases, i.e., with and without involving the differential braking controller, respectively. A driver is involved to evaluate the controller by operating the vehicle simulator. Note that in the modeling and simulation of the vehicle system, the system parameters take the values shown in the offered nomenclature.

Two test maneuvers are simulated, a 50m radius circular path following and a double lane change on a path with 80m long in longitudinal direction and a 3.5m lateral offset. For both maneuvers, the vehicle is driven at a constant speed of 80km/h. Simulation results are presented and compared in terms of vehicle sideslip angle, yaw rate and vehicle trajectory in the global X-Y coordinate system.

Fig 6 shows the results in the circular path following, and the time history of the vehicle sideslip angle, yaw rate and trajectory are illustrated in Fig 6 (a)-(c), respectively. Without the controller, the sideslip angle is significantly deviated from the desired value, and the yaw rate is unable to follow the desired one, even after a transit period in the beginning of the simulation. Compared with the case without the controller, in terms of the steady state results, the controller can reduce the side slip angle from 0.08 to 0.03 radians, and the yaw rate from 0.72 to 0.28rad/s. Moreover, the controller makes the SUV closely follow the designated path.

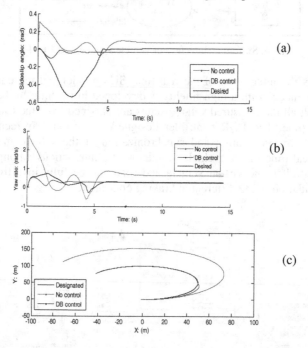

**Fig. 6.** Comparison of SUV performance for the 50m circular scenario

Fig 7 shows the simulation results in the double lane change scenario. Compared with the case without the controller, the controller reduces the sideslip angle from 0.05 to 0.01radians and the yaw rate from 0.5 to 0.16rad/s. Furthermore, the controller make the vehicle follow the specified path accurately.

It is also noticeable that the driver's operation is very important and different operations may lead to significant test result fluctuation. In the testing, the driver repeated driving the virtual SUV and only the best results are presented in Figs 6 and 7. Improper or clumsy driving operations interacted with a given controller may adversely deteriorate the overall vehicle stability and path-following performance.

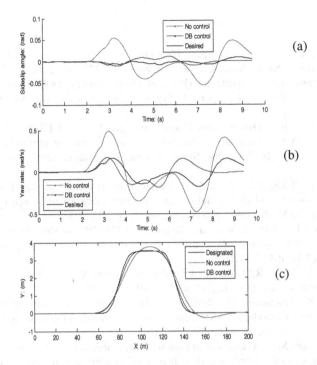

**Fig. 7.** Comparison of SUV performance for the double lane change scenario

# 6    Conclusions

This paper presents a design and validation method for differential braking controllers of SUVs using driver-in-the-loop real-time simulations. A linear yaw plane model is generated to derive the differential braking controller. To validate and improve the controller design, the real-time version of the controller and the SUV model are reconstructed; with the integration of the controller and SUV model, the real-time simulations are implemented on a vehicle simulator.

Simulations show that the differential braking controller can effectively manipulate the yaw moment to improve the stability and maneuverability of the SUV. With the effective coordination between the driving operation of the driver and the action of the controller, the overall performance of the SUV can be improved. With the driver-in-the-loop real-time simulations, the interactions among the driver, differential braking controller, and SUV model are well exposed and can be fully investigated for improving designs. The vehicle simulator provides a cost-effective way for vehicle stability control system evaluation prior to in-vehicle road testing.

# References

1. Palkovics, L., Fries, A.: Intelligent Electronic Systems in Commercial Vehicles for Enhanced Traffic Safety. Vehicle System Dynamics 35, 227–289 (2001)
2. US Department of Transportation Office of Public Affairs: DOT Requires Upgraded Rollover Warning Label for Sports Utility Vehicles. Press Releases No. NHTSA 8-99 (1999)
3. Rajamani, R.: vehicle Dynamics and Control. Springer, New York (2006)
4. Van Zanten, A.T.: Evolution of electronic control systems for improving the vehicle dynamic behavior. In: Proc. Int. Symp. Advanced Vehicle Control, vol. 20, pp. 7–15 (2002)
5. Zhang, S.Q., Zhang, T.X., Zhou, S.W.: Vehicle stability control strategy based on active torque distribution and differential braking. In: International Conference on Measuring Technology and Mechatronics Automation, vol. 1, pp. 922–925 (2009)
6. Barbarisi, O., Palmieri, G., Scala, S., Glielmo, L.: LTV-MPC for yaw rate control and side slip control with dynamically constrained differential braking. European Journal of Control 15(3-4), 468–479 (2009)
7. MacAdam, C., Ervin, R.: Differential Braking for Limited-Authority Lateral Maneuvering, IDEA Program Final Report, Report No. UMTRI-98-43 (1998)
8. Friedman, K., Hutchinson, J.: Review of existing repeatable vehicle rollover dynamic physical testing methods. In: ASME International Mechanical Engineering Congress and Exposition, vol. 16, pp. 51–59 (2009)
9. Short, M., Pont, M.J.: Assessment of high-integrity embedded automotive control systems using hardware in the loop simulation. Journal of Systems & Software 81(7), 1163–1183 (2008)
10. Chen, B., Peng, H.: Differential-Braking-Based Rollover Prevention for Sport Utility Vehicles with Human-in-the-Loop Evaluations. Vehicle System Dynamics 36(4-5), 359–389 (2001)
11. Huang, A., Chen, C.: A low-cost driving simulator for full vehicle dynamics simulation. IEEE Transactions on Vehicular Technology 52(1), 162–172 (2003)
12. Pilutti, T., Ulsoy, G., Hrovat, D.: Vehicle steering intervention through differential braking. In: Proceedings of the 1995 American Control Conference, pp. 1667–1671 (1995)

## Nomenclature

| Symbol | Definition | Value |
|--------|-----------|-------|
| $c_f$ | Front cornering stiffness | -68420 N/rad |
| $c_r$ | Rear cornering stiffness | -68420 N/rad |
| $d$ | Axle tread | 1.575m |
| $F_{xfl}$ | Longitudinal force of front-left tire | |
| $F_{xfr}$ | Longitudinal force of front-right tire | |
| $F_{xrl}$ | Longitudinal force of rear-left tire | |
| $F_{xrr}$ | Longitudinal force of rear-right tire | |
| $H$ | Height of CG | 0.72m |
| $I_z$ | Yaw moment of inertia | 2488kg·m$^2$ |
| $k_c$ | Rear brake proportioning coefficient | 0.75 |
| $k_{bf}$ | Brake gain of the front tires | 400 N/MPa |
| $l_f$ | Distance from CG to front axle | 1.18m |
| $l_r$ | Distance from CG to rear axle | 1.77m |
| $m$ | Vehicle mass | 1592kg |
| $M_y$ | SUV yaw moment | |
| $n_1$ | Steer gear ratio | 20.5 |
| $n_2$ | Transmission gear ratio | 4.1 |
| $P_{bfl}$ | Brake pressure of front-left tire | |
| $P_{bfr}$ | Brake pressure of front-right tire | |
| $R_e$ | Effective tire radius | 0.38m |
| $T_t$ | Driving axle shaft torque | 200N·m |
| $U$ | SUV longitudinal velocity | |
| $V$ | SUV lateral velocity | |
| $\alpha_f$ | Front tire slip angle | |
| $\alpha_r$ | Rear tire slip angle | |
| $\beta$ | Sideslip angle of Vehicle body | |
| $\gamma$ | Yaw rate of vehicle body | |
| $\delta_f$ | Vehicle steering angle | |
| $\mu$ | Tire-road friction coefficient | 0.85 |

# Optimization of Measurement Configurations for Geometrical Calibration of Industrial Robot

Alexandr Klimchik[1,2], Anatol Pashkevich[1,2], Yier Wu[1,2],
Benoît Furet[2], and Stephane Caro[2]

[1] Ecole des Mines de Nantes, 4 rue Alfred-Kastler, Nantes 44307, France
[2] Institut de Recherche en Communications et Cybernétique de Nantes, 44321 France
{alexandr.klimchik,anatol.pashkevich,yier.wu}@mines-nantes.fr,
{benoit.furet,stephane.caro}@irccyn.ec-nantes.fr

**Abstract.** The paper is devoted to the geometrical calibration of industrial robots employed in precise manufacturing. To identify geometric parameters, an advanced calibration technique is proposed that is based on the non-linear experiment design theory, which is adopted for this particular application. In contrast to previous works, the calibration experiment quality is evaluated using a concept of the user-defined test-pose. In the frame of this concept, the related optimization problem is formulated and numerical routines are developed, which allow user to generate optimal set of manipulator configurations for a given number of calibration experiments. The efficiency of the developed technique is illustrated by several examples.

**Keywords:** industrial robot, calibration, design of experiments, industry-oriented performance measure, test-pose based approach.

## 1 Introduction

In the usual engineering practice, the accuracy of robotic manipulator depends on a number of factors. Usually, for the industrial applications where the external forces/torques applied to the end-effector are relatively small, the prime source of the manipulator inaccuracy is the *geometrical errors*, which are responsible for about 90% of the total position error [1]. These errors are associated with the differences between the nominal and actual values of the link/joint parameters. Typical examples of them are the differences between the nominal and the actual length of links, the differences between zero values of actuator coordinates in the real robot and the mathematical model embedded in the controller (joint offsets) [2]. They can be also induced by the non-perfect assembling of different links and lead to shifting and/or rotation of the frames associated with different elements, which are normally assumed to be matched and aligned. It is clear that the errors in geometrical parameters do not depend on the manipulator configuration, while their effect on the position accuracy depends on the last one. At present, there exists various sophisticated calibration techniques that are able to identify the differences between the actual and the nominal

C.-Y. Su, S. Rakheja, H. Liu (Eds.): ICIRA 2012, Part I, LNAI 7506, pp. 132–143, 2012.

geometrical parameters [3,4], however the problem of optimal selection of measurement configurations is still in the focus of robotic experts.

The primary motivation of this research area is the possibility of essential reduction the measurement error impact. From point of view of classical experiment design theory [5] this goal can be achieved by proper selection of measurement poses that differ from each other as much as possible. However, in spite of potential advantages of this approach and potential benefits to improve the identification accuracy significantly, only few works addressed to the issue of the best measurement pose selection [6-8]. Related works focus on optimization of some abstract performance measures [9-12] (condition number of the aggregated Jacobian matrix, its determinant, etc.) which are not directly related to the robot precision for particular industrial application. In contrast, this work operates with an industry-oriented performance measure that is directly related to the robot position accuracy in a given workspace location (corresponding to so-called test configuration). Using this idea, in the following sections the problem of calibration experiment design is formulated as a constrained optimization problem (taking into account some specific technological requirements) and is solved for serial manipulators with 2 and 6 degrees of freedoms.

## 2    Problem of Geometrical Calibration

Let us consider a serial robotic manipulator whose end-effector position $\mathbf{p}$ is computing using the geometrical model

$$\mathbf{p} = g(\mathbf{q}, \mathbf{\Pi}) \tag{1}$$

which includes the vector of the unknown parameters $\mathbf{\Pi}$ to be identified and where the vector $\mathbf{q}$ aggregates all joint coordinates. Usually the most essential components of the vector $\mathbf{\Pi}$ are the deviations of the robot link lengths $l_i$ and the offsets $\Delta q_j$ in the actuated joints, but in some cases it may also include inclinations of the joint axes, etc. In practice, the above defined function $g(.)$ can be extracted from the product of homogeneous transformation matrices

$$\mathbf{T} = \mathbf{T}_{\text{base}} \left( \prod_{i=1}^{n} \mathbf{T}_i(q_i, \mathbf{\Pi}_i) \right) \mathbf{T}_{\text{tool}} \tag{2}$$

which are widely used in robotic kinematics. Here, $\mathbf{T}_{\text{base}}$ and $\mathbf{T}_{\text{tool}}$ denote the 'Base' and 'Tool' transformations respectively, $\mathbf{T}_i(q_i, \mathbf{\Pi}_i)$ defines transformations related to the $i$-th actuated joint. Here, $\mathbf{T}$, $\mathbf{T}_i$, $\mathbf{T}_{\text{base}}$, $\mathbf{T}_{\text{tool}}$ are $4 \times 4$ matrices that are computed as a product of simple translation/rotation matrices, for which the number of multipliers and their order is defined by robot geometrical model. Since the deviations of geometrical parameters $\Delta \mathbf{\Pi}$ are usually relatively small, calibration usually relies on the linearized model [8]

$$\mathbf{p} = g(\mathbf{q}, \mathbf{\Pi}_0) + \mathbf{J}(\mathbf{q}, \mathbf{\Pi}_0) \Delta \mathbf{\Pi} \tag{3}$$

which includes the Jacobian $\mathbf{J}(\mathbf{q}, \mathbf{\Pi}_0) = \partial g(\mathbf{q}, \mathbf{\Pi}_0)/\partial \mathbf{\Pi}$ computed for the nominal parameters $\mathbf{\Pi}_0$.

In the frame of this work, the following assumptions concerning the manipulator model and the measurement equipment limitations are accepted:

**A1**: *each calibration experiment produces two vectors* $\{\mathbf{p}_i, \mathbf{q}_i\}$, which define the robot end-effector position and corresponding joint angles;

**A2**: the calibration relies on the *measurements of the end-effector position only* (i.e. Cartesian coordinates x, y, z; such approach allows us to avoid the problem of different units and to use three points with position instead of one with position and orientation);

**A3**: *the measurements errors* are treated as independent identically distributed random values with zero expectation and standard deviation $\sigma$.

Because of the measurement errors, the unknown parameters $\mathbf{\Pi}$ are always identified approximately and their estimates $\hat{\mathbf{\Pi}}$ can be also treated as random values. For this reason, the "identification quality" is usually evaluated via the covariance matrix $\mathrm{cov}(\hat{\mathbf{\Pi}})$, whose elements should be as small as possible. However, this approach does not provide the final user with a clear engineering characteristic of the accuracy improvement, which is achieved due to calibration. Thus, it is proposed to use another performance measure that directly evaluates the robot accuracy after compensation of the geometrical errors, which in the frame of the adopted above notations can be expressed as.

$$\varepsilon_p(\mathbf{q}) = g\left(\mathbf{q}, \hat{\mathbf{\Pi}}\right) - g\left(\mathbf{q}, \mathbf{\Pi}\right) \tag{4}$$

where $\mathbf{q}$ defines the manipulator configuration. Further, to take into account particularities of the considered technological application, it is reasonable to limit the possible configurations set by a single one $\mathbf{q}_0$, which is treated as a typical for the manufacturing task. It is obvious that definition of $\mathbf{q}_0$ ("test-pose") is a non-trivial step that completely relies on the user experience and his/her understanding of the technological process. The main substantiation for this approach is to take into account that all geometrical errors have different influence on the end-effector position and this influence varies throughout the workspace. However, in practice, high accuracy is required in the neighborhood of the prescribe trajectory only.

Taking into account that the geometric parameter estimate $\hat{\mathbf{\Pi}}$ is computed via the best fitting of the data set $\{\mathbf{p}_i, \mathbf{q}_i\}$ by the function (1), the expectation of the position errors after compensation is equal to zero, i.e. $E(\varepsilon_p) = 0$. However, the standard deviation $E(\varepsilon_p^T \varepsilon_p)$ essentially depends on the measurement configurations (which, from point of view of the experiment design theory, can be treated as the plan of the calibration experiments). This allows us to present the considered problem in the following way:

**Problem:** *For a given number of experiments* $m$ *, find a set of measurement configurations* $\{\mathbf{q}_1, \ldots \mathbf{q}_m\}$ *defined by the vectors of the joint variables* $\mathbf{q}_i$ *that ensures minimum value of the position error s.t.d. for the test configuration* $\mathbf{q}_0$ :

$$E\left(\| g(\mathbf{q}_0, \hat{\mathbf{\Pi}}) - g(\mathbf{q}_0, \mathbf{\Pi}) \|^2\right) \to \min_{\{\mathbf{q}_1 \cdots \mathbf{q}_m\}} \tag{5}$$

*where* $\|\mathbf{\varepsilon}_p\|$ *denotes the Euclidian norm of the vector* $\mathbf{\varepsilon}_p$ .

In the following sections this optimization problem will be solved subject to the additional constraints imposed by the application area.

# 3    Influence of Measurement Errors

For comparison purpose, let us first evaluate the influence of the measurement errors on the accuracy of the geometrical parameters identification. Using the linear approximation of the geometrical model (3), the deviation of the desired parameters with respect to their nominal values $\Delta\mathbf{\Pi} = \hat{\mathbf{\Pi}} - \mathbf{\Pi}_0$ can be obtained from the minimum least-square formulation

$$\sum_{i=1}^{m} \left(\mathbf{J}_i \Delta\mathbf{\Pi} - \Delta\mathbf{p}_i\right)^T \left(\mathbf{J}_i \Delta\mathbf{\Pi} - \Delta\mathbf{p}_i\right) \to \min_{\Delta\mathbf{\Pi}} \tag{6}$$

which yields expression

$$\Delta\hat{\mathbf{\Pi}} = \left(\sum_{i=1}^{m} \mathbf{J}_i^T \mathbf{J}_i\right)^{-1} \cdot \left(\sum_{i=1}^{m} \mathbf{J}_i^T \Delta\mathbf{p}_i\right) \tag{7}$$

where $\Delta\mathbf{p}_i = \mathbf{p}_i - \mathbf{p}_{0i}$ denotes the shift of the end-effector position $\mathbf{p}_i$ for the $i$-th experiment with respect to the location corresponding to the nominal geometrical parameters $\mathbf{\Pi}_0$ and measurement configuration $\mathbf{q}_i$ . To increase the identification accuracy, the foregoing linearized procedure has to be applied several times, in accordance with the following iterative algorithm:

**Step 1.** Carry out experiments and collect the input data in the vectors of generalized coordinates $\mathbf{q}_i$ and end-effector position $\mathbf{p}_i$. Initialize $\Delta\mathbf{\Pi} = 0$.

**Step 2.** Compute end-effector position via direct kinematic model (1) using initial generalized coordinates $\mathbf{q}_i$

**Step 3.** Compute residuals and unknown parameters $\Delta\mathbf{\Pi}$ via (7)

**Step 4.** Modify mathematical model and generalized coordinates $\mathbf{\Pi}$ and $\mathbf{q}_i$ .

**Step 5.** If required accuracy is not satisfied, repeat from Step 2.

Further, to integrate the measurement errors $\mathbf{\varepsilon}_i$ in equation (7), $\Delta\mathbf{p}_i$ can be expressed as

$$\Delta\mathbf{p}_i = \mathbf{J}_i \Delta\mathbf{\Pi} + \mathbf{\varepsilon}_i \tag{8}$$

where $\varepsilon_i$ are assumed to be independent identically distributed (i.i.d.) random values with zero expectation $E(\varepsilon_i) = 0$ and the variance $E(\varepsilon_i^T \varepsilon_i) = \sigma^2$. Hence, as follows from (7), the geometric parameters estimate $\hat{\Pi}$ can be presented as the sum

$$\hat{\Pi} = \Pi_0 + \left( \sum_{i=1}^{m} \mathbf{J}_i^T \mathbf{J}_i \right)^{-1} \left( \sum_{i=1}^{m} \mathbf{J}_i^T \varepsilon_i \right) \tag{9}$$

where the first term corresponds to the expectation of this random variable. From the latter expression, the covariance matrix of $\hat{\Pi}$, which defines the identification accuracy, can be computed as

$$\mathrm{cov}(\hat{\Pi}) = \left( \sum_{i=1}^{m} \mathbf{J}_i^T \mathbf{J}_i \right)^{-1} E\left( \sum_{i=1}^{m} \mathbf{J}_i^T \varepsilon_i \varepsilon_i^T \mathbf{J}_i \right) \left( \sum_{i=1}^{m} \mathbf{J}_i^T \mathbf{J}_i \right)^{-1}. \tag{10}$$

So, considering that $E\left( \varepsilon_i \varepsilon_i^T \right) = \sigma^2 \mathbf{I}$, the desired covariance matrix can be simplified to:

$$\mathrm{cov}(\hat{\Pi}) = \sigma^2 \left( \sum_{i=1}^{m} \mathbf{J}_i^T \mathbf{J}_i \right)^{-1} \tag{11}$$

where $\sigma$ is the s.t.d. of the measurement errors. Hence, the impact of the measurement errors on the identified values of the geometric parameters is defined by the matrix sum $\sum_{i=1}^{m} \mathbf{J}_i^T \mathbf{J}_i$ that is also called the information matrix.

It should be stressed that most of the related works [9-11] reduce the calibration experiment design problem to the problem of covariance matrix minimization, which is evaluated by means of the determinant, Euclidian norm, trace, singular values, etc. However, because of some essential disadvantages mentioned in the previous section, this approach may provide a solution, which does not guarantee the best position accuracy for typical manipulator configurations defined by the manufacturing process. This motivates another approach presented below.

## 4      Test-Pose Based Approach

To overcome the above mentioned difficulty, it is prudent to introduce another performance measure, which is directly related to the robot accuracy after compensation of the geometrical errors. Besides, to take into account that the desired accuracy should be achieved for rather limited workspace area, it is proposed to limit possible manipulator configurations by a single one (corresponding to joint variables $\mathbf{q}_0$), which further will be referred to as a test-pose. It is evident that this performance measure is attractive for practicing engineers and also allows to avoid the multiobjective optimization problem that arises while minimizing all elements of the covariance matrix (11) simultaneously. In addition, using this approach, it is possible to find a balance between accuracy of different geometrical parameters whose influence on the final robot accuracy is unequal.

In more formal way, the proposed performance measure $\rho_0$ may be defined as the s.t.d. of the distance between the desired end-effector position and its real position achieved after application of the geometrical error compensation technique.

Using the notations from the previous section, this distance may be computed as the Euclidean norm of the vector $\delta\mathbf{p} = \mathbf{J}_0 \delta\mathbf{\Pi}$, where the subscript '0' is related to the test pose $\mathbf{q}_0$ and $\delta\mathbf{\Pi} = \hat{\mathbf{\Pi}} - \mathbf{\Pi}$ is the difference between the estimated and true values of the robot geometrical parameters. It can be proved that the above presented identification algorithm provides an unbiased compensation, i.e. $\mathrm{E}(\delta\mathbf{p}) = \mathbf{0}$, while the standard deviation of the compensation error $\mathrm{E}(\delta\mathbf{p}^T \delta\mathbf{p})$ can be expressed as

$$\rho_0^2 = \mathrm{E}\left( \delta\mathbf{\Pi}^T \mathbf{J}_0^T \mathbf{J}_0 \delta\mathbf{\Pi} \right) \tag{12}$$

Taking into account geometrical meaning of $\rho_0$, this value will be used as a numerical measure of the error compensation quality (and also as a quality measure of the related plan of calibration experiments). This expression can be simplified by presenting the term $\delta\mathbf{p}^T \delta\mathbf{p}$ as the trace of the matrix $\delta\mathbf{p}\delta\mathbf{p}^T$, which yields

$$\rho_0^2 = \mathrm{trace}\left( \mathbf{J}_0 \mathrm{E}\left( \delta\mathbf{\Pi}\delta\mathbf{\Pi}^T \right) \mathbf{J}_0^T \right) \tag{13}$$

Further, taking into account that $\mathrm{E}(\delta\mathbf{\Pi}\delta\mathbf{\Pi}^T)$ is the covariance matrix of the geometrical parameters estimate $\hat{\mathbf{\Pi}}$, the proposed performance measure (13) can be presented in the final form as

$$\rho_0^2 = \sigma^2 \mathrm{trace}\left( \mathbf{J}_0 \left( \sum_{i=1}^{m} \mathbf{J}_i^T \mathbf{J}_i \right)^{-1} \mathbf{J}_0^T \right) \tag{14}$$

As follows from this expression, the proposed performance measure $\rho_0^2$ can be treated as the weighted trace of the covariance matrix (11), where the weighting coefficients are computed using the test pose coordinates. It has obvious advantages compared to previous approaches, which operate with "pure" trace of the covariance matrix and involve straightforward summing of the covariance matrix diagonal elements, which may be of different units.

Using this performance measure, the problem of calibration experiment design can be reduced to the following optimization problem

$$\mathrm{trace}\left( \mathbf{J}_0 \left( \sum_{i=1}^{m} \mathbf{J}_i^T \mathbf{J}_i \right)^{-1} \mathbf{J}_0^T \right) \rightarrow \min_{\{\mathbf{q}_1 \ldots \mathbf{q}_m\}} \tag{15}$$

whose solution gives a set of the desired manipulator configurations $\{\mathbf{q}_1, \ldots \mathbf{q}_m\}$. It is evident that here an analytical solution can hardly be obtained, so a numerical approach is the only reasonable one. An application of this approach for the design of the manipulator calibration experiments and its advantages are illustrated below. Geometrical interpretation of the proposed approach is presented in Fig. 1, where the performance measure $\rho_0$ defines the position error for the target point after calibration.

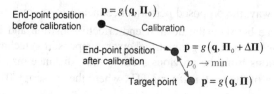

**Fig. 1.** Geometrical interpretation of the test-pose based approach

# 5    Illustrative Example

Let us illustrate the advantages of the test-pose-based approach by an example of the geometrical calibration of the 2-link manipulator. For this manipulator, the end-effector position can be computed as

$$x = (l_1 + \Delta l_1)\cos q_1 + (l_2 + \Delta l_2)\cos(q_1 + q_2)$$
$$y = (l_1 + \Delta l_1)\sin q_1 + (l_2 + \Delta l_2)\sin(q_1 + q_2) \tag{16}$$

where $x$ and $y$ define the end-effector position, $l_1, l_2$ and $\Delta l_1, \Delta l_2$ are nominal link lengths and their deviations (that should be identified), $q_1$, $q_2$ are the joint coordinates that define manipulator configuration. It can be proved that, in the case of $\Delta\Pi = (\Delta l_1, \Delta l_2)$ the parameter covariance matrix does not depend on the angles $q_{1i}$ and can be expressed as:

$$\text{cov}(\Delta\hat{\Pi}) = \frac{\sigma^2}{m^2 - \left(\sum_{i=1}^{m}\cos q_{2i}\right)^2}\begin{bmatrix} m & -\sum_{i=1}^{m}\cos q_{2i} \\ -\sum_{i=1}^{m}\cos q_{2i} & m \end{bmatrix} \tag{17}$$

where $m$ is the number of experiments and $i = 1,...m$.

For comparison purposes the design of experiment problem was solved using both the known approaches and the proposed one. It can be shown that here it is not reasonable to use the A-criterion (the goal of A-criterion is to minimize the trace of the covariance matrix) because the trace of the relevant information matrix does not depend on the plan of experiments. Further, it was proved that the criteria that operate with the covariance matrix determinant (D and D* criteria, [8]; the goal of D-criterion is to minimize the determinant of the covariance matrix, the goal of D*-criterion is to ensure independence of the identified parameters and to minimize the determinant of the covariance matrix that is diagonal) lead to minimization of $\left|\sum_{i=1}^{m}\cos q_{2i}\right|$. This solution provides good accuracy on average, but not for the test configuration $(q_{10}, q_{20})$.

For the proposed performance measure $\rho_0^2$, the basic expression (14) can be transformed to

$$\rho_0^2 = 2\sigma^2 \left( m - \cos q_{20} \sum_{i=1}^{m} \cos q_{2i} \right) \Bigg/ \left( m^2 - \left( \sum_{i=1}^{m} \cos q_{2i} \right)^2 \right) \tag{18}$$

Here, the minimum value of $\rho_0^2$ is achieved when

$$\sum_{i=1}^{m} \cos q_{2i} = m\left(1 - |\sin q_{20}|\right) \Big/ \cos q_{20} \tag{19}$$

and is equal to

$$\rho_{0\min}^2 = \left(\sigma^2/m\right)\cos^2 q_{20} \Big/ \left(1 - |\sin q_{20}|\right) \tag{20}$$

It is evident that general solution of equation (19) for $m$ configurations can be replaced by the decomposition of the whole configuration set by the subsets of 2 and 3 configurations (while providing the same identification accuracy). This essentially reduces computational complexity and allows user to reduce number of different configurations without loss of accuracy.

Compared with other approaches, it should be mentioned that in the test pose $(q_{10}, q_{20})$, the D-criterion insures the accuracy $\rho_D^2 = 2\sigma^2/m$ only. Corresponding loss of the accuracy is presented in Table 1. It is shown that the test-pose based approach allows us to improve the accuracy of the end-effector position up to 41%.

**Table 1.** Accuracy comparison for D-based and test-pose based approaches

| $|q_{20}|$, deg | 0° | 30° | 60° | 90° | 120° | 150° | 180° |
|---|---|---|---|---|---|---|---|
| $\rho_D^2/\sigma^2$ | 1 | 1 | 1 | 1 | 1 | 1 | 1 |
| $\rho_0^2/\sigma^2$ | 0.5 | 0.75 | 0.83 | 1 | 0.83 | 0.75 | 0.5 |
| $\rho_D/\rho_0$, % | 41 | 15 | 10 | 0 | 10 | 15 | 41 |

To illustrate advantages of the proposed approach, Fig. 2 presents three plots showing geometrical error compensation efficiency for different calibration plans. These results correspond to the manipulator parameters $l_1 = 1\,\mathrm{m}$, $l_2 = 0.8\,\mathrm{m}$, two measurement configurations $m = 2$, the test pose $\mathbf{q}_0 = (-45°, 20°)$, and s.t.d. of the measurement errors $\sigma = 10^{-3}\,\mathrm{m}$. The calibration experiment has been repeated 100 times. In the case (a), the plan of experiments corresponds to $\mathbf{q}_1 = (0°, -10°)$ and $\mathbf{q}_2 = (0°, 10°)$. In the case (b), the measurement configurations are $\mathbf{q}_1 = (0°, -90°)$ and $\mathbf{q}_2 = (0°, 90°)$ and insure that $\sum_{i=1}^{2} \cos q_{2i} = 0$. And for the case (c), the measurement configurations $\mathbf{q}_1 = (0°, -46°)$ and $\mathbf{q}_2 = (0°, 46°)$ were computed using equation (19). These results show that the proposed approach allows us to increase accuracy of the end-point location on average by 18% comparing to the calibration using D-optimal plan and by 48% comparing to the calibration using non-optimal plan.

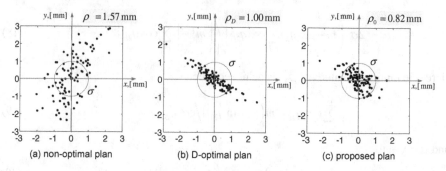

**Fig. 2.** The accuracy of geometrical error compensation for different plans of calibration experiments: identification of parameters $\Delta l_1, \Delta l_2$ for measurement errors with $\sigma = 10^{-3}$ m

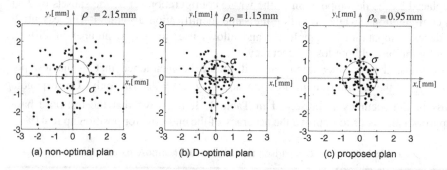

**Fig. 3.** The accuracy of geometrical error compensation for different plans of calibration experiments: identification of parameters $\Delta l_1, \Delta l_2, \Delta q_1, \Delta q_2$ for measurement errors with $\sigma = 10^{-3}$ m

In the frame of this example, it was also studies the case of the joint offsets calibration, where $\Delta\Pi = (\Delta q_1, \Delta q_2)$. It has been proved that expressions (18)-(20) are also valid in this case . This allows us to suggest a hypothesis that a more general case of simultaneous calibration of the link lengths and joint offsets $\Delta\Pi = (\Delta l_1, \Delta l_2, \Delta q_1, \Delta q_2)$ can be also solved using the same expressions. This hypothesis has been confirmed by the simulation results presented in Fig. 3, where calibration was based on three measurements ( $m = 3$ ). Here, case (a) employees the configurations $q_1 = (0°, -10°)$ , $q_2 = (0°, 0°)$ and $q_3 = (0°, 10°)$; case (b) uses the configurations $q_1 = (0°, -120°)$ , $q_2 = (0°, 0°)$ and $q_3 = (0°, 120°)$ ; and case (c) is based on the optimal configurations $q_1 = (0°, -57°)$ , $q_2 = (0°, 0°)$ and $q_3 = (0°, 57°)$ . As follows from these results, here the proposed approach allows us to increase the robot accuracy by 18% compared to D-optimal plan and by 56% compared to non-optimal plan of experiments.

# 6     Application Example: Calibration of Kuka KR270

Now let us present a more sophisticated example that deals with calibration experiments design for the industrial robot KUKA KR-270 (Fig. 4a). The geometrical model and parameters of the robot are presented in Fig. 4b [13]. For this case study, the parameters $d_0$, $d_5$, $\Delta q_6$ do not affect the robot accuracy. For this reason, they are eliminated from the list of parameters used in the experiment design.

Accordingly, the optimization problem (15) associated with the calibration experiment plans for $m \in \{3,4,12\}$ has been solved. While solving this problem, it was assumed that the end-effector position is estimated using FARO laser tracker (Fig 3c) [14], for which the measurement errors can be presented as unbiased random values with s.t.d. $\sigma = 0.03\,mm$. For the computations, the workstation Dell Precision T7500 with two processors Intel® Xeon® X5690 (Six Core, 3.46GHz, 12MB Cache12) and 48 GB 1333MHz DDR3 ECC RDIMM has been used. Since the optimisation problem (15) is quite sensitive to the starting point, parallel computing with huge number of the initial points were used. To increase robustness of the proposed approach, the starting points were selected taking into all constraints. Besides, filtering of the points that correspond to the high values of $\rho_0$ has been applied.

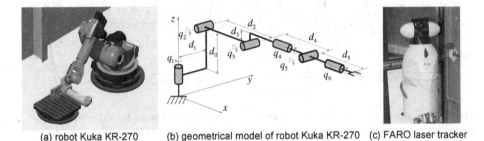

(a) robot Kuka KR-270     (b) geometrical model of robot Kuka KR-270   (c) FARO laser tracker

**Fig. 4.** Robot Kuka KR-270, its geometrical model and FARO laser tracker

The obtained results and comparison study with random plan are summarized in Table 2. Here, random plans have been generated 20 000 times using joints and workspace limits. Table 2 includes maximum, minimum and mean values of the performance measure $\rho_0$ for the generated sets of configurations. It has been shown that within the proposed plan of experiments, the calibration is much more efficient and high accuracy can be achieved using 3-4 measurement configurations only. Table 2 also includes some additional results obtained by multiplication of the measurement configurations, which show that it is not reasonable to solve optimization problem for 12 configurations (that produce 72 design variables). However, almost the same accuracy of the error compensation can be achieved by carrying out 12 measurements in 4 different configurations only (3 measurements in each configuration).

For comparison purposes, Fig 5 presents simulation results obtained for different types of calibration experiments. Here, each point corresponds to a single calibration experiment with random measurement errors. As follows from the obtained results, any optimal plan (obtained for the case of three, four or twelve calibration experiments) improves the accuracy of the compliance error compensation in the given test pose by about 75% comparing to the random plan. Also, it is shown that repeating experiments with optimal plans obtained for the lower number of experiments provides almost the same accuracy as the "full-dimensional" optimal plan. Thus, this idea of the reduction of the measurement pose number looks very attractive for the engineering practice.

**Table 2.** Accuracy of the error compensation $\rho_0$,[m$\times 10^{-6}$] for different plans of experiments

| Number of experiments | | 3 | 4 | 3×4 | 4×3 | 12 |
|---|---|---|---|---|---|---|
| | max | $47.1\times10^6$ | 8078 | $23.6\times10^6$ | 2693 | 144 |
| Random plan | min | 101 | 76.2 | 50.0 | 44.0 | 44.3 |
| | mean | $0.49\times10^6$ | 375 | $0.24\times10^6$ | 217 | 67.2 |
| Proposed plan | | 63.7 | 52.1 | 31.9 | 30.1 | 30.0 |

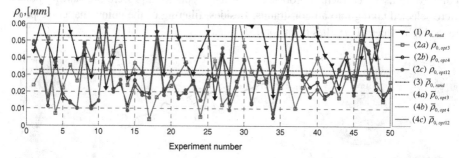

**Fig. 5.** The accuracy of errors compensation in the test configuration for different plans of calibration experiments for Kuka KR-270 robot for $\sigma = 0.03 mm$ : (1) random plan $\rho_{0, rand}$ ; (2a) four experiments for optimal plan obtained for three calibration experiments $\rho_{0, opt3}$ , (2b) three experiments for optimal plan obtained for four calibration experiments $\rho_{0, opt4}$ , (2c) experiments for optimal plan obtained for twelve calibration experiments, $\rho_{0, opt12}$ ; (3) expectation for the plan (1) $\bar{\rho}_{0, rand} = 52.7 \cdot 10^{-3} mm$ ; (4a) expectation for the plan (2a) $\bar{\rho}_{0, opt3} = 32.7 \cdot 10^{-3} mm$ ; (4b) expectation for the plan (2b) $\bar{\rho}_{0, opt4} = 30.3 \cdot 10^{-3} mm$ ; (4c) $\bar{\rho}_{0, opt12} = 29.8 \cdot 10^{-3} mm$ ;

# 7    Conclusions

The paper presents a new approach for the design of calibration experiments for robotic manipulators that allows essentially reducing the identification errors due to proper selection of the manipulator configurations. In contrast to other works, the quality of the calibration experiment plan is estimated using a new performance measure that evaluates the efficiency of the error compensation in the given test-pose. This approach ensures the best position accuracy for the given test configuration.

The advantages of the developed technique are illustrated by two examples that deal with the calibration experiment design for 2 d.o.f. and 6 d.o.f. manipulators. The results show that the combination of the low-dimension optimal plans gives almost the same accuracy as the full-dimension plan. This heuristic technique allows user to reduce essentially the computational complexity required for the calibration experiment design. In a future work, an additional investigation will be performed for the experiment design for the set of the test poses (or for a long machining path).

**Acknowledgments.** The work presented in this paper was partially funded by the ANR, France (Project ANR-2010-SEGI-003-02-COROUSSO).

# References

1. Elatta, A.Y., Gen, L.P., Zhi, F.L., Daoyuan, Y., Fei, L.: An Overview of Robot Calibration. Information Technology Journal 3, 74–78 (2004)
2. Veitchegger, W.K., Wu, C.H.: Robot accuracy analysis based on kinematics. IEEE Journal of Robotics and Automation 2, 171–179 (1986)
3. Khalil, W., Dombre, E.: Modeling, identification and control of robots. Hermes Penton, London (2002)
4. Hollerbach, J., Khalil, W., Gautier, M.: Chapter: Model identification. In: Springer Handbook of robotics, pp. 321–344. Springer (2008)
5. Atkinson, A., Done, A.: Optimum Experiment Designs. Oxford University Press (1992)
6. Daney, D.: Optimal measurement configurations for Gough platform calibration. In: IEEE International Conference on Robotics and Automation (ICRA), pp. 147–152 (2002)
7. Daney, D., Papegay, Y., Madeline, B.: Choosing measurement poses for robot calibration with the local convergence method and Tabu search. The International Journal of Robotics Research 24, 501–518 (2005)
8. Klimchik, A., Wu, Y., Caro, S., Pashkevich, A.: Design of experiments for calibration of planar anthropomorphic manipulators. In: IEEE/ASME International Conference on Advanced Intelligent Mechatronics (AIM), pp. 576–581 (2011)
9. Khalil, W., Gautier, M., Enguehard, C.: Identifiable parameters and optimum configurations for robots calibration. Robotica 9, 63–70 (1991)
10. Sun, Y., Hollerbach, J.M.: Observability index selection for robot calibration. In: IEEE International Conference on Robotics and Automation (ICRA), pp. 831–836 (2008)
11. Borm, J.H., Menq, C.H.: Determination of optimal measurement configurations for robot calibration based on observability measure. J. of Robotic Systems 10, 51–63 (1991)
12. Imoto, J., Takeda, Y., Saito, H., Ichiryu, K.: Optimal kinematic calibration of robots based on maximum positioning-error estimation (Theory and application to a parallel-mechanism pipe bender). In: Proc. of the 5th Int. Workshop on Computational Kinematics, pp. 133–140 (2009)
13. KUKA Industrial Robots, http://www.kuka-robotics.com/
14. FARO Laser Tracker, http://www.faro.com/lasertracker/

# Multi-line Fitting Using Two-Stage Iterative Adaptive Approach

Junli Liang, Ding Liu, Yue Zhao, and Nianlong Song

School of Automation and Information Engineering,
Xi'an University of Technology, 710048, China
laingjunli@xaut.edu.cn

**Abstract.** A new multi-line fitting algorithm using two-stage iterative adaptive approach (IAA) is proposed in this paper. The key points and main contributions are: i) The proposed algorithm decouples the multi-line fitting problem into two-stage spectral estimation problems; ii) In the first stage, it formulates the binary image into virtual far-field array signals with a single snapshot, and estimates the incoming angles using the iterative adaptive approach; iii) In the second stage, it formulates the binary image into multiple near-field signals, and estimates the offsets of these lines using IAA. Simulation and experimental (lane detection) results show that the proposed algorithm is an alternative multi-line fitting approach.

**Keywords:** Multi-Line fitting, iterative adaptive approach.

## 1  Introduction

Line fitting is the process of determining the angles and offsets of straight lines in an image, and is widely applied into many fields such as image processing and computer vision. For example, in the field of the mobile robotics, the line fitting technique can be used for self-localization and robot orientation [1]. In addition, it is one of the key techniques in the vehicle autonomous navigation system, in which it recognizes roads by detecting lane edges [12].

The line fitting problem can be described as follows: given an image which contains a number of discrete "1" pixels lying on a "0" background, the objective is to estimate the angles and offsets of these straight lines that fit groups of collinear "1" pixels [2]. Several classical approaches have been proposed for solving this problem [2-6]. As one of the most excellent line fitting methods, the Hough-transform (HT) method [3-5] applies a special Radon transform to all points in the image and then accomplishes a two-dimensional search to find the maxima in the angle-offset plane. Another classical algorithm is the Subspace-based LIne DEtection (SLIDE) method [2,6], which skillfully makes an analogy between each line in an image and a planar propagating wavefront radiating on a sensor array [7].

Motivated by that the iterative adaptive approach (IAA) is an efficient nonparametric spectral estimation algorithm, being applied into passive array processing [8], underwater acoustic communications[9], and MIMO radar imaging[10], this paper

C.-Y. Su, S. Rakheja, H. Liu (Eds.): ICIRA 2012, Part I, LNAI 7506, pp. 144–153, 2012.
© Springer-Verlag Berlin Heidelberg 2012

considers fitting multiple lines in an image using IAA. It is worthwhile to highlight several aspects of the proposed approach here:

i) The proposed algorithm decouples the multi-line fitting problem into two-stage spectral estimation problems;

ii) In the first stage, it formulates the binary image into virtual far-field array signals [12] with a single snapshot, and estimates the incoming angles using the iterative adaptive approach (IAA);

iii) In the second stage, it formulates the binary image into multiple near-field signals with a single snapshot [12], and estimates the offsets of these lines using IAA.

The rest of this paper is organized as follows. The problem is described in Section 2. A new multi-line fitting algorithm using two-stage iterative adaptive approach is developed in Section 3. Experimental results are presented in Section 4. Conclusions are drawn in Section 5.

## 2      Problem Formulation

Consider a binary image with size $M \times M$, in which only "1" and "0"-valued pixels are contained. The "1" pixels represent collinear those in a finite number of groups (or noise), while the "0" pixels correspond to the background [2,6]. For convenient to describe, we take a single line for example, as shown in Fig.1. Each line is characterized by its x-axis offset $\tilde{x}$ and angle $\theta$, and the related equation is given by

$$x = y \tan \theta + \tilde{x} \tag{1}$$

The objective of this paper is to estimate the parameters of multiple lines $(\tilde{x}_1, \tilde{x}_2, \cdots, \tilde{x}_d)$ and $(\theta_1, \theta_2, \cdots, \theta_d)$, where $d$ stands for the number of lines in the given image $\mathbf{D}$.

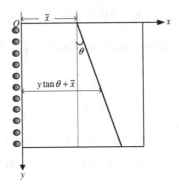

**Fig. 1.** The line model used in this paper

## 3      Proposed Algorithm

To distinguish multiple lines in an image uniquely, it is necessary to determine their angles and offsets. In this section, we consider estimating angles and offsets consequently.

## 3.1 The First Stage

Let $\mathbf{u} = \begin{bmatrix} 1 & e^{j\mu} & e^{j2\mu} \cdots e^{j(M-1)\mu} \end{bmatrix}^T$, and define:

$$
\begin{aligned}
\mathbf{z} &= \mathbf{D}\mathbf{u} \\
&= \left[ \sum_{i=1}^{d} e^{j\mu(0\times\tan\theta_i + \tilde{x}_i)} \quad \sum_{i=1}^{d} e^{j\mu(1\times\tan\theta_i + \tilde{x}_i)} \quad \cdots \quad \sum_{i=1}^{d} e^{j\mu((M-1)\times\tan\theta_i + \tilde{x}_i)} \right]^T \\
&= \sum_{i=1}^{d} \mathbf{a}(\theta_i) s_i
\end{aligned}
\tag{2}
$$

where $s_i = e^{j\mu\tilde{x}_i}$, and

$$
\mathbf{a}(\theta_i) = \begin{bmatrix} 1 & e^{j\mu\tan\theta_i} & e^{j2\mu\tan\theta_i} & \cdots & e^{j(M-1)\mu\tan\theta_i} \end{bmatrix}^T
\tag{3}
$$

Obviously, via the transform above the binary image $\mathbf{D}$ is transformed into virtual single-snapshot far-field array signals $\mathbf{z}$ with amplitude $s_i$, where the virtual sensor array is a uniform linear array (ULA) consisted of $M$ sensors [17,18]. Note that $\mu|\tan\theta_i| \le \pi$ is required to ensure the unique estimation [2,6].

To estimate $\theta_i$ from the single snapshot $\mathbf{z}$, we consider formulating the angle estimation problem as a sparse representation problem [10]. Let $(\tilde{\theta}_1, \tilde{\theta}_2, \cdots, \tilde{\theta}_{N_\theta})$ be a sampling grid of all angles of interest in the range $[-90°, 90°]$, and the number of potential angles $N_\theta$ must be even larger than the number of incoming array signals $d$. Construct an over-complete dictionary $\mathbf{A} = [\mathbf{a}(\tilde{\theta}_1) \ \mathbf{a}(\tilde{\theta}_2) \cdots \mathbf{a}(\tilde{\theta}_{N_\theta})] \in C^{M \times N_\theta}$ where the atom $\mathbf{a}(\tilde{\theta}_i), i = 1, 2, \cdots, N_\theta$ has the same form as Eq. (3), and thus $\mathbf{z}$ can be represented by the $N_\theta$ signals with amplitudes $(\tilde{s}_1, \tilde{s}_2, \cdots, \tilde{s}_{N_\theta})$ and angles $(\tilde{\theta}_1, \tilde{\theta}_2, \cdots, \tilde{\theta}_{N_\theta})$ as follows:

$$
\mathbf{z} = \mathbf{A}\mathbf{s} + \mathbf{n}
\tag{4}
$$

Where $\mathbf{s} = \begin{bmatrix} \tilde{s}_1 & \tilde{s}_2 \cdots \tilde{s}_{N_\theta} \end{bmatrix}^T$, $\mathbf{n}$ is the noise. In $\mathbf{s}$, when the $i$ th element $\tilde{s}_i$ is related to one of the $d$ incoming array signals, it is nonzero; otherwise, it equals to zero.

To estimate $\mathbf{s}$, we develop the following iterative adaptive approach (IAA):

**Step 1:** Initialize $(\tilde{s}_1 \ \tilde{s}_2 \ \cdots \ \tilde{s}_{N_\theta})$ with the matched filter, i.e.,

$$
\tilde{s}_i(0) = \frac{\mathbf{z}^H \mathbf{a}(\tilde{\theta}_i)}{\mathbf{a}^H(\tilde{\theta}_i)\mathbf{a}(\tilde{\theta}_i)}, \quad i = 1, 2, \cdots, N_\theta,
\tag{5}
$$

**Step 2:** For $j = 1, 2, \cdots$

For $i = 1, 2, \cdots, N_\theta$

Iteratively solving the following weighted least squares problem:

$$\min_{\tilde{s}_i(j)} \quad \left\| \mathbf{z} - \tilde{s}_i(j) \mathbf{a}(\tilde{\theta}_i) \right\|^2_{\mathbf{Q}_M^{-1}(\tilde{\theta}_i)}$$
$$= \left( \mathbf{z} - \tilde{s}_i(j) \mathbf{a}(\tilde{\theta}_i) \right)^H \mathbf{Q}_M^{-1}(\tilde{\theta}_i) \left( \mathbf{z} - \tilde{s}_i(j) \mathbf{a}(\tilde{\theta}_i) \right) \tag{6}$$

Where

$$\mathbf{Q}_M(\tilde{\theta}_i) = \mathbf{R}(j-1) - p_i(j-1) \mathbf{a}(\tilde{\theta}_i) \mathbf{a}^H(\tilde{\theta}_i) \tag{7}$$

$$p_i(j-1) = \left| \tilde{s}_i(j-1) \right|^2 \tag{8}$$

$$\mathbf{R}(j-1) = \mathbf{A} \mathbf{P}(j-1) \mathbf{A}^H \tag{9}$$

$$\mathbf{P}(j-1) = \text{diag}\{ p_i(1), p_i(2), \cdots, p_i(N_\theta) \} \tag{10}$$

The solution to Eq. (6) is given by:

$$\tilde{s}_i(j) = \frac{\mathbf{a}^H(\tilde{\theta}_i) \mathbf{Q}_M^{-1}(\tilde{\theta}_i) \mathbf{z}}{\mathbf{a}^H(\tilde{\theta}_i) \mathbf{Q}_M^{-1}(\tilde{\theta}_i) \mathbf{a}(\tilde{\theta}_i)} \tag{11}$$

Based on Matrix Inversion Lemma, i.e.,

$$\mathbf{Q}_M^{-1}(\tilde{\theta}_i) = \left( \mathbf{R}(j-1) - p_i(j-1) \mathbf{a}(\tilde{\theta}_i) \mathbf{a}^H(\tilde{\theta}_i) \right)^{-1}$$
$$= \mathbf{R}^{-1}(j-1) + \frac{p_i(j-1) \mathbf{R}^{-1}(j-1) \mathbf{a}(\tilde{\theta}_i) \mathbf{a}^H(\tilde{\theta}_i) \mathbf{R}^{-1}(j-1)}{1 - p_i(j-1) \mathbf{a}^H(\tilde{\theta}_i) \mathbf{R}^{-1}(j-1) \mathbf{a}(\tilde{\theta}_i)} \tag{12}$$

Eq. (11) can be represented in another form as

$$\tilde{s}_i(j) = \frac{\mathbf{a}^H(\tilde{\theta}_i) \left[ \mathbf{R}^{-1}(j-1) + \dfrac{p_i(j-1) \mathbf{R}^{-1}(j-1) \mathbf{a}(\tilde{\theta}_i) \mathbf{a}^H(\tilde{\theta}_i) \mathbf{R}^{-1}(j-1)}{1 - p_i(j-1) \mathbf{a}^H(\tilde{\theta}_i) \mathbf{R}^{-1}(j-1) \mathbf{a}(\tilde{\theta}_i)} \right] \mathbf{z}}{\mathbf{a}^H(\tilde{\theta}_i) \left[ \mathbf{R}^{-1}(j-1) + \dfrac{p_i(j-1) \mathbf{R}^{-1}(j-1) \mathbf{a}(\tilde{\theta}_i) \mathbf{a}^H(\tilde{\theta}_i) \mathbf{R}^{-1}(j-1)}{1 - p_i(j-1) \mathbf{a}^H(\tilde{\theta}_i) \mathbf{R}^{-1}(j-1) \mathbf{a}(\tilde{\theta}_i)} \right] \mathbf{a}(\tilde{\theta}_i)}$$
$$= \frac{\mathbf{a}^H(\tilde{\theta}_i) \mathbf{R}^{-1}(j-1) \mathbf{z}}{\mathbf{a}^H(\tilde{\theta}_i) \mathbf{R}^{-1}(j-1) \mathbf{a}(\tilde{\theta}_i)} \tag{13}$$

Based on $\tilde{s}_i(j)$, one can compute the virtual spectrum of array signals $\mathbf{p}_{spec} \in R^{1 \times N_\theta}$, the $i$ th element of which is defined as follows:

$$\mathbf{p}_{spec}(i) = \left\| \tilde{s}_i(j) \right\|^2 \tag{14}$$

Thus, the $d$ highest peaks of the spectrum $\mathbf{p}_{spec}$ indicate the estimated angles $\left( \hat{\theta}_1, \hat{\theta}_2, \cdots, \hat{\theta}_d \right)$.

## 3.2    The Second Stage

Based on a new parameter $\mu_1$, another snapshot of a new near-field source-type array manifold [12] can be formed as follows:

$$\mathbf{r} = \sum_{l=1}^{d} \mathbf{A}(\theta_l) \mathbf{b}(\tilde{x}_l) \tag{15}$$

Where

$$\mathbf{A}(\theta_i) = \operatorname{diag}\left\{ 1, e^{j\mu_1 \tan \theta_k}, e^{j4\mu_1 \tan \theta_k}, \cdots, e^{j(M-1)^2 \mu_1 \tan \theta_k} \right\} \tag{16}$$

$$\mathbf{b}(\tilde{x}_i) = \left[ 1 \quad e^{j\mu_1 \tilde{x}_k} \quad e^{j2\mu_1 \tilde{x}_k} \quad \cdots \quad e^{j(M-1)\mu_1 \tilde{x}_k} \right]^T \tag{17}$$

and the output of the $i$-th virtual sensor can be given by

$$\begin{aligned}
\mathbf{r}(i) &= \sum_{k=1}^{d} e^{j\mu_1 i x_{i,j}} = \sum_{k=1}^{d} e^{j\mu_1 i(i\tan\theta_k + \tilde{x}_k)} \\
&= \sum_{k=1}^{d} e^{j(i^2 \mu_1 \tan\theta_k + i\mu_1 \tilde{x}_k)} = \sum_{k=1}^{d} e^{ji^2 \mu_1 \tan\theta_k} e^{ji\mu_1 \tilde{x}_k}
\end{aligned} \tag{18}$$

For each angle $\hat{\theta}_i$, assume the offsets of interest (OI) are $\left( \tilde{x}_{i,1}, \tilde{x}_{i,2}, \cdots, \tilde{x}_{i,N_i} \right)$. Construct an over-complete dictionary $\mathbf{B} = [\mathbf{B}_1 \ \mathbf{B}_2 \ \cdots \mathbf{B}_d]$, where the sub-dictionary has the same form as

$$\begin{aligned}
\mathbf{B}_i &= \left[ \mathbf{A}(\theta_i)\mathbf{b}(\tilde{x}_{i,1}) \ \mathbf{A}(\theta_i)\mathbf{b}(\tilde{x}_{i,2}) \ \cdots \mathbf{A}(\theta_i)\mathbf{b}(\tilde{x}_{i,N_i}) \right] \\
&= \mathbf{A}(\theta_i) \left[ \mathbf{b}(\tilde{x}_{i,1}) \ \mathbf{b}(\tilde{x}_{i,2}) \ \cdots \mathbf{b}(\tilde{x}_{i,N_i}) \right]
\end{aligned} \tag{19}$$

Thus, the received signal $\mathbf{r}$ can be represented by the $\sum_{i=1}^{d} N_i$ atoms as:

$$\mathbf{r} = \mathbf{B}\mathbf{s} + \mathbf{n} \tag{20}$$

Where $\mathbf{s} = \begin{bmatrix} s_1 & s_2 & \cdots & s_{\tilde{N}} \end{bmatrix}^T$ and $\tilde{N} = \sum_{i=1}^{d} N_i$.

Similar to Eq. (4), $\mathbf{s}$ can be solved by the similar IAA as those of Eq. (5)-(14). Once $\mathbf{s}$ is obtained, the $d$ highest peaks of the spectral values indicate the estimated offsets.

# 4    Simulation and Experimental Results

To verify the performance of the proposed method, it is compared with the conventional HT and SLIDE approaches [2-6].

## 4.1    The First Experiment Without Noise

In this experiment, we consider a $(256 \times 256)$-dimensional image (with zero-mean white and homogeneous Gaussian noise) with two lines, as shown in Fig.2 (a), which are characterized by $(\theta_1 = 15°, \tilde{x}_1 = 30)$ and $(\theta_2 = 50°, \tilde{x}_2 = -20)$, respectively. After threshold segmentation, a binary image is obtained in Fig. 2 (b). Based on the binary image, $\mu = 0.6$ and $\mu_1 = 0.004$ are applied to yield two virtual single -snapshot 256 -sensor array signals, which consist of two incoming waves. The sampling grid is uniform with $1°$ in the range $[-90°, 90°]$, i.e., $N_\theta = 181$ . In addition, let the sampling grid of offsets be uniform with 1 pixel in the range $[-50, 200]$ . The HT method, SLIDE method, and the proposed method are used to estimate the angles and offsets of the lines in the resulted binary image. From results of the three algorithms listed in Table 1, it can be seen that the SLIDE algorithm performs poor under this case while the proposed method and the HT method still perform well. As shown in Figs. 3 and 4, the proposed algorithm can detect the angles and offsets of the two lines accurately.

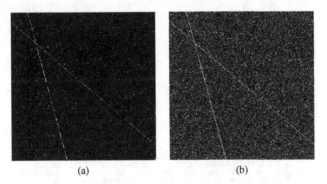

(a)                                    (b)

**Fig. 2.** (a) an image with Gaussian noise (zero-mean and standard deviation $\sigma = 0.15$),(b)the binary image from threshold segmentation (Threshold value 225)

**Table 1.** Estimation results from different algorithms

| Method | $\hat{\theta}_1$ | $\hat{\tilde{x}}_1$ | $\hat{\theta}_2$ | $\hat{\tilde{x}}_2$ |
|--------|------------------|---------------------|------------------|---------------------|
| Proposed | $15\,^\circ$ | 30 | $50\,^\circ$ | -20 |
| HT | $15\,^\circ$ | 30 | $50\,^\circ$ | -20 |
| SLIDE | $15.16\,^\circ$ | 31.07 | $50.03\,^\circ$ | -19.11 |

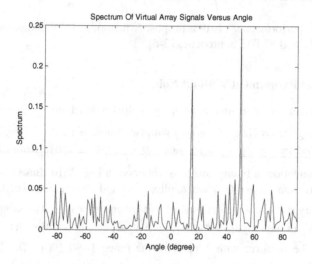

**Fig. 3.** The spectral values versus angle

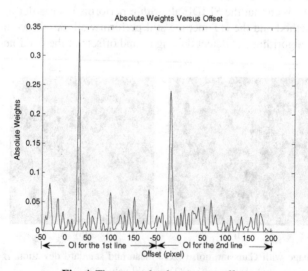

**Fig. 4.** The spectral values versus offset

## 4.2    The Second Experiment with Parallel Lines

This experiment explores the capability of the proposed algorithm to detect parallel lines, which is an important difficulty in the multi-line fitting problem [6]. In Fig. 5, there are three lines with the same angle $\theta = -20°$ but different offsets $(\tilde{x}_1 = 80, \tilde{x}_2 = 90, \tilde{x}_3 = 110)$. Table 2 lists the estimation results using all three algorithms. These results show that the proposed algorithm can distinguish parallel lines well in the second stage.

**Fig. 5.** Three lines with the same angle

**Table 2.** Estimation results under parallel line case

| Method | $\hat{\theta}_1$ | $\hat{\tilde{x}}_1$ | $\hat{\tilde{x}}_2$ | $\hat{\tilde{x}}_3$ |
|--------|------------------|---------------------|---------------------|---------------------|
| Proposed | $-20°$ | 80 | 90 | 110 |
| HT | $-20°$ | 80 | 90 | 110 |
| SLIDE | $-20.07°$ | 83.64 | -304.83 | 108.87 |

## 4.3    The Third Experiment for Lane Detection

Line fitting is one of the key techniques in the vehicle autonomous navigation system. In this experiment, we use the proposed algorithm for detecting the lane markers and recognizing roads [11].

A gray-level image (Fig.6) with size $200 \times 400$ is applied in this experiment. Via the watershed transform-based segmentation (separating the background), threshold segmentation (threshold value 200), Morphology processing (including Corrosion and Thinning), the proposed algorithm fits the lines in a binary image, and the fitted results are given in Fig. 7. In addition, Table 3 lists all experimental results from the three algorithms, from which it can be seen that the SLIDE method has a huge deviation.

**Fig. 6.** A lane image

**Table 3.** Estimation results for lane markers

| Method | $\hat{\theta}_1$ | $\hat{\tilde{x}}_1$ | $\hat{\theta}_2$ | $\hat{\tilde{x}}_2$ |
|---|---|---|---|---|
| Proposed | -64 ° | 419 | 45 ° | 185 |
| HT | -64 ° | 416 | 45 ° | 184 |
| SLIDE | -64 ° | -216.16 | 46.26 ° | 179.98 |

**Fig. 7.** The fitting results from all three methods (the proposed algorithm and the HT method (marked in red), the SLIDE method (marked in blue))

The above-mentioned experiments show that the proposed algorithm is an alternative multi-line fitting method, which can distinguish the lines in a noisy image, and multiple parallel lines.

## 5    Conclusion

A new multi-line fitting algorithm using two-stage iterative adaptive approach IAA) is proposed in this paper. It formulates the binary image with lines into virtual far-field and near-field single-snapshot signals to estimate angles and offsets of lines, respectively. Simulation and experimental results show that the proposed algorithm is an alternative multi-line fitting approach.

**Acknowledgement.** This work was supported in part by the National Science Foundation of China under Grants 61172123, 60901059, and 61075044; by the Young Research Star of Shaanxi Province under Grant 2012KJXX-35; by the Educational Department Foundation of Shaanxi Province under Grant 12JK0526; by the China Postdoctoral Science Foundation Funded Project under Grants 201003679 and 20100481355.

# References

[1] Inigo, R.M., McVey, E.S., Berger, B.J., Wirtz, M.J.: Machine vision applied to vehicle guidance. IEEE Trans. Pattern Analysis and Machine Intelligence 6(7), 820–826 (1984)

[2] Aghajan, H.K., Kailath, T.: Sensor array processing techniques for super resolution multi-line-fitting and straight edge detection. IEEE Trans. Image Processing 2(4), 454–465 (1993)

[3] Hough, P.: Method and means for recognizing complex patterns. U. S. Patent 3 069 654 (1962)

[4] Duda, R.O., Hart, P.E.: Use of the Hough transform to detect lines and curves in pictures. Comm. ACM 15, 11–15 (1972)

[5] Jain, A.K.: Fundamentals of Digital Image Processing. Prentice-Hall, Englewood Cliffs (1989)

[6] Aghajan, H.K., Kailath, T.: SLIDE: subspace-based line detection. IEEE Trans. Pattern Analysis and Machine Intelligence 16(1), 1057–1073 (1994)

[7] Krim, H., Viberg, M.: Two decades of array signal processing research: The parameter approach. IEEE Signal Process. Mag 13(4), 67–94 (1996)

[8] Yardibi, T., Li, J., Stoica, P., Xue, M., Baggeroer, A.B.: Source localization and sensing: A nonparametric iterative approach based on weighted least squares. IEEE Trans. Aerospace and Electronic Systems 46, 425–433 (2010)

[9] Ling, J., Yardibi, T., Su, X., He, H., Li, J.: Enhanced channel estimation and symbol detection for high speed multi-input multi-output underwater acoustic communications. Journal of the Acoustical Society of America 125, 3067–3078 (2009)

[10] Roberts, W., Stoica, P., Li, J., Yardibi, T., Sadjadi, F.A.: Iterative adaptive approaches to MIMO radar imaging. IEEE Journal of Selected Topics in Signal Processing 4(1), 5–20 (2010)

[11] Assidiq, A.A.M., Khalifa, O.O., Islam, R., Khan, S.: Real time lane detection for autonomous vehicles. In: International Conference on Computer and Communication Engineering, pp. 82–88 (2008)

[12] Liang, J., Liu, D.: Passive localization of mixed near-field and far-field sources using two-stage MUSIC algorithm. IEEE Trans. Signal Processing 58(1), 108–120 (2010)

# Collaborative Training Mechanism Design for Wireless Sensor and Actuator Networks[*]

Lei Mo and Bugong Xu[**]

Key Laboratory of Autonomous Systems and Network Control,
Ministry of Education,
College of Automation Science and Engineering,
South China University of Technology,
Guangzhou 510641, P.R. China
aubgxu@scut.edu.cn

**Abstract.** Wireless sensor and actuator networks (WSANs) combine a large number of sensor nodes and a lower number of actuator nodes that are connected with wireless medium, providing distributed sensing and executing appropriate tasks to the events monitored in a special region of interest. The design of coordination mechanisms among nodes is considered in this paper. First, we formulate the mathematical models for WSANs system. Then, a strategy is proposed to assign proper tasks to actuators based on the characteristics of current events. Finally, according to system requirements, a distributed PID neural network control scheme is adopted to take coordinated actions of actuators on the given tasks. The simulations demonstrate the effectiveness of our proposed methods.

**Keywords:** Wireless sensor and actuator networks, Coordination mechanisms, PID neural network.

## 1 Introduction

Wireless sensor and actuator networks (WSANs) can be seen as an important evolution of wireless sensor networks (WSNs) [1]. Sensors are resource-constrained nodes with limited power, computation and communication capabilities. Their purpose is to monitor the field and operate with duty cycle to save energy, while the resource-rich actuator nodes can process the sensing data to make decisions, and then, perform appropriate actions [2]. Currently, tremendous effort has been dedicated toward the nodes coordination problems. This is because (1) the amount, resource and the traffic load are nonsymmetrical between sensors and actuators, (2) the whole system exists in a dubious wireless environment with external disturbances, and (3) the WSANs must satisfy the

---

[*] This work was supported by the National Natural Science Foundation of China under grant 61174070 and the Specialized Research Fund for the Doctoral Program under grant 20110172110033.
[**] Corresponding author.

C.-Y. Su, S. Rakheja, H. Liu (Eds.): ICIRA 2012, Part I, LNAI 7506, pp. 154–163, 2012.

real time and reliable applications requirements [3]. Thus, in this paper, we focus on the nodes coordination problems for multi-actuator control in WSANs.

In the event-triggered control, instead of periodically updating the control input, the update instants are generated by the violation of a condition on the state of the plant. Many researchers have shown a renewed interest on these techniques [4-5]. The main idea of these methods lies in formulate the control and schedule problem as an optimization problem and then obtained optimal solutions through optimization algorithms seeking to determine schedules maximizing the performance criterion. In [6], the authors propose a centralized control scheme and a distributed control scheme in WSANs for building-environment control systems. In [7], a new distributed estimation and collaborative control scheme is proposed for industrial control systems with WSANs, which can achieve a robust control against inaccurate system parameters. Our work is motivated by the above studies. The key difference is that we introduce an event-driven task allocation mechanism into the nodes collaborative process.

WSANs have many promising applications in industrial fields. In order to meet those requirements, we attempt to develop an application-level design methodology for WSANs in control applications. The most popular control algorithm in the control community is the proportional-integral-derivative (PID) control [8]. However, the conventional PID algorithm is hard to obtain desired performance for the WSANs systems due to their unsymmetrical multi-variable structures. Based on the online training and the updating abilities, neural network (NN) is a promising intelligent control approach which does not require the mathematical model of the controlled plant and can match the WSANs system effectively. PID neural network (PIDNN) utilizes the advantage of both PID control and neural network [9], it can learn online, adjust the connection weights and change the gains of P, I and D in strong or weak according to the system response, so to achieve superior dynamic and static properties.

The remainder of this paper is organized as follows: Section 2 presents a model of WSANs architecture. Section 3 introduces the structure, the forward and the back-propagation algorithms of the PIDNN. Section 4 provides a node coordination mechanism. Finally, the results of simulations conducted to explore the performance of proposed algorithm are demonstrated in Section 5.

## 2 System Models

We consider the WSANs that are employed to the industrial instrumentation and control applications. The control object is to adjust the system state variables to meet our requirements. We assume that there are $n_s$ sensors and $n_a$ actuators spread throughout the region of interest (ROI) to detect and track $n_p$ system states and take necessary actions in that area.

Consider following dynamic process with a discrete-time state space model:

$$X(k+1) = AX(k) + BU(k) + \omega(k) \tag{1}$$

where $X(k) = [x_1(k), ..., x_{n_p}(k)]^T$ is the system state, $U(k) = [u_1(k), ..., u_{n_a}(k)]^T$ is the control input to the actuators, and $\omega(k)$ is the process noise. The $(i,j)$th entry of matrix $A$, $a_{ij} \neq 0$ if $x_i$ and $x_j$ are adjacent so that their state are correlated, otherwise, $a_{ij} = 0$. Here, we assume that the dynamics of $x_i$ is not interconnected with others. $B$ is a $n_p \times n_a$ input matrix whose element $b_{ij}$ represents the influence of actuator $A_j^a$ exerts on system state $x_i$:

$$b_{ij} = \begin{cases} g_j(1 - \dfrac{d_{ij}}{r_a}), d_{ij} < r_a \\ 0, \qquad d_{ij} \geq r_a \end{cases} \tag{2}$$

where $d_{ij}$ represents the Euclidean distance between $x_i$ and $A_j^a$, $r_a$ is the action range of actuator, $g_j$ is a gain coefficient measuring $A_j^a$'s input and output. Here, we consider a scenario with homogenous actuators. Due to the actuator's physical constraints, its output cannot change freely. Thus, $u_j$ is bounded. We set $u_j \in [\underline{u}, \overline{u}]$.

To be more precise, let

$$y_i(k) = c_i x_i(k) + \nu_i(k) \tag{3}$$

be the sensing model of sensor $S_i$, where $c_i$ and $\nu_i(k)$ are observation item and measurement noise, respectively. Assume that $\omega(k)$ and $\nu_i(k)$ are Gaussian, uncorrelated, white, zero mean with $E\{\omega(k)\} = 0$, $E\{\nu_i(k)\} = 0$, $E\{\omega(k)\omega^T(l)\} = Q(k)\delta_{kl}$, $E\{\nu_i(k)\nu_j^T(l)\} = r_i(k)\delta_{kl}\delta_{ij}$, where $\delta_{kl} = 1$ if $k = l$, and $\delta_{kl} = 0$, otherwise.

According to the structure of $A$ and $B$, WSANs can be modeled as the following block diagonal system:

$$A = \begin{bmatrix} A_1 & \cdots & 0 \\ 0 & \cdots & 0 \\ 0 & \cdots & A_m \end{bmatrix}, B = \begin{bmatrix} B_1 & \cdots & 0 \\ 0 & \cdots & 0 \\ 0 & \cdots & B_m \end{bmatrix}, X = \begin{bmatrix} X_1 \\ \cdots \\ X_m \end{bmatrix} \tag{4}$$

where $A_i \in \mathbb{R}^{n_i \times n_i}$, $B_i \in \mathbb{R}^{n_i \times l_i}$, $X_i \in \mathbb{R}^{n_i \times 1}$, $i \in \{1, ..., m\}$, and $\sum_{i=1}^m n_i = n_p$, $\sum_{j=1}^m l_j = n_a$. Then, the whole system is said to be partitioned into $m$ individual subsystem: $\{GS_1 = (A_1, B_1, X_1), ..., GS_m = (A_m, B_m, X_m)\}$. $GS_i = (A_i, B_i, X_i), i \in \{1, ..., m\}$ is an isolated subsystem due to the actuators in $B_i$ are not influence the system states in $X_j, j \neq i$.

## 3   The PIDNN Approach

PIDNN is a multi-layer forward neural network. It consists of proportional neuron, integral neuron and derivative neuron and their connective weights are adjusted by the back-propagation (BP) algorithms. For a $p$ inputs $\times$ $q$ outputs multi-variable system, PIDNN is a three layers ($2q \times 3q \times p$) forward network, its output is regulated by the difference of system setting and sensing data. The structure of PIDNN is shown in Fig.1.

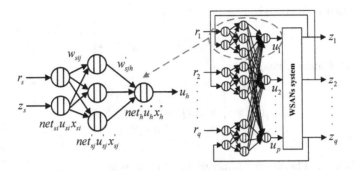

**Fig. 1.** The structure of PIDNN

## 3.1 PIDNN Structure

**Input Layer.** The input layer has 2 neurons which receive system setting $r_s(k)$ and sensing data $z_s(k)$:

$$\begin{cases} net_{s1}(k) = r_s(k) \\ net_{s2}(k) = z_s(k) \end{cases} \tag{5}$$

The input layer neuron's state is:

$$u_{si}(k) = net_{si}(k), i = 1, 2 \tag{6}$$

The output of input layer neuron is:

$$x_{si}(k) = \begin{cases} \overline{u}, & u_{si}(k) > \overline{u} \\ u_{si}(k), \underline{u} \le u_{si}(k) \le \overline{u} \\ \underline{u}, & u_{si}(k) < \underline{u} \end{cases} \tag{7}$$

where $s = 1, 2, ..., q$ represent sub-network's serial number.

**Hidden Layer.** The hidden layer is the key layer of PIDNN, the relationship of hidden layer is:

$$net'_{sj}(k) = \sum_{i=1}^{2} w_{sij}(k)x_{si}(k), j = 1, 2, 3 \tag{8}$$

There have three kinds of hidden layer states.
    Proportional neuron's state is:

$$u'_{s1}(k) = net'_{s1}(k) \tag{9}$$

Integral neuron's state is:

$$u'_{s2}(k) = u'_{s2}(k-1) + net'_{s2}(k) \tag{10}$$

Derivative neuron's state is:

$$u'_{s3}(k) = net'_{s3}(k) - net'_{s3}(k-1) \tag{11}$$

The output of hidden layer neuron is:

$$x'_{sj}(k) = \begin{cases} \overline{u}, & u'_{sj}(k) > \overline{u} \\ u'_{sj}(k), & \underline{u} \le u'_{sj}(k) \le \overline{u} \\ \underline{u}, & u'_{sj}(k) < \underline{u} \end{cases} \tag{12}$$

**Output Layer.** The input of output layer neuron is:

$$net''_h(k) = \sum_{s=1}^{q} \sum_{j=1}^{3} w'_{sjh}(k)x'_{sj}(k) \tag{13}$$

where $w'_{s1h}(k)$, $w'_{s2h}(k)$ and $w'_{s1h}(k)$ are the connective weights between hidden layer and output layer, which can be seen as the proportional gain $K_P$, integral gain $K_I$, and derivative gain $K_D$, respectively.

The state of output layer neuron is:

$$u''_h(k) = net''_h(k) \tag{14}$$

The output of output layer neuron is:

$$x''_h(k) = \begin{cases} \overline{u}, & u''_h(k) > \overline{u} \\ u''_h(k), & \underline{u} \le u''_h(k) \le \overline{u} \\ \underline{u}, & u''_h(k) < \underline{u} \end{cases} \tag{15}$$

where $h = 1, 2, ..., p$ is output neurons' serial number. According to the mutual cross-coupling between hidden layer and output layer, PIDNN realizes the decoupling control of unsymmetrical multi-variable system.

Finally, the output of PIDNN equals output layer neurons:

$$u_h(k) = x''_h(k) \tag{16}$$

## 3.2    PIDNN Controller

The arm of the PIDNN algorithm is to minimize:

$$J(k+1) = \frac{1}{2} \sum_{l=1}^{k+1} \sum_{s=1}^{q} [r_s(l) - z_s(l)]^2 = \frac{1}{2} \sum_{l=1}^{k+1} e^2(l) \tag{17}$$

The connective weights of PIDNN is changed by the gradient algorithms in an on-line training process. Hence, after the $k$th training step, the connective weights from hidden layer to output layer are:

$$w'_{sjh}(k+1) = w'_{sjh}(k) - \eta' \frac{\partial J(k+1)}{\partial w'_{sjh}(k)} = w'_{sjh}(k) + \Delta w'_{sjh}(k) \tag{18}$$

By using the BP method:

$$\frac{\partial J(k+1)}{\partial w'_{sjh}(k)} = \sum_{s=1}^{q} \frac{\partial J(k+1)}{\partial z_s(k+1)} \frac{\partial z_s(k+1)}{\partial u_h(k)} \frac{\partial u_h(k)}{\partial x''_h(k)} \frac{\partial x''_h(k)}{\partial u''_h(k)} \frac{\partial u''_h(k)}{\partial net''_h(k)} \frac{\partial net''_h(k)}{\partial w'_{sjh}(k)} \quad (19)$$

So, the connective weight $w'_{sjh}(k)$ is updated by the amount:

$$\Delta w'_{sjh}(k) = -\eta' \frac{\partial J(k+1)}{\partial w'_{sjh}(k)} = \eta' \sum_{s=1}^{q} \delta'_{hs}(k) x_{sj}(k) \quad (20)$$

where $\eta'$ is a learning step and

$$\delta'_{hs}(k) = [r_s(k+1) - z_s(k+1)] sgn \frac{z_s(k+1) - z_s(k)}{u_h(k) - u_h(k-1)} \quad (21)$$

On the same way, the connective weights from input layer to hidden layer are:

$$w_{sij}(k+1) = w_{sij}(k) - \eta \frac{\partial J(k+1)}{\partial w_{sij}(k)} = w_{sij}(k) + \Delta w_{sij}(k) \quad (22)$$

By using the BP method:

$$\frac{\partial J(k+1)}{\partial w_{sij}(k)} = \sum_{s=1}^{q} [\frac{\partial J(k+1)}{\partial z_s(k+1)} \sum_{h=1}^{p} \frac{\partial z_s(k+1)}{\partial u_h(k)} \frac{\partial u_h(k)}{\partial w_{sij}(k)}] \quad (23)$$

Then, the connective weight $w_{sij}(k)$ is updated by the following equation:

$$\Delta w_{sij}(k) = -\eta \frac{\partial J(k+1)}{\partial w_{sij}(k)} = \eta \sum_{s=1}^{q} \sum_{h=1}^{p} \delta_{sjh}(k) x_{si}(k) \quad (24)$$

where $\eta$ is a learning step and

$$\delta_{sjh}(k) = \delta'_{hs} w'_{sjh} sgn \frac{u'_{sj}(k) - u'_{sj}(k-1)}{net'_{sj}(k) - net'_{sj}(k-1)} \quad (25)$$

## 4   Nodes Coordination

### 4.1   Event-Driven Task Allocation

Assume an event $ex_i$ occurs, i.e. if system state $x_i$ varies from the set point $x_i^*$, the event-triggered schedule turn on the corresponding actuators: $\{A_j^a | b_{ij} \neq 0\}$, remain them in active state till the error signal $e_i = x_i - x_i^*$ becomes zero. When there is no event occurs, the nodes follow a static sleep schedule. Regular data collection is done using the sensors periodically and the actuators are completely off. When $b_{ii} \neq 0, b_{ij} \neq 0, j \neq i$, we refer $ex_i$ as a coordination-base event. To this event, the Actuator-Actuator coordination is always necessary since the problem of actuator schedule and design a proper control strategy should be taken into consider in the purpose of compensating the overlapping actuation [7]. When $b_{ii} \neq 0, b_{ij} = 0, j \neq i$, we refer $ex_i$ as a coordination-free event. For such case, the coordination problem simplifies to the correspond actuator processes all incoming data and initiates appropriate actions without any involvement of other actuators.

## 4.2   Sensor-Sensor Coordination

When an event $ex_i$ occurs, the sensors whose sensing range cover it will be activated, these nodes organize themselves into local cluster, and the sensor remains a higher energy level will be selected as the cluster head. According to the sensing data $\{y_i^1(k), ..., y_i^m(k)\}$ received from its cluster members, the cluster head performs following data aggregation: (1) calculates the mean value $\bar{y}_i(k)$ in the set $V_i = \{y_i^1(k), ..., y_i^m(k)\}$; (2) removes the value $y_i^l(k), l \in \{1, ..., m\}$ such as that $|y_i^l(k) - \bar{y}_i(k)| > \epsilon_{th}$ from $V_i$; (3) calculates the mean value $y_i(k)$ of the set $V_i$; (4) relays $y_i(k)$ to the coordinator.

## 4.3   Sensor-Actuator and Actuator-Actuator Coordination

After the initial nodes deployment, each sensor $S_i$ and actuator $A_j^a$ have their static position $p_i^s$ and $p_j^a$, respectively. By using Voronoi cells method [10], we can divide the ROI into $n_a$ partitions $\{P_1, P_2, ..., P_{n_a}\}$, where all sensors in the partition $P_j$ are closer to the position $p_j^a$ of $A_j^a$ than to the positions of all other actuators $A_i^a, i \neq j$. $A_j^a$ will then be responsible only for the sensors in its own partition and periodically perform data collection task for sensors in $P_j$.

In our framework, the coordinator can be defined as an actuator which roles as a mediator between the associated sensors and other actuators. For sensor's coordinator is the nearest actuator, since the closer the actuator to the sensor is, the earlier the actuator is informed, thus the quicker the actuator reacts and the earlier action to be initiated. So, the Voronoi cells method mentioned above can be used to select the coordinator.

From section 3, we could see that PIDNN is an error-driven control algorithm, measurement noise $\nu(k)$ will not only degrade the system performance, but also destabilize the system. A very natural thing is to design an observer to estimate system state for the control design. Hence, a sample Kalman filter can be performed by the coordinator to estimate the system state:

$$x_i(k|k-1) = a_{ii}x_i(k-1|k-1) + \sum_{j \in B_i} b_{ij}u_j(k-1) \tag{26}$$

$$p_i(k|k-1) = a_{ii}p_i(k-1|k-1)a_{ii} + q_{ii}(k-1) \tag{27}$$

$$m_i(k) = p_i(k|k-1)c_i[c_i p_i(k|k-1)c_i + r_i(k)]^{-1} \tag{28}$$

$$x_i(k|k) = x_i(k|k-1) + m_i(k)[y_i(k) - c_i x_i(k|k-1)] \tag{29}$$

$$p_i(k|k) = [1 - m_i(k)c_i]p_i(k|k-1) \tag{30}$$

Then the coordinator will broadcast the sensing data $z_i(k) = x_i(k|k)$ to other actuators in the same subsystem. After information exchange, each actuator in $GS_i$ accesses their responsible system states $X_i(k|k)$ and implements PIDNN mentioned above to calculate the control law $U_i(k)$.

## 5 Simulation

We consider a WSANs system for temperature control with $n_p = 3$, $n_a = 4$ and $n_s = 30$. The nodes are deploy in a $150m \times 150m$ ROI to detect events and take necessary actions. Each actuator has an action radius $r_a = 30m$. The action bound to the actuator such that $u_i \in [-10, 10]$. Here, we assume there is no sensor uncoveraged holes due to the large deploy number. The control arm is to meet the set points $X^* = [24(°C), 25(°C), 26(°C)]^T$, and the system model parameters are:

$$A = \begin{bmatrix} 0.9 & 0 & 0 \\ 0 & 0.9 & 0 \\ 0 & 0 & 0.9 \end{bmatrix}, B = \begin{bmatrix} 0.3 & 0.4 & 0 & 0 \\ 0 & 0.5 & 0.3 & 0 \\ 0 & 0.4 & 0 & 0.3 \end{bmatrix}, C = \begin{bmatrix} 1 & 0 & 0 \\ 0 & 1 & 0 \\ 0 & 0 & 1 \end{bmatrix}$$

Based on the $(A, B, C)$ established, a 3-input $\times$ 4-output PIDNN is applied to control actuators. The initial values of $w_{sij}(0)$ are: $w_{s1j}(0) = 1, w_{s2j}(0) = -1, s = 1, ..., n_p, j = 1, 2, 3$, and $w'_{sjh}(0)$ are randomly select between 0 and 0.1. Learning steps are $\eta = 0.00001$ and $\eta' = 0.000001$, respectively. In the simulations, all the system noise sequences, i.e., $\{\omega_i(k), \nu_j(k)\}$ are set to have the same amplitude: $q_{ii}(k) = r_i(k) = 0.1$.

The system response after collaborative training process are shown in Fig.2. The system state curves show that the PIDNN control scheme has a good system performance, which can achieve quick responses, small overshoot and steady state error. After undergoes 200 times of studies, the objective function $J(k)$ has been met our desired requirements.

In Fig.3, the results illustrate the control law of actuators under the PIDNN control scheme. In this case, we can easily see that the control system is stable. In our Actuator-Actuator coordination framework, the action will take place when an event is detected. Actuators will modulate their outputs according to the objective function $J(k)$. At the beginning, due to the initial set system state

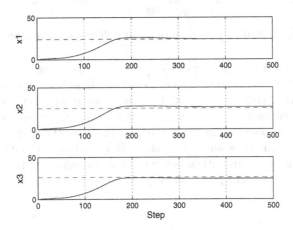

**Fig. 2.** Dynamic system response

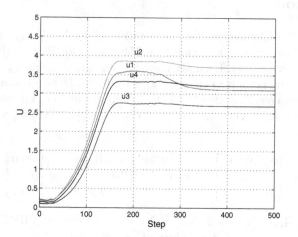

**Fig. 3.** Control law of actuators

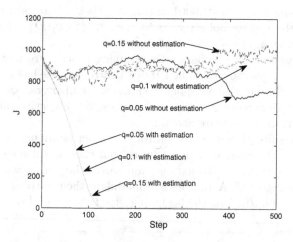

**Fig. 4.** System performance under different system noise

$(X(0))$ and connective weights $(w_{sij}(0), w'_{sjh}(0))$, the initial error $e(k)$ is big, but as the error on-line training process, $e(k)$ will tend to be zero eventually.

Fig.4 compares the evolutions of $J(k)$ the system with and without state estimation are able to achieve under different system noise levels. It can be seen that, without state estimation, $J(k)$ vary violently as the increment of noise power and thus leads to a unstable system. If we utilize estimation algorithm to filter sensor data, it can mitigates the detrimental effects of the system noise and improves system performance greatly.

# 6   Conclusion

This paper deals with the design of WSANs for control applications. The related challenge to design such a system is to perform an effective collaborative processing mechanism among nodes within this network. First, an event-driven task allocation mechanism based on the characteristics of events is introduced to model actuator schedule. Then, according to the control requirements, a distributed PIDNN control strategy is applied to coordinate nodes' actions to accomplish effective tasks. While performing such strategy, in order to improve the control accuracy, Kalman filter is applied to estimate system state from noisy measurement. Simulation results demonstrate that the proposed method has a well adaptability, strong robustness and satisfactory system performance.

# References

1. Akyildiz, I.F., Kasimoglu, I.H.: Wireless Sensor and Actor Networks: Research Challenges. Ad Hoc Networks 2, 351–367 (2004)
2. Yuan, H.D., Ma, H.D., Liao, H.Y.: Coordination Mechanism in Wireless Sensor and Actor Networks. In: The First International Multi-Symposiums on Computer and Computational Sciences, pp. 627–634. IEEE Press, New York (2006)
3. Xu, Z.H., Wang, Y., Zou, Q.Y., Tang, J.: Adaptive Kalman Filtering Based Location Coordination Algorithm For Wireless Sensor And Actor Networks. In: International Forum on Information Technology and Applications, pp. 264–267. IEEE Press, New York (2009)
4. Melodia, T., Pompili, D., Gungor, V.C., Akyildiz, I.F.: Communication and Coordination in Wireless Sensor and Actor Networks. IEEE Trans. on Mobile Computing 6, 1116–1129 (2007)
5. Melodia, T., Pompili, D., Akyildiz, I.F.: Handing Mobility in Wireless Sensor and Actor Networks. IEEE Trans. on Mobile Computing 9, 160–173 (2010)
6. Cao, X.H., Chen, J.M., Xiao, Y., Sun, Y.X.: Building-environment Control With Wireless Sensor and Actuator Networks: Centralized Versus Distributed. IEEE Trans. on Industrial Electronics 57, 3596–3606 (2010)
7. Chen, J.M., Cao, X.H., Chen, P., Xiao, Y., Sun, Y.X.: Distributed Collaborative Control for Industrial Automation With Wireless Sensor and Actuator Networks. IEEE Trans. on Industrial Electronics 57, 4219–4229 (2010)
8. Ang, K.H., Chong, G., Li, Y.: PID Control System Analysis, Design, and Technology. IEEE Trans. on Control System Technology 13, 559–576 (2005)
9. Shu, H.L., Guo, X.C., Shu, H.: PID Neural Networks in Multivariable Systems. In: the 2002 IEEE International Symposium on Intelligent Control, pp. 440–444. IEEE Press, New York (2002)
10. Aurenhammer, F.: Voronoi Diagrams-A Survey of a Fundamental Grometric Data Structure. ACM Comput. Surv. 23, 345–405 (1991)

# A Practical Calibration Method
# for Spray Painting Robot in Factory

Xiaoping Zhang[1], Wenyu Yang[1], Xuegang Cheng[2], and Wei Zhu[2]

[1] State Key Lab of Digital Manufacturing Equipment and Technology,
Huazhong University of Science and Technology, Wuhan, China, 430074
[2] Industrial Robot Research Center Co. Ltd., Kunshan, China, 215347
shoppinggre@gmail.com, mewyang@mail.hust.edu.cn,
{xg.cheng,w.zhu}@huahengweld.com

**Abstract.** Calibration techniques played an essential role of improving
the pose accuracy of the industrial robot before delivery. Due to the
intense competition among the industrial robot market, numerous complicated calibration approaches, which were classified into 3 levels, had
been successfully developed. Yet, in practical, level-1 and level-2 calibration, other than higher level, were often used in factory for the sake of
cost-effective matter. And most of the researches and applications were
focused on enhancing the position accuracy while the orientation accuracy was neglected. Considering the requirement of painting process
and efficiency of calibration, we proposed a practical level-2 calibration
method for a spray painting robot which was designed by Industrial
Robot Research Center Co. Ltd. The measuring system consisted of API
laser tracker and an orientation testing End-Effector. After identification and compensation process, we found this method was more effective
compares to Zero-Offset method and Direct Calibration method with the
relatively competitive consumption time.

**Keywords:** Robot Calibration, D-H parameters, MD-H, POE, Zero-
Offset, Direct Calibration, Singularity, Least Squares programming.

## 1 Introduction

Thanks to the flexibility and capability of reprogramming, robot manipulator has
shown us a quite economic and environmental solution in a variety of industries.
Due to the intense competition of robot market, there are strong demands for
high pose accuracy [1] and delivery efficiency among enterprises. Thus, a simple
and practical offline calibration process, which make the robot ready to use with
an acceptable accuracy for clients, is needed before shipping..

The calibration methods have been used to improve the pose accuracy of the
robot through a soft way to avoid increasing the mechanical cost. For decades,
many efforts have been made in this research area. Early in 1987, Roth [2]
categorized the robot calibration methods into 3 levels, which are 'joint level'
calibration, 'kinematic model based' calibration and 'non-geometric' calibration,

C.-Y. Su, S. Rakheja, H. Liu (Eds.): ICIRA 2012, Part I, LNAI 7506, pp. 164–173, 2012.
© Springer-Verlag Berlin Heidelberg 2012

respectively. Later, Elatta et al. [3] replenished the contributions during the interval. However, level-1 [4] and level-2 [5], [6], [7], [8], [9], [10], [11] calibration methods were proved to be more popular in factory, owing to their excellent cost-efficiency. Level-3 calibration [12], [13], which enables the online fast trajectory tracking, yet, is rarely used due to the high cost of measuring.

The level-1 calibration, previously, was to identify the model between the output of transducer and joint displacement. And it was simply achieved by introducing the mechantronic instruments to measure the absolute displacement of joints at specified configuration, such as the Kuka's emt [14]. However, when the mechanical fixture is wear, this method will lose accuracy to a certain extent. In addition, it requires the experienced workers and the process appears to be tedious and dangerous. To improve the effectiveness of level-1 calibration, researchers proposed the level-2 calibration method. By means of using the Least-squares programming, the actual geometric parameters are identified through the kinematic models and measuring data. Owing to its generality, this method has been popular used until now and extent to parallel robots [15] and the robot systems with external cells [16]. Pertinent application software has emerged like Dynacal from Dynalog [17] as well. The main issue of level-2 calibration [5], [6] has been the singularities of the kinematic model, which breaks the effectiveness of Least-squares programming. Then, several rectifications were made, such as MD-H model [7], S-model [8], and POE model [9], [10], [11]. The MD-H model is widely used because of its convenience of introducing the extra rotational parameters. But the issue transformed and lied in the difficulties to have a proportional and complete model. Whereas the S-model meets the completeness condition, its measuring process seems to be lengthy. The POE model is proved to be complete and proportional in theory, but the efficiency of the identification process appears to be non-competitive. To note, the hybrid methods of level-1 and level-2 became to attract the eyeballs with appearance of the updates of measuring method like using laser tracker. A direct calibration method [18], which is model free and combines the measuring and identification process, is developed. In terms of rotating each link, the actual geometric parameters are obtained. But, this method appears to be time-consuming as well.

Due to the requirement of spray painting process and compromise of the measuring cost, the orientation accuracy which was neglected by almost all the researches is demanded. As a direct factor that results unevenly spraying, the orientation accuracy shows to be very important for the quality of painting.

In this paper, we propose an effective and efficient calibration method for practical use in factory. In priority, we focus on improving the pose accuracy in terms of extending the MD-H model, in which full pose differentials are derived. In addition, an orientation testing tool and the API laser tracker are introduced to help completing the pose measuring. After that, Least-Squares programming is used to identify the geometric parameters. To compare with other methods, we try the Zero-Offset method [19] and the Direct method, as well. Finally, the

post-correction results are analyzed and compared, which will show the reason
why the method we proposed is more practical and competitive.

## 2   General Model of Kinematic Error

The previous studies of rigid kinematics allow us to describe the pose of End-
Effector of a general manipulator through a series of consecutive transformations.
Each transformation, expressed in a $4 \times 4$ homogeneous matrix, describes the
kinematic relationship between adjacent frames attached to each link. In terms
of D-H method [20], without losing the generality, the standard transformation
matrix, derived by Paul [21], is described as follows.

$$_{i-1}^{i}\mathbf{A} = \mathbf{R}(\mathbf{z}_{i-1},\theta_i) \cdot \mathbf{T}(0,0,d_i) \cdot \mathbf{T}(a_i,0,0) \cdot \mathbf{R}(\mathbf{x}_i,\alpha_n) . \tag{1}$$

Considering the singularity issue, we apply the Modified Denavit-Hartenberg
Model, which is singular free. An extra rotation $\beta_n$ around current axis $\mathbf{y}_n$ is
added that (1) is updated to

$$_{i-1}^{i}\mathbf{A} = \begin{bmatrix} -s\alpha_i s\beta_i s\theta_i + c\beta_i c\theta_i & -c\alpha_i s\theta_i & s\alpha_i c\beta_i s\theta_i + s\beta_i c\theta_i & a_i c\theta_i \\ s\alpha_i s\beta_i c\theta_i + c\beta_i s\theta_i & c\alpha_i c\theta_i & -s\alpha_i c\beta_i c\theta_i + s\beta_i s\theta_i & a_i s\theta_i \\ -c\alpha_i s\beta_i & s\alpha_i & c\alpha_i c\beta_i & d_i \\ 0 & 0 & 0 & 1 \end{bmatrix} . \tag{2}$$

where $s(\cdot) = sin(\cdot)$ and $c(\cdot) = cos(\cdot)$. Then, the kinematics can be represented
as:

$$_{0}^{n}\mathbf{A} = \prod_{i=1}^{n} {}_{i-1}^{i}\mathbf{A} \qquad i = 1,\ldots,6 . \tag{3}$$

Further, the transformation of the tool frame $\{\mathbf{T}\}$ relative to base frame $\{\mathbf{0}\}$ is
described as:

$$_{0}^{tool}\mathbf{A}(\Omega) = {}_{0}^{6}\mathbf{A} \cdot \begin{bmatrix} {}_{6}^{tool}\mathbf{R} & {}_{6}^{tool}\mathbf{p} \\ \mathbf{0} & 1 \end{bmatrix} = \begin{bmatrix} \mathbf{n} & \mathbf{o} & \mathbf{a} & \mathbf{p} \\ 0 & 0 & 0 & 1 \end{bmatrix} . \tag{4}$$

where $\Omega = \left[\theta_i, d_i, \alpha_i, a_i, \beta_i, {}_{6}^{tool}\mathbf{R}, {}_{6}^{tool}\mathbf{p}\right]_{42 \times 1}^{T}$, $i = 1,\ldots,6$, are the nominal geometric parameters. By differentiating every column of (4), we obtain:

$$\Delta\mathbf{p} = \mathbf{p}_{mea} - \mathbf{p}_{nom} = \sum_{j=1}^{42} \frac{\partial\mathbf{p}}{\partial\Omega_j}\Delta\Omega_j = \left[\frac{\partial\mathbf{p}}{\partial\Omega_1},\cdots,\frac{\partial\mathbf{p}}{\partial\Omega_{42}}\right]\Delta\Omega = \mathbf{H}_p \cdot \Delta\Omega . \tag{5}$$

$$\Delta\mathbf{n} = \mathbf{n}_{mea} - \mathbf{n}_{nom} = \sum_{j=1}^{42} \frac{\partial\mathbf{n}}{\partial\Omega_j}\Delta\Omega_j = \left[\frac{\partial\mathbf{n}}{\partial\Omega_1},\cdots,\frac{\partial\mathbf{n}}{\partial\Omega_{42}}\right]\Delta\Omega = \mathbf{H}_n \cdot \Delta\Omega . \tag{6}$$

$$\Delta\mathbf{o} = \mathbf{o}_{mea} - \mathbf{o}_{nom} = \sum_{j=1}^{42} \frac{\partial\mathbf{o}}{\partial\Omega_j}\Delta\Omega_j = \left[\frac{\partial\mathbf{o}}{\partial\Omega_1},\cdots,\frac{\partial\mathbf{o}}{\partial\Omega_{42}}\right]\Delta\Omega = \mathbf{H}_o \cdot \Delta\Omega . \tag{7}$$

$$\Delta \mathbf{a} = \mathbf{a}_{mea} - \mathbf{a}_{nom} = \sum_{j=1}^{42} \frac{\partial \mathbf{a}}{\partial \Omega_j} \Delta \Omega_j = \left[ \frac{\partial \mathbf{a}}{\partial \Omega_1}, \cdots, \frac{\partial \mathbf{p}}{\partial \Omega_{42}} \right] \Delta \Omega = \mathbf{H}_a \cdot \Delta \Omega . \quad (8)$$

$\Delta \mathbf{p}$, $\Delta \mathbf{n}$, $\Delta \mathbf{o}$ and $\Delta \mathbf{a}$ are the position and orientation errors to be measured. In addition, we write (5), (6), (7) and (8) together, and obtain:

$$\Delta \mathbf{E} = \mathbf{H} \cdot \Delta \Omega . \quad (9)$$

Where $\Delta \mathbf{E} = \left[ \Delta \mathbf{p}^T \, \Delta \mathbf{n}^T \, \Delta \mathbf{o}^T \, \Delta \mathbf{a}^T \right]^T$, $\mathbf{H} = \left[ \mathbf{H}_p^T \, \mathbf{H}_n^T \, \mathbf{H}_o^T \, \mathbf{H}_a^T \right]^T$ is referred as the Jacobian matrix and $\Delta \Omega = \left[ \Delta \theta_i, \Delta d_i, \Delta \alpha_i, \Delta \beta_i, \Delta_6^{tool} \mathbf{R}, \Delta_6^{tool} \mathbf{p} \right]$ is the geometric errors to be identified.

Further, for $z - y - z$ Euler angle, the orientation errors are expressed as:

$$\Delta a = atan2(\mathbf{R}_{mea}(2,1), \mathbf{R}_{mea}(1,1)) - a_{nom} . \quad (10)$$

$$\Delta b = atan2(-\mathbf{R}_{mea}(3,1), \sqrt{\mathbf{R}_{mea}^2(1,1) + \mathbf{R}_{mea}^2(2,1)}) - b_{nom} . \quad (11)$$

$$\Delta c = atan2(\mathbf{R}_{mea}(3,2), \mathbf{R}_{mea}(3,3)) - c_{nom} . \quad (12)$$

Where $\mathbf{R}_{mea} = [\mathbf{n}_{mea}, \mathbf{o}_{mea}, \mathbf{a}_{mea},]$ is the measured orientation of $\{\mathbf{T}\}$.

## 3  Measuring Setup

### 3.1  Position and Orientation Measuring

The position and orientation, namely the pose, of the robot is referred as x, y, z, a, b, c values. To measure the position accuracy, according to ISO 9283, an example End-Effector is provided [1]. However, it is incapable of testing the orientation

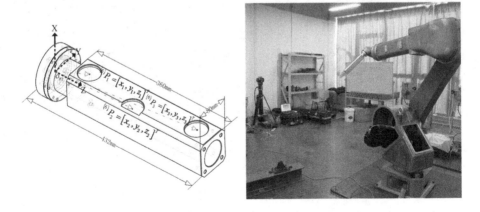

**Fig. 1.** The spray painting robot assembled with orientation testing tool

of the robot unless a deterministic frame is built. Actually, the orientation of the robot can be measured in terms of using the optional 6-dimensional laser tracking sensor, which is costly and only available from Automated Precision Inc. [22]. Considering the financial effects, we designed a new economic end effector [23] to measure the robot poses with API 3-dimensional laser tracker, see in Fig.1. There are 3 holes, designed to fix the Spherically Mounted Retro-reflector (SMR) in terms of $3 \times \phi 50.20mm$ dedicated bases, on the top surface of the effector to establish the tool frame $\{T\}$. After assembling the end effector onto the end of the robot, we can use the 3D API laser tracker to measure the positions of these 3 points. A line, which is constructed by $P_1$ and $P_3$ and supposed to be parallel to the Z axis of frame $\{6\}$, is the Z axis. In addition, we can make a plane, in terms of $P_1$, $P_2$ and $P_3$, the normal (or its inverse) of which is set to be the X axis. Then, the tool frame $\{T\}$, whose origin is located at $P_1$, can be established through the orthogonal method. Hence, we can read $\mathbf{R}_{mea}$ of the tool pertinent to the frame $\{0\}$ from the Spatial Analyzer, which is the software package of API laser tracker.

## 3.2    Measuring Details and Sampling Strategy

In order to identify the geometric errors, enough and effective sampling data should be gathered to establish a Least-Squares programming, in the case of which a unique estimation could be obtained. Considering that only 6 independent equations are provided for each pose, we should at least test 7 non-singular poses to get the Least-Squares solution. Thus, we choose 49 different poses, which are depicted in Fig.2 and enough to eliminate the random noise from the repeatablity of the robot and other factors in testing enviroment as well.

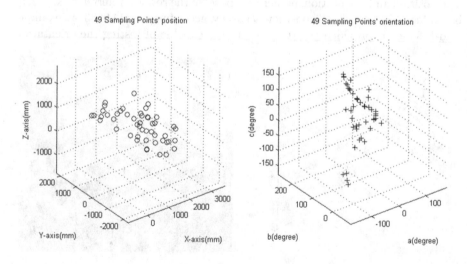

**Fig. 2.** 49 Nominal poses to be measured

During measurement, we command the robot to wait 18 seconds at each pose so that the API laser tracker can measure the pose data in a smooth manner. The entire setup and measurement process is less than 30 minutes.

## 4    Identification Process

The spray painting robot we calibrate is designed by Industrial Robot Research Centre Co. Ltd. The kinematic parameters are described in Table.1, in which we find axis 2 and axis 3 are designed to be paralleled. According to [7], the extra parameter $\beta_2$ is only needed to avoid singularity issue. Meanwhile, the controller system we apply to the robot is KEBA Ketop T50 and KeMotion, in which $\alpha_i$ ($i = 1, 2, 3$) can't be written. Therefore, the parameter $\Delta\Omega$ to be estimated is 34 dimensional. After checking $\mathbf{H}^T \cdot \mathbf{H}$ is non-singular, the Least-Squares programming is finely established that $\Delta\Omega$ can be estimated as

$$\Delta\hat{\Omega} = (\mathbf{H}^T \cdot \mathbf{H})^{-1} \cdot \mathbf{H}^T \cdot \Delta\mathbf{E} . \tag{13}$$

In terms of using commands of *jacobian* and *subs* in Symbolic math toolbox of MATLAB, we obtain real value of $(\mathbf{H}^T \cdot \mathbf{H})^{-1} \cdot \mathbf{H}^T$ from current geometric configuration. Then, we substitute (13) with the nominal D-H parameters and measuring data, and apply the commands of *lsqlin* and *lsqnonlin* in optimization toolbox. Through both algorithms, we obtain the same results, shown in Table.2. and Table.3. We note that the whole computation process is within 5 minutes.

The results show that the modification of tool's orientation is just rotate the nominal tool frame around $\omega = [0.4013, 0.3255, 0.8562]^T$ with 1.3244e-4 degrees, and are consistent with the POE method stated in [6].

Moreover, to compare with other identification methods, we run the Zero-Offset method and Direct Calibration method. The results are depicted in Table.4 and Table.5, respectively.

## 5    Errors Correction and Results comparison

Whereas the correction process can be completed within a minute for Zero-offset method, the correction of all geometric parameters needs rewrite of the kinematic configuration in KEBA controller and reboot of the robot system, which take about 5 minutes. However, comparing to the Direct calibration method, which takes more than 1 hour, the correction time is fairly reasonable. After correction, we re-measure the errors, depicted in Fig.3 and Fig.4.

The results show that the calibration method we applied is more effective than others. The 49 pose errors after calibration follow tighter normal distributions with smaller standard deviations. The range of position errors shrinks to [0.3545, 1.7076] mm. The standard deviation of orientation errors are down to [0.0044, 0.0096, 0.0349] degree. Further, the comparison of calibration time, depicted in Fig.5, shows the calibration method we used is relatively competitive.

**Table 1.** D-H parameters for Spray Painting Robot

| Link $i$ | $a_i\,(mm)$ | $\alpha_i\,(degree)$ | $d_i\,(mm)$ | $\theta_i\,(degree)$ |
|---|---|---|---|---|
| 1 | 270 | 90 | 0 | $\theta_1$ |
| 2 | 1300 | 0 | 0 | $\theta_2$ |
| 3 | 42.5 | 90 | 0 | $\theta_3$ |
| 4 | 0 | 70 | 1300 | $\theta_4$ |
| 5 | 0 | -70 | 108.9 | $\theta_5$ |
| 6 | 0 | 0 | 82 | $\theta_6$ |

**Table 2.** The Estimated errors of D-H parameters

| Link $i$ | $\Delta a_i\,(mm)$ | $\Delta\alpha_i\,(degree)$ | $\Delta d_i\,(mm)$ | $\Delta\theta_i\,(degree)$ |
|---|---|---|---|---|
| 1 | -1.9719 | 0 | -0.2069 | -0.0569 |
| 2 | 2.1750 | 0 | -0.9600 | -0.0877 |
| 3 | 0.3612 | 0 | -0.9594 | 0.0257 |
| 4 | 0.3002 | -0.0764 | 0.1390 | 0.0138 |
| 5 | -0.0032 | 0.0637 | 0.0728 | 0.0829 |
| 6 | 0.0839 | 0.0718 | 0.5111 | 0 |

**Table 3.** The Estimated errors of Tool parameters

| Tool | $\Delta p\,(mm)$ | $\Delta_6^{tool}R_x\,(radian)$ | $\Delta_6^{tool}R_y\,(radian)$ | $\Delta_6^{tool}R_z\,(radian)$ |
|---|---|---|---|---|
| x | 0.0003 | 1.0675e-17 | 1.9486e-6 | 6.9915e-7 |
| y | 0 | -2.1163e-6 | 5.2149e-18 | -1.0443e-6 |
| z | 0.0004 | -7.1453e-7 | 9.1147e-7 | 3.7762e-24 |

**Table 4.** The identified Zero-Offset angle errors for 6 joints

| $\Delta\theta_1(degree)$ | $\Delta\theta_2(degree)$ | $\Delta\theta_3(degree)$ | $\Delta\theta_4(degree)$ | $\Delta\theta_5(degree)$ | $\Delta\theta_6(degree)$ |
|---|---|---|---|---|---|
| -0.0046 | -0.0388 | 0.0255 | 0.1558 | -0.2297 | 0 |

**Table 5.** The identified Geometric errors through Direct Calibration method

| $\Delta\theta_1(degree)$ | $\Delta\theta_2(degree)$ | $\Delta\theta_3(degree)$ | $\Delta\theta_4(degree)$ | $\Delta\theta_5(degree)$ | $\Delta\theta_6(degree)$ |
|---|---|---|---|---|---|
| -0.0294 | -0.0589 | 0.0317 | 0.0245 | -0.1822 | 0 |

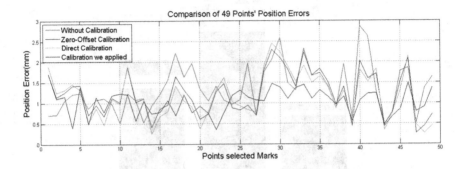

**Fig. 3.** Comparison of Position Errors for 49 Points

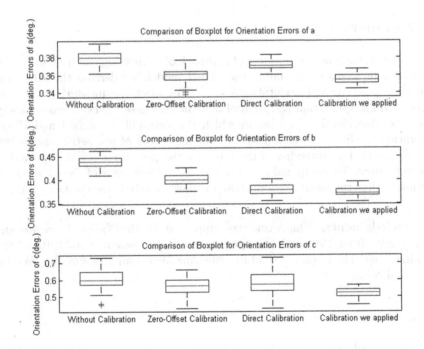

**Fig. 4.** Comparison of Orientation Errors 49 Points

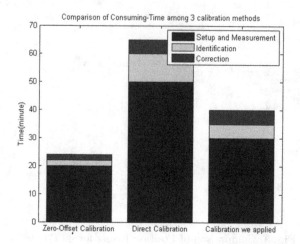

**Fig. 5.** Comparison of Consuming-Time among 3 calibration method

## 6    Summary

In this paper, we provided a practical approach of calibrating the spraying paint-ing robot. In terms of extending the MD-H model, we derived the kinematic model for position and orientation errors. To collect the measuring data, we introduced an orientation testing tool and the API laser tracker, economically. After the identification process, in which the Zero-Offset method and Direct calibration method are attempted as well, the errors of geometric parameters were obtained. By correcting of these errors, the pose accuracy is improved to different extent. We compared the effectiveness and efficiency of these 3 methods and found that the method we proposed is more practical for the factory use.

**Acknowledgments.** This work was supported by the National Science and Technology Major Project '15kg spraying robot equipment' (No.2010zx04008-041) in China. The authors would like to thank Wanchun Yan and Tao Wen for their kind help.

## References

1. International Organization for Standardization: Manipulating industrial robots-performance criteria and related test methods, BS EN ISO 9283 (1998)
2. Roth, Z., Mooring, B.W., Ravani, B.: An over view of robotic calibration. IEEE Journal of Robotic and Automation 3, 377–385 (1987)
3. Elatta, A.Y., Li, P.G., Fan, L.Z., Yu, D.Y.: An over view of robot calibration. Information Technology Journal 3(1), 74–82 (2004)
4. Whitney, D.E., Lozinski, C.A., Rourke, J.M.: Industrial robot forward calibration method and results. ASME J. Dynamic Syst., Meas. Contr. 108, 1–8 (1986)

5. Motta, J.: An investigation of singularities in robot kinematic chains aiming at building robot calibration models for off-line programming. J. Braz. Soc. Mech. Sci. Eng. 27, 200–204 (2005)
6. Wang, H., Shen, S., Lu, X.: A screw axis identification method for serial robot calibration based on poe model. Industrial Robot 39 (2012)
7. Hayati, S.: Robot arm geometric link parameter estimation. In: 22nd IEEE Conf. Decision and Control, pp. 1477–1483 (1983)
8. Stone, H.: Statistical performance evaluation of the s-model arm signature identification technique. In: IEEE Conf. Robot and Automation, pp. 939–946 (1988)
9. He, R.B., Zhao, Y.J., Yang, S.N., Yang, S.Z.: Kinematic-parameter identification for serial-robot calibration based on poe formula. IEEE Transactions on Robotics 26(3), 411–423 (2010)
10. Mustafa, S.K., Yang, G., Yeo, S.H., Lin, W.: Kinematic calibration o f a 7-dof self-calibrated modular cable-driven robotic arm. In: IEEE Conf. Robotics and Automation, Pasadena, CA, USA, pp. 1288–1293 (2008)
11. Chen, I., Yang, G., Tan, C., Yeo, S.: Local poe model for robot kinematic calibration. J. Mech. Mach. 36(11) (2001)
12. Becquet, M.: Analysis of flexibility sources in robot structure. In: IMACS/IFAC. Symp. Modeling and Simulation of Distributed Parameters, Hiroshima, Japan, pp. 419–424 (1987)
13. Meng, L., Shah, D.K.: Dynamic analysis of a three-degrees-of-freedom, in-parallel actuated manipulator. IEEE J. Robotics and Automation 4, 361–367 (1988)
14. KUKA Robot Group's corporate, http://www.kuka-robotics.com
15. Lubrano, E., Bouri, M., Clavel, R.: Ultra-high-precision industrial robots calibration. In: IEEE Conf. Robotics and Automation, pp. 228–233 (2011)
16. Li, X., Zhang, B.: Towards general industrial robot cell calibration. In: IEEE Conf. Robotics, Automation and Mechantronics, pp. 137–142 (2011)
17. Robot Calibration for Dynalog, http://www.dynalog-us.com
18. Motta, S., Carvalho, G., Mcmaster, S.: Robot calibration using a 3d vision-based measurement system with a single camera. Robot and Computer-Integrated Manufacturing 17, 487–497 (2001)
19. Chen, H., Fuhlbrigge, T., Choi, S., Wang, J., Li, X.: Practical industrial robot zero offset calibration. In: IEEE Conf. Auto. Sci. and Eng., pp. 516–521 (2008)
20. Denavit, J., Harterberg, R.S.: A kinematic notation for lower-pair mechanisms based on matrices. ASME J. Applied Mechanics 22(6), 215–221 (1955)
21. Richard, P.: Robot manipulators: mathematics, programming, and control: the computer control of robot manipulators. MIT Press, Cambridge (1981)
22. API automated Precision, http://www.apisensor.com
23. Zhang, X.P., Yan, W.C., Zhu, W., Wen, T.: A design of end effector for measuring robot orientation accuracy and repeatability. Applied Mechanics and Materials 137, 382–386 (2011)

# Study on a New Bridge Crack Detection Robot Based on Machine Vision

Qijing Yu, Jie Guo, Shuyu Wang, Qinmiao Zhu, and Bo Tao

State Key Laboratory of Digital Manufacturing Equipment and Technology,
Huazhong University of Science and Technology,
Wuhan, 430074, P.R. China
Yuqijing888@gmail.com

**Abstract.** In this article, a robot designed to detect fissure underneath the bridge is presented. While the robot is working, it actually walks on a the truss stretches from a truck, automatically avoiding obstacles ahead in aid of the sensors and micro-controller. The whole device, equipped with CCD camera, can agilely move with the three degree mechanical structure. Moreover, the system performs brilliantly in identifying cracks from the complex view under the bridge and providing exact parameter related to it such as length, width and position by utilizing improved algorithm. This machine can also be operated by man directly to adjust the camera's position, once the fissure was discovered.

**Keywords:** bridge detection, robot, machine vision, image processing, crack detection.

## 1 Introduction

There is a large number of bridges in China, however, according to statistics, 40% of the bridges have been built for a very long time and the number is growing. Detection of the bridge has become an important topic among bridge managers, but detection system of bridges faces the problems of inadequate detection 、 maintenance system、 poor technology and equipment、 lack of senior inspectors in China at present, so it is necessary to develop a new bridge detection technology.

The bridge detection technology is developing rapidly. In terms of software, Beijing Jiaotong University uses MATLAB as a development platform to do some researches such as grayscale, image enhancement, thresholding to remove noise , calculating the eigenvalues , automatically identifying cracks by the value of the multi-feature matching algorithms and storing calculated data. In terms of hardware, it is mainly about detection carrier and it is divided into deck carrier and underbridge carrier. Deck carrier is project vehicle, which is driven on the decks to detect with the measuring instruments. Underbridge carrier is always a project truck with hydraulic robot arm which detects under the bridge, for example bridge detection vehicle, it provides a closer inspection and testing platform for inspectors to detect the slab concrete strength, the size and appearance of cracks of any parts under the bridge. It changes the past

C.-Y. Su, S. Rakheja, H. Liu (Eds.): ICIRA 2012, Part I, LNAI 7506, pp. 174–184, 2012.

detection way of hanging with a rope to the bridge for testing, making detection and make it faster, more accurate, easier and safer to detect. Currently there are many detection vehicles be bought to detect the bridges in Wuhan, Guangzhou, Nanchang, Fuzhou, Xiamen, Nanjing, Shenzhen [8].

Though the bridge detection technology is developing rapidly, but there are some limitations. MIT postgraduate students in school of mechatronics developed the bridge detection robot under the guidance of Dr. Harry Asada, the robot detect the bridge under the bridge with magnetic force, however, it can only be used for steel bridges, not for concrete bridge which occupies the majority. [2]. The software designed by Beijing Jiaotong University which is mentioned above cannot be used to automatically determine whether it is cracks, it need step-by-step pictures photographed by inspectors. It is mainly used for analysis of the various features of cracks such as width, length, roundness, aspect ratio, area, cracks mean gray etc., but it cannot be applied to scan under bridge, determining whether there are cracks and calculating a variety of eigenvalue of the cracks.

## 2    Profile of Detection Robot

The robot is designed to detect fissure underneath the bridge. While the robot is working, it actually walks on a truss stretch from a truck. The whole device equipped with CCD camera can agilely move with the three degree mechanical structure. Moreover, the system performs brilliantly in identifying cracks from the complex view under the bridge and providing exact parameter related to it such as length, width and position by utilizing improved algorithm. System schematic are shown in Fig.1.

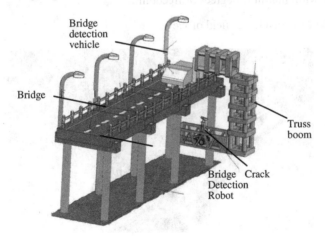

**Fig. 1.** System schematic

### 2.1    Mechanical Structure

This robot primarily consists of three parts, its system module unit is shown in Fig.2.

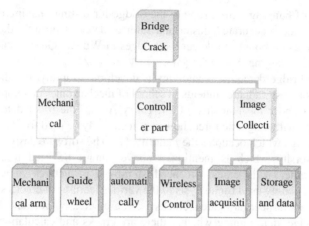

**Fig. 2.** System module unit

(1)Guide roller

This ensures the stability of the movement and to keep it in straight line.

(2) Lifting lever

Assisted by sensors, the lever's movement is controlled by the single-chip microcomputer, so the distance lies in the bridge bottom and the camera could be adjusted accordingly.

(3) Platform with multitude degrees of freedom

It endows the camera a better field of view.

**Fig. 3.** Model diagram of mechanical structure

## 2.2    Controller Part

This part is mainly divided into two parts: a wireless controller manipulated by human in distance and Single-chip Microcomputer to help avoid obstacles. The hardware in controller part is shown in Figure 4.

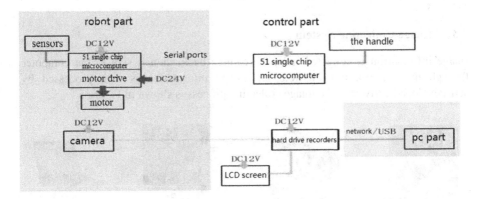

**Fig. 4.** Hardware in controller part

(1)Wireless controller

When a significant fissure is spotted through the camera, the robot could be totally controlled by it. In this way, the observer could get the suitable angle to scrutinize and analysis the wreck with more time and effort by order it rotate or move closer.

The devices used are one emitter with four buttons, controlling a range of 200M and the receiver named 2272.

(2) The part that single-chip microcomputer control

A. Hardware

The circuits are made up of a single-chip microcomputer, drive for motor, circuit of the sensors, a camera, a DC motor with 24Volts and a serial communications port.

The type of the single-chip microcomputer is SST-51, with 8-bit CPU and 4k bytes of ROM, 128 bytes of RAM, 21 special function registers, 32 I / O lines, addressing 64k bytes of external data and program storage space, two 16-bit timer counter and interrupt structure, with two priority, five interrupt sources and a full dual-port serial port for bit addressing function.

Also there are three infrared ray distance sensor located in front of the back and top, they can detect obstacle within 1 meter distance and then the signal is transmitted to the control system. Besides two DC drive motors are placed in it to increase and decrease the height of the platform and drive it forward or backward.

## B. Working process

If impediment is encountered when moving forward on the guide roller, the robot, after received the signal from the sensor would stop or return; the exact movement has to be decided by its algorithm. If the lever is blocked by obstacles under the uneven bridge bottom, the lever can automatically descend to avoid them; while the distance to bottom is out of reach (80CM-100CM), the lever can stretch out to offset it.

## 2.3    Image Collecting System

Image information is collected from the camera back, then is sent to the computer through the network transmission, the image information is then processed by self-developed software. The image collecting process is shown in Figure 5.

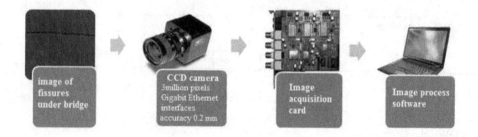

**Fig. 5.** Image collecting process

(1)  CCD (charged couple device) camera is made by high-sensitivity semiconductor, it will convert the light into charge, and then the analog signal is converted to digital signal.

The German Basler CCD camera is selected in the product. This CCD camera has the following advantages: i. small size and light weight; ii. low operating voltage; iii. durable in shock and vibration,  iv. high sensitivity . These features provide a solid foundation for the acquisition of the bridge bottom image. The specific parameters of industrial cameras are as the following form

(2)   Image acquisition card

The image acquisition card is able to collect the video data and transform it into a readable form for computers, so later it could be processed there.

(3)   Design of the software

The software, programmed in Open CV (Open Source Computer Vision Library), finally identifies and measures the fissures.

**Table 1.** The specific parameters of industrial cameras

| definition | parameters |
|---|---|
| Camera model | scA1300-32gm |
| Resolution | 1296X996 |
| Camera frame rate | 30fps |
| The size of the target surface | 1/3 |
| Pixel size | 3.75X3.75um |
| Trigger mode | External trigger |
| CCD Type | SonyICX445 CCD |
| Lens Mount | C interface |
| Data interface | Gigabit Ethernet interfaces |

The whole software is divided into five modules:

A. The main module: in response to a variety of events from users.

B. Interactive control module: Set the parameters of the hardware and software in order to meet the users' demand.

C. The image display module: display the video collected from the camera on the computer screen, so that users could spot the continuous view under the bridge.

D. The image process module: carry out actions as filtering noise, image segmentation, feature matching and so on.

E. Data storage module: save the collected data about the schism for future analysis or investigation

The interface of the software is shown in Figure 6.

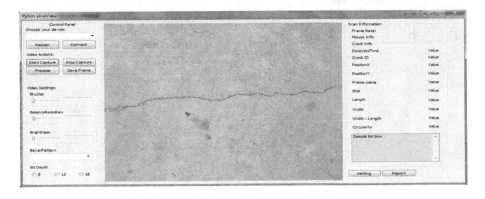

**Fig. 6.** User Interface of Crack Inspection System

Adjustment of the camera and setting the overall effect lies in the left part. The image display part is in the middle, where the image or the video is shown. The data acquisition part is on the right, and users are able to obtain the parameters such as width, length there.

Apart from these, the parameters that set the threshold of a schism can also be altered correspondingly. The crack information is shown in Table II.

**Table 2.** Crack information

| Crack Number | 1 | |
|---|---|---|
| Length/mm | 60.1192 | |
| Width/mm | 61.6519 | |
| Area/mm$^2$ | 0.9824 | |
| Circularity | 0.0729 | |
| Aspect Ratio | 62.8820 | |

## 2.4    Crack Analysis

The most important part in our system is the crack analysis. Its process is shown in Fig.7

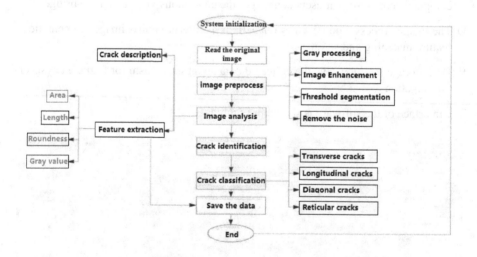

**Fig. 7.** Flow chart of crack processing

### 2.4.1  Image Preprocessing[3]

1)  Gray processing

Because there is a difference in the situation of sunshine in different shooting place, the brightness of the image can be very different, so we use the following formula to finish gray processing:

$$I(R,G,B)=0.299*R+0.587*G+0.144*B \tag{1}$$

In the formula (1) R,G,B refers to the value of red, green and blue. We can increase the efficiency of image processing by this way and it won't lose any data

2)  Removal of image noise

In this example we use median filter and Gaussian filter to remove the image noise efficiently which is produced in collecting and transmitting.

Before that, we use the following formula to process every pixel:

$$G(x, y) = \min\left\{ \frac{(255 - f(x, y))^2}{f(x, y)}, 255 \right\} \tag{2}$$

In this formula (2), f (x, y) refers to the value of input gray scale, and g(x, y) refers to the output gray scale.

The following formula to achieve Gaussian filter [6] :

$$F(x) = \begin{cases} 0\,(black) & f(x, y) \le T \\ 255(white) & f(x, y) > T \end{cases} \tag{3}$$

By this Non-linear formula (3), we can make the differences of each pixel in the image more remarkable

$$g(x, y) = \begin{cases} 1 & f(x, y) < x1) \\ \beta * f(x, y) + \gamma & x1 \le f(x, y) \le x2 \\ 254 & f(x, y) > x2 \end{cases} \tag{4}$$

3)  Binary image conversion: in this process we transform the gray image to binary image in order to calculate the eigenvalues of the cracks in the image. The formula to finish binary image conversion as follows [4]:

The T in the formula (4) refers to the threshold which is used in the identification of cracks. The final effect of image preprocessing is shown in Fig. 8.

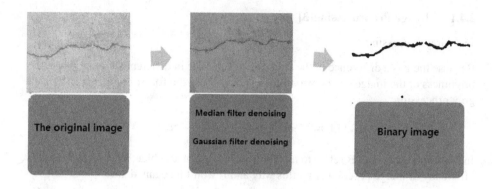

**Fig. 8.** The effect of image preprocessing

### 2.4.2    Image Analysis

Binaryzation image is obtained through threshold segmentation and noise is still in the image. Because of the shadow of the dark background, some cracks are considered to be value zero. Thus, the problems should be settled. In this paper, the extract image values have to be calculated. After threshold segmentation and image denoising, each connection areas left are marked as suspected crack area. The parameters for identifying the cracks as follows:

a. region area

b. boundary perimeter:$F = 4\pi \times \frac{A}{c^2}$

c. circularity

d. ratio of the major axis to minor axis of an external elliptic

According the results of experiments, characteristic values of several hundreds of crack pictures are took into statistics analysis. The features of crack area as follows:

1) the circular degrees of crack targets is very small, and 90% of them are smaller than 0.01;
2) the ratios of the major axis to minor axis of an external elliptic are large, 80% of the ratios are bigger than 7;
3) the grayscale of crack area is obvious different with average gray of external elliptic, the difference bigger than 30 is 85%.

### 2.4.3    Fracture Discrimination

From several typical characteristics of the empirical counting values of fissure image, the crack images can be recognized largely according to the characteristics of the definition conditions above.

### 2.4.5    The Actual Effect

According to the experiment results of different methods, which are as shown in Fig.11, it is obvious that the proposed method is better than other methods.

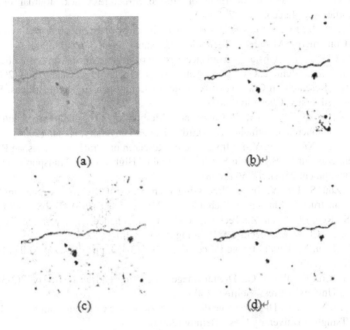

**Fig. 9.** Results of different methods (a)original image (b)proposed method  (c) adaptive threshold  (d)  region growing arithmetic

## 3    Conclusions

Inspection robot based on machine vision technology is safe and effective to detect the bridge. Using software and image processing technology, and with the reliable mechanical structure and control system, it can perform well in detecting task of bridge test automatically for crack information. And the calculated crack information and parameters are transmitted to PC database management system, providing reference for maintenance. The inspection robot proposed in this paper can get good effect in actual process.

## References

1.  Shu, A.: Study on the Arm Structure and Hydraulic System of Intelligent Bridge_detection Vehicle, Guangzhou (2006)
2.  Ding, Y., Wang, M.: Interview of meeting for early warning of dangerous bridge-2004 international conference on the bridge structure assessment. Construction Science and Technology 21, 33 (2004)

3. Yang, Z.: Analysis for Causes of Cracking in Concrete Box Girder. Southwest Jiaotong University, Chengdu (2005)
4. Zhang, W., Liu, M., Yang, M.: Bridge Crack Detection Technology Based on Digital Image Processing. Modern Transportation Technology 5, 34–36 (2008)
5. Kai, Y.-W.: Test and Counterplan of Bridge Structure Crack. Journal of Zhejiang Transportation College 4, 16–17 (2006)
6. Du, W., Zhu, S., Liu, Y.: Image Processing Technology of Highroad Asphaltum Pavement Crack. Construction Machinery Technology & Management 3, 65–68 (2006)
7. Zou, A.: Research on Obstacle-avoidance System of Performance Arm of Intelligent-video Bridge-detection Vehicle. Guangdong University of Technology, Guangzhou (2005)
8. Zhang, F.: Research on Cracking Box Girder of Long-Span Concrete Bridges. Southwest Jiaotong University, Chengdu (2004)
9. Yuan, T.: Analysis of Crack Cause and Method of Consolidation Maintenance of Prestressed Concrete Continuous Box-girder. Hunan University, Hunan (2006)
10. Wang, G.-L., Xie, J., Fu, Y.-F.: Investigalion Research on Crack of Long-span Prestressed Concrete Box Girder Bndges in Service. Journal of Highway and Transportation Research and Development 25(8), 53–56 (2008)
11. Du, W., Zhu, S., Liu, Y.: Image Processing Technology of Highroad Asphaltum Pavement Crack. Construction Machinery Technology & Management 19(3), 65–68 (2006)
12. Yang, S., Ren, M., Chen, Z.: Technical code of maintenance for city bridge CJJ 99-2003, vol. 2, p. 25. China Architecture & Building Press, Beijing (2004)
13. Guo, W., Hou, Y.: Digital Image Processing, vol. 5(3-18), pp. 195–197. Xidian University Press, Xi'an (2009)
14. Gong, S., Liu, C., Wang, Q.: Digital image processing and analysis, vol. 7(2-3), p. 177. Tsinghua University Press, Beijing (2006)
15. Lan, Z., Li, Y., Li, A.: Digital Image Processing and Image Communication, vol. 3(5-6), pp. 56–60. Tsinghua University Press, Beijing (2009)
16. Wu, Y.-M.: Method for calculating areas of multiple regions in image based on freeman chain code. Computer Engineering and Applications 44(15), 199–201 (2008)
17. Zhang, G.: Study on the Concrete Bridge Bottom Crack Inspection Method Based on Image Processing, vol. 6, pp. 52–53. Beijing Jiaotong University, Beijing (2010)

# Robust Gaussian-Based Template Tracking

Hadi Firouzi and Homayoun Najjaran

Okanagan School of Engineering,
The University of British Columbia, Kelowna BC, Canada
{hadi.firouzi,h.najjaran}@ubc.ca

**Abstract.** In this paper a visual object tracking method is presented which is robust against changes in the object appearance, shape, and scale. This method is also able to track objects being occluded temporarily in cluttered environments. It is assumed the target object moves freely through an unpredicted pattern in a dynamic environment where the camera may not be stationary. The proposed method models the object representation by an adaptive and deformable template which consists of several Gaussian functions. A 5 degree-of-freedom transformation function is employed to map the pixels from the template reference frame to the image reference frame. Moreover, the object localization method is based on a robust probabilistic optimization algorithm which is performed at every image frame to estimate the transformation parameters. The comparisons of the results obtained by the proposed tracker and several state-of-the-art methods with the manually labeled ground truth data demonstrate higher accuracy and robustness of the proposed method in this work.

**Keywords:** Visual Tracking, functions, non-rigid object, adaptive template.

## 1 Introduction

Efficiency and reliability of many robotic and computer vision applications such as automated visual surveillance systems [1] and intelligent preventive safety systems [2] highly depend on their visual object tracking algorithm. In general, a visual tracker consists of two main components which are object representation model and localization method. Object model can be represented either based on its features or image region. Different feature descriptors including silhouette, contour , texture , Haar-like features , and histograms have been used to model the objects. Although feature-based representation models such as SIFT [3] can suitably handle the appearance non-rigidity and scale variations, they are hampered in real-world applications due to the high computational cost of feature extraction and matching. Moreover, a suitable feature extraction method must be chosen before hand depending on the application. On the other hand, as a region-based model, object template is a well-studied technique which represents the object by its pixel values. Since early methods [4,5], the accuracy and efficiency of the template-based trackers have been improved in different ways

C.-Y. Su, S. Rakheja, H. Liu (Eds.): ICIRA 2012, Part I, LNAI 7506, pp. 185–195, 2012.

using a more general template transformation [6], linear appearance variation [7], and Active Appearance Models (AAMs) to model non-rigid appearance [8]. Moreover, low-dimensional sub-space representation models such as Principal Component Analysis (PCA) and Probabilistic PCA have been used in [9,10] to improve the robustness of the template trackers against illumination changes, outliers, and noise.

Apart from the representation model, object localization method also plays a crucial role in the performance of a visual tracker. Gradient-based searches and non-gradient methods such as sampling algorithms are two main approaches for finding the object location. Sequential Monte Carlo (SMC) methods such as Condensation algorithm [11] estimate the likelihood distribution of the object state using a sampling algorithm. SMC methods usually require a large number of samples (or particles) to obtain a satisfactory accuracy and robustness against large and complex object motion, scale, and appearance variations. In the case of tracking with no information about motion dynamics (although target motion dynamics can be estimated during the time, it is not reliable due to the unpredicted and complex target and camera motion), localization based on the target appearance and representation model is the key to develop a robust tracking method. On the contrary, in gradient-based methods such as Lucas-Kanade algorithm [12,13] and Mean-Shift method [14], a similarity measure as a cost function is optimized to find the next object location based on the motion model.

In this paper a robust template tracking method based on the sum of Gaussian errors between the object template and the candidate sub-image is proposed. The proposed method is capable of tracking non-rigid objects with variable appearance, shape, and scale in cluttered environments. A probabilistic optimization algorithm is used to minimize the error function. Moreover, several Gaussian functions are used to model the object template. At every frame, the template is adaptively updated so that it can handle both the object appearance changes and the "drift" problem[1]. It is assumed that the object bounding rectangle is specified manually or automatically (by any existing object detection method) at the first frame and the main goal is to track the object without any prior knowledge about the object appearance and motion dynamic.

The rest of this paper is organized as follows. In section 2, the template-based visual tracking problem will be defined, and then the formulation and the algorithm of the proposed robust Gaussian-based template tracking method will be explained in detail. In Section 3, the proposed tracker will be applied on a challenging video and its results will be compared with several state-of-the-art methods as well as the ground truth data. Concluding discussion and potential extensions for future work will be provided in Section 4.

---

[1] The problem of gradually updating the object appearance model with irrelevant information such as background pixel values [12]

## 2    Robust Template Tracking

Template matching is a powerful machine vision approach which has been introduced in [5] for the task of visual tracking. In this approach, the object specified at the first image $I^1$ is considered as the object template $T(X)$ where $X = \{x, y\}$ is the pixel coordinates and then the tracking task is to find the best match to the template in an image sequence. If the object dynamic is modeled by a transformation function $W(X; \Theta)$ where $\Theta = (\theta_1, .., \theta_K)$ are the template transformation parameters, one can define the squared error between the template and the next image $I^n$ as the similarity measure to find the best match. In [5], a non-linear optimization algorithm is introduced to solve Eq. 1.

$$\Theta^n = \arg \min_{\Theta} \sum_{X \in T} [I^n(W(X; \Theta)) - T(X)]^2 \tag{1}$$

In this work, as shown in Fig. 1, the object region is specified by a deformable bounding box. This box is defined by five parameters as $R = \{x_c, y_c, w, h, \beta\}$ where $x_c$ and $y_c$ are the center pixel coordinates of the object, $w$ and $h$ are the width and height of the region, and $\beta$ is the rotation in the image plane.

**Fig. 1.** Object region definition based on a deformable bounding box

In the proposed method, an adaptive deformable template based on several Gaussian functions is designed to represent the object appearance. The template consists of the object region intensity values, each template pixel $T(X)$ is modeled by a Gaussian distribution function $G_X$ defined by an adaptive mean $\mu_X$ and variance $\sigma_X$. The adaptive Gaussian functions used for the object template enhance the ability of the representation model to handle appearance variations, illumination changes, cluttered background, and occlusion. Also the proposed template is robust against the "drift" problem by considering the irrelevant pixels as outliers. In fact, an outlier region can be rejected by assigning a high value of the variance to the corresponding Gaussian functions. The deformable object region on the other hand, can manage the shape and scale changes as well as different poses. Moreover, a gradient-based search is used to locate the object region in the image sequence. The proposed localization algorithm is based on a probabilistic optimization method which minimizes the sum of Gaussian errors between the template and the candidate sub-image to find the template transformation parameters $\Theta^t$.

Although a generic transformation matrix with more parameters (e.g., 6-DOF affine transformation map used in [15]) can offer more flexibility to the task of object localization, a large number of parameters being estimated may increase the uncertainty and convergence speed as well as the computational cost. A more suitable transformation function should be defined based on the object representation model. Considering the proposed representation model, we used a 5-DOF[2] transformation function $W(X; \Theta)$ to map the pixel $X$ in the coordinate frame of the template to the pixel located at $W(X; \Theta)$ in the coordinate frame of the image. As shown in Eq. 2, the transformation function is composed of translation, rotation, and scale transformations.

$$W(X;\Theta) = \begin{bmatrix} \cos(\beta) & -\sin(\beta) & d_x \\ \sin(\beta) & \cos(\beta) & d_y \end{bmatrix} \begin{bmatrix} s_x \times x \\ s_y \times y \\ 1 \end{bmatrix} \tag{2}$$

where $d_x$ and $d_y$ are the object translation in x and y axises, $s_x$ and $s_y$ are the scale factor in x and y axises respectively, and $\beta$ is the object rotation in the image plane.

---

**Algorithm 1.** Summary of the proposed tracking algorithm

---

1: Specify the first object region ($R^1 = \{x_c, y_x, w, h, \beta\}$) either manually or by an object detection method
2: Initialize the object template based on Eq. 3
3: Estimate the object location using Eq. 10
4: Update the templates based on Eq. 11
5: Go to step 3 until the end of image sequences

---

Based on the experimental results, it is shown that the 5-DOF transformation function employed in this work outperforms the popular 6-DOF affine transformation function used in [15]. A summary of the proposed tracking algorithm is shown in Algorithm 1. In the following subsections, different parts of this algorithm are explained in detail.

## 2.1    Template Initialization

The template is first initialized from the object region $R^1 = \{x_c^1, y_c^1, w^1, h^1, \beta^1\}$ at the first image $I^1$. As mentioned in the previous section, the template $T$ consists of the object image where each pixel $T(X)$ is modeled by a Gaussian function $G_X = \{\mu_X, \sigma_X\}$. The parameters of each Gaussian function are initialized based on Eq. 3.

$$\mu_X = I^1\left(W(X; \Theta^1)\right) \; ; \; \sigma_X = \{1\}_{w^1 \times h^1} \tag{3}$$

---

[2] Degree of freedom

where $\mu_X$ and $\sigma_X$ are the mean and variance values for the Gaussian function corresponding to the pixel X in the coordinate of the template, $\{1\}$ is a matrix of "1"s, and also the transformation parameters are initialized based on the object region as $\Theta^1 = \{\beta^1, s_x = 1, s_y = 1, d_x^1 = 0, d_y^1 = 0\}$.

## 2.2   Object Localization

In general, visual tracking task consists of two different processes which are called Target Representation and Localization (TRL), and Filtering and Data Association (FDA). In the latter process, the object is tracked through the estimation of its motion dynamics; however, in TRL, the object is located based on the object appearance and shape. In many real-world applications, localizing the object based on the estimated object dynamic model is not robust due to the complex and unpredicted object motion. Therefore, in this work a gradient-based algorithm which minimizes the sum of Gaussian errors between the template and the candidate sub-image is proposed to locate the object. In the following subsections, the proposed localization method is explained in detail. Also, for the sake of clarity, the time instant is not specified within the equations.

**Formulation.** The localization problem can be viewed as an optimization task. As the proposed object template is composed of Gaussian functions, we considered the sum of Gaussian errors (SGE) between the template and the candidate sub-image as the optimization cost function. Minimizing the SGE function defined in Eq. 4, we obtain the new transformation parameters $\Theta^*$.

$$SGE = \sum_{X \in R} \exp \left( -\frac{1}{2} \left( \frac{I_{W(X;\Theta^*)} - \mu_X}{\sigma_X} \right)^2 \right) \tag{4}$$

where the new transformation parameters $\Theta^*$ are found from the previous values $\Theta$ plus the parameters change $\Delta\Theta$. Also using the Taylor series, we can expand the transformed candidate sub-image $I_{W(X;\Theta^*)}$ based on Eq. 5.

$$I_{W(X;\Theta+\Delta\Theta)} = I_{W(X;\Theta)} + \nabla I_{W(X;\Theta)} \frac{\partial W}{\partial \Theta} \Delta\Theta \tag{5}$$

By substituting Eq. 5 into Eq. 4, the SGE is defined as:

$$SGE = \sum_{X \in R} \exp \left( -\frac{\left( I' + \nabla I' \frac{\partial W}{\partial \Theta} \Delta\Theta - \mu_X \right)^2}{2\sigma_X^2} \right) \tag{6}$$

where $I' = I_{W(X;\Theta)}$.

Taking derivative of the transformation function $W$ with respect to its parameters $\Theta$, we obtain:

$$\frac{\partial W}{\partial \Theta} = \begin{bmatrix} -xs_x S_\beta - ys_y C_\beta & xC_\beta & -yS_\beta & 1 & 0 \\ xs_x C_\beta - ys_y S_\beta & xS_\beta & yC_\beta & 0 & 1 \end{bmatrix} \tag{7}$$

where $S_\beta$ and $C_\beta$ are $\sin(\beta)$ and $\cos(\beta)$ respectively.

The change in transformation parameters $\Delta\Theta$ is estimated by taking derivative of Eq. 6 with respect to $\Delta\Theta$ and set the equation to zero.

$$\Delta\Theta = H^{-1} \sum_X \left[ \nabla I' \frac{\partial W}{\partial \Theta} \right]^T \left( \mu_X - I' \right) \tag{8}$$

where the Hessian matrix is:

$$H = \sum_X \left[ \nabla I' \frac{\partial W}{\partial \Theta} \right]^T \left[ \nabla I' \frac{\partial W}{\partial \Theta} \right] \sigma_X^2 \tag{9}$$

According to Eq. 9, the Hessian matrix needs to be calculated in every image frame which is not possible in many real-time applications. Nevertheless, having the independency assumption, we can calculate the transformation parameters based on Eq. 10.

$$\Delta\theta_k = \frac{\sum_X \left[ \nabla I' \frac{\partial W}{\partial \theta_k} \right]^T \left( \mu_X - I' \right)}{\sum_X \left[ \nabla I' \frac{\partial W}{\partial \theta_k} \right]^T \left[ \nabla I' \frac{\partial W}{\partial \theta_k} \right] \sigma_X^2} \tag{10}$$

where $\Theta = \{\theta_k\}_{k=1:K}$ and $K$, the number of parameters, is six.

Note that in Eq. 10, $\frac{\partial W}{\partial \theta_k}$ and $\nabla I'$ are $[2 \times 1]$ and $[1 \times 2]$ vectors; therefore, no matrix inversion is required which significantly increases the efficiency of the localization task.

## 2.3   Template Updating

After localizing the object, the template $T^t$ at time instant $t$ is updated from the sub-image specified by the transformation function $W(X; \Theta^t)$ with the new parameters $\Theta^t$. As shown in Eq. 11, an adaptive forgetting factor $\alpha_\mu \in [0, 1]$ is used to update the mean value of the Gaussian functions corresponding to the template pixel values. Also the variance of each Gaussian is empirically estimated from the error between the template and the sub-image $e_X^t$. In fact, those pixel which have been changed more than others will have a higher variance and consequently they are considered as outliers by the localization algorithm, see Eq. 10.

According to the mentioned properties, the proposed object representation model can improve the tracking robustness against different object poses, cluttered scenes, partial occlusion, and drifting.

$$e_X^t = I^t \left( W(X; \Theta^t) \right) - \mu_X^{t-1}$$
$$\mu_X^t = \mu_X^{t-1} + \alpha_\mu^t \times e_X^t$$
$$\sigma_X^t = \frac{1}{t} \left( (t-1)\sigma_X^{t-1} + e_X^{t\,2} \right) \tag{11}$$

Experimentally, the forgetting factor is defined based on the root mean square (RMS) error of the template and the sub-image. As a result, the proposed adaptive template is able to handle both short-term and long-term appearance changes by only updating the template from the high confident samples.

$$\alpha_\mu^t = \frac{1 - \sqrt{\frac{1}{N_X} \sum_X \left(\mu_X^{t-1} - I^t(X;\Theta^t)\right)^2}}{100} \tag{12}$$

where $N_X$ is the number of Gaussians representing the template and also $\alpha_\mu^t = 0$ if $\alpha_\mu^t < 0$.

## 3   Experimental Results

In this section, a challenging video studied in [16] has been used. This video consists of 1140 gray-scale images which are recorded at 30 frame per second with the size of $360 \times 240$. Also, the pixel values are scaled to $[0, 30]$.

The accuracy and robustness of the proposed tracking method have been verified by comparing its performance with several state-of-the-art methods. Also the ground truth data is used to validate the comparison. In Fig. 2, the object bounding box obtained by the proposed method using 5-DOF transformation map (bold dashed red box) and affine transformation map (bold dashed blue box), the ground truth data (bold dotted yellow box), the Mean-shift [14] (dash-dot cyan box), the Fragment-based Tracker [17] (solid magenta box), and the Color-Texture based Mean-shift [18] (dashed green box) for 6 sample frames are illustrated. Based on this figure, the proposed method is robust to track the target object in several challenging situations including: different poses (e.g., 4, 355, 962), scaling (e.g., 4, 962, 1081), illumination changes (e.g., 355, 828, 962), shape deformation (e.g., 355, 828), and temporary occlusion (e.g., 208, 355). In contrast to the typical template tracking methods, the proposed method is robust to the "drift" problem and can track the object where its appearance is changed significantly (e.g., 208).

Fig. 2 shows that the target object has been tracked accurately and robustly by the proposed method in different image sequences whereas other methods occasionally failed to locate the target at several frames. For instance, the Mean-shift method failed to track the object at frames 828, 962, and 1081, the Fragment-based tracker failed at frames 962 and 1081, and the Color-texture based Mean-shift could not locate the object at frames 208, 355, and 962. Based on this comparison the proposed method outperformed others in most frames. In early frames, the Fragment based tracker was the best tracker; however this method had significant drift at several frames (e.g., frame 962 and 1081), due to the large object motion, changes in the object appearance and lighting. The Mean-Shift tracker generally performed poorly especially in cluttered scenes where the object and background pixel values are mixed. Although the

Color-Texture based Mean-shift outperformed the typical Mean-shift method, it could not track the object precisely and it was not robust against occlusion and appearance changes.

**Fig. 2.** A comparison of the proposed tracker using 5-DOF transformation map (bold dashed red box) and affine transformation map (bold dashed blue box) with the ground truth (bold dotted yellow box), the Mean-shift (dash-dot cyan box), the Fragment-based Tracker (solid magenta box), and the Color-Texture based Mean-shift (dashed green box)

## 3.1    Quantitative Comparison

The root mean square (RMS) error between the object bounding box provided by the manually-labeled ground truth data and other methods is used to evaluate the precision of the proposed tracking method in comparison with the other methods.

As shown in Fig. 3 (b), the average RMS error between the ground truth object bounding box and the estimated bounding box obtained by the proposed method using the 5-DOF transformation is less than the others's average RMS errors, also based on Fig. 3, the RMS error obtained by the proposed method is smaller than other's error in most image frames. Although the RMS error of the proposed tracker (5-DOF transformation map) is not the least at all frames (e.g., between frames 300 and 600), the proposed method is more reliable than other methods in different situations where the object appearance and scale are changed.

Moreover, according to the quantitative results illustrated in figure 3 (a), the 5-DOF transformation map used in this paper outperformed a 6-DOF affine transformation map. In fact, not always a more general transformation function with more parameters provides a better tracking result.

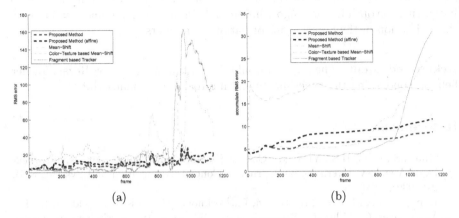

**Fig. 3.** The (a) immediate and (b) accumulated RMS error between the ground truth data and other tracking methods

## 4   Conclusions

This paper presents a probabilistic formulation to solve the visual tracking problem in complex environments where the object may be occluded and its shape, scale, and appearance are changing. In the proposed method the object is specified by a deformable bounding box which is represented by an adaptive template. Each pixel in the object template is modeled by an adaptive Gaussian function. The new location of the object is estimated by minimizing the sum of Gaussian errors between the template and the candidate sub-image. Based on the experimental results in section 3, the proposed method is robust against object appearance, shape, and scale variations and it is also able to handle partial and full occlusions (e.g, image frame 208 in Fig. 2). In addition, a 5-DOF transformation map is used for object transformation based on the object representation model. As shown in figure 3, the results obtained by the 5-DOF transformation map are more accurate and robust than the results of a more general 6-DOF affine transformation map.

The accuracy and robustness of the proposed tracking method are the result of using several adaptive Gaussian functions, the proper transformation function, and the probabilistic localization method. More precisely, Gaussian functions can manage outliers, noise, and appearance variations. Also the template is updated by a dynamic forgetting factor to improve the tracking reliability and solve the "drift" problem by rejecting outliers and occluded sub-images. In comparison with several state-of-the-art trackers, the proposed method can track a non-rigid object more accurately and robustly. However it occasionally drifts from the target object especially where the object deformation and motion are significant. As a solution, the localization algorithm can be performed in multi-resolution from coarse to fine to locate the object when it has moved significantly. Also initializing the optimization algorithm from different starting points can improve the estimation of the object transformation parameters.

**Acknowledgment.** The authors would like to thank Dr. Golriz Rezaei for her help on conducting the experiments and improving the manuscript.

# References

1. Kim, I.S., Choi, H.S., Yi, K.M., Choi, J.Y., Kong, S.G.: Intelligent visual surveillance A survey. International Journal of Control, Automation and Systems 8(5), 926–939 (2010)
2. Hampapur, A., Bobbitt, R., Brown, L., Desimone, M., Feris, R., Kjeldsen, R., Lu, M., Mercier, C., Milite, C., Russo, S., et al.: Video analytics in urban environments. In: 2009 Advanced Video and Signal Based Surveillance, pp. 128–133 (2009)
3. Lowe, D.D.G.: Distinctive image features from scale-invariant keypoints. International Journal of Computer Vision 60(2), 91–110 (2004)
4. Barnea, D.I., Silverman, H.F.: A Class of Algorithms for Fast Digital Image Registration. IEEE Transactions on Computers C-21(2), 179–186 (1972)
5. Lucas, B., Kanade, T.: An iterative image registration technique with an application to stereo vision. In: International Joint Conference on Artificial Intelligence, vol. 3, pp. 674–679 (1981)
6. Bergen, J.R., Anandan, P., Hanna, J., Hingorani, R.: Hierarchical Model-Based Motion Estimation. In: Sandini, G. (ed.) ECCV 1992. LNCS, vol. 588, pp. 237–252. Springer, Heidelberg (1992)
7. Black, M., Jepson, A.: Eigentracking: Robust matching and tracking of articulated objects using a view-based representation. International Journal of Computer Vision 26(1), 63–84 (1998)
8. Cootes, T., Edwards, G., Taylor, C.: Active appearance models. IEEE Transactions on Pattern Analysis and Machine Intelligence 23(6), 681–685 (2001)
9. Ross, D.A., Lim, J., Lin, R.-S., Yang, M.-H.: Incremental Learning for Robust Visual Tracking. International Journal of Computer Vision 77(1-3), 125–141 (2007)
10. Gai, J., Stevenson, R.: Studentized Dynamical System for Robust Object Tracking. IEEE Transactions on Image Processing 20(1), 186–199 (2011)
11. Isard, M., Blake, A.: Condensation - conditional density propagation for visual tracking. International Journal of Computer Vision 29(1), 5–28 (1998)
12. Matthews, I., Ishikawa, T., Baker, S.: The template update problem. IEEE Transactions on Pattern Analysis and Machine Intelligence 26(6), 810–815 (2004)
13. Silveira, G., Malis, E.: Unified direct visual tracking of rigid and deformable surfaces under generic illumination changes in grayscale and color images. International Journal of Computer Vision 89(1), 84–105 (2010)
14. Comaniciu, D., Ramesh, V., Meer, P.: Kernel-based object tracking. IEEE Transactions on Pattern Analysis and Machine Intelligence 25(5), 564–577 (2003)
15. Lim, J., Ross, D., Lin, R.: Incremental learning for visual tracking. Advances in Neural Information Processing 17(1), 793–800 (2004)

16. Jepson, A., Fleet, D., El-Maraghi, T.: Robust online appearance models for visual tracking. IEEE Transactions on Pattern Analysis and Machine Intelligence 25(10), 1296–1311 (2003)
17. Adam, A., Rivlin, E., Shimshoni, I.: Robust Fragments-based Tracking using the Integral Histogram. In: 2006 IEEE Computer Society Conference on Computer Vision and Pattern Recognition (CVPR 2006), vol. 1, pp. 798–805. IEEE (2006)
18. Ning, J., Zhang, L., Zhang, D., Wu, C.: Robust Object Tracking Using Joint Color-Texture Histogram. International Journal of Pattern Recognition and Artificial Intelligence 23(07), 1245 (2009)

# Combined Online and Offline Information for Tracking Facial Feature Points

Xin Wang[1], Yequn Zhang[2], and Chunlei Chai[3]

[1] College of Computer Science and Technology,
Zhejiang University of Technology,
Hangzhou, China
[2] College of Information Engineering,
Zhejiang University of Technology,
Hangzhou, China
[3] College of Computer Science and Technology,
Zhejiang University,
Hangzhou, China
xinw@zjut.edu.cn, zhangyequnsun@163.com, dishengchai@126.com

**Abstract.** This paper proposes a novel real-time facial feature points tracking method. A 3D geometric face model is used to give a robust tracking which includes offline information that the movement constraints of facial feature points in 3D space. The iterative frame-to-frame tracking method with Gabor wavelet is used to give a high accuracy which is robust to homogeneous illumination changing and affine deformation of the face image. The former tracking method based offline information and the latter tracking method based on online information are integrated with the bundle adjustment method. We compare our method with three other typical methods. The experimental results show that it can be used for robust, real-time and wide-angle facial feature tracking.

**Keywords:** Facial Feature, Gabor Wavelet, 3D Tracking, Bundle Adjustment.

## 1    Introduction

Real-time and automatic facial feature points tracking is a fundamental and challenging problem in computer vision research area. To solve that problem, many researchers have proposed various approaches, which can be generally sorted into top-down and bottom-up approaches [1]. The top-down approach is based on the image features of all the facial organs, and the typical models are Active Appearance Models (AAM) proposed by Cootes et al [2][3], Direct Appearance Models(DAM) proposed by Hou et al [4]. The bottom-up approach tracks part of facial organs, combines with the position relation between the organs, and optimize the tracking results further. Typically, Jin Cheng et al [1] proposed the bottom-up facial feature localization, and RS Feris et al [5] proposed facial feature tracking method based on Gabor wavelet networks.

C.-Y. Su, S. Rakheja, H. Liu (Eds.): ICIRA 2012, Part I, LNAI 7506, pp. 196–206, 2012.
© Springer-Verlag Berlin Heidelberg 2012

The previous types of facial feature tracking methods [1-7] only used 2D facial image information. For example, ASM(Active Shape Model) model [6] used the 2D facial global shape information and feature points' local texture information; AAM model [2] used the 2D facial global shape information and texture information; the methods based on Gabor wavelet make use of all the texture information around the facial feature points. In fact, except the nearby area of the eyes and mouth, the movement of every facial feature point is approximately equal to the movement of 3D point of rigid body, and the constraint relationships between these points remain unchanged. 3D constraint relationships between facial feature points can be used to solve the problem of tracking points loss when the rotation angle is too large. In this paper, by referring to ideas of 3D tracking algorithm based on offline and online information proposed by Vacchetti L. et al [10], we propose a facial feature tracking method based on 3D model and Gabor wavelet. According to the characters of real-time facial tracking, we use a tracking algorithm based-on Gabor wavelet [8] in frame-by-frame tracking , and an algorithm proposed in the algorithm [10-12] in the 3D model aided tracking.The two tracking methods are integrated to get the final tracking result by bundle adjustment.

## 2    Flowchart of the Tracking Algorithm

The method proposes in this paper is illustrated in Fig.1, from which we can see that the tracking algorithm is mainly composed of three parts: construction of initial key frame, frame-by-frame tracking based on Gabor wavelet, and integrated tracking based on 3D model.

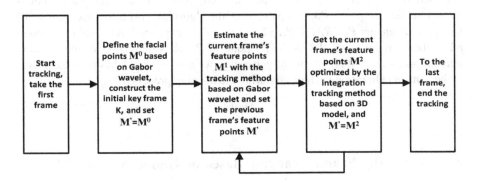

**Fig. 1.** Flowchart of the tracking method

## 3    Construction of the Initial Key Frame

There are 14 feature points used in this paper as shown in Fig.2 (a). These points are obvious features of the human face, so we can locate the corresponding points better by the trained Gabor wavelet Jets. The specific matching method will be described in the next section. As the Candide-1 facial model is simple, 3D vertices of grid has a clear geometric meaning, we make it as generalized 3D facial model in this paper, named as $F$. Between the 3D vertices of $F$ and the 2D facial feature points $p2$, we can easily build one-to-one correspondence as shown in Figure 2 (b).

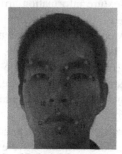     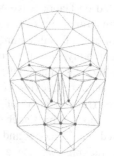

(a)   2D facial feature points          (b)   3D facial feature points

**Fig. 2.** 2D&3D facial feature points

In order to get the height-width ratio of the face in current frame, this paper adopts a face detection method proposed by Paul Viola et al [13] to quickly obtain facial area. Based on the ratio, this paper performs a global scaling transformation on $F$ to make the ratio of $F$ the same with the ratio of the current face. Finally, in order to align $F$ with the 2D feature points $p2$, we use the piece-wise affine warping method to deform $F$, so we can make the 3D facial organs distribution be consistent with 2D facial organs' distribution in current frame.

After above deformation, $F$ is a novel 3D face model whose facial point's distribution is very similar with 2D face structure. Based on 2D facial feature points $p2$ and 3D feature points $P3$, this paper uses the algorithm [14] to get the current 3D face pose parameter $P_k=[R_k|T_k]$. $P_k$, $p2$ and $P3$ can be expressed as formula (1), where $p2^i$ is the $i$th point of $p2$, $P3^i$ is the $i$th point of $P3$, $A$ is the matrix of the camera's internal parameters. Without loss of generality, we assume that $A$ has been calculated in the camera calibration unchanged during the tracking process.

$$p2^i = AP_k P3^i \tag{1}$$

## 4     Frame-by-Frame Tracking Based on Gabor Wavelet

The Gabor function, proposed by Dennis Gabor, has obvious biological sense for its structure is similar to the structure of the function of the retinal cells' perception area, which is widely applied to the field of computer vision. In fact, Gabor function is the product of Trigonometric Function and Gaussian Function. 1D Gabor function expression is as follows:

$$W(t, t_0, \omega) = e^{-\sigma(t-t_0)^2} e^{i\omega(t-t_0)} \tag{2}$$

Corresponding wavelet transformation is defined as:

$$C(x(t))(t_0, \omega) = \int_{-\infty}^{+\infty} x(t) W(t, t_0, \omega) dt \tag{3}$$

We consider the 2D Gabor function as the Generating function of the wavelet transform, and the 2D Gabor function is defined as formula (4).

$$W(x, y, \theta, \lambda, \varphi, \sigma, \gamma) = e^{-\frac{x'^2 + \gamma^2 y'^2}{2\sigma^2}} \cos(2\pi \frac{x'}{\lambda} + \varphi) \tag{4}$$

$$x' = x\cos\theta + y\sin\theta .$$
$$y' = -x\sin\theta + y\cos\theta .$$

Where $\theta$ is the orientation of 2D Gabor, $\lambda$ is the wavelength of 2D Gabor, $\varphi$ is the phrase of 2D Gabor, $\sigma$ is the radius of Gaussian function, $\gamma$ is the height-width ratio of 2D Gabor. The different combinations of the five parameters above constitute different 2D Gabor wavelet function. The experiment results [9] indicate that the different combination of $\theta$ and $\lambda$ can express the 2D facial feature information enough. We assign 8 directions to $\theta$, 5 values to $\lambda$, so the Gabor wavelet functions have 40 different combinations of Gabor wavelet function. With these functions, the Wavelet transform can be performed in the facial feature points in image. As a result, each image point can obtain 40 plurals, namely 80 parameters which are so-called Gabor Jet [9]. The Gabor Jet can express the facial points feature well.

For the initial positioning problem of facial feature points, during the training process, we calculate the Jet set $S$ of each facial feature points in various typical cases. When tracking the first video frame, namely constructing the initial key frame, we can detect the face area by the method proposed by Paul Viola et al [13]. In this area, according to the experience of facial organs' distribution, we can roughly get every feature point's distribution area $R$. We calculate every point's Jet in the $R$, comparing it with the trained Jet set $S$, and the most matching point is the most likely facial feature point.

Supposing that we are aware of the facial feature points' location of the frame $i$, according to the formula (5) about the Jet similarity of phase correlation proposed in the work [9], if there are two points making the formula obtain the maximum value, we can conclude that the two points are most probably the same point of the two consecutive frames. Based on the conclusion above, if we want to detect the feature point's location in frame $i+1$, we can detect it in the frame $i$. Assuming that the center of the circle is the feature point, and that the length of the radius is 8 pixels. Thus what we should do is to detect the most similar point to Jet of the previous frame in the circle so as to get the point in the frame $i+1$.

$$S_\phi(J, J') = \frac{\sum_j a_j a'_j \cos(\phi_j - \phi'_j - d k_j)}{\sqrt{\sum_j a_j^2 \sum_j a_j'^2}} \tag{5}$$

There are various search strategies in circular area. Experiments show that the exhaustive method has minimum error. So we adopt the exhaustive method while it costs lots of time. To achieve real-time tracking, we make use of the following approximate equation (6) to accelerate the calculation

$$a' \approx a \bullet . \phi' \approx \phi + k \cdot d \tag{6}$$

Where $\alpha$ and $\phi$ are the amplitude and the phase angle of the jet of the feature point $P$ in the frame $i$. $\alpha'$ and $\phi'$ are the amplitude and the phase angle of the evaluated point $P'$. $d$ is the distance vector between $P$ and $P'$, $k$ is a vector of the same direction as Gabor function and of the same amplitude equal to trigonometric frequency. $d$ and $k$ can be calculated as follows:

$$d = \begin{bmatrix} dx \\ dy \end{bmatrix} \bullet k = \begin{bmatrix} \dfrac{2\pi \cos\theta}{\lambda} \\ \dfrac{2\pi \sin\theta}{\lambda} \end{bmatrix} . \tag{7}$$

# 5     Integration of Tracking Based on 3D Model

With the frame-by-frame tracking method based on Gabor wavelet, we can use of the facial feature points in frame $i$ to predict the feature points in frame $i+1$. Although the frame-by-frame method based on Gabor wavelet can overcome the light changes, pose changes and other effects, to obtain some good tracking results, it only used the information in previous frame while not taking advantage of the 3D face global constraint information. According to the conclusions in the reference [15], only using spatial and temporal continuity information between successive frames to track often leads to error accumulation, and gradually causes the drift. This problem can be resolved by integrating the information of the key frame information of object. The information of the key frame used in this paper is the information of the key frame K stored in the initial construction stage.

Supposed we have tracked to the frame $i$, then the 2D facial points' information and 3D face pose parameters of each frame before frame $i$ is already known. The face pose parameters of frame $i-1$ is $P_{i-1}=[R_{i-1}|T_{i-1}]$, and we can define a planar homographic transformation $H$ based on $P_{i-1}$ and $P_k$. Using the $H$ we can transform the 2D image of key frame face into a similar face images with the frame $i-1$, which also is the human face image similar with the 2D face image in frame $i$. Matrix $H$ is defined as formula (8):

$$H = A(\delta R - \frac{\delta t \cdot \vec{n}'^{T}}{d'})A^{-1} . \tag{8}$$

Where $\delta R = R_{i-1} R_k^{T}$; $\delta t = -R_{i-1} R_k^{T} T_k + T_{i-1}$;

$$\vec{n}'^{T} = R_k \bar{n};\, ; d' = d - T_k^{T}(R_k \bar{n}) \cdot \tag{9}$$

This paper takes the 30 pixels × 30 pixels image area around each facial points as image block before transformation. These points not in any of those blocks have no value, set consistently as pure black, and the whole image is marked as $I_k$. After each pixel in $I_k$ is transformed by $H$, we get a new image $I'_{i-1}$. $I'_{i-1}$ is actually constituted by 14 sub-regions of 30 pixels × 30 pixels image. Each sub-region corresponds to a facial feature points which is marked as $I'_{i-1} = \{R_j | j=1,2,\ldots,14\}$. In this paper, the method to use the key frame information $K$ is to find a sub-region $R'_j$, within a 50 pixels × 50 pixels region, which is most similar to $R_j$ in the frame of $i$. $R'_j$ and $R_j$ have the same center point. The center of $R'_j$ is the $j$th facial feature points based on the key frame information. Specific sub-region similarity calculation method is the normalized cross correlation [16] as criteria for the similarity measure.

The 14 facial feature points based on key frame information $K$ are marked as $P^k_j$.

$$P^k_i = \{p^k_i(j) \mid j=1,2,\ldots,14\}. \tag{10}$$

$P^k_j$ contains the constraints information on 3D face, and the next step we should combine the facial feature points $P^k_j$ tracked by key frame $K$ with the facial feature points $P^g_i$ tracked by Gabor wavelet, removing the error data, making the tracking results smooth and eliminating error accumulation.

As for the integration of two point sets, we use bundle adjustment [17], which is frequently used in the field of 3D reconstruction. We aim to find 3D facial pose parameters $P_i$ which can minimize remapping error. We mark the remapping error as $r_i$, which is defined as follows:

$$r_i = \sum_{j=1}^{28} \rho_{\text{TUK}} \left( \left\| m^j_i - \phi(P_i, M^{f(j)}_i) \right\|^2 \right). \tag{11}$$

where $m^j_i \in \{P^k_i \cup P^g_i\}$, $M^{f(j)}_i$ is 3D point in $F$ corresponding to $m^j_i$, $f(j) = \begin{cases} j & ; \text{ if } j \leq 14 \\ j-14; & \text{if } j > 14 \end{cases}$, $P_i$ is 3D face pose parameters for the frame $i$ estimated. Function $\rho_{\text{TUK}}$ is Tukey M-Estimator, with which the mismatched points can be removed. The $\phi$ is a mapping function which uses the pose parameters to map the 3D facial point $M^{f(j)}_i$ to 2D feature points. Considering the temporal and spatial continuity between successive frames, this paper designs objective optimization function as formula (12):

$$g(P_i, P_{i-1}) = \min_{P_i, P_{i-1}} (r_i + r_{i-1}). \tag{12}$$

As for such an optimization problem, using the Levenberg-Marquardt algorithm [15], we can quickly get the solution $P_i$ of the most optimal function. The optimized facial feature points set $p2'$ of the frame $i$ can be directly obtained based on the optimal solution $P_i$, the map function $\phi$ and facial feature points $P3$. $p2'$ is the final facial feature point tracking results in frame $i$.

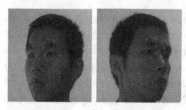

Fig. 3. Moving in the left-right direction    Fig. 4. Moving in the up-down direction

Fig. 5. Face swaying in the plane    Fig. 6. Changes of facial expression

## 6    Experiment Results

In the phrase of training Gabor wavelet Jets library, face image databases of 100 human were used with different skin colors, illumination, facial expressions and pose properties.

In the aspect of tracking speed, this method can achieve 25fps. In the aspect of tracking effect, Figure 3 shows the case of left and right rotation around the face, figure 4 shows the case of up and down rotation around the face, figure 5 shows the case of before and after move of the face, figure 6 shows the case of facial expression changed.

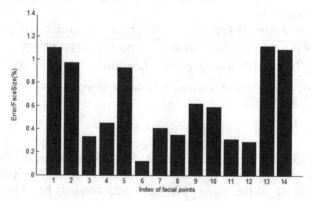

Fig. 7. Localization error of each point

In ordinary laboratory light environment, typically the above five types of facial movement, this paper collects 100 motion data of five different people in each type of movement. For this $5 \times 5 \times 100$ frame data, the average statistics error between the results of this paper's tracking method and the ideal location is shown in Figure 7. Abscissa axis of Figure 7 is 14 individual facial feature point index. The vertical axis of figure 7 is the average face positioning error of each feature point relative to the size of face.

In addition, we selected 10 typical video data from the UCSD/Honda face video database [21] to validate the algorithm's tracking performance. The key frame sequence diagrams of tracking results with wearing glasses, a beard, a little hair shelter and other special circumstances are shown in Figure 8. It can be seen that in glasses, beard, a little hair shelter and other cases, our method can still track each feature point accurately. Figure 8(d) also shows some examples of the failure to track, mainly because of face rotation angle being too large or facial expression rapid changing.

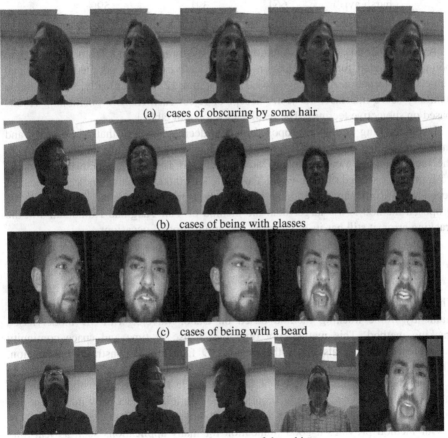

(a)   cases of obscuring by some hair

(b)   cases of being with glasses

(c)   cases of being with a beard

(d)   cases of unsuccessful tracking

**Fig. 8.** Tracking results in special cases

**Table 1.** Results on UCSD/Honda database

| Video Name | Total frame number | Accept frame number | Accept ratio |
|---|---|---|---|
| behzad.avi | 384 | 261 | 68% |
| james.avi | 314 | 220 | 70% |
| joey.avi | 336 | 235 | 73% |
| yokoyama.avi | 329 | 247 | 75% |
| ming.avi | 390 | 254 | 65% |
| saito.avi | 437 | 253 | 58% |
| fuji.avi | 291 | 230 | 79% |
| danny.avi | 368 | 305 | 83% |
| rakesh.avi | 390 | 335 | 86% |
| harsh.avi | 664 | 391 | 59% |
| hector.avi | 419 | 314 | 75% |

As UCSD/Honda does not have the frame-by-frame Ground Truth facial feature point data needed for the evaluation of the effectiveness. We adopted the artificial subjective evaluation method proposed in literature [22]. Specifically, with a simple auxiliary score interface, the tester accept or reject each frame's positioning results based on subjective feelings. The results are shown in table 1.

In the tracking error, the proposed method decreases 8% of that of Cootes's, and increases 6% that of the Yan Tang and Romdhani's. In computing time efficiency, in the same computing environment (Intel Core2 Duo T5870), this method can handle 25 frames per second of data, while Yan Tang's method can only handle 7 frames per second, and Romdhani method can handle only 2 frames per second. Thus, while the proposed method is 6% larger than the method of Yan Tang and Romdhani's in the tracking error, it still has its advantages and application of occasions.

# 7    Conclusion

This paper proposes a novel facial feature points tracking method that combined frame by frame tracking method based on Gabor wavelet with 3D model based tracking method. This method not only makes use of time and space continuity between frames, but also uses the human 3D face global constraint information. Thereby avoiding the jitter and drift phenomenon.

Experimental results showed that for large-angle face posse transformation, our method still has a good tracking accuracy, and can tolerate face yaw movement and pitch movement in the range of 45 degrees, roll movement of 60 degrees.

Our method provides a good foundation for many applications such as real-time 3D face recognition, face-based intelligent human computer interaction et al. Our method can be used to track not only facial points but also other rigid body objects in real-time tracking.

**Acknowledgments:** This work was supported by Natural Science Foundation of Zhejiang Province (Y1110882, Y1110688, R1110679), Department of Education of Zhejiang Province (Y200907765, Y201122434), and Doctoral Fund of Ministry of Education of China (20113317110001).

# References

1. Jin, C., Bu, J.-J., Chen, H., et al.: Human face detection and feature tracking in a bottom-up way. Journal of Zhejiang University (Engineering Science) 42(5), 794–799 (2008)
2. Cootes, T., Walker, K., Taylor, C.: View-based active appearance models. In: Proceedings of Fourth IEEE International Conference on Automatic Face and Gesture Recognition, Grenoble, French, pp. 227–232 (2000)
3. Chen, S.Y., Zhang, J., Guan, Q., Liu, S.: Detection and amendment of shape distortions based on moment invariants for active shape models. IET Image Processing 5(3), 273–285 (2011)
4. Hou, X., Li, S., Zhan, G.H., et al.: Direct appearance models. In: Proceedings of IEEE Computer Society Conference on Computer Vision and Pattern Recognition(CVPR 2001), Hawaii, pp. 828–833 (2001)
5. Feris, R.S., Cesar Jr., R.M.: Tracking Facial Features Using Gabor Wavelet Networks. In: Proceedings of XIII Brazilian Symposium on Computer Graphics and Image Processing, Gramado, pp. 22–27 (2000)
6. Li, Y., Lai, J.-H., Yuen, P.-C.: Multi-Template ASM and Its Application in Facial Feature Points Detection. Journal of Computer Research and Development 41(1), 133–140 (2007)
7. Duan, H., Cheng, Y.-M., Wang, Y.-X., et al.: Tracking Facial Feature Points Using Kanade-Lucas-Tomasi Approach. Journal of Computer-Aided Design & Computer Graphics 16(3), 279–283 (2004)
8. Yan, J.-G., Pan, L.-D.: Tracking Facial Feature with Gabor Wavelet. Computer Applications 24(7), 50–51 (2004)
9. Wiskott, L., Fellous, J.M., Kruger, N., et al.: Face Recognition by Elastic Bunch Graph Matching. IEEE Transaction on Pattern Analysis and Machine Intelligence 19(7), 775–779 (1997)
10. Vacchetti, L., Lepetit, V., Fua, P.: Stable real-time 3D tracking using online and offline information. IEEE Transactions on Pattern Analysis and Machine Intelligence 26(10), 1385–1391 (2004)
11. Chen, S.Y., Wang, Z.J.: Acceleration Strategies in Generalized Belief Propagation. IEEE Transactions on Industrial Informatics 8(1), 41–48 (2012)
12. Chen, S., Zhang, J.H., Li, Y.F., Zhang, J.W.: A Hierarchical Model Incorporating Segmented Regions and Pixel Descriptors for Video Background Subtraction. IEEE Transactions on Industrial Informatics 8(1), 118–127 (2012)
13. Viola, P., Jones, M.: Rapid Object Detection Using a Boosted Cascade of Simple Features. In: Proceedings of 2001 IEEE Computer Society Conference on Computer Vision and Pattern Recognition( CVPR 2001), Hawaii, pp. 511–518 (2001)
14. Dementhon, D.F., Davis, L.S.: Model-Based Object Pose in 25 Lines of Code. International Journal of Computer Vision 15(1-2), 123–141 (1995)
15. Vacchetti, L., Lepetit, V., Fua, P.: Fusing Online and Offline Information for Stable 3D Tracking in Real-time. In: Proceedings of 2003 IEEE Computer Society Conference on Computer Vision and Pattern Recognition(CVPR 2003), Wisconsin, vol. 2, pp. 241–248 (2003)

16. Cross Correlation [EB/OL], http://en.wikipedia.org/wiki/Cross-correlation#Normalized_cross-correlation (May 31, 2009)
17. Triggs, B., McLauchlan, P., Hartley, R., et al.: Bundle Adjustment-A Modern Synthesis. In: Proceedings of International Workshop on Vision Algorithms (ICCV 1999), pp. 298–372 (1999)
18. Chen, S.: Kalman Filter for Robot Vision: a Survey. IEEE Transactions on Industrial Electronics 59(11), 4409–4420 (2012)
19. Chen, S.Y., Tong, H., Cattani, C.: Markov models for image labeling. Mathematical Problems in Engineering 2012, AID 814356, 18pages (2012)
20. William, H.P., Brian, P.F., Saul, A.T., et al.: Numerical Recipes in C, 2nd edn. Cambridge University Press
21. Lee, K.C., Ho, J., Yang, M.H., Kriegman, D.: Visual tracking and recognition using probabilistic appearance manifolds. Computer Vision and Image Understanding 99(3), 303–331 (2005)
22. Song, G., Ai, H.-Z., Xu, G.-Y.: Texture Constrained Facial Point Tracking. Journal of Software 15(11), 1607–1615 (2004)

# Extracting Minimalistic Corridor Geometry
# from Low-Resolution Images

Yinxiao Li*, Vidya N. Murali*, and Stanley T. Birchfield

Department of Electrical and Computer Engineering,
Clemson University, USA
{yinxial,vmurali,stb}@clemson.edu

**Abstract.** We propose a minimalistic corridor representation consisting of the orientation line (center) and the wall-floor boundaries (lateral limit). The representation is extracted from low-resolution images using a novel combination of information theoretic measures and gradient cues. Our study investigates the impact of image resolution upon the accuracy of extracting such a geometry, showing that accurate centerline and wall-floor boundaries can be estimated even in texture-poor environments with images as small as $16 \times 12$. In a database of 7 unique corridor sequences for orientation measurements, less than 2% additional error was observed as the resolution of the image decreased by 99%. One of the advantages of working at such resolutions is that the algorithm operates at hundreds of frames per second, or equivalently requires only a small percentage of the CPU.

**Keywords:** Low-Resolution, Robot Navigation, Geometry Estimation.

## 1 Introduction

Psychological studies have shown that while driving or walking human beings tend to focus their eye gaze on the direction of the goal and also along tangent points in roadways/hallways to steer toward. Land and Tatler in their classic paper [5] speak of the tendency of race car drivers to steer along the direction of the goal while allowing the bend points (tangent points) to hold their gaze intermittently to judge the future steering angle. In indoor environments, this phenomenon loosely translates into pedestrians having a tendency to look near wall-floor boundaries when nearing a corner.

While working on visual sensing for robot navigation/exploration, the question of what resolution is sufficient for basic navigation tasks is an inherent question. Psychological studies have shown that the human visual system does not require high-resolution images to ascertain information about the environment for basic navigation. The "selective degradation hypothesis", developed by Leibowitz [7], states that some visual abilities such as vehicle steering and speed control remain relatively easy despite loss in visual acuity and color vision. Torralba *et al.* [13,14] in their recent work have presented convincing psychovisual evidence that $32 \times 24$ bit images are sufficient for humans to successfully performs basic scene classification, object segmentation, and

---

* Indicates equal contribution.

C.-Y. Su, S. Rakheja, H. Liu (Eds.): ICIRA 2012, Part I, LNAI 7506, pp. 207–216, 2012.

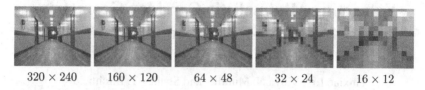

$$320 \times 240 \qquad 160 \times 120 \qquad 64 \times 48 \qquad 32 \times 24 \qquad 16 \times 12$$

**Fig. 1.** A typical corridor image at five different resolutions. Even at $32 \times 24$ resolution, it is easy to see the structure of the corridor. For display purposes, the downsampled images were upsampled to ensure that they are all at the same size.

identification. The work of Tovar *et al.* [15] and O'Kane and LaValle [11] focuses on identifying simple and generic solutions to basic robot exploration/navigations tasks, with emphasis on minimalistic representations.

Motivated by this idea, we describe a system to develop a minimalistic structural representation of an indoor corridor for basic navigation tasks by a mobile robot. We also show that the recovered critical steering information does not degrade significantly with reduction in resolution. The corridor is represented by three lines: the center of the corridor, the left wall-floor boundary, and the right wall-floor boundary. While in theory the center line is redundant (it is simply the vertical line passing through the intersection of the two wall-floor boundary lines), it is helpful to keep it distinct, particularly when the robot is not looking straight down the corridor. To detect this representation, we combine and extend two previous approaches. In previous work, Murali and Birchfield presented the use of ceiling lights for determining the center of the corridor using low-resolution techniques [10]. We extend this work by using other metrics like maximum entropy and maximum symmetry to estimate the center of the corridor when ceiling lights are not visible. Li and Birchfield [8] deveoped a method for extracting wall-floor boundaries for indoor environments that is much more computationally efficient than previous approaches to perform geometric reasoning on images [4,6]. We extend this work by detecting wall-floor boundaries of typical indoor office environments using low-resolution images. Fig. 1 shows a typical indoor corridor image varying from high resolution to low resolution, from which it can be seen that structural information in the scene is visually discernible even at very low resolutions.

## 2   Orientation Line Estimation

We model the structure of a corridor by three lines in the image. A vertical line indicates the orientation line, or centerline, of the corridor, which passes through the vanishing point. The wall-floor boundary is then captured by two diagonal lines that meet at the same point on the orientation line. (As mentioned above, the vertical line is redundant in theory but helps in the case when both diagonal lines are not visible.) Our approach consists of two steps: First we estimate the orientation line in the image by combining multiple cues, then we estimate the wall-floor boundary.

In this section we describe the orientation line estimation. Our approach is adapted from the work done by Murali and Birchfield [10], which uses the median of bright pixels (ceiling lights), maximum entropy, and maximum symmetry measures in the corridor image to determine its center and therefore the orientation. This approach has several advantages over existing techniques: It is simple, computationally efficient, and yields good results even for low-resolution images.

## 2.1 Median of Bright Pixels

The ceiling lights, which are usually symmetric with respect to the main corridor axis, provide an important cue. When lights are not in the center of the corridor, we can use the $k$-means algorithm to overcome this difficulty, where $k = 2$. The median horizontal position of the brighter of the two regions is calculated, yielding an estimate of the center position. In order to overcome specular reflections of the walls, we use Ullman's formula for local contrast [16]. The horizontal coordinate is transformed to an angle by applying the same scalar factor using the equation $f_l(I) = \psi(\text{med}\{x : (x,y) \in \mathcal{R}_{bright}\})$, where $I$ is the image, $\mathcal{R}_{bright}$ is the set of bright pixels, med is the median, and $\psi = \alpha x$ converts from pixels to degrees, where the factor $\alpha$ is determined empirically. Sample results of orientation line estimation using bright pixels are shown in Fig. 2.

**Fig. 2.** Variation of bright pixels and corresponding orientation estimate in corridor images with resolution of $32 \times 24$

## 2.2 Maximum Entropy

Empirically, entropy is maximum when the camera is pointing down the corridor [10]. The reason for this perhaps surprising result is that such an orientation causes scene surfaces from a variety of depths to be visible, yielding an increase of image information at this orientation. A similar observation has been noted by other researchers in the context of using omnidirectional images [2,3]. We divide the image into overlapping vertical slices and computing the graylevel entropy of the image pixels in each slice. The maximum entropy along the horizontal axis is then used to estimate the orientation. Sample results of orientation line estimation using entropy are shown in Fig. 3.

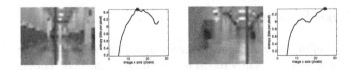

**Fig. 3.** Variation of entropy and corresponding orientation estimate in corridor images with resolution of $32 \times 24$

## 2.3 Symmetry by Mutual Information

Another important feature of corridors is symmetry. One easy way to find symmetry is to compare the two regions using mutual information by calculating entropy. As with entropy, for each horizontal coordinate $x$ a column of pixels $\mathcal{C}(x)$ is considered. The column is divided in half along its vertical center into two columns $\mathcal{C}_L(x)$ and $\mathcal{C}_R(x)$. The normalized graylevel histograms of these two regions are used as the two probability mass functions (PMFs), and the mutual information between the two functions is computed:

$$MI(x) = \sum_{v \in \mathcal{V}} \sum_{w \in \mathcal{V}} p(v, w) \log \frac{p(v, w)}{p_L(v) p_R(w)}, \tag{1}$$

where $p(v, w)$ is the joint PMF of the intensities, and $p_L(v)$ and $p_R(w)$ are the PMFs computed separately of the intensities of the two sides. As before, the orientation estimate is given by $f_s(I) = \psi(\arg\max_x MI(x))$. Sample results of orientation line estimation using mutual information are shown in Fig. 4.

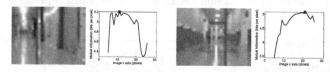

**Fig. 4.** Variation of symmetry and corresponding orientation estimate in corridor images with a resolution of $32 \times 24$

## 2.4 Combining the Metrics

We combine the estimates as a weighted average: $f(I) = \alpha_l(I) f_l(I) + \alpha_h(I) f_h(I) + \alpha_s(I) f_s(I)$. Because of the reliability of the bright pixels, we set $\alpha_l = 0.8$, $\alpha_h = \alpha_s = 0.1$. An example result obtained for different resolutions is shown in Fig. 5.

| $320 \times 240$ | $160 \times 120$ | $64 \times 48$ | $32 \times 24$ | $16 \times 12$ |

**Fig. 5.** The orientation line estimate (vertical green line) for the images shown in Fig. 1. The results remain essentially unchanged from the original resolution down to a resolution of $16 \times 12$

## 3 Wall-Floor Boundary

We use the idea of the floor segmentation method introduced by Li and Birchfield [8] which has been shown to be fairly robust to reflections on the floor. For the seven different resolutions, we compute the minimum acceptance length of the horizontal line segments $l_h$ as $l_h = \log \eta d$, where $d = \sqrt{w^2 + h^2}$ is the length of the diagonal of the image, $w$ and $h$ are the width and height of the image, respectively, $\eta = 5$ is a scaling factor, and $\log$ is the natural logarithm.

According to the floor segmentation method [8], there are three different scores (structure score, homogeneous score, and bottom score) that contribute to the final wall-floor boundary detection. When applying the method to different resolutions, we noticed the structure score always shows the best accuracy, while the bottom score always fails when decreasing the resolution. Therefore, we adapt the weights for the three scores according to the resolution so that $\Phi_{total}(\ell_h)$ is relatively high for line segments near the wall-floor boundary. At the same time, when combining with the orientation line, we compute the intersection of the orientation line and the wall-floor boundary, which is considered as the vanishing point. Then we apply the line-fitting algorithm to both half wall-floor boundaries separated by the vanishing point. Using the slopes and the computed vanishing point, it is easy to find the two terminal points on the image border. Finally, we connect the vanishing point, two terminal points, as well as the orientation line and obtain the structure of the corridor. The sample results are shown in Fig. 10 and the second row of Fig. 6.

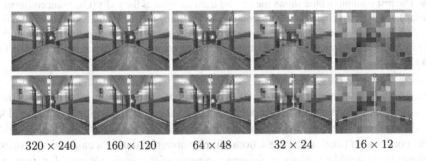

$$320 \times 240 \qquad 160 \times 120 \qquad 64 \times 48 \qquad 32 \times 24 \qquad 16 \times 12$$

**Fig. 6.** TOP: The wall-floor boundary found by the algorithm described in [8] for the different resolution images of Fig. 1. The accuracy degrades slightly until the resolution of $32 \times 24$, after which the errors become more pronounced. BOTTOM: The three-line model estimate of the corridor found by combining the orientation line with the wall-floor boundary, on the same images. As before, the structure of the corridor remains intact even in the resolution of $32 \times 24$, with only slight errors visible in $16 \times 12$.

## 4  Experimental Results

For orientation, we collected data for 4 different buildings, 8 unique corridors (1 training + 7 for testing). For every unique corridor, at equally spaced intervals along the corridor (4.5m), we rotated the robot from $-20°$ to $+20°$ and collected corresponding odometry (heading), laser readings (span of $-90°$ to $+90°$) and images. We ran the entropy detector, light detector, and symmetry detector on the images and compared with ground truth (odometry and/or laser). Since a linear relationship exists between the detected pixel location corresponding to the center of the corridor and the robot orientation as explained in previous sections, we use either the estimate $f_l$ or $(f_h + f_s)/2$.

For wall-floor boundary and corridor reconstruction, we collected data for 11 distinct corridors in 6 different buildings. We drove the robot three times (middle, left, right separated by 0.5 m) along each corridor and collected images along with their

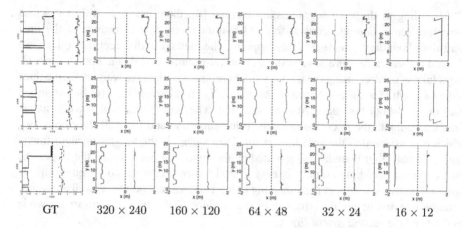

GT          320 × 240     160 × 120     64 × 48      32 × 24      16 × 12

**Fig. 7.** Corridor structure reconstruction from the wall-floor boundary, displayed as a top-down view. The first column in blue shows the ground truth location of the walls (Cartesian conversion of polar laser readings), and the next 5 columns in red show the reconstruction results from the wall-floor boundaries on different resolution images. Each row represents a different run of the robot in the same corridor, with the robot placed at a different lateral position in the corridor for each run.

corresponding laser readings ($-90°$ to $+90°$ sweep). The position of the orientation line with respect to the wall-floor boundaries gives the lateral position in the corridor. The distance between the two end-points in the wall-floor boundary yields the width of the corridor (in pixels). We use a homography obtained during a calibration process to transform to world coordinates. Several examples of the recovered corridor structure are shown in Fig. 7. The robot's position was determined using an image to top-down view calibration procedure utilizing a homography between a square pattern on the floor of the corridor and the image of its four corners. Ground truth was provided by laser readings, which were converted from polar to Cartesian coordinates to yield a top-down measurement of the corridor for every image in the sequence. Using the detected wall-floor boundary and applying a homography to get the top-down structure of the corridor and the lateral position, we achieved the reconstruction shown in Fig. 7. The Normalized Root Mean Square Error (NRMSE) between ground truth (laser) and predicted values of estimated corridor width and lateral position was calculated for each of the 7 resolutions considered ($320 × 240, 160 × 120, 80 × 60, 64 × 48, 32 × 24, 16 × 12$ and $8 × 6$), for three trials in a corridor. The results are shown in Fig. 8.

The parameters for a linear fit between the location of the orientation line and predicted orientation were estimated by using one of the corridors as a training set. Using the trained parameters, the orientations for all the other data for the remaining 7 test corridors ($\theta$) were predicted from the mean pixel locations using the above equations. The Normalized Root Mean Square Error between ground truth (laser) and predicted values of heading was calculated for each of the 7 resolutions considered. The results are shown in Fig. 9.

In Fig. 10 we show a variety of corridors in which our results are successful, including one without ceiling lights, where the result is based only on maximum symmetry

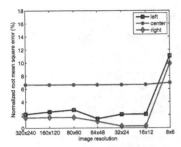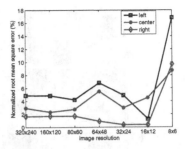

**Fig. 8.** LEFT: NRMSE for estimating the lateral position of the robot for three runs in a single corridor. The structure was accurately captured in all three cases. RIGHT: Mean NRMSE for the estimation of the corridor width. There is not much difference in estimation error rates across the different resolutions, and in fact the error drops in some cases for $32 \times 24$ and $16 \times 12$ sizes due to the removal of noise and artifacts by downsampling.

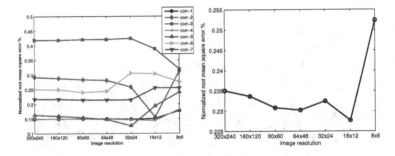

**Fig. 9.** Minimalistic geometric information is obtained by the algorithm at very low image resolutions. LEFT: NRMSE for all 7 test corridors. RIGHT: Mean NRMSE for the corridors. The orientation estimation error remains relatively stable across different image resolutions. In fact, the error drops for a few corridors at $32 \times 24$ and $16 \times 12$, primarily due to the fact that downsampling removes artifacts such as reflections and other noise on the walls and floor.

and maximum entropy.[1] In addition, empirically we found that when approaching the end of a corridor, the angle between the two wall-floor boundary lines increases toward 180°, thus providing some indication of the distance to the end of the corridor. Fig. 11 shows normalized error in continuous frames with resolutions of $320 \times 240$ and $32 \times 24$. We also found that entropy decreases sharply when the robot reaches the end of the corridor [10]. Therefore, these could be used to detect the end of a corridor.

Estimating the pose of the robot or the orientation of the robot in a typical indoor corridor is one of the necessary tasks for robot exploration/navigation. While many authors have approached this problem by estimating vanishing points in a corridor [1,9,12], we have discovered that the approach of clustering detected lines performs poorly in low-resolution and textureless images because lines are not easily detected in such images. A more recent approach by Kong *et al.* [4] approaches the problem similarly but uses

---

[1] See http://www.ces.clemson.edu/~stb/research/
minimalistic_corridor for videos of the results.

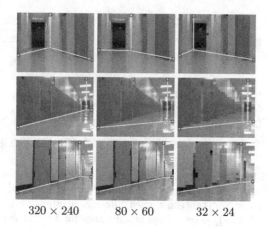

$$320 \times 240 \qquad 80 \times 60 \qquad 32 \times 24$$

**Fig. 10.** Additional results for other corridors, including one without ceiling lights

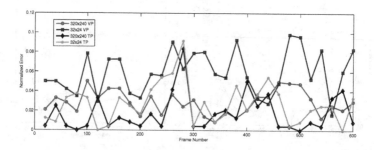

**Fig. 11.** Normalized error of vanishing point (VP) and terminal points (TP) in *Sirrine Hall* video sequence compared with ground truth. Results do not change significantly when 99% of the pixels are discarded.

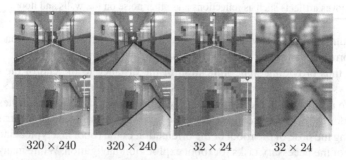

$$320 \times 240 \qquad 320 \times 240 \qquad 32 \times 24 \qquad 32 \times 24$$

**Fig. 12.** Comparison between our results (three yellow lines) and those of Kong *et al.* [4] (pink region). Our algorithm achieves more accurate estimation of both the orientation line and the wall-floor boundary in indoor scenes, particularly at low resolutions.

texture orientation rather than explicit line detection. In their approach, Gabor filters yield texture estimates, and an adaptive voting scheme allows pixels to decide the confidence of an orientation. Not only is their approach much more computationally intensive than ours, but with indoor low-resolution images the results are significantly less accurate. See Fig. 12 for some examples.

## 5 Conclusion

We have proposed an algorithm to extract a minimalistic geometric representation of a typical indoor corridor environment using low resolution images. Motivated by the "selective degradation hypothesis", our approach exploits the redundancy of image information in order to extract useful information for mobile robotic tasks with minimal processing. Our algorithm combines two ideas: extracting the wall-floor boundary by combining intensity edges and specular reflection removal, and centerline estimation using a combination of information theoretic cues and bright pixel estimation. Previous approaches for these problems have been extended and modified to facilitate low resolution processing. The proposed algorithm was tested on images from several different corridors, showing that the accuracy of the estimation of the orientation line or corridor geometry changed very little even when more than 99% of the original information was discarded by downsampling the image to an extremely low resolution. Our approach can be seen as an exploration into identifying how much information is needed for basic mobile robot tasks such as corridor exploration and navigation. By reducing the resolution required for these basic tasks, the CPU time is freed for other tasks that potentially require higher resolutions and more involved processing.

**Acknowledgments.** The authors greatly acknowledge the support of NSF grant IIS-1017007.

## References

1. Bayramoglu, E., Andersen, N., Kjolstad Poulsen, N., Andersen, J., Ravn, O.: Mobile robot navigation in a corridor using visual odometry. In: International Conference on Advanced Robotics, pp. 1–6 (June 2009)
2. Bonev, B., Cazorla, M., Escolano, F.: Robot navigation behaviors based on omnidirectional vision and information theory. Journal of Physical Agents 1(1), 27–35 (2007)
3. Escolano, F., Bonev, B., Suau, P., Aguilar, W., Frauel, Y., Saez, J., Cazorla, M.: Contextual visual localization: cascaded submap classification, optimized saliency detection, and fast view matching. In: IEEE International Conference on Intelligent Robots and Systems (2007)
4. Kong, H., Audibert, J.Y., Ponce, J.: General road detection from a single image. In: IEEE Conference on Computer Vision and Pattern Recognition (2009)
5. Land, M.F., Tatler, B.W.: Steering with the head: The visual strategy of a racing driver. Current Biology 11(15), 1215–1220 (2001)
6. Lee, D., Hebert, M., Kanade, Y.: Geometric reasoning for single image structure recovery. In: IEEE Computer Society Conference on Computer Vision and Pattern Recognition, CVPR (2009)

7. Leibowitz, H.W., Rodemer, C.S., Dichgans, J.: The independence of dynamic spatial orientation from luminance and refractive error. Perception & Psychophysics 25(2), 75–79 (1979)
8. Li, Y., Birchfield, S.T.: Image-based segmentation of indoor corridor floors for a mobile robot. In: IROS (2010)
9. McLean, G., Kotturi, D.: Vanishing point detection by line clustering. IEEE Transactions on Pattern Analysis and Machine Intelligence 17, 1090–1095 (1995)
10. Murali, V.N., Birchfield, S.T.: Autonomous exploration using rapid perception of low-resolution image information. Autonomous Robots 32(2), 115–128 (2012)
11. O'Kane, J.M., LaValle, S.M.: Almost-sensorless localization. In: Proc. IEEE International Conference on Robotics and Automation (2005)
12. Segvic, S., Ribaric, S.: Determining the absolute orientation in a corridor using projective geometry and active vision. IEEE Transactions on Industrial Electronics 48(3), 696–710 (2001)
13. Torralba, A.: How many pixels make an image? Visual Neuroscience 26(01), 123–131 (2009)
14. Torralba, A., Fergus, R., Freeman, W.T.: 80 million tiny images: A large data set for non-parametric object and scene recognition. IEEE TPAMI 30(11), 1958–1970 (2008)
15. Tovar, B., Guilamo, L., Lavalle, S.M.: Gap navigation trees: Minimal representation for visibility-based tasks. In: Proceedings of the Workshop on the Algorithmic Foundations of Robotics, pp. 11–26 (2004)
16. Ullman, S.: On visual detection of light sources. Biological Cybernetics 21, 205–212 (1976)

# Triangulation-Based Plane Extraction
# for 3D Point Clouds

Tobias Kotthäuser and Bärbel Mertsching

GET Lab., University of Paderborn
Pohlweg 47 - 49, 33098 Paderborn, Germany
{kotthaeuser,mertsching}@get.uni-paderborn.de

**Abstract.** The processing of point clouds for extracting semantic knowledge plays a crucial role in state of the art mobile robot applications. In this work, we examine plane extraction methods that do not rely on additional point features such as normals, but rather on random triangulation in order to allow for a fast segmentation. When it comes to an implementation in this context, typically the following question arises: *RANSAC or Hough transform?* In this paper, we examine both methods and propose a novel plane extraction approach based on the randomized 3D Hough transform. Our main concerns for improvement are extraction time, accuracy, robustness as well as memory consumption.

**Keywords:** Triangulation-based plane extraction, RANSAC, randomized Hough transform.

## 1 Introduction

When deployed in domestic indoor environments, such as offices, hallways and living rooms, it is becoming more and more important for state of the art robotic systems to acquire a semantic understanding of the environment in order to solve context-dependent tasks. Due to the increased availability of affordable and accurate distance measurement sensors, three-dimensional perception mechanisms have gained importance for mobile robot applications. In this work, we are concerned with the processing of unordered point clouds as acquired from actuated laser range finders. In order to gain semantic knowledge from this kind of data, it is instrumental to consult a meaningful abstraction which can be expeditiously established. The topology of interior environments is generally dominated by planar surfaces, most notably wall, floor and ceiling segments. Even objects located within a scene, e.g. table tops, doors and cabinets usually possess highly planar portions. An obvious approach is therefore, to partition points into homogeneous planar surface patches, i.e. to perform a segmentation (see Fig. 1). Approximating planar point segments by their geometric plane representations reduces the amount of data without suffering a loss of information content and accuracy and allows for an efficient post-processing.

Raw points acquired from laser range devices or depth images registered from multiple views occur in high quantities and are usually unordered, that is, there is

C.-Y. Su, S. Rakheja, H. Liu (Eds.): ICIRA 2012, Part I, LNAI 7506, pp. 217–228, 2012.
© Springer-Verlag Berlin Heidelberg 2012

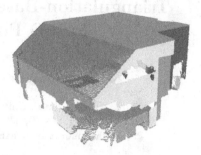

**Fig. 1.** A point cloud (aprox. 1.4 million points) acquired from a cluttered indoor environment and its planar segmentation

no information about point neighborhoods available. Many of the segmentation techniques consulted in literature require the estimation of additional features, such as point normals, which generally involve a huge computational overhead. We would like to avoid additional data structures or preceding sorting approaches as we aim to determine planes without additional costs.

In recently published work involving the extraction of planes, the RANSAC approach found extensive applications. Yet the qualities of the 3D randomized Hough transform hold high potential for its practical application. In the following, we propose enhancements to 3D RHT aiming to compensate for its shortcomings and to further advance its conveniences. Our main concerns are extraction time, accuracy, robustness as well as memory consumption.

The remainder of this paper is organized as follows. Sec. 2 gives an overview of existing plane extraction methods, in Sec. 3 we formulate the extraction problem, briefly introduce the Hough transform and RANSAC for 3D point clouds and propose a set of improvements for the 3D RHT. Finally, we evaluate our enhancements in Sec. 4.

## 2    Related Work

A large number of techniques for the reconstruction of planar surfaces from featureless point clouds has been proposed. A technique that does not rely on additional point features is the Hough transform (HT) [1], an established method for the extraction of curves, especially straight lines from 2D images. Analogously, the HT can be deployed to extract planes from 3D point cloud data. Early applications of the HT for extracting planar surfaces are presented by Vosselman et al. [2],[3] pursuing a reconstruction of building roofs from aerial depth images. Rabbani et al. [4] used the HT to extract cylindrical objects from point clouds. They propose a sequential HT partitioning the detection into two consecutive steps: determining strong hypotheses for the cylinder orientation using a Gaussian sphere and estimating position and radius using a 3D HT. Sarti et al. [5] used the HT for the detection and characterization of planar fractures in rock masses acquired from 3D tomography. A more recent application for the automatic detection of planar roofs from aerial data is presented by [6], providing a brief comparison between the standard HT and RANSAC-based approaches. Borrmann *et al.* [7] adapted an accumulator for a 3D randomized Hough transform (RHT) [8], accomplishing uniform cell sizes in the Hough space, and yielding more precise results.

Another technique is the RANSAC (*Random Sample Consensus*) algorithm [9], a popular method for robust fitting of models in the presence of many data outliers. In the context of 3D point cloud segmentation, RANSAC was widely deployed to extract planes [10] but also other geometric primitives [11] from point clouds. Apart from computational costs a major drawback when deploying RANSAC for plane extraction is that the detection succeeds when a predefined number of inliers fulfilling the model was found. This may lead to the problem that the identified inliers are located within a minimum distance to some plane, but this plane does not necessarily correspond to a real planar surface within the point cloud (false positive). This problem can be tackled by introducing additional constraints such as a comparison of point normals or curvature [12],[13].

Other recent works focus on the plane extraction from 3D cameras, where the point clouds can be assumed to be ordered. Holz *et al.* introduced a fast segmentation for point clouds acquired from RGB-D cameras [14]. They exploit neighborhoods in the image space to access the local neighborhood of points in order to estimate their surface normals. Oehler *et al.* [15] proposed a multi-resolution approach for segmenting 3D point clouds using RANSAC and a standard HT.

## 3   Plane Extraction

### 3.1   Definition and Prerequisites

Particularly in indoor environments the availability of plane representations plays a role in many subsequent processes. The aim of the extraction process is to determine the number of planes, their geometric representations and the association of points to planes. The resulting set of planes should enable the approximation of appearance and significance of the original point set. In the following, the extraction of planes from a given point cloud $P$ is regarded as a segmentation process partitioning $P$ in $N_s$ segments $P_i$, such that

$$P \supset P_i \neq \emptyset, \ P_i \cap P_j = \emptyset, \ \forall i \neq j \in \{1, \ldots, N_s\}. \tag{1}$$

The way in which individual points are arranged into a segment $S_i$ relies on auxiliary information available for each of the points as well as the particular segmentation strategy. Depending on the acquisition technique, various information about the spatial arrangement of points or point features may be available that could be deployed for the extraction of planes.

An alternative method is to determine geometric plane representations by repeatedly applied fitting, for instance, by randomly selecting points. Once a plane representation has been found, the plane inliers can be removed from $P$ and the

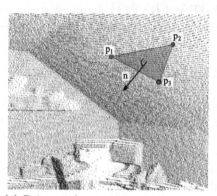

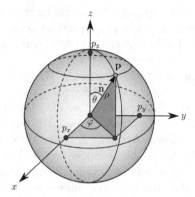

(a) Point triplet spanning a plane sampled from a point cloud and its normal

(b) Normal sphere depicting the spherical coordinates used to describe a Cartesian plane

**Fig. 2.** From points to planes: Sampled points forming a plane (a) and a plane representation in the normal sphere (b)

fitting process re-initiated. To enforce the planar nature of the segment definition of (1), the consistency of each segment can be formulated as maximizing the amount of inliers of each segment

$$\arg\max_{(\mathbf{n},\varrho)} |P^I_{(\mathbf{n},\varrho)}|. \tag{2}$$

The inliers located within a maximum distance $\varepsilon$ to a plane given by a normal vector $\mathbf{n} \in \mathbb{R}^3$ and its distance $\varrho \in \mathbb{R}$ to the origin are defined by

$$P^I_{(\mathbf{n},\varrho)} := \{\mathbf{p} \in P \ : \ |\mathbf{p} \cdot \mathbf{n} - \varrho| < \varepsilon\}. \tag{3}$$

The most prominent techniques of this category are RANSAC and the 3D Hough transform. Their advantage lies in the low requirements with respect to the input data and its features.

## 3.2 Random Access Triangulation

If the local neighborhood of points is unknown, random sampling from the entire point set provides a straightforward strategy to access nearly all areas of the point cloud. However, if applied at one instance without altering the point set, random sampling tends to favor points in areas featuring high point densities, such as surfaces which are located closer to the sensor during acquisition. Consequently, inliers of already identified planes need to be consecutively inhibited or removed from the point cloud in order to raise the chance for points from sparser areas to be selected. The lack of access to local point neighborhoods impedes the use of surface homogeneity criteria to discriminate between points. An alternative to locally approximate the point cloud's surface can be achieved by triangulation. Thereby, we expect that each randomly sampled triple $\mathbf{p}_1, \mathbf{p}_2, \mathbf{p}_3$ defines a plane

$$\varrho = \mathbf{n} \cdot \mathbf{p}_1 = (\mathbf{p}_3 - \mathbf{p}_2) \times (\mathbf{p}_1 - \mathbf{p}_2) \cdot \mathbf{p}_1 \tag{4}$$

conforming to a planar surface actually existing in the cloud (see Fig. 2(a)). Obviously, that claim is not met by every triangle. To enhance the triangulation process we introduce a parameter $\delta_t$ regulating the maximum point-to-point distance for each triangle. An analysis on influences of $\delta_t$ is given in Sec. 4.1.

### 3.3    3D Hough Transform

The Hough transform (HT) can be deployed for the extraction of features having incomplete occurrences. Its main concept is to map points that are considered as part of a required feature onto the combinations of parameters which describe the feature located in that point. In order to determine the occurrence of the parameter combinations, the parameter space is discretized and each cell is individually associated with a counting index. The corresponding data structure is also known as *accumulator*. The counting indices of the cells that are touched by the combination of parameters are incremented respectively. By determining the local maximum from the accumulator, parameters of the respective feature candidates can be extracted.

Several variants of the HT have been proposed for the extraction of diverse models under varying circumstances. The randomized Hough transform (RHT) introduced by [8] pursues a strategy that accommodates the triangulation requirements elaborated in section 3. Instead of successively transforming individual points into an $m$-dimensional parameter space for a curve with $m$ parameters, $m$ points are randomly drawn and mapped into one point in the parameter space. As the access to the point cloud is made solely by random triangulation, the 3D RHT can be regarded as a quantitative evaluation (histogram) of the plane parameters.

Each plane can be characterized by a parameter triple $(\theta, \varphi, \varrho)$, where the inclination angle $\theta \in [-\frac{\pi}{2}, \frac{\pi}{2}]$ denotes the angle between the normal $\mathbf{n}$ and the $z$ coordinate, the azimuth angle $\varphi \in [0, 2\pi)$ is the angle of the projection of $\mathbf{n}$ on the $xy$ plane and the $x$ axis and $\varrho \in \mathbb{R} \geq 0$ the normal vector's length as illustrated in Fig. 2(b). The normal vector $\mathbf{n} \in \mathbb{R}_3$ can then be denoted in a spherical representation yielding the following notation of a plane

$$\varrho = \mathbf{p} \cdot \mathbf{n} = p_x \cdot \cos \varphi \cdot \sin \theta + p_y \cdot \sin \theta \sin \varphi + p_z \cdot \cos \theta \tag{5}$$

Solving eq. (5) for the Cartesian points $p_x, p_y, p_z$ then yields a map into sinusoidal curves in the parameter space.

The applicability of the RHT for the extraction of planes from point clouds was recently ascertained by Bormann *et al.* [7]. Their work provides a detailed evaluation of various HT variants in combination with different accumulator designs. They conclude that a fusion of RHT and a ball accumulator design outperforms other HT-design combinations with respect to runtime and precision. For the implementation of the ball accumulator an irregular discretization of the azimuth angle is adopted, such that each cell on the unit sphere bears the same size with respect to the angular division. This scheme overcomes the discrimination of smaller cells located at the poles of the sphere.

## 3.4  RANSAC

In the presence of outliers, standard fitting approaches, such as least squares, tend to break down as they assume a normal distribution of the errors. The RANSAC algorithm iteratively determines a subset of the input points from which the outliers have been removed and thus, fulfills the given model [9]. In the beginning of each RANSAC iteration step, $n$ data points are randomly sampled from the input data set, assuming that non is an outlier. Here, $n$ corresponds to the number of values that are necessary to calculate the respective model parameters (in the case of a plane model $n = 3$). All points of the input data set whose distance from the model falls below a predefined threshold value support the model and form the *consensus set.*

**Table 1.** Brief comparison between RANSAC and 3D RHT

|              | RANSAC | 3D RHT |
|--------------|:------:|:------:|
| Accuracy     | ⊕      | ⊖      |
| Runtime      | ⊖      | ⊕      |
| Memory Cons. | ⊕      | ⊖      |
| Multiple Models | ⊖   | ⊕      |

At first, the quality of the computed model is derived from the size of the consensus set. The more points support the model, the more likely that the 3 randomly selected values do not contain outliers. Secondly, the respective model parameters are calculated based on the consensus set and evaluate how well the new model fits these points.

These steps - random data sampling, model fitting, determining and evaluating the supporting consensus set - are performed for each iteration. The best consensus set and its corresponding model are stored respectively. The solution can be estimated from the final consensus set, which ideally no longer contains outliers, with the help of traditional balancing methods.

## 3.5  Proposed 3D RHT Enhancements

Without carrying out a sophisticated evaluation, a few general performance characteristics for both methods can be outlined: As the cell size of the RHT is discrete, so are the extracted parameter triples, possibly yielding to discretization errors. As with most HT types, there is a *precision vs. memory consumption* tradeoff, regulated by the accumulator discretization. Due to the relatively large number of accumulator cells, the RHT tends to possess a higher memory consumption than RANSAC. The average runtime of the RHT is potentially lower, as the occurrences of parameter configurations are continuously gathered without respectively examining its inliers. Finally, the RHT can extract multiple models at the same instance, while RANSAC can only extract one. A brief overview of these aspects is summarized in Tab. 1.

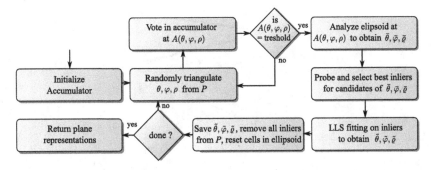

**Fig. 3.** Flowchart visualizing our enhancements of the 3D RHT algorithm

One advantage of the HT over RANSAC is that further characteristics of planes can be derived during the extraction directly from the accumulator. Due to noise and potential discretization errors, the local maxima tend to disperse to ambient accumulator cells as visualized in Fig. 4. To cope with these adverse effects, we extend the extraction of triples to not only withdraw the parameters of one overflowing cell. We further examine the cells contained in an ellipsoidal neighborhood of the overflowing cell, yielding to a more robust description of the plane parameters $(\bar{\theta}, \bar{\varphi}, \bar{\varrho})$ (see Fig. 3). By estimating the dispersion $\sigma$ of the occupied cells contained in the volume of the ellipsoid, we can draw a conclusion about the peculiarities among the 3D points in the corresponding plane. Accordingly, it is possible to determine the distance $\varepsilon$ for each plane individually before extracting its inliers. This enables us to incorporate planes with particular surface properties or distinct sensor characteristics.

A time-critical aspect when dealing with very large point clouds are operations that involve iterations over *all* existing points in $P$. A prominent example is the determination of plane inliers, a crucial operation for plane extraction procedures as described in eq. (3). As to the inlier extraction, we are facing a problem if the correctness of the input planes becomes unforeseeable. If the plane parameters are corrupt, obtaining the inlier set does not contribute to the overall progress while we are losing valuable time. In order to avoid useless calculations for ambiguous plane representations, as they appear for some accumulator configurations, we define a score $\xi = |\tilde{P}^I_{(\mathbf{n},\varrho)}|$ for each plane candidate. $\xi$ is the number of inliers for a randomly sampled and notably smaller set $\tilde{P} \subset P$. A final extraction of inliers is now only applied to the plane candidate having the highest value of $\xi$, or multiple candidate combinations if they score within the same maximum range. This way, corrupt plane parameters can be obviated before an iteration over a large set of points is initiated. Moreover, the probe points $\tilde{P}^I_{(\mathbf{n},\varrho)}$ reconstitute a representation of a plane in $P$. Due to noise in $(\bar{\theta}, \bar{\varphi}, \bar{\varrho})$ the plane parameters may indeed describe a proper plane; its parameters may, however, still be inaccurate. Therefore, we use a linear least squares fitting on the partial inlier set $\tilde{P}^I_{(\mathbf{n},\varrho)}$ in order to enhance the accuracy of the present plane parameters. After fitting, the new parameters $(\tilde{\theta}, \tilde{\varphi}, \tilde{\varrho})$ have been matched

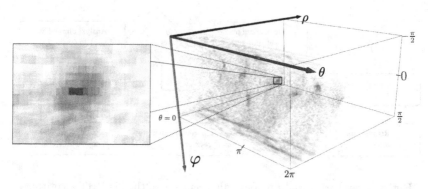

**Fig. 4.** The cells of the spherical 3D accumulator mapped into a Cartesian coordinate frame. Opaque red color is associated to relatively high cell counting indices, transparent blue correspond to low counts (best viewed in color).

to an actual plane existing in the point cloud and therefore, are more likely to accurately describe that plane. Whereas the discretization of the accumulator with fixed boundaries and resolution appears justifiable for angular parameters $\varphi$ and $\theta$, the specification for $\varrho$ is more intricate. Choosing a small range for $\varrho$ provides a memory preserving performance. If our point cloud contains planes that are located further away from the origin, the detection might, however, be severely restricted. Assigning, on the other hand, a wide range for $\varrho$ encourages a comprehensive detection of planes, but requires an extensive use of memory. Examining the occurrence of votes for $\varrho$ reveals a sparse accumulator allocation (compare Fig. 4). In fact, our experiments on real world data revealed a cell usage of less than six percent for a discretization of $(N_\theta = 45, N_\varphi = 90, \Delta \varrho = 0.1)$ and even less than one percent for $(N_\theta = 90, N_\varphi = 180, \Delta \varrho = 0.05)$ while providing minimum range utilization. For this reason, we adapted our accumulator implementation by associative arrays instead of using static pre-allocated cells. We discretize $\varrho$ by means of the given resolution and only store these values in conjunction with the corresponding voting count.

## 4    Experiments

For our experiments we have made use of point clouds acquired from a robot platform equipped with a laser range finder for taking 360° scans in interior environments. The examined rooms are cluttered and possess irregular shapes as illustrated in Fig. 7. In order to investigate the performance of the plane extraction algorithms, we further examined simulated point clouds imitating typical interior environments. The scenes portray a set of rooms containing an arrangement of planes with different sizes and orientations as well as the corresponding ground truth information.

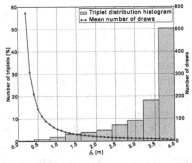
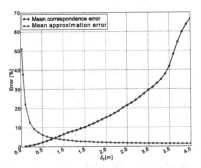
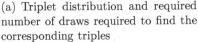

(a) Triplet distribution and required number of draws required to find the corresponding triples

(b) Mean Assignment and triangulation errors with respect to the maximum point-to-point distance

**Fig. 5.** Triangulation analysis for the point cloud acquired from simulation. Fig. (a) illustrates a histogram for the distribution of triangles restricted to $\delta_t = 4.0$ m as well as the mean number of draws that have to be carried out in order to triangulate a triple with a point-to-point distance of $\delta_t$. Fig. (b) illustrates the two errors occurring in dependence on the maximum point-to-point distance. The mean correspondence error expresses in how many of the cases the points are assigned to different logical surfaces, the mean approximation error expresses the deviation of the triangle orientation with respect to the orientation of the surface to which the three points correspond.

### 4.1 Evaluating Triangulation Characteristics

The choice of $\delta_t$ directly affects runtime, stability as well as accuracy of the triangulation process and thus, the performance of RANSAC and the 3D RHT. The histogram in Fig. 5(a) discloses a comparatively minor appearance of triangles with slender $\delta_t$ values. Consequently, the smaller $\delta_t$ is presupposed within the given range, the lower is the probability that a triple (satisfying this distance criterion) is instantaneously found. This coherence is reflected by the mean number of draws which directly correlate to the run-time of the triangulation.

From the accuracy point of view we can differentiate approximation and correspondence errors (see Fig. 5(b)). The approximation of surface patches with only three points cannot be performed as robustly as, for instance, the estimation of surface normals, where the approach is supported by a multitude of points and least-square fitting methods. In particular small triangles, naturally having relatively small point-to-point distances, tend to exhibit erroneous surface approximations. To ascertain the dependency of the approximation error, the ground truth normal vector $\mathbf{n}_g$ for each plane is provided by the simulation framework in which the point clouds have been acquired. Hence, the approximation error $e_a$ can be quantified by the angle between $\mathbf{n}$ and $\mathbf{n_g}$, e.g. $e_a = \cos^{-1}(\mathbf{n} \cdot \mathbf{n}_g)$. From the plot, we can see that the larger the minimum point-to-point distance is defined, the lower the mean triangulation error will be. For this connection, we assume that the three points actually belong to the same plane.

This correspondence-related aspect leads to the correspondence error. Choosing a high $\delta_t$ may lead to the risk that the three points are no longer adjacent and thus, correspond to different surface patches. This could lead to the consequence that the resulting triangle approximates a surface erroneously or is mistakenly spanned at locations that do not conform to an actual surface. This behavior is reinforced in the presence of clutter, or when the triangulation occurs nearby junctions of disparately oriented regions. The probability of mismatching declines with decreasing $\delta_t$. The trade-off that needs to be considered for $\delta_t$ with respect to both types of errors is expressed in Fig. 5(b). Based on our experiments, we have found values of $0.5\,\mathrm{m} < \delta_t < 1.5\,\mathrm{m}$ to deliver satisfying results for most of the examined real world scenes with respect to runtime and margin of error.

## 4.2    Evaluating 3D RHT Extensions

In order to assess how the accumulator resolution affects runtime efficiency and error behavior, we performed several tests with multiple discretizations. We applied the default 3D RHT and our implementation on a set of point clouds providing 13.6 planes on average. In Fig. 6, we can see that our method outperforms the default 3D RHT with respect to angular error and runtime. Further, we can observe the expected tendency that the angular error declines with decreasing resolution. The small increase in runtime with increasing discretization can be traced back to the additional maintenance of associative array that came into operation.

For experiments with RANSAC, we used a modified method for RANSAC from the PCL[16], extended by additional triangulation constraints in accordance with Sec. 4.1. From Tab. 2 we can see that, although the improvements showed promising results with respect to the angular error, RANSAC still yields slightly better accuracies. However, at over 900 ms, the execution time of RANSAC exceeds both RHT implementations by far (68 ms and 48 ms respectively). The maximum cell allocation of the accumulator using associative arrays for this test was less then one percent of the default accumulator size.

**Table 2.** Comparison of the examined plane extraction methods: RANSAC vs. 3D RHT vs. our method. For both RHT implementations we used the reference accumulator discretization of ($N_\theta = 90, N_\varphi = 180, \Delta\varrho = 0.05$).

|  | RANSAC | 3D RHT | 3D RHT Ext. |
|---|---|---|---|
| Runtime | 934 ms | 68 ms | 48 ms |
| Angular Error | 0.093° | 0.76° | 0.13° |
| Cell Allocation | - | 100% | < 1% |

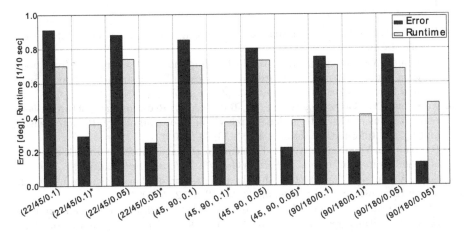

**Fig. 6.** Errors and runtime for selected accumulator resolutions given by the cell discretization $(N_\theta, N_\varphi, \Delta\varrho)$. Results from our method are marked respectively (*).

**Fig. 7.** Results for our plane extraction on real world point clouds. Black points correspond to non-planar outliers. Left: 26 planes, ~360 ms. Right: 24 planes, ~370 ms.

## 5  Conclusion

In this paper, we proposed a plane extraction method based on the RHT that allows for an efficient extraction of planes from 3D point clouds, without estimating additional features. Compared to the existing 3D RHT approach, we reduced the overall extraction time by introducing a score, based on a preliminary inlier inspection. The accuracy of the extracted plane representations was enhanced by correcting the plane parameters with an intermediate fitting procedure on the examined inlier subset. We improved the robustness of the accumulator by incorporating the cells in ellipsoidal proximities of the overflowing cell for parameter extraction and accumulator resetting. Finally, an accumulator based on associative arrays was adopted to noticeably cut down the memory consumption during the plane extraction. We conducted experiments on real as well as ground truth data and compared our results with those of the 3D RHT and RANSAC. In future work, we will consider the extraction of more complex models from 3D data.

# References

1. Hough, P.: Method and means for recognizing complex patterns, US Patent 3,069,654 (1962)
2. Vosselman, G., Dijkman, S., et al.: 3d building model reconstruction from point clouds and ground plans. International Archives of Photogrammetry Remote Sensing and Spatial Information Sciences 34(3/W4), 37–44 (2001)
3. Vosselman, G., Gorte, B., Sithole, G., Rabbani, T.: Recognising structure in laser scanner point clouds. International Archives of Photogrammetry, Remote Sensing and Spatial Information Sciences 46(8), 33–38 (2004)
4. Rabbani, T., Van Den Heuvel, F.: Efficient hough transform for automatic detection of cylinders in point clouds. ISPRS WG III/3, III/4 3, 60–65 (2005)
5. Sarti, A., Tubaro, S.: Detection and characterisation of planar fractures using a 3d hough transform. Signal Processing 82(9), 1269–1282 (2002)
6. Tarsha-Kurdi, F., Landes, T., Grussenmeyer, P.: Hough-transform and extended ransac algorithms for automatic detection of 3d building roof planes from lidar data. Science and Technology 36(1), 407–412 (2007)
7. Borrmann, D., Elseberg, J., Lingemann, K., Nüchter, A.: The 3d hough transform for plane detection in point clouds: A review and a new accumulator design. 3D Research 2(2), 32 (2011)
8. Xu, L., Oja, E., Kultanen, P.: A new curve detection method: randomized hough transform (rht). Pattern Recognition Letters 11(5), 331–338 (1990)
9. Fischler, M., Bolles, R.: Random sample consensus: a paradigm for model fitting with applications to image analysis and automated cartography. Communications of the ACM 24(6), 381–395 (1981)
10. Rusu, R., Marton, Z., Blodow, N., Holzbach, A., Beetz, M.: Model-based and learned semantic object labeling in 3d point cloud maps of kitchen environments. In: IEEE/RSJ International Conference on Intelligent Robots and Systems, IROS 2009, pp. 3601–3608. IEEE (2009)
11. Schnabel, R., Wahl, R., Klein, R.: Efficient ransac for point-cloud shape detection. In: Computer Graphics Forum, vol. 26, pp. 214–226. Wiley Online Library (2007)
12. Bretar, F., Roux, M.: Extraction of 3d planar primitives from raw airborne laser data: a normal driven ransac approach. In: MVA 2005, pp. 452–455 (2005)
13. Dorninger, P., Nothegger, C.: 3d segmentation of unstructured point clouds for building modelling. International Archives of the Photogrammetry, Remote Sensing and Spatial Information Sciences 35(3/W49A), 191–196 (2007)
14. Holz, D., Holzer, S., Rusu, R.B., Behnke, S.: Real-time plane segmentation using rgb-d cameras. In: Proc. of the 15th Robo Cup International Symposium (2011)
15. Oehler, B., Stueckler, J., Welle, J., Schulz, D., Behnke, S.: Efficient Multi-resolution Plane Segmentation of 3D Point Clouds. In: Jeschke, S., Liu, H., Schilberg, D. (eds.) ICIRA 2011, Part II. LNCS, vol. 7102, pp. 145–156. Springer, Heidelberg (2011)
16. Rusu, R., Cousins, S.: 3d is here: Point cloud library (pcl). In: 2011 IEEE International Conference on Robotics and Automation (ICRA), pp. 1–4. IEEE (2011)

# Evolutionary Computation for Intelligent Self-localization in Multiple Mobile Robots Based on SLAM

Yuichiro Toda[*], Shintaro Suzuki, and Naoyuki Kubota

Tokyo Metropolitan University, Graduate School of System Design,
6-6 Asahigaoka, Hino, Tokyo, Japan
{toda-yuuichirou,suzuki-shintaro}@sd.tmu.ac.jp, kubota@tmu.ac.jp

**Abstract.** The localization is one of the most important capabilities for mobile robots. However, other robots can be considered as unknown objects when a mobile robot performs localization, because other robots can enter the sensing range of a mobile robot. Therefore, we propose a method of intelligent self-localization using evolutionary computation for multiple mobile robots based on simultaneous localization and mapping (SLAM). First, we explain the method of SLAM using occupancy grid mapping by a single mobile robot. Next, we propose an intelligent self-localization method using multi-resolution map and evolutionary computation based on relative position of other robots in the sensing range. The experimental results show the effectiveness of the proposed method.

**Keywords:** SLAM, Multi-robot, Intelligent Robotics.

## 1 Introduction

Recently, various types of sensors such as laser range finders, visual sensors, and 3D infrared range sensors have been applied to robots. The sensors can measure large size of data in one scan, but it takes much computational time and cost to extract meaningful and important information from the measured spatiotemporal data. Therefore, intelligent technologies are required for information extraction. Simultaneous Localization and Mapping (SLAM) is a fundamental task for searching the unknown environments and decision making of an autonomous robot.

Various types of methods for SLAM have been proposed such as Extended Kalman Filter (EKF) SLAM, Graph SLAM, visual SLAM. The EKF SLAM algorithm applies the EKF to online SLAM using maximum likelihood data associations. In the EKF SLAM, feature-based maps are used with point landmarks [1]. Graph SLAM solves a full SLAM problem in offline using all data obtained until the current time, e.g., all poses and all features in the map. Therefore, Graph SLAM has access to the full data when building the map [2,3]. In our previous work, we proposed a topological map building method based on a growing neural network as a

---

[*] Corresponding author.

C.-Y. Su, S. Rakheja, H. Liu (Eds.): ICIRA 2012, Part I, LNAI 7506, pp. 229–239, 2012.

topological approach. A growing neural network can add neurons and their connections to the network. We applied a steady-state genetic algorithm (SSGA) to update the estimated self-position of a mobile robot by using the measured distance and topological map [4]. Furthermore, cooperative SLAM (C-SLAM) has been also discussed in the study of multi-robot systems.

Multi-robot systems have been applied to various problems such as autonomous guided vehicles, soccer robots, and search and rescue system [5-7]. However, the robots must localize the self-position in order to search for unknown area such as a disaster site. There have been proposed three main approaches of C-SLAM. The first one is a map merging approach. In the method, each robot independently conducts SLAM, and the built maps are merged according to the matching degree between two maps. This approach is a simple extension of standard SLAM, but the preciseness of the merged map strongly depends on the characteristics of sensors equipped with each robot. Therefore, the same type and properties of sensors should be equipped with each robot in order to improve the performance of SLAM. The second one is a map sharing approach. In the method, a leader robot builds a map based on SLAM. Other follower robots share the built map, and independently perform self-localization [8-12]. If each robot has different types of sensors, it is easy for follower robots to obtain the feasible performance of localization. The last one is a multi-robot sensor integration approach. In this method, the measured data are cooperatively integrated to build a map. The interdependency of the multi-robot sensor integration approach is the highest in these three approaches.

We proposed a self-localization method of multi-robot system based on the map sharing approach [13]. In the proposed method, first of all, one leader robot performs SLAM based on occupancy grid mapping. Both of localization and map building are performed by SSGA. The other robots receive and share the map information from the leader robot and perform the self-localization using the shared map. However, other robots can be considered as unknown objects when a mobile robot performs localization, if other robots enter the sensing range of a mobile robot. Therefore, we propose a method of intelligent self-localization using evolutionary computation for multiple mobile robots. Therefore, if a mobile robot detects other robots in the sensing range, their corresponding measurement data are not used for the intelligent self-localization.

This paper is organized as follows. Section 2 explains the method of SLAM using the occupancy grid mapping by a single mobile robot. Section 3 proposes an intelligent self-localization method using multi-resolution maps for multiple mobile robots. Next, we propose a method of self-localization using evolutionary computation based on relative position of other robots in the sensing range. Finally, we show several experimental results of self-localization of multi-robot system based on SLAM.

# 2    SLAM

## 2.1    Mobile Robots

To begin with, we explain the hardware specification of a mobile robot (Table 1). We use an omni-directional robot with four omni-wheels and DC motors. The robot can move to different omni-direction by changing the combination of output levels to motors. Basically, the action outputs of the robot are direct forward movement and rotation at the same position to avoid the slip appeared as noise in SLAM. Furthermore, the robot changes the moving direction only when the robot conducts obstacle avoidance. In addition, we use a laser range finder (LRF, URG04-LN) for SLAM and self-localization. Figure 1 shows the omni-directional mobile robot.

Figure 2 shows an example of multiple mobile robots. Sometimes, a mobile robot can enter the sensing range of other mobile robots (Fig.2 (a)). As a result, it is very difficult for the mobile robot to perform self-localization using a shared grid map (Fig.2 (b), because other robots appeared in the sensing range can be considered as unknown objects.

**Table 1.** Specification of Omni-directional mobile robot

| Diameter | 300 mm |
|---|---|
| Height | 177 mm |
| Weight | 8 kg (approximately) |
| Maximal Speed | 1.5 km/h |
| Operating Time (Battery) | 1 hour |
| Maximal Payload Weight | 15 kg |
| Communication Method | Wi-Fi (2.4 GHz) |

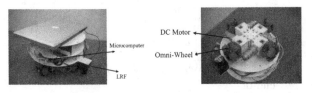

**Fig. 1.** Omni-directinal mobile robot

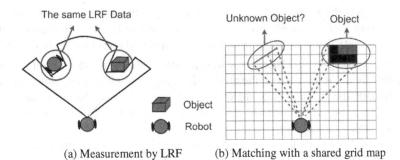

(a) Measurement by LRF     (b) Matching with a shared grid map

**Fig. 2.** A problem in self-localization of multiple mobile robots

## 2.2     Procedure for SLAM

In the proposed method, we use the occupancy grid mapping [14, 15]. Figure 3 shows the concept of the occupancy grid map. The value of each discrete cell is represented by

$$map_0(x, y) = \begin{cases} 1 & \text{(occupied)} \\ 0.5 & \text{(partially occupied)} \\ 0 & \text{(unknown)} \\ -1 & \text{(empty)} \end{cases}. \tag{1}$$

Here the value of all cells is initialized at 0. The measurement data is represented by $(d_i, \theta_i)$, $i=1,2, ..., M$, $j=1,2, ..., L$, where $d_i$ is measurement distance from LRF; $\theta_i$ is the angle of the measurement direction; $M$ is the number of total measurement directions; $L_i$ $(= [\alpha^{Res} \cdot d_i])$ is the number of resolution for the map building by the occupancy grid model. Therefore, the map is updated by following procedure

| Algorithm 1. Map-update |
|---|
| for $i=1$ to $M$ do |
| $\qquad$ for $j=1$ to $L_i$ do |
| $$u_{i,j} = \frac{j}{L_i}\left(d_i \cos(\theta_i + r_p)\right) + x_p$$ $$v_{i,j} = \frac{j}{L_i}\left(d_i \sin(\theta_i + r_p)\right) + y_p \tag{2}$$ $$x_{i,j} = \left[\alpha^{Map} \cdot u_{i,j}\right]$$ $$y_{i,j} = \left[\alpha^{Map} \cdot v_{i,j}\right] \tag{3}$$ $$map_0(x_{i,j}, y_{i,j}) = f(map_0(x_{i,j}, y_{i,j}), j) \tag{4}$$ |
| $\qquad$ endfor |
| endfor |

where $(x_p, y_p)$ is the position of the mobile robot; $r_p$ is the posture; $d_i$ is measurement distance from LRF in the $i$th direction; $\theta_i$ is the angle of the measurement direction; $\alpha^{MAP}$ is the scale factor mapping from the real world to the grid map; $f(\cdot)$ in (9) is a function according to IF-THEN rules shown in the Table 2. If the position and angle of the mobile robot are correct, the above map is updated efficiently. However, if the estimation of the position and angle is not correct, the map building results in a failure. Therefore, the position and angle should be corrected. Table.1 shows the state transition table of the map-update.

We apply SSGA for the correction of the position and angle. As one stream of evolutionary computing, genetic algorithms (GAs) have been effectively used for optimization problems in robotics [16]. GAs can produce a feasible solution, not necessarily an optimal one, with less computational cost. The main role of GAs in robotics is the optimization in modeling or problem-solving. SSGA simulates the continuous model of the generation, which eliminates and generates a few individuals in a generation. A candidate solution is composed of numerical parameters of revised values to the current position ($g_{k,x}$, $g_{k,y}$) and rotation ($g_{k,r}$). In the SSGA, only a few existing solutions are replaced with the candidate solution generated by the crossover and mutation. We use the elitist cross over and adaptive mutation. Elitist crossover randomly selects one individual and generates an individual by incorporating genetic information from the selected individual and best individual in order to obtain feasible solutions rapidly. Next, the following adaptive mutation is performed to the generated individual,

$$g_{k,h} \rightarrow g_{k,h} + \left( \alpha^{SSGA} \cdot \frac{f_{max} - f_k}{f_{max} - f_{min}} + \beta^{SSGA} \right) \cdot N(0,1) \tag{5}$$

where $f_k$ is the fitness value of the $k$th individual, $f_{max}$ and $f_{min}$ are the maximum and minimum of fitness values in the population; $N(0,1)$ indicates a normal random value; $\alpha^{SSGA}$ and $\beta^{SSGA}$ are the coefficient and offset, respectively. A Fitness value of the $k$th candidate solution is calculated by the following equation,

$$fit_k^{Loc} = \sum_{i=1}^{M} map_0(x_{i,L}, y_{i,L}) \tag{6}$$

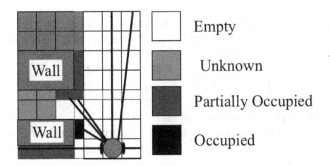

**Fig. 3.** Concept image of the occupancy grid map

**Table 2.** State Transition of Map-update

| Condition | | Output |
|---|---|---|
| $j$ | $map_0(x,y)$ | |
| $j < L$ | 0 | -1 |
| $j < L$ | 1 | 0.5 |
| $j = L$ | 0 | 1 |
| $j = L$ | -1 | 0.5 |

# 3    Intelligent Self-localization for Multiple Mobile Robots

## 3.1    Multi-resolution Map

This subsection explains how to generate a multi-resolution map from the original map based on the measurement data. The values of the original map built by the

SLAM are $\{-1, 0, 0.5, 1\}$, but we consider a partially occupied cell as an occupied cell in the 1st level of map as follows;

$$map_1(x_1, y_1) = \begin{cases} 1 & \text{if } map_0(x, y) = 0.5 \\ map_0(x, y) & \text{otherwise} \end{cases}, \tag{7}$$

where $(x_k, y_k)$ is the position of the mobile robot in the $k$th layer. Figure 4 shows the basic concept of multi-resolution map. Basically, since the map should be built as precisely as possible. If the original size of map is used for the search, it takes much computational cost owing to the large size of cell space. Therefore, first, we re-build the map by reducing the granularity of a map, and we obtain the lower resolution map. A value of the lower resolution map is calculated from the higher resolution map in the following;

$$map_{k+1}(x_{k+1}, y_{k+1}) = \sum_{i=0}^{1} \sum_{j=0}^{1} map_k(x_k + i, y_k + j)$$
$$x_k = 0, k^2, 2k^2, ..., X, \quad y_k = 0, k^2, 2k^2, ..., Y, \quad k = 1, 2, ..., K \tag{8}$$

As the increase of $k$, the map information becomes sparse. In this paper, we get the low-resolution map that is built by substituting $k$ to equation (8). The information of $map_k(x_k, y_k)$ is the following equation,

$$map_k(x_k, y_k) \in \left\{ -2^{2(k-1)}, -2^{2(k-1)} + 1, ..., -1, 0, 1, ..., 2^{2(k-1)} - 1, 2^{2(k-1)} \right\}, \tag{9}$$

where the number of possible values is $2k+1$.

Next, we normalize the value of $map_k(x_k, y_k)$ in order to calculate the state of each cell such as empty state, occupied state, and uncertain state;

$$n_k(x_k, y_k) = \frac{1}{2^{2(k-1)}} map_k(x_k, y_k). \tag{10}$$

Basically, if the state of a cell is uncertain, the value of $map_k(x_k, y_k)$ approaches 0. However, The value of $map_k(x_k, y_k)$ can be 0 in some cases in addition to the unknown state, since the $map_k(x_k, y_k)$ is determined by the simple summation. Therefore, in order to extract the unknown state from uncertain states, we define a $map^{Unk}_k(x_k, y_k)$ by the following equation.

$$map^{Unk}_{k+1}(x_k, y_k) = \sum_{i=0}^{1} \sum_{j=0}^{1} \left| map_k(x_k + i, y_k + j) \right| \tag{11}$$

Furthermore, we define the degree of unknownness in the search,

$$n^{Unk}_k(x_k, y_k) = \frac{1}{2^{2(k-1)}} map^{Unk}_k(x_k, y_k). \tag{12}$$

We can obtain the small size of abstract map for self-localization by reducing the search space.

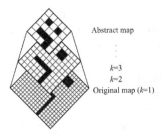

Abstract map

$k$=3
$k$=2
Original map ($k$=1)

**Fig. 4.** Conceptual image of multi-resolution map

## 3.2    Intelligent Self-localization

We apply a multi-resolution map for intelligent self-localization for multiple mobile robots. To begin with, we must discriminate occupied cell and empty cell on the multi-resolution map for self-localization. As mentioned above, we use two different types of multi-resolution maps based on the uncertainty and unknownness. By using these values, we can obtain the state of the cell easily as the following equation,

$$s_k(x_k,y_k) = \begin{cases} 1 & (if \ \ o_k(x_k,y_k) > \alpha^{State}) \\ 0 & (otherwise) \end{cases}, \tag{13}$$

$$o_k(x_k,y_k) = n_k(x_k,y_k) + n_k^{Unk}(x_k,y_k) \tag{14}$$

where $\alpha^{State}$ indicates the threshold value. If $s_k(x_k,y_k)$ is 1, then the state of the cell means an occupied cell. Figure 5 shows an extraction result of occupied cells drawn in blue at each resolution map.

Next, we explain an intelligent self-localization method. The initial self-localization is done by $(\mu+\lambda)$-ES where $\mu$ and $\lambda$ indicate the number of parent population and the number of offspring population produced in a single generation, respectively. Algorithm 2 shows the procedure of our initial self-localization. The $k$ indicates the level of the multi-resolution map; $n$ indicates the number of steps; $N$ indicates the maximal number of generations (search iterations). A candidate solution is composed of numerical parameters of revised values to the current position ($g^l_{i,x}$, $g^l_{i,y}$) and the current direction angle of the robot ($g^l_{i,r}$). The fitness value $fit^l_i$ of the $i$th individual is calculated by the following equation,

$$fit^l_i = \frac{hit}{hit + err} \tag{15}$$

$$\begin{pmatrix} hit \leftarrow hit + 1 & if \ s_k(x_k,y_k) = 1 \\ err \leftarrow err + 1 & if \ s_k(x_k,y_k) = 0 \end{pmatrix}.$$

In the step 5 and step 12, the weight $w^l_i$ is calculated by the following equation,

$$w^l_i = \frac{fit^l_i}{\sum\limits_{j=1}^{\mu} fit^l_j}. \tag{16}$$

After the initial self-localization, the self-localization of the robots is calculated by the SSGA in order to perform the local search. In this way, the robots can estimate the current position as precisely as possible.

| Algorithm 2. Initial self-localization |
| --- |
| Initialization of Algorithm 2:<br>Step1: Initialize $\mu$ parents and $n = 0$.<br>Step2: Measurement the LRF data and<br>Step3: Estimate other robots position according to the pose of each individual.<br>Step4: -If other robots appear in the sensing range,<br>      then the corresponding LRF data are not used in step 5.<br>Step5: Calculate fitness value $fit^l_i$ and the weight $w^l_i$.<br><br>Iteration Process:<br>Step6: Produce $\lambda$ offspring depending on $w^l_i$.<br>Step7: Measurement the LRF data.<br>Step8: Estimate other robots position according to the pose of each individual.<br>Step9: -If other robots appear in the sensing range,<br>      then the corresponding LRF data are not used in step 10.<br>Step10: Calculate the fitness value $fit^l_i$.<br>Step11: The top $\mu$ candidates are selected as next parent.<br>Step12: Calculate the weight $w^l_i$.<br>Step13: -If the best fitness value is higher than $\alpha^h$,<br>      then $k \leftarrow k-1$ and $n = 0$.<br>    -Otherwise, go to step 10.<br>Step14: -If $n > N$ and the best fitness value is lower than $\alpha^s$,<br>      then $k \leftarrow k+2$ and $n = 0$.<br>Step15: -If $k = 1$, then finish the initial self-localization.<br>    -Otherwise, go to step 6 and $n \leftarrow n+1$. |

(a) Original map        (b) $k = 3$               (c) $k = 5$

**Fig. 5.** Extraction the occupied cells at each resolution map

## 4    Experimental Results

We conduct an experiment of the proposed intelligent self-localization method in our laboratory. The parameters used for self-localization are shown in the following. The numbers of parent candidates ($\mu$) are 1000 and the numbers of offspring candidates ($\lambda$)

are 500; $\alpha^{State}$ = 0.01; $\alpha^h$ = 0.75; $\alpha^s$ = 0.5; the initial resolution level $k$ of the multi-resolution map is 2. Figure 6 and 7 show experimental results of initial self-localization. In Fig.6 (a), the candidates spread all over the map in order to estimate the current robot position (The candidates are drawn by purple). However, the best fitness value stays low for 20 generations, because the change of fitness value is very sensitive to the change of the estimated position in the high-resolution map ($k$ = 2). Therefore, the robot updates the resolution level to $k$ = 4 in Fig.6 (b). When the resolution level is low ($k$ = 4), the best fitness value is higher than 0.9 in Fig.7. In the low-resolution map, it is easy to roughly estimate the robot position because the low-resolution map has the wide acceptable error range. By estimating the robot position in the low-resolution map, the best fitness value is high after downgrading the resolution level. In this way, the robot can estimate the current position by using the multi-resolution map where the best candidate is drawn by the red triangle in Fig.6 (d).

Next, we show an experimental result of intelligent self-localization for multiple mobile robots where a red triangle and green triangle indicate a self-position and the position of other robots, respectively (Fig.8). In Fig.8 (a), the robot performs self-localization by using all of measurement data, because other robots don't exist in the sensing range of LRF equipped with the robot. After that, the robot A turns right. As a result, two other robots appear in the sensing range of LRF equipped with the robot. In Fig.8 (b), the fitness value for the intelligent self-localization is calculated without using measurement data of the area depicted by blue lines. In this way, the mobile robot can estimate the self-position with adequate preciseness.

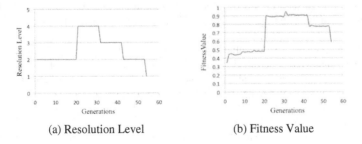

(a) $t = 0$ ($k = 2$)    (b) $t = 25$ ($k = 4$)    (c) $t = 45$ ($k = 3$)    (d) $t = 53$

**Fig. 6.** An experimental result of initial self-localization

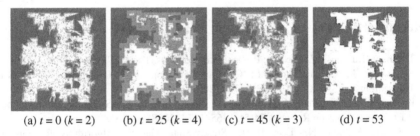

(a) Resolution Level                (b) Fitness Value

**Fig. 7.** Resolution level and the best fitness value in each generation

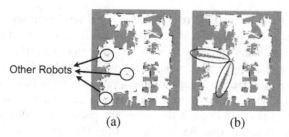

**Fig. 8.** An experimental result of intelligent self-localization

## 5     Summary

In this paper, we proposed our SLAM based on the occupancy grid mapping. Our SLAM method uses the SSGA in order to estimate the current robot position. Next, we proposed our self-localization method using the multi-resolution map. The initialize self-localization is based on the evolutionary strategy (ES) for global optimization. The other part is based on the SSGA for local optimization. The experimental results showed the effectiveness of the proposed self-localization method based on the multi-resolution map. However, our self-localization depends on some hard-coded threshold values. Therefore, we should discuss these parameters. Furthermore, we will apply our self-localization method to the multi-robot systems such as the formation behavior.

## References

1. Thrun, S., Burgard, W., Fox, D.: Probabilistic Robotics. The MIT Press (2005)
2. Folkesson, J., Christensen, H.I.: Closing the Loop With Graphical SLAM. IEEE Transactions on Robotics 23(4), 731–741 (2007)
3. Kaess, M., Ranganathan, A., Dellaert, F.: iSAM: Incremental Smoothing and Mapping. IEEE Transactions on Robotics 24(5), 1365–1378 (2008)
4. Woo, J., Kubota, N., Lee, B.-H.: Steady-State Genetic Algorithms for Growing Topological Mapping and Localization. In: Zhang, B.-T., Orgun, M.A. (eds.) PRICAI 2010. LNCS (LNAI), vol. 6230, pp. 558–569. Springer, Heidelberg (2010)
5. Sugawara, K., Hayakawa, Y., Mizuguchi, T., Sano, M.: Collective Motion of Multi-Robot System based on Simple Dynamics, p. 522. Itech Education and Publishina (September 2007)
6. Kubota, N., Aizawa, N.: Intelligent Control of A Multi-agent System based on Multi-objective Behavior Coordination, In: Proc (CD-ROM) of 7th IEEE International Symposium on Computational Intelligence in Robotics and Automation (CIRA 2007), Jacksonville, Florida, USA, pp. 184–189 (June 2007)
7. Vig, L., Adams, J.A.: Multi-Robot Coalition Formation. IEEE Transactions on Robotics 22(4), 637–649 (2006)
8. Huang, G.P., Trawny, N., Mourikis, A.I., Roumeliotis, S.I.: Observability-based consistent EKF estimators for multi-robot cooperative localization. Journal Autonomous Robots 30(1) (January 2011)

9. Pinheiro, P., Wainer, J.: Planning for Multi-robot Localization. In: da Rocha Costa, A.C., Vicari, R.M., Tonidandel, F. (eds.) SBIA 2010. LNCS, vol. 6404, pp. 183–192. Springer, Heidelberg (2010)
10. Choi, J., Choi, M., Nam, S.Y., Chung, W.K.: Autonomous topological modeling of a home environment and topological localization using a sonar grid map. Journal Autonomous Robots 30(4) (May 2011)
11. Roumeliotis, S.I., Bekey, G.A.: Distributed Multirobot Localization. IEEE Transaction on Robotics and Automation 18(5), 781–795 (2002)
12. Prorok, A., Bahr, A., Martinoli, A.: Low-Cost Collaborative Localization for Large-Scale Multi-Robot Systems. In: IEEE International Conference on Robotics and Automation, ICRA (2012)
13. Toda, Y., Suzuki, S., Kubota, N.: Self-localization of Multi-robot System based on Simultaneous Localization and Mapping. In: Proc (CD-ROM) of International Symposium on Advanced Intelligent Systems (ISIS 2011), Suwon, Korea, September 28 - October 1 (2011)
14. Thrun, S.: Learning Occupancy Grid Maps With Forward Sensor Models. Autonomous Robots 25(2), 111–127 (2003)
15. Lee, K., Chung, W.K.: Effective Maximum Likelihood Grid Map with Conflict Evaluation Filter using Sonar Sensors. IEEE Transactions on Robotics 25(4), 887–901 (2009)
16. Fogel, D.B.: Evolutionary Computation. IEEE Press (1995)

# Optimum Design of a Planar 3-DOF Parallel Manipulator for Good Motion and Force Transmissibility

JieYang[1] and Yongzhi Hua[2]

[1] School of Mechanical Engineering, Hebei University of Technology, Tianjin, China
[2] Department of Precision Instruments, Tsinghua University, Beijing, China
yangjie871@yahoo.com.cn,
huayz10@mails.tsinghua.edu.cn

**Abstract.** Since motion and force transmissibility is the inherent characteristic of a closed-chain manipulator, the design of a parallel manipulator should take into account this performance. This paper presents the optimum design of a 3-RRR parallel manipulator by considering motion and force transmission performance. Based on the screw analysis of the manipulator, some performance indices, such as *good transmission workspace* (GTW) and *global transmission index* (GTI), are then defined as the criterion for the design of the manipulator. By using the parameter design space, the corresponding performance atlases are plotted to illustrate the relationship between indices and geometrical parameters. The optimum design result, which is actually an optimum region, is then reached. The designed manipulator is far from singularity and has good motion and force transmissibility in its workspace.

**Keywords:** parallel manipulator, screw theory, motion and force transmissibility, optimum design.

## 1    Introduction

Compared with serial manipulators, parallel manipulators have the advantages of a compact structure, high stiffness, low moving inertia, high load/weight ratio, especially, high speed and payload capability. So, motion and force transmissibility is the main performance of such manipulators. Actually, motion and force transmission analysis has been the focus of many studies. Several indices, such as the transmission angle, the pressure angle, and the transmission factor have been proposed to evaluate motion/force transmission. For example, Yuan et al. [1] used Ball's virtual coefficient [2] between the *transmission wrench screw* (TWS) and the *output twist screws* (OTS) as a transmission factor to evaluate the transmission performance of spatial mechanisms. Tsai and Lee [3] introduced *generalized transmission wrench screw* (GTWS) to characterize transmission properties of mechanisms. They defined the transmissibility and the manipulability, and investigated the transmission performance of a variable lead screw mechanism (VLSM). By fixing all but one of the inputs of the 6-RSS parallel manipulator, Takeda et al. [4] developed a transmission index based

C.-Y. Su, S. Rakheja, H. Liu (Eds.): ICIRA 2012, Part I, LNAI 7506, pp. 240–249, 2012.
© Springer-Verlag Berlin Heidelberg 2012

on the minimum value of the cosine of the pressure angle between the leg and the moving platform. Lin et al. [5] proposed the *force transmission index* (FTI) for general single-DOF linkage mechanisms. They also developed the *mean force transmission index* (MFTI) as an extended definition of the FTI. Chen and Angeles [6] proposed a generalized transmission index for spatial mechanisms which is applicable to single-loop spatial linkages with fixed output and single or multiple degrees of freedom. Recently, Wang, Wu and Liu [7] proposed a unified analysis and evaluation method of the motion and force transmission for fully parallel mechanisms and introduced several indices for the design of such kinds of mechanisms.

For the issue of optimal design of parallel manipulators, there are two approaches in general. One is first to develop an objective function and then to achieve the result using the numerical method with an algorithm [8]. The other is first to plot performance charts, and then to identify the result with the intersection of these charts with specified constraints [9]. The design solutions of the two methods are different, i.e. the result of the former one is only one solution, while that of the later one is actually an optimum region which includes some solutions.

In the field of parallel manipulators, the planar 3-DOF parallel manipulator with three revolute joints in each of its legs is a typical parallel structure which has been studied by many scholars [10, 11, and 12]. In this paper, the motion and force transmissibility of the manipulator will be investigated and the indices for optimum design will be defined. After plotting the performance charts, by using the optimum design approach introduced in [9], the design process will be presented and an optimal design result will be given as an example.

## 2    Twist Screw and Wrench Screw Analysis

A planar three-DOF 3-RRR parallel manipulator is shown in Fig. 1a, where the moving platform is connected to the base by means of three legs, each of which includes three revolute joints and two bars. This manipulator is used to position and orient the gripper in the plane. The position of the center $O'$ of the moving platform can be described by $(x, y)$ with respect to the global coordinate system $O$-$xy$, and the orientation of the moving platform can be described by the angle $\varphi$ measured counterclockwise from the $x$-axis to the $x'$-axis of the local coordinate system which is attached to the moving platform. The three revolute joints A, D and G fixed on the base are actuated, represented by the angle $\theta_i$ as shown in Fig. 1b, and they are equally distributed at a nominal angle of 120° on a circle whose center is the origin $O$ and radius is $r_4$. The moving platform has the shape of an equilateral triangle, the circumcircle of which has a radius of $r_3$. The parameter $r_1$ is the length of the input links AB, DE, and GH, and $r_2$ the length of the coupler links BC, EF, and HI.

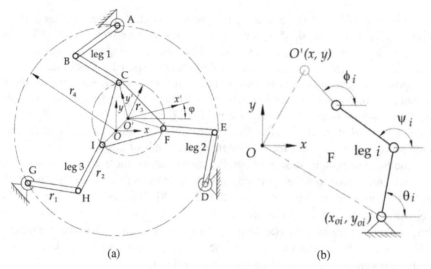

**Fig. 1.** A 3-RRR parallel manipulator **(a)** the whole sketch **(b)** one leg

Fig. 1 (b) shows one of the three legs of the 3-RRR parallel manipulator, in which each leg has three revolute joints with one DOF, respectively. With respect to the coordinate system O-xy, there are three motion screws which can be expressed as

$$\$_1 = (0,0,1; m_1, n_1, 0) \tag{1}$$

$$\$_2 = (0,0,1; m_2, n_2, 0) \tag{2}$$

$$\$_3 = (0,0,1; m_3, n_3, 0) \tag{3}$$

where $m_i, n_i$ $(i = 1,2,3)$ are constants related to the instantaneous position of every kinematic pair in the corresponding coordinate system. By analyzing the linear correlation among the three motion screws briefly, we can see that they are linearly independent which compose a three-DOF leg. Meanwhile, we can get a three-order screw system as

$$U_3 = \{\$_1, \$_2, \$_3\} \tag{4}$$

As the first revolute joint is the actuated joint, the corresponding motion screw is the input twist screw $\$_I$, which can be expressed as

$$\$_I = \$_1 = (0,0,1; m_1, n_1, 0) \tag{5}$$

It is clear to find that there are three input twist screws $\$_I$ in the 3-RRR parallel manipulator, as shown below

$$\$_{Ii} = (0,0,1; m_{1i}, m_{1i}, 0) \quad i = 1,2,3 \tag{6}$$

Assuming that the actuation joint is locked, we can remove $\$_1$ from the motion screw system. And a new passive joint screw system can be then achieved as $U_2$, i.e.,

$$U_2 = \{\$_2, \$_3\} \tag{7}$$

Now we can find a new screw, namely, the *transmission wrench screw* (TWS), which is reciprocal to all the passive joint screws in $U_2$, represented as

$$\$_T \circ \$_i = 0 \quad i = 2, 3 \tag{8}$$

As there is only one actuator in each of its legs, such a manipulator is usually referred to as a fully parallel manipulator. Each leg has its own TWS which indicates the motion and force transmission performance from the input members to its output members. From Eq. (8), we can get

$$\$_{Ti} = (f_i, h_i \times f_i) \quad i = 1, 2, 3 \tag{9}$$

where $f_i$ is a pure force vector with the direction through the two passive joints' centers, and $h_i$ represents a position vector to the origin of the proposed coordinate system. Here we can notice that the axis of $\$_{Ti}$ $(i = 1, 2, 3)$ always passes through two passive joints' centers along the related passive leg.

As to a three-DOF parallel manipulator at a certain configuration, when fixing all of its input joints except the one in the $i-$th leg $(i = 1, 2, 3)$, the instantaneous unit motion of the moving platform can be represented by a unit twist screw $\$_{oi}$. In this case, only the transmission wrench represented by $\$_{Ti}$ can contribute to the moving platform, while all other transmission wrenches apply no work to the moving platform. Hereby, we may get

$$\$_{Tj} \circ \$_{oi} = 0 \quad j = 1, 2, 3, i \neq j \tag{10}$$

From Eq. (10), three output twist screws $\$_{oi}$ $(i = 1, 2, 3)$ can be obtained.

By calculating the proposed motion and force transmission functions based on screw theory, one can give the analysis to every leg of 3-RRR parallel manipulator. Then one can get three input twist screws $\$_{Ii}$ $(i = 1, 2, 3)$, transmission wrench screws $\$_{Ti}$ $(i = 1, 2, 3)$ and output twist screws $\$_{oi}$ $(i = 1, 2, 3)$, accordingly, which can be used as the prerequisites for the performance analysis of the parallel manipulator.

## 3     Performance Index

In this section, using the analysis results of section 2, several transmission indices are introduced for the evaluation of motion and force transmission performance of the 3-

RRR parallel manipulator. The mathematical foundation of screw theory has already been shown in Ref. [12].

## 3.1　Local Transmission Index (LTI)

(a) Input Transmission Index (ITI).

As analyzed in last section, the studied 3-RRR manipulator has three input twist screws $\$_I$ , three transmission wrench screws, and three output twist screws $\$_O$ , respectively. The power coefficient between input twist screw of leg $i$ and its TWS can be defined as its ITI. This index is represented by

$$\lambda_i = \frac{\left|\$_{Ti} \circ \$_{Ii}\right|}{\left|\$_{Ti} \circ \$_{Ii}\right|_{max}} \quad i = 1,2,3 \tag{11}$$

By submitting Eqs. (6) and　(9) to Eq.(11), one may get

$$\lambda_i = \left|\sin(\psi_i - \theta_i)\right| \quad i = 1,2,3 \tag{12}$$

where $\psi_i, \theta_i$ are the angles as shown in Fig. 1b.

(b) Output Transmission Index (OTI).

The power coefficient between the TWS of leg $i$ and the corresponding output twist screw can be defined as its OTI. This index of leg $i$ is represented by

$$\eta_i = \frac{\left|\$_{Ti} \circ \$_{Oi}\right|}{\left|\$_{Ti} \circ \$_{Oi}\right|_{max}} \quad i = 1,2,3 \tag{13}$$

where $\$_{Oi}$ can be obtained from Eq. (10).

It may be seen from Eq. (13) that $\eta_i$ is independent of any coordinate system, and $0 \le \eta_i \le 1$. Since $\left|\$_{Ti} \circ \$_{Oi}\right|_{max}$ is constant at a certain configuration, $\eta_i$ should be as large as possible in order to transmit more power to the output member.

(c) Local Transmission Index (LTI).

It is concluded that both input transmission index and output transmission index of every leg should be as large as possible to obtain a good transmission performance. For an integrated 3-RRR parallel manipulator with three legs, therefore, when the transmission indices $\lambda_i$ and $\eta_i$ $(i = 1,2,3)$ are both large enough, it is said to have a good motion and force transmission performance; and if any one of them is small, the manipulator has poor motion and force transmissibility. For these reasons, a transmission index is defined as below

$$\gamma = \min\{\lambda_i, \eta_i\} \quad i = 1,2,3 \tag{14}$$

Since the values of $\gamma$ may be different at different configurations, it is referred to as the *Local Transmission Index* (LTI). LTI equals to the minimum one of ITI and OTI, which are both frame-free, and ranging from 0 to 1, so the LTI is also independent from the coordinate system and its value range can be expressed by

$$0 \leq \gamma \leq 1 \qquad (15)$$

### 3.2  Good Transmission Workspace (GTW)

In order to evaluate the transmission performance of the studied manipulator, a limit to the LTI should be defined to indicate the quality of the motion and force transmission performance. Thus the set of pose points satisfying a specified condition or the LTI being no less than a specified value is called the *good transmission workspace* (GTW) of the manipulator.

In experience, for the purpose of high speed and high payload capability [13], the limit of the LTI can be specified as $\sin \pi/4 \approx 0.7$. If LTI $\geq 0.7$, the manipulator can propose a good motion and force transmission ability in the local configuration; otherwise LTI$<0.7$, the manipulator has a poor motion and force transmission.

In normal, different manipulators have different good transmission workspaces, so the area of GTW, denoted as GTW_area, can be applied directly to the analysis and design of parallel manipulators.

### 3.3  Global Transmission Index (GTI)

Considering the fact that the good transmission workspace might be the same for manipulators with different geometric parameters, it is therefore impossible to determine the better manipulator based on only the value of GTW_area.

To evaluate the global motion and force transmissibility when the manipulator works in the proposed GTW, the GTI is defined based on the LTI value as

$$\Gamma = \frac{\int_W \gamma \, dW}{\int_W dW} \qquad (16)$$

where $W$ is the GTW, and $\gamma$ the LTI value which has no relation to the selected frame coordinate and its value ranges from 0 to 1. The range of GTI is $\Gamma_{min} < \Gamma < 1$ ( $\Gamma_{min} = \sin \pi/4 \approx 0.7$ ), and the GTI is also a frame-free index. In normal, the larger $\Gamma$ is, the better the motion /force transmission ability of the manipulator will be.

## 4    Optimum Design of the Manipulator

The optimum design based on the performance charts of a manipulator was introduced in Ref. [9] for a general case. For the parallel manipulator studied here, the design process can be described as follows.

### 4.1  Parameter Design Space

Parameter design space is a useful tool to present the relationship between performances and link lengths of a mechanism. Considering the studied parallel manipulator shown in Fig. 1a, if the manipulator can be assembled and has workspace, the condition for the four geometrical parameters should be

$$\begin{cases} r_3 \le r_4 \\ r_1 + r_2 + r_3 \ge r_4 \end{cases} \tag{17}$$

It is difficult to illustrate the performance index in the design space of a manipulator with more than four parameters. In this paper, we take a special case for an example to present how illustrating the link lengths affect the GTW and GTI. So, here we let the length of two legs be equal, i.e. $r_1 = r_2$. There then leaves three design parameters $r_1$, $r_3$ and $r_4$. The design space can then be obtained as shown in Fig. 2(a), which can be mapped into a planar space as shown in Fig. 2(b). Every point in the design space corresponds to a 3-RRR parallel manipulator with specified values of $r_1(r_2)$, $r_3$ and $r_4$. Thus, the proposed design space can be used to show the relationship between GTW or GTI and the link lengths $r_1$, $r_3$ and $r_4$ in the subsequent section. The mapping functions between $(s,t)$ and $(r_1, r_3, r_4)$ can be expressed as

$$\begin{cases} s = r_1 \\ t = -\dfrac{\sqrt{3}}{3} r_3 + \dfrac{\sqrt{3}}{3} r_4 \end{cases} \tag{18}$$

which can be used to plot the performance atlas in Fig. 2(b) when the geometric parameters $r_1$, $r_3$ and $r_4$ are given.

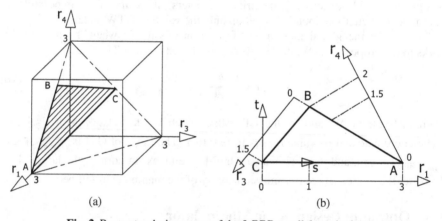

(a)                              (b)

**Fig. 2.** Parameter design space of the 3-RRR parallel manipulator

## 4.2    Performance Charts of GTW and GTI

According to the definition of GTW and GTI introduced in section 3, the performance charts of the 3-RRR parallel manipulator in the parameter design space can be generated as shown in Figs.3 and 4. It is noteworthy that the 3-RRR parallel manipulator has three DOFs, which combines the position $(x, y)$ with rotational angle $\varphi$. Figs. 3 and 4 show the special case of positional workspace by fixing the orientation as $\varphi = 20°$. From the two charts, one may see that when $r_4$ is specified, the GTW or GTI is inverse proportional to $r_3$. Especially, the GTW of a manipulator reaches its best when $r_3 = 0$. This result can be explained by the fact that when $r_3 = 0$ the 3-RRR parallel manipulator is degenerated as a redundant 2-DOF parallel manipulator with three RRR legs. Such a manipulator has a larger workspace.

### 4.3    Optimum Design Result

The performance charts of GTW and GTI obtained in section 4.2 can be used to identify the design result. Here, two cases will be given. The first case can be identified by letting $GTW \geq 0.4$ and $GTI \geq 0.9$. This leads to the optimum region as shown in Fig. 5 (a) (the shaded region). Any point within this region represents a non-dimensional manipulator with parameters $r_1 = r_2$, $r_3$, and $r_4$, whose GTW and GTI are no less than 0.4 and 0.9, respectively. For example, picking up a mechanism with $r_1 = r_2 = 0.86$, $r_3 = 0.50$ and $r_4 = 1.64$ from the region, its GTW and GTI are 0.6648 and 0.9001, respectively. The distribution of LTI within its workspace is shown in Fig. 6 (a), where the blue edge curve is the input transmission singularity loci. The region enclosed by the blue edge curve is the useable workspace, while the area bounded by curve with 0.7 is the GTW.

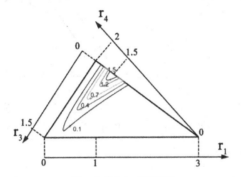

**Fig. 3.** Atlas of GTW

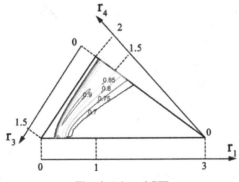

**Fig. 4.** Atlas of GTI

The second case can be identified by letting $GTW \geq 1.2$ and $GTI \geq 0.88$. This results in the optimum region shown as the shaded region in Fig. 5 (b). Picking up a mechanism with $r_1 = r_2 = 1.25$, $r_3 = 0.1$ and $r_4 = 1.65$ from the region, its GTW and GTI are 1.5594 and 0.8886, respectively. The distribution of LTI within its workspace is shown in Fig. 6 (b), where the region bounded by the curve with 0.7 is its GTW.

From the two cases, one may see that with different GTW and GTI constraints or different requirements the optimum regions are different. A manipulator of the first case has a smaller GTW and better GTI, while a manipulator of the second case has a larger GTW but a little worse GTI. Usually, we hope the workspace to be as large as possible. Under this requirement, the optimum result of the second case is preferred.

For the page limit, here the special case when $\varphi = 20°$ is only investigated and the optimum design is introduced accordingly. One can study other cases such as $\varphi = 10°$, $\varphi = 30°$, and so on by using the same method.

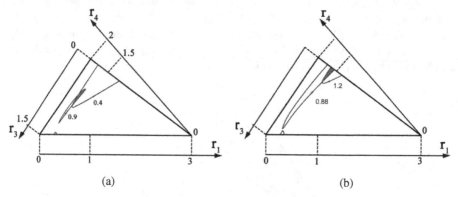

(a)                                                            (b)

**Fig. 5.** An optimal region defined by (a) $GTW \geq 0.4$ and $GTI \geq 0.90$, (b) $GTW \geq 1.2$ and $GTI \geq 0.88$

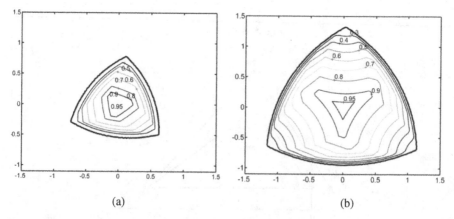

(a)                                                            (b)

**Fig. 6.** The LTI distribution of a 3-RRR parallel manipulator (a) with $r_1 = r_2 = 0.86$, $r_3 = 0.50$ and $r_4 = 1.64$ (b) with $r_1 = r_2 = 1.25$, $r_3 = 0.1$ and $r_4 = 1.65$

# 5    Conclusion

This paper addresses the optimum design of a planar 3-DOF parallel manipulator considering the motion and force transmissibility. To this end, the motion/force transmission analysis of the studied manipulator was firstly presented. Some performance indices such as ITI, OTI, and LTI, and two design indices GTW and GTI were then defined as the motion and force transmission evaluation criterion. Based on these indices, the performance charts have been plotted in the design space to illustrate relationship between the performances and the geometrical parameters of the manipulator. Finally, two cases of optimum design were introduced. Any one of the designed manipulators has good motion/force transmissibility. Moreover, the manipulator of the second case has a larger GTW. The paper provides a solution to design optimally the manipulator.

# References

1. Yuan, M.S.C., Freudenstwin, F., Woo, L.S.: Kinematic analysis of spatial mechanism by means of screw coordinates. Journal of Engineering for Industry, Transaction ASME, Series B 91, 67–73 (1971)
2. Ball, R.S.: A Treatise on the Theory of Screws. Cambridge University Press, Cambridge (1990)
3. Tsai, M.J., Lee, H.W.: Generalized evaluation for the transmission performance of mechanisms. Mechanism and Machine Theory 29, 607–618 (1994)
4. Takeda, Y., Funabashi, H., Ichimaru, H.: Development of spatial in-parallel actuated manipulators with six degrees of freedom with high motion transmissibility. JSME International Journal, Series C 40, 299–308 (1997)
5. Lin, C.C., Chang, W.T.: The force transmissibility index of planar linkage mechanisms. Mechanism and Machine Theory 37(12), 1465–1485 (2002)
6. Chen, C., Angeles, J.: Generalized transmission index and transmission quality for spatial linkages. Mechanism and Machine Theory 42(9), 1225–1237 (2007)
7. Wang, J., Wu, C., Liu, X.-J.: Performance evaluation of parallel manipulators: Motion/force transmissibility and its index. Mechanism and Machine Theory 45(10), 1462–1476 (2010)
8. Ryu, J., Cha, J.: Volumetric error analysis and architecture optimization for accuracy of HexaSlide type parallel manipulators. Mechanism and Machine Theory 38(3), 227–240 (2003)
9. Liu, X.-J., Wang, J.: A new methodology for optimal kinematic design of parallel mechanisms. Mechanism and Machine Theory 42(9), 1210–1224 (2007)
10. Gosselin, C.M., Angeles, J.: The optimum kinematic design of a planar three-degree-of-freedom parallel manipulator. ASME, J. Mechanisms, Trans. Auto. Design 110(1), 35–41 (1988)
11. Liu, X.-J., Wang, J., Gao, F.: Performance atlases of the workspace for planar 3-DOF parallel manipulators. Robotica 18(5), 563–568 (2000)
12. Bonev, I.A., Zlatanov, D., Gosselin, C.M.: Singularity analysis of 3-DOF planar parallel mechanisms via screw theory. ASME Journal of Mechanical Design 125(3), 573–581 (2003)
13. Tao, D.C.: Applied Linkage Synthesis. Addison-Wesley, Reading (1964)

# Singularity Analysis of the Planar 3-RRR Parallel Manipulator Considering the Motion/Force Transmissibility

Xiang Chen, Fugui Xie, and Xin-jun Liu

The State Key Laboratory of Tribology & Institute of Manufacturing Engineering, Department of Precision Instruments and Mechanology, Tsinghua University, Beijing 100084, China
Chenxiang10@mails.tsinghua.edu.cn

**Abstract.** Singularity is an inherent characteristic of a closed-chain manipulator. This paper presents an approach to singularity analysis of the planar 3-RRR parallel manipulator. On the basis of screw theory, the motion/force transmission analysis of the manipulator is first achieved. The singularity is classified into three types: constraint singularity, input transmission singularity, and output transmission singularity, in which the last two ones can be investigated by two indices correspondingly. By using the proposed method, not only can all types of possible singularity configurations and their singular loci be identified, but their physical meanings are also explained in terms of their motion/force transmission performances, which make 3-RRR parallel manipulator more comprehensible.

**Keywords:** parallel manipulator, singularity analysis, motion/force transmissibility.

## 1  Introduction

Singularity analysis of parallel manipulator has been investigated by many researchers as one of the most important issues. As is well known, a parallel manipulator would almost lose control at its singular configuration. Two effects generally occurs: (1) the manipulator gains one or more unwanted degrees of freedom (DOFs), thereby degrading the natural stiffness and diminishing load capacity in the direction of the additional DOF; (2) the manipulator loses one or more DOFs, and lies at a dead point. In practice, we should identify all possible singular configurations of parallel manipulator and avoid them as far as we can.

Singularity is one of the inherent characteristics of parallel manipulators. It influences a considerable number of performance factors, including workspace, dexterity, stiffness and load capacity. In the past three decades, many researchers have studied singularity in parallel manipulators. The methods typically used to identify singularity can be divided into two categories: analytical and geometric methods. In the analytical method, the Jacobian matrix of every chain in the parallel manipulator is derived to identify singularity. Using the Jacobian matrix, Gosselin and Angeles [1] analyzed singularity in the closed-loop chains of parallel manipulators, and classified

C.-Y. Su, S. Rakheja, H. Liu (Eds.): ICIRA 2012, Part I, LNAI 7506, pp. 250–260, 2012.

the singularity into three main groups: inverse singularity, forward singularity, and combined singularity. In the geometric method, screw theory and line geometry are commonly used to solve singularity problem [2]. Hunt [3] laid down a general framework for using screw theory in analyzing singularity in parallel manipulators. Then, Huang et al. [4] conducted a more detailed analysis of closed-chain singularities by using the concept of reciprocity in screw theory. Merlet [5] noticed that it is possible to identify all singular configurations via the line geometric. More recent approaches to singularity analysis are discussed by Park and Kim [6], Davidson and Hunt [7], Ma and Angeles [8] and Tsai [9].

Undoubtedly, efforts should be devoted not only to accurately identifying singular configurations, but also to explaining their physical meanings. In this paper, we address the singularity analysis to the planar 3-RRR (R refers to revolute joint) parallel manipulator from three classified singular styles by using a screw theory-based approach, which considers the motion/force transmissibility. Numerous researchers have studied this type of parallel manipulator, but few have extensively applied singularity analysis to it. The current study contributes to literature in that it facilitates the understanding of singularity in the 3-RRR manipulator, thereby facilitating its optimal use [10], [11], [12].

The rest of the paper is organized as follows. The screw theory-based analysis of the motion/force transmissibility in 3-RRR parallel manipulator is addressed in Section 2. In section 3, we introduce our approach to classifying and identifying all possible singularities in terms of motion/force transmissibility. Finally, some conclusions drawn are provided in the last section.

# 2    Motion/Force Transmissibility Analysis

The essential function of a parallel manipulator is to transmit motion and force from its input members to its output member. Normally, the input members are the actuators, and the output member is the moving platform. In this section, the motion/force transmissibility analysis of the 3-RRR parallel manipulator will be presented, which can be used as bases for the singularity analysis.

## 2.1    Architecture

The kinematic scheme of a planar three-DOF parallel manipulator is presented in Fig. 1. The mobile platform is connected to the base by three identical RRR limbs, each with three revolute joints and two bars. In each leg, the revolute joint attached to the base is active. The base and mobile platform have circles, whose centers are origins $O$ and $O'$, respectively. All the joints connected to the base and mobile platform are symmetrically distributed at a nominal angle of $120°$ on the circles. The lengths of input links AB, DE, and GH equal one another, denoted as $r_1$; $r_2$ represents the equal lengths of coupler links BC, EF, and HI. The radii of the mobile platform and base are $r_3$ and $r_4$, respectively. A short analysis reveals that the parameters should satisfy some inequalities to constitute a complete 3-RRR parallel manipulator, i.e., $r_3 \leq r_4$, and $r_1 + r_2 + r_3 \geq r_4$.

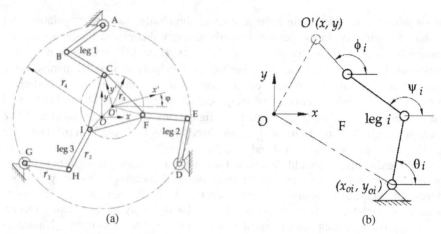

**Fig. 1.** Sketch of 3-RRR parallel manipulator (a) the whole manipulator, and (b) one RRR leg

## 2.2     Twist Screw and Wrench Screw

Fig. 1-(b) shows that each leg has three revolute joints with one DOF each. With respect to coordinate system O-xy, three twist screws exist, expressed as

$$\$_1 = (0,0,1; a_1, b_1, 0),\qquad(1)$$

$$\$_2 = (0,0,1; a_2, b_2, 0),\qquad(2)$$

and

$$\$_3 = (0,0,1; a_3, b_3, 0),\qquad(3)$$

where $a_i$, $b_i$, $(i = 1, 2, 3)$ are constants related to the instantaneous position of every kinematic pair in the corresponding coordinate system. A brief analysis of the linear correlation among the three twist screws reveals that, the twist screws are linearly independent, constituting a three-DOF leg. Meanwhile, a three-order twist screw system can be derived as follows

$$U_3 = \{\$_1, \$_2, \$_3\}.\qquad(4)$$

Because the first revolute joint is the active joint, the corresponding twist screw is the *input twist screw* (ITS), which can be expressed as

$$\$_I = \$_1 = (0,0,1; a_1, b_1, 0).\qquad(5)$$

Three ITSs   are found in the 3-RRR parallel manipulator, as shown below:

$$\begin{aligned}\$_{Ii} &= (0,0,1; a_{1i}, b_{1i}, 0)\\ &= (0,0,1; -r_4 \sin(\pi/2 + 2(i-1)/3), -r_4 \cos(\pi/2 + 2(i-1)/3), 0)\quad i = 1, 2, 3\end{aligned}\qquad(6)$$

Here, we can obtain three linearly independent screws $\$_j^r$ $(j=1,2,3)$, which are reciprocal to all the screws in $U_3$.

$$\$_j^r \circ \$_i = 0 \quad i = j = 1,2,3 . \tag{7}$$

Thus,

$$\$_1^r = (0,0,1;0,0,0), \tag{8}$$

$$\$_2^r = (0,0,0;1,0,0), \tag{9}$$

And

$$\$_3^r = (0,0,0;0,1,0), \tag{10}$$

where $\$_j^r$ $(j=1,2,3)$ are the unit reciprocal screws of the $i$-th leg.

In terms of physical meanings, each screw $\$_j^r$ $(j=1,2,3)$ can represent a *constraint wrench screw* (CWS) that the kinematic leg chain provides for the moving platform. Given the centrally symmetrical property of the 3-RRR manipulator, all the three leg chains provide the same CWSs, which can be expressed as $\$_{Cp}$ $(p=1,2,3)$. Thus, all the CWSs of the manipulator form a three-order constraint wrench screw system, denoted as

$$U_C = \left\{ \$_1^r \ \$_2^r \ \$_3^r \right\} = \left\{ \$_{C1} \ \$_{C2} \ \$_{C3} \right\} . \tag{11}$$

Among these screws, the first $\$_{C1}$, indicates a pure force which restricts the translational DOF, whereas the remaining screws, $\$_{C2}$ and $\$_{C3}$, indicate pure moments that constrain the two rotational DOFs.

As there is only one actuator in each of its legs, such a manipulator is usually referred to as a fully non-redundant parallel manipulator. As for the $i$-th leg, assuming that the actuation joint is locked, we can remove $\$_{Ii}$ from twist screw system $U_3$. Accordingly, a new passive joint screw system can be derived, i.e.,

$$U_2 = \{\$_2, \$_3\} . \tag{12}$$

We can then identify a new screw, namely, the *transmission wrench screw* (TWS), which is reciprocal to all the passive joint screws in $U_2$ and all the wrench screws in $U_C$, expressed as

$$\begin{cases} \$_T \circ \$_m = 0 & m = 2,3 \\ \$_T \circ \$_{Cn} = 0 & n = 1,2,3 \end{cases}, \tag{13}$$

where $\$_T$ is the TWS of the $i$-th leg.

Thus, we have

$$\$_{T1} = (\cos\psi_1, \sin\psi_1, 0; 0, 0, C_1), \tag{14}$$

$$\$_{T2} = (\cos\psi_2, \sin\psi_2, 0; 0, 0, C_2), \tag{15}$$

and

$$\$_{T3} = (\cos\psi_3, \sin\psi_3, 0; 0, 0, C_3), \tag{16}$$

Where
$$C_1 = (r_1\cos\theta_1)\sin\psi_1 - (r_4 + r_1\sin\theta_1)\cos\psi_1, \tag{17}$$

$$C_2 = [(-\sqrt{3}/2)r_4 + r_1\cos\theta_2]\sin\psi_2 - [(-1/2)r_4 + r_1\sin\theta_2]\cos\psi_2, \tag{18}$$

$$C_3 = [(\sqrt{3}/2)r_4 + r_1\cos\theta_3]\sin\psi_3 - [(-1/2)r_4 + r_1\sin\theta_3]\cos\psi_3, \tag{19}$$

Among the above equations, $\theta_i$ $(i=1,2,3)$ are the angles between the corresponding active legs and x-axis in the global coordinate system, and $\psi_i$ $(i=1,2,3)$ denote the angles between the corresponding passive legs and x-axis [Fig. 1-(b)].

As for the 3-RRR parallel manipulator, all its input joints except for that in the $i$-th leg $(i=1,2,3)$ are assumed to be fixed at a certain configuration. In this case, only the transmission wrench represented by $\$_{Ti}$ can contribute to the moving platform, whereas all other transmission wrenches apply no work to the moving platform. The instantaneous unit motion of the moving platform can be represented by a unit *output twist screw* (OTS) $\$_{Oi}$. Thus, we derive

$$\$_{Tj} \circ \$_{Oi} = 0 \quad (i = 1, 2, 3, \; j \neq i) \tag{20}$$

From Eq. (20), three related OTSs $\$_{Oi}$ $(i = 1, 2, 3)$ can be obtained.

By analyzing the motion/force transmissibility of 3-RRR parallel manipulator on the basis of screw theory, we can derive three ITSs, denoted as $\$_{Ii}$ $(i = 1, 2, 3)$; three TWSs, denoted as $\$_{Ti}$ $(i = 1, 2, 3)$; and three OTSs, denoted as $\$_{Oi}$ $(i = 1, 2, 3)$, respectively. These screws can be used as the bases for the singularity analysis of the 3-RRR parallel manipulator.

## 3    Singularity Analysis

In the motion/force transmission process of a limited-DOF parallel manipulator, there always exist the TWSs and CWSs, which constitute the transmission wrench screw system and constraint wrench screw system, respectively. Hereby, the singularity problem of a parallel manipulator is conducted from two aspects as transmission singularity and constraint singularity, among which the transmission singularity can be further subdivided into the input and output transmission singularity. Thus, the singularities of a parallel manipulator can be classified into three types: constraint singularity, input transmission singularity, and output transmission singularity.

We propose two indices for analyzing transmission singularity. A manipulator transmits motion and force via the interaction among ITSs, TWSs, and OTSs.

By locking all the actuators except for the $i$-th actuator, the manipulator becomes of single-DOF type. Thus, the $i$-th chain corresponds to an ITS, TWS, and OTS, which are denoted by $\$_{Ii}$, $\$_{Ti}$, and $\$_{Oi}$, respectively. The reciprocal product of the TWS and ITS is taken as the *input transmission power* (ITP) of the $i$-th chain in the manipulator. Similarly, the reciprocal product of the TWS and OTS is taken as the *output transmission power* (OTP). We then obtain

$$\text{ITP} = \$_{Ii} \circ \$_{Ti} \quad i = 1, 2, 3 , \tag{21}$$

$$\text{OTP} = \$_{Ti} \circ \$_{Oi} \quad i = 1, 2, 3 . \tag{22}$$

The physical meanings of the two proposed indices ITP and OTP indicate the power between the transmission wrench and input twist, and that between the transmission wrench and output twist, respectively. If ITP equals zero, the power between ITS and TWS will vanish, indeed, the motion from the corresponding actuator cannot be transmitted by its transmission wrench. In this case, a type of transmission singularity occurs: input transmission singularity. If OTP equals zero, the external wrench along the axis of $\$_O$ cannot be counterbalanced by any transmission wrench. Therefore, the manipulator suffers from another type of transmission singularity, namely, output transmission singularity. If any value of the ITP or OTP in three chains of the parallel manipulator equals zero, input transmission singularity or output transmission singularity occurs, respectively.

**Constraint Singularity.** As previously stated, there exist three constraint wrench screws $\$_{Ci}$ ($i = 1, 2, 3$) in each chain of 3-RRR manipulator, among which two screws are unit moments, and the remaining one is a pure unit force. Normally, they are linear independent with each other and constraint two rotational DOFs and one translational DOF. Thus, we conclude that the 3-RRR parallel manipulator does not suffer from constraint singularity [13].

**Input Transmission Singularity.** Here, we use the proposed index ITP to describe this singularity. The manipulator is centrally symmetrical; hence, using only one leg in the analysis is sufficient.

Substituting Eqs. (6) and (14) to Eq. (21), one may obtain

$$\text{ITP} = \$_{I1} \circ \$_{T1} = r_1 \cos \theta_1 \sin \psi_1 - (2r_4 + r_1 \sin \theta_1) \cos \psi_1 , \tag{23}$$

from which one may see that, ITP equals zero if and only if $\theta_1 = 90°$ and $\psi_1 = 90°$ or $270°$. At these configurations, therefore, the manipulator stays at the input singular points, as shown in Fig. 2-(a) and (b). An in-depth analysis of these configurations reveals that a small rotation on the actuator does not cause the mobile platform to generate any output motion. In terms of motion/force transmissibility, the motion cannot be transmitted from the input member to the output member at such an input transmission singularity. The mobile platform degenerates the translational DOF along the axis of $\$_{T1}$. Input singularity in the other two legs can be analyzed using the same method, but the analysis is not discussed in this paper.

The singularity loci are comprised of a series of continuous singularity points. Accordingly, input singularity loci are made up of all input singular dead points. It is obvious that, singularity loci found in a definite manipulator, and vary as the parameters of the 3-RRR manipulator change. We describe the input singularity loci of a kinematic optimized 3-RRR manipulator, with parameters $r_1 = r_2 = 1.25$, $r_3 = 0.10$, and $r_4 = 1.65$ (Fig. 3). The blue curve in Fig. 3 is the input transmission singular loci with its rotational angle $\varphi$ equals zero. The loci are centrally symmetrical as in the case of their structure characteristics.

**Output Transmission Singularity.** The index OTP is used to describe this type of singularity. If any value of OTP equals zero, output transmission singularity occurs in the manipulator. As analyzed above, the 3-RRR parallel manipulator has three TWSs, denoted as $\$_{Ti}\ (i = 1, 2, 3)$, each presenting a pure force along the corresponding axis of the passive bar (the bar connected by two passive joints). A comprehensive analysis of the geometric properties of the screw system in Ref [3] reveals that the three TWSs typically span a three-order TWS system. However, these TWSs can only form a two-order line screw system in two cases, i.e., the three TWSs intersect at one point, and those are parallel to one another in the same plane. To use OTP, one or more OTP values of all the legs equal to zero at such two cases. We conclude that when the rank of the TWS system degenerates from three to two or one, the minimum OTP value equals zero, thereby causing output transmission singularity.

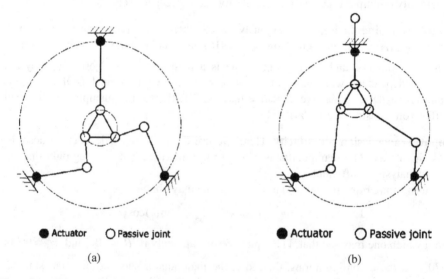

|  | Actuator | ◯ Passive joint | | Actuator | ◯ Passive joint |

(a)                                                        (b)

**Fig. 2.** Input transmission singularity (a) when $\theta_1 = 90°, \psi_1 = 90°$ and (b) when $\theta_1 = 90°, \psi_1 = 270°$

The configuration of output transmission singularity depends not only on the configuration of the mobile platform, but also on the positional relationships among the three passive legs. The workspace of the manipulator has uncountable configurable points, but considering all these points is impossible and unnecessary. Thus, we take only point of origin $(x, y) = (0,0)$ as an example in analyzing this type of output singularity. Fig. 4 shows the relationship between the OTP value and rotational degree of mobile platform $\varphi$ at the same manipulator parameters as before ($r_1 = r_2 = 1.25$, $r_3 = 0.10$, and $r_4 = 1.65$).

Fig. 4 illustrates that the OTP value of the 3-RRR manipulator varies as rotation degree $\varphi$ varies between $(-180°, 180°]$. The value equals zero when $\varphi_1 = -48°$ and $\varphi_2 = 132°$, corresponding to two output singular configurations as shown in Fig. 5-(a) and (b), respectively. It is worth noting that, there always exist two complementary degrees that result in the output transmission singularity in which the mobile platform is located in the usable workspace, as in $|\varphi_1 - \varphi_2| = 180°$ when the mobile platform is located at the point of origin.

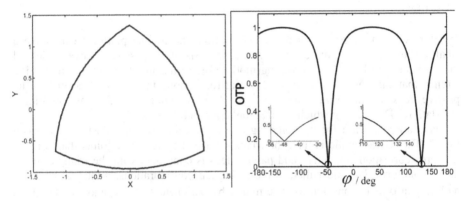

**Fig. 3.** Input singularity loci with parameters $r_1 = r_2 = 1.25$, $r_3 = 0.10$, and $r_4 = 1.65$

**Fig. 4.** Relationship between OTP value and rotational angle $\varphi$ in which the mobile platform is located at point of origin $(x, y) = (0,0)$

Fig. 5 shows that at such configurations, the mobile platform can still perform a small rotation about the convergence point even when all the actuators are locked. When the motion/force transmission performance is considered, this output transmission singularity stems from the three corresponding planar TWSs converging to one point. The external torque about the axis of the convergence point cannot be counterbalanced by any transmission wrench. That is, no transmission force can transmit power that enables the moving platform to rotate about the related axis. This manipulator generates an unwanted rotational DOF, along which poor stiffness arises.

As stated above, another condition of output transmission singularity is that all the three TWSs are parallel to one another in the same plane (Fig. 6). Thus, the TWS system degenerates to a two-order system, which comprises three planar parallel wrench screws $\$_{Ti}$ ($i = 1, 2, 3$). The minimum OTP value of the manipulator is

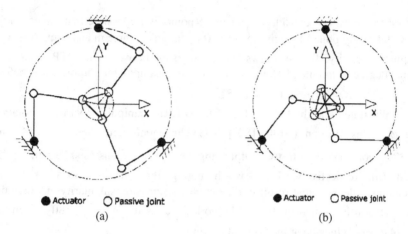

**Fig. 5.** Output transmission singularity configurations (a) when $\varphi_1 = -48°$ and (b) when $\varphi_2 = 132°$

therefore equal to zero. At such a configuration, the mobile platform can move a small distance along the direction normal to the axis of the passive leg even when all the actuators are locked. Considering motion/force transmissibility, no transmission wrench that can counterbalance the external force along the direction normal to the passive legs in the same plane exists. This manipulator gains an additional translational DOF, along which the manipulator exhibits poor stiffness.

One particular case for the referring output transmission singularity is shown in Fig. 7. The characteristic is that, the triangle formed by the three joints that connect the three corresponding active and passive legs is congruent with the triangle in the mobile platform. It is clear that, in these singular configurations, rotational angle of mobile platform is constant, as determined by parameters $r_1$, $r_3$ and $r_4$. The blue curve in Fig. 7 denotes its singular loci of this kind of output transmission singularity which is a circle located at the central point of the base platform.

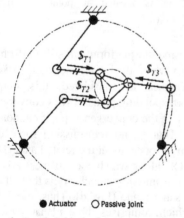

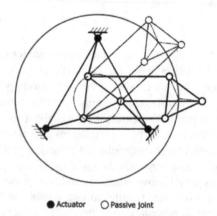

**Fig. 6.** Another kind of output transmission singularity

**Fig. 7.** Output transmission singularity and its loci

Three points should be noted: (a) not all 3-RRR manipulators with any geometric parameters exhibit this kind of output transmission singularity; and (b) the singularity depends not only on the position of the mobile platform, but also on the orientation of it; (c) because of the symmetrical characteristics of the 3-RRR parallel manipulator, singular configurations would always arise in three symmetrical cases as well.

# 4    Conclusion

This paper addresses the singularity analysis of the planar 3-DOF parallel manipulator. To this end, a method considering the motion/force transmissibility based on screw theory has been presented. Two indices ITP and OTP have been proposed to identify the input transmission singularity and output transmission singularity, respectively. From the theoretical and practical singularity analysis to the parallel manipulator, the conclusions drawn are summarized as follows:

(a)  It is an effective and general method to deal with the singularity problem in a closed-chain manipulator on the basis of screw theory.
(b)  The proposed method can not only identify all possible singularities as far as we can, but also explain their physical meanings in terms of the motion/force transmission performances—a highly important issue in closed-chain manipulators.
(c)  Three types of singularities are identified, including a group of complex output transmission singularities, which can further elucidate the 3-RRR manipulator and enable the resolution of singularity problems.

**Acknowledgement.** This work was supported by the National Natural Science Foundation of China under Grants 51075222 and 51135008.

# References

1. Gossenlin, C., Angeles, J.: Singularity analysis of closed-loop kinematic chains. IEEE Transactions on Robotics and Automation 6(2), 281–290 (1990)
2. Yang, G.L., Chen, I.M., et al.: Singularity analysis of three-legged parallel robots based on passive-joint velocities. IEEE Transactions on Robotics and Automation 17(4), 413–422 (2001)
3. Hunt. K.H.: Kinematic geometry of mechanisms. Oxford University Press (1978)
4. Huang, Z., Zhao, Y.S., Zhao, T.S.: Advanced spatial mechanism. China Higher Education Press, Beijing (2005) (in Chinese)
5. Merlet, J.P.: Singularity configurations of parallel robots and Grassmann geometry. International Journal of Robotics Research 8(5), 45–56 (1989)
6. Park, D.C., Kim, J.W.: Singularity analysis of closed kinematic Chains. Journal of Mechanical Design 121(1), 32–38 (1999)
7. Davidson, J.K., Hunt, K.H.: Robots and screw theory: applications of kinematics and statics to robotics. Oxford University Press, London (2004)
8. Ma, O., Angeles, J.: Architecture singularities of parallel manipulators. The International Journal of Robotics and Automation 7(1), 23–29 (1992)

9. Tsai, L.W.: Robot Analysis: The mechanics of serial and parallel manipulators. Wiley-Interscience Publication, New York (1999)
10. Liu, X.-J., Wang, J., Gao, F.: Performance atlases of the workspace for planar 3-DOF parallel manipulators. Robotica 18(5), 563–568 (2000)
11. Marc, A., Roger, B.: The synthesis of three-degree-of–freedom planar parallel mechanisms with revolute joints (3-RRR) for an optimal singularity-free workspace. Journal of Robotic Systems 21(5), 259–274 (2004)
12. Daniali, H.R., Murray, P.J., Angeles, J.: Singularity analysis of a general class of planar parallel manipulators. In: IEEE International Conference on Robotics and Automation, pp. 1547–1552 (1995)
13. Zlatanov, D., Bonev, O.A., Gosselin, C.M.: Constraint singularities of parallel mechanisms. In: Proceedings of the IEEE International Conference on Robotics and Automation, Washington, DC, pp. 496–502 (2002)

# Dimensional Synthesis of a Planar Parallel Manipulator for Pick-and-Place Operations Based on Rigid-Body Dynamics

Binbin Lian, Yimin Song[*], Gang Dong, Tao Sun, and Yang Qi

Key Laboratory of Mechanism Theory and Equipment Design of Ministry of Education,
Tianjin University, Tianjin300072, China
{lianbinbin016,qiyang1900}@163.com, {ymsong,dg_tju}@tju.edu.cn,
suntaotju@gmail.com

**Abstract.** This paper presents a linear driven 2 degree-of-freedoms (DoFs) Parallel Manipulator (PM) for pick-and-place operation in the light industry, and its dynamic dimensional synthesis is carried out. Inverse kinematics and rigid-body dynamics are formulated to propose a dynamic performance index, which is to minimize the maximum driving force of a single link. The index is associated with dimensional and inertial parameters and can be expressed as function of transmission angles. Then performance constraints are considered by investigating the relationship between singular values of Jacobian matrix and mapping characteristics of velocity, accuracy and stiffness. The approach is illustrated in detail through an example and the optimized dimensional parameters are obtained for high performance throughout the entire workspace.

**Keywords:** parallel manipulator, pick-and-place operation, rigid-body dynamic, dynamic performance index.

## 1 Introduction

In recent years, high-speed PMs with less than 6 DoFs have been found wide applications in electronics, pharmacy packaging and many other light industries, which is exemplified successfully by Adept robot [1], Delta robot [2-3], Diamond robot [4-5] and so on. High-speed PMs with lower mobility possess the potentials of good accuracy, high velocity and excellent dynamics compared with serial manipulators [6-7]. In order to obtain better performance, the scholars and the engineers lay great interest in the optimal design of high-speed PMs [8]. It's necessary to focus on two issues in the optimal design, one is performance evaluation index [9] and another is optimal design method [10-11].

In most cases, the mathematical characteristics of Jacobian matrix are adopted as performance evaluation index, such as condition number, determinant, singular value, etc [12-15]. Considering power dissipation and dynamic performance of PMs in the high-speed environment, the performance evaluation index mentioned above is not

---

[*] Corresponding author.

C.-Y. Su, S. Rakheja, H. Liu (Eds.): ICIRA 2012, Part I, LNAI 7506, pp. 261–270, 2012.

suitable. Therefore it's important to formulating the appropriate performance index for high-speed PMs. With respect to the optimal design method, the traditional way [16-17] is to regard the performance evaluation index as the objective function and the corresponding geometric limit as the constraint condition, and then the optimum values are achieved by solving the nonlinear equations including geometric limits. However, as to the optimal design of high-speed PMs, only geometric limits in the constraint conditions are not enough, other performances reflected by objective function should be considered necessarily.

Zhang [18-19] studies the performance evaluation index and the optimal design flow of the well-known Delta manipulator. As the extension of his method, this paper focuses on the optimal design of a kind of planar parallel manipulator which can be applied in the pick-and-place operations. The novel planar 2-DoF parallel manipulator actuated by linear motors possesses the high-speed, good accuracy and perfect dynamic capabilities.

The remainder of this paper is as follows, Section 2 is devoted to the inverse kinematics of the 2-DoF PM. In Section 3, rigid-body dynamic is carried out by means of virtual work principle, followed by the dynamic dimensional synthesis. Section 4 gives an example and the conclusions are drawn in Section 5.

## 2     Inverse Kinematics

As shown in Fig. 1a), the 2-DoF PM is symmetrical and composed of a fixed base, a moving platform and two identical kinematic chains. Each kinematic chain consists of a set of parallelogram formed by two passive links and a bracket. Driven by the linear motors situated on the base, the moving platform can translate along two directions in its moving plane. The module can be integrated with screw-lead cell to form a 3-DoF hybrid robot which is especially suitable for long distance and relatively slow or step motion in the direction normal to the working plane (see Fig. 1b)).

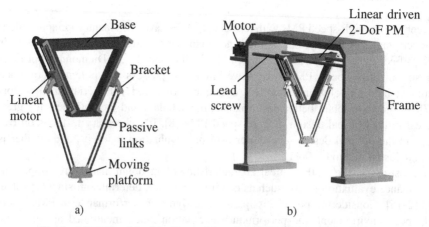

**Fig. 1.** a) CAD model of the linear driven 2-DoF PM; b) 3-DoF hybrid robot

The moving platform is represented by its central point named reference point $O'$ as shown in the schematic diagram of the proposed mechanism in Fig. 2. In the $O\text{-}XY$ coordinate system, the position vector $r$ of point $O'$ is calculated as

$$r = \text{sgn}(i)be_1 + d_iu_i + lw_i \qquad i=1,2. \tag{1}$$

Where $r = (x \quad y)^T$; $b$ is the distance between $O$ and $A_i$; $e_1$ is the unit vector of axis $X$; $d_i$ is the displacement of the $i$th linear motor; $u_i$ is the unit vector in the direction of the $i$th slider; $l$ is the length of the passive link; $w_i$ is the unit vector of the $i$th passive link; and $\text{sgn}(i) = \begin{cases} 1 & i=1 \\ -1 & i=2 \end{cases}$.

The inverse position analysis gives

$$d_i = -\sqrt{E_{1i}^2 - E_{2i}} - E_{1i} \qquad i=1,2. \tag{2}$$

Where $E_{1i} = \left[\text{sgn}(i)x - b\right]\sin\dfrac{\theta}{2} + y\cos\dfrac{\theta}{2}$; $E_{2i} = \left[x - \text{sgn}(i)b\right]^2 + y^2 - l^2$; $\theta$ is the angle between $u_1$ and $u_2$.

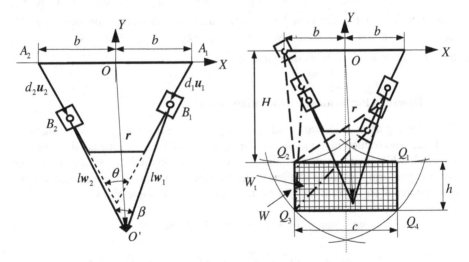

**Fig. 2.** Diagram and workspace of the linear driven 2-DoF PM

Differentiating Eq. (1) with respect to time and write in matrix form

$$\dot{d}_i = Jv. \tag{3}$$

Where $v$, $\dot{d}_i$ are the vector velocity of point $O'$ and that of linear motors, respectively. $J = \left[\dfrac{w_1}{w_1^T u_1} \quad \dfrac{w_2}{w_2^T u_2}\right]^T$ is referred to as the Jacobian matrix.

Differentiating Eq. (3) in the same way yields

$$\ddot{d}_i = Ja + f(v).$$

(4)

Where $a$, $\ddot{d}_i$ are the vector acceleration of point $O'$ and that of linear motor,

respectively. $f(v) = \left[ v^{\mathrm{T}} \dfrac{u_1^{\mathrm{T}} u_1}{l \left( u_1^{\mathrm{T}} w_1 \right)^2} v \quad v^{\mathrm{T}} \dfrac{u_2^{\mathrm{T}} u_2}{l \left( u_2^{\mathrm{T}} w_2 \right)^2} v \right]^{\mathrm{T}}$.

## 3     Dynamic Dimensional Synthesis

### 3.1     Workspace and Design Parameter

The reachable workspace of the robot is the set of all the locations of point $O'$ that can reach when linear motors move in the range $[0, d_{max}]$. As shown in Fig. 2, the reachable workspace $W$ can be formed once $l$, $b$ and $\theta$ are determined. A rectangle $W_t$ is selected as the task workspace, which intersects the boundary of $W$ at $Q_1$, $Q_2$, $Q_3$, $Q_4$. The distance between $X$ axis and the upper boundary of $W_t$ is $H$. In order to find out the effects of dimensional parameters on dynamic performance, $H$ and $b$ are normalized by $l$ such that $\lambda_H = H / l$, $\lambda_b = b / l$. So $\lambda_H$, $\lambda_b$, $\theta \in (0, \pi)$ are chosen as the design parameters.

### 3.2     Dynamic Performance Evaluation Index

The following assumptions are made in formulating the inverse rigid-body dynamics: (1) There's no friction in the joints. (2) The moments of inertia of the passive links are negligible while their masses are concentrated to the two endpoints. (3) The mass of the moving platform including the end-effector and load can be represented by the concentrated mass of point $O'$. Thus, the virtual work principle gives

$$\left( -ma - mge_2 \right)^{\mathrm{T}} \delta r + \left( F - m_{\mathrm{B}} \ddot{d}_i - F_{\mathrm{Bg}} \right)^{\mathrm{T}} \delta d_i = 0.$$

(5)

Where $m$ is the mass concentrated on point $O'$; $e_2 = (0 \ \ 1)^{\mathrm{T}}$; $F = (F_1 \ \ F_2)^{\mathrm{T}}$ is the driving force of linear motors; $m_{\mathrm{B}}$ is the mass concentrated on point $B_i$; $F_{\mathrm{Bg}} = (m_1 g \ \ m_2 g)^{\mathrm{T}}$ is the gravity; and $\delta r$, $\delta d_i$ are the virtual displacement of point $O'$ and that of linear motors, respectively.

Taking Eq. (3) and Eq. (4) into account, Eq. (5) can be rewritten as

$$F = m_{\mathrm{B}} Ga + m_{\mathrm{B}} f(v) + F_g.$$

(6)

Where $G = \eta J^{-\mathrm{T}} + J$; $F_g = mg J^{-\mathrm{T}} e_2 + F_{\mathrm{Bg}}$; $\eta = m / m_{\mathrm{B}}$.

Previous researches [5, 20-21] have shown that inertia force is dominant during accelerating or decelerating period. Then the gravity can be ignored when considering the maximum of the driving forces. So the inverse dynamic equation is expressed as

$$F = F_a + F_v , \quad F_a = m_B Ga , \quad F_v = m_B v^T vH . \tag{7}$$

Where $G = \begin{bmatrix} \eta \dfrac{\left(w_1^T u_1\right) w_2^T Q}{w_2^T Q w_1} + \dfrac{w_1^T}{w_1^T u_1} \\[2ex] \eta \dfrac{\left(w_2^T u_2\right) Q w_1}{w_2^T Q w_1} + \dfrac{w_2^T}{w_2^T u_2} \end{bmatrix}$, $Q = \begin{bmatrix} 0 & -1 \\ 1 & 0 \end{bmatrix}$, $H = \begin{bmatrix} \dfrac{1}{l\left(u_1^T w_1\right)^2} \\[2ex] \dfrac{1}{l\left(u_2^T w_2\right)^2} \end{bmatrix}$.

$F_a$ and $F_v$ are linear independent, then the maximum driving force of single active joint is the sum of $F_{a\max}$ and $F_{v\max}$. According to inner product operation, $F_{i\max}$ can be determined by

$$F_{i\max} = m_B \sqrt{G_i G_i^T} + m_B \sqrt{H_i H_i^T} = m_B \left( \sqrt{\eta^2 \frac{\cos^2 \alpha_i}{\sin^2 \beta_i} + \frac{1}{\cos^2 \alpha_i} + 2\eta} + \frac{1}{l \cos^2 \alpha_i} \right). \tag{8}$$

Where $G_i$ and $F_i$ denote the $i$th row of $G$ and $F$, respectively; $\alpha_i$, $\beta$ are the transmission angles within a limb and between the limbs, $\cos \alpha_i = w_i^T u_i$, $\sin \beta = w_2^T Q w_1$. The minimum of $F_{i\max}$ in the feasible workspace is chosen as the dynamic performance optimization objective $F_M$

$$\min_z F_M = \max_{r \in W_t} \left\{ F_{i\max} (r, z) \right\}. \tag{9}$$

Where $z = \left(\lambda_H, \lambda_b, \theta\right)$ is the design parameters.

## 3.3    Constraint Conditions

**Dimension Constraint.** In order to make the general structure compact relative to the workspace, the workspace to machine dimension ratio should be $\lambda_c / \lambda_b \leq 1$, where $\lambda_c = c / l$.

**Velocity Constraint.** Based on the principle of singular value decomposition, the minimum singular value of $J^{-1}$ should be big enough to ensure the moving platform achieving high velocity. It is easy to proved that

$$\min_{r \in W_t} \sigma_{\min} \left(J^{-1}(r, z)\right) \geq b_u \iff \max_{r \in W_t} \sigma_{\max} \left(J(r, z)\right) \leq b_u. \tag{10}$$

**Accuracy Constraint.** The mapping relation between position error $\Delta r$ and actuated joint error $\Delta d$ is expressed as $\Delta r = J^{-1} \Delta d$, which leads to

$$\max_{r \in W_t} \sigma_{\max} \left(J^{-1}(r, z)\right) \leq b_1 \iff \min_{r \in W_t} \sigma_{\min} \left(J(r, z)\right) \geq b_1. \tag{11}$$

**Stiffness Constraint.** Assumed that the equivalent stiffness of actuated joints is constant $k_i$, the driving force can be written as $F = \mathrm{diag}(k_i)\Delta d$. The deformation of point $O'$ is produced by the external forces $f_e$, which is determined by $f_e = K\Delta r$. Since $f_e = J^T F$, $\Delta r = J^{-1}\Delta d$, it is easy to derive that $K = J^T \mathrm{diag}(k_i) J$. $K$ is the total stiffness matrix of the mechanism and it is required to be bigger in order to get better stiffness, which leads to the maximizing of minimum eigenvalue of matrix $J^T J$. The problem is equivalent to determine the minimum of $\sigma_{\min}(J)$, which is the same as the accuracy constraints.

Then, Eq. (10) and (11) are chosen as the performance constraints for the optimal design. As for the proposed linear driven 2-DoF PM, the singular value of Jacobian matrix can be calculated as

$$\sigma_{\max,\min}(J) = \frac{1}{\sqrt{2}|q_1||q_2|}\sqrt{\left(q_1^2 + q_2^2\right) \pm \left[\left(q_1^2 - q_2^2\right)^2 + \left(2q_1 q_2 t\right)^2\right]^{\frac{1}{2}}}. \tag{12}$$

Where $q_i = w_i^T u_i = \cos\alpha_i$, $t = w_1^T w_2 = \cos\beta$. For a well performance of velocity, accuracy and stiffness, $\alpha_i$ and $\beta$ are not allowed to be $\pi/2$. And when $\alpha_i \to \pi/2$, $\beta \to 0$, $F_{i\max}$ tends to be infinite from equation(8). So $\alpha_i$, $\beta$ should fall in the range $\alpha_i \in [0, \theta_E]$, $\beta \in [\theta_F, \theta_G]$. $b_u$ in the equation (10) and $b_l$ in the equation (11) can be written as

$$b_u = \frac{1}{\sqrt{2}\cos^2\theta_E}\sqrt{2\cos^2\theta_E + \left(2\cos^4\theta_E + 2\cos^4\theta_E\left(2\cos^2\theta_G - 1\right)\right)^{\frac{1}{2}}}$$

$$b_l = \left(1 - \frac{\sqrt{2}}{2}|\cos\theta_F|\right)^{\frac{1}{2}}.$$

## 4    Example Discussion

The task workspace $W_t$ is designed as a rectangle of $c = 600\,\mathrm{mm}$ in width and $h = 180\,\mathrm{mm}$ in height. $m_d$ is the mass of payload and the movable platform while $m_e$ is the mass of linear motor and the bracket. Assuming that the rods are in constant section and $\mu = 0.125\,\mathrm{g/mm}$ is the mass per unit length, the inertial parameters of the mechanism are listed in Table 1.

**Table 1.** Inertial Parameters (Unit: kg )

| $m_d$ | $m_e$ | $m_B$ | $m$ |
|-------|-------|-------|-----|
| 1.2 | 4.488 | $1.2 + \mu l$ | $4.488 + 2\mu l$ |

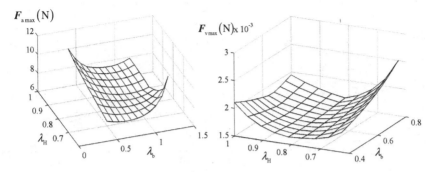

**Fig. 3.** Variation of $F_{a\,max}$, $F_{v\,max}$ versus $\lambda_b$ and $\lambda_H$ ($\theta=\pi/3$)

As shown in Fig. 3, $F_{v\,max}$ is much smaller than $F_{a\,max}$ in the entire workspace, which allows $F_{max} = F_{a\,max}$ without taking the effect of $F_{v\,max}$ into account.

It has been found in Fig. 4 that $F_M$ decreases with the increase of $\theta$. For a given $\theta$, $F_M$ increases as $\lambda_b$, $\lambda_H$ climb up, and folds in the space. Then there is a set of $\lambda_b$, $\lambda_H$ which is approximately in linear relation to make sure that $F_M$ gets the minimum value.

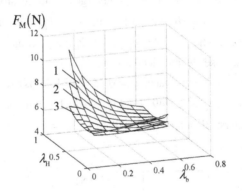

**Fig. 4.** Variation of $F_M$ versus $\lambda_b$, $\lambda_H$ and $\theta$ (1: $\theta=\pi/3$, 2: $\theta=\pi/2$, 3: $\theta=2\pi/3$)

When $\theta = \pi/3$, the variation of $\min\sigma_{min}$, $\max\sigma_{max}$ versus $\lambda_b$, $\lambda_H$ is presented in Fig. 5. It is easy to find out that a series of constraint plane are formed when $b_1$, $b_u$ are different, which would limit the range of $\lambda_b$ and $\lambda_H$. When $b_1$ increases, the feasible region of $\lambda_b$, $\lambda_H$ get smaller, and $\lambda_b$ would first reach its boundary. $\min\sigma_{min}$ becomes bigger with the increase of $\lambda_b$, and the effect of $\lambda_H$ is in curve shape. The change of $\max\sigma_{max}$ is just the opposite of that of $\min\sigma_{min}$. $\max\sigma_{max}$ becomes bigger as $\lambda_b$ monotonously increases, and it presents as concave curve when it comes to the effect of $\lambda_H$. The feasible region of $\lambda_b$, $\lambda_H$ get smaller with the decrease of $b_u$, and $\lambda_H$ would first get to the boundary.

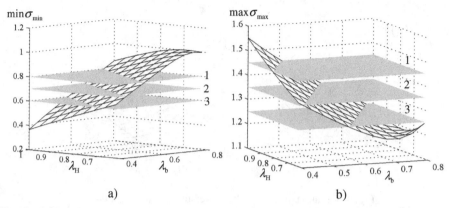

**Fig. 5.** a) Variation of $\min\sigma_{\min}$ versus $\lambda_b$, $\lambda_H$ and $b_l$ (1: $b_l = 0.8$, 2: $b_l = 0.6$, 3: $b_l = 0.4$), b) Variation of $\max\sigma_{\max}$ versus $\lambda_b$, $\lambda_H$ and $b_u$ (1: $b_u = 1.3$, 2: $b_u = 1.4$, 3: $b_u = 1.5$). $\theta = \pi/3$ in both figures.

It can be found in Fig. 6 that $F_M^*$ monotonously decreases with the increase of $\theta$, and the position of interval $[b_l, b_u]$ can also influence $F_M^*$. When $[b_l, b_u]$ shift to the right, which means $b_l$, $b_u$ get bigger, $F_M^*$ converges to the feasible region boundary of $\lambda_b$. On the contrary, when $[b_l, b_u]$ shift to the left, $F_M^*$ converges to the feasible region boundary of $\lambda_H$. The feasible region of $\lambda_b$, $\lambda_H$ would be narrowed down when attempting to increase $b_l$ and decrease $b_u$.

Considering the given task workspace, $b_l = 0.75$, $b_u = 1.45$ is chosen for the prototype design. When $\theta = \pi/3$, $F_M^*$ is 7.3749 N in Fig. 6, which determines $\lambda_b$, $\lambda_H$. It is easy to get the scale parameters: $\theta^* = \pi/3$, $l^* = 800$ mm, $b^* = 544$ mm, $H^* = 762$ mm.

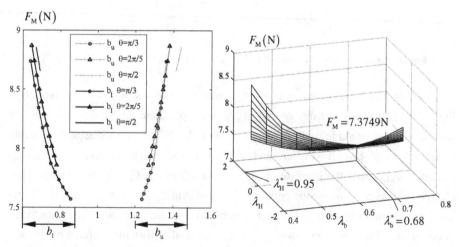

**Fig. 6.** Variation of $F_M$ versus $b_l$, $b_u$; Variation of $F_M$ versus $\lambda_b$, $\lambda_H$ ($\theta = \pi/3$)

# 5    Conclusions

This paper presents an approach of dimensional synthesis which combines performance of kinematic and rigid-body dynamic for the proposed linear driven 2-DoF PM. The maximum driving force of single active link $F_M$ is chosen as the optimization objective, which can be expressed as a function associate with dimensional and inertial parameters, transmission angles in a limb and between limbs. By setting a set of constraints in terms of velocity, accuracy and stiffness performance, optimized dimensional parameters for achieving minimum $F_M$ is obtained. It has been found that there is a set of $\lambda_b$, $\lambda_H$ which is approximately in linear relationship to make sure that $F_M$ gets the minimum value when $\theta$ is determined.

**Acknowledgments.** The research is supported by the National Natural Science Foundation of China (No. 51075295, No. 51135008), and the Tianjin Science and Technology Program (No. 11JCZDJC22700).

# References

1. Adept Technology Inc., http://adept.com
2. Clavel, R.: Device for the Movement and Positioning of an Element in Space. Patent number: US 4976582 (1990)
3. Rey, L., Clavel, R.: The Delta Parallel Robot. In: Boer, C.R., Molinari-Tosatti, L., Smith, K.S. (eds.) Parallel Kinematic Machine: Theoretical Aspects and Industrial Requirements, pp. 401–417. Springer, New York (1999)
4. Huang, T., Li, M., Li, Z.X., et al.: Optimal Kinematic Design of 2-DOF Parallel Manipulators with Well-shaped Workspace Bounded by a Specified Conditioning Index. IEEE Transactions on Robotics and Automation 20, 538–542 (2004)
5. Huang, T., Mei, J.P., Li, Z.X.: A Method for Estimating Servomotor Parameters of a Parallel Robot for Rapid Pick-and-Place Operations. ASME Journal of Mechanical Design 127, 596–601 (2005)
6. Weck, M., Staimer, D.: Parallel Kinematic Machine Tools: Current State and Future Potentials. Annals of the CIRP 51, 671–683 (2002)
7. Merlet, J.P.: Solid Mechanics and Its Applications, 2nd edn., vol. 128. Springer, The Netherlands (2006)
8. Francois, P., Vincent, N., Sebastien, K., et al.: Optimal Design of a 4-DOF Parallel Manipulator: From Academic to Industry. IEEE Transactions on Robotic 25(2), 213–224 (2009)
9. Liu, X.J., Wu, C., Wang, J.S.: A New Index for the Performance Evaluation of Parallel Manipulators: A Study on Planar Parallel Manipulators. In: The 7th World Congress on Intelligent Control and Automation, Chongqing, China, pp. 353–357 (2008)
10. Kim, S.G., Ryu, J.: Optimal Design of 6-DOF Parallel Manipulators Using Three Point Coordinate. In: IEEE/RSJ International Conference on Intelligent Robots and Systems, Hawaii, USA, pp. 2178–2183 (2001)

11. Wang, Z.F., Ji, S.M., Wan, Y.H., et al.: Optimal Design of Parallel Robot for the Prescribed Regular Dexterous Workspace. In: IEEE International Conference on Automation and Logistics, Jinan, China, pp. 565–568 (2007)
12. Merlet, J.P.: Jacobian, Manipulability, Condition Number, and Accuracy of Parallel Manipulators. Journal of Mechanical Design 128, 199–206 (2006)
13. Ma, O., Angeles, J.: Optimum Architecture Design of Platform Manipulator. In: IEEE Int. Conf. Robotics and Automation, pp. 1131–1135 (1991)
14. Ranjbaran, F., Angeles, J., Kecskemethy, A.: On the Kinematic Conditioning of Robotic Manipulators. In: IEEE International Conference on Robotics and Automation, Minneapolis, Minnesota, pp. 3167–3172 (1996)
15. Pott, A., Boye, T., Hiller, M.: Parameter Synthesis for Parallel Kinematic Machines From Given Process requirements. In: IEEE/ASME International Conference on Advanced Intelligent Mechatronics Monterey, California, USA, pp. 753–758 (2005)
16. Kim, H.S., Tsai, L.W.: Design Optimization of a Cartesian Parallel Manipulator. ASME Journal of Mechanical Design 125, 43–51 (2003)
17. Liu, X.J., Jin, Z.L., Gao, F.: Optimum design of 3-DOF spherical parallel manipulators with respect to the conditioning and stiffness indices. Mechanism and Machine Theory 35, 1257–1267 (2000)
18. Zhang, L.M., Song, Y.M.: Optimal Design of the Delta Robot Based on Dynamics. In: IEEE International Conference on Robotic and Automation, Shanghai, China, pp. 336–341 (2011)
19. Zhang, L.M., Mei, J.P., Zhao, X.M., et al.: Dimensional Synthesis of the Delta Robot Using Transmission Angle Constraints. Robotica, 1–7 (2011)
20. Codourey, A.: Dynamic Modeling of Parallel Robots for Computed-torque Control Implementation. Int. J. Robot. Res. 17, 1325–1336 (1998)
21. Choi, H., Konno, A., Uchiyama, M.: Inverse Dynamic Analysis of a 4-DOF Parallel Robot H4. In: IEEE International Conference on Intelligent Robotic Systems, Sendai, Japan, pp. 3501–3506 (2004)

# Analytical Forward Kinematics
# for Two Kinds of Typical Tripods
# Part I: Closed-Form Solutions
# for Forward Kinematics Methods

You-Nan Xu[1,2], Xin-Jun Liu[1], and Jin-Song Wang[1]

[1] Department of Precision Instruments and Mechanology, Tsinghua University,
Beijing, P.R. China, 100084
[2] Mechanical & Electronical Engineering, East China Jiaotong University,
Nanchang, Jiangxi, P.R. China, 330013

**Abstract.** The articulated A/B-axis tool heads with parallel structure behave better than the traditional tool heads with serial structure in terms of saving machine processing time and reducing the deformation of the workpiece when they are used in thin wall machining applications for structural aluminium aerospace components. The 3-$\underline{P}_V P_H S$ and 3-$\underline{P}_V SP$ parallel mechanisms (where P, R, and S standing for prismatic, revolute, and spherical joints, respectively, and the subscripts V and H indicating that the direction of the P joint is vertical or horizontal, and the joint with underline symbol means the joint is active) are two typical mechanisms that can be applied to articulated A/B-axis tool heads with parallel structure. This paper focuses on these two kinds of typical tripods. Their analytic forward kinematics methods are discussed respectively, and their closed-form solutions for forward kinematics are derived. Further study will disclose that the proposed methods are of high precision, stability and efficiency, and are easy to use, when dealing with the location and error analysis in on line real-time control and the prediction or analysis of their mechanical characteristics.

**Keywords:** tripod, closed-form solution for forward kinematics, articulated A/B-axis tool head.

## 1 Introduction

To save the machine processing time and reduce the deformation of the workpiece, the articulated A/B-axis tool heads with parallel structure behave better in thin wall machining applications for structural aluminium aerospace components[1], for which, several such tool heads have been developed, e.g., the Sprint Z3[2] tool head developed by DS Technologie [German], the 5H tool head[3] by FATROMIK [Spanish], and the 3-$\underline{P}$RS tripod for polishing[4] by Ryerson University [Canada]. Each of the mechanisms used in those tool heads has three degrees of freedom, which are the movement along the Z-axis, and the rotations about the A-axis and B-axis.

C.-Y. Su, S. Rakheja, H. Liu (Eds.): ICIRA 2012, Part I, LNAI 7506, pp. 271–281, 2012.

The 3-$P_VP_HS$ and 3-$\underline{P}_VS\underline{P}$ parallel mechanisms are also such kinds of mechanisms. The two kinds of typical tripods would be able to make a five-axis hybrid mechanism by combing with a X-Y motion platform, and enjoys the advantages of both serial and parallel mechanisms[6].

This paper will study the closed form solutions algorithm of forward kinematics of the two kinds of typical tripods, then study their workspace properties in order to disclose their natures of zero-torsion and Z-axis motion invariance, which would build theoretical foundation for the application of the articulated A/B-axis tool heads.

The forward kinematics of parallel mechanism has played an important role in the mechanical movement control and the movement error prediction, and received a continuous effort from a lot of researchers[5, 11], which is mainly about the study of 6-S$\underline{P}$S Steward platform. The algorithms for forward kinematics could be divided into numerical method and analytical one according to their principles. The analytical method includes the closed form solution[13-14] and the polynomial equation[15-17]. The numerical method includes linear algorithms (for example, J-matrix iteration algorithm) and nonlinear programming algorithms[18-19]. Usually the closed-form solutions are expected, but they can be found only for simple parallel mechanisms. The polynomial algorithms would get all solutions (the feasible or unfeasible solutions, and the real or imaginary solutions), but the high order polynomial equations themselves are hard to be solved by analytical algorithms. The nonlinear algorithms are easy to build their optimal models, but have difficulties in convergence. And the J-matrix iteration algorithm is not only inefficient, but also unstable around the singularity configurations[20]. Refs. [16] and [17] focus on the forward kinematics of the 3-PRS and 3-RPS mechanisms, the Bezout elimination method is used to calculate the nonlinear equations, and finally an one-variable-sixteen-order polynomial equations are derived. This algorithm has been put forward by Merlet[21] and its order was reduced to an eight-order polynomial, which is the simplest result by now. The polynomial equation has a problem in efficiency and in the distinguishing of real solutions and imaginary ones. Besides, homotopy function algorithm[22-23], using the homotopy between two groups nonlinear equations and searching up to 256 homotopic paths according to known solutions of the homotopic functions, can get all needed solutions, including real or imaginary ones. But this algorithm cannot be directly applied in real-time conditions due to lower calculating efficiency.

In a word, the algorithms of direct kinematics of parallel mechanisms are complicated and diversiform. Each of them has its advantages in calculation speed, precision, stability, suitability and simplicity. The multidisciplinary modeling and analyzing method used in Ref. [6] overcame the disadvantages resulting from a singly theory or unified method used. The comparison results show that the algorithm using numerical method to do on-line forward kinematic analyzing is one of the fastest, the most efficient and the most stable algorithms. The proposed algorithm here, which employed a combination of the advantages of both geometry and algebra methods, is based on the above research frame.

This paper will study the forward kinematics for the 3-PPS and the 3-PSP mechanisms. Firstly their kinematic models will be built, secondly their basic kinematics equations and kinematic constraint equations will be derived, finally their analytical solutions will be given. Further study about their workspaces, singularities and characters of the forward kinematics will be given in Ref. [24], and will disclose their performances for precision, stability and efficiency of the proposed methods.

## 2    Kinematic Models of the Mechanisms

### 2.1    The Physical Models of Kinematics

The kinematic structures of the 3-$P_VP_HS$ and 3-$P_VSP$ mechanisms are shown in Fig. 1. The mechanisms are at dressed locations, each of them is composed by the MP (Moving Platform) $B_1B_2B_3$, the BP (Based Platform or Fixed Platform) $A_1A_2A_3$, and three kinematics-chains $A_i - B_i - C_i$ that attach to the MP and the BP. $A_i$ and $B_i$ are located in two circles centered on point $O$ and $P$, and their radius are $r_a$ and $r_b$ respectively. The first joint $A_i$ is a active joint and its motion parameter is represented by the leg lengths $A_i C_i$, that is, $l_i$. For convenience sake, the two mechanisms are called the 3-PPS and 3-PSP mechanisms in shortly. To depicture their configurations, a fixed coordinate system $O$-$xyz$ and a moving coordinate system $P-x'y'z'$ are built and are attached to the BP and the MP, respectively.

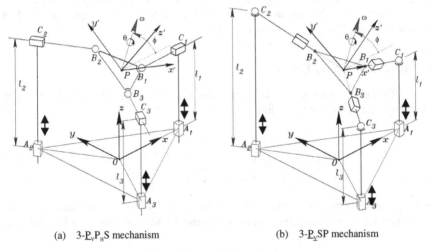

(a)   3-$\underline{P}_VP_HS$ mechanism          (b)   3-$\underline{P}_VSP$ mechanism

**Fig. 1.** The parallel mechanisms

To depicture the poses of the MP, the reference point $P$ and the reference orientation $R$ are used. Where $P$ is the centre point of the MP, and represents the position of the MP; $R$ is the rotary matrix of the MP, formed with rotation axis $\omega$ and rotation angle $\theta$, and represents the orientation of the MP. Assuming that both the moving platform and the fixed platform are equilateral triangles, the three points of the joints are arranged in counterclockwise order and are numbered starting at X-axis, take

$$\begin{cases} [\alpha_1 \ \ \alpha_2 \ \ \alpha_3] = [0° \ \ 120° \ \ -120°] \\ [\beta_1 \ \ \beta_2 \ \ \beta_3] = [0° \ \ 120° \ \ -120°] \end{cases}, \quad U = [U_1 \ \ U_2 \ \ U_3] = \begin{bmatrix} 1 & -1/2 & -1/2 \\ 0 & \sqrt{3}/2 & -\sqrt{3}/2 \\ 0 & 0 & 0 \end{bmatrix} \quad (1)$$

where $\alpha_i$ and $\beta_i$ represent the oriental angles of point $A_i$ in the FP and point $B_i$ in the MP, respectively. Then point $A_i$ and point $B_i$ in each local coordinate system can be expressed as:

$$A = [A_1 \ \ A_2 \ \ A_3] = r_a \begin{bmatrix} \cos\alpha_1 & \cos\alpha_2 & \cos\alpha_3 \\ \sin\alpha_1 & \sin\alpha_2 & \sin\alpha_3 \\ 0 & 0 & 0 \end{bmatrix} = r_a U \quad (2)$$

$$B = [B_1 \ \ B_2 \ \ B_3] = r_b \begin{bmatrix} \cos\beta_1 & \cos\beta_2 & \cos\beta_3 \\ \sin\beta_1 & \sin\beta_2 & \sin\beta_3 \\ 0 & 0 & 0 \end{bmatrix} = r_b U \quad (3)$$

For the physical models built above, $\{ r_a, r_b, \alpha_i, \beta_i, \}$ are structural parameters, and $\{ l_i \}$, $\{P, R, \omega, \theta \}$ are motion parameters. The motion parameters are not independent, for example, among the nine parameters of the rotary matrix $R$, only three of them are independent, two in three parameters of $\omega$ are independent, furthermore $P$ and $R$ are not independent either.

## 2.2    Basic Kinematics Equations

For the 3-PPS mechanism in Fig. 1(a), by using of the geometrical relationship among the leg lengths and the joint positions, we get

$$\begin{cases} l_i = e_3 \cdot (RB_i + P - A_i) \\ \dfrac{s\alpha_i}{c\alpha_i} = \dfrac{e_2 \cdot (RB_i + P - A_i)}{e_1 \cdot (RB_i + P - A_i)} \end{cases}, i = 1,2,3 \quad (4a)$$

where $e_1$ represents the unit vector of $x$ axis, and so on; $s\alpha_i$ and $c\alpha_i$ are $\sin\alpha_i$ and $\cos\alpha_i$ in simplified form, respectively. Similarly, for the 3-PSP mechanism in Fig. 1(b), we get

$$\begin{cases} A_{ix} = e_1 \cdot (RC_i + P) \\ A_{iy} = e_2 \cdot (RC_i + P) \quad i = 1,2,3 \\ l_i = e_3 \cdot (RC_i + P) \end{cases} \quad )$$

Eqs. (4a) and (4b) are the basic kinematics equations needed of the mechanisms, where $C_i = r_i U_i (i = 1,2,3)$ represent the coordinates of points $C_i(i=1,2,3)$ in local coordinate system $P - x'y'z'$.

As shown in Fig. 1 and the basic kinematic Eqs. (4a) and (4b), when driving each leg equally, the platform would only move along the Z-axis. This conclusion shows that both of the two kind of mechanisms discussed here have the same behave of Z-axis motion invariance.

## 2.3    Kinematic Constraint Equations

For the 3-PSP mechanism, when respecting the first sub-equation of Eq. (4b), we can get six kinematics equations in six unknown variables. So Eq. (4b) is decoupled partially. By eliminating $r_i$, we get

$$\frac{r_a \sin \alpha_i - y_p}{r_a \cos \alpha_i - x_p} = \frac{e_2 \cdot RU_i}{e_1 \cdot RU_i}, i = 1,2,3 \tag{5}$$

This is equal to

$$m_{2i}x_p - m_{1i}y_p = r_a(m_{2i}c\alpha_i - m_{1i}s\alpha_i) \begin{cases} m_{ij} = e_i^T RU_j \\ C_j = r_j U_j \end{cases} i,j = 1,2,3 \tag{6}$$

Above equations are the linear equations come from the nonlinear ones. There are three equations in total, where $(x_p, y_p)$ are the base variables, i.e. independent variables, and $m_{2i}(i = 1,2,3)$ are dependent variables, which have relationship with $R$ impliedly. For there are only two independent variables in three linear equations, there must follows the linear algebra theory, i.e. the determinant of the coefficient matrix must be zero if there exists a feasible solution. Thus, we get

$$\begin{vmatrix} m_{21} & -m_{11} & r_a(m_{21}c\alpha_1 - m_{11}s\alpha_1) \\ m_{22} & -m_{12} & r_a(m_{22}c\alpha_2 - m_{12}s\alpha_2) \\ m_{23} & -m_{13} & r_a(m_{23}c\alpha_3 - m_{13}s\alpha_3) \end{vmatrix} = 0 \tag{7}$$

Follow the determinant calculating regulation of the linear algebra, adding the last two rows to the first one in the above equation, its determinant is invariance, so

$$\begin{vmatrix} \sum_{i=1}^{3} m_{2i} & -\sum_{i=1}^{3} m_{1i} & \sum_{i=1}^{3} r_a(m_{2i}c\alpha_i - m_{1i}s\alpha_i) \\ m_{22} & -m_{12} & r_a(m_{22}c\alpha_2 - m_{12}s\alpha_2) \\ m_{23} & -m_{13} & r_a(m_{23}c\alpha_3 - m_{13}s\alpha_3) \end{vmatrix} = 0 \tag{8}$$

For $\sum_{i=1}^{3} m_{1i} = 0$, and $\sum_{i=1}^{3} m_{2i} = 0$, so

$$\sum_{i=1}^{3} r_a(m_{2i}c\alpha_i - m_{1i}s\alpha_i) = 0 \tag{9}$$

This is equal to

$$e_2^T R \sum_{i=1}^{3} (U_i \cdot c\alpha_i) = e_1^T R \sum_{i=1}^{3} (U_i \cdot s\alpha_i) \tag{10}$$

Simplifying above equation, we get

$$e_2^T R \left( \frac{3}{2} e_1^T \right) = e_1^T R \left( \frac{3}{2} e_2^T \right) \tag{11}$$

where $R = [(r_{ij})]$, so

$$r_{21} = r_{12} \tag{12}$$

From above equation, we can simplify the rotary matrix $R$ of the Moving Platform

$$R = Rot(\omega, \theta) = E + \hat{\omega}^2 (1 - \cos\theta) + \hat{\omega}\sin\theta \tag{13}$$

where $\quad \omega = \begin{Bmatrix} \omega_x \\ \omega_y \\ \omega_z \end{Bmatrix} = \begin{Bmatrix} \cos\phi \\ \sin\phi \\ 0 \end{Bmatrix}, \quad \hat{\omega} = \begin{bmatrix} 0 & 0 & \sin\phi \\ 0 & 0 & -\cos\phi \\ -\sin\phi & \cos\phi & 0 \end{bmatrix}.$

For the 3-PPS mechanism, the above equation is available also[1]. Because of $\omega_z = 0$, the 3-PSP parallel mechanism belongs to zero-torsion mechanisms, just like the 3-PPS mechanism, but there exists parasitic motion $\{x_p, y_p\}$ companying with the major movements $\{\theta_x, \theta_y, z_p\}$. For the 3-PPS mechanism,

$$\begin{Bmatrix} x_p \\ y_p \end{Bmatrix} = \frac{1}{2} r_b \begin{Bmatrix} \cos 2\varphi \\ -\sin 2\varphi \end{Bmatrix} (1 - \cos\theta)^{[1]} \tag{14}$$

where $\varphi$ is the orientation angle and $\theta$ is rotation angle of the Moving Platform. While, for the 3-PSP mechanism, from Eq. (6), we get

$$\begin{Bmatrix} x_p \\ y_p \end{Bmatrix} = \frac{r_a}{2(r_{12}r_{21} - r_{11}r_{22})} \begin{bmatrix} r_{11} & r_{12} \\ r_{21} & r_{22} \end{bmatrix} \begin{Bmatrix} r_{22} - r_{11} \\ r_{12} + r_{21} \end{Bmatrix} \tag{15}$$

Simplifying above equation, we get

$$\begin{Bmatrix} x_p \\ y_p \end{Bmatrix} = \frac{1}{2} r_a \begin{Bmatrix} \cos 2\varphi \\ -\sin 2\varphi \end{Bmatrix} \frac{(1 - \cos\theta)}{\cos\theta} + \frac{1}{2} r_a \begin{Bmatrix} -\cos\varphi \\ \sin\varphi \end{Bmatrix} \sin 3\phi \frac{(1 - \cos\theta)^2}{\cos\theta} \tag{16}$$

The parasitic motions related to orientation angle and rotation angle are shown in Fig. 2. The circular lines in Fig. 2(a) represent the relationship between the parasitic motions and the rotation angles for the 3-PPS tripod. The inclines in Fig. 2(a) represent the relationship between the parasitic motions and the orientation angles for the 3-PPS tripod. The heart-shaped lines in Fig. 2(b) and Fig. 2(c) represent the relationship between the parasitic motions and the rotation angles for the 3-PSP tripod.

The radial line in Fig. 2(b) and Fig. 2(c) represent the relationship between the parasitic motions and the orientation angles for the 3-PSP tripod. Fig. 2 shows that 3-PPS mechanism's parasitic motions are identical in different orientations, and are similar in different rotation angles, but 3-PSP mechanism are not. While the rotation angles are limited to a small range ( $\theta < 30°$ ), their properties are very close.

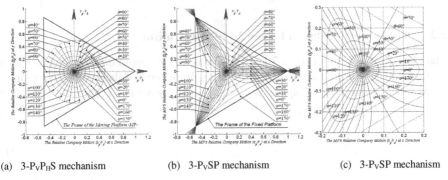

(a)  3-P$_V$P$_H$S mechanism          (b)  3-P$_V$SP mechanism          (c)  3-P$_V$SP mechanism

**Fig. 2.** Parasitic motions of the moving platform

## 3      Forward Kinematics

The forward kinematics problem of the 3-PPS and 3-PSP mechanisms can be described as: Given the leg lengths $l=\{l_1, l_2, l_3\}$, to solve their position $P(x_p, y_p, z_p)$, and the orientation $R(\omega, \theta)$ of the MPs. Among the parameters to be solved, there are only three independent parameters. All the parameters meet the requirements in Eqs. (14) and (16).

### 3.1      Closed-Form Solution for the 3-PPS Mechanism

For the 3-PPS mechanism in Fig. 1(a), there is $z' \perp \Delta B_1 B_2 B_3$ , so we get

$$C_i = \{r_a c\alpha_i \quad r_a s\alpha_i \quad l_i\}^T , \quad z_{bi} = z_{ci} , \quad i = 1, 2, 3 \tag{17}$$

Firstly substituting above equations into Eq. (4a), then summing all the three sub-equations, and finally we get

$$z_p = P \cdot e_3 = (l_1 + l_2 + l_3)/3 = \overline{l} \tag{18}$$

Substituting above equation into Eq. (4a), we get

$$\begin{cases} r_{31} = -\sin\phi\sin\theta = (l_1 - z_p)/r_b \\ r_{32} = \cos\phi\sin\theta = \sqrt{3}/3(l_2 - l_3)/r_b \end{cases} \tag{19}$$

Solving above equations, we get

$$\begin{cases} \theta = \pm \sin^{-1}(\sqrt{r_{31}^2 + r_{32}^2}) \\ \varphi = tg^{-1}(\mp r_{31}, \pm r_{32}) \end{cases} \tag{20}$$

Above equations will result two group solutions, but the poses of the MP are just the same. So, the positive rotation angle can be selected in the real algorithm.

## 3.2    Closed-Form Solution for the 3-PSP Mechanism

The closed-form solution for a 3-PSP mechanism is far more difficult than a 3-PPS mechanism. To overcome the difficulty in the elimination of the redundant variables in the kinematics equations, spatial analytical geometry method is employed. Because of $z' \perp \Delta C_1 C_2 C_3$, we get

$$\begin{cases} Z' = \overrightarrow{C_1 C_2} \times \overrightarrow{C_2 C_3} \\ z' = Z' / \|Z'\| \end{cases} \tag{21}$$

Where $C_i = \{r_a c\alpha_i \quad r_a s\alpha_i \quad l_i\}^T$ are the coordinates expressed in $O - xyz$.

Fig. 3 is the vertical project configuration of the 3-PSP mechanism along the $z'$-axis attached to the MP.

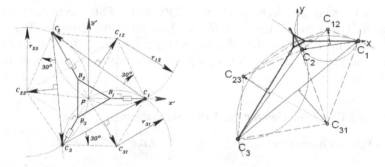

(a)  When the rotary angles are small        (b)  When the rotary angles are large

**Fig. 3.**    The project configuration of the 3-PSP mechanism along the $z'$-axis

For Fig. 3(a), there is $\angle C_1 P C_2 = 120°$. Letting $C_{12}$ be the center of the circumcircle of points $C_1$, $P$ and $C_2$ i.e. $C_{12}$ is located at the perpendicular bisector of line sections $C_1 C_2$, $PC_1$, and $PC_2$, then

$$C_{12} = \frac{(C_1 + C_2)}{2} + \frac{\sqrt{3}}{6} \overrightarrow{C_1 C_2} \times z' \tag{22a}$$

For the sake of the same reason, we get

$$C_{23} = \frac{(C_2 + C_3)}{2} + \frac{\sqrt{3}}{6}\overrightarrow{C_2 C_3} \times z' \tag{22b}$$

$$C_{31} = \frac{(C_3 + C_1)}{2} + \frac{\sqrt{3}}{6}\overrightarrow{C_3 C_1} \times z' \tag{22c}$$

Linking $C_{12}$, $C_{23}$ and $C_{31}$ in Fig. 3(a) respectively will form a equilateral triangle $\Delta C_{12} C_{23} C_{31}$. For $C_{12} C_{31} // y'$, thus we get

$$\begin{cases} Y' = C_{12} - C_{31} \\ y' = Y' / \|Y'\| \end{cases} \tag{23}$$

Finally, according to condition of the orthogonal coordinate system, we get

$$x' = y' \times z' \tag{24}$$

According to Eqs. (21), (23) and (24), we get

$$R(\varphi, \theta) = [x' \quad y' \quad z'] \tag{25}$$

Above equations are the closed-form solutions for the 3-PSP mechanism, when the rotary angle is small. The triangle $\Delta C_1 C_2 C_3$ will become an obtuse angle, and the center point $P$ will locate out of the triangle when the rotary angle is large, $\Delta C_1 C_2 C_3$, while the geometrical conditions are still the same, i.e. Eqs. (21)~(24) are suitable for this case also. By the use of Eq. (20), we can solve the orientation angle $\varphi$ and the rotation angle $\theta$ first. By the use of Eq. (15) or Eq. (16), then we can solve the parasitic variable $\{x_p, y_p\}$. By the use of Eq. (4b), finally we get

$$\begin{cases} r_i = \dfrac{a_{ix} - x_p}{E_1^T R U_i}, \quad or \quad \dfrac{a_{iy} - y_p}{E_2^T R U_i} (i = 1, 2, 3) \\ z_p = l_i - r_i E_3^T R U_i (i = 1, 2, 3) \end{cases} \tag{26}$$

By now, all the necessary equations for the closed-form solutions of the 3-PSP mechanism are gotten. Next, we will use the proposed methods to analysis the workspaces of those kinds of mechanisms, and do some comparisons to illustrate the advantages of the proposed methods.

## 4    Conclusion

The closed-form forward kinematics methods of two kinds of parallel mechanisms, the 3-PPS and the 3-PSP mechanisms, are studied in this paper. Firstly their kinematic models are built, secondly their basic kinematics equations and kinematic constraint equations are derived, finally their analytical solutions are given.

   To get the closed-form solutions of the 3-PPS mechanism, the geometric equations and its constraint equations are combined together, and are solved perfectly. To get the closed-form solutions of the 3-PSP mechanism, firstly the nonlinear equations are transferred into a linear ones by variable substituting, and three linear equations about $(x_p, y_p)$ are gotten. Then following the linear algebra theory, the constraint equation is gotten by the condition of solving a group of linear equations. Finally the closed-form solutions are derived by geometrical condition.

For the 3-PPS and the 3-PSP mechanisms, the researching results in this paper show that both of the 3-PPS and the 3-PSP mechanisms are zero-torsion, and have Z-axis movement invariance.

Further study about their workspaces, singularity configurations and performances of the forward kinematics in Ref. [24] will disclose that the proposed methods are of high precision, stability and efficiency, and are easy to use, when dealing with the location and error analysis in on line real-time control and the prediction or analysis of their mechanical characteristics.

Based on which, we know that the two mechanisms are available for articulated A/B-axis tool heads, but their workspaces are slightly different. The algorithms in this paper have combined the advantages both geometry method and detection method, and have solved the conflict between the efficiency and simplicity of kinematic forward displacement algorithm. Hopefully, a further study would possibly be able to put forward the forward kinematics algorithm of tripods.

**Acknowledgement.** This work was supported by the National Natural Science Foundation of China under Grant 51175174.

# References

1. Liu, X.J., Bonev, L.A.: Orientation Capability, Error Analysis, and Dimensional Optimization of Two Articulated Tool Heads With Parallel Kinematics. ASME, Journal of Manufacturing Science and Engineering 130, 011015-1–011015-9 (2008)
2. Wahl, J.: Articulated Tool Head, WIPO Patent No. WO 00/25976 (2000)
3. Bonev, I.A.: Geometric Analysis of Parallel Mechanisms, Ph.D. thesis, Laval University, Quebec (2002)
4. Xi, F., Han, W., Marcel, V., Ross, A.: Development of a Sliding-leg Tripod as an Add-on Device for Manufacturing. Robotica 18, 285–294 (2000)
5. Lee, K.M., Shah, D.K.: Kinematic Analysis of a Three-Degree-of-Freedom in-Parallel Actuated Manipulator. IEEE J. Rob. Autom. 4(3), 354–360 (1988)
6. Xu, Y.N., Xi, F.: A Realtime Method for Solving the Forward Kinematics of a Tripod with Fixed-length Legs. Journal of Manufacturing Science and Engineering Transaction of ASME 128(2), 204–212 (2006)
7. Carretero, J.A., Nahon, M.A., Podhorodeski, R.: Workspace Analysis and Optimization of a Novel 3-DOF Parallel Manipulator. IEEE Trans. Rob. Autom. 15(4), 178–188 (2000)
8. Pond, G.T., Carretero, J.A.: Kinematic Analysis and Workspace Determination of the Inclined PRS Parallel Manipulator. In: Proc. of 15th CISMIFToMM Symposium on Robot Design, Dynamics, and Control, Paper No. Rom04-18, Montreal (2004)
9. Liu, X.J., Pruschek, P., Pritschow, G.: A New 3-DOF Parallel Mechanism With Full Symmetrical Structure and Parasitic Motions. In: Proc. of International Conf. on Intelligent Manipulation and Grasping, Genoa, Italy, pp. 389–394 (June 2004)

10. Liu, X.J., Wang, J., Kim, J.: Determination of the Link Lengths for a Spatial 3-DoF Parallel Manipulator. ASME J. Mech. Des. 128, 365–373 (2006)
11. Dasgupta, B., Mruthyunjaya, T.S.: The Stewart Platform Manipulator: a Review. Mechanical and Machine Theory 35, 15–40 (2000)
12. Fichter, E.F.: A Stewart Platform-Based Manipulator: General Theory and Practical Construction. The International Journal of Robotics Research 15(2), 157–182 (1986)
13. Merlet, J.P.: Closed-Form Resolution of the Direct Kinematics of Parallel manipulator Using Extra Sensor Data. In: Proc. IEEE Int. Robotics and Automation Conf., Altanta, GA, pp. 200–204 (1993)
14. Sreenivasan, S.V., Waldron, K.J.: Closed-Form Direct Displacement Analysis of a 6-6 Stewart Platform. Mech. Mach. Theory 29(6), 855–864 (1994)
15. Innocenti, C.: Forward Kinematics in Polynomial Form of the General Stewart Platform. J. Mech. Des. 123, 254–260 (2001)
16. Tsai, M.S., Shiau, T.N., Tsai, Y.J., Chang, T.H.: Direct Kinematic Analysis of a 3-PRS Parallel Mechanism. Mech. Mach. Theory 38, 71–83 (2003)
17. Jinwook, K., Park, F.C.: Direct Kinematic Analysis of 3-RPS Parallel Mechanisms. Mech. Mach. Theory 36, 1121–1134 (2001)
18. Lee, T.Y., Shim, J.K.: Forward Kinematics of the General 6-6 Stewart Platform using Algebraic Elimination. Mech. Mach. Theory 36, 1073–1085 (2001)
19. Wen, F.A., Liang, C.G.: Displacement analysis of the 6-6 Stewart platform mechanisms. Mech. Mach. Theory 29(4), 547–557 (1994)
20. Monsarrat, B., Gosselin, C.: Singularity Analysis of a Three-Leg Six-degree-of-Freedom Parallel Platform Mechanism Based on Grassman Line Geometry. Int. J. Robot. Res. 20(4), 312–328 (2001)
21. Merlet, J.P.: Direct Kinematics and Assembly Modes of Parallel Manipulators. Int. J. Robot. Res. 11(2), 150–162 (1992)
22. Wu, T.M.: A study of convergence on the Newton- homotopy continuation method. Applied Mathematics and Computation 168, 1169–1174 (2005)
23. Varedi, S.M., Daniali, H.M., Ganji, D.D.: Kinematics of an offset 3-UPU translational parallel manipulator by the homotopy continuation method. Nonlinear Analysis: Real World Applications 10, 1767–1774 (2009)
24. Xu, Y.N., Liu, X.J., Wang, J.S.: Analytical Forward Kinematics for Two Kinds of Typical Tripods. Part II: Analyzing for Their Workspaces, and Performances of the Forward Kinematics. In: Su, C.-Y., Rakheja, S., Liu, H. (eds.) ICIRA 2012, Part I. LNCS (LNAI), vol. 7506, pp. 282–293. Springer, Heidelberg (2012)

# Analytical Forward Kinematics
# for Two Kinds of Typical Tripods
# Part II: Analyzing for Their Workspaces,
# and Performances of the Forward Kinematics

You-Nan Xu[1,2], Xin-Jun Liu[1], and Jin-Song Wang[1]

[1] Department of Precision Instruments and Mechanology, Tsinghua University,
Beijing, P.R. China, 100084
[2] Mechanical & Electronical Engineering, East China Jiaotong University,
Nanchang, Jiangxi, P.R. China, 330013

**Abstract.** The 3-$\underline{P}_V P_H S$ and 3-$\underline{P}_V SP$ parallel mechanisms (where P, R, and S standing for prismatic, revolute, and spherical joints, respectively, and the subscripts V and H indicating that the direction of the P joint is vertical or horizontal, and the joint with underline symbol means the joint is active) are two typical mechanisms that can be applied to articulated A/B-axis tool heads with parallel structure. This paper focuses on the applications of the forward kinematic for these two kinds of typical tripods. Based on their analytic forward kinematics methods, their workspaces with geometrical constraints are analyzed, their performances are compared with the J-matrix iteration methods in terms of precision, stability and efficiency. The results show that the proposed methods are of high precision, stability and efficiency, and are easy to use, when dealing with the location and error analysis in on line real-time control and the prediction or analysis of their mechanical characteristics.

**Keywords:** tripod, workspace with geometrical constraint, closed-form solution for forward kinematics, articulated A/B-axis tool head.

## 1 Introduction

To save the machine processing time and reduce the deformation of the workpiece, the articulated A/B-axis tool heads with parallel structure behave better in thin wall machining applications for structural aluminum aerospace components[1]. The 3-PPS and 3-PSP parallel mechanisms are two kinds of typical tripods, which can be functioned as the articulated A/B-axis tool heads. The two typical parallel mechanisms have some closing behaviors like the Sprint Z3[2] tool head developed by DS Technologie [German], the 5H tool head[3] by FATROMIK [Spanish], and the 3-$\underline{P}$RS tripod for polishing[4] by Ryerson University [Canada]. Each of the mechanisms used in those tool heads has three degrees of freedom, and is of Z-axis zero-torsion. All of these kinds of tripods would be able to make a five-axis hybrid mechanism by combing with an X-Y motion platform, and enjoys the advantages of both serial and parallel mechanisms[5]. Based on the closed-form solutions for the 3-$P_V P_H S$ and the 3-$P_V SP$ mechanisms[6], the workspace for the two typical mechanisms

C.-Y. Su, S. Rakheja, H. Liu (Eds.): ICIRA 2012, Part I, LNAI 7506, pp. 282–293, 2012.

will be studied here. Furthermore, their performances for precision, stability and efficiency of the proposed methods will be disclosed.

The workspace, a most important property[7] of the parallel kinematic machine, is used as design and analysis purposes[8-10] generally. Kumar[11] classified it into reachable workspace, dexterous workspace, and workspace with constraint orientation. while, You-Lun Xiong(2002) classified it into five categories: whole workspace, position workspace, orientation workspace, position workspace with fixed orientation, and orientation workspace with fixed position. Traditionally, the workspaces analysis methods are divided into the analytical methods[12, 13] and the numerical ones[14-17]. The Gosselin geometrical method[12] is a typical analytical example, but the numerical methods, such as Grid method, Monte Carlo method, and optimal method, etc, are widely used currently, though they need great amount calculating work. To enhance the calculating efficiency, this paper will studied the workspace with geometrical constraints, and do some mapping work between the joint workspace and the workspace of the moving platform.

## 2    Kinematic of the Two Typical Parallel Mechanisms

The kinematic structures of the 3-PPS and 3-PSP mechanisms are shown in Fig. 1. To depicture their configurations, a fixed coordinate system $O$-$xyz$ and a moving coordinate system $P-x'y'z'$ are built and are attached to the Base Platform (BP) and the Moving Platform (MP), respectively (See Ref. [6] for details).

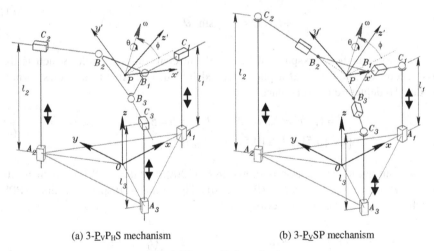

(a) 3-P̲vP̲HS mechanism          (b) 3-P̲vSP mechanism

**Fig. 1.** The parallel mechanisms

The forward kinematics problem of the 3-PPS and 3-PSP mechanisms [6] can be described as: Given the leg lengths $l=\{l_1, l_2, l_3\}$, to solve their position $P(x_p, y_p, z_p)$, and the orientation $R(\omega, \theta)$ of the MPs. So the forward kinematics method can be logically expressed as (See Ref. [6] for details)

$$[\theta, \varphi, P] = FK(l_1, l_2, l_3) \tag{1}$$

where $FK()$ standing the forward kinematic method. Similarly, their reverse kinematic methods[6] can be defined as: Given their position $P(x_p, y_p, z_p)$, and the orientation $R(\omega, \theta)$ of the MPs, to solve their leg lengths $\{l_1\ l_2,\ l_3\}$. So the reverse kinematics method can be logically expressed as (See Ref. [6] for details)

$$[l_1, l_2, l_3] = RK(\theta, \varphi, P) \tag{2}$$

where $RK()$ standing the reverse kinematic method.

# 3    Workspace Analysis

## 3.1    Analysis for the Joint Workspace

Here the definition domains of joint variables of the 3-PPS and 3-PSP mechanisms will be discussed. Those domains will form the joint spaces. According to their Z-axis movement invariance characters, i.e. when the MP moves along the Z-axis, their orientation angles, rotary angles, and parasitic motions will be the same. So, we can assume $z_p = 0$, and exam their constraint joint spaces only. For the 3-PPS mechanism, from Eq. (4a) in Ref. [6], summing all the leg lengths and their squares, we get

$$\begin{cases} l_1 + l_2 + l_3 = 0 \\ l_1^2 + l_2^2 + l_3^2 = \dfrac{3}{2} r_b^2 \sin^2 \theta \end{cases} \tag{3}$$

which shows that the workspace of the 3-PPS mechanism is a circle, which is the cross section of a sphere and a plane defined by Eq. (3). All those circles form a cylinder. To depicture its workspace, take

$$\begin{cases} r_b = 1, \quad r_a = 2.5 = 2.5 r_b, \quad l_{i\max} = 5 = 5 r_b \\ l_1 \in [0,5], \quad l_2 \in [0,5] \quad l_3 \in [0,5] \end{cases} \tag{4}$$

Thus, we can get its workspace as shown in Fig. 2(a). For the 3-PSP mechanism, its joint workspace is just a cubic (Fig. 2(b)). The joint workspace of the 3-PPS mechanism (Fig. 4(a)) can be described as

$$\begin{cases} (l_1^2 - \overline{l}^2) + (l_2^2 - \overline{l}^2) + (l_3^2 - \overline{l}^2) \le \dfrac{3}{2} r_a^2, \quad \overline{l} = \dfrac{1}{3}(l_1 + l_2 + l_3) \\ l_1 \in [0, l_{i\max}] \quad l_3 \in [0, l_{i\max}] \quad l_3 \in [0, l_{i\max}] \end{cases} \tag{5}$$

And the joint workspace of the 3-PSP mechanism (Fig. 4(b)) can be described as

$$l_1 \in [0, l_{i\max}] \quad l_3 \in [0, l_{i\max}] \quad l_3 \in [0, l_{i\max}] \tag{6}$$

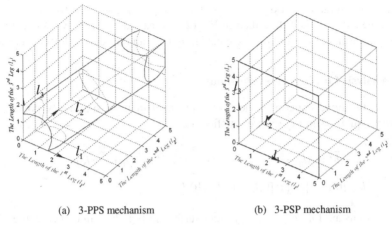

(a)  3-PPS mechanism                    (b)  3-PSP mechanism

**Fig. 2.** Joint workplaces of the mechanisms

## 3.2    Analysis for the MPs' Workspaces

To get the MP's workspace of the 3-PPS mechanism, we just need use the proposed forward kinematic method described in Eq. (1) to trace six line sections and six curves lie on the cylinder surface in Fig. 2(a), twelve curves in total are gotten in Fig. 3(a), and the majority of the workspace is a cylinder. There, the cylindrical coordinates system is defined as: the radial lines are orientation angles, the circular lines are rotation angles, and the vertical coordinate is $z_p$.

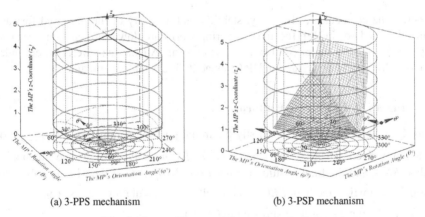

(a) 3-PPS mechanism                    (b) 3-PSP mechanism

**Fig. 3.** The workspaces of the moving platforms

Similarly, to get the workspace of the 3-PSP mechanism, we just need to trace twelve line sections in Fig. 2(b), twelve curves in total are gotten in Fig. 3(b) also, and the workspace is a six-surface cubic.

Based on the proposed analytic joint workspaces, and the closed-form kinematics algorithms described in Eq. (1), the 3-PPS and 3-PSP mechanisms' workspaces, including their singular workspace of the later, are gotten conveniently. By the use of reverse kinematic method described in Eq. (2), we can also get the workspace of the moving platform, but must pay more calculating time and in relative lower precisions.

## 3.3    Analysis for Singularity Positions

According to above equations, the 3-PPS mechanism is in singularity poses when equivalent equations in Eq. (5) are satisfied. i.e.

$$\begin{cases} (l_1^2 - \overline{l}^2) + (l_2^2 - \overline{l}^2) + (l_3^2 - \overline{l}^2) = \dfrac{3}{2} r_a^2, \quad \overline{l} = \dfrac{1}{3}(l_1 + l_2 + l_3) \\ l_1 \in [0, l_{i\max}] \quad l_3 \in [0, l_{i\max}] \quad l_3 \in [0, l_{i\max}] \end{cases} \tag{7}$$

Those positions are located on the cylinder surface in Fig. 2(a). In that case, the MP is located at the perpendicular positions, and the rotary angle is 90°. Those positions are located on the cylinder surface in Fig. 3(a).

$$\theta = 90° \tag{8}$$

The 3-PSP mechanism can meet those requirements only when the differences of two leg lengths are infinite, i.e. the singularity poses would not exist in the finite area of the 3-PSP mechanism.

# 4    Properties of the Proposed Forward Kinematics Methods

To verify the correctness, efficiency, stability and usability of the proposed forward kinematics methods in Ref. [6], the comparing works are down through some relative programs developed under Matlab 7.0 environment. All the data were gotten under Windows XP operating system on HP Compaq 2100CA laptop computer.

## 4.1    Errors of the Moving Platforms

To analyze the errors of the MP, firstly the initial position parameters $(\theta_0, \phi_0, z_{p0})$ of the MP are given, Then the leg lengths $\{l_1, l_2, l_3\}$ are solved by reverse kinematics method $RK()$, and the final position parameters $(\theta_f, \phi_f, P_f)$ of the MP are solved by forward kinematics method $FK()$, and finally the calculating errors $(\delta\theta, \delta\varphi)$ are gotten. All the three steps are expressed in Eq. (9).

$$\begin{cases} [l_1, l_2, l_3, P] = RK(\theta_0, \varphi_0, z_p) \\ [\theta_f, \varphi_f, P_f] = FK(l_1, l_2, l_3) \\ [\delta\theta, \delta\varphi] = [\theta_f - \theta_0, \phi_f - \phi_0] \end{cases} \tag{9}$$

Based on above equations, the entire workspace for the MP of the 3-PPS mechanism is tested. Its rotary angle errors and orientation angle errors of the MP are shown in Fig. 4 and Fig. 5, respectively. There the angle errors are defined as

$$
\begin{cases}
E_\theta = \log_{10} |\delta\theta| \\
E_\varphi = \log_{10} |\delta\varphi|
\end{cases}
\tag{10}
$$

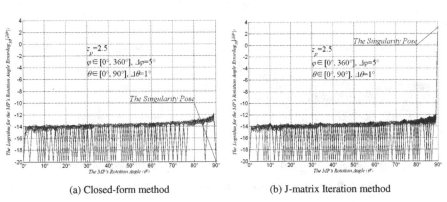

(a) Closed-form method      (b) J-matrix Iteration method

**Fig. 4.** Rotary angle errors of the MP of the 3-PPS mechanism

The rotary angle errors of the MP of the 3-PPS mechanism are shown in Fig. 4. The results show that the closed-form method can get high precisions in the entire workspace, but the J-matrix iteration method has convergent problem at the singularity poses (Fig.4(b)).

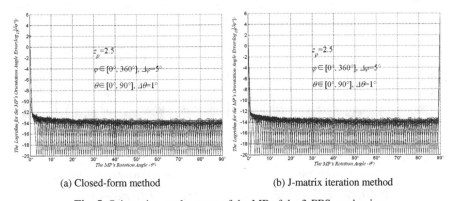

(a) Closed-form method      (b) J-matrix iteration method

**Fig. 5.** Orientation angle errors of the MP of the 3-PPS mechanism

The orientation angle errors of the MP of the 3-PPS mechanism are shown in Fig. 5. The results show that neither of the two methods can get high precisions when rotary angles are very small (or near zero). Furthermore, the J-matrix iteration method still has convergent problem at the singularity poses (Fig. 5(b)).

Using the same method, the angle errors of the moving platform of the 3-PSP mechanism are analyzed also, and the results are depictured in Fig.6 and Fig. 7. The results in Fig.6 show that the closed-form method can get high precisions except the singularity poses (Fig. 6(a)), but the J-matrix iteration method even has convergent problem near the singularity poses (Fig. 6(b)).

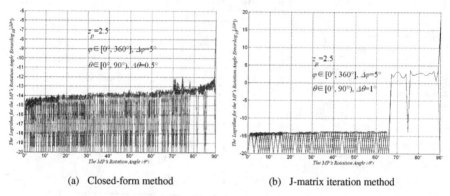

(a)  Closed-form method                    (b)  J-matrix iteration method

**Fig. 6.** Rotation angle errors of the MP of the 3-PSP mechanism

The orientation angle errors of the MP of the 3-PSP mechanism are shown in Fig. 7. The results show that both of the two methods cannot get high precision when rotary angles are very small, furthermore the closed-form method has convergent problem at the singularity poses only (Fig. 7(a)), and J-matrix iteration method still has convergent problem near the singularity poses (Fig. 7(b)).

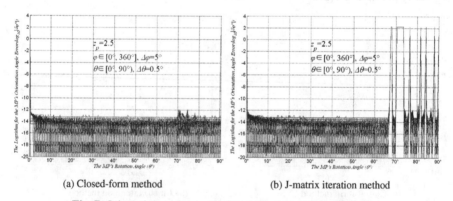

(a) Closed-form method                    (b) J-matrix iteration method

**Fig. 7.** Orientation angle errors of the MP of the 3-PSP mechanism

## 4.2    Errors of the Leg Lengths

To analyze the errors of the driving joints, firstly the initial leg lengths $(l_{10}, l_{20}, l_{30})$ are given, then the position parameters $(\theta, \phi, P)$ of the MP are solved by forward kinematics method $FK()$, and then the final leg lengths $(l_{1f}, l_{2f}, l_{3f})$ are solved by reverse kinematics method $RK()$, finally the leg length errors $\delta l_i\, (i = 1, \cdots, n)$ are gotten. All the three steps are expressed in Eq. (11).

$$\begin{cases} [\theta, \varphi, P] = FK(l_{10}, l_{20}, l_{30}) \\ [l_{1f}, l_{2f}, l_{3f}, P] = RK(\theta, \varphi, z_p) \\ \delta l_i = l_{if} - l_{i0}, i = 1, 2, 3 \end{cases} \qquad (11)$$

Based on above equations, the entire joint workspaces for the MPs of the 3-PPS and 3-PSP mechanisms are tested. Their leg length errors are shown in Fig. 8 and Fig. 9, respectively. There the leg length errors are defined as

$$E_{li} = \log_{10} |\delta \varphi| \qquad (12)$$

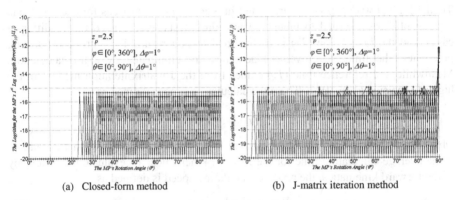

(a)  Closed-form method        (b)  J-matrix iteration method

**Fig. 8.** Leg length errors of the 3-PPS mechanism

The leg length errors of the 3-PPS mechanism parallel mechanisms are depictured in Fig. 8. The results show that the closed-form method can get high precisions in entail work space (Fig. 8(a)), but the J-matrix iteration method has convergent problem at the singularity poses (Fig. 8(b)).

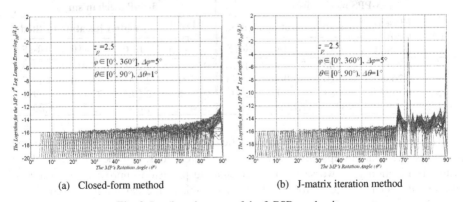

(a)  Closed-form method        (b)  J-matrix iteration method

**Fig. 9.** Leg length errors of the 3-PSP mechanism

The leg length errors of the 3-PSP mechanism are shown in Fig. 9. The results show that the closed-form method can get high precisions except the singularity poses (Fig. 9(a)), but the J-matrix iteration method has convergent problem near the singularity poses (Fig. 9(b)).

## 4.3    Efficiencies of the Proposed Algorithms

To illustrate the efficiencies of the proposed algorithms, the entire workspaces are searched and the calculating times for the forward kinematics methods are tested in this section. The calculating grids are set by

$$\begin{cases} \theta \in [0°, \quad 90°], \quad \Delta\theta = 0.5° \\ \varphi \in [0°, \quad 360°], \quad \Delta\varphi = 5° \end{cases} \tag{13}$$

Total 12960 (180×72) points were tested in theoretical workspaces for each test, and their results are recorded in table 1. There three tests were carried out in different cases, and the fastest one $(T_F)$ is as the final testing result. To improve the testing precisions, the times for reverse kinematics are eliminated by extra calculating. Meanwhile, the reference time $(T_R)$ comes from the J-matrix iteration method in the highest precision $(1.0\times10^{-15})$. There the calculating time is defined as

$$T_F = \min\{T_{F1}, T_{F2}, T_{F3}\} \tag{14}$$

where $T_{Fi}$ is the average calculating time of the $i^{th}$ test for forward kinematics, and $T_F$ is the average calculating time for the forward kinematics. To evaluate the efficiency of the forward kinematics, the relative calculating speed is defined as

$$V_{Ratio} = T_R / T_F \tag{15}$$

where, $V_{Ratio}$ is the index to evaluate the efficiency of the forward kinematics. The higher of the $V_{Ratio}$ index, the higher of the efficiency of the forward kinematics.

**Table 1.** Average calculating Times of the forward kinematics in theoretical workspace (ms)

| ID | 3-PPS mechanism | | | | 3-PSP mechanism | | | |
|---|---|---|---|---|---|---|---|---|
| | Closed form method | J-matrix iteration method | | | Closed form method | J-matrix iteration method | | |
| | | 10-6 | 10-10 | 10-15 | | 10-6 | 10-10 | 10-15 |
| 1 | 0.2531 | 6.1202 | 7.2317 | 8.1216 | 0.7493 | 2.2793 | 2.7911 | 3.7963 |
| 2 | 0.2638 | 6.1220 | 7.2283 | 8.1705 | 0.6731 | 2.2904 | 2.4980 | 3.8037 |
| 3 | 0.2592 | 6.1083 | 7.2531 | 8.2402 | 0.6806 | 2.2920 | 2.5111 | 3.7998 |
| $V_{Ratio}$ | 32.09 | 1.33 | 1.12 | 1.00 | 5.64 | 1.67 | 1.52 | 1.00 |

The results in Table 1 show that the efficiencies of the J-matrix iteration method have distinct relationships with their calculating precisions, and the efficiency of the J-matrix iteration goes worse when its calculating precision improves. According to the tested data in Table 1, for the 3-PPS mechanism, the calculating speed of the closed-form method is five times more than that of the J-matrix method; for the 3-PSP mechanism, the calculating speed of the closed-form method is thirty times more than that of the J-matrix method; for the closed-form methods, the calculating speed of the 3-PPS mechanism is near triple than that of the PSP mechanism. So the efficiencies of the closed-form methods are far higher than that of the J-matrix iteration methods; the efficiency of the closed-form method for the 3-PPS mechanism is far higher than that of the 3-PSP mechanism, because of their different complexity.

The same tests were done in the joint workspaces, 9261 (21×21×21) points in total were calculated. The testing grids are set by Eq. (15), and the testing results are recorded in Table 2.

$$l_i \in [0, \quad 5], \quad \Delta l_i = 0.25 \quad i = 1, 2, 3 \tag{16}$$

**Table 2.** Average calculating times of the forward kinematics in joint workspace (ms)

| | 3-PPS mechanism | | | | 3-PSP mechanism | | | |
|---|---|---|---|---|---|---|---|---|
| ID | Closed-form method | J-matrix iteration method | | | Closed-form method | J-matrix method | | iteration |
| | | $10^{-6}$ | $10^{-10}$ | $10^{-15}$ | | $10^{-6}$ | $10^{-10}$ | $10^{-15}$ |
| 1 | 0.0595 | 24.2049 | 24.4072 | 24.6787 | 0.6185 | 2.2179 | 2.3217 | 3.2700 |
| 2 | 0.0638 | 24.4065 | 24.3445 | 24.5640 | 0.6262 | 2.1335 | 2.3930 | 3.2137 |
| 3 | 0.0606 | 24.4312 | 24.2829 | 24.5878 | 0.6661 | 2.1931 | 2.3400 | 3.2289 |
| $V_{Ratio}$ | 412.84 | 1.01 | 1.01 | 1.00 | 5.20 | 1.51 | 1.38 | 1.00 |

The same laws are shown in table 2 just like table 1, except the efficiency of the forward kinematics for the 3-PPS mechanism is much high. We should notice the sharp contrast between the calculating time taken by the J-matrix iteration and the closed-form method, the main reason is that most test points are located outside the joint workspace. The closed-form method shares a clearly advantage, which can rapidly check out the points that are not in the workspace, which cost a lot of calculating time, while the J-matrix iteration method can not. According to the tested data in Table 1, the calculating speed of the 3-PPS mechanism is decuple more than that of the PSP mechanism, due to their different calculating complexities.

The efficiencies were tested by Matlab in a relatively slower computer (CPU 1.66 GHz, 32 bit system), and had reach a speed about 4 kHz and 1.5 kHz to the calculating frequencies of the 3-PPS and 3-PSP, respectively. The efficiencies are well enough for simulation, analyses and the majority of on-line control cases. When a faster computer, for example a 3.0 GHz CPU with 4 cores and 8 threads run under 64-bit system, is used and a more efficient program language C or C++ is employed, the speeds would reach 20-100 times faster, this would satisfy almost all the application demands so far.

# 5    Conclusion

Based on the analytical forward kinematics methods and their closed-form solutions of two typical kinds of parallel mechanisms, the joint workspaces and MP's workspaces for the 3-PPS and 3-PSP mechanisms are analyzed, respectively. Several examples are given to verify the precision, efficiency and stability of the proposed forward kinematics methods in Ref. [6]. And the singularity configurations are given out briefly.

To analyze the workspaces and singularity configurations, the analytical methods are employed. To verify the performances of the proposed forward kinematics methods, the analytical forward kinematics methods and reverse kinematics methods are employed. Through several testing examples for the forward kinematics methods, some laws are disclosed, and the researching results in this paper show that

(1) The efficiencies of the closed-form methods are far higher than that of the J-matrix methods. The efficiency of the closed-form method for the 3-PPS mechanism is far higher than that for the 3-PPS mechanism because of their different complexities.
(2) The closed-form methods have the highest precisions, and the J-matrix iteration method can reach high precisions also, but would take further more calculating times.
(3) The closed-form solutions for the 3-PPS mechanism is available in entire work space, but the J-matrix method is not available in the singularity poses; and the closed-form solutions for the 3-PSP mechanism is not available in singularity poses, but the J-matrix method is not available even near singularity poses. Thus, the closed-form methods have higher stability than the J-matrix iteration method.

For the 3-PPS and 3-PSP mechanisms, the researching results in this paper show that

(1) The joint workspace of the 3-PSP mechanism is a full cubic, but the joint workspace of the 3-PPS mechanism is the section of a full cubic and an inclined cylinder. The former is much larger than the later.
(2) The MP's workspace of the 3-PPS mechanism is near a full cylinder, but the MP's workspace of the 3-PSP mechanism is a deformation cubic like a diamond. The former is much larger than the later, especially in rotation angles. To get a more large rotation angle, its leg lengths must big enough for a 3-PSP mechanism.
(3) The 3-PPS mechanism will locate in singularity poses, when rotation angle is equal to 90°, but the 3-PSP mechanism cannot reach these singularity poses in limited leg length.

Though, the two mechanisms are available for articulated A/B-axis tool heads, but their workspaces are slightly different. The analytical forward kinematic methods employed in this paper have ensured all the testing examples are done perfectly with height precision, efficiency and stability.

**Acknowledgement.** This work was supported by the National Natural Science Foundation of China under Grant 51175174.

# References

1. Liu, X.J., Bonev, L.A.: Orientation Capability, Error Analysis, and Dimensional Optimization of Two Articulated Tool Heads With Parallel Kinematics. ASME, Journal of Manufacturing Science and Engineering 130, 011015-1–011015-19 (2008)
2. Wahl, J.: Articulated Tool Head, WIPO Patent No. WO 00/25976 (2000)

3. Bonev, I.A.: Geometric Analysis of Parallel Mechanisms, Ph.D. thesis, Laval University, Quebec (2002)
4. Xi, F., Han, W., Marcel, V., Ross, A.: Development of a Sliding-leg Tripod as an Add-on Device for Manufacturing. Robotica 18, 285–294 (2000)
5. Xu, Y.N., Xi, F.: A Realtime Method for Solving the Forward Kinematics of a Tripod with Fixed-length Legs. Journal of Manufacturing Science and Engineering Transaction of ASME 128(2), 204–212 (2006)
6. Xu, Y.N., Liu, X.J., Wang, J.S.: Analytical Forward Kinematics for Two Kinds of Typical Tripods. Part I: Closed-Form Solutions for Forward Kinematics Methods. In: Su, C.-Y., Rakheja, S., Liu, H. (eds.) ICIRA 2012, Part I. LNCS (LNAI), vol. 7506, pp. 282–293. Springer, Heidelberg (2012)
7. Luh, C., Adkins, F.A., Haug, E.J.: Working Capability Analysis of Stewart Platforms. Journal of Mechanical Design, Transactions of the ASME 118(2), 220–227 (1996)
8. Merlet, J.P.: Design a Parallel Manipulator for a Special Worksapce. International Journal of Robotics Research 16(4), 545–556 (1997)
9. Stamper, R.E., Tsai, L.W., Walshg, G.C.: Optimization of a Three DOF Translational Platform for Well-Conditional Workspace. In: Procdings of the 1997 IEEE International Conference on Robotics and Automation, Albuquerque, New Mexico, pp. 3250–3255 (1997)
10. Carretero, J.A., Nahon, M.A., Podhorodeski, R.: Workspace Analysis and Optimization of a Novel 3-DOF Parallel Manipulator. IEEE Trans. Rob. Autom. 15(4), 178–188 (2000)
11. Kumar, V.: Characterization of Workspaces of Parallel Manipulators. Journal of Mechanical Design 14(3), 368–375 (1992)
12. Gosselin, C.M.: Determination of the Workspace of 6-DOF Parallel Manipulators. Journal of Mechanical Design 112(3), 331–336 (1990)
13. Kim, D.I., Chung, W.K., Youm, Y.: Geometrical Approach for the Workspace of 6-DOF Parallel Manipulators. In: Proceedings of the 1997 IEEEE International Conference on Robotics and Automation, Albuquerque, New Mexco, pp. 2986–2991 (1997)
14. Pond, G.T., Carretero, J.A.: Kinematic Analysis and Workspace Determination of the Inclined PRS Parallel Manipulator. In: Proc. of 15th CISMIFToMM Symposium on Robot Design, Dynamics, and Control, Paper No. Rom04-18, Montreal (2004)
15. Haug, E.J., Luh, C., Adkins, F.A.: Numerical Alogrithms for Mapping Boundaries of Manipulators Worksapces. Journal of Mechanical Design, Transactions of the ASME 118(2), 228–234 (1996)
16. Adkins, F.A., Haug, E.J.: Operational Envelope of a Spatial Stewart Platform. Journal of Mechanical Design, Transactional of the ASME 119(2), 330–332 (1997)
17. Marco, C., Massimo, S.: The Effects of Design Parameters on the Workspace of a Turin Parallel Robot. The International Journal of Robotics Research 17(8), 886–902 (1998)

# Robust Sliding Mode Control Law Design
# for Unmanned Gyroplane

Jingchao Lu and Wei Chen

Department of Automatic Control, Northwestern Polytechnical University,
Xi'an, Shaanxi, 710072, China

**Abstract.** Based on a gyroplane T-S fuzzy model in whole flight envelope, the equivalent control law, which is dependent on a set of available feedback control law parameters, is implemented using parameter robust design method according to the design requirements and the constraints of measurable states, sliding manifold parameters of the system is confirmed correspondingly, and the sliding mode control law, designed for the unmanned gyroplane in whole flight envelope, is realized. The simulation result shows that the system satisfies the dynamic performance with strong anti-interference ability, and the design method is feasible and effective.

**Keywords:** gyroplane, T-S fuzzy model, sliding mode, design, control law, robustness (control systems), feedback control, simulation.

## 1    Introduction

As gyroplane has bad static stability, obvious cross-linkage and nonlinear characteristics, with aerodynamic characteristic seriously affected by flight velocity and height, pilot is needed to implement stability augmentation control. So it is necessary to design control law to make the gyroplane meet quality index requirements in whole flight envelope with strong robustness.

T-S fuzzy model has good universal approximation[1], which reflects whole flight envelope characteristic of the system by a synthesis of little perturbation information at different design points. In the same way, whole flight envelope control laws based on parallel distributed compensation algorithm can be realized by a synthesis of control law parameters meeting quality index at different design points.

Sliding mode control earns widespread respect in flight control design because of its arbitrary robustness to uncertainties[2]. However, traditional sliding manifold, which is confined in a dimension reduced state subspace, is mismatched with the natural attribute of practical controlled system, so it is difficult to characterize the quality index of the system, and more control energy and longer time is needed to drive the system to sliding manifold. Integral sliding mode can increase orders of the sliding mode equation, maintain the consistency of sliding mode system and nominal system, and ensure the compatibility between the sliding mode control design and the flight quality requirements[3]. In this condition, parameter region mapping approach is developed to

C.-Y. Su, S. Rakheja, H. Liu (Eds.): ICIRA 2012, Part I, LNAI 7506, pp. 294–301, 2012.
© Springer-Verlag Berlin Heidelberg 2012

design equivalent control law; integral sliding manifold parameters in corresponding state are fixed so as to provide conditions for switching control law design. So parameter robust design and sliding mode control methods are organically combined, and both the quality index requirements and robustness can be satisfied at the end of the design.

## 2    Modeling of Gyroplane Control System

Fig.1 shows the structure of longitudinal control system of the unmanned gyroplane, and $\vartheta_g$ is the given pitching angle.

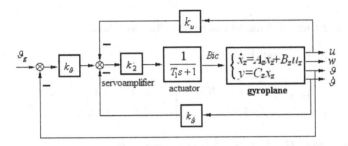

**Fig. 1.** Configuration of the longitudinal control system

Where, the elements of state vector $x_z = [u \quad w \quad \vartheta \quad \dot{\vartheta}]^T$ are respectively the increments of forward and normal velocity, pitching angle and pitching angle rate, among which $\vartheta$, $\dot{\vartheta}$ and $u$ are measurable.

State variables of the gyroplane equations are rearranged according to whether they are measurable, and the longitudinal input $Bic$ is added as a new state variable by appending the servo model to the longitudinal gyroplane model. Then the state equation of the longitudinal gyroplane control system can be expressed as follows:

$$\begin{cases} \dot{x} = A\dot{x} + Bv \\ y = Cx \end{cases} \tag{1}$$

Where $x = [\vartheta \quad \dot{\vartheta} \quad u \quad w \quad Bic]^T$, $v = [\vartheta_g]$, $y = [\vartheta \quad \dot{\vartheta} \quad u]^T$, and $A, B, C$ are the matrices with relevant dimension.

Eq.(1) is the little perturbation equation which describes the gyroplane only at a certain flight state. In order to design the flight control law within the whole flight envelope, nonlinear model should be built to describe the global character of the gyroplane. Aerodynamic characteristic variation with flight height and velocity is fitted using universal approximation of the T-S fuzzy model by synthesizing little perturbation information at certain design points.

Choose $H$ and $V$ as the linguistic variables, Gaussian function as the membership function, and divide $H$ into 3 fuzzy sets while $V$ into 6 fuzzy sets according to the design points distribution in the flight envelope. The two-dimensional representation is shown in Fig.2.

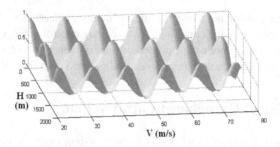

**Fig. 2.** Membership function for $H$ , $V$

Using if-then rules, T-S model can be described as follows:

Rule $l$ : if $H$ is $F_{l1}$ , and $V$ is $F_{l2}$ ,

$$\text{then} \quad \begin{cases} \dot{x} = A_l x + B_l v \\ y = Cx \end{cases} \quad \begin{cases} l = 6(i-1) + j = 1, 2, \cdots, 18 \\ i = 1, 2, 3 \quad\quad j = 1, 2, \cdots, 6 \end{cases} \tag{2}$$

Given a flight state ( $H$ , $V$ ), then T-S model output is:

$$\dot{x}(t) = \frac{\displaystyle\sum_{l=1}^{18} \alpha_l(z)\left[A_l x(t) + B_l u(t)\right]}{\displaystyle\sum_{l=1}^{18} \alpha_l(z)} = \sum_{l=1}^{18} \mu_l(z)\left[A_l x(t) + B_l u(t)\right] \tag{3}$$

Where

$$z = [H \ V], \quad \alpha_l(z) = \prod_{k=1}^{2} F_{lk}(z_k), \quad \mu_l(z) = \frac{\alpha_l(z)}{\displaystyle\sum_{l=1}^{18} \alpha_l(z)}$$

$F_{lk}(z_k)$ is the value of membership function $F_{lk}$ at the point $z_k$ , $\mu_l$ is the weight for rule $l$ . Thus, the system model can be synthetically described as:

$$\begin{cases} \dot{x} = \displaystyle\sum_{l=1}^{18} \mu_l\left[A_l x + B_l v\right] = \left(\sum_{l=1}^{18} \mu_l A_l\right)x + \left(\sum_{l=1}^{18} \mu_l B_l\right)v \\ y = Cx \end{cases} \tag{4}$$

Obviously, Eq.(4) is the nonlinear interpolating expression in whole flight envelope based on little perturbation linear models at design points. T-S model is built to get smooth fitting of the gyroplane global model using local information. Thus linear state equation can be obtained when the flight height and velocity are fixed so as to employ linear system theorem to design flight control law in whole flight envelope.

# 3    Equivalent Control Law Design

Design requirement is described as following dynamic response specifications:

$$\sigma\% \leq 20\%, \quad t_s \leq 5.$$

Where $\sigma\%$ is the overshoot and $t_s$ is the settling time.

According to the requirement, we can derive the range of the corresponding damping ratio and natural frequency for the short period poles as follows:

$$\begin{cases} \xi_d \geq 0.456 \quad (\beta_d \leq 62.87°) \\ \omega_{nd} \geq 1.535 \end{cases} \tag{5}$$

We've put an upper bound to $\omega_{max}$ to make sure the control system will satisfy the operating efficiency requirement and the frequency band of the system will not be so wide. Thus, we can ascertain a region in s-plane where the short period poles of the control system will guarantee satisfactory system performance. This region shapes is a sector $\Gamma$, as it shows in Fig.3.

Total pole assignment can not be used, because there are only three measurable state variables: pitching angle $\vartheta$, pitching angle rate $\dot{\vartheta}$ and forward velocity $u$. The feedback gain is carved up as follows:

$$K_E = \begin{bmatrix} K_a & K_b \end{bmatrix} \tag{6}$$

Where $K_a = \begin{bmatrix} k_\vartheta & k_{\dot{\vartheta}} & k_u \end{bmatrix}$ is the undetermined parameter, and $K_b = \begin{bmatrix} k_w & k_{Bic} \end{bmatrix} = \begin{bmatrix} 0 & 0 \end{bmatrix}$. According to the character specifications, the long period pole corresponding to forward velocity is fixed appropriately at negative real axis of s-plane and the short period poles at the region $\Gamma$. Taking advantage of J.Ackermann theorem[4], the feedback parameter vector $K_a$ can be determined during to the three poles. Parameter mapping is done at the boundary of short period poles region $\Gamma$, then the boundary of feedback parameters region $K_\Gamma$ can be confirmed accordingly (Fig.4). Thus correspondence between feedback parameters and short period poles is set up, which provides advantage to design control law in whole flight envelope.

Move the long period pole to another advisable point, and parameter mapping is repeated. Then the three-dimensional parameter region which corresponds to the three poles (two short period poles and one long period pole) can be obtained.

When the short period poles are assigned to desired place by parameter $K_a$, other two poles of the system are confirmed as well. These poles should be examined according to the character specifications. So the suitable range of the short period poles in the sectorial region is restricted, that is the usable feedback parameter is a subset of $K_\Gamma$.

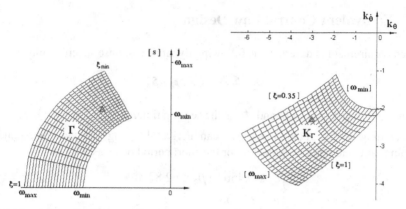

**Fig. 3.** Grid for short period poles region Γ    **Fig. 4.** Grid for feedback parameters region $K_\Gamma$

Similar mapping is performed for all the design points in flight envelope, and the practicable parameter sets are painted respectively in parameter space. Controller parameters chosen from the intersection of the practicable parameter sets can guarantee the system stability and dynamic performance requirements. The distributing regularity of the practicable parameter sets at each design points are valuable for the equivalent control law design.

There is a small scale practicable parameter intersection at the 18 design points for gyroplane longitudinal model. Though a fixed-parameter controller can be obtained during the intersection, it is not ideal for some states, so an adaptable parameters-tuning controller is designed.

According to the character requirements, the short period poles are assigned to $\lambda_{1,2} = -0.9216 \pm j1.3466$, and forward velocity pole is assigned to $\lambda_3 = -0.0772$. Fig.5 shows the distribution of control law parameters in parameter subspace $(k_\vartheta, k_{\dot\vartheta})$ at each design points.

RBF network parameters-tuning controller (T-S form) is trained using the control law parameter samples at the design points, with whose universal approximation, the control law obtained by parameter robust method is fitted. Given a discretional flight state (height and velocity), the control law parameters can be obtained accordingly. Thus dynamic performances of the gyroplane can be always corresponding to the assigned poles in whole envelope.

Similar to Eq.(2), according to parallel distributed compensation algorithm[5], the control rule of the T-S form parameters-tuning controller can be described as follows:

$$\text{rule } l: \text{if } H \text{ is } F_{l1}, \text{ and } V \text{ is } F_{l2}, \text{ then } K_a = K_{la} \tag{7}$$

The control law parameter samples $k_\vartheta$, $k_{\dot\vartheta}$ and training data of the T-S form parameter-tuning controller output are shown in Fig.6. The equivalent control law in whole flight envelope can be described as:

$$u_e = -\left(\sum_{l=1}^{18} \mu_l K_a\right)\begin{bmatrix}\vartheta & \dot\vartheta & u\end{bmatrix}^T = -\left(\sum_{l=1}^{18} \mu_l k_\vartheta\right)\vartheta - \left(\sum_{l=1}^{18} \mu_l k_{\dot\vartheta}\right)\dot\vartheta - \left(\sum_{l=1}^{18} \mu_l k_u\right)u \tag{8}$$

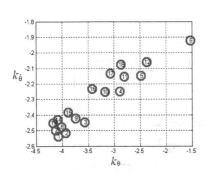

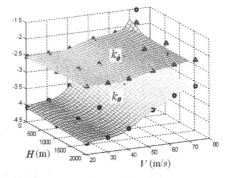

**Fig. 5.** Distribution graph of control law parameters at each design points

**Fig. 6.** Surface of training data of pitching control law parameters

## 4    Sliding Manifold and Switching Control Law Design

Full state information is needed to drive the system states to the sliding manifold which is under constraint of the equivalent control law. The switching control law can be constructed by design sliding mode observer[6]. Using integral sliding mode, the sliding manifold coefficient vector $C_s$ is determined by the characteristic polynomial which is computed from the assigned poles and the other two poles, so that the sliding manifold is matched with system character in favor of avoiding the chattering. The sliding mode equation is

$$s(x) = [C_s T \;\; 1]x^* = [\bar{C}_s \;\; 1]\hat{x}^*$$
$$= \bar{C}_1 \int_0^t \hat{x}_1 dt + \bar{C}_2 \hat{x}_1 + \bar{C}_3 \hat{x}_2 + \bar{C}_4 \hat{x}_3 + \bar{C}_5 \hat{x}_4 + \hat{x}_5 \tag{9}$$

Where $T$ is linear transform matrix which can turn the original state equation to controllability canonical form, $\hat{x}^* = [\int \hat{x}_1 dx \;\; \hat{x}_1 \;\; \hat{x}_2 \cdots \hat{x}_5]^T$ is phase variable form of the state vector. Then the switching control law based on full states can be designed. Under uniform reaching law, the switching control is

$$u_v = -k \cdot \mathrm{sgn}(s(x)) \tag{10}$$

The variation law of the vector $\bar{C}_s = [\bar{C}_1 \; \bar{C}_2 \cdots \bar{C}_5]$ with flight height and velocity is fitted using RBF network (T-S form). Then the switching control in whole flight envelope is realized as follows:

$$u_v = -k(CB)^{-1} \mathrm{sgn}\left[\left(\sum_{l=1}^{18} \mu_l CT\right)x\right] \tag{11}$$

Considering Eq.(8) and Eq.(11), longitudinal sliding mode control law in the whole flight envelope based on parallel distributed compensation algorithm is realized, and the corresponding structure of control system is shown in Fig.7.

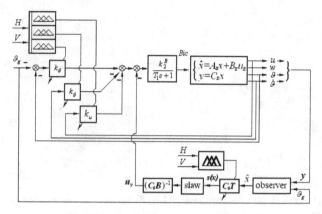

**Fig. 7.** The structure of gyroplane longitudinal robust sliding mode control system

# 5    Simulation

We choose the state H=1000m, V=40m/s, give the system initial pitching angle $\vartheta(0) = 5\,(°)$ , initial pitching angle rate $\dot\vartheta(0) = 5\,(°/s)$ , and exert disturbance $r(t) = 10\sin(\pi t)/57.3$. Dynamic response curves of the gyroplane are shown in Fig.8. From the response of the pitching angle, we can see that the system should return to its original state in no more than 5 seconds with 10% overshoot, which satisfies the dynamic index requirements. Fig.9 shows the corresponding dynamic curves of sliding mode rate $\dot s(t)$, output of sliding mode function $s(t)$ and switching control $u_v(t)$. It is obvious that the system can reach the sliding manifold in less than 0.2 seconds with strong robustness in sliding mode which can be concluded from nearly superposition of the dynamic curves with and without disturbance.

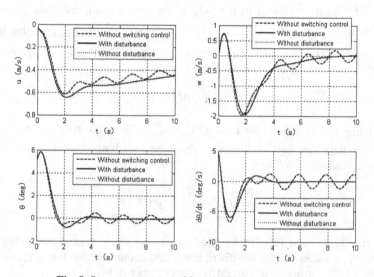

**Fig. 8.** System responses with and without disturbances

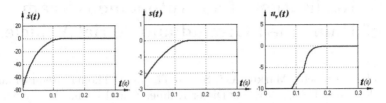

**Fig. 9.** Curves of corresponding $\dot{s}(t)$, $s(t)$ and $u_v(t)$

# 6    Conclusion

In this paper, advantages of parameter robust design and sliding mode control methods are combined to design flight control system. The equivalent control law for gyroplane longitudinal control system is implemented using parameter mapping method according to the requirements of system performance, integral sliding manifold parameters is confirmed at the same time, at last the switching control law is designed. On this basis, gyroplane little perturbation models and the corresponding controllers at each design points are integrated in the form of T-S fuzzy model. Thus the sliding mode control law in the whole flight envelope based on parallel distributed compensation algorithm is realized.

Simulation result shows that the system dynamic character satisfies the index demand with strong anti-interference ability, and the design method is feasible and effective.

# References

1. Cao, S.G., Rees, N.W., Feng, G.: Analysis and Design for A Class of Complex Control Systems. Parts I: Fuzzy Modeling and Identification. J. Automatica 33(6), 1017–1028 (1997)
2. Tong, X.T., Zhao, H.C., Feng, G.H.: Adaptive Global Terminal Sliding Mode Control for Anti-Warship Missiles. In: Proc. of 6th World Congress on Intelligent Control and Automation, pp. 1962–1966 (2006)
3. Bartolini, G., Punta, E., Zolezzi, T.: Simplex Methods for Nonlinear Uncertain Sliding-Mode Control. IEEE Trans. Automat Contr. 49(6), 922–933 (2004)
4. Ackermann, J.: Robust flight control: a design example. J. Guid Control 4(6), 597–605 (1981)
5. Erbatur, K., Kaynak, O.: Use of Adaptive Fuzzy Systems in Parameter Tuning of Sliding-Mode Controllers. IEEE/ASMIE Trans. on Mechatronics 6(4), 474–482 (2001)
6. Xiang, J., Su, H.Y., Chu, J.: Sliding-mode observer design for a class of uncertain system. Control Theory & Applications 23(6), 996–1000 (2006)

# Realization of an Autonomous Team
# of Unmanned Ground and Aerial Vehicles

Marco Langerwisch[1], Markus Ax[2], Stefan Thamke[2], Thomas Remmersmann[3],
Alexander Tiderko[3], Klaus-Dieter Kuhnert[2], and Bernardo Wagner[1]

[1] Leibniz Universität Hannover, Real Time Systems Group (RTS),
Appelstr. 9A, D-30167 Hannover, Germany
{langerwisch,wagner}@rts.uni-hannover.de
[2] University of Siegen, Institute of Real-Time Learning Systems (EZLS),
Hölderlinstr. 3, D-57068 Siegen, Germany
{markus.ax,stefan.thamke}@uni-siegen.de, kuhnert@fb12.uni-siegen.de
[3] Fraunhofer Institute for Communication, Information Processing
and Ergonomics (FKIE)
Neuenahrer Straße 20, D-53343 Wachtberg, Germany
{thomas.remmersmann,alexander.tiderko}@fkie.fraunhofer.de

**Abstract.** The paper presents work that has been done by three different research institutions. The aim was to realize an autonomous team of heterogeneous unmanned ground and aerial vehicles performing certain reconnaissance and surveillance tasks, where the tasks were set by an operator at a team level instead of controlling each vehicle seperately. To overcome the lack of a common middleware, the interfaces between vehicles and graphical user interface have been defined using Robot Operating System (ROS) and Battle Management Language (BML). We present approaches for autonomous control of the vehicles, focussing on the unmanned ground vehicle. Moreover, we conducted some large field experiments and present the results.

**Keywords:** Unmanned ground vehicle (UGV), unmanned aerial vehicle (UAV), field testing, robot operating system (ROS), battle management language (BML), autonomous vehicles.

## 1 Introduction

Complex tasks for robots provide numerous challenges for both, the robots and and the human operator. In case of autonomous reconnaissance and surveillance, the deployment of an integrated multi-robot team consisting of heterogeneous robots might provide advantages compared to strict homogeneous compositions. Unmanned Ground Vehicles (UGV) offer the opportunity to carry a multitude of different sensors into known or unknown environment, having usually a very restricted field of view and a constrained mobility in case of non-holonomic vehicles and cluttered environment. In contrast, Unmanned Aerial Vehicles (UAV) can move almost unconstrained, having thus a large operating space. On the other hand, they have usually a very low payload, being only capable of transporting

C.-Y. Su, S. Rakheja, H. Liu (Eds.): ICIRA 2012, Part I, LNAI 7506, pp. 302–312, 2012.

sensors like a GPS receiver or a lightwight camera. Deploying a combination of UGV and UAV, a UAV might have a look behind a wall limiting an UGV, for example. Moreover, a human operator controlling a team of robots should not be forced to control each unit sperately. Instead, he should be able to formulate a task to the team without taking care of the creation of seperate tasks for each individual robot. In addition, the sensor data should be fed back to the control station.

In this paper, we will present the results of work conducted by three different research institutions. Instead of using a unified middleware, each institution applies its own software and communication system. We will present the necessarily well defined interfaces between all components of the multi-robot team. To keep the possibility to integrate further robots or other components in the future, existing and established standards have been used. The aim of our work is to realize an autonomous team of an UGV and two UAV, namely quadrocopters, that receives reconnaissance and surveillance tasks by a single human operator using a graphical user interface. Depending on the specific task, the vehicles move either seperate or together. All units contribute to the reconnaissance results by sending their sensor data back to the control station. This phase of the research work was completed by a field test, demonstrating all abilities. The vehicles, the communication interfaces, some used approaches, and results of the field test will be presented in this paper. Here, the focus lies on the UGV. Detailed descriptions and results regarding GUI and UGV are published seperately.

Not much work has been done in the area of autonomous teams of UGV and UAV. Usually, research work focuses on single aspects of UGV/UAV cooperation. For example, [1] deals with the common localization of a quadrocopter, while the authors of [2] describe their approach to control the formation of all robots. In [3], a UGV is accompanied by an UAV ("Flying Eye") to detect negative obstacles like holes or steep slopes. To the best of our knowledge, the only work that deals with the complete realization of a UGV/UAV team and a real field test is presented in [4]. In contrast to our work, the aerial vehicles have been used only to identify possible regions of interest, so that ground vehicles can start approaching these regions and fulfill their tasks.

The paper is organized as follows: The following section presents the communication architecture and all used interfaces. In Sec. 3, the participating vehicles are described, while Sec. 4 illustrates the graphical user interface. The control of the UGV and the UAV is part of Sec. 5, while Sec. 6 presents results of our field experiments. The paper ends with a conclusion.

## 2    Communication Architecture

Because three research institutions were involved in the presented work, it has been agreed on clearly defined interfaces between all parties. Three subsystems can be identified: the aerial vehicles, the ground vehicle, and the control station with the graphical user interface (GUI). To connect the GUI with the vehicles, a markup language called Battle Management Language (BML) was used. It will be described in Sec. 2.1. As both types of vehicles were using different operating systems, middlewares, and communication protocols, it was decided to use the Robot Operating System (ROS) [5] as a communication standard between the vehicles. ROS offers well-defined data types for most kinds of data, is open source and hence freely available, and has a constantly growing community contributing to the software repository. The integration of ROS into the corresponding middlewares is described in Sec. 3. To connect the ROS system of the vehicles with the GUI, a ROS component called BMLConnector has been developed in Python. It is subject of Sec. 2.2.

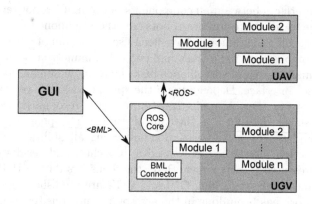

**Fig. 1.** Communication architecture of the whole system. Blue: ROS, red: proprietary middleware, green: BML.

The communication architecture is depicted in Fig. 1. The GUI is communicating with the UGV via BML. The vehicles are communicating through ROS among themselves. As can be seen, one ROSCore and one BMLConnector have been used. The advantage is the reduced complexity of the whole system. As a consequence, all BML tasks have to be transmitted via the UGV. Alternatively, multiple ROSCores and BMLConnectors (one on each vehicle) could have been used, having the communication between the vehicles encapsulated in BML again.

During the field testing, a continuous IEEE 802.11 (WiFi) connection between all participants was assured.

## 2.1 Battle Management Language

In order to express commands to be pushed from the user to the vehicles we use Battle Management Language (BML) [6] because it is human readable, unambiguous, and in standardization process of Simulation Interoperability Standards Organization (SISO). BML can be used to express tasks, reports, and requests between command and control systems (C2 systems), simulation systems and real units. In addition, BML also may be used to interact with robotic units. Thus, it allows C2 systems and their users to interact with robot systems in the same way as with real units or units simulated in simulation systems. For example, in [7] the authors describe how to control robots running the middleware RoSe by using BML.

BML must be unambiguous to allow automatic processing. Therefore, BML has been designed as a formal language. A formal language is the set of all sentences generated by a formal grammar. A formal grammar consists of a lexicon (the words of the language) and a set of rules (how to combine the words). In the case of BML, this grammar is the Command and Control Lexical Grammar (C2LG) [8]. To be more precise, the lexicon contains the attributes and values provided by the Joint Consultation Command and Control Information Exchange Data Model (JC3IEDM) [9]. This set of rules incorporates the idea of the 5Ws (Who, What, Where, When, Why) for individual BML expressions.

### 2.2   BML Connector

The communication between the C2LG GUI and the ROS nodes is done by translating between BML Messages and ROS messages. To handle the translation we implemented a ROS node called BMLConnector. The BMLConnector has a TCP connection to the C2LG GUI. The received BML commands are translated to a defined ROS message, called BmlTask. The BmlTask message is then published as a ROS topic. For status reports, the ROS messages will be translated back to BML. Currently only the robot positions are translated to BML reports and are used for visualization. For other sensor data, particularly with regard to binary data such as images, video, or lidar data, there is currently no representation in BML. In this case, the ROS message is converted to an XML format. For the transmission to the C2LG GUI an additional TCP connection is used.

Since not all sensor data is required on C2LG GUI, only the data of particular ROS topics are forwarded to the C2LG GUI. For setup purposes, the BMLConnector comes with an XML-RPC interface. This can be used to add or remove topics, which are forwarded to the C2LG GUI. It is especially useful if new nodes are running on one of the robots, or if a robot is added or removed from the group.

## 3   Vehicles

Two different types of vehicles took part in the experiments, a car-like UGV, and two quadrocopter drones. All will be described in the following two sections.

### 3.1   UGV RTS-HANNA

The unmanned ground vehicle RTS-HANNA (see Fig. 2) is based on an off-the-shelf Kawasaki Mule 3010 Diesel chassis. It has been retrofitted with a drive-by-wire interface and is fully street-licensed when driven manually. The maximum velocity is 40 km/h, and the maximum payload is 600 kg.

**Fig. 2.** UGV RTS-HANNA

The vehicle platform can be equipped with a multitude of possible sensors. For environmental perception, two continuously rotating 3D laser rangefinders RTS-ScanDriveDuo, one Velodyne HDL-64E, one Ibeo Lux, and a Microsoft Kinect are mounted on the vehicle. For the navigation, odometry, a gyroscope, and two GPS receivers are available. The vehicle can communicate either by IEEE 802.11 (WiFi) channels, a 433 Mhz serial link, or by GSM/UMTS.

Five embedded PCs are used for processing the sensor data, navigation and control of the vehicle. All PCs are running a Linux operating system with the real time extension Xenomai, and are connected via the real time ethernet stack RTnet [10]. The software is developed using the robotic framework RACK. As described in Sec. 2, at least one embedded PC has to be capable of executing ROS components. Therefore, we cross-compiled ROS for our Linux distribution and made the ROS libraries and API available to our middleware RACK. To let the RACK components communicate with ROS components, a kind of gateway module has been implemented. The module is part of the RACK communication system, but is also able to publish and subscribe to ROS topics. It receives the BML tasks and organizes the execution, and publishes further tasks for the UAV and sensor data for the GUI as ROS topics. As depicted in Fig. 1, the UGV is running the ROSCore and the BMLConnector in ROS context, the gateway module ("Module 1") in both worlds, and the rest of the software components in RACK.

### 3.2    UAV Psyche 1000

The UAV Psyche 1000 (see Fig. 3) are modified drones MD4-1000 by Micro-drones. They are electronically driven helicopters with four rotors, so called quadrocopters, providing a maximum flight weight of 6 kg. The UAV have a high precision position stabilization and location estimation system. Using a GPS receiver, accelerometers, gyroscopes, a magnetometer and a barometer, the manufacturer provides the user a filtered position estimation. The drones are equipped with a system on a chip running a specialized embedded Linux distribution. The control module running on the system utilizes the localization and attitude estimations provided by the manufacturer, and generates signals that are fed back into the proprietary control software of the drone. This allows us to make use of all position stabilization functionalities provided by the manufacturer. ROS has been integrated into the middleware to make communication to other ROS components possible.

**Fig. 3.** UAV Psyche 1000

The UAV are equipped with two communication channels. A bi-directional low-bandwidth, but high distance 2.4 GHz link can be used to connect to a remote control for manual operation. The second channel is a 5 GHz IEEE 802.11 connection, handling the communication to other drones and robots.

Moreover, the UAV are equipped with a 14.7 MP zoom camera each, mounted in a moveable frame deflected by two servos. Pictures are either available as live video preview that is normally used on the camera display (320 × 240 pixels, average file size 9kB, available at 25Hz), or by the high resoltion single picture mode (up to 4416 × 3312 pixels, average file size 4 MB).

## 4   Graphical User Interface

We use a Graphical User Interface (GUI), the Command and Control Lexical Grammar (C2LG) GUI, to enter the tasks for our robot system. The C2LG GUI is used in other projects to test interoperability with simulation systems. The GUI supports the user generating the tasks. It allows selecting objects from a list or to pick them from the integrated map. Geographical features like areas can be created on the map as well. These features then can be referenced. The GUI also visualizes the robots' reports. In particular, the robots themselves are shown in the map due to their periodic position reports. Moreover, the camera and map feedback of the robots can be visualized.

The GUI is depicted in Fig. 4. The main window contains the control elements and the integrated map, where geographical features can be added. It also contains the current positions of the vehicles (blue symbols) and their travelled paths. The smaller windows on the right side show the live camera streams of the three vehicles. Below the main window, high resolution camera images taken by the UAV can be visualized.

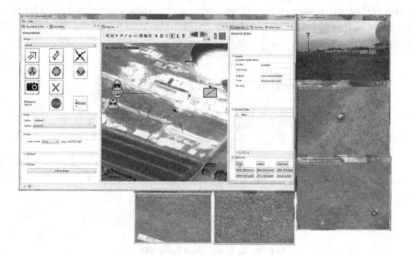

**Fig. 4.** Graphical User Interface C2LG GUI

## 5    Control of the Vehicles

As the UGV receives a new task via BML message, it is responsible to assign seperate tasks to itself and the UAV. We will exemplarily have a look on two possible task assignments: patrolling a given path, and reconnaissance of a certain area.

The patrol task contains a list of waypoints. The goal is, that the UGV patrols these waypoints periodically, and the UAV accompany it while orbiting the ground vehicle and keeping their cameras aligned towards it to let the operator keep track of the vehicle's environment. Having received the patrol task, the UGV initiates its MOVE behaviour to the next waypoint, as described below. While executing the MOVE behavior, a patrol task is submitted to the drones with a frequency of 1 Hz, including the current position of the ground vehicle. The drones receive the patrol task and calculate their orbit positions self dependent. As soon as one waypoint is reached, the process repeats with the next one, and so on.

In contrast to the patrol task, the BML message for reconnaissance contains an area described by its corner points. At first, the UGV calculates the centroid of the area and initiates a MOVE behavior to that point. A move task is submitted to the drones with a frequency of 1 Hz, including the current position of the ground vehicle. The drones receive the move task and calculate their own positions for a fix formation to follow the vehicle self dependent. As soon as the vehicle pulls into the area, a RECCE behavior is initiated as described below. One drone keeps receiving a move task periodically to follow the UGV, and one drone receives a reconnaissance task and starts to fly along the borders of the area.

The MOVE and the RECCE behaviors of the vehicles will be described below. A detailed description of the control of the quadrocopter drones, including collision avoidance and formation control, is published seperately.

## 5.1  MOVE Behavior

The road network at the test site is known in advance and is available in OpenStreetMap (OSM) format, while the vehicle localizes itself via differential GPS. When a MOVE behavior is initiated, a path from the robot's current location to the desired goal point is calculated. This is done by a simple A* search for a shortest path in the OSM geodata. If an obstacle occurs that cannot be avoided reactively, the corresponding way segment is marked as blocked, and a global path replanning is performed. A detailed description can be found in [11]. To follow the planned path, a hybrid feedback controller, introduced in [12], is applied. It includes reactive obstacle avoidance and local path replanning.

## 5.2  RECCE Behavior

The RECCE behavior is initiated once the UGV has reached the desired area. The aim of the behavior is to navigate on all ways in that area, and to build an obstacle map, namely an occupancy grid map. Therefore, a path that passes all ways has to be calculated. At first, the OSM map is reduced to all way segments, that have a non-empty intersection with the designated area. Way segments that are not completely contained in the area are cut along the area's border. The result is a reduced OSM road network. Afterwards, the problem of finding a way traversing all OSM nodes can be seen as a Travelling Salesman Problem (TSP). Because the graph is symmetric and it is allowed to pass an OSM node twice, a distance graph of all included OSM nodes is computed. Subsequently, a simple nearest neighbour heuristic is applied. During field testing, the heuristic turned out to be very fast and efficient enough for our purposes. Another, more efficient, heuristic could be easily applied here. Moreover, the approach avoids to travel into dead-end ways when they are in sensor range, because they have already been mapped.

The approach results in a path that traverses each OSM node in the designated area at least once. The vehicle follows the path using an hybrid feedback controller as described above. When an unavoidable obstacle occurs, the way segment is marked as blocked, and all previous OSM nodes are marked as visited. A new TSP is solved, resulting in a new path avoiding the blocked way and not necessarily traversing again already visited nodes.

# 6   Experimental Results

To finish this phase of our research work and to present the feasibility of our approaches, we conducted a large field test, where all scenarios were tested and presented. The test site consisted of an outdoor area with gravel roads, fences, bushes, muddy ground, and some smaller buildings. The size of the site was appr. 300m × 120m. In the following, the results of the patrol and the reconnaissance scenarios will exemplarily be presented. The desired behaviors of the vehicles have been described in Sec. 5. Other scenarios like the observation of a specific point or a designated area have also been presented successfully.

## 6.1   Patrol Scenario

During the patrol scenario, the team of unmanned ground and aerial vehicles received some waypoints that had to be travelled periodically and autonomously. The drones had to orbit the ground vehicle, keeping their cameras focused at the ground vehicle. Fig. 5 shows a detail of the GUI during the scenarion. The starting point of all vehicles was at the black arrowhead. The black arrow marks the waypoints in their order. The travelled path of the ground vehicle is marked in purple, the paths of the two quadrocopters are marked in light and dark blue. One can see, that the UGV travelled along the way up to its current position (light blue vehicle symbol), and that the UAV were orbiting the UGV, observable by the loops in the light and dark blue lines. In Fig. 4, the same situation is depicted in the complete GUI. The two lower windows on the right side show the live video stream of the drones, both focused at the ground vehicle. During the whole test run, there was no manual intervention.

## 6.2   Reconnaissance Scenario

After having received the reconnaissance task, the team moved into the desired reconnaissance area autonomously. Afterwards, they started the reconnaissance of the area as described in Sec. 5. Results of the reconnaissance scenario are depicted in Fig. 6. On the left side, the known road network is painted in blue. The desired area has been marked in light red. The resulting obstacle map (occupancy grid map) taken by the environmental sensors of the UGV is depicted on the right side. It is overlayed with the road network in blue.

It has been shown, that the team of robots was able to reconnoiter a certain area fully autonomous and, again, without any manual intervention. A path has been planned that traverses each way node of the area at least once. Apart from the video stream delivered by the UAV, the UGV created an obstacle map and transferred it back to the operator station.

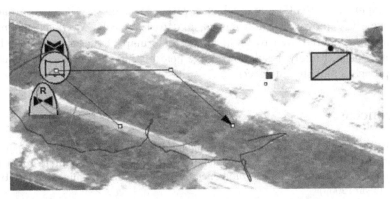

**Fig. 5.** Travelled paths during the patrol scenario. Path of the ground vehicle painted in purple, paths of quadrocopter drones painted in dark and light blue, sequence of the patrol waypoints marked by black arrow.

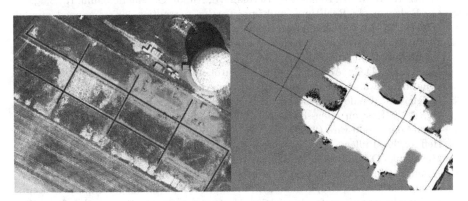

**Fig. 6.** Results of the reconnaissance scenario. Left: aerial image of the test site, known road network painted in blue, desired reconnaissance are marked in light red. Right: created obstacle map of the desired area, road network painted in blue.

## 7    Conclusions

We presented our approach to realize an autonomous team of unmanned ground (UGV) and aerial vehicles (UAV) that was developed by three different research institutions. Two heterogeneous types of vehicles, and a graphical user interface (GUI) were involved. The approach lets an operator define tasks at a team level instead of defining seperate tasks for each individual vehicle. To overcome the lack of common middleware and communication standards, it has been agreed on well defined interfaces for the communication between the vehicles and the GUI. The interfaces were based on the well-known Robot Operating System (ROS), and the Battle Management Language (BML), which is currently in standardization process.

312 M. Langerwisch et al.

The paper presented GUI and vehicles, with a focus on the UGV. Approaches to let the UGV move to a destination, and to let the UGV travel all known paths in a designated area to build an obstacle map of the environment have been introduced. Finally, results of a large field testing showed the feasibility of our approaches and the interfaces.

# References

1. Zhang, T., Li, W., Achtelik, M., Kuhnlenz, K., Buss, M.: Multi-sensory motion estimation and control of a mini-quadrotor in an air-ground multi-robot system. In: IEEE International Conference on Robotics and Biomimetics (ROBIO), pp. 45–50 (2009)
2. Michael, N., Fink, J., Kumar, V.: Controlling a team of ground robots via an aerial robot. In: IEEE/RSJ International Conference on Intelligent Robots and Systems, pp. 965–970 (2007)
3. Stentz, A., Kelly, A., Rander, P., Herman, H., Amidi, O., Mandelbaum, R., Salgian, G., Pedersen, J.: Real-time, multi-perspective perception for unmanned ground vehicles. In: AUVSI Unmanned Systems Symposium 2003 (2003)
4. Hsieh, M.A., Cowley, A., Keller, J.F., Chaimowicz, L., Grocholsky, B., Kumar, V., Taylor, C.J., Endo, Y., Arkin, R.C., Jung, B., Wolf, D.F., Sukhatme, G.S., MacKenzie, D.C.: Adaptive teams of autonomous aerial and ground robots for situational awareness. Journal of Field Robotics 24(11-12), 991–1014 (2007)
5. Quigley, M., Conley, K., Gerkey, B.P., Faust, J., Foote, T., Leibs, J., Wheeler, R., Ng, A.Y.: Ros: an open-source robot operating system. In: ICRA Workshop on Open Source Software (2009)
6. Heffner, K., Pullen, J.M., Simonsen, K.J., Schade, U., Reus, N.D., Khimeche, L., Mevassvik, O.M., Brook, A., Veiga, R.G.: NATO MSG-048 C-BML final report summary. In: Fall Simulation Interoperability Workshop (2010)
7. Remmersmann, T., Brüggemann, B., Frey, M.: Robots to the ground. In: Concepts and Implementations for Innovative Military Communications and Information Technologies, pp. 61–68. Military University of Technology (September 2010)
8. Schade, U., Hieb, M.R., Frey, M., Rein, K.: Command and control lexical grammar (C2LG) specification. Technical report, Fraunhofer FKIE, Neuenahrer Straße 20, 53343 Wachtberg (July 2010)
9. Gerz, M., Schade, U.: Das Joint Consultation Command and Control Information Exchange Data Model. In: Grosche, J., Wunder, M. (eds.) Verteilte Führungsinformationssysteme, pp. 219–233. Springer (2009)
10. Kiszka, J., Wagner, B.: Rtnet - a flexible hard real-time networking framework. In: 10th IEEE Conference on Emerging Technologies and Factory Automation, vol. 1, pp. 449–456 (2005)
11. Hentschel, M., Wagner, B.: Autonomous robot navigation based on OpenStreetMap geodata. In: 13th International IEEE Conference on Intelligent Transportation Systems, pp. 1645–1650 (September 2010)
12. Hentschel, M., Wulf, O., Wagner, B.: A hybrid feedback controller for car-like robots - combining reactive obstacle avoidance and global replanning. Integr. Comput. Aided Eng. 14(1), 3–14 (2007)

# Design of Helicopter Cable-Orientation Control System Based on Finite-Element Modeling

Xiaoyan Wang, Xinmin Wang, Rong Xie, and Yi Zheng

School of Automation, Northwestern Polytechnical University, Xi'an, China
wxy2029@126.com, {wxin,xierong}@nwpu.edu.cn
zhengy1968@163.com

**Abstract.** The cable model is established based on the finite-element method to describe actual dynamic characteristics of cable dipping sonar system. The definition of reference cable angle is proposed and an adaptive Fuzzy-PID cable-orientation controller is designed. The controller designed in this paper combines the variable universe Fuzzy controller and PID controller together appropriately. The segment control strategy of Fuzzy control and PID control is used. The cable dynamic equations and cable-orientation controller are designed as the outer loop, while the helicopter equation and ground speed maintenance mode work as the inner loop. Through the control of helicopter's ground speed in hovering mode, cable-orientation can remain at an expected angle value under different wind speed or ocean current interference. Simulation results show that the cable-orientation controller designed in this paper has a good performance. Cable angles can track and keep the reference values accurately when helicopter is hovering over the sea, indicating that the adaptive Fuzzy-PID method for the cable-orientation control system is effective and has good robustness.

**Keywords:** Helicopter, Cable-orientation, Finite element, Fuzzy PID, Adaptive.

## 1    Introduction

Anti-submarine helicopter should keep hovering state and drop dipping sonar into the sea to detect submarines by mooring cable [1][2]. The sonar must be dropped into water perpendicularly and avoid dragging so that it can detect targets and locate the position accurately. The effects of sea waves or other disturbances should be inhibited. So the helicopter motion should be controlled to adjust the cable-orientation which is the angle between fuselage and cable. The dipping sonar attitude control is realized indirectly through the control of helicopter's ground speed. It is important to study the dynamic characteristics and establish the cable model, which is the difficult point of cable-orientation control system design. The accuracy of the model affects the performance of the controller directly. Document [1] presents two kinds of cable model, one is cable equations based on curve fitting and the other is simplified static model. Document [2] establishes the dynamic model of cable according to moment balance.

C.-Y. Su, S. Rakheja, H. Liu (Eds.): ICIRA 2012, Part I, LNAI 7506, pp. 313–322, 2012.

The dynamic characteristics of dipping sonar system are complicated. Cable is at a zero damping state when the system is in balance state, while the damping becomes bigger when the cable slip angle is bigger [3]. To approach the real dynamic characteristic of the cable dipping sonar system, finite element method is used to analysis the cable model.

Based on the finite element model, the adaptive Fuzzy PID controller is designed to control the cable-orientation while hovering. This controller combines the advantages of Fuzzy control and PID control method. The cable-orientation can be well controlled under different winds or other disturbances.

## 2     Finite Element Modeling

### 2.1     Cable Coordinate System

Set the point where the cable dropping from the helicopter as the origin point, establish a right hand coordinate system $O_l X_l Y_l Z_l$ whose axis are parallel to the axis of ground coordinate system $O_d X_d Y_d Z_d$. It is shown in Fig.1.

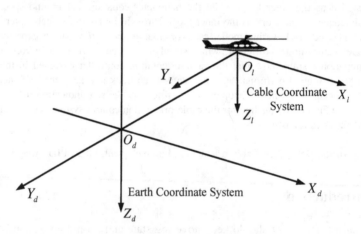

**Fig. 1.** Cable Coordinate System

### 2.2     Cable Modeling

According to finite element theory, cable-element is regarded as a steel resistance bar with well distributed physical parameters (or a bar whose quality is concentrated on one point). There is no bending moment between cable-elements and no transport of torque's hinge joint [3]. At this circumstance, the movement form of cable-element is rotation and its pulling force is calculated by centripetal force formula. The dynamic equation of cable-element is described by motion parameters in vector form. So, it is easy to be derived from physical concept directly. The motion of cable-element coordinate is described in quaternion form. This method simplifies the movement analysis.

The accuracy is better as the partitioned sections increase, but the computational complexity will increase. In view of the practical situation, we divide the cable into 3 segments. One segment is over the sea face and the other two are under sea face. It is shown in Fig.2. $\theta_1$ $\theta_2$ $\theta_3$ are longitudinal misalignment angles and $\varphi_1$ $\varphi_2$ $\varphi_3$ are lateral misalignment angles. These angles are used as the motion parameters of cable.

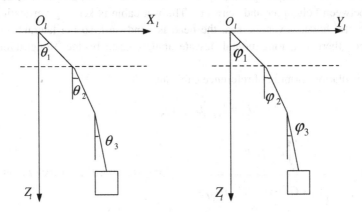

**Fig. 2.** Cable segmentation

Force condition is analyzed for every section respectively so that the differential equation of each section is established. Then the linearized motion equations of the cable can be derived. The longitudinal motion equation is:

$$\dot{x}_1 = A_1 x_1 + B_{11} u_1 + B_{12} d \tag{1}$$

The lateral motion equation is:

$$\dot{x}_2 = A_2 x_2 + B_2 u_2 \tag{2}$$

Where,

$$x_1 = \begin{bmatrix} \dot{\theta}_1 & \dot{\theta}_2 & \dot{\theta}_3 & \theta_1 & \theta_2 & \theta_3 \end{bmatrix}^T, u_1 = \begin{bmatrix} u_d & \dot{u}_d \end{bmatrix}^T, \quad d = \begin{bmatrix} u_{wind} \end{bmatrix}^T,$$

$$x_2 = \begin{bmatrix} \dot{\varphi}_1 & \dot{\varphi}_2 & \dot{\varphi}_3 & \varphi_1 & \varphi_2 & \varphi_3 \end{bmatrix}^T, u_2 = \begin{bmatrix} v_d & \dot{v}_d \end{bmatrix}^T$$

Where, $u_d$ and $v_d$ are the projections of helicopter ground speed on longitudinal axis and lateral axis of ground coordinate system, respectively; $u_{wind}$ is the steady-state wind on the sea face; $A_1$, $B_{11}$ and $B_{12}$ are the state matrix, input matrix and perturbation input matrix of cable longitudinal motion equations, respectively. $A_2$ and $B_2$ are the state matrix and input matrix of cable lateral motion equations, respectively.

# 3    Design of Cable-Orientation Control System

## 3.1    Reference Cable Angle Calculation

Define the balanced state of the cable. To simplify the question, assume the seawater speed is zero, the helicopter ground speed is controlled to zero and there is no relative motion between helicopter and seawater. The wet cable is keeping verticality. When the helicopter hovers over the sea, the head is windward, so the lateral wind speed is zero and there is a longitudinal deviate angle caused by the   longitudinal wind speed.

The calculation formula of reference cable angle is:

$$\theta_{eq} = k_{eq} \cdot \left| U_f \right| \cdot u_{wind} \tag{3}$$

where $k_{eq} = \dfrac{\int_0^{l_{AB}} k_f \cdot l \cdot dl}{(\frac{1}{2}G_1 + G_2 + G_3 + G_M) \cdot l_{AB}}$ ,   $k_{f1} = \dfrac{1}{2}\rho_1 \cdot C_{f1} \cdot d_s$ ,   where   $\rho_1$   is the air

density, $C_{f1}$ is the drag coefficient of the cable in the air, $d_s$ is the diameter of the cable. $G_i$ (i=1,2,3) is the weight of the i-th section of the cable , $G_M$  is the weight of the sonar. $U_f$  is the nominal inflow speed.

The wind speed on the sea face is variable so that it is hard to get its exact information. However, the helicopter's airspeed is measurable and contains the wind speed information. So replace the $u_{wind}$ by $-u$ and get the reference cable angle calculation formula:

$$\theta_{eq} = -k_{eq} \cdot \left| U_f \right| \cdot u \tag{4}$$

If the helicopter's hovering speed is not zero, the sonar operator may modify the cable-orientation error caused by ocean current through fine turning knob.

## 3.2    Cable-Orientation Controller Design Principle

The cable-orientation is required to keep at the expected value quickly when the helicopter uses the dipping sonar for searching submarine. Because of the complicated nonlinear characteristics, it is hard to get a good control result using PID design method based on linear model [5]. So, adaptive fuzzy PID control scheme is chosen to realize the control of cable-orientation. That is to use the strategy of PID and Fuzzy stepwise control. When  | e | ≥e0, Fuzzy controller is used to improve the system's rapidity; when  | e | <e0, it is switched to PID controller to remove the static error. The principle diagram is shown in Fig.3:

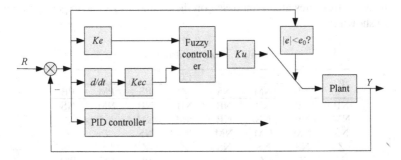

**Fig. 3.** Adaptive fuzzy PID controller principle diagram

When closed-loop system switches from one control mode to another one, it is necessary to keep the system output continuous. That is to say, when system switches from Fuzzy control to PID control, the initial output of PID controller must be equal to the last output of Fuzzy controller. Because these two control modes do not run simultaneously, the effects of coupling are avoided so that the Fuzzy controller and PID controller can be designed seperately.

### 3.3  Fuzzy Controller Design

To improve the control accurate and rapidity, the Fuzzy controller has two inputs and one output. The inputs are error $e$ and error derivative $\dot{e}$, while the output is control variable $u$. Their fuzzy sets are $E$, $EC$, $U$, respectively.

Define their fuzzy subsets and corresponding universes.

$E$, $EC$ and $U$ have the same fuzzy sets as:

$$\{NB, \ NM, \ NS, \ Z, \ PS, \ PM, \ PB\}$$

where NB、NM、NS、Z、PS、PM、PB means Negative Big, Negative Medium, Negative Small, Zero, Positive Small, Positive Medium, Positive Big, respectively.

$E$、$EC$ and $U$ have the same universe:

$$\{-6, \ -5, \ -4, \ -3, \ -2, \ -1, \ 0, \ 1, \ 2, \ 3, \ 4, \ 5, \ 6\}$$

The Gauss membership functions are used for the fuzzification of $E$, $EC$ and $U$ which are shown in Fig.4.

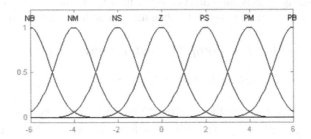

**Fig. 4.** Membership functions of $E, EC, U$

The fuzzy control rules are given based on the data analysis and expert experiences, which are shown in Tab.1.

**Table 1.** Fuzzy control rules

| E | EC | | | | | | |
|----|----|----|----|----|----|----|----|
|    | NB | NM | NS | Z | PS | PM | PB |
| NB | NB | NB | NB | NB | NB | NM | NS |
| NM | NB | NB | NB | NM | NM | NS | Z |
| NS | NM | NM | NM | NS | NS | Z | Z |
| Z  | NS | NS | NS | Z | Z | PS | PS |
| PS | Z | Z | Z | Z | PS | PM | PM |
| PM | Z | Z | PS | PM | PM | PB | PB |
| PB | PS | PS | PM | PM | PB | PB | PB |

According to Tab.1, the parameter tuning rule can be written in fuzzy conditional statement:

If $E$ is $A_i$ and $EC$ is $B_i$, Then $U$ is $C_i$.

where Ai, Bi and Ci are relevant fuzzy sets.

The Mamdani's method associated with the max-min composition is used to undertake fuzzy operate. For example: if $e=a$, $\dot{e}=b$, then the fuzzy inference result of $U$ is:

$$\mu_U(Z_U) = \bigvee_{i=1}^{56} \omega_i \wedge \mu_{C_i}(Z_U) \tag{5}$$

Where $\omega_i = \mu_{A_i}(a) \wedge \mu_{B_i}(b)$

According to Tab.1 and formula (5), the membership of control variable $u$ under the circumstance of different error $e$ and its derivative $\dot{e}$ can be obtained, then the weighted average method for defuzzification is used to calculate the accurate value of $u$:

$$u = \frac{\sum_j \mu_{U_j}(Z_U) \cdot Z_{U_j}}{\sum_j \mu_{U_j}(Z_U)} \tag{6}$$

## 3.4    Variable Universe Contraction-Expansion Factor

"Variable universe" means the universe will adjust while the variable changes. The initial universes of $e$, $\dot{e}$ and $u$ are [-6,6], then their variable universes are:

$$E(e) = [-\alpha_1(e) \times 6, \alpha_1(e) \times 6] , \ EC(\dot{e}) = [-\alpha_2(\dot{e}) \times 6, \alpha_2(\dot{e}) \times 6]$$

$$U(u) = [-\beta(u) \times 6, \beta(u) \times 6]$$

Where $\alpha_1(e)$, $\alpha_2(\dot{e})$, $\beta(u)$ are the universe contraction-expansion factors of inputs $e$, $\dot{e}$ and output $u$, respectively. The following formulas are adopted to calculate the universe contraction-expansion factors:

$$\alpha_1(e) = 1 - \xi \exp(-ke^2), 0 < \xi < 1, k > 0 \qquad (7)$$

$$\alpha_2(\dot{e}) = 1 - \xi \exp(-k\dot{e}^2), 0 < \xi < 1, k > 0 \qquad (8)$$

$$\beta(u) = 1 - \xi \exp(-ku^2), 0 < \xi < 1, k > 0 \qquad (9)$$

Select $\xi = 0.9$, $k = 0.5$. Then the universe contracts when the error decreases. That means the control rules are increased on the local universe. As a result, the control accuracy will be improved.

### 3.5    PID Controller Design

The conventional PID controller is:

$$u(t) = K_p e(t) + K_i \int_0^t e(\tau)d\tau + K_d \frac{de(t)}{dt} \qquad (10)$$

Where $e(k)$、 $u(k)$ is the input and output of PID controller respectively. The control variable $u$ can be got from the sum of error's proportion、 integration、 differential. $K_P$、 $K_i$、 $K_d$ is the coefficient of proportion、 integration、 differential respectively.

### 3.6    Switching Conditions

Fuzzy controller is equal to a PD controller. There is no differential block, so the static error cannot be eliminated [6]. Fuzzy controller transforms the error signal to a integer value in the universe:

$$m = \text{int}(k_e e^* + 0.5) \qquad (11)$$

where $m$ is the integer value in the universe domain transformed from error signal, $e^*$ is the error signal at a certain moment, $k_e$ is error quantization factor. When $m=0$, the system will enter the stage of stable state. Then, $\text{int}(k_e e^* + 0.5) = 0$, that is to say:

$$|e^*| < 0.5/k_e \qquad (12)$$

Assume that error actual variation range is $[-e,e]$, the fuzzy universe domain of error is $\{n, -n-1,\ldots,-1,0,1,\ldots,n-1,n \}$. The quantization factor $k_e = n/e$ is substituted into expression (12), and then:

$$|e^*| < 0.5e/n \qquad (13)$$

The value of $n$ is always 6. The control accuracy improves while n increases, but the control rules become more complex. So, when $n=6$, it can be derived:

$$|e^*| < 8\%e \qquad (14)$$

That is to say, the fuzzy controller can not eliminate the steady-state error when $|e^*| < 8\%e$.

# 4    Simulation Analysis

## 4.1    Simulation Structure

The combination point of helicopter and cable is the ground speed of the helicopter. The cable-orientation can be adjusted though controlling the ground speed of helicopter. Through the control of helicopter's ground speed in hovering mode, cable-orientation can remain at an expected angle value under different wind speed and interference. So the cable dynamic equations and cable orientation controller are conducted as the outer loop of the cable-orientation control system, and the helicopter equation and ground speed maintenance mode work as the inner loop. The cable-orientation error is used to modify helicopter's ground speed so that to realize the control of cable-orientation. The projections of helicopter's longitudinal velocity and lateral velocity in ground coordinate system are static decoupling. The cable's longitudinal and lateral motion equations are mutually independent. So the helicopter-cable system can be regarded as two SISO systems and be designed respectively [5]. According to the design idea of fuzzy PID controller, the feedback cable-orientation signal is compared with the reference signal to get an error. This error signal is used to be the input of fuzzy PID controller to calculate the control variable for helicopter's ground speed control system. The simulation structure is shown in Fig.5.

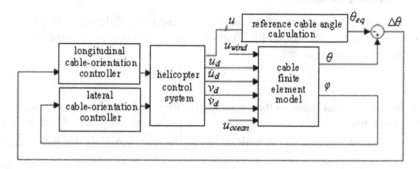

**Fig. 5.** Cable-orientation control system simulation structure

## 4.2    Simulation Analysis

The simulations are carried out in all kinds of circumstances. There are only two representative simulations results are shown in this paper.

First, the simulation of the designed system is carried out at the situation of $u_{wind}$ =-20m/s, which is an atrocious sea condition. The reference cable angle can be calculated by formula (8) ,that is $\theta_{eq}$ =-3.8°, the initial cable angle $\theta_0$ =-7.8°, $\varphi_0$ =0°, then $\Delta\theta_0 = \theta_0 - \theta_{eq}$ =-4°, initial helicopter's ground speed is $u_d = 0$ m/s. Then the cable response is shown in Fig.6.

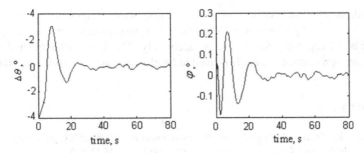

**Fig. 6.** Response curves of cable angle

From Fig.6, it can be seen that when the helicopter is hovering over the sea and turns on the cable-orientation control mode, the cable angles will response correspondingly, and will get to the steady state within 25s. The error between reference cable angle and real cable angle is almost zero. Because of the sea wave noise effects and coupling between cable-orientation control loop and cable-height control loop, there is a little volatility of cable angles, but it is so small that can be accepted.

There is another simulation carried out to verify the robustness of the control system. At the stable state of the cable-orientation control system, gust disturbance is put to the helicopter after 30s simulation. The cable angles response as shown in Fig.7.

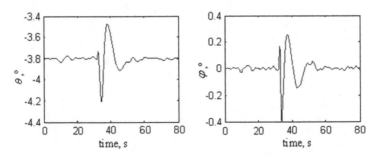

**Fig. 7.** Response curves of cable angle under gust disturbance

The simulation figure shows that when disturbed by the vertical gust disturbance, the system can hold the expected cable angles. The system proved to have a good anti-wind -interference performance.

## 5    Conclusions

The finite-element method is used to establish the nonlinear model of cable. Based on this model, an adaptive Fuzzy-PID cable-orientation controller is designed to get not only good dynamic performance but also high steady state accuracy. The segment control strategy of Fuzzy control and PID control is used and the switch conditions are derived. Simulation results show that the cable-orientation controller designed in this paper has a good performance. When there is a gust disturbance, cable angles can also track and keep the reference value accurately. The Fuzzy-PID method for the cable- orientation control system is proved to be effective and has good robustness.

## References

1. Zhongjian, L., Jinwen, A.: Simulation of Anti-submarine Helicopter's Cable-orientation and Cable-height Control System. J. Flight Dynamics 18(3), 72–75 (2000)
2. Ning, D.: Design and Simulate the Helicopter Anti-submarine Control System. J. Helicopter Technique 134, 23–26 (2003)
3. Gang, C., Fuhai, D., Chang'an, H.: Finite - element Modeling and Simulation for Helicopter Cable & Dipping Sonar System. J. Computer Simulation 20(2), 13–16 (2003)
4. Ider, S.K.: Finite - element based recursive formulation for real time dynamic simulation of flexible multibody systems. J. Computer & Structures 4, 939–945 (1991)
5. Kadmiry, B., Driankov, D.: A fuzzy flight controller combining linguistic and model-based fuzzy control. J. Elsevier Fuzzy Sets and Systems 146, 313–347 (2004)
6. Sasaki M., Ishida H., Katsuno T.: Learning fuzzy logic controller for hovering a helicopter. J. North American Fuzzy Information Processing Society 25–28(1998)
7. Yidong, Y.: Helicopter flight control. National Defense Industry Press, Beijing (2007)

# Research on Alignment of Camera and Receptacle during the Autonomous Aerial Refueling

Qiuling Jia[1], Shuzheng Shi[2], Yaohong Qu[1], and Guangwen Li[1]

[1] College of Automation ,Northwestern Polytechnical University, Xi'an,
Shanxi Province, China
jiaqiuling@nwpu.edu.cn
[2] The second artillery Sergeant School, QingZhou, ShanDong Province, China

**Abstract.** The technique of the boom docking into the receptacle of the receiver is a difficult problem in the procedure of autonomous aerial refueling. The technique by image tracking is a hot solution to the problem and appropriate image information is required to calculate the coordinates of the target rigidly. A camera platform control system based on CamShift algorithm merged with Current Statistical model is proposed in this paper to adjust camera angle for the target tracking. The position and dimensions of the tracked target could be acquired by the CamShift algorithm, accordingly the camera can be controlled to turn to the target. To solve the background interference and occlusion problem, frame interpolation and tracking model are introduced. The simulation results show that the camera by the control way introduced in this paper is able to aim at the target when the speed of the target is in the required limit.

**Keywords:** platform control, image tracking, CamShift algorithm, autonomous aerial refueling.

## 1 Introduction

The technique of air refueling is an important way to increase the aircraft combat radius, the load of the bombs, and to solve contradiction between the takeoff weight and flight performance[1]. Because the manual operation of air refueling is restricted to the pilot's psychology, physiology , technical and tactical status, the study on the autonomous aerial refueling is urgently needed. But the alignment of the boom and the receptacle is a hard problem against which a lot of methods based on GPS navigation, passive vision, active vision and so on are studied and discussed[2]. More and more attentions have been paid to the image processing technique because of its high speed and less disturbance. The camera needs to aim at the receptacle to get enough image information. Considering more disturbances and more frequent speed variety in the air, merging CamShift with Current Statistical(CS) model, a method of controlling the camera to aim at the receptacle is proposed. Aiming at the background interference and occlusion problem, Frame interpolation and tracking model are introduced and the hardware in the loop is built to simulate the camera aiming at the receptacle.

C.-Y. Su, S. Rakheja, H. Liu (Eds.): ICIRA 2012, Part I, LNAI 7506, pp. 323–330, 2012.

This paper is organized as follows. In Sections 2, the trajectory prediction algorithm is designed. In Section 3, video tracking algorithm is designed. In section 4, experimental platform is built and the simulation results are obtained.

## 2    Trajectory Prediction Algorithm Design

Under the air refueling circumstance, the target is always in the maneuvering state because of too many affective factors. As the Current Statistical model(CS model) characterize the acceleration with non-zero mean and revised Rayleigh distribution, the acceleration is more realistic. The CS[3],[4] has a solid theoretical foundation and artful conception which considers that the random maneuvering acceleration complys with first order time-related model which is given as follows:

$$\ddot{x}(t) = \overline{a}(t) + a(t)$$
$$\dot{a}(t) = -\alpha a(t) + w(t)$$

(1)

The state equation of the CS model derived from (1) is given by:

$$\begin{bmatrix} \dot{x}(t) \\ \ddot{x}(t) \\ \dddot{x}(t) \end{bmatrix} = \begin{bmatrix} 0 & 1 & 0 \\ 0 & 0 & 1 \\ 0 & 0 & -\alpha \end{bmatrix} \begin{bmatrix} x(t) \\ \dot{x}(t) \\ \ddot{x}(t) \end{bmatrix} + \begin{bmatrix} 0 \\ 0 \\ \alpha \end{bmatrix} \overline{a} + \begin{bmatrix} 0 \\ 0 \\ 1 \end{bmatrix} w(t)$$

(2)

Combined with CS model, adaptive kalman filter equation is given by:

$$X(k/k) = \hat{X}(k/k-1) + K(k)[Y(k) - H(k)\hat{X}(k/k-1)]$$
$$K(k) = P(k/k-1)H^{T}(k)[H(k)P(k/k-1)H^{T}(k) + R(k)]^{-1}$$
$$P(k/k-1) = \phi(k,k-1)P(k-1/k-1)\phi^{T}(k,k-1) + Q(k-1)$$
$$\hat{X}(k/k-1) = \phi(k,k-1)X(k-1/k-1) + U(k)\overline{a}(k)$$
$$P(k/k) = [I - K(k)H(k)]P(k/k-1)$$

(3)

Where $H(k)$ is the observe matrix, $\alpha$ is the maneuvering frequency, $T$ is the sampling period, $R$ is the system noise, $W(k)$ is discrete-time white noise sequence.

A large number of experimental results and literatures show that the algorithm does well in tracking maneuvering targets .The parameters are adjusted according to different situations. In this paper, the parameters are defined as follows:

$$H(k) = \begin{bmatrix} 1 & 0 & 0 \end{bmatrix} ; \ \alpha = 1/20 ; \ a_{max} = 50 ; a_{-max} = -50; R = 4; \ T = 0.1$$

$$Q(k) = E[W(k)W^{T}(k)] = 2\alpha\delta_{a}^{2} \begin{bmatrix} q_{11} & q_{12} & q_{13} \\ q_{2} & q_{22} & q_{23} \\ q_{13} & q_{12} & q_{33} \end{bmatrix}$$

(4)

$$q_{11} = \frac{1}{2\alpha^5}\left[1 - e^{-2\alpha T} + 2\alpha T + \frac{2\alpha^3 T^3}{3} - 2\alpha^2 T^2 - 4\alpha T e^{-\alpha T}\right]; \quad q_{33} = \frac{1}{2\alpha}\left[1 - e^{-2\alpha T}\right]$$

$$q_{12} = \frac{1}{2\alpha^4}\left[e^{-2\alpha T} + 1 - 2e^{-\alpha T} + 2\alpha T e^{-\alpha T} - 2\alpha T + \alpha^2 T^2\right]; \quad q_{13} = \frac{1}{2\alpha^3}\left[1 - e^{-2\alpha T} - 2\alpha T e^{-\alpha T}\right]$$

$$q_{22} = \frac{1}{2\alpha^3}\left[4e^{-\alpha T} - 3 - e^{-2\alpha T} + 2\alpha T\right]; \quad q_{23} = \frac{1}{2\alpha^2}\left[e^{-2\alpha T} + 1 - 2e^{-\alpha T}\right]$$

$$\delta_a^2 = \frac{2\alpha(4 - \pi)}{\pi}(\mp a_{max} \pm E[a(t)/Y(t)])^2 \tag{5}$$

## 3    Video Tracking Algorithm Design

### 3.1    Camshift Algorithm

Meanshift algorithm displays excellent robustness and high processing speed in solving the bottom problem of the computer vision, so it gets lots of attentions in the field of computer vision. A powerful tool is offered by the development of Meanshift algorithm for solving the stability and real-time problem. CamShift algorithm was obtained by extending MeanShift algorithm to a continuous image sequence. Assuming $(x, y)$ is the pixel location in the search window, and $I(x, y)$ is the pixel value of the $(x, y)$ in the projection image. The search window's zero-order moment $M_{00}$, second-order moment $M_{02}, M_{20}$ are defined by :

$$M_{00} = \sum_x \sum_y I(x, y)$$

$$M_{20} = \sum_x \sum_y x^2 I(x, y)$$

$$M_{02} = \sum_x \sum_y y^2 I(x, y) \tag{6}$$

$$M_{11} = \sum_x \sum_y xyI(x, y)$$

set $a = \dfrac{M_{20}}{M_{00}} - x_c^2$ ; $b = 2(\dfrac{M_{11}}{M_{00}} - x_c y_c)$ ; $c = \dfrac{M_{02}}{M_{00}} - y_c^2$

The direction angle of the major axis in the target is given by:

$$\theta = \frac{1}{2}\tan^{-1}(\frac{2b}{a^2 - c^2}) \tag{7}$$

The length of the major and minor axis in the image is given by:

$$l = \sqrt{\frac{(a + c) + \sqrt{b^2 + (a - c)^2}}{2}} \tag{8}$$

$$w = \sqrt{\frac{(a+c) - \sqrt{b^2 + (a-c)^2}}{2}} .$$

The size of the search window is adjusted according to $M_{00}$. Move the center of the search window to the centroid, if the migration length is greater than the threshold fixed, recalculate the window's centroid. A new round of position calculations and size adjustments is underway.

## 3.2     Occlusion Problem Research

The CamShift algorithm[7],[8]has better robustness to the external disturbance and changes of the shape and size because its search window size is able to adjust itself, it uses the color information as features and it has clustering analysis ability. The targets can be tracked by the CamShift algorithm when there is partial occlusion, but the target will get lost if the targets are completely covered or their most part are covered.

A method to judge the occlusion situations has to be proposed. The method designed in this paper can tell occlusion situations by comparing the position predicted by the CS model with the position obtained by CamShift algorithm.

The location components of the $\hat{X}(k)$ predicted by CS model are $\hat{x}(k)$ and $\hat{y}(k)$, the observed position values of the camshift algorithm are $Y(k) = (x(k) \quad y\ (k))^\tau$ ,the interpolation value between location components of $\hat{X}(k)$ and $Y(k)$ are given as follows:

$$d(k) = \sqrt{(x(k) - \hat{x}(k))^2 + (y(k) - \hat{y}(k))^2} \qquad (8)$$

Generally speaking, in the first few frames after initialization, $d(k)$ is small. the value of $d(k)$ will get bigger with the growing occlusion part. The serious occlusion will be regarded to happen when the $d(k)$ is greater than a certain threshold and the kalman filter has to be stopped. The next frame's possible starting position will be predicted by the CS model according to the frames before and the target location in the current frame will be inquired by the camshift algorithm. If $d(k)$ is smaller than the threshold, the kalman filter will work again, or repeat the process above.

In order to get more accurate detection of the occlusion situations, the adaptive adjustment is introduced to revise the value of the threshold $D(k)$ as follows:

$$D(k) = v(k)T + 1/2 a(k)T^2 \qquad (9)$$

Therefore, the speed and acceleration need to be estimated separately.

Considering the one step prediction $\hat{\ddot{x}}(k/k-1)$ of $\ddot{x}(t)$ as the current acceleration, combined with the CS[5],[6] model described in part 2, the acceleration mean adaptive algorithm can be obtained as follows:

$$\hat{X}(k/k-1) = \phi(k/k-1)\hat{X}(k-1/k-1) + U(k-1)\hat{\ddot{x}} . \qquad (10)$$

$$\phi(k-1/k)=\begin{bmatrix} 1 & T & \dfrac{1}{\alpha^2}(-1+\alpha T+e^{-\alpha T}) \\ 0 & 1 & \dfrac{1}{\alpha}(1-e^{-\alpha T}) \\ 0 & 0 & e^{-\alpha T} \end{bmatrix} \quad ; \quad U(k-1)=\begin{bmatrix} \dfrac{1}{\alpha}(-T+\dfrac{\alpha T^2}{2}+\dfrac{1-e^{-\alpha T}}{\alpha}) \\ T-\dfrac{1-e^{-\alpha T}}{\alpha} \\ 1-e^{-\alpha T} \end{bmatrix}$$

The speed and acceleration can be estimated by:

$$v(k)=\hat{x}(k/k-1).$$

$$a(k)=\hat{\ddot{x}}(k/k-1).$$

(11)

### 3.3 Background Interference Research

The tracking results of the camshift algorithm are inaccurate when the similar color background interference emerges, the position information obtained by the camshift and the realistic position is different.

In order to enhance the capacity of resisting disturbance caused by the similar color background, interpolation operations between the search window of the camshift and the initialized are made from the second circle. The serious disturbance is thought to happen when the size change of the window exceeds the threshold.

$$\rho(k)=\sqrt{(r(k)-\hat{r}(k))^2} \ .$$

(12)

The search window can be reset by frame interpolation method. The radius of the track window is compared with the radius predicted by the CS model, if the background interferences are serious enough, the variation of the radius will exceed the threshold, and then the size and position of the search widow will be decided by the CS model. Keep comparing the radius predicted by CS model and that obtained by camshift, if the variation is smaller than the threshold, adopt the size obtained by camshift algorithm. In this way, the interference caused by similar color can be held back effectively.

## 4    The Building of Experimental Platform

### 4.1    System Build

The experimental platform is set up after the camera, tripod head, Ethernet, pc, power source are chosen. Based on camshift and CS model, the system is set up. The application program is programmed by VC++6.0 with OpenCv function library, and run on the Windows Xp platform. Finally, the system is tested.

## 4.2    Experimental Results

**Fig. 1.** CamShift algorithm tracking performance under the occlusion condition. The simulation results show that when the most part is covered, the accuracy of the state information of the current frame obtained by the CamShift algorithm is very low.

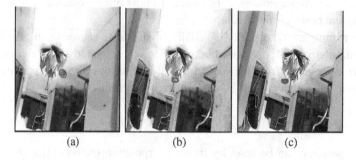

**Fig. 2.** Improved algorithm track performance under occlusion condition. It can be found that the tracking performance of the improved algorithm has been highly promoted in the tracking fig.2. when the serious occlusion happens, just like fig.2. (b), the choose box adopts the predicted value. When the serious occlusion is over, like figure 2(c), the camshift algorithm value is adopted again.

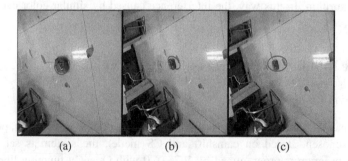

**Fig. 3.** Track performance under background interference. It can be seen from the simulation results that the tracking performance is very bad when the similar color background emerges.

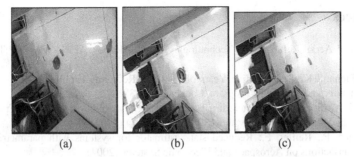

(a)           (b)           (c)

**Fig. 4.** Improved algorithm track performance under background interference condition. Compared with fig.3., it can be seen in fig.4. that the performance of the improved camshift is much better when the similar color interference emerges.

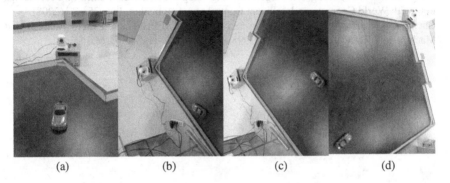

(a)         (b)         (c)         (d)

**Fig. 5.** The consequences of the alignment of the camera and the target. Run the hardware in the loop, and the effects of the alignment of the camera and the target are shown in the figure above.

**Table 1.** Image - camera angle table

| figure | (a) | (b) | (c) | (d) |
|---|---|---|---|---|
| horizontal angle (°) | 0.0 | -15.2 | 3.4 | -8 |
| pitching angle (°) | -1 | -0.5 | -0.6 | -0.3 |

It can be seen from fig.5 and the table 1. that the camera is able to aim at the target once video information of the target can be given enough.

## 5  Conclusion

A method merging camshift with CS model is developed and applied to control the camera to aim at the target. The occlusion problem and background interference problem are solved successfully by the method developed.A hardware in the loop is set up and the simulation results show that the system works very well.

# References

1. Automated Aerial Refuel(AAR) Technologies and Challenges. AFRL- VA -WP-TP -2004-314
2. Smith Richard, K.: Seventy- five Years of In- flight Refueling Highlights(1923-1998). Air Force History and Museu ms Program, Lockland (1998)
3. Rong Li, X.: Survey of Maneuvering Target. Part 1: Dynamic Models, IEEE Transactions on Aerospace and Electronic Systems 39(4), 1337–1364 (2003)
4. Mookerjee, P., Reifler, F.: Reduced state estimator for systems with parametric inputs. IEEE Transactions on Aerospace and Electronic Systems (2004)
5. Bar-Shalom, Y., Fortmann, T.E.: Tracking and Data Association. Academic press (1988)
6. Lee, D.-J.: Nonlinear Bayesian filtering with applications to estimation and navigation. Chonbuk National University (2005)
7. Yang, B., Zhou, H., Wang, X.: Target Tracking using Predicted Cam Shift. In: Proceedings of the 7th World Congress on Intelligent Control and Automation, June 25 - 27 (2008)
8. Cheng, Y.: Mean Shift, mode seeking and clustering. IEEE Trans. Pattern Analysis and Machine Intelligence 17(8), 790–799 (1995)

# Consensus Algorithms in a Multi-agent Framework to Solve PTZ Camera Reconfiguration in UAVs

Jose Luis Alarcon Herrera* and Xiang Chen

University of Windsor, Windsor, Ontario, Canada
{alarconj,xchen}@uwindsor.ca

**Abstract.** A method for PTZ camera reconfiguration is presented. The objective of this work is to improve target tracking and surveillance applications in unmanned vehicles. Pan, tilt, and zoom configurations are computed transforming the visual constraints, given by a model of visual coverage, into geometric constraints. In the case of multiple targets the camera configurations are computed by a consensus algorithm. The approach is defined in a multi-agent framework allowing for scalability of the system, and cooperation between the cameras. Experimental results show the performance of the approach.

**Keywords:** Camera reconfiguration, consensus algorithms, multi-agents, wireless sensor networks.

## 1    Introduction

The interest for surveillance systems has grown over the last decade, reflected in part by the intensive research done in this area. Hu et al. [8] and Weinland et al. [25] present surveys of visual surveillance and action recognition, respectively. In these surveys, the authors agree on the importance of the task of tracking a target by estimating its $3D$ pose. In recent years vision systems have found new applications in the filed of unmanned autonomous vehicles [6]. Surveillance systems can benefit from the flexibility in mobility provided by autonomous vehicles. On the other hand, autonomous vehicles can also benefit from vision applications. Vision systems in unmanned autonomous vehicles allow the identification and pose estimation of targets in real time. Examples of this kind of work are presented in the work of Vidal et al. [24], the authors present a pursuit-evasion game with unmanned vehicles where $3D$ pose estimations of targets and occlusions are used to build the navigation map. Kontitsis et al. [10] present a vision system for airborne surveillance of forest fires. Merino et al. [18] propose a vision system to estimate the relative motion of unmanned aerial vehicles (UAV) using

---

* This research was supported in part by the National Council of Science and Technology of Mexico (CONACyT), and by the University of Windsor through the international doctoral tuition scholarship. Corresponding author: Prof. Xiang Chen, xchen@uwindsor.ca

C.-Y. Su, S. Rakheja, H. Liu (Eds.): ICIRA 2012, Part I, LNAI 7506, pp. 331–340, 2012.
© Springer-Verlag Berlin Heidelberg 2012

feature matching between the images of different vehicles. Similarly, Bethke et al. [3] design a system for cooperative tracking using multiple UAVs, the images are transmitted to a central computer and the pose estimations are refined using a kalman filter.

Pan-tilt-zoom (PTZ) cameras provide flexibility in the design of vision systems. In that, unlike static cameras, PTZ cameras can change their focusing distance and field of view, thus making the internal and external camera parameters vary over time. Moreover, surveillance systems are expected to perform in dynamic scenarios where the targets are not static and the objectives are constantly varying. For these reasons, the dynamic nature of PTZ cameras makes them a suitable tool in target tracking and activity recognition applications. In this case the question of how to control the camera is not new, and many methodologies have been proposed [21,22]. To this day, the more interesting question is how to optimize the control or self-reconfiguration process of the cameras. Vision systems with reconfigurable cameras have been used in unmanned vehicles, as in Ludington et al. [11]. Where the authors present target tracking module for UAV, by tracking the target on the image plane the camera is configured to keep the target centered in the image. Hrabar et al. [7] use a PTZ camera to estimate the pose and track a UAV as it moves around the camera, the authors show how this can aid the built in positioning system of the UAV. Huang at al. [9] develop a vision system to robustly track a region of interest in the image by predicting the location of the region of interest in the new images using a kalman filter and considering the motion of the region of interest in the image.

The purpose of the current brief is to present a self-configuring PTZ camera system. In order to compute the camera configurations for improved visual coverage for multiple targets, we use a combination of consensus algorithms in Euclidian space and the group of rotations $SO(3)$. Additionally, we develop our work in the multi-agent framework to allow cooperation between the camera agents. The objective of the system is to improve the performance of a target tracking application. The remainder of this paper is organized as follows: In Section 2 we define the problem and some relevant concepts. Section 3 presents a high level overview of the proposed solution. Section 4 presents the consensus-based approach in detail. In Section 5 we show the validity of our approach through experiments. Finally, conclusions and some comments on future work are given in Section 6.

## 2    Problem Statement

The coverage model of a vision system models multiple cameras, the environment, and the task. The camera system is approximated using the pin hole model [14], which accounts for the sensor's properties, and the coverage model additionally considers the lens' properties. The geometric environment model is a set of three-dimensional surfaces and it accounts for static occlusion in the scene. The task is modeled using a set of directional points, which are three-dimensional points with a direction component, and a set of task parameters.

The directional points model the target to an arbitrary degree of precision, and the task parameters model the visual requirements of the task; for example minimum resolution, maximum allowed blur, and maximum view angle. The coverage function $C(\mathbf{p})$ is bounded to the range $[0, 1]$ and it represents the grade of coverage at a point $\mathbf{p}$. In order to represent the grade of relevance of each point to the task, the relevance function $R(\mathbf{p})$ is used and it is also bound to the range $[0, 1]$. Finally the coverage performance of the sensor system with respect to the task is given by

$$F(C, R) = \frac{\sum_{\mathbf{p} \in \langle R \rangle} C(\mathbf{p}) R(\mathbf{p})}{\sum_{\mathbf{p} \in \langle R \rangle} R(\mathbf{p})} \tag{1}$$

For the full definition about the coverage model and its validation we refer the reader to the work of Mavrinac et al. [15, 16, 17] and Alarcon et al. [2].

We assume that the $3D$ pose of the target is available and we use it to re-configure the PTZ parameters to keep the target in the field of view and with the required resolution and focus. This is not an unrealistic assumption because there has been advances in the field of human pose estimation from single views. Examples include the work of Agarwal and Triggs [1], and Lv and Nevatia [12].

We are given a network of PTZ smart cameras, a model of the scene with an initial configuration of internal and external camera parameters, an application capable of providing a pose estimation for the targets, and the task requirements $\{\mathcal{T}\}$. Each camera agent is expected to make coordinated decisions to improve its own local objectives. The problem is to find the vector x that satisfies the task requirements so that the coverage performance $F_n$ of every new configuration improves with respect to the initial performance $F_i$.

$$\text{Find } x : F_n \geq F_i \; \forall \mathbf{p} \in S \text{ subject to } \{\mathcal{T}\} \tag{2}$$

where $\mathbf{p}$ is an interest point in the scene $S$, and $\{\mathcal{T}\}$ is the set of task requirements. The solution takes the form of a vector $x = [\theta, \phi, \zeta]$. The pan and tilt angles are represented by $\theta$ and $\phi$, respectively. $\zeta$ represents the zoom configuration of the lens.

## 3   Solution Strategy

The visual requirements to improve are: visibility, resolution, and focus. The pan and tilt parameters enable the improvement of visibility since they control the orientation of the camera. The zoom and focus parameters of the lens can improve the resolution and focus.

### 3.1   Visibility

The principal axis of the camera, or the $z$ axis, determines the orientation of the camera. In order to improve visibility, the $z$ axis has to pass through the target. In the case where the optical center of the camera is the same as the center of rotation of the servomotors, the pan and tilt configurations can be computed from the angles between the optical axis and the normal of the surface tangent to the target. However, in this work we address the more complicated case where the optical center is not the same as the center of rotation. As shown in Figure 1, the optical center of the camera is constrained to a sphere at the center of rotation $o_r$ with radius equal to the magnitude of vector $\overrightarrow{o_r o_c}$. Then, the objective is to find a new point in the sphere that yields an optical axis that passes through the point **p**. Since the target **p** and the center of rotation $o_r$ are known, and the angle $\alpha$ is constant, we can use this angle as a constraint to find the new viewpoint. The new point in the sphere yields a new vector $\overrightarrow{o_r o_c}'$ which represents the new camera orientation.

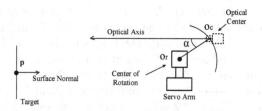

**Fig. 1.** Side view of the PTZ camera

## 3.2 Resolution and Focus

The resolution and focus components of the coverage model are both functions of the distance along the optical axis of the camera. The limits at which the resolution occurs, specified by the task parameters, is given by (3) substituting the ideal resolution $R_i$ and the acceptable resolution $R_a$ for $R$. The pair of distances $(z_\triangleleft, z_\triangleright)$, and $(z_n, z_f)$ are the near and far limits of the depth of field as given by (4), substituting the ideal $c_i$ and acceptable $c_a$ blur circle diameters, respectively for $c$.

$$z_R(R) = R \min \left( \frac{w}{\tan \alpha_l + \tan \alpha_r}, \frac{h}{\tan \alpha_t + \tan \alpha_b} \right) \tag{3}$$

where $R$ is the required resolution in millimeters per pixel, $w$ and $h$ are the image dimensions in pixels, $\alpha_l$ and $\alpha_r$ are left and right angles, and $\alpha_t$ and $\alpha_b$ are top and bottom angles. From the optical axis $\alpha_l$, $\alpha_r$, $\alpha_t$, and $\alpha_b$ spawn the filed of view.

$$z(c) = \frac{A f z_S}{A f \pm c(z_S - f)} \tag{4}$$

where $A$ is the aperture diameter of the lens in millimeters, $f$ is the focal length in millimeters, $c$ is the diameter of the blur circle in pixels, and $z_S$ is the distance, in millimeters, at which a point in the scene maps to a point in the image plane.

The objective of the resolution and focus optimization is to find the zoom-lens configuration that zooms and focuses the lens to image a point $\mathbf{p}$ such that $z_\triangleleft < \mathbf{p}.z < z_\triangleright$ and $\mathbf{p}.z \leq z_R(R_i)$. Using (3) and (4) we find the appropriate distances at which to zoom and focus, and the zoom and focus configurations are found using lens calibration for motorized lenses. To this end we make use of a calibrated lookup table that contains the internal parameters of the lens for all the zoom and focus configurations. This is a significant advantage because it gives us real time access to the internal camera parameters of the lens, which would be unavailable otherwise or would require unfeasible calibration of the lenses after every change in the zoom and focus configurations. The lens calibration was implemented following the work of Chen et al. [5].

## 4   Consensus Algorithm

We propose a new application of consensus algorithms, to solve the problem of finding the viewpoint of a camera that improves the coverage performance of a set of targets. Let $C_i \in \mathcal{C}$ be a camera agent in the network, and $T^l \in T'$ be the target updated from the tracking application. For each target $T^l$ there is a PTZ configuration that improves the coverage performance $(F)$ with respect to $T^l$. This configuration is considered as a viewpoint yielding a new camera pose. Let $\{P|R\}$ be the current viewpoint of the camera agent $C_i$, then $\{P^l|R^l\}$ is the viewpoint that improves the coverage performance of camera agent $C_i$ for target $T^l$. With these viewpoints as the initial configurations, the final viewpoint is found when the viewpoint $\{P|R\}$ is updated to equal the average of all viewpoints $\{P^l|R^l\}$. We use a consensus algorithm in $\mathbb{R}^3$ to update the position $P$ as the average of $P^l$ for all $T^l$, and a consensus algorithm in $SO(3)$, as presented by Tron et al. [23], to update the rotation $R$ as the average along the geodesic between every $R^l$. Consensus on individual spaces $\mathbb{R}^3$ and $SO(3)$ has been reported in the work of Ma et al. [13] and Moakher. [19]. Similarly, Soto et al. [22], and Song et al. [4] use a distributed Kalman consensus algorithm to compute the mean of positions as a method for sensor fusion. To the best of our knowledge there have not been any attempts to use a consensus algorithm to compute camera viewpoints for improved visual coverage. The consensus algorithm in Euclidean space and the group of rotations are given by (5) and (6).

$$P_j^{(k+1)} = P_j^{(k)} + \frac{1}{|T|} \sum_{j=1}^{|T|} a_{lj}(P_l^{(k)} - P_j^{(k)}) \tag{5}$$

where $P_j^{(k)}$ is the consensus estimate, at step $k$, of the average of the positions $P_l^{(k)}$ for all $T^l$, and $a_{lj}$ denotes the entry of the adjacency matrix.

$$R_j^{(k+1)} = R_j^{(k)} \exp\left(\frac{1}{|T|} \sum_{j=1}^{|T|} a_{lj} \log(R_j^{(k)^\top} R_l^{(k)})\right) \tag{6}$$

where log() denotes the exponential map from $SO(3)$ to $so(3)$ and exp() denotes the exponential map from $so(3)$ to $SO(3)$ as given by the Rodrigues' rotation formula [14]. For simplicity of notation $R_l^{(k)}$ is the rotation of the viewpoint corresponding to $T^l$. $k$ denotes the iteration step of the consensus algorithm, $R_j^{(k)}$ is the consensus estimate of the average of all the targets $T^l$. $a_{lj}$ denotes the entry of the adjacency matrix.

In our multi-agent framework, the camera agents know their locations with respect to each other (though camera calibration), in the case of UAV systems this is commonly addressed by the built-in global positioning system. Furthermore, the camera agents can communicate with each other and broadcast the pose of all targets, being tracked by the network, with respect to a common reference frame. This communication is advantageous because a camera agent can use the consensus algorithm to compute the PTZ parameters for multiple targets, even if some of the targets are not in its field of view. With the pose information provided by other camera agents the coverage model is used to evaluate the performance of a new PTZ configuration, Thus enabling the camera agent to make coordinated decisions about which targets to track.

## 5   Experimental Results

The validation of the proposed solution is divided in two parts. First, we evaluate the reconfiguration capability of the camera, for this we analyze the capability of the system to extend its visual coverage by zooming onto a target as it is being tracked, and we test the ability of the system to follow the target as it moves around the scene, and thus, test its ability to reconfigure its own pan and tilt parameters. Second, we show through software simulations the ability of the camera to reconfigure its parameters to track multiple targets at the same time.

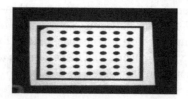

**Fig. 2.** Target used for $3D$ pose estimation

The application that performs the pose estimation in this experiment was implemented using the machine vision libraries HALCON [20]. The target itself is a plate with some marks of well known geometry, shown in Figure 2, and it is placed at a known distance from the camera. And then, the experiment is carried out with the zoom and focus reconfiguration functions disabled. Afterwards, the reconfiguration functionality is enabled and the experiment is repeated. For both cases the target is moved along the $z$ axis and away from the camera in increments of 0.01 m. Table 1 shows the comparison between the two cases. The section of the table left from the ground truth shows the results with the reconfiguration functions disabled, and the right side shows results with the reconfiguration functions enabled. The results indicate that the system was able to provide a good coverage performance while keeping track of the target.

**Table 1.** Tracking Error and Coverage Performance

| Coverage Performance | Distance $z$ (m) | Ground Truth (m) | Distance $z$ (m) | Coverage Performance |
|---|---|---|---|---|
| 1.0 | 1.181 | 1.18 | 1.183 | 1.0 |
| 1.0 | 1.181 | 1.19 | 1.197 | 1.0 |
| 1.0 | 1.191 | 1.20 | 1.207 | 1.0 |
| 1.0 | 1.203 | 1.21 | 1.212 | 1.0 |
| 1.0 | 1.214 | 1.22 | 1.214 | 1.0 |
| 1.0 | 1.224 | 1.23 | 1.235 | 1.0 |
| 1.0 | 1.236 | 1.24 | 1.245 | 1.0 |
| 0.9968 | 1.248 | 1.25 | 1.256 | 1.0 |
| 0.8592 | 1.256 | 1.26 | 1.266 | 1.0 |
| 0.5996 | 1.267 | 1.27 | 1.277 | 1.0 |
| 0.2936 | 1.280 | 1.28 | 1.289 | 1.0 |
| 0.0 | NA | 1.29 | 1.305 | 1.0 |
| 0.0 | NA | 1.30 | 1.311 | 1.0 |
| 0.0 | NA | 1.31 | 1.322 | 1.0 |
| 0.0 | NA | 1.32 | 1.330 | 1.0 |
| 0.0 | NA | 1.33 | 1.354 | 1.0 |

The pan and tilt capabilities of the system are tested by moving the target around the scene, the camera then reconfigures its parameters to follow the target and keep it at the center of the image. Figure 3 shows that once the camera is aware of the target, the camera can follow it and reconfigure its parameters to maintain a good coverage performance, which is close to 1.

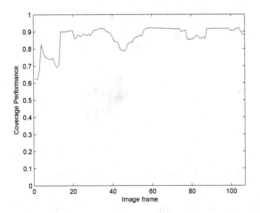

**Fig. 3.** Coverage performance of the system

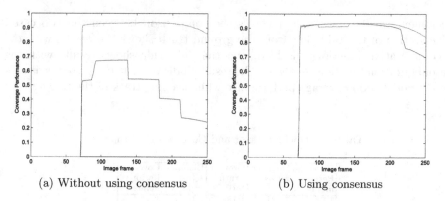

(a) Without using consensus     (b) Using consensus

**Fig. 4.** Coverage performance of the simulated system

Next, we show the more interesting case where the camera has two targets within its range. We compare the performance of the system, when the camera is assigned to track one of the targets, with the performance of the system when the camera is assigned to track both targets and use the consensus algorithm to compute the appropriate PTZ parameters. The results are shown in Figure 4. Initially, the moving targets are outside the field of view of the camera, eventually the camera is informed of the pose of the targets and it carries out the reconfiguration process for the two cases described above. As seen in Figure 4a the performance of the system for one of the targets is considerably low because the camera is configured to track the other target. On the other hand, Figure 4b shows that the system is able to keep track of both targets and provide a good coverage performance when the consensus algorithm is applied. Figure 5 shows the simulation of the camera as it keeps both targets at the center of the frustum of the field of view. The simulation is performed using our Adolphus[1] simulation software.

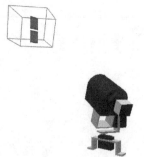

**Fig. 5.** Simulation of the PTZ camera

---

[1] Adolphus is free software licensed under the GNU General Public License. Python source code and documentation are available at http://github.com/ezod/adolphus

It is important to note that although the tracking application used in these experiments tracks a simple target, our solution works with any application that can output a pose estimate for the target. The target can be a vehicle on the scene or a human. Thus, we do not restrict the usefulness of the proposed approach in this paper.

## 6   Conclusions

In this work we have addressed the problem of computing the pan, tilt, and zoom configurations for PTZ cameras using a consensus algorithm. The algorithm was used to reach an agreement in the geometric constraints required by the visibility, resolution, and focus criteria. The methodology was framed so that each camera is considered as an independent agent. The results show the efficacy of the method to enable single cameras with reconfigurability to track multiple targets. In future work we plan to apply this method to the multi-agent case with protocols for agent interactions so that the camera agents can pursue a global utility by first optimizing the local utilities as shown in this work.

## References

1. Agarwal, A., Triggs, B.: Recovering 3D Human Pose from Monocular Images. IEEE Transactions on Pattern Analysis and Machine Intelligence 28(1), 44–58 (2006)
2. Alarcon-Herrera, J.L., Mavrinac, A., Chen, X.: Sensor Planning for Range Cameras via a Coverage Strength Model. In: IEEE/ASME International Conference on Advanced Intelligent Mechatronics, pp. 838–843 (2011)
3. Bethke, B., Valenti, M., How, J.: Cooperative Vision Based Estimation and Tracking Using Multiple UAVs. In: Proc. of the 7th Int. Conf. on Cooperative Control and Optimization, pp. 179–189 (2007)
4. Bi, S., Kamal, A.T., Soto, C., Chong, D., Farrell, J.A., Roy-Chowdhury, A.K.: Tracking and Activity Recognition Through Consensus in Distributed Camera Networks. IEEE Transactions on Image Processing 19(10), 2564–2579 (2010)
5. Chen, Y., Shih, S., Hung, Y., Fuh, C.: Simple and Efficient Method of Calibrating a Motorized Zoom Lens. Image and Vision Computing 19(14), 1099–1110 (2001)
6. He, Z., Iyer, R., Chandler, P.: Vision-Based UAV Flight Control and Obstacle Avoidance. In: American Control Conference, pp. 1–5 (2006)
7. Hrabar, S., Corke, P., Hilsenstein, V.: PTZ Camera Pose Estimation by Tracking a 3D Target. In: Proc. IEEE Intl. Conf. on Robotics and Automation, pp. 240–247 (2011)
8. Hu, W., Tan, T., Wang, L., Maybank, S.: A Survey on Visual Surveillance of Object Motion and Behaviors. IEEE Transactions on Systems, Man, and Cybernetics, Part C: Applications and Reviews 34(3), 334–352 (2004)
9. Huang, C., Chou, C., Hsu, Y., Shih, M.: Real-Time Multi-Camera Air Surveillance System Using a Simultaneous Estimation, Filtering and Rejection Tracking Algorithm. In: Visual Communications and Image Processing, pp. 1–4 (2011)
10. Kontitsis, M., Valavanis, K., Tsourveloudis, N.: A UAV Vision System for Airborne Surveillance. In: Proc. IEEE Intl. Conf. on Robotics and Automation, pp. 77–83 (2004)

11. Ludington, B., Johnson, E., Vachtsevanos, G.: Augmenting UAV autonomy. IEEE Robotics Automation Magazine 13(3), 63–71 (2006)
12. Lv, F., Nevatia, R.: Single View Human Action Recognition using Key Pose Matching and Viterbi Path Searching. In: IEEE Conference on Computer Vision and Pattern Recognition, pp. 1–8 (2007)
13. Ma, Y., Kosecká, J., Shankar, S.: Optimization Criteria and Geometric Algorithms for Motion and Structure Estimation. International Journal of Computer Vision 44(3), 219–249 (2001)
14. Ma, Y., Soatto, S., Kosecka, J., Sastry, S.: An Invitation to 3-D Vision: From Images to Geometric Models. Springer (2004)
15. Mavrinac, A., Alarcon-Herrera, J.L., Chen, X.: A Fuzzy Model for Coverage Evaluation of Cameras and Multi-Camera Networks. In: Proc. 4th ACM/IEEE Intl. Conf. on Distributed Smart Cameras, pp. 95–102 (2010)
16. Mavrinac, A., Alarcon-Herrera, J.L., Chen, X.: Evaluating the Fuzzy Coverage Model for 3D Multi-Camera Network Applications. In: Proc. 3rd Int. Conf. Intelligent Robotics and Applications, pp. 692–701 (2010)
17. Mavrinac, A., Chen, X.: Optimizing Load Distribution in Camera Networks with a Hypergraph Model of Camera Topology. In: Proc. 5th ACM/IEEE Int. Conf. Distributed Smart Cameras (2011)
18. Merino, L., Wiklund, J., Caballero, F., Moe, A., De Dios, J., Forssen, P.E., Nordberg, K., Ollero, A.: Vision-Based Multi-UAV Position Estimation. IEEE Robotics Automation Magazine 13(3), 53–62 (2006)
19. Moakher, M.: Means and Averaging in the Group of Rotations. SIAM Journal on Matrix Analysis and Applications 24(1), 1–16 (2002)
20. MVTec Software GmbH: HALCON, http://www.mvtec.com/halcon
21. Piciarelli, C., Micheloni, C., Foresti, G.: Automatic Reconfiguration of Video Sensor Networks for Optimal 3D Coverage. In: Proc. 5th ACM/IEEE Intl. Conf. on Distributed Smart Cameras, pp. 1–6 (2011)
22. Soto, C., Bi, S., Roy-Chowdhury, A.: Distributed Multi-Target Tracking in a Self-Configuring Camera Network. In: IEEE Conference on Computer Vision and Pattern Recognition, pp. 1486–1493 (June 2009)
23. Tron, R., Vidal, R., Terzis, A.: Distributed Pose Averaging in Camera Networks via Consensus on SE(3). In: Second ACM/IEEE International Conference on Distributed Smart Cameras, vol. (3) (2008)
24. Vidal, R., Rashid, S., Sharp, C., Shakernia, O., Jin, K., Sastry, S.: Pursuit-Evasion Games with Unmanned Ground and Aerial Vehicles. In: Proc. IEEE Intl. Conf. on Robotics and Automation, pp. 2948–2955 (2001)
25. Weinland, D., Ronfard, R., Boyer, E.: A Survey of Vision-Based Methods for Action Representation, Segmentation and Recognition. Computer Vision and Image Understanding 115(2), 224–241 (2011)

# Detection and Tracking of Underwater Object Based on Forward-Scan Sonar

Shaorong Xie[1], Jinbo Chen[1], Jun Luo[1], Pu Xie[2], and Wenbin Tang[1]

[1] School of Mechatronic Engineering and Automation, Shanghai University,
No.149 YanChang Rd. Shanghai, China
{srxie,jbchen,luojun}@shu.edu.cn, wenbin.derek.tang@gmail.com
[2] Department of Mechanical &Aerospace Engineering, New Mexico State University,
Las Cruces, NM 88003, USA
jackyxie@nmsu.edu

**Abstract.** Underwater object detection is critical in a lot of applications in maintenance, repair of undersea structures, marine sciences, and homeland security. However, because optics camera is subject to the influence of light and turbidity, its visibility is very poor in underwater environment. Therefore, forward-scan sonar is widely applied to the underwater object detection in recent years. But there are still some problems such as: Forward-scan sonar imaging, which is different from optics imaging, processes echo information from acoustic signal in the water. Generally, sonar images are with high noise and low contrast. It is difficult for the operator to identify underwater objects from the images. In addition, the surveillance of underwater objects is tedious and time consuming, and it is easy to make mistakes due to the fatigue and distraction of the operator. To solve the above problems, an image processing strategy to detect and track the underwater object automatically is presented. Firstly, the sonar images are enhanced by the Gabor filter. And then underwater objects are extracted. Finally the tracking method based on Kalman filter is adopted. The experimental results validate that the presented methods are valid.

**Keywords:** Forward-scan sonar, Underwater object detection and tracking, Sonar image enhancement.

## 1    Introduction

Underwater object detection is critical in a lot of applications in maintenance, repair of undersea structures, marine sciences, and homeland security. For example, the surveillance and inspection of underwater pipelines (such as cables for energy and telecommunication) with optics camera are presented in [1-5].

However, because optics camera is subject to the influence of light and turbidity, its visibility is very poor in underwater environment. Therefore, forward-scan sonar is widely applied to the underwater object detection in recent years [6-7].

But there are still some problems such as: Forward-scan sonar imaging, which is different from optics imaging, processes echo information from acoustic signal in the water. Generally, sonar images are with high noise and low contrast. It is difficult for the operator to identify underwater objects from the images. In addition, the

C.-Y. Su, S. Rakheja, H. Liu (Eds.): ICIRA 2012, Part I, LNAI 7506, pp. 341–347, 2012.

surveillance of underwater objects is tedious and time consuming, and it is easy to make mistakes due to the fatigue and distraction of the operator.

To solve the above problems, an image processing strategy to detect and track the underwater object automatically is presented. Our previous work is shown in [8] (in Chinese). Firstly, the sonar images are enhanced by the Gabor filter. It is similar to human vision system that two-dimensional Gabor wavelet filter represents image features in frequency and direction. So Gabor filter has been applied in different vision [9-10], such as edge detection, image texture analysis and facial recognition etc. And then underwater objects are extracted. Finally the tracking method based on Kalman filter is adopted. The experimental results validate that the presented methods are valid.

## 2     Sonar Image Enhancement

### 2.1     Principle of Sonar Imaging

In this paper, Dual-Frequancy IDentification SONar (DIDSON) [11] is applied to detect underwater objects. Figure 1 shows the geometry schematic of sonar imaging. The imaging point of P(x, y, z) in the sonar coordinates system is (u, v). According to the principle of sonar imaging, its imaging coordinate transformation is:

$$u = r \times \sin\theta = x\sqrt{1 + \tan^2 \beta}$$
$$v = r \times \cos\theta = y\sqrt{1 + \tan^2 \beta}$$

(1)

Where, $r = \sqrt{x^2 + y^2 + z^2}$, $\theta = \sin^{-1}(x/r_{xy})$, $r_{xy} = \sqrt{x^2 + y^2}$; $\beta$ is the inclined angle between vector OP and imaging plane.

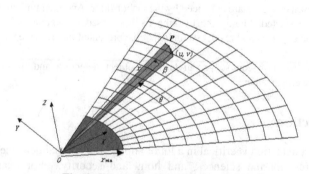

**Fig. 1.** Geometry schematic of sonar imaging

### 2.2     Sonar Image Enhancement by Gabor Filter

Two-dimensional Gabor filter can be represented as combined sine signal modulated by Gaussian function. A two-dimensional Gabor filter can be written as:

$$g(x, y) = \frac{1}{2\pi\sigma_x\sigma_y} \exp\left[-\frac{1}{2}(\frac{x'^2}{\sigma_x^2} + \frac{y'^2}{\sigma_y^2})\right] \exp[2\pi w_0 x']$$

(2)

$$\begin{cases} x' = x\cos\theta + y\sin\theta \\ y' = -x\sin\theta + y\cos\theta \end{cases} \tag{3}$$

Where, $\sigma_x$ and $\sigma_y$ represent two-dimensional Gauss transformation variance in the directions of two coordinates respectively; x and y denote positions of spatial pixels; $w_0$ is centre frequency; $\theta$ represents the direction of Gabor wavelet.

With regard the variability of Gabor wavelet in frequency and direction, a lot of valuable information can be picked up through filtering image in different frequency and direction.

Sonar images are filtered by convolution method in Gabor wavelet. If sonar image can be represented by $I(x, y)$, Gabor wavelet transform of image in $(x_0, y_0)$ can be represented by convolution of formula 3. Then the formula is given by:

$$\begin{aligned} F(\omega, \sigma, \theta) &= I(x, y) \bullet G(x, y)\,|_{x=x_0, y=y_0} \\ &= \iint I(x, y)G(x - x_0\Delta x, x - y_0\Delta y)dxdy \end{aligned} \tag{4}$$

Where, $\Delta x$ and $\Delta y$ are sampling intervals.

Because the Gabor wavelet is non-orthogonal, redundant information will be produced after image filtering. Therefore, proper frequency and direction should be selected when design Gabor filter. In order to enhance object image by Gabor filtering transform, according to experimental results, total 20 Gabor filters are selected in 10 different directions with 2 different frequencies in each direction, then $\sigma$ of Gabor filter is:

$$\sigma = \frac{1.177(2^\phi + 1)}{(2^\phi - 1)\omega} \tag{5}$$

Where, $\phi$ represents bandwidth of Gabor filter in different frequency.

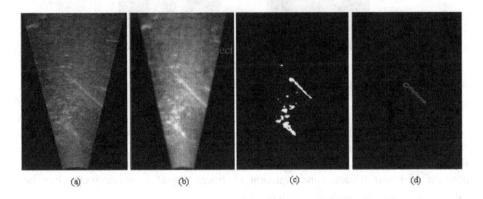

(a)   (b)   (c)   (d)

**Fig. 2.** Original sonar image and post-processing images

The enhanced image can be obtained by calculating weighted L2 norm of convolutions of original images and multi Gabor filters.

Original image is shown in Figure 2(a), and it is high noise and low contrast. Enhanced image is shown in Figure 2(b). The detected object is highlighting.

## 3    Object Extraction

Many underwater objects are linear, e.g. pipelines, cables, and undersea structures. Therefore, linear underwater objects are extracted and tracked in this paper.

After Gabor filtering, the binary image as Figure 2(c) can be achieved. And then contour feature of linear object can be extracted by Canny edge extraction, as shown in Figure 2(d).

The line can be extracted by Hough transform with contour feature of linear object. Hough transform as a simple and efficient line extraction algorithm is very effective in border discontinuous straight line extraction, because it is insensitive to the noise, and an interrupt is allowed. Based on regularization parameters Hough transform, angle between normal vector of a straight line and x-axis and distance between the line and origin is definite [12]. So any point on given line can be formulated:

$$\rho = x_i \cos\theta + y_i \sin\theta \tag{6}$$

Point $(x_i, y_i)$ is the point that lies on the line given in formula (6). It only needs to solve $(\rho, \theta)$ of line equation.

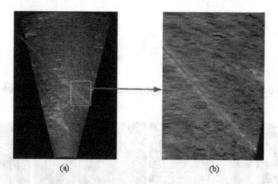

(a)                                      (b)

**Fig. 3.** Extraction result of linear underwater object

Line equation in image can be obtained by Hough transform, and extraction result is shown in Figure 3(a). But many similar lines will appear around pipeline during the extraction processing. After the area of white frame in figure 3(a) being blown up, as shown in Figure 3(b), there are a number of lines and even bifurcation passing the position of linear object. Line equation of linear object in sonar image can be calculated by statistic method, which is $(\rho, \theta)$.

## 4    Object Tracking

Although the position and direction of linear object can be obtained by image processing, searching linear object is time-consuming in the entire image. In order to reduce the required computation, it needs to track linear object. Tracking linear object is based on the fact that parameters of linear object change continuously between the neighboring images. The search region can be confirmed by predicting position of linear object and giving allowable range, which will reduce the range of image processing. Linear Kalman filter is adopted to predict parameters of linear object, because the motion of forward-scan sonar is unknown for water disturbances and the motion of its carrier. Then model of Kalman filter is given by:

$$X = (\rho, \theta)$$
$$X(t+1) = X(t) + v \qquad (7)$$
$$Z(t+1) = X(t+1) + w$$

Where, $v$ is systematical error and $w$ is observation error.

Predictive value can be obtained by calculating. In consideration of tolerance $\Delta X = (\Delta \rho, \Delta \theta)$, the new range of searching linear object is :

$$R(t+1) = X(t+1) + \Delta X \qquad (8)$$

It only needs tracking linear object in $R(t+1)$ in next image, which will reduce the range of image processing and required computation, and improve detecting velocity.

## 5    Experimental Results

In order to validate the applicability of the method, an interesting experiment on ROV was performed, and a forward-scan sonar DIDSON was installed in central position of ROV.

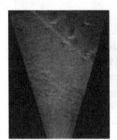   

**Fig. 4.** Experimental results of underwater object extracting in sonar images in different states of sonar and ROV

The dynamic change of ROV by the water disturbances will cause the position and posture of image sonar is unceasingly changed. So sonar images will be in different states.

During the experiments, results show that the method in this paper can effectively achieve underwater object detecting by tracking linear object in different directions and distances. The experimental results are shown in Figure 4. Frame rate of forward-scan sonar image is about 10 frames per second, and the resolution is $512 \times 256$. The algorithms can meet real-time requirements.

# 6     Conclusion

In view of existing problems such as: Forward-scan sonar images are with high noise and low contrast, and it is difficult for the operator to identify underwater objects from the images; In addition, the surveillance of underwater objects is tedious and time consuming, and it is easy to make mistakes due to the fatigue and distraction of the operator, the image processing strategy to detect and track the underwater object automatically is presented. Firstly, the sonar images are enhanced by the Gabor filter. And then underwater objects are extracted. Finally the tracking method based on Kalman filter is adopted. The experimental results validate that the presented methods are valid, and can meet real-time detection and tracking requirements.

Because many underwater objects are linear, e.g. pipelines, cables, and undersea structures, linear underwater objects are extracted and tracked in this paper. Detecting and tracking underwater objects of more complex shapes are more difficulty. They will be studied in our future work.

**Acknowledgement.** This paper is supported by Innovation Program of Shanghai Municipal Education Commission (No. 10ZZ060), " Shu Guang " project supported by Shanghai Municipal Education Commission and Shanghai Education Development Foundation (No. 09SG37), and Shanghai Municipal Science and Technology Commission Project (No. 10170500400). The authors also gratefully acknowledge the helpful comments and suggestions of the reviewers, which have improved the presentation.

# References

1. Narimani, M., Nazem, S., Loueipour, M.: Robotics vision-based system for an underwater pipeline and cable tracker. In: OCEANS 2009 - EUROPE, pp. 1–6 (May 2009)
2. Ortiz, A., Simó, M., Oliver, G.: A vision system for an underwater cable tracker. Machine Vision and Application 13, 129–140 (2002)
3. Antich, J., Ortiz, A.: Underwater Cable Tracking by Visual Feedback. In: Perales, F.J., Campilho, A.C., Pérez, N., Sanfeliu, A. (eds.) IbPRIA 2003. LNCS, vol. 2652, pp. 53–61. Springer, Heidelberg (2003)
4. Antich, J., Ortiz, A.: A behaviour-based control architecture for visually guiding an underwater cable tracker. In: Proceeding of the IFAC Workshop GCUV (2003)
5. Marani, G., Choi, S.: Underwater Target Localization. IEEE Robotics & Automation Magazine 17(1), 64–70 (2010)

6. Negahdaripour, S., Sekkati, H., Pirsiavash, H.: Opti-Acoustic Stereo Imaging: On System Calibration and 3-D Target Reconstruction. IEEE Transactions on Image Processing 18(6), 1203–1214 (2009)
7. Matthew, W., Franz, H., John, L.: SLAM for Ship Hull Inspection using Exactly Sparse Extended Information Filters. In: 2008 IEEE International Conference on Robotics and Automation, Pasadena, CA, USA, pp. 1463–1470 (2008)
8. Chen, J., Gong, Z., Li, H., Xie, S.: A Detection Method Based on Sonar Image for Underwater Pipeline Tracker. In: 2011 Second International Conference on Mechanic Automation and Control Engineering (MACE), Hohhot, China, pp. 3766–3769 (2011)
9. Sun, Z., Bebis, G., Miller, R.: On-Road vehicle detection using evolutionary Gabor filter optimization. IEEE Transactions on Intelligent Transportation System 6, 125–136 (2005)
10. Hong, C., Nanning, Z., Chong, S.: Boost Gabor Features Applied to Vehicle Detection. In: ICPR 2006, pp. 662–666 (September 2006)
11. http://www.soundmetrics.com/
12. Gonzalez, R.C., Woods, R.E.: Digital Image Processing. Prentice-Hall (2008)

# Structural Design and Analysis of 3-DOF Bionic Eye Based on Spherical Ultrasonic Motor

Jun Luo[1], Chaojiong Huang[1], Hengyu Li[1], Shaorong Xie[1], and Youmin M. Zhang[2]

[1] School of Mechatronic Engineering and Automation, Shanghai University,
No.149 YanChang Rd. Shanghai, China
{luojun,hcj,lihengyu,srxie}@shu.edu.cn
[2] Department of Mechanical & Industrial Engineering, Concordia University,
1515 St. Catherine West, Montreal, Quebec, H3G 1M8, Canada
ymzhang@encs.concordia.ca

**Abstract.** Vision system is crucial for autonomous robots. In order to realize some visual performances by complicated eye movements, like tracking target, image stabilization and vestibulo-ocular reflex, we present the mechanism and simulation of a robot bionic eye based on spherical ultrasonic motor (SUSM) with three rotational degrees of freedom (3-DOF). SUSM is a compact mechanism occupying little space but good responsiveness, high positioning accuracy, high torque at low speed and strong magnetic field compatibility. So based on SUSM, the bionic eye is fit to solve the problem of vision instability during robots' working. The bionic eye is constructed of three annular stators adhered with several piezoelectric elements and a spherical rotor as a camera actuator. The rotor is driven by frictional forces from the three stators accompanying with same preload generated by the deformations of specialized coil springs. Through simulation by a virtual prototype to analyze the rotational speed, torque and responsiveness, our mechanical design is verified to be reasonable and effective preliminary.

**Keywords:** Bionic eye, spherical ultrasonic motor, 3-DOF, mechanical design, simulation and analysis.

## 1 Introduction

There is no doubt that eye is the most significant sensor for human beings, because more than 80% of our information perception is acquired by eyes. Correspondingly, it is very important for autonomous robots, especially bionic robots to have a kind of human eye, which we call it "bionic eye". Researching bionic eye could improve the detecting technology significantly [1]. As is well-known, human being's eye can rotate about the spherical center, which means it has three degrees of freedom (3-DOF) to make eye movement more flexible and quick. It's better for robots to have multi-DOF eyes, with some supplementary stabilization to get good subjective image quality and resolution [2-3]. But it is common to see most robots only have two DOF bionic eyes, which are the rotation around X axis (Pitch) and the rotation around Y axial (Yaw). Adding another rotation around Z axis (Roll) makes bionic eye like human eye with one spherical center of rotation.

C.-Y. Su, S. Rakheja, H. Liu (Eds.): ICIRA 2012, Part I, LNAI 7506, pp. 348–356, 2012.

Many research groups have attempted the development of robot eyes to achieve gaze stabilization, among which 3-DOF robot vision devices are better to realize accurate images, becoming a focus of research. An agile eye was developed by Gosselin and his colleagues, which by six sets of links can also be adapted to robotic vision system. However, the link mechanism surrounds the end effectors and suggests some difficulty encasing the device behind a layer of a humanoid face [4-5]. To overcome this drawback, Y. B. Bang et al. presented a 3-DOF anthropomorphic oculomotor system that reproduced realistic human eye movements for human-sized humanoid applications [6]. Unlike the agile eye, the anthropomorphic oculomotor simulator was built with bent link segments, whose design maintain motion path behind the eyeball. Professor Xuan Wang [7] raised a concept that 3-DOF eyeball mechanism is actuated by six the pneumatic artificial muscles functioning as related six eye muscles, but it requires compressed air.

We also develop a 3-DOF bionic eye based on spherical ultrasonic motor (SUSM), which is our first attempt to apply SUSM into bionic eye and whose aim is to simulate the human eye movements like tracking target, image stabilization, vestibulo-ocular reflex (VOR), etc. There are several advantages for applying SUSM into a bionic eye: (1) the bionic eye has a simple and compact structure with no reduction gears, (2) SUSM exhibits a high output torque at low speed and high responsiveness, (3) SUSM has holding torques for braking if the electricity is turned off or the robot is moving in bumpy environment, (4) the principle of SUSM allows bionic eye to be smaller than the human eye if the camera size is suited, also with good performances.

As a compact mechanism but with good responsiveness, high positioning accuracy, high torque at low speed and strong magnetic field compatibility, SUSM has been applied into robot manipulator like a surgical robot's manipulator designed by T. Mashimo and S. Toyama [8], camera actuator like a pip inspection robot's head unit developed by M. Hoshina [9], also artificial limb like an artificial arm developed by N. FUKAYA et al [10]. The present paper reports a novel SUSM application as a bionic eye. The rest of this paper is organized as follows. Section 2 depicts the principle of the traveling wave type SUSM, including its mechanism and driving model. In section 3 we show the structural design of our bionic eye. Then some evaluation results by virtual prototype technology are presented in section 4.

## 2    Principle of Spherical Ultrasonic Motor

### 2.1    Mechanism of the SUSM

The SUSM is constructed of three annular stators and a spherical rotor, and produces an angular velocity vector of the spherical rotor with 3-DOF by the arrangement of the three stators. The definition of a general orthogonal coordinate is shown in Fig.1(a). The three stators make an angle $\alpha$ to the $x$-$y$ plane and are placed at 120° intervals around the $z$-axis as shown in Fig.1(b). The composition vector by three angular velocity vectors resulting from the stators has a component vectors in each $x$, $y$, and $z$ axial direction. Consequently, the rotor can rotate around these axes with freedom.

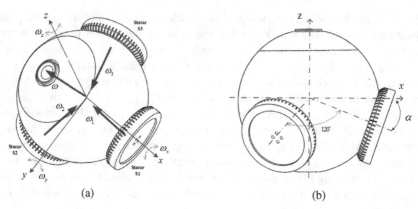

**Fig. 1.** Mechanism of the SUSM: (a) angular velocity vector from 3 stators of the spherical rotor and (b) placement of 3 stators from x-z plane

The target angular velocity vector $\omega$, obtained by processing videos from camera, is equal to the sum of three angular velocity vectors $\omega_1$, $\omega_2$ and $\omega_3$ resulting from three stators:

$$\omega = \omega_1 + \omega_2 + \omega_3 \tag{1}$$

$$\omega_1 = \omega_1[-\cos\alpha \quad 0 \quad \sin\alpha]^T \tag{2}$$

$$\omega_2 = \omega_2\left[-\frac{1}{2}\cos\alpha \quad -\frac{\sqrt{3}}{2}\cos\alpha \quad \sin\alpha\right]^T \tag{3}$$

$$\omega_3 = \omega_3\left[\frac{1}{2}\cos\alpha \quad \frac{\sqrt{3}}{2}\cos\alpha \quad \sin\alpha\right]^T \tag{4}$$

Where the scalar quantities $\omega_1$, $\omega_2$ and $\omega_3$ are determined by the magnitude, frequency and phase differences of the voltages applied to the stators. From (1)-(4), the desired angular velocity vector $\omega$ is expressed as

$$\omega = \begin{bmatrix} \omega_x \\ \omega_y \\ \omega_z \end{bmatrix} = \begin{bmatrix} \left(-\omega_1 + \frac{1}{2}\omega_2 + \frac{1}{2}\omega_3\right)\cos\alpha \\ \left(-\frac{\sqrt{3}}{2}\omega_2 + \frac{\sqrt{3}}{2}\omega_3\right)\cos\alpha \\ \left(\omega_1 + \omega_2 + \omega_3\right)\sin\alpha \end{bmatrix} \tag{5}$$

## 2.2    Driving Model of the SUSM

We apply the traveling wave ultrasonic motor with a spherical rotor into the bionic eye. The driving model of the traveling wave ultrasonic motor at the geometry of the stators and the spherical rotor is described to calculate the motion of the SUSM, as shown in Fig.2.

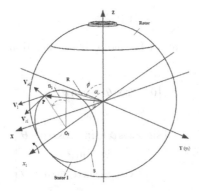

**Fig. 2.** Geometrical relationship on the contact area of the rotor and the stator

Taking a fundamental coordinate system $\sigma(OXYZ)$ with the origin at the center of the rotor and the $z$-axis as the vertical, the plane that intersects the origin perpendicular to the $z$-axis is the $x$-$y$ plane. We take the $x$-axis to be the line from the origin passing through the stator $S1$ and the $y$-axis as the line passing through the origin perpendicular to the x-axis and $z$-axis. Meanwhile, we build a coordinate system $\sigma_1(Ox_1y_1z_1)$ with its $x_1$-axis coinciding with the shaft axis of stator $S1$ and its $y_1$-axis coinciding with the $y$-axis. So we get the transfer matrix $A_{01}$ from $\sigma_1$ to $\sigma$.

$$A_{01} = \begin{bmatrix} \sin\alpha & 0 & -\cos\alpha \\ 0 & 1 & 0 \\ \cos\alpha & 0 & \sin\alpha \end{bmatrix} \quad (6)$$

An arbitrary contact point $P_1$ between the rotor and the stator $S1$ is expressed in the $\sigma_1$ as

$$P_1 = R\begin{bmatrix} \sin\phi & -\cos\phi\sin\theta & \cos\phi\cos\theta \end{bmatrix}^T \quad (7)$$

And $P$ is the same point expressed in the $\sigma$ as

$$P = A_{01}P_1 = R\begin{bmatrix} \sin\alpha\sin\phi - \cos\alpha\cos\phi\cos\theta \\ -\cos\phi\sin\theta \\ \cos\alpha\sin\phi + \sin\alpha\cos\phi\cos\theta \end{bmatrix} \quad (8)$$

When the rotor is rotating with a target angular velocity vector $\omega$, the velocity vector $V_1$ of point P is expressed as

$$V_1 = \omega \times P \quad (9)$$

Here we decompose $V_1$ to two sub vectors $V_{t1}$ and $V_{n1}$. $V_{t1}$ is the tangential subvector with the same direction with $S1$'s crest velocity vector $V_{s1}$ and $V_{n1}$ is the vertical subvector. They are expressed as

$$V_{n1} = \left(V_1^T n_p\right) \cdot n_p \quad (10)$$

$$V_{t1} = \left(V_1^T t_p\right) \cdot t_p \tag{11}$$

Where $t_p$ is the direction vector of $V_{t1}$ and $n_p$ is the direction vector of $V_{n1}$. They are calculated as

$$t_p = A_{01}\begin{bmatrix} 0 & -\cos\theta & -\sin\theta \end{bmatrix}^T \tag{12}$$

$$n_p = \frac{P}{|P|} \times t_p = \begin{bmatrix} \sin\alpha\cos\phi + \sin\phi\cos\alpha\cos\theta \\ \sin\phi\sin\theta \\ \cos\alpha\cos\phi - \sin\alpha\sin\phi\cos\theta \end{bmatrix} \tag{13}$$

The driving force $F_d$ is produced by the vibration of stators along the tangential direction of frictional circle. Meanwhile the frictional resistance $F_f$ between stator and rotor is engendered by their relative motions. At the contact point $P$ in stator $S1$, the driving force and the frictional resistance are given by

$$F_{d1} = \mu\left(V_{s1} - V_{t1}\right)N \tag{14}$$

$$F_{f1} = -\mu V_{n1} N \tag{15}$$

Where $\mu$ is the friction coefficient and $N$ is the preload.

So we can get the driving torque and frictional torque of stator $S1$:

$$T_{d1} = \frac{n}{2\pi}\int_0^{2\pi} P \times F_{d1} d\theta \tag{16}$$

$$T_{f1} = \frac{n}{2\pi}\int_0^{2\pi} P \times F_{f1} d\theta \tag{17}$$

Where $n$ is the count of wave crests in a contact circle. In addition, Stator $S2$ and Stator $S3$ produce driving torques $T_{d2}$, $T_{d3}$ and frictional torques $T_{f2}$, $T_{f3}$ to the rotor, which are calculated by the same method. Consequently, when the rotor rotates, its driving torque is

$$T = T_{d1} + T_{d2} + T_{d3} + T_{f1} + T_{f2} + T_{f3} \tag{18}$$

## 3     Design of Bionic Eye Using a SUSM

### 3.1     Eyeball

Our bionic eye uses SUSM as a camera actuator and a rotor as its eyeball. Our aim to design a bionic eye is to get a novel agile PTZ and achieve some similar eye movements controlled by our oculomotor control model. So the outer rotor-type SUSM [8] is not suit for our application because of its big moment of inertia and low response. Here the spherical rotor is a shell structure holding a camera and a MEMS sensor to, driven by three vibrating stators. We use an industrial high-definition camera combining with image processing technology to obtain good videos. The sensor is a miniature attitude heading reference system (AHRS), utilizing which we get a feedback signal to achieve loop control of the eyeball's attitude, and it is also a good measuring device to measure the SUSM's angle, rotational speed and response time, depending on its good performance.

In addition, the rotor is split up to two parts for assembling a camera and a sensor into it. Its surface will meet the requirement of friction drive from three stators when besmeared with friction material. Here the diameter of rotor is 60mm, limited by the dimensions of the camera and the sensor but with no impact of the compactness of the bionic eye.

## 3.2    Driving Stators

The stator is a key part to determine the performance of SUSM, which is an annular metallic body whose one side is equally spaced dentalation and another side is adhered by several piezoelectric elements. When AC voltages at a resonance frequency are applied to the piezoelectric elements, the piezoelectric element expands or contracts depending on the pole direction. Traveling waves are generated by the combination of 2 stationary waves, each having position difference and temporal phase difference of $\pi/4$. The stator transmits energy to the rotor through contact with stators.

Generally the material of stators is tin bronze which is a kind of non-magnetic metallic elastomer with good conductivity and thermal conductivity.We use ANSYS Workbench to analyze the modal frequencies of a stator for optimization design, and finally we select the modal $B_{09}$ with $49603Hz$ in Fig.3(a) and $49607Hz$ in Fig.3(b)as two approximate resonance frequencies. Then we get an optimal working frequency through the harmonic response analysis by exerting sine potentials. Fig.4 shows a stator's result of harmonic response analysis and we can see the maximum amplitude is generated on the working frequency of $49605Hz$.

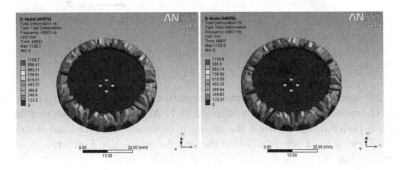

(a) $49603Hz$ of modal $B_{09}$                    (b) $49607Hz$ of modal $B_{09}$

**Fig. 3.** The model $B_{09}$ of a stator

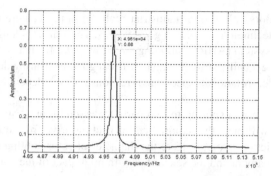

**Fig. 4.** The result of harmonic response analysis

## 3.3    Preloaded Apparatus

From the above analysis, we get the maximum amplitude of each vibrating stator, only 0.68μm, which means that the inside edges of stators must be in contact with the rotor. According to the driving model of SUSM, it is easy to control the SUSM when three preloads have a same value and symmetrical directions all through the center of rotor. So the following preloaded apparatus is added, as shown in Fig.5 (a). The stator is fixed to the center hole of a coil spring via a shaft, which is limited to move along the axial direction of stator by a ball-bushing.

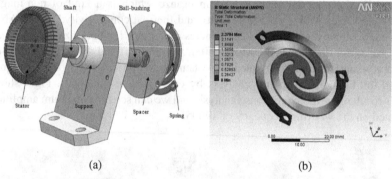

(a)                                                        (b)

**Fig. 5.** The preloaded apparatus (a) and the coil spring's displacement analysis for the case in which 50N is preloaded (b)

The coil spring has three Archimedes spirals and three pins fixed on the stator support. The result of static analysis obtained by FEM in Fig.5 (b) shows that the stator generates a preload of 50N when the spring is deflected to 2.3784mm at axis. This structure of spring has a benefit to adjust the rotor automatically. Furthermore, we add a spacer to regulate the actual preload by changing its thickness.

## 4    Simulation and Analysis of Bionic Eye's Virtual Prototype

In this section, a virtual prototype is used to predict the performance of our bionic eye in ADAMS, with its setup shown in Fig.6, and its parameters are given in Table.1. It is

**Fig. 6.** Parameter setup of virtual prototype

**Table 1.** Parameters for the simulation of SUSM

| Quantity | Symbol | Value |
|---|---|---|
| Radial of the rotor | R | 37mm |
| Inner radial of the stator | $r_s$ | 16mm |
| Outward radial of the stator | $R_s$ | 20mm |
| Tilted angle of the stators | $\alpha$ | 105° |
| Number of the dentalation | $n_d$ | 60 |
| Height of the dentalation | H | 3.5mm |
| Coefficient of friction | $\mu$ | 0.15 |
| Number of the waves | n | 9 |
| Resonance frequency | f | Hz |
| Amplitude of the travelling wave | $A_f$ | 0.68$\mu m$ |
| Preload | N | 50N |

necessary and beneficial to improve the design scheme and reduce mistakes before physical prototype.

SUSM can be controlled by the phase difference of two impressed AC voltages, electrodes A and B. We choose three phase differences of 30°, 60° and 90° to simulate and analyze the relationship between Torque and rotational speed from each twelve sets of results from ADAMS Postprocessor, as shown in Fig.7, indicating that it is linear and the phase difference controllability is effective. If we choose the phase difference 90°to get the best performance, we can get that the rotational speed is 60*rpm*, good enough, when the torque 80*mNm* meets the demand of holding torque in some bumpy environments. Obviously SUSM's performance is suit for the application of bionic eye.

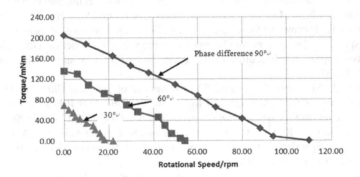

**Fig. 7.** Torque and rotational speed characteristics

# 5    Conclusion

We have presented the design of a novel bionic eye based on SUSM, which has compactness, superior responsiveness and high accuracy because of no reduction gear and little moment of inertia only from a spherical rotor. Benefitted from SUSM, our bionic eye shows a good performance from its virtual prototype. Next, we will do some experiments on a real prototype and use the oculomotor control model developed by our research group to realize some complicated eye movements.

**Acknowledgement.** This work was supported by the National Science Foundation of China (Grant No.50975168), Shanghai Municipal Science and Technology Commission Project (No.10170500400), and "Shu-guang" Project supported by Shanghai Municipal Education Commission and Shanghai Education Development Foundation (No.09SG37). The authors also gratefully acknowledge the helpful comments and suggestions of the reviewers, which have improved the presentation.

# References

1. Li, H.Y., Luo, J., et al.: A novel landing method for subminiature robot helicopters based on binocular vergence eye movements. J. Chinese High Technology Letters 18(10), 1047–1052 (2007)
2. Lenz, A., Balakrishnan, T., Melhuish, C.: An adaptive gaze stabilization controller inspired by the vestibulo-ocular reflex. Bioinspiration & Biomimetics 3(035001), 1–11 (2008)
3. Lenz, A., Anderson, S.R., Pipe, A.G., Melhuish, C.: Cerebellar-Inspired Adaptive Control of a Robot Eye Actuated by Pneumatic Artificial Muscles. IEEE Transactions on systems, Man, and Cybernetics-part B: Cybernetics 39(6), 1420–1432 (2009)
4. Gosselin, C.M., St-Pierre, E., Gagne, M.: On the development of the agile eye. IEEE Robotics & Automation Magazine 3(4), 29–37 (1996)
5. Gosselin, C.M., St-Pierre, E.: Development and experimentation of a fast 3-DOF camera-orienting device. International Journal of Robotics Research 16(5), 619–630 (1997)
6. Bang, Y.B., Paik, J.K.B., Shin, H., Lee, C.: A Three-Degree-of - Freedom Anthropomorphic Oculomot or Simulator. International Journal of Control, Automation, and Systems 4(2), 227–235 (2006)
7. Wang, X.U., et al.: Design and Kinematic Analysis of a Novel Humanoid Robot Eye Using Pneumatic Artificial Muscles. J. Journal of Bionic Engineering 5(3), 264–270 (2008)
8. Mashimo, T., Toyama, S.: Development of an MRI compatible surgical assist manipulator using spherical ultrasonic motor (1st report) - Prototype of the spherical ultrasonic motor. Seimitsu Kogaku Kaishi/Journal of the Japan Society for Precision Engineering 73(2), 275–280 (2007)
9. Hoshina, M., Mashimo, T., Toyama, S.: Development of Spherical Ultrasonic Motor as a Camera Actuator for Pipe Inspection Robot. In: Proc. of 2009 IEEE/RSJ International Conference on Intelligent Robots and Systems (IROS 2009), pp. 2379–2384 (2009)
10. Fukay, N., Sawada, K., Oku, H., Wada, H., Toyama, S.: Development of an Artificial Arm by Using a Spherical Ultrasonic Motor. Journal of the Japan Society of Precision Engineering 67, 654–659 (2011)
11. Li, H.Y., Luo, J., et al.: Active Compensation Method of Robot Visual Error Base on Vestibulo-ocular Reflex. J. Robot. 33(1) (2011)

# Cooperative Control for UAV Formation Flight Based on Decentralized Consensus Algorithm[*]

Yaohong Qu[1], Xu Zhu[1], and Youmin M. Zhang[2]

[1] School of Automation, Northwestern Polytechnical University, Xi'an, 710129, China
[2] Department of Mechanical and Industrial Engineering,
Concordia University, Montreal, H3G 2W1, Canada

**Abstract.** Decentralized consensus algorithm is suggested to maintain a specified formation configuration of multiple Unmanned Aerial Vehicles (UAVs). As no explicit leader exists in the team, only the local neighbor-to-neighbor information between vehicles is needed for the proposed control strategy. Position of the virtual leader and attitude of each UAV is the convergence state variable chosen for the algorithm. Communication limits and measurement errors are also considered to improve robustness. Besides, the motion synchronization technology is incorporated to achieve coordinated control of the UAVs, such that coupled relative position errors are used to calculate the trajectory modification. Finally, conclusion is conducted based on the testing results with simulation examples.

**Keywords:** Unmanned Aerial Vehicle (UAV), formation control, decentralized consensus, synchronization technology.

## 1    Introduction

Formation flight control of multiple Unmanned Aerial Vehicles has been an active topic in recent years[1-5] since it promises many practical applications, such as reconnaissance, surveillance, atmospheric study, communication relaying and search and rescue. Some of these tasks may be dangerous and will not be recommended for human pilots, thus making them ideal for autonomous unmanned vehicles.

Recently, there are many research methods suggested on multiple UAVs control, such as leader following[6], behavior based approach[7], virtual leader[8] and artificial potential function[9]. In these methods, virtual leader is much reliable in modern war. Comparing with the traditional real leader, the virtual one can be never destroyed in physics. Moreover, there is a big problem in formation control that how to make full use of neighbor-to-neighbor information communication. Because using the information could improve synchronization of the entire formation. In the virtual leader approach used in this paper, decentralized consensus is induced to the entire formation is treated as a single entity. It can evolve as a rigid body in a given direction with some

---

[*] This work is supported by the National Natural Sciences Foundation (NNSF) of China under Grant 60974146.

C.-Y. Su, S. Rakheja, H. Liu (Eds.): ICIRA 2012, Part I, LNAI 7506, pp. 357–366, 2012.

given orientation and maintain the geometric relationship among multiple vehicles base on a reference point in the virtual leader structure. For more specific formation flight problem of aircraft, a consensus is that the vehicles should be able to achieve tracking for given velocity, heading, and altitude commands[9,10] in order for a formation controller to be developed for the aircraft. An autopilot model that provides tracking capabilities for the three commands and the method of trajectory command modifications based on relative position errors is used as part of the control algorithm in this note. This method is coupled with the virtual leader approach to achieve formation flights for research.

This paper is outlined as follows. In Section 2, the virtual leader structure is defined followed by distributed consensus formation algorithm. In Section 3, communication limits is analyzed and the synchronization technology is incorporated into the controller to suppress measurement errors. Simulation results on formation control of multiple flying wings are given in Section 4. At last, Section 5 offers conclusions and future research possibilities.

## 2     Formation Control for UAVS

Consider the formation of $n$ identical UAVS, and each is denoted by $U_i$. They constitute of a graph $G = \{V, E\}$, where $V = \{1, 2, \cdots, n\}$ is the set of nodes. $E \subseteq V \times V$ is the set of edges, and an edge of the graph $G$ is denoted by $e_{ij} = (i, j)$, i.e., $e_{ij}$ is a directed edge from $i$ to $j$. The set of neighbors for node $i$ is denoted by $N_i = \{j \in V : (i, j) \in E\}$. $U_i$ does not send information to $j \in N_i$. Therefore $N_i$ is endowed with a neighboring unidirectional relation. That is, when $j \in N_i$, a directed edge $(j, i)$ exists such that $j \rightarrow i$, which means that sensory data comprised of position and velocity for $j$ flowing from $j$ to $i$.

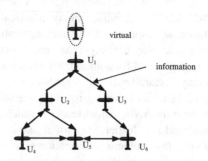

**Fig. 1.** Virtual leader structure

Formation stabilization obtained with the controller presented in the next section is guaranteed under the assumption that $G$ is a connected digraph. The formation geometry is defined by prescribed line-of-sight angle and relative distance between $i$

and $j$ that are communicated from one node to another according to the graph. For brevity, morphing of the formation is not considered here; that is, relative distances are assumed time invariant. Finally, the formation comprises a virtual leader vehicle, which tracks a certain reference trajectory $I_{xyz}$.

**Assumption 1.** UAV formation is kept in a fixed geometry during the whole flight envelope, and each team member does not change its relative position in formation with time.

Vehicle positions are attained with respect to an inertial frame $I_{xyz}$. Each agent UAV is a rigid body with inertial position $\rho_i$, which is constructed by three dimensions.

$$\rho_i = (x_i, y_i, z_i)^T \tag{1}$$

Velocity and heading angle of $U_i$ can be represented as $V_i$ and $\psi_i$, respectively.

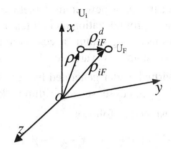

**Fig. 2.** Virtual leader generated by $U_i$

The virtual leader is defined as $U_F$ with initial position $\rho_{iF}$, which is generated by each UAV. In the autonomous cooperation, virtual leader is generated by each UAV. $\rho_{iF}^d$ is desired distance from $U_i$ to the virtual leader. If each desired distance is given, the team geometry is identified to keep formation maneuvering. Figure 2 shows the relation of $e_{xi} = -\sum_{j \in N_i} a_{ij}[(x_i^* + x_{iF}^d) - (x_j^* + x_{jF}^d)]$, $\rho_{iF}$ and $\rho_{iF}^d$ considered in this study.

$$\rho_{iF} = \rho_i + \rho_{iF}^d \tag{2}$$

Relative distance between UAVS is denoted by $\rho_{ij}, j \in N_i$. Assume that the formation maintains fixed geometry during flight, and similarly relative desired distance $\rho_{ij}^d, j \in N_i$ between UAVS is fixed. The control objective of the team is that $\rho_{ij} \to \rho_{ij}^d$ as $t \to \infty$. Navigation equations for each UAV are selected as

$$
\begin{aligned}
\dot{x}_i &= V_i \cos \mu_i \cos \varphi_i \\
\dot{y}_i &= V_i \cos \mu_i \sin \mu_i \\
\dot{z}_i &= V_i \sin \mu_i
\end{aligned}
\tag{3}
$$

where $\mu_i$ and $\varphi_i$ are flight path angle and azimuth track angle, respectively. If $U_i$ obtains information from $U_j$, then kinematics equations is represented as follows

$$\dot{x}_{ij} = V_j \cos\mu_j \cos\varphi_j - V_i \cos\mu_i \cos\varphi_i$$
$$\dot{y}_{ij} = V_j \cos\mu_j \sin\varphi_j - V_i \cos\mu_i \sin\varphi_i \qquad (4)$$
$$\dot{z}_{ij} = -V_j \sin\mu_j + V_i \sin\mu_i$$

It can be easily seen that the position $\rho_i = [x_i, y_i, z_i]^T$ is adjusted by trajectory commands $T_i = [V_i, \varphi_i, \mu_i]^T$. In order to control the distance between UAVs, the control law of $V_i, \varphi_i, \mu_i$ is designed to realize cooperation.

## 2.1 Distributed Consensus Formation Control Algorithm

Distributed consensus algorithm is a new control method with complete autonomy, which casts off dependence of ground station and all team members take participation in decision-making. Consensus algorithm needs common variables to achieve synchronization. $\rho_F$ is the common variable. In the consensus algorithm, $\rho_{iF}$ represents the position of virtual leader generated by each UAV, which is different at the beginning. As time going on, consensus algorithm makes $\rho_{iF} \to \rho_{jF}$ as $t \to \infty$. Specific control laws are designed as follows.

$$\dot{V}_{xi} = -\sum_{j\in N_i} a_{ij}[(x_i + x_{iF}^d) - (x_j + x_{jF}^d) - \gamma\dot{x}_{ij}]$$
$$\dot{V}_{yi} = -\sum_{j\in N_i} a_{ij}[(y_i + y_{iF}^d) - (y_j + y_{jF}^d) - \gamma\dot{y}_{ij}] \qquad (5)$$
$$\dot{V}_{zi} = -\sum_{j\in N_i} a_{ij}[(z_i + z_{iF}^d) - (z_j + z_{jF}^d) - \gamma\dot{z}_{ij}]$$

where $\gamma$ is a positive constant, and $a_{ij}$ is determined by the Laplacian graph. Let $x_{iF} = x_i + x_{iF}^d$, $y_{iF} = y_i + y_{iF}^d$ and $z_{iF} = z_i + z_{iF}^d$, where $\rho_{iF} = (x_{iF}, y_{iF}, z_{iF})^T$. Therefore, the control algorithm of $V_i$ is obtained that

$$\dot{V}_i = (\sqrt{V_{xi}^2 + V_{yi}^2 + V_{zi}^2})' = \frac{V_{xi}\dot{V}_{xi} + V_{yi}\dot{V}_{yi} + V_{zi}\dot{V}_{zi}}{V_i} \qquad (6)$$

where $\dot{V}_i$ is a second consensus algorithm consists of both position information and velocity information. In the design of attitude control, first consensus is capable of synchronization.

$$\dot{\varphi}_i = -\sum_{j\in N_i} a_{ij}(\varphi_i - \varphi_j) \qquad (7)$$

$$\dot{\mu}_i = -\sum_{j\in N_i} a_{ij}(\mu_i - \mu_j) \qquad (8)$$

The objective of consensus algorithm is to guarantee that $V_i \rightarrow V_j$, $\varphi_i \rightarrow \varphi_j$, $\varphi_i \rightarrow \varphi_j$, as $t \rightarrow \infty$, which means that the formation fight can be realized. The Laplace matrix of digraph $G$ is defined as

$$L = [l_{ij}], l_{ii} = \sum_{j \in N_i} a_{ij} \ and \ l_{ij} = -a_{ij}, \forall i \neq j \tag{9}$$

and $L$ is a positive definite matrix. Let $X_F = [x_{1F}, x_{2F}, \cdots, x_{nF}]^T$, $Y_F = [y_{1F}, y_{2F}, \cdots, y_{nF}]^T$, $Z_F = [z_{1F}, z_{2F}, \cdots, z_{nF}]^T$, $V = [V_1, V_2, \cdots, V_n]^T$, $\varphi = [\varphi_1, \varphi_2, \cdots, \varphi_n]^T$, and $\mu = [\mu_1, \mu_2, \cdots, \mu_n]^T$.

Then, the control algorithm (5), (7) and (8) change into

$$\dot{V}_x = -L(X_F + \gamma \dot{X}); \quad \dot{V}_y = -L(Y_F + \gamma \dot{Y}); \quad \dot{V}_z = -L(Z_F + \gamma \dot{Z}) \tag{10}$$

$$\dot{\varphi} = -L\varphi \tag{11}$$

$$\dot{\mu} = -L\mu \tag{12}$$

(10), (11) and (12) are matrix forms of the distributed consensus algorithm.

## 2.2    Flight Path Control

Flight path control is designed to control the trajectory of formation. The desired flight path angle is defined as $\varphi_d$. All UAVs in the formation aim to follow $\varphi_d$. Such that the control law of $\varphi_i$ is modified, which will not only realize synchronization for formation maneuver, but also complete trajectory planning.

$\varphi_d$ is considered as a reference state in the consensus algorithm, which is the terminal convergence value for all $\varphi_i$. Then, new control law for $\varphi_i$ is generated with reference state.

$$\dot{\varphi}_i = -\sum_{j \in N_i} a_{ij}(\varphi_i - \varphi_j) - (\varphi_i - \varphi_d) \tag{13}$$

## 2.3    Consensus Stability

Equation (6) is a second-order consensus algorithm, though equation (7) and (8) are both first-order consensus algorithms. In literature [11], first-order consensus algorithm achieving convergence only needs a directed spanning tree in communication graph.

However, if second-order consensus algorithm reach consensus, a directed spanning tree is just a precondition, where $\gamma$ should be properly chosen as well. Now, $\gamma$ should be chosen properly such that the control algorithm can reach convergence. It can't be too small in order to avoid positive poles arising in the system[11]. According to our previous work [12], a sufficient condition is given that the polynomial with coefficient $[1\ \gamma]^T$ should be Hurwitz. When communication topology has a directed spanning tree and $\gamma > 1$, $V_{xi}$, $V_{yi}$ and $V_{zi}$ could achieve convergence.

It is assured that $V_{xi} \rightarrow V_{xj}$, $V_{yi} \rightarrow V_{yj}$ and $V_{zi} \rightarrow V_{zj}$ as $t \rightarrow \infty$. In another word, $\dot{V}_{xi} \rightarrow 0$, $\dot{V}_{yi} \rightarrow 0$ and $\dot{V}_{zi} \rightarrow 0$ as $t \rightarrow \infty$. Submitting them into (6), it is easy to concluded that $\dot{V}_i \rightarrow 0$ as $t \rightarrow \infty$. Consequently, control algorithm (6) can also achieve convergence at finite time.

# 3    Robustness of Control Algorithm

## 3.1    Communication Topology

Considering the measurements from sensors with limited fields of views or random communication data loss, a unidirectional or bidirectional information flow topology can be considered. On account of low cost for miniature UAVs and a spot of airborne communication equipment, bidirectional ring communication topology is chosen to overcome these limits. Figure 3 depicts this communication topology.

If there are communication faults between certain UAVs such as bidirectional communication changing into directional one, a directed spanning tree still exists in the topology. Only when bidirectional information flow is both invalid, consensus stability is completely destroyed.

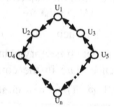

**Fig. 3.** Bidirectional ring communication topology

## 3.2    Synchronization Technology

Another objective in this project is to incorporate the motion synchronization technology to achieve coordinated control of the UAVs. Thus, the next step is to apply this technology in the controller.

On the influence of navigation and range finding, position data $\rho$ contains measurement errors.

$$x_i^* = x_i + \tilde{x}_i; \quad y_i^* = y_i + \tilde{y}_i; \quad z_i^* = z_i + \tilde{z}_i \qquad (14)$$

Such that the measurement values $x_i^*, y_i^*, z_i^*$ are used to replace the values $x_i, y_i, z_i$, where $\tilde{x}_i, \tilde{y}_i, \tilde{z}_i$ are measurement errors. Substitute (14) into (5) to get that

$$\dot{V}_{xi} = -\sum_{j \in N_i} a_{ij}[(x_i^* + x_{iF}^d) - (x_j^* + x_{jF}^d) - \gamma \dot{x}_{ij}]$$

$$\dot{V}_{yi} = -\sum_{j \in N_i} a_{ij}[(y_i^* + y_{iF}^d) - (y_j^* + y_{jF}^d) - \gamma \dot{y}_{ij}] \quad (15)$$

$$\dot{V}_{zi} = -\sum_{j \in N_i} a_{ij}[(z_i^* + z_{iF}^d) - (z_j^* + z_{jF}^d) - \gamma \dot{z}_{ij}]$$

For simplicity, $x$ channel is chosen to analysis the control algorithm. The strategy uses the cross coupling concept to synchronize the relative position tracking motion of the aircraft. It utilizes synchronization errors $e_{xi} = -\sum_{j \in N_i} a_{ij}[(x_i^* + x_{iF}^d) - (x_j^* + x_{jF}^d)]$, which incorporates error information from different UAVs in the system, to identify the performance of synchronization. The cross coupled error $e_{xi}^*$ then couples the error $\tilde{x}_i$ and synchronization error $e_{xi}$ through a positive synchronization gain $\beta_i$.

$$e_{xi}^* = \tilde{x}_i + \beta_{xi} e_{xi} \quad (16)$$

The objective of the synchronization strategy is to drive $e_{xi}^*$ of each UAV in (16) to 0 by choosing the proper gain values, implying that both $\tilde{x}_i$ and $e_{xi}$ are driven to 0 as well. In another word, the team uses information from each other to eliminate the errors synchronously.

The coupled relative position errors from (16) are used to calculate the trajectory modification $\Delta \dot{V}_{xi}^*$ and the new modified trajectory command that will be passed to the controller of the UAVs is $\dot{\overline{V}}_{xi}^* = \dot{V}_{xi} + \Delta \dot{V}_{xi}^*$, where $\Delta \dot{V}_{xi}^*$ is a PID controller.

$$\Delta \dot{V}_{xi}^* = k_{Px} e_{xi}^* + k_{Ix} \int_0^t e_{xi}^* dt + k_{Dx} e_{xi}^{*\prime} \quad (17)$$

where $k_{Px}, k_{Ix}, k_{Dx}$ are proportional, integral and differential coefficients. The controllers for $y, z$ channel are designed in the same way. Then, the control law for $V_i$ is concluded

$$\dot{V}_i = \frac{V_{xi} \dot{\overline{V}}_{xi}^* + V_{yi} \dot{\overline{V}}_{yi}^* + V_{zi} \dot{\overline{V}}_{zi}^*}{V_i} \quad (18)$$

## 4    Simulation Evaluations

The formation flight control system's response to the virtual leader maneuvers is simulated using nonlinear models of UAVs. Six aircrafts are taken for our simulation, where all UAVs are considered similar. Flight path commands are decided by the virtual leader and performance of the whole formation UAVs are analyzed. Figure 4 shows a communication network which has a directed spanning tree, which consists of six UAVs. An edge from UAV $j$ to UAV $i$ means that UAV $i$ can receive information from UAV $j$.

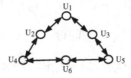

**Fig. 4.** Communication topology

Simulations are performed on a maneuver followed by straight line travel for UAVs in a flight formation. An autopilot model developed for a MAGICC lab flying- wing UAV is used in the simulations. All the UAVs have to maintain an equilateral triangular formation, where every three adjacent UAVs constitute a small equilateral triangular with side length of 4m. Besides, they do not fly at an identical altitude. $U_2$ and $U_3$ maneuver 4m lower than $U_1$, while $U_4$, $U_5$ and $U_6$ are 8m lower than $U_1$. The virtual leader is in the front of $U_1$ with the distance of 4m. However, the team does not start at the desired positions at the beginning of the flight. No collision avoidance algorithm is implemented.

The initial position of each UAV are $\rho_1 = [30,20,1200]^T$, $\rho_2 = [20,10,1195]^T$, $\rho_3 = [10,0,1190]^T$, $\rho_4 = [0,-10,1185]^T$, $\rho_5 = [-10,-20,1180]^T$ and $\rho_6 = [-20,-30,1175]^T$. Initial flight path angle and azimuth track angle are selected as $\mu = [-5°,0°,5°,-5°,10°,-5°]^T$ and $\varphi = [45°,0°,65°,75°,20°,40°]^T$, respectively. There are white Gaussian noises in the measurement of position with mean value of 0 and variance of 0.5m.

Formation control is then implemented for the UAVs based on virtual leader approach and trajectory modifications as proposed in Section 3. The setup for the simulation is the same as before and the gains used for the trajectory PID controllers are given in Table 1.

**Table 1.** Control Gains of PID Controller

| Parameter | Value | Parameter | Value | Parameter | Value |
|---|---|---|---|---|---|
| $K_{Px}$ | 5 | $K_{Ix}$ | 0.5 | $K_{Dx}$ | 0.3 |
| $K_{Py}$ | 0.005 | $K_{Iy}$ | 0.0005 | $K_{Dy}$ | 0.0003 |
| $K_{Pz}$ | 1 | $K_{Iz}$ | 0.005 | $K_{Dz}$ | 0.003 |

The synchronization technology in Section 3 is incorporated in the controller. The synchronization gains $\beta_{xi}$, $\beta_{yi}$ and $\beta_{zi}$ for these vehicles are being set to 1. Applying the suggested control law, Figs. 5-7 illustrate the flight path angle, the azimuth track angle and the velocity of the team, which show that each information variable achieves consensus quickly for the bidirectional ring structure.

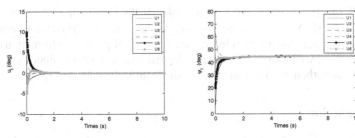

**Fig. 5.** Flight path angle of UAVs     **Fig. 6.** Azimuth track angle of UAVs

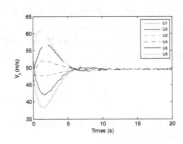

**Fig. 7.** Velocity of UAVs

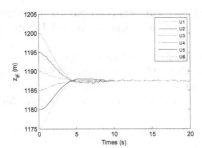
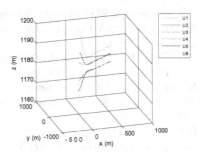

**Fig. 8.** $x$ position for $U_F$     **Fig. 9.** $y$ position for $U_F$

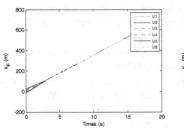
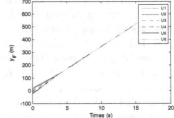

**Fig. 10.** $z$ position for $U_F$     **Fig. 11.** Trajectory responses of UAVs

Figs. 8-10 are $\rho_{iF}$ states in the first seconds. At the beginning, the virtual leader generated by each UAV is at different position. As time goes on, the positions coincide. It can also be seen that disturbances in the measurement of position information can be depressed by the synchronization strategy. Distributed consensus algorithm is still effective with disturbances. The trajectory of the team is depicted as Fig. 11.

# 5    Conclusions

A distributed consensus formation control strategy is proposed for multiple UAVs in this paper. In the proposed strategy, neighbor-to-neighbor information communication affects maneuvers of each UAV. To improve the robustness of communication, bidirectional ring topology is chosen to suppress communication limits. Moreover, a synchronized PID controller is suggested to deal with measurement errors. Our future work will focus on formation control with time-varying geometry.

# References

[1] Giulietti, F., Pollini, L., Innocenti, M.: Autonomous formation flight. IEEE Control Systems Magazine 20(6), 34–44 (2006)
[2] Pachter, M., D'Azzo, J.J., Proud, A.W.: Tight formation flight control. Journal of Guidance, Control, and Dynamics 24(2), 246–254 (2001)
[3] Gu, Y., Seanor, B., Campa, G., Napolitano, M.R., Rowe, L., Gururajan, S., Wan, S.: Design and flight testing evaluation of formation control laws. IEEE Transactions on Control Systems Technology 14(6), 1105–1112 (2006)
[4] Shan, J., Liu, H.T.: Close-formation flight control with motion synchronization. Journal of Guidance, Control and Dynamics 28(6), 1316–1320 (2005)
[5] Lawton, J.R.T., Beard, R.W., Young, B.J.: A decentralized approach to formation maneuvers. IEEE Transactions on Robotics and Automation 19(6) (2003)
[6] Ye, H., Miao, C., Lei, X.: Formation method and flight test of multiple UAVs based on leader-follower pattern. Robot 32(4), 505–510 (2005)
[7] Kim, S., Kim, Y.: Three dimensional optimum controller for multiple UAV formation flight using behavior-based decentralized approach. Control, Automation and Systems 12, 1387–1392 (2007)
[8] Ren, W., Beard, R.W.: Virtual structure based spacecraft formation control with formation feedback. In: AIAA Guidance, Navigation, and Control Conference and Exhibit, pp. 2002–4963 (2002)
[9] Song, Y.D., Li, Y., Liao, X.H.: Orthogonal transformation based robust adaptive close formation control of multi-UAV. In: American Control Conference, pp. 2983–2988 (2005)
[10] Kumar, R., Kabamba, P.T., Hyland, D.C.: Controller design using adaptive random search for close-coupled formation flight. Journal of Guidance, Control, and Dynamics 28(6), 1323–1325 (2005)
[11] Ren, W., Beard, R.W.: Distributed Consensus in Multi-vehicle Cooperative Control: Theory and Applications. Springer (2007)
[12] Zhu, X., Yan, J., Qu, Y.: Consensus problems for high-order multi-agent systems. Advanced Materials Research 403-408(11), 2736–2739 (2011)

# Segmentation and Classification of Side-Scan Sonar Data

Mahesh Khidkikar and Ramprasad Balasubramanian

Department of Computer and Information Science
University of Massachusetts Dartmouth
Dartmouth, MA 02747, USA
{mkhidkikar,r.bala}@umassd.edu

**Abstract.** Side scan sonar is an acoustic sensor which uses sound waves to generate side scan sonar images. Most adaptive behavior of AUVs would require that the vehicle be able sense the environment, detect objects of interest, localize and then change its current behavior. The first step toward this process would be the real time processing of its sensor data for object identification. In this paper we present an approach to real time processing of side scan sonar data using texture segmentation and classification. Given a side scan sonar image, texture is used to classify the image into four major categories - rocks, wreckage, sediments and sea floor. The image is first broken into relevant areas based on edge density and edge orientation statistics. Laws texture energy measures are then computed on these areas. The texture energy feature vector for each sub region is then classified using clustering algorithms.

**Keywords:** Side-scan images, AUVs, Texture, Clustering.

## 1    Introduction

An autonomous underwater vehicle (AUV) is a robot which travels underwater without requiring input from an operator. These AUVs are generally used for commercial, military, and research purposes. AUVs rely on multiple sensors to gather information about its environment. Some of these sensors include - Side scan sonar, Doppler Velocity Log (DVL) and forward looking sonar. A side scan sonar array is used to efficiently create an acoustic image of large areas of the sea floor. Side scan sonar data is also used to detect debris and other objects of interest in underwater environments. Most common use of side scan sonar data is via post-mission processing to locate objects of interest through manual inspection. Typical applications include the detection and tracking of pipelines, cables and mine like objects.

This paper proposes an approach to performing real time processing of side scan sonar data for feature extraction, detection and classification of objects of interest in an underwater environment. The approach proposed in this paper can also be used to address the simultaneous localization and mapping (SLAM) problem. Simultaneous localization and mapping is used by robots and autonomous vehicles to build a map

C.-Y. Su, S. Rakheja, H. Liu (Eds.): ICIRA 2012, Part I, LNAI 7506, pp. 367–376, 2012.
© Springer-Verlag Berlin Heidelberg 2012

within an unknown environment or to update a map within a known environment while localizing itself in the map.

The scope of this paper involves presenting a framework for real time processing of side scan sonar data in order to extract and classify objects. The implementation of this approach works on an input which is an accumulated side scan sonar data stream. The raw data captured by side scan sonar is converted into image format before being fed into the algorithm. The logging of side scan sonar sensor data is assumed to be one column every second (most side-scan sensors operate at 1Hz).

Extraction and classification of underwater images would have multiple applications, including but not limited to adaptive behaviors, detection of mine-like objects and identifications of wreckage etc. In this paper we make the assumption that the number of classes of objects that we are classifying is known a priori. This assumption is required and reasonable as making any algorithm capable of large number of classification intractable. Also computing capabilities on-board AUVs typically tend to be limited.

Results presented in this paper on side scan sonar images are obtained from SportScan, YellowFin and Klein on an Iver-2 AUV. Figure 1 shows a sample side-scan image with two 2 textures - rock and sediments, manually segmented.

**Fig. 1.** Manually Segmented Sediment from a Klein 3500 Side Scan Image

## 2    Previous Work

The processing of side scan sonar images, in order to study seabed, riverbed is most often performed via post processing. Here we review some papers that relate to underwater image processing. Daniel, Le Leannec, and Roux presented a method for the matching of real world images in underwater images, acquired with acoustic sensors. As a final objective, the system aims at matching data from two-dimensional scenes [1]. The proposed approach uses hypothetical reasoning based on objects, represented by shadows and echoes in the sonar images. Using qualitative representation for robust features, measures which are invariant to changes in sonar settings and noise characteristics is addressed [1]. The approach developed does not work in real time. Another approach developed by Celik and Tjahjadi attempts to extract features using an unsupervised multistage seabed segmentation algorithm from side scan sonar images. Feature vectors are created using multi-resolution inter- and intra-scale data [2]. But there no real-time approach to performing such tasks is presented. Performing these tasks real time would help to minimize the time and cost of every operation. One of the approaches to identify underwater lengthy objects like cables and pipelines uses Hough transform in [3] and [4]. These approaches require the complete side scan sonar image to find lengthy objects. Hough transforms also tend be very expensive in terms of time and space, as it involves exhaustive search of the parameter space.

Finding active contours is one of the highly researched areas in side scan sonar processing. The basic idea in active contour models or snakes is to evolve a curve, subject to constraints from a given image, in order to detect objects in that image. For instance, starting with a curve around the object to be detected, the curve moves toward its interior normal and has to stop on the boundary of the object [8].

There are several approaches to performing texture segmentation, but there are limited algorithms in the literature for finding texture boundaries in real images in the absence of prior models of the specific textures present. One such method is to compute large binary objects by convolving the image with a Laplacian of Gaussian (LoG) of small sigma, finding attributes of these blobs, and using statistical tests to identify local properties of blob attributes [6]. Voorhees and Poggio talk about finding texture boundaries in images based on a computational model of human texture perception [5]. Texture classification with the help of spectral histogram is one the highly used methods.

Based on a local spatial/frequency representation, Liu and Wang employ a spectral histogram as a feature statistic for texture classification. Using a filtering stage and a histogram stage local structure of images and the global appearance of texture are extracted. The distance between two spectral histograms is measured using $\chi 2$-statistic. The spectral histogram with the appropriate distance measure shows several key properties that are important for classification using texture [7].

Unlike the previous approaches described, the framework proposed in this paper works real time on side scan sonar images. The algorithm presented in this paper uses input accumulated from side scan sonar sensor to find objects of interest. Edge statistics of an object and texture energy measures are used to extract features from the input stream. Texture segmentation is performed based on edge statistics and texture energy measures. Texture classification is performed on the segmented regions. Clustering algorithms are used in order to classify them into different categories. Fuzzy C-means and K-mean clustering algorithms are used to perform classification.

# 3    Approach

The algorithm presented in this paper is divided into two parts, texture segmentation and texture classification. Texture segmentation is performed using edge statistics. Calculating texture energy measures using Laws Texture Energy is the intermediate step between segmentation and classification. Texture classification is the last part of the algorithm which is performed using a Fuzzy C-means clustering algorithm. Figure 2 shows the steps involved in this approach.

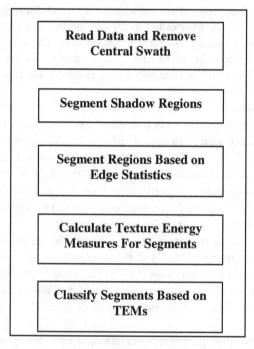

**Fig. 2.** Real Time Segmentation and Classification of Side Scan Sonar Images

The algorithm begins by reading the real time input data as it comes from the side-scan sonar. In the paper we are simulating the real time reading process by reading 50 columns at a time of an input data (converted into jpeg format). The image read has central swath (the shadow directly below the vehicle) in it. Side scan sonar sensors are typically mounted on the side of the AUV which cannot capture the region directly below the AUV. After reading the input data first step is to remove this central swath. The central swath is removed by starting from the center of the image and scanning in either direction till actual data is found. Then data on either side is stitched together. After removing central swath the image is used for segmentation.

The next step is the detection of shadows in the image. Existence of shadow represents presence of objects in nearby area. Segmenting shadow regions is therefore first step towards locating objects of interest. The regions having pixel intensity value less than 30 are marked as shadow pixels. Remaining regions are used in the next step - calculating edge statistics. Regions are segmented based on edge density and edge orientation values. Edge density corresponds to total number of edges in a specific area. Edge orientation corresponds to direction of those edges in that specific area. There are four possible directions for an edge, diagonal up, diagonal down, vertical and horizontal. This step is performed to identify regions of (edge) activities for both segmentation and classification. Essentially this step is performed to segment foreground objects (rocks, sediment and wreckage) from the background (seafloor).

Based on these edge statistics, the image is segmented. The next step involves computing Law's Texture Energy measures. Law's texture energy measures are calculated for segmented foreground regions. It uses the following 1-dimensional kernels to calculate texture energy measures.

$$
\begin{array}{lcl}
\text{L5 (Level)} & = & [1\ 4\ 6\ 4\ 1] \\
\text{E5 (Edge)} & = & [-1\ -2\ 0\ 2\ 1] \\
\text{S5 (Spot)} & = & [-1\ 0\ 2\ 0\ 1] \\
\text{R5 (Ripple)} & = & [1\ -4\ 6\ -4\ 1] \\
\text{W5 (Wave)} & = & [-1\ 2\ 0\ -2\ 1]
\end{array}
$$

2-dimensional kernels are created by cross multiplying complement of 1-dimensional kernel with all other kernels.

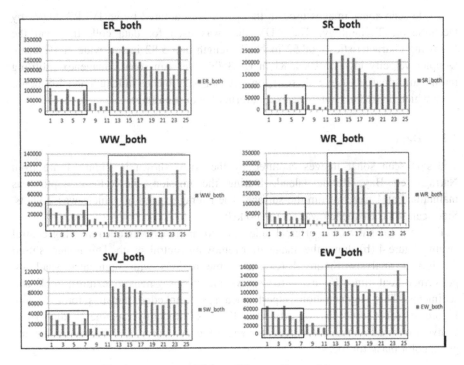

**Fig. 3.** Histogram of Selected Texture Energy Measures

Using the 14 texture energy measures, Information Content analysis was performed and narrowed to 6 features to be used for classification. Information Content provides a numeric representation of 'information' contained in a feature with respect to a feature. Features that contribute very little to classification were eliminated. As the feature we are trying to segment is known a priori, calculating the information content is relatively straight forward. Figure 3 shows the histograms of 6 selected texture energy measures. Each chart represents a 2-d kernel feature applied to samples belonging to rock data (1-7), samples belonging to sediment data (8-11) and samples belonging to wreckage data (12-25). These six kernels provide statistically the largest difference between the samples. Based on this difference between values we can classify them into separate categories.

Classification is a two-step process. In first step we are using Fuzzy C-means clustering algorithm to create separate clusters for input segments. In the second step we identify these cluster based on a priori knowledge of representative cluster feature vectors.

# 4     Results

## 4.1     OceanServer's Iver2 AUV

The side scan sonar images used in this paper are captured by an IVER2 AUVs by OceanServer Technology. The AUV that was used for data collection had the following characteristics - 68.52 inches in length and 5.82 inches wide, a 10 Beam Doppler velocity log (DVL), a Klein L3 3500 side scan sonar, Imagenex profiling multibeam sonar sensors. Side scan sonar sensor is 22 inches in length and 1.6 inches wide which is used to capture seabed in form of acoustic images.

## 4.2     Data

The side scan sonar images captured by the AUV shown in Figure 4 are from Narragansett Bay, Rhode Island. During the mission, the vehicle depth was maintained at 4 meters from the surface. The average speed of vehicle was 2 knots. Side scan sonar frequency was set to 900 kHz.

Figure 4 (a) shows the original side scan sonar image without removing central swath. Figure 4 (b) shows the image after removing central swath. This image is used for further analysis. Figure 4 (c) shows the regions with segmented shadows, performed real time. Figure 4 (d) shows the two segmented textures, rock and sediments. This segmentation is performed based on edge statistics for a region. Figure 4 (e) shows the objects classified as wreckage, sediments and rock. Convention used is blue color mask for wreckage, red color mask for sediments and green color mask for rocks.

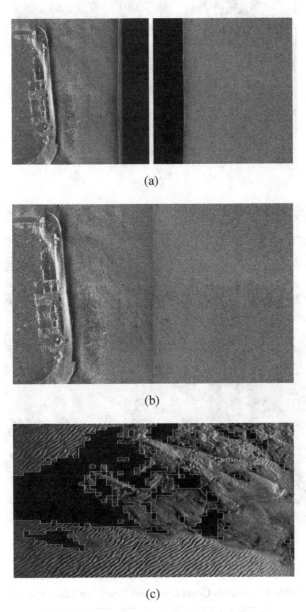

(a)

(b)

(c)

**Fig. 4.** Segmentation and Classification Results

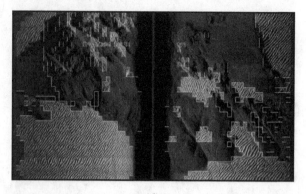

(d)

(e)

**Fig. 4.** (*continued*)

**Table 1.** Raw Data Count Confusion Matrix for Classification

|  | Total Count | Rock | Wreckage | Sediment | Shadow | Floor |
|---|---|---|---|---|---|---|
| **Rocks** | 750 | 639 | 55 | 40 | 0 | 16 |
| **Wreckage** | 900 | 67 | 791 | 14 | 0 | 26 |
| **Sediment** | 370 | 33 | 0 | 330 | 0 | 7 |
| **Shadow** | 450 | 10 | 17 | 0 | 432 | 0 |
| **Floor** | 880 | 25 | 24 | 8 | 0 | 823 |

Table 1, column1 shows the total instances of rocks, sediments, wreckage, shadows and seafloor based on manually identifying 50 x 50 (pixels) regions of the side-scan images that were used for testing the presented approach. These are from multiple runs of the AUV in the same region over the wreckage.

Table 1 also presents the raw classification numbers of our approach. The columns rocks, wreckages, sediments, shadow and floor displays the occurrences found out by the algorithm. For example in first row out of 750 occurrences of rocks 645 were classified as rocks, 52 were classified as wreckage, 38 were classified as sediments, 0 were classified as shadow and 15 were classified as floor. Classification results between rock, wreckage, and sediment overlaps with each other.

The confusion matrix is shown in the Table 2 as percentage of correct classification. The shadow and floor classification towards itself is 95% and 96% respectively. Classification results between rock, wreckage, and sediment overlaps with each other.

**Table 2.** Confusion Matrix for Percentage Classification

|  | Rock | Wreckage | Sediment | Shadow | Floor |
|---|---|---|---|---|---|
| **Rock** | 85.20 | 7.33 | 5.33 | 0 | 2.13 |
| **Wreckage** | 7.44 | 87.89 | 1.55 | 0 | 2.89 |
| **Sediment** | 8.91 | 0 | 89.18 | 0 | 1.89 |
| **Shadow** | 2.22 | 3.77 | 0 | 96 | 0 |
| **Floor** | 2.84 | 2.72 | 0.91 | 0 | 93.53 |

Table 3 shows the amount of under and over segmentation done for every class. Under and over segmentation usually happens at the boundary of the object. For example given wreckage, if algorithm classifies wreckage part as a floor it is said to be under segmentation for wreckage and over segmentation for floor.

**Table 3.** Under and Over Segmentation

| Class | Under Segmentation | Over Segmentation |
|---|---|---|
| **Rock** | 14.80% | 5.19% |
| **Wreckage** | 12.11% | 3.91% |
| **Sediment** | 10.82% | 2.08% |
| **Shadow** | 4.00% | 0.00% |
| **Floor** | 6.47% | 1.98% |

The under segmentation column for rock is the percentage of area which was under rock category but it was not classified as rock. It may be classified as wreckage, sediment, shadow or floor. Under segmentation for wreckage, sediment, shadow and floor was calculated in a similar fashion. The issue of under segmentation where the application is missing some of the features due to window size of 50x50 can be improved by choosing appropriate smaller window size. Over segmentation column for rock is the percentage of area which was not under rock category but still classified as rock. The issue of over segmentation is not significant with a maximum error under 6%. Overall the performance of the algorithm for segmentation is shown to be very effective for the classification of wreckage, sediment, rocks, shadows and floor.

# 5    Conclusion

Autonomous Underwater Vehicles (AUVs) are being deployed to perform complex tasks requiring very high degrees of accuracy and precision. Any sort of adaptive behavior will require on-board processing. Side-scan sonar sensors are capable of producing high-quality acoustic images of the seabed. Being able to process these images quickly would prove to be invaluable to researchers. In this paper we present an approach to real-time segmentation and classification of side-scan data. Effective classification can lead to elegant solution to the SLAM problem as well as creating adaptive behaviors in AUVs.

# References

[1] Daniel, S., Le Leannec, F., Roux, C.: Side Scan Sonar Image Matching. Proceedings IEEE Journal of Oceanic Engineering 3(3), 245–259 (1998)
[2] Celik, T., Tjahjadi, T.: A Novel Method for Side scan Sonar Image Segmentation. Proceedings IEEE Journal of Oceanic Engineering 36(2), 186–194 (2011)
[3] Bagnitsky, A., Inzartsev, A., Pavin, A.: Side Scan Sonar using for Underwater Cables & Pipelines Tracking by Means of AUV, Underwater Technology (UT). In: IEEE Symposium on 2011 Workshop on Scientific Use of Submarine Cables and Related Technologies (SSC), France (April 2011)
[4] Petillot, Y.R., Reed, S.R., Bell, J.M.: Real time AUV Pipeline Detection and Tracking using Side Scan Sonar and Multi-beam Echo-sounder. In: Oceans 2002 MTS/IEEE, vol. 1, pp. 217–222 (2002)
[5] Voorhees, H., Poggio, T.: Computing Texture Boundaries from Image. Nature 333, 364–367 (1988)
[6] Malik, J., Perona, P.: A Computational Model of Texture Segmentation. In: Proceedings CVPR 1989, IEEE Computer Society Conference on Computer Vision and Pattern Recognition, pp. 326–332 (June 1989)
[7] Liu, X., Wang, D.: Texture Classification using Spectral Histograms. IEEE Transactions on Image Processing 12(6), 661–670 (2003)
[8] Karoui, I., Fablet, R., Boucher, J., Augustin, J.: Seabed Segmentation using Optimized Statistics of Sonar Textures. IEEE Transactions on Geoscience Remote Sensor 47(6), 1621–1631 (2009)

# Vision Guidance System for AGV Using ANFIS

Kyunghoon Jung, Inseong Lee, Hajun Song, Jungmin Kim, and Sungshin Kim[*]

School of Electrical Engineering, Pusan National University, Busan, 609-735, Korea
{hooraring,islee,darkhajun,kjm16,sskim}@pusan.ac.kr

**Abstract.** This paper presents a study of vision guidance system of AGV using ANFIS(adaptive network fussy inference system). The vision guidance system is based on driving method that recognize obvious characteristic object like driving line and landmark. It has an advantage in its ability to get more data points than other induction sensor of AGV. However, it is hard to build such a system because the camera used for vision guidance system is severely affected by disturbance factor caused by varying brightness of light. Therefore, we have designed and created a dark-room environment to minimize this disturbance factor. However, due to the reduction of viewing-angle by minimized dark-room design, it is difficult to control using PID which is commonly used in driving control, on fast converted driving line. Therefore, this paper proposes vision guidance method of AGV using ANFIS. AGV modeling is done through kinematic analysis for camera and created dark-room environment. Steering angle by double wheel input is revised through FIS. This data is trained by hybrid ANFIS training method, and it is used for driving control. To do performance test of proposed method, we have conducted series of experiments by creating a simulation model of AGV. We also conducted a comparative analysis of proposed method with PID control.

**Keywords:** vision guidance system, AGV, PID, ANFIS, driving control.

## 1 Introduction

AGV is used at various applications to do tasks that are normally hard, even impossible to be completed by human. Due to these particular features, various industrial automation systems use AGV for loading, unloading, transporting and automating various tasks that normally require human intervention. The development of various automation processes and techniques for industrial production particularly reduced the cost associated to distribution of many industrial goods adding an competitive edge to overall production and distribution scheme. The increasing importance of the AGV in industrial applications contributed the growing number of studies for localization and driving control techniques as well as exploring new guidance system technology related to AGV [1-2].

The AGV guidance method, as a key element of AGV technology is divided into two parts: one is wireless guidance method and the other is wired guidance method. In

---

[*] Corresponding author.

C.-Y. Su, S. Rakheja, H. Liu (Eds.): ICIRA 2012, Part I, LNAI 7506, pp. 377–385, 2012.
© Springer-Verlag Berlin Heidelberg 2012

wireless guidance method, the position of the AGV is calculated by triangulation using the receiver or the transmitter which are installed on the wall, the ceiling and the pillar. However, wireless guidance method is affected by the disturbance element from the environment which introduces the significant level of errors when the receiver or the transmitter processes incoming and transmission signals. Wire guidance method is based on a guided line that is laid on the surface of the floor which the vehicle follows. This method is frequently used in the payload delivery system due to its safety feature. However, the drawback of this method is that it requires the high cost to lay the guiding line. Another drawback of this method is that it has the low-flexibility in reconfiguring itself to adapt to newly changed environment - the guide line needs to be laid again according to new path configuration. Recently, there are growing interests in finding new vision guidance system that is cost-effective. Vision guidance system distinguishes the landmark or guide line from the input image from AGV camera and uses this landmark to guide the AGV. In the past, problem associated with computer processing time of vast amount of image information was the major stumbling block in choosing the right model. However, in recent days, the difficulty in this area has seen major improvement due to the advances of computer technology [3-5].

After the AGV based on optical guidance system obtains images from mounted camera, images get decomposed and feature guidelines and landmarks from the surround environment are identified using image transformation routine. However, due to the limitation inherent to the camera in its ability to resolve different elements of images at varying brightness of the light, some information within image is lost. This paper proposes a noble vision guidance system less affected by disturbance factors caused by different brightness of the light. To achieve this goal, darkroom environment is designed and set up in such way uniform brightness level is maintained throughout the room. The type of controls established for the driving are P control, PI control and PD control. However, they each have the problem. Therefore, the driving control method has been used mainly PID control that integrated advantages. However, PID control method is simple structure and efficient in the linear system, whilst that is difficult to apply in nonlinear environment and varying System. In this paper, optical guidance system using ANFIS(Adaptive neuro-fuzzy inference system) is proposed for effective driving control of AGV according to the driving line to the rapidly changing.

ANFIS commonly is used to optimization in control and prediction because it is possible function approximation of input value and output value. Proposed method measure guide line in acquired image from camera with AGV and then it input to ANFIS calculated center error of AGV and inclination. It learns input value using hybrid learning method and control drive of AGV through output value.

## 2      Model of Vision Guidance System

To verify the proposed method, we designed the simulator of AGV based on vision system as Fig. 1.

Driving method of the AGV model is to use differential wheels that speed difference of two wheels decides to drive AGV whether in a straight line or around a curve. This AGV is controlled after acquiring image that has a constant brightness. However, a general image has a problem of light disturbance which is disadvantage of the camera. To minimize the problem, a camera is equipped with a darkroom in this paper. The kinematic analysis of AGV's movement is required for driving control of AGV. Figure2 shows the analyzed kinematic model of the used AGV.

In Fig. 2, $W_L$ and $W_R$ are angular velocities of each wheel that were calculated from encoders on the AGV. $v_L$ and $v_R$ as linear velocities of each wheel can be derived by Eq. (1) that is composed of angular velocity of each wheel and the wheel radius.

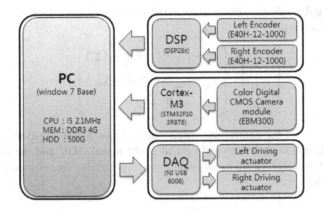

**Fig. 1.** System configuration of used AGV

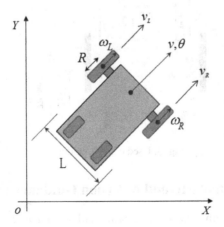

**Fig. 2.** Kinematics of experimental AGV

$$v_L = w_L \times R, v_R = w_R \times R$$

(1)

Linear velocity of AGV can be calculated by Eq. (2) that is composed of values obtained from a breeding Eq. (1).

$$v_k = \frac{v_L + v_R}{2} \tag{2}$$

Angular velocity of AGV can be obtained by calculating Eq. (3) is composed of L, $v_L$ and $v_R$. L means the rotation axis of left-wheel to rotation axis of right-wheel the distance.

$$\Omega_k = \tan^{-1}\left(\frac{v_R - v_L}{L}\right) \tag{3}$$

Using the angular velocity, linear velocity of AGV has moved to distance and angle of Eq. (4) is shown in.

$$\begin{bmatrix} x_{k+1} \\ y_{k+1} \\ \theta_{k+1} \end{bmatrix} = \begin{bmatrix} x_k + v_{Lk} \times \cos(\theta_k + \Omega_k) \\ y_k + v_{Rk} \times \sin(\theta_k + \Omega_k) \\ \theta_k + \Omega_k \end{bmatrix} \tag{4}$$

Eq. (4) can be used for controlling speed value of two-wheel, position value can be determined. Installed darkroom and optical in the actual AGV and the devices were manufactured miniaturization to facilitate mounting. Driving line is used for detection as shown in Fig. (3).

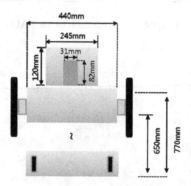

**Fig. 3.** Used camera module

## 3     Driving Control Method of Vision Guidance System

The AGV which contains the camera with darkroom has a short view, and the information of guidance line is changed quickly. Because of this, PID controller doesn't correspond with the control system which considers the error of the AGV's center position and the slope of guidance line. In this paper, to solve such problem, we proposed the driving control method of AGV using ANFIS algorithm [6-8].

### 3.1    Detecting Method of Guidance Line

To control accurately driving of the vision guidance AGV, both the current position of the AGV and target position are required. In this paper, we extract the current position of the AGV and the target position on the guidance line after detecting the guidance line from the image obtained by camera. Fig. 4 shows the detecting method which calculates center error of AGV and the slope of the guidance line.

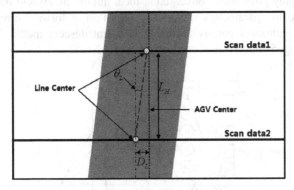

**Fig. 4.** The used method for detecting a guidance line

The center position error presents the distance between the center of the guidance line and the center of AGV, and the slope of a guidance line presents the slope of a guidance line based on the heading of AGV. The center position and the slope of guidance line are calculated by Eq. (5).

$$\theta_L = \tan^{-1}\left(\frac{D_L}{L_H}\right) \tag{5}$$

$$D_L = AGV_{center} - Line2_{center}$$

### 3.2    PID Controller

$$V_d = K_p(D_L + \theta_L) + K_i \int D_L dt \tag{6}$$

PID controller can be made by using center position and the slope of guidance line calculated from captured image. Eq. (6) represents about the equation for PID control used in the paper [9]. $V_d$ is velocity-difference on reference voltage related to velocity. Eq. (7) shows that $V_d$ is used for calculating velocity of wheels on both side.

$$V_R = V_{reference} + V_d$$
$$V_L = V_{reference} - V_d \tag{7}$$

## 3.3    ANFIS Algorithm

ANFIS algorithm was proposed by Jang in 1993, it has excellent performance for function approximation. Recently, it was broadly applied to time series prediction and system control. Optimization methods of ANFIS parameters include gradient training method and hybrid training method. In this paper, hybrid training method which is a combination of different two training rules is used instead of gradient method that is slow and has highly possibility converged at local minimum. Hybrid training method optimizes conclusion parameters using LSE algorithm at forward-direction training and optimizes conditional parameters using Gradient descent method at backward-direction [10]. Fig. 5 show overall configuration of ANFIS.

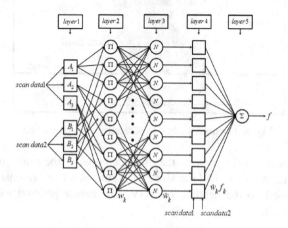

**Fig. 5.** Structure of ANFIS

Rule1 : if SD1 = M, AND SD2 = M, then z = 0.0003799*SD1 + 0.01567*SD2 − 0.07959

Rule2 : if SD1 = M, AND SD2 = L, then z = -0.01267*SD1 + 0.03142*SD2 − 0.6641

Rule3 : if SD1 = L, AND SD2 = M, then z = -0.01268*SD1 - 0.006715*SD2 − 0.2415

Rule4 : if SD1 = L, AND SD2 = L, then z = -0.001255*SD1 − 0.009251*SD2 + 0.7071

Rule5 : if SD1 = VL, AND SD2 = M, then z = -0.04593*SD1 + 0.141*SD2 − 2.67

Rule6 : if SD1 = VL, AND SD2 = L, then z = 0.007312*SD1 + 0.05564*SD2 − 2.077

**Fig. 6.** If-then rule of Sugeno type

If-then rules of used ANFIS are shown in Fig. 6 where SD1 is center position and SD2 is angle of guide line. Data are linguistic variables that has next set {M(middle),L(left),VL(very left)}. Z is input value of double wheel for SD1 and SD2. In this paper, training data are scan-line data and velocity-related voltage gap as input-output data of ANFIS. It is attained by driving AGV through PID control.

# 4    Experimental Result

## 4.1    Experimental Environment

To experiment, we installed two cameras in front of AGV as Fig. 7. First camera slantingly is installed to control PID. Second camera is installed in dark-room to vertical direction from ground.

**Fig. 7.** Experimental AGV

Experiment space is 360 cm × 360 cm. We attached guide line as Fig. 8 and were driving AGV at the speeds of about 16 cm/s. In addition, Experiment separate to get learning data and to recognition learned algorithm.

**Fig. 8.** Experimental environment

## 4.2    Extraction of Learning Data

Experiments are conducted on the same guidance line as PID controller's through the simulation what we designed. The driving result of proposed method is shown in Fig. 9.

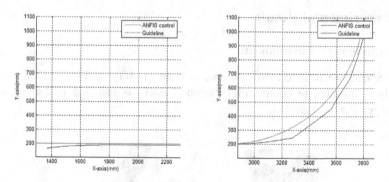

**Fig. 9.** Experimental result

Table 1 shows max value of the error distance and error angle in curved drive which proposed method is applied to.

**Table 1.** Performance of ANFIS control

|  | Traveling angle | Error of the AGV's center |
|---|---|---|
| Max | 15.18 degree | 38mm |

Experimental results show that proposed method can drive stably without the derailment.

## 5    Conclusion

This paper presented the guidance method of AGV using vision guidance system. To develop the vision guidance system, we designed and used the AGV of differential driving type and the camera module. To reduce the disturbance from the brightness of the light for the weakness of the camera, we used the darkroom to detect the guidance line. To track the quickly changed guidance line on the driving effectively, ANFIS algorithm with hybrid learning algorithm is used for the driving control. We analyzed the performance of proposed method through the simulator with the modeling of AGV after the learning that used the measured data based on the PID controller. The experimental results based on the curve-driving which is occurred the most error, we verify the result that proposed method enables AGV to drive stably with reducing the error and no derailment.

**Acknowledgments.** This research was supported by the MKE(The Ministry of Knowledge Economy), Korea, under the Human Resources Development Program for Specialized Navigation/Localization Technology Research Center support program supervised by the NIPA(National IT Industry Promotion Agency) (NIPA-2012-H1502-12-1002).

# References

1. Dogandzic, A., Riba, J., Seco, G., Lee Swindle-hurst, A.: Positioning and Navigation with Applications to Communications. IEEE Signal Proc. Magazine 22(4), 10–11 (2005)
2. Le-Anh, T., De Koster, M.: A review of design and control of automated guided vehicle system. Eur. J. Oper. Res. 171, 1–23 (2006)
3. Vis, I.A.: Survey of Research in the Design and Control of Automated Guided Vehicle Systems. European Journal of Operational Research 170(3), 677–709 (2006)
4. Schulze, L., Wullner, A.: The Approach of Automated Guided Vehicle Systems. Service Operations and Logistics, and Informatics, pp. 522–527 (2006)
5. Crowley, J.: Navigation for an intelligent mobile robot. IEEE Journal of Robotics and Automation, 31–41 (2002)
6. Kim, Y., Kim, S., Lee, K.: Auto Steering Control of Unmanned Container Transport(UCT) with Vision System and Cell-Mideated Immune Algorithm Controller. In: 30th IECON, vol. 3(2), pp. 2987–2991 (2004)
7. Butdee, S., Suebsomran, A.: Automatic Guided Vehicle Control by Vision System. Industrial Engineering and Engineering Management, 694–697 (2009)
8. Lee, Y., Suh, J., Lee, J.: Driving control of an AGV for an automated container terminal using an immunized PID controller based on cell-mediated immunity. Artificial Life and Robotics 9(2), 90–95 (2005)
9. Lee, J., Kim, J., Lee, Y., Lee, K.: A Study on Recognition of Lane and Movement of Vehicles for port AGV Vision System. In: Proceeding of the 2002 IEEE International Symposium on Industrial Electronics, vol. 2, pp. 463–466 (2002)
10. Jang, J.-S.R.: ANFIS: Adaptive-Network-Based Fuzzy Inference System. IEEE Transactions on Systems, Man and Cybernetics 23(3), 665–685 (1993)

# Payload Drop Application of Unmanned Quadrotor Helicopter Using Gain-Scheduled PID and Model Predictive Control Techniques

Iman Sadeghzadeh, Mahyar Abdolhosseini, and Youmin M. Zhang*

Department of Mechanical and Industrial Engineering, Concordia University,
Montreal, QC, Canada
{i_sade,ma_abdol,ymzhang}@encs.concordia.ca
http://users.encs.concordia.ca/~ymzhang/

**Abstract.** In this paper two useful control techniques are applied to a Quadrotor helicopter to control the height and while carrying a payload weighing one-fourth of its total weight as well as dropping the payload at a predetermined time. The first technique used in this paper is the Gain Scheduled Proportional Integral Derivative (GS-PID) control and the Model Predictive Control (MPC) algorithm is studied secondly. Both algorithms showed a very promising performance. Finally, both algorithms are successfully implemented on an unmanned quadrotor helicopter testbed (known as Qball-X4) available at the Networked Autonomous Vehicles Lab (NAVL) of Concordia University for height control to demonstrate effectiveness and stability of the two techniques. The results are presented and compared at the last section of this paper.

**Keywords:** Unmanned Aerial Vehicle (UAV), Payload Drop, Gain-Scheduled PID (GS-PID), Model Predictive Control (MPC).

## 1 Introduction

Unmanned helicopters have become increasingly popular platforms for Unmanned Aerial Vehicles (UAVs). Initially started with linear control algorithms such as PID control [1] or LQR control [2], linear control methods proved not to be promising for the nonlinear quadrotor system. The problem of nonlinear control design has been addressed using several methods such as feedback linearisation [3], sliding mode control [4], Model Predictive Control [5], and back-stepping control [6]. Nevertheless, among these studies, maximum take-off weight has always been assumed to be constant with flight time and the effects of either gradual or abrupt mass variation over the period of flight have not been well investigated in the corresponding literature. The issue of maximum take-off weight variation is of much concern since for some specific applications like search and rescue or firefighting to name but a few, abrupt or gradual mass variation is inevitable. Lack of publication in this area was the main motivation of this work.

---

* Corresponding author.

C.-Y. Su, S. Rakheja, H. Liu (Eds.): ICIRA 2012, Part I, LNAI 7506, pp. 386–395, 2012.
© Springer-Verlag Berlin Heidelberg 2012

Airdrop is a very useful and common manoeuvre (technique) for flying vehicles for different civil and military applications such as: firefighting, delivery of supplies to ground forces and also flight test of hypersonic and glider-type experimental airplanes which need to be mounted on another flying vehicle and to be released in the air. During the recent earthquake in Japan, military helicopters were dumping seawater on a stricken nuclear reactor in north-eastern Japan to cool overheated fuel rods inside its core. Also U.S. Joint Forces Command continues to develop the Joint Precision Airdrop System (JPAS) with new ways of delivering supplies to ground forces while minimizing risks to soldiers. A joint military utility assessment team recently observed and rated airdrops of cargos of 6,000 to 10,000 pounds at Yuma Proving Ground, Ariz [7].

Proportional-Integral-Derivative (PID) controllers are the most widely used controllers in industry. PID controllers are reliable and easy to use and to tune. Gain-Scheduled PID (GS-PID) is a useful technique which can be used for the times when the parameters or the state of the plant can change rapidly. In aerospace application, different portions of the flight envelope can be considered which needs properly tuning the controller gains.

Model Predictive Control is one of the rarest advanced control techniques that is capable of systematic consideration of operational constraints that exist on: Amplitude of the Control Signal, Rate of Change of the Control Signal, and Control Systems Outputs/State Variables. An extensive study of the literature reveals that the era of model predictive control can be broken down into three decades of developments and achievements, rendering the third decades main focus on the development of fast MPC [9].

This paper is structured as follows: Qball-X4, the quadrotor helicopter used in the flight tests is described in Section 2 in terms of system hardware and system software. Equations of motion governing dynamics of the vehicle are also presented. Section 3 explains the GS-PID Control algorithm and discusses how it can be applied to the control of an unmanned quadrotor helicopter over the phase of payload drop. The structure of a discrete-time MPC framework and its implementation is detailed in Section 4. Experimental results are presented in Section 5, followed by conclusions and future work.

## 2    Description and Dynamics of the Quadrotor UAV System

The quadrotor UAV available at the Networked Autonomous Vehicle (NAV) Laboratory in the Department of Mechanical and Industrial Engineering at Concordia University is the Quanser Qball-X4 system shown in "Fig. 1". The quadrotor UAV is enclosed within a protective carbon fiber ball-shape cage (therefore a name of Qball-X4) to ensure safe operation. It features four $10 \times 4.7$ inch propellers and standard RC motors and speed controllers. The user interface to the Qball-X4 is MATLAB/Simulink with QuaRC. The controllers are developed in Simulink environment with QuaRC on the host computer, and these models/controllers are compiled into executable codes and downloaded on the target (Gumstix) seamlessly. The system is composed of three main parts. The subsequent sections describe the corresponding mathematical model for each of the three parts. More information regarding system's hardware and software in [10].

***Electronic Speed Controllers, DC Motors, and Propellers***—The actuators of the Qball-X4 are out-runner brushless motors. The generated thrust $T_i$ of the $i^{th}$ motor is related to the $i^{th}$ PWM input $u_i$ by a first-order linear transfer function

$$T_i = K \frac{\omega}{s + \omega} u_i \qquad (1)$$

where $i = 1\ 2\ 3\ 4$ and $K$ is a positive gain and $\omega$ is the motor bandwidth. $K$ and $\omega$ are theoretically the same for the four motors but this may not be the case in practice. It should be noted that $u_i = 0$ corresponds to zero thrust and $u_i = 0.05$ corresponds to the maximal thrust that can be generated by the $i^{th}$ motor.

***Geometry***—A schematic representation of the Qball-X4 is given in "Fig. 2". The motors and propellers are configured in such a way that the back and front (1 and 2) motors spin clockwise and the left and right (3 and 4) spin counterclockwise. Each motor is located at a distance $L$ from the center of mass $o$ and when spinning, a motor produces a torque $\tau_i$ which is in the opposite direction of that of the motor as shown in "Fig. 2".

The relations between the lift/torques and the thrusts are

$$u_z = T_1 + T_2 + T_3 + T_4; \quad u_\theta = L(T_1 - T_2); \quad u_\phi = L(T_3 - T_4); \quad u_\psi = \tau_1 + \tau_2 + \tau_3 + \tau_3 \qquad (2)$$

The torque $\tau_i$ produced by the $i^{th}$ motor is directly related to the thrust $T_i$ via the relation of $\tau_i = K_\psi T_i$ with $K_\psi$ being a constant. In addition, by setting $T_i = K u_i$ from (1), the relations (2) can be written in a compact matrix form as

$$\begin{bmatrix} u_z \\ u_\theta \\ u_\phi \\ u_\psi \end{bmatrix} = \begin{bmatrix} K & K & K & K \\ KL & -KL & 0 & 0 \\ 0 & 0 & KL & -KL \\ KK_\psi & KK_\psi & -KK_\psi & -KK_\psi \end{bmatrix} \begin{bmatrix} u_1 \\ u_2 \\ u_3 \\ u_4 \end{bmatrix} \qquad (3)$$

where $u_z$ is the total lift generated by the four propellers and applied to the quadrotor UAV in the z-direction (body-fixed frame). $u_\theta$, $u_\phi$, and $u_\psi$ are respectively the applied torques in $\theta$, $\phi$, and $\psi$ directions as illustrated in "Fig. 2". $L$ is the distance from the center of mass to each motor.

***Dynamics of the Quadrotor***—A commonly employed quadrotor UAV model is

$$m\ddot{x} = u_z(\cos\phi \sin\theta \cos\psi + \sin\phi \sin\psi)$$
$$m\ddot{y} = u_z(\cos\phi \sin\theta \sin\psi + \sin\phi \cos\psi)$$
$$m\ddot{z} = u_z(\cos\phi \cos\theta) - mg \qquad (4)$$

where x, y and z are the coordinates of the quadrotor UAV center of mass in the earth-fixed frame. $\theta$, $\phi$, and $\psi$ are the pitch, roll and yaw Euler angles

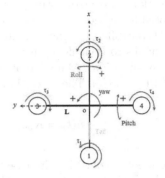

**Fig. 1.** The Qball-X4 quadrotor UAV (Quanser, 2010)

**Fig. 2.** Schematic representation of the Qball-X4

respectively. $m$ is the mass. If we fix the yaw angle to zero ($\psi = 0$) and consider the roll and pitch angles to be very small then a simplified linear model can be obtained in hovering conditions [11]. Therefore the linear model that can be used for control design is given by

$$\ddot{x} = \phi g; \qquad \ddot{y} = -\phi g; \qquad \ddot{z} = \frac{u_z}{m} - g \qquad (5)$$

***The Payload Releasing Mechanism***—For the purpose of payload drop, a servo motor is used in a simple configuration and is installed under the quadrotor battery bay. The PWM signal generated by Gumstix computer controls the servo motor to push/pull the metallic rod attached to servo horn. On the other hand, the payload is hooked to the above mentioned metallic rod and can be released at the desired time.

## 3   Gain-Scheduled Proportional Integral Derivative (GS-PID) Controller

In view of the advantages of widely used Proportional-Integral-Derivative (PID) controller and gain scheduling control strategy in aerospace and industrial

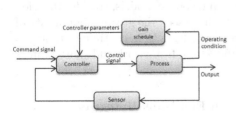

**Fig. 3.** Gain scheduling control structure

**Fig. 4.** Servo based payload releasing mechanism

applications, a control strategy by using gain scheduling based PID controller is proposed for payload drop using the UAV test-bed Qball-X4.

PID controllers are the standard tool in current industrial automation experience thanks to their flexibility making the PID controller capable of being used in many situations. Many simple control problems can be handled very well by using PID control. The algorithm of the PID controller is shown as following

$$u(t) = K_p e(t) + K_I \int_0^t e(\tau)d\tau + K_D \frac{de(t)}{dt} \tag{6}$$

where $u$ is the control variable, $e$ the tracking error defined as $e = u_c - y$ where $u_c$ is the desired output and $y$ is the real output of the system. $K_P$, $K_I$, and $K_D$ are controller gains associated with proportional $(P)$, integral $(I)$, and derivative $(D)$ actions, respectively [12].

Generally, if the change of dynamics in a system/process with the operating condition is known, then it is possible to change the parameters of the controller by monitoring the operating conditions of the process. This approach is called gain scheduling because the scheme was originally used to accommodate changes in process gain only. A block diagram of a control system with gain scheduling mechanism is shown in "Fig. 3".

The idea of relating the controller parameters to auxiliary variables is not new, but the implementation of gain scheduling is still challenging in practice. In this work, for GS-PID controller, a set of pre-tuned gains are applied to the controllers under both payload carrying and payload drop conditions. In order to obtain the best stability and performance of Qball-X4 under both conditions, specially in payload drop scenario, the switching action from one set of pre-tuned PID gains to another set plays a vital role in performance of the helicopter at the moment of releasing the payload. In other words, if this transient (switching) time is held long (more than one second) it can cause the Qball-X4 to overshoot abruptly and cause a crash.

## 4    Discrete-Time Model Predictive Control

In this section the structure of discrete-time Model Predictive Control with integral action is discussed using the state-space methods. There are three general approaches to predictive control design, each featuring a unique model structure. Among finite impulse response and step response models, transfer function models, and state-space models, recent years have seen the growing popularity of predictive control design using state-space methods, both in continuous time and discrete time mainly due to simplicity of the design framework and shortcomings of other mathematical modellings.

### 4.1    State-Space Internal Models with Embedded Integrator

As mentioned previously, model predictive control systems are designed based on a mathematical model of the plant. In this approach, the model to be used in the control system design is taken to be a state-space model. By using a state-space model, the current information required for predicting ahead is represented by the state variable at the current time.

It is assumed that the underlying plant is described by

$$x_m(k+1) = A_m x_m(k) + B_m u(k) , \qquad (7)$$

$$y(k) = C_m x_m(k) , \qquad (8)$$

where $u$ is the control signal or input variable, $y$ is the process output, and $x_m$ is the state variable vector with assumed dimension $n_1$. To meet the offset-free tracking requirement, it is desired to change the model to suit our design purpose in which an integrator is embedded.

Taking a difference operation on both sides of (7) and (8) followed by substitution of (7) in (8) leads to the following state-space model

$$\begin{bmatrix} \Delta x_m(k+1) \\ y(k+1) \end{bmatrix} = \begin{bmatrix} A_m & o_m^T \\ C_m A_m & 1 \end{bmatrix} \begin{bmatrix} \Delta x_m(k) \\ y(k) \end{bmatrix} + \begin{bmatrix} B_m \\ C_m B_m \end{bmatrix} \Delta u(k)$$

$$y(k) = \begin{bmatrix} o_m & 1 \end{bmatrix} \begin{bmatrix} \Delta x_m(k) \\ y(k) \end{bmatrix} , \qquad (9)$$

where $o_m = [0\ 0\ \dots\ 0]$ contains $n_1$ zero entries. The triplet $(A, B, C)$ is called the augmented model, which will be used in the design of predictive control.

## 4.2 Eigenvalues of the Augmented Model

Considering a system of $p$ inputs and $q$ outputs, the characteristic polynomial equation of the augmented model is

$$\rho(\lambda) = det \begin{bmatrix} \lambda I - A_m & o_m{}^T \\ -C_m A_m & (\lambda - 1)I_{q \times q} \end{bmatrix} = (\lambda - 1)^q det(\lambda I - A_m) = 0 , \qquad (10)$$

where the property that the determinant of a block lower triangular matrix equals the product of the determinants of the matrices on the diagonal has been used. Equation (10) illustrates how the eigenvalues of the augmented model are the union of the eigenvalues of the plant model and the $q$ eigenvalues, $\lambda = 1$. This means that there are $q$ integrators embedded into the augmented design model. This is the means by which the integral action is incorporated into an MPC system.

## 4.3 Prediction of State and Output Variables

Upon formulation of the mathematical model, the next step is to calculate the predicted plant output with the future control signal as the adjustable variables. Here, it is assumed that the current time is $k_i$ and the length of the optimization window is $N_p$ as the number of samples. It has been assumed that at the sampling instant $k_i$, $k_i > 0$, the state variable vector $x(k_i)$ is available through measurement; this provides the current plant information. Based on the augmented state-space model $(A, B, C)$, the predicted future state variables, the predicted plant output with the future control signal in a compact matrix form is

$$Y = Fx(k_i) + \Phi \Delta U , \qquad (11)$$

where

$$F = \begin{bmatrix} CA \\ CA_2 \\ CA^3 \\ \vdots \\ CA^{N_p} \end{bmatrix} ; \quad \Phi = \begin{bmatrix} CB & 0 & 0 & \cdots & 0 \\ CAB & CB & 0 & \cdots & 0 \\ CA^2B & CAB & CB & \cdots & 0 \\ & \vdots & & & \\ CA^{N_p-1}B & CA^{N_p-2}B & CA^{N_p-3}B & \cdots & CA^{N_p-N_c}B \end{bmatrix} .$$

## 4.4 Optimization

Having defined a set-point signal $r(k_i)$ or a desired output, the objective of the model predictive controller at sample time $k_i$ is to bring the predicted output as close as possible to the set-point signal, where it is assumed that the set-point signal remains constant over the prediction horizon, or the optimization window. That is to say

$$min \; J = (R_s - Y)^T (R_s - Y) + \Delta U^T \bar{R} \Delta U , \qquad (12)$$

where $J$ denotes the cost function in which the first term is linked to the objective of minimizing the discrepancy between the set-point signal and the predicted output, whereas the second term refers to reducing the control effort while achieving this objective, and $R_s$ is the data vector that contains information regarding the set-point signal. Also, in this expression $\bar{R}$ is a diagonal matrix in the form of $\bar{R} = r_w I_{N_c \times N_c}$  $(r_w \geq 0)$ where $r_w$ acting on the control effort, is used as a tuning parameter for the desired closed-loop performance.

Next is consideration of operational constraints that are frequently encountered in the design of control systems. This is where Model Predictive Control lends itself to; *the systematic handling of operational constraints*. Such constraints are usually presented as linear equalities and inequalities of the control and plant variables. In practice, there are three major types of constraints frequently encountered on the Control Variable Incremental Variation, Amplitude of the Control Variable, and Outputs or State Variables. Finally, the Model Predictive Control in the presence of hard constraints is proposed as finding the parameter vector $\Delta U$ that minimizes

$$J = (R_s - Fx(k_i))^T (R_s - Fx(k_i)) - 2\Delta U^T \Phi^T (R_s - Fx(k_i)) + \Delta U^T (\Phi^T \Phi + \bar{R}) \Delta U ,$$
$$(13)$$

subject to the inequality constraints

$$\begin{bmatrix} M_1 \\ M_2 \\ M_3 \end{bmatrix} \Delta U \leq \begin{bmatrix} N_1 \\ N_2 \\ N_3 \end{bmatrix} , \qquad (14)$$

where the data matrices are

$$M_1 = \begin{bmatrix} -C_2 \\ C_2 \end{bmatrix}; \qquad N_1 = \begin{bmatrix} -U^{min} + C_1 u(k_i - 1) \\ U^{max} - C_1 u(k_i - 1) \end{bmatrix}; \qquad M_2 = \begin{bmatrix} -I \\ I \end{bmatrix};$$

$$N_2 = \begin{bmatrix} -\Delta U^{min} \\ \Delta U^{max} \end{bmatrix}; \qquad M_3 = \begin{bmatrix} -\Phi \\ \Phi \end{bmatrix}; \qquad N_3 = \begin{bmatrix} -Y^{min} + Fx(k_i) \\ Y^{min} - Fx(k_i) \end{bmatrix}. \qquad (15)$$

In principle, all the constraints are defined within the prediction horizon; this allows modifying each at the beginning of each optimization window. However, in order to reduce the computational load it is sometimes preferred to keep the constraints invariant with time and chose a smaller set of sampling instants at which to impose the constraints, instead of all the future samples [13].

## 4.5 A Numerical Solution Using Quadratic Programming

The standard quadratic programming problem has been extensively studied in the literature [14], and this is a field of extensive investigation in its own right. The required numerical optimization solution for the Model Predictive Control is often viewed as an obstacle in the application of MPC due to limited computational power available, Nevertheless, Hildreths Quadratic Programming Procedure proves to be computationally effective. This procedure was proposed for solving a group of problems collectively referred to as *Primal-Dual* to which the family of active set methods belongs [15]. If the active set could be identified in advance, then the iterative procedure would be shortened; hence in the specific structure of the Hildreths QP procedure deployed in this work, it has been tries to address this pre-identification requirement.

## 5 Experimental Results

In this paper two control techniques are studied and implemented in real time on a quadrotor UAV for performance comparison, and to demonstrate effectiveness of the control algorithms a number o experiments are set up. In the first set of experiments, focus is on the PID control, starting with a single PID controller to take over control of the quadrotor over the phases of take-off, flight with payload onboard, payload drop, and finally landing. Although the single PID controller was capable of keeping the desired height,it was not able to eliminate undesired overshoot at the moment of payload drop. Hence, the single PID controller is replaced by the GS-PID controller to improve performance of the system at that specific moment, i.e. payload drop.

For the same objective to evaluate performance of the quadrotor helicopter the third experiment is conducted and flight tested using the MPC controller. The take-off and payload carrying flight phases were better than a single PID and GS-PID in terms of offset-free tracking and takeoff overshoot, but compared to GS-PID the overshoot was 3.4% more at the time of payload drop as shown in "Fig. 5". This can be decreased by proper tuning of the controller using the

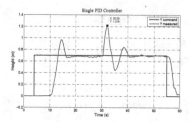
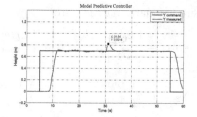

**Fig. 5.** Flight testing result with single PID control

**Fig. 6.** Flight testing result with MPC

controllers' design parameters such as the prediction horizon $N_p$, the control horizon $N_c$, and control change penalizing parameter $r_w$ in the cost function. As illustrated in "Fig. 5" for the case of a single PID controller the quadrotor does maintain the desired height but is not satisfactory in performance since 73% of overshoot happens over the course of payload drop. On the other hand, the MPC controller noticeably improves system's reaction to payload drop as shown in "Fig. 6", eliminating vertical jerk at the instant of payload dump with 17% of overshoot at the moment of payload drop. Despite, the best performance is achieved using GS-PID with 13.6% of overshoot at the time of release as presented in "Fig. 7".

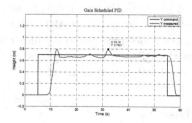

**Fig. 7.** Flight testing result with gain-scheduled PID control

## 6    Conclusion and Future Work

Among all the three controllers studied in this paper, the GS-PID is suggested for the scenario of payload drop. However fine tuning of gains as well as healthy and fully charged Li-Po batteries are two essential factors affecting system's behavior. For instance, not fully charged battery packs can have a direct effect on the performance of fine tuned controller gains and deviate them from the desired values. Also, due to the nature of non model-based switching techniques such as the GS-PID, there is no guarantee of system stability. Therefore, the future work will be mainly focused on application of Linear Parameter Varying (LPV) technique to the quadrotor helicopter in order to address the issue of control system's stability and performance. In addition, the MPC control technique proved to perform well. However, in this work treatment of the setpoint as a constraint on the state variable or output was not practised because of limited computational power onboard the Qball-X4 quadrotor helicopter; hence, an extension to this work will be implementation of hard constraints on the control system's output, i.e. its height.

**Acknowledgments.** This work is partially supported by the Natural Sciences and Engineering Research Council of Canada (NSERC) through a Strategic Project Grant and a Discovery Project Grant.

# References

1. Erginer, B., Altug, E.: Modeling and PD Control of a Quadrotor VTOL Vehicle. In: IEEE Intelligent Vehicles Symposium, pp. 894–899 (2007)
2. Oner, K., Cetinsoy, E., Unel, M., Aksit, M., Kandemir, I., Gulez, K.: Dynamic Model and Control of a New Quadrotor UAV with Tilt-wing Mechanism. In: World Academy of Science, Engineering and Technology (2008)
3. Efe, M.O.: Robust Low Altitude Behavior Control of a Quadrotor Rotorcraft Through Sliding Modes. In: Mediterranean Conf. on Control and Automation (2007)
4. Bouadi, H., Bouchoucha, M., Tadjine, M.: Sliding Mode Control Based on Backstepping Approach for an UAV Type-quadrotor. In: World Academy of Science, Engineering and Technology (2007)
5. Abdolhosseini, M., Zhang, Y., Rabbath, C.A.: An Efficient Model Predictive Control Scheme for an Unmanned Quadrotor Helicopter. In: International Conference on Unmanned Aircraft Systems (2012)
6. Madani, T., Benallegue, A.: Backstepping Control for a Quadrotor Helicopter. In: International Conference on Intelligent Robots and Systems, pp. 3255–3260 (2006)
7. Soldiers Magazine (2007),
   http://findarticles.com/p/articles/mi_m00XU/is_5_62/ai_n27236124/
8. Maciejowski, J.M.: Predictive Control with Constraints. Prentice-Hall (October 2000)
9. Lee, J.H.: Model Predictive Control: Review of the Three Decades of Development. International Journal of Control, Automation, and Systems 9(3), 415–424 (2011)
10. Quansers Rapid Control prototyping (QuaRC), http://www.quanser.com/quarc
11. Sadeghzadeh, I., Mehta, A., Chamseddine, A., Zhang, Y.: Active Fault-Tolerant Control of a Quadrotor UAV Based on Gain-Scheduled PID Control. In: IEEE Canadian Conference on Electrical and Computer Engineering (2012)
12. Astrom, K.J., Wittenmark, B.: Adaptive Control, 2nd edn. Dover (2008)
13. Wang, L.: Model Predictive Control System Design and Implementation Using MATLAB. Springer, London (2009)
14. Fletcher, R.: Practical Methods of Optimization, 2nd edn. John Wiley & Sons (1987)
15. Dimitrov, D., Wieber, P.B., Stasse, O., Ferreau, H.J., Diedam, H.: An Optimized Linear Model Predictive Control Solver, pp. 309–318. Springer (2010)

# UAV Flight Performance Optimization Based on Improved Particle Swarm Algorithm

Rong Xie, Xiaoyan Wang, Xinmin Wang, and Hongshen Wei

School of Automation, Northwestern Polytechnical University,
710129, Xi'an, China

**Abstract.** As the energy problem becomes more and more serious, it is necessary to do research on energy saving. In order to achieve the desired height economically and quickly, the two key factors of fuel consumption and time cost are considered. First, the mathematical model of UAV's climbing trajectory is established, the fuel consumption and time cost are considered as the performance optimization indexes. Second, the UAV's performance optimization method based on the improved particle swarm algorithm is proposed, then the problem of UAV's performance optimization is turned into the problem of constrained multi-parameter optimization, and the climbing trajectory with the optimal comprehensive index is determined. Finally, the proposed method is used in a certain type of UAV, and the simulation results show, compared with the conventional method, the proposed method saves more operation costs and has better superiority.

**Keywords:** UAV, climbing trajectory, performance optimization, improved particle swarm algorithm.

## 1 Introduction

In the recent years, the energy problem is becoming more and more serious, and the aerial fuel's price is keeping increasing, fuel saving has became one of the important goals of the flight performance optimization, so it is necessary to study how to improve the operating efficiency and decrease the time cost are very important. As the flight velocity, fuel consumption and time cost of the climbing trajectory have great influence on the whole flight process, the climbing trajectory is taken as the research object. The task of the climbing trajectory performance optimization is to design the best reference climbing trajectory.

There are some research results in trajectory performance optimization. An optimization technique based on the improved genetic algorithm was studied to calculate the fastest climbing trajectory[1], A genetic algorithm was used to design the optimization trajectory in the vertical flight in order to saving the fuel[2].But all the methods are devoted to find the optimization trajectory based on single index, it is difficult to achieve the goal that get the shortest climbing time and the least fuel consumption in the same time.

C.-Y. Su, S. Rakheja, H. Liu (Eds.): ICIRA 2012, Part I, LNAI 7506, pp. 396–403, 2012.
© Springer-Verlag Berlin Heidelberg 2012

The rate of UAV's fuel consumption increases rapidly with the velocity increasing. If only use the fastest climbing rate as the optimization performance index may lead to the climbing rate becomes too fast, and the fuel consumption becomes too high; Contrary to the above situation, if only use the least fuel consumption as the optimization performance, the climbing rate becomes too slow, and the climbing time becomes long. As the result, the climbing time and the fuel consumption are comprehensively considered in this paper, and the weighted sum (comprehensive operation cost) are used as the performance index to optimize the UAV's climbing trajectory.

The entire climbing trajectory can be divided into several parts according to the constant attitude $\Delta h$, the parameter of each height is optimized using the particle swarm algorithm. Particle swarm optimization (PSO) is an optimization method based on the swarm intelligence, it is widely used in various optimization fields as it has following advantages: flexible, efficient and easy to find the global optimal solution[3,4]. An improved particle swarm optimization (IPSO) is used to optimize the UAV's climbing trajectory in this paper, and the optimal reference climbing trajectory is determined according to the specific optimization task.

## 2    Mathematic Model

Assume the UAV doing no-sideslip particle motion in this period, and ignore the influence of the wind, the UAV's dynamic equations are:

$$m\frac{dv}{dt} = T\cos\alpha - L\sin\alpha - D - mg\sin\gamma \tag{1}$$

$$mv\frac{d\gamma}{dt} = T\sin\alpha + L\cos\alpha - mg\cos\gamma \tag{2}$$

and the kinematic equations are:

$$\frac{dx}{dt} = v\cos\gamma \tag{3}$$

$$\frac{dm}{dt} = q_h \tag{4}$$

In the above equations, $m$ is the weight of the UAV, $x$ and $h$ are the horizontal voyage and the climb height respectively, $v$ is the airspeed of the UAV (As ignoring the influence of the wind, the airspeed is the ground speed ), $\theta$, $\alpha$ and $\gamma$ are pitch angle, angle of attack and flight-path angle respectively, $L$, $D$ and $T$ are the lift force, resistance and side force respectively, and $q$ is the rate of fuel consumption per unit time at the height $h$.

The climb trajectory can be divided into several parts according to the equal height $\Delta h$. Assume the UAV flies from point $h_i$ to point $h_{i+1}$, the change of airspeed and the path tilt angle are: $v_i \rightarrow v_{i+1}$, $\gamma_i \rightarrow \gamma_{i+1}$ $\Delta t_i$, $\Delta x_i, \Delta W_{f_i}$ are the flight time, horizontal displacement and the fuel consumption respectively:

$$\Delta t_i = \frac{m(v_{i+1} - v_i)}{T \cos \alpha_i - L \sin \alpha_i - D - mg \sin \gamma_i} \tag{5}$$

$$\Delta x_i = \frac{1}{2}(v_i + v_{i+1})\Delta t_i \cos \gamma_i \tag{6}$$

$$\Delta W_{f_i} = \frac{1}{2}(q_{h_i} + q_{h_{i+1}})\Delta t_i \tag{7}$$

$c_t$ and $c_f$ are the flight cost weight of the time and the fuel consumption, and the flight cost of the climbing trajectory is:

$$J_i = c_t \Delta t_i + c_f W_{f_i} \tag{8}$$

Because the value of the angle of attack is small (usually less than $10°$), so the equation (5) can be simplified as:

$$\Delta t_i = \frac{m(v_{i+1} - v_i)}{T_i - D_i - mg \sin \gamma_i} \tag{9}$$

So the time cost $t$ of the climbing trajectory, the total horizontal voyage $x$, and the total fuel consumption $W$ are be expressed respectively as:

$$t = \sum_{i=1}^{n} \Delta t_i, \; x = \sum_{i=1}^{n} \Delta x_i, \; W_f = \sum_{i=1}^{n} \Delta W_{f_i} \tag{10}$$

The minimum value of $J$ in equation (10) can be used as the optimization performance index:

$$J = \min \sum_{i=1}^{n} J_i \tag{11}$$

## 3    Optimization of the Climbing Trajectory Based on the IPSO

### 3.1    Improvement of the PSO

In the PSO, every member of the swarm, namely particle flies in the multi-dimensional search space at a certain speed, and keeps updating the information of its own position and velocity based on its own inertia, experience and social experience.

The dimension of the particle swarm is the dimension of the search space; each dimension represents a parameter which is preparative optimized.

Assuming the number of the search space's dimension is $n$, the position and the velocity of particle $i$ at time $t$ can be expressed as[5]:

$$X_i(t) = [x_{i1}(t),...x_{ij}(t), x_{i,j+1}(t),...x_{in}(t)] \tag{12}$$

$$V_i(t) = [v_{i1}(t),...v_{ij}(t), v_{i,j+1}(t),...v_{in}(t)] \tag{13}$$

The exon $j$ dimension position updating formula of particle $i$ at time $t+1$ is:

$$x_{ij}(t+1) = x_{ij}(t) + v_{ij}(t+1) \tag{14}$$

In the PSO, $y_i$ is used to record the optimal search position of the particle $i$, and the $j$ th dimension velocity updating formula of particle $i$ can be expressed as:

$$v_{ij}(t+1) = v_{ij}(t) + c_1 r_{1j}(t)[y_{ij}(t) - x_{ij}(t)] + c_2 r_{2j}(t)[\hat{y}_j(t) - x_{ij}(t)] \tag{15}$$

In the equation (15), $c_1$ and $c_2$ are the accelerating constant of the cognitive portion and the social portion respectively, they are also optional parameter; $r_{1j}$ and $r_{2j}$ are the random number of interval [0,1], which satisfies uniform distribution.

To ensure the PSO has a good convergence, the inertial weight $w$ can be introduced to improve the PSO, then the equation (14) can be changed to:

$$v_{ij}(t+1) = w v_{ij}(t) + c_1 r_{1j}(t)[y_{ij}(t) - x_{ij}(t)] + c_2 r_{2j}(t)[\hat{y}(t) - x_{ij}(t)] \tag{16}$$

To ensure the algorithm have good convergence and strong exploration ability, the dynamic method of linear reduction is used to set $w$, and the changing formula is[6]:

$$w(t) = (w(0) - w(n_t)) \frac{(n_t - t)}{n_t} + w(n_t) \tag{17}$$

In the equation (17), $n_t$ is the maximum step of the algorithm execution iteration time, $w(0)$ is the final inertial weight (the value of it is small), $w(t)$ is the weight at time $t$, and $w(0) > w(n_t)$.

The flow chart of the IPSO is as follows:

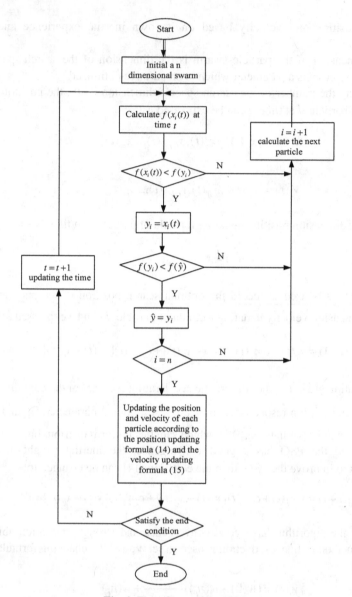

**Fig. 1.** Flow Chart of the IPSO

## 3.2    Climbing Trajectory Optimization Based on IPSO

If the global optimization is made to the entire climbing trajectory, the whole optimization parameters of the entire height will be included; this may lead to the dimension of the particle swarm become too large. For example, if the number of preparative optimization parameters is $m$, and the entire height is divided into $n$ parts, then the number of preparative optimization parameters in the entire climbing trajectory is $m * n$ ,it is also the dimension of the particle swarm. If the dimension of the particle swarm is too large, it will increase the complexity of the algorithm, decrease the search speed, and even not find the optimal solution.

In this paper, the parameter is optimized in each part, so the dimension of the particle swarm is $m$ , the dimension of the particle swarm is greatly reduced from $m * n$ to $m$ .The optimization problem of the climbing trajectory should be converted into the optimization problem of the equation (18):

$$J = \min \sum_{i=1}^{n} J_i \approx \sum_{i=1}^{n} (\min J_i) \tag{18}$$

In order to make the UAV climb to the target height as soon as possible, the maximum thrust climbing method is used in this research, the specific steps of the optimization algorithm is as follows:

(1) The initial speed is known, aiming at the first part $(h_0, h_1)$, the initial speed $v_1$ in the next part $(h_1, h_2)$ can be obtained by optimizing the value of $(v_1, \gamma_0)$;

(2) $\Delta x_0$ and $\Delta W_{f_0}$ can be obtained according to equation (6) and (7), then the comprehensive cost $J_0$ in the first part $(h_0, h_1)$ can be calculated by equation (18);

(3) To every part $(h_i, h_{i+1})$, repeat step (1);

(4) Repeat step (2), the optimal climbing trajectory can be obtained by optimizing and synthesizing every part of height.

## 4    Simulation and Analysis

The proposed method is used in a certain type of UAV to optimize its climbing trajectory. The UAV climbs from $1000\,m$ to $10000\,m$ at the initial speed of $0.4\,Ma$ , and the constraint conditions are:

$$\begin{cases} 0.4 \leq Ma \leq 0.7 \\ 0° \leq \alpha \leq 10° \\ 0° \leq \theta \leq 11° \end{cases}$$

The optimization step chosen in this paper is $\Delta h = 500m$ , and the optimization results are shown in Fig.2 and Fig.3:

Compared with the high altitude, the fuel consumption is higher in the low altitude, so the climbing rate in the low altitude should grow quickly, and climb at the high flight-path angle so that the UAV can deorbits the low altitude area which has higher fuel consumption. As shown in the Fig.2, the climb rate is highest in the

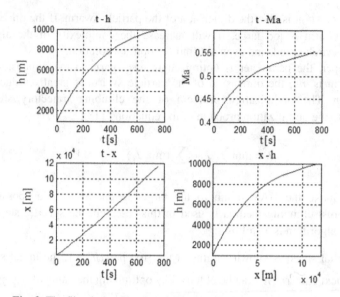

**Fig. 2.** The Simulation Results of Climbing Trajectory Based on IPSO

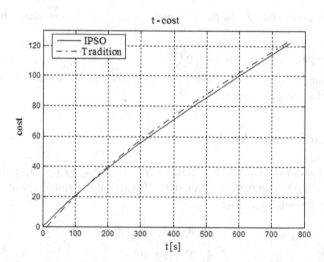

**Fig. 3.** Comparison of Climbing Trajectory Cost by Using the IPSO and the Traditional Algorithm

low altitude, and decreases gradually with the height increasing; The climb rate decreases quickly when the UAV reaches a certain height in order to determine the optimal climbing trajectory according to the performance index. The analysis conclusions verify the reliability of the results and the feasibility of the research method.

As shown in the Fig.3, at the beginning in climbing, the cost of IPSO is slightly larger than the cost of the traditional algorithm; After 200s, the cost of IPSO is smaller than the cost of the traditional algorithm. As a whole, the cost of IPSO is smaller than the cost of the traditional algorithm about 2.3%.

## 5     Conclusion

In this paper, the IPSO is researched to solve the optimization problem of the UAV's climbing trajectory, the time cost and fuel consumption are considered synthetically. The operation cost of the UAV's climbing trajectory is saved to a certain degree, and the climbing speed is also increased. The reliability and superiority of the IPSO is verified by example calculation.

## References

1. Tsuchiya, T.: Real-time Flight Trajectory Optimization and Its Verification in Flight. Journal of Aircraft 46(4), 1468–1470 (2009)
2. Yong, E.-M., Tang, G.-J., Chen, L.: Rapid Trajectory Optimization for Hypersonic Reentry Vehicle via Gauss Pseudo Spectral Method. Yuhang Xuebao/Journal of Astronautics 29(6), 1766–1772 (2008)
3. Pidaparti, R.M.: Aircraft Structural Integrity Assessment through Computational Intelligence Techniques. Journal of Aircraft 2, 131–147 (2006)
4. El-Zonkoly, A.M.: Optimal Tinning of Lead-lag and Fuzzy Logic Power System Stabilizers using Particle Swarm Optimization. Expert Systems with Applications 36(2), 2097–2106 (2009)
5. Liu, Z.-X., Liang, H.: Parameter Setting and Experimental Analysis of the Random Number in Particle Swarm Optimization Algorithm. Control Theory and Applications 27(11), 1489–1496 (2010)
6. Cai, J., David Pan, W.: On Fast and Accurate Block-based Motion Estimation Algorithms using Particle Swarm Optimization. Information Sciences 197(1), 53–64 (2012)

# Trajectory Optimization of Unmanned Aerial Vehicle in Vertical Profile

Jianying Gong and Rong Xie

School of Automation, Northwestern Polytechnical University,
710129, Xi'an, China

**Abstract.** The new optimization algorithm of UAV's vertical profile is proposed in this paper. The optimization model of the UAV is established. The optimization index functions are constructed using the Hamilton function. As the problem of high dimensional two-point boundary value which cannot be solved by the analytical method, but solved by means of an appropriate numerical method, an improved deepest descent algorithm based on the steepest descent method and the Newton method is proposed. The flight trajectory optimization problem is solved by using the proposed new algorithm, the gradient descent method is improved and the convergence rate is accelerated. Finally, the feasibility and the effectiveness of the flight trajectory optimization algorithm are verified by the simulation.

**Keywords:** UAV, trajectory optimization, improved steepest descent algorithm, Newton method, steepest descent method.

## 1    Introduction

In some cases, the problem of UAV's trajectory optimization in vertical profile is very complex [1][2]. Numerical algorithms which have constraint computational parameters are often used to solve the problem. The goal of trajectory optimization is to determine the best optimal way for an object to move from Point A to Point B while both minimizing the performance indexes and according with the object's basic equations of motion. The optimal parameters of the flight performance are speed, altitude and thrust setting, etc. These optimal parameters constitute the optimal flight path, and directly affect the economic costs [3][4]. Flight performance optimization can be expressed as an optimal control problem, which needs to limit the boundaries of the restrictions of the objective function [5].

In the indirect optimization method, there is a problem of high dimensional two-point-boundary-value model and the value of time integral variable is no longer equal after the iterative calculation [6][7]. To solve this problem, an improved deepest descent algorithm based on the steepest descent method and the Newton method is proposed, the algorithm can improves the gradient descent method and accelerates the convergence rate by introducing the energy to simplify UAV mathematical equations.

The aircraft model represents by a set of simplified component models which are derived from the experimental data. A simplification to the aircraft model is required in order to convert the problem to an optimization problem of sufficient scope to

C.-Y. Su, S. Rakheja, H. Liu (Eds.): ICIRA 2012, Part I, LNAI 7506, pp. 404–410, 2012.

reach the generalize conclusions. The optimization model is transformed into a nonlinear programming problem, and the constrained problem could be change into an unconstrained problem by introducing the generalized Lagrange multiplier method.

## 2    Mathematic Models

### 2.1    UAV Model

To simply the problem of flight path optimization, the UAV's flight path is constrained only in vertical profile. Using a flat earth coordinate system, the aircraft's equations of motion are as follows [4][8]:

$$\frac{dV}{dt} = \frac{T\cos\alpha - D}{m} - g\sin\gamma \tag{1}$$

$$\frac{d\gamma}{dt} = \frac{T\sin\alpha + L}{mV} - \frac{g\cos\gamma}{V} \tag{2}$$

$$\frac{dx}{dt} = V\cos\gamma \tag{3}$$

$$\frac{dh}{dt} = V\sin\gamma \tag{4}$$

$$\frac{dm}{dt} = -f \tag{5}$$

where $\alpha$ is the angle of attack, $\gamma$ is the flight path angle, $x$ and $h$ are represent the position of the UAV, $V$ is the velocity, $m$ is the mass of the UAV, $f$ is the fuel flow rate, and $T$ is the engine thrust.

The lift $L$ and the resistance $D$ are defined as follows [4][9]:

$$L \approx 0.5\rho V^2 SC_L \tag{6}$$

$$D \approx 0.5\rho V^2 SC_D \tag{7}$$

where $C_L$ and $C_D$ are the lift coefficient and resistance coefficient respectively. They are both assumed to be continuous function of the angle of attack $\alpha$.

### 2.2    Objective Function

In the flight performance optimization, the vertical profile needs to be optimized according to the fixed distance, initial positions, velocity, and flight path angle.

Because the value of the angle of attack is small (usually less than $10°$ ), so the equation (1) can be simplified as:

$$\Delta t_i = \frac{m(v_{i+1} - v_i)}{T_i - D_i - mg \sin \gamma_i} \tag{8}$$

Therefore the objective function can be expressed as the minimum time in the fixed distance[10]:

$$J = \int_0^{t_f} \frac{m(v_{i+1} - v_i)}{T_i - D_i - mg \sin \gamma_i} dt \tag{9}$$

where $t_f$ is the terminal time.

# 3    Optimization

## 3.1    Optimization Model

The necessary conditions for trajectory optimization and flight control are derived from the Hamiltonian system which defined as follows:

$$H(X, u, \lambda, t) = \lambda_V \dot{V} + \lambda_\gamma \dot{\gamma} + \lambda_x \dot{x} + \lambda_h \dot{h} + \lambda_m \dot{m} \tag{10}$$

where $X = \begin{bmatrix} V & \gamma & x & h & m \end{bmatrix}$, $\lambda = \begin{bmatrix} \lambda_V & \lambda_\gamma & \lambda_x & \lambda_h & \lambda_m \end{bmatrix}$, $\lambda_V$, $\lambda_\gamma$, $\lambda_x$, $\lambda_h$, $\lambda_m$ are the Lagrangian coefficients; $u = \begin{bmatrix} \alpha & T \end{bmatrix}$, $u$ is the control vector.

In order to solve the resulting optimal control problem, the state, co-state and the optimal conditions and the required boundary conditions are developed.

The state differential equation can be expressed as:

$$\dot{X} = \frac{\partial H(X, u, \lambda, t)}{\partial \lambda} \tag{11}$$

The co-state differential equation can be expressed as:

$$\lambda = -\frac{\partial H(X, u, \lambda, t)}{\partial X} = \begin{bmatrix} \dfrac{\lambda_V}{m} \dfrac{\partial D}{\partial V} + \dfrac{\lambda_\gamma}{mV^2} \dfrac{\partial L}{\partial V} - \lambda_x \cos \gamma - \lambda_h \sin \gamma \\[2mm] \lambda_V g \cos \gamma - \dfrac{\lambda_\gamma g \sin \gamma}{V} - \lambda_x V \sin \gamma + \lambda_h V \cos \gamma \\[2mm] 0 \\[2mm] 0 \\[2mm] -\dfrac{T \cos \alpha - D}{m^2} - \dfrac{T \sin \alpha + L}{m^2 V} \end{bmatrix} \tag{12}$$

The control equation is formulated as:

$$\frac{\partial H\left(X,u,\lambda,t\right)}{\partial u}=\frac{\left[\frac{\lambda_{\gamma}}{mV}\left[\frac{\partial L}{\partial \alpha}+T\cos\alpha\right]-\frac{\lambda_{V}}{m}\left(T\sin\alpha+\frac{\partial D}{\partial \alpha}\right)\right]}{\frac{\cos\alpha}{m}\lambda_{V}+\frac{\sin\alpha}{mV}\lambda_{\gamma}}=0 \tag{13}$$

The state and control path constraints are:

$$h_{L}\leq h\left(x,u,t\right)\leq h_{H}$$

and the state and control variable box constraints are:

$$x_{L}\leq x\left(t\right)\leq x_{H}$$

$$u_{L}\leq u\left(t\right)\leq u_{H}$$

## 3.2    The Improve Steepest Descent Algorithm

The optimization model can be transformed into the unconstrained nonlinear programming by using the generalized multiplier method. The objective function is converted to a non-quadratic convex function. An Improved deepest descent algorithm based on the steepest descent method and the Newton method is adopted here to solve the resulting optimal control problem.

The iterative function $\{x_{k}\}$ is defined as follows:

$$x_{k+1}=x_{k}-\lambda_{k}f\left(x_{k},t\right) \tag{14}$$

Where the function $f\left(x_{k},t\right)$ can be expressed as:

$$f\left(x_{k},\tau\right)=\begin{cases} g_{k}=\nabla f\left(x_{k},t\right) & \dfrac{g_{k}}{g_{k-1}}>0 \\[2mm] g_{k}G_{k}^{-1} & \dfrac{g_{k}}{g_{k-1}}\leq 0 \end{cases} \tag{15}$$

where the $g_{k}$ is the grads of the function $f\left(x_{k},t\right)$. $G_{k}=\nabla g_{k}(x_{k})$, and $G_{k}$ is the grads of the $g_{k}$ at the $x_{k}$.

The limitation of iterative step $\lambda_{k}$ is defined as follows:

$$H\left(x_{k}+\lambda_{k}f\left(x_{k},t\right)\right)=\min_{\lambda\geq 0} H\left(x_{k}+\lambda f\left(x_{k},t\right)\right) \tag{16}$$

The steps of the proposed algorithm of iteration are designed as follows:

Step 1: Select the initial point $x_0$ and $g_0$, give the termination error $\varepsilon > 0$, and set $k = 0$.

Step 2: Calculate the value of $g_k$, if $\|g_k\| \le \varepsilon$, then stop and output the $x_k$, otherwise go to Step 3.

Step 3: Calculate the value of $G_k$, search the solution of the function $f(x_k, \tau)$ and $\lambda_k$, then letbe $x_{k+1} = x_k - \lambda_k f(x_k, t)$ and $k = k+1$.

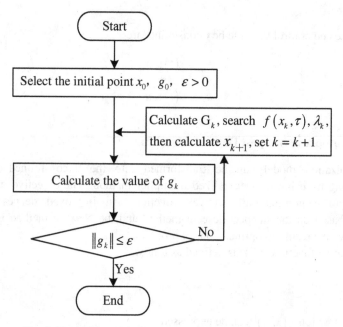

**Fig. 1.** Flow Chart of the Improved Deepest Descent Algorithm

## 4    Simulation and Analysis

Simulation conditions are given, and the initial and terminal conditions of the aircraft are:

$h(0) = 1\,\text{km}, \quad \gamma(0) = 0.1\,\text{rad}, \quad V(0) = 100\,\text{m/s},$

$x(0) = 0\,\text{km}, \quad m(0) = 100\,\text{kg},$

$h(t_f) = 10\,\text{km}, \quad V(t_f) = 160\,\text{m/s}.$

The flight distance is 100km; the change of height is 9km.

The simulation results of the vertical profile are shown as follows:

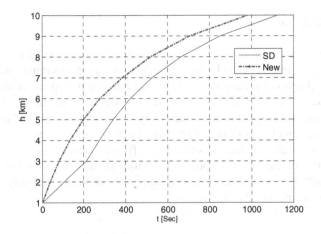

**Fig. 2.** The Simulation Results of $t - h$ using the Steepest Descent Algorithm (SD) and the Improved Steepest Descent Algorithm (NEW))

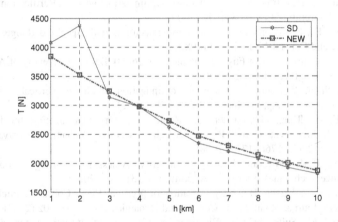

**Fig. 3.** The Simulation Results of $T - h$ using the Steepest Descent Algorithm (SD) and the Improved Steepest Descent Algorithm (NEW))

The optimal trajectory of both methods is consistent with the actual flight characteristic. To achieve optimal climbing results of UAV, the climbing rate should grow quickly in the low altitude but grow slowly in the high altitude. As shown in Fig.2, the curve of the climbing rate is accordance with the trend by using the ISD, at the beginning of the curve of the climbing rate doesn't meet with the trend by using SD. The flight time of 1121.3s by using SD method, compared with the flight time is 892.1s using the ISD to achieve the target height about 10km, which means the climbing time is shorter by using ISD than SD.

With the high increment, the ideal curve of the trust should increases relatively smooth. As shown in the Fig.3, compared with the curves simulated by using SD, the curve of trust by using the ISD is smoother.

# 5    Conclusion

The trajectory optimization problem is transformed into a nonlinear programming problem in this paper. The problem is changed into a unconstrained non-quadratic programming problem by using the generalized Lagrange multiplier method, and look for the optimal solution with improved steepest descent algorithm. The proposed optimization method is feasible and effective by theoretical analysis and mathematical simulation. The simulation results show that the ISDA has the advantages of good generality, less calculation, high velocity, high efficiency and etc.

The research of the UAV's optimal trajectory should not only limit on purely theory, the further work which needs to be done is to do some relatively experiments to verify to correctness of the algorithm .

# References

1. Tsuchiya, T.: Real-time Flight Trajectory Optimization and Its Verification in Flight. Journal of Aircraft 46(4), 1468–1470 (2009)
2. Erzberger, H., Lee: Constrained Optimum Trajectories with Specified Range. Journal of Guidance and Control 13(1), 78–85 (1980)
3. Fang, Z.: Aviation Aircraft Flight Dynamics, pp. 26–30. Beijing University of Aeronautics and Astronautic Press, Beijing (2010)
4. Wu, S., Shen, Y., Guo, S.: Trajectory optimization of aircraft vertical flight profile. Control Theory and Applications 9(4), 380–386 (1992)
5. Yong, E.-M., Tang, G.-J., Chen, L.: Rapid Trajectory Optimization for Hypersonic Reentry Vehicle via Gauss Pseudo Spectral Method. Yuhang Xuebao/Journal of Astronautics 29(6), 1766–1772 (2008)
6. Pidaparti, R.M.: Aircraft Structural Integrity Assessment through Computational Intelligence Techniques. Journal of Aircraft 2(3), 131–147 (2006)
7. Komduur, H.J., Visser, H.G.: Optimization of Vertical Plane Cobralike Pitch Reversal Maneuvers. Journal of Guidance, Control and Dynamics 25(4), 693–702 (2002)
8. L'Afflitto, A., Sultan, C.: Applications of Calculus of Variations for aircraft and Spacecraft Path Planning. In: Proc. AIAA Guidance Navigation and Control Conference, Chicago, IL (August 2009)
9. Lizzagra, M.I.: Spatially Deconflicted Path Generation for Multiple UAVs in a Bounded Airspace. In: Position, Location and Navigation Symposium, 2008 IEEE/ION (2008)
10. Wu, S., Guo, S.: Research on Civil aircraft flight performance optimization. Civil Aircraft Design and Resarch (3), 1–5 (1990)

# Trajectory Tracking with Model Predictive Control for an Unmanned Quad-rotor Helicopter: Theory and Flight Test Results

Mahyar Abdolhosseini, Youmin M. Zhang, and Camille Alain Rabbath

Department of Mechanical and Industrial Engineering, Concordia University,
Montreal, QC, Canada
{ma_abdol,ymzhang}@encs.concordia.ca, rabbath@bell.net
http://users.encs.concordia.ca/~ymzhang/

**Abstract.** In this paper, by effective use of a fast Quadratic Programing solver known as Hildreth's Quadratic Programing Procedure, as well as adaptation of an Integral-Action-Embedded Model Predictive controller, it has been tried to design an autopilot control system for the purpose of three-dimensional trajectory tracking of an unmanned quad-rotor helicopter. Eventually, to demonstrate effectiveness and performance of the designed autopilot in addition to the simulation results, the suggested constrained MPC framework is successfully implemented on an unmanned quad-rotor helicopter testbed (known as Qball-X4) available at the Networked Autonomous Vehicles Lab. (NAVL) of Concordia University for three-dimensional autonomous flights of the system.

**Keywords:** Trajectory Tracking, Model Predictive Control (MPC), Offset-free Tracking, Quad-rotor Helicopter.

## 1 Introduction

With the abilities such as hovering and taking-off and landing vertically, unmanned helicopters have become increasingly popular platforms for Unmanned Aerial Vehicles (UAVs). For the control of a quad-rotor helicopter, various control techniques have been proposed. Initially started with linear control algorithms such as PID control [1] or LQR control [2], linear methods proved not to be promising for the nonlinear quad-rotor system. The problem of nonlinear control design has been addressed using several methods such as feedback linearization [3], sliding mode control [4], and back-stepping control [5]. Nevertheless, among those nonlinear control methods, capability of explicitly dealing with operational constraints prevalent in a control system is yet hardly achievable.

Model Predictive Control, or Model-Based Predictive Control (MPC or MBPC as it is sometimes known), is one of the rarest advanced control techniques that is capable of systematic consideration of operational constraints that exist on: Amplitude of the Control Signal, Rate of Change of the Control Signal, and Control Systems' Outputs/State Variables [6].

C.-Y. Su, S. Rakheja, H. Liu (Eds.): ICIRA 2012, Part I, LNAI 7506, pp. 411–420, 2012.
© Springer-Verlag Berlin Heidelberg 2012

Due to the specific structure of MPC which will be explained in the following sections, its successful implementation is highly dependent on availability of sufficient computational power [7]. Furthermore, MPC strongly relies on an internal precise mathematical model of the vehicle under control. Since the real plant is invariably nonlinear, there exists always some degree of discrepancy between the mathematical model and the plant itself; therefore implementation of offset-free tracking control system with MPC is seldom attainable in UAVs. In some literature it has been tried to meet the requirement of offset-free tracking by incorporating an integral-action controller in the outermost control loop so as to compensate for model uncertainties. Basically this control structure is a decentralized design which simply adds control inputs from both the MPC and the Integral algorithms [8]. Although the steady state error can be eliminated by integral gain tuning, this control structure is incapable of constraint handling since the integrator dynamics is not included in QP formulation [9]. In this work, by deployment of a fast QP solver known as Hildreths Quadratic Programing Procedure, as well as adaptation of an Integral-Action-Embedded MPC controller, it has been tried to address the main two drawbacks of MPC just mentioned.

This paper is structured as follows. Qball-X4, the quad-rotor helicopter used in the flight tests is described in Section 2, in terms of system hardware, system software; equations of motion governing dynamics of the vehicle are also presented. In Section 3 the structure of a discrete-time model predictive control framework and its implementation are detailed. Simulation results reflecting hard operational constraints corresponding to the specific hardware of the quad-rotor under study will be discussed in Section 4. Finally, experimental results are presented in Section 5, followed by concluding remarks and future work in Section 6.

## 2    Qball-X4: An Unmanned Quad-rotor Helicopter

### 2.1    Non-linear Model of the Quad-rotor Helicopter

As detailed in [10], based on the balance of forces and moments, equations of motion governing dynamics of a quad-rotor helicopter with respect to an earth-fixed coordinate system can be represented in matrix form as:

$$\ddot{x} = \frac{(\sin\psi\sin\phi + \cos\psi\sin\theta\cos\phi)u_1 - K_1\dot{x}}{m}$$

$$\ddot{y} = \frac{(\sin\psi\sin\theta\cos\phi - \cos\psi\sin\phi)u_1 - K_2\dot{y}}{m}$$

$$\ddot{z} = \frac{(\cos\phi\cos\theta)u_1 - K_3\dot{z}}{m} - g \tag{1}$$

$$\ddot{\phi} = \frac{(u_3 - K_4\dot{\phi})l}{I_z}; \qquad \ddot{\theta} = \frac{(u_2 - K_5\dot{\theta})l}{I_y}; \qquad \ddot{\psi} = \frac{(u_4 - \tilde{K}_6\dot{\psi})}{\tilde{I}_z} \tag{2}$$

where $K_i$, $i = 1$, $2$, $\ldots$, $6$ are the drag coefficients associated with the aerodynamic drag force, $l$ is the distance between the center of gravity of the quad-rotor and the center of each propeller, and $c$ is the thrust-to-moment scaling factor. Note that the drag coefficients are negligible at low speeds. Also, $I_x$, $I_y$, and $I_z$ represent the moments of inertia along $x$, $y$, and $z$ directions. For computational convenience the inputs to the system $u_i$, $i = 1$, $2$, $3$, $4$ are defined as:

$$\begin{bmatrix} u_1 \\ u_2 \\ u_3 \\ u_4 \end{bmatrix} = \begin{bmatrix} 1 & 1 & 1 & 1 \\ 0 & -1 & 0 & 1 \\ -1 & 0 & 1 & 0 \\ 1 & -1 & 1 & -1 \end{bmatrix} \begin{bmatrix} F_1 \\ F_2 \\ F_3 \\ F_4 \end{bmatrix} \tag{3}$$

The actuators of the quad-rotor helicopter are brushless DC motors. The relation between the thrust and the PWM input is:

$$F_i = K_{motor} \frac{w_{motor}}{s + w_{motor}} u_{PWM} \tag{4}$$

where $K_{motor}$ is a positive gain and $w_{motor}$ represents the actuator bandwidth.

## 2.2  Model Reduction to Minimize Computational Demands

In this section, to reduce the burden of calculations in order to render application of the MPC to unmanned aerial systems feasible, it has been tried to decouple the six-degree-of-freedom equations of motion governing dynamics of the quad-rotor so that the system is described by four second-order differential equations, in which the translational longitudinal displacement $x$ is coupled with the rotational pitching motion $\theta$, the translational lateral displacement $y$ is coupled with the rotational rolling motion $\phi$, and the translational vertical displacement along the normal axis $z$ is treated separately and independently from the other two. That is to say:

$$\ddot{x} = \frac{u_1 \sin \theta}{m}; \; \ddot{y} = \frac{u_1 \sin \phi}{m}; \; \ddot{z} = \frac{u_1}{m} - g; \quad \ddot{\phi} = \frac{u_3 l}{I_x}; \; \ddot{\theta} = \frac{u_2 l}{I_y}; \; \ddot{\psi} = \frac{u_4}{I_z} \tag{5}$$

With this new subset of equations, $\sin \theta$, $\sin \phi$, and $\frac{u_1}{m} g$ will be taken as manipulated inputs of their corresponding equations of 5. Next, the new versions of equations are discretized with a proper discretization time step, preserving dynamics of the quad-rotor system.

## 2.3  Qball-X4: System's Software vs. Hardware

The Quansers Qball-X4 is a quad-rotor helicopter platform suitable for a wide variety of UAV research and development applications. This innovative rotary wing vehicle design is propelled by four DC motors fitted with 10 inch propellers. The entire system is enclosed within a spherical protective carbon fiber cage of 68 cm as shown in Fig. 1. The protective cage is a crucial feature of such a system, since this unmanned vehicle was designed for use in an indoor laboratory where there are typically many close-range hazards (including other vehicles).

To have sensor measurements on-board and drive the motors, the Qball-X4 utilizes Quanser's onboard avionics data acquisition card (DAQ), the HiQ, and the embedded single-board computer, Gumstix. QuaRC, Quanser's real-time control software, the interface to the Qball-X4 in MATLAB/Simulink environment, allows researchers and developers to rapidly develop and test controllers on actual hardware through the MATLAB/Simulink interface [11].

**Fig. 1.** The Quanser Qball: A Quad-rotor Helicopter Platform

# 3   Discrete-Time Model Predictive Control

In this section the structure of discrete-time MPC with integral action is discussed using the state-space model.

## 3.1   State-space Internal Models with Embedded Integrator

As mentioned previously, model predictive control systems are designed based on a mathematical model of the plant. In this approach, the model to be used in the control system design is taken to be a state-space model. By using a state-space model, the current information required for predicting ahead is represented by the state variable at the current time.

It is assumed that the underlying plant is described by

$$x_m(k+1) = A_m x_m(k) + B_m u(k) \,, \tag{6}$$

$$y(k) = C_m x_m(k) \,, \tag{7}$$

where $u$ is the control signal or input variable, $y$ is the process output, and $x_m$ is the state variable vector with assumed dimension $n_1$. To meet the offset-free tracking requirement, it is desired to change the model to suit our design purpose in which an integrator is embedded as inspired by the work in [12].

Taking a difference operation on both sides of (6) and (7) followed by substitution of (6) in (7) leads to the following augmented state-space model

$$\begin{bmatrix} \Delta x_m(k+1) \\ y(k+1) \end{bmatrix} = \begin{bmatrix} A_m & o_m^T \\ C_m A_m & 1 \end{bmatrix} \begin{bmatrix} \Delta x_m(k) \\ y(k) \end{bmatrix} + \begin{bmatrix} B_m \\ C_m B_m \end{bmatrix} \Delta u(k)$$

$$y(k) = \begin{bmatrix} o_m & 1 \end{bmatrix} \begin{bmatrix} \Delta x_m(k) \\ y(k) \end{bmatrix} , \tag{8}$$

where $o_m = \begin{bmatrix} 0 & 0 & \dots & 0 \end{bmatrix}$ contains $n_1$ zero entries. This augmented model will be used in the design of predictive control.

## 3.2   Eigenvalues of the Augmented Model

Considering a system of $p$ inputs and $q$ outputs, the characteristic polynomial equation of the augmented model is

$$\rho(\lambda) = det \begin{bmatrix} \lambda I - A_m & o_m{}^T \\ -C_m A_m & (\lambda - 1)I_{q \times q} \end{bmatrix} = (\lambda - 1)^q det(\lambda I - A_m) = 0 , \tag{9}$$

where the property that the determinant of a lower triangular block matrix equals the product of the determinants of the matrices on the diagonal has been used. Equation (9) illustrates how the eigenvalues of the augmented model are the union of the eigenvalues of the plant model and the $q$ eigenvalues, $\lambda = 1$. This means that there are $q$ integrators embedded into the augmented design model. This is the means by which the integral action is incorporated into an MPC system.

## 3.3   Prediction of State and Output Variables

Upon formulation of the mathematical model, the next step is to calculate the predicted plant output with the future control signal as the adjustable variables. Here, it is assumed that the current time is $k_i$ and the length of the optimization window is $N_p$ as the number of samples. It has been assumed that at the sampling instant $k_i$, $k_i > 0$, the state variable vector $x(k_i)$ is available through measurement; this provides the current plant information. Based on the augmented state-space model $(A, B, C)$, the predicted future state variables, the predicted plant output with the future control signal in a compact matrix form is

$$Y = Fx(k_i) + \Phi \Delta U , \tag{10}$$

where

$$F = \begin{bmatrix} CA \\ CA_2 \\ CA^3 \\ \vdots \\ CA^{N_p} \end{bmatrix} ; \quad \Phi = \begin{bmatrix} CB & 0 & 0 & \dots & 0 \\ CAB & CB & 0 & \dots & 0 \\ CA^2B & CAB & CB & \dots & 0 \\ \vdots & & & & \\ CA^{N_p-1}B & CA^{N_p-2}B & CA^{N_p-3}B & \dots & CA^{N_p-N_c}B \end{bmatrix} .$$

## 3.4  Optimization

Having defined a set-point signal $r(k_i)$ or a desired output, the objective of the model predictive controller at sample time $k_i$ is to bring the predicted output as close as possible to the set-point signal, where it is assumed that the set-point signal remains constant over the prediction horizon, or the optimization window. That is to say

$$min \ J = (R_s - Y)^T(R_s - Y) + \Delta U^T \bar{R} \Delta U \ , \tag{11}$$

where $J$ denotes the cost function in which the first term is linked to the objective of minimizing the discrepancy between the set-point signal and the predicted output, whereas the second term refers to reducing the control effort while achieving this objective, and $R_s$ is the data vector that contains information regarding the set-point signal. Also, in this expression $\bar{R}$ is a diagonal matrix in the form of $\bar{R} = r_w I_{N_c \times N_c}$   $(r_w \geq 0)$ where $r_w$ acting on the control effort, is used as a tuning parameter for the desired closed-loop performance.

Next is consideration of operational constraints that are frequently encountered in the design of control systems. This is where Model Predictive Control lends itself to; *the systematic handling of operational constraints*. Such constraints are usually presented as linear equalities and inequalities of the control and plant variables. In practice, there are three major types of constraints frequently encountered on the Control Variable Incremental Variation, Amplitude of the Control Variable, and Outputs or State Variables. Finally, the Model Predictive Control in the presence of hard constraints is proposed as finding the parameter vector $\Delta U$ that minimizes

$$J = (R_s - Fx(k_i))^T(R_s - Fx(k_i)) - 2\Delta U^T \Phi^T(R_s - Fx(k_i)) + \Delta U^T(\Phi^T\Phi + \bar{R})\Delta U \ , \tag{12}$$

subject to the inequality constraints

$$\begin{bmatrix} M_1 \\ M_2 \\ M_3 \end{bmatrix} \Delta U \leq \begin{bmatrix} N_1 \\ N_2 \\ N_3 \end{bmatrix} \ , \tag{13}$$

where the data matrices are

$$M_1 = \begin{bmatrix} -C_2 \\ C_2 \end{bmatrix}; \qquad N_1 = \begin{bmatrix} -U^{min} + C_1 u(k_i - 1) \\ U^{max} - C_1 u(k_i - 1) \end{bmatrix}; \qquad M_2 = \begin{bmatrix} -I \\ I \end{bmatrix};$$

$$N_2 = \begin{bmatrix} -\Delta U^{min} \\ \Delta U^{max} \end{bmatrix}; \qquad M_3 = \begin{bmatrix} -\Phi \\ \Phi \end{bmatrix}; \qquad N_3 = \begin{bmatrix} -Y^{min} + Fx(k_i) \\ Y^{min} - Fx(k_i) \end{bmatrix}. \tag{14}$$

In principle, all the constraints are defined within the prediction horizon; this allows modifying each at the beginning of each optimization window. However, in order to reduce the computational load it is sometimes preferred to keep the constraints invariant with time and chose a smaller set of sampling instants at which to impose the constraints, instead of all the future samples [13].

## 3.5   A Numerical Solution Using Quadratic Programming

The standard quadratic programming problem has been extensively studied in the literature [14], and this is a field of extensive investigation in its own right. The required numerical optimization solution for the MPC is often viewed as an obstacle in the application of MPC due to limited computational power available, Nevertheless, Hildreths Quadratic Programming Procedure proves to be computationally effective. This procedure was proposed for solving a group of problems collectively referred to as *Primal-Dual* to which the family of active set methods belongs [15]. If the active set could be identified in advance, then the iterative procedure would be shortened; hence in the specific structure of the Hildreths QP procedure deployed in this work, it has been tried to address this pre-identification requirement.

## 4   Simulation and Experimental Results

*Simulation*—As mentioned previously, there are four effectors in the form of four brushless DC motors that provide the helicopter with lift as well as directional thrust. These DC motors each, receives a PWM signal changing with time within the range of 0 to 0.1 for nominal operation.

The lateral and longitudinal controllers' manipulated variables are $\sin\phi$ and $\sin\theta$, respectively. Since the model reduction technique employed is based on the assumption that these angles stay within the vicinity of zero in almost all flight maneuvers-except for some really abrupt changes of direction or orientation which is not the case-it is crucial to keep Euler angles within the tight presumed range as close as possible to zero. Otherwise, the reduced model will not precisely represent the non-linear dynamics of the quad-rotor helicopter, thus rendering the control system unstable or stable but with degraded performance. Fig. 2 illustrates system's performance.

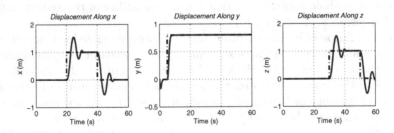

**Fig. 2.** Simulation Results - 3D Tracking Performance of the MPC Autopilot Control System

*Experiment*—In this section, except for some fine tuning parameters which have been slightly changed, the very same simulated controller is implemented onto the ball-X4 unmanned quad-rotor helicopter available at the Networked

Autonomous Vehicles Lab without any major modification. (NAVL) of Concordia University for three-dimensional autonomous flight of the unmanned system. The same square trajectory has been fed into the control system as a predefined track to follow.

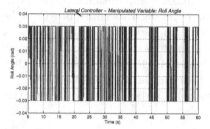
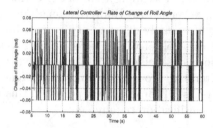

**Fig. 3.** Constraints on the Amplitude of the Control Variable - Lateral/Longitudinal Controller

**Fig. 4.** Constraints on the Control Variable Incremental Variation - Lateral/Longitudinal Controller

Generally speaking, implementation of hard constraints on the control variable incremental variation $\Delta U$ is considered if there is limitation on how fast an actuator can respond to a change of the setpoint signal; which is the case in almost all practical applications. However, this type of constraint may be implemented exclusively tighter than what the actuators manufacturer has just mentioned for their designed effector. This tight treatment of constraints on rate of change of control, as long as not jeopardizing stability of the control system, makes a plant respond smoothly to the setpoint signal changes. This has been practiced in the design of this autopilot. As stated earlier, $\sin \phi$ ad $\sin \theta$ are the manipulated variables of the lateral and longitudinal controllers, respectively. In order to guarantee smooth flight, they are confined to stay within a range of -0.03 to +0.03 as shown in Fig. 4. In contrast, this constraint has been removed for the altitude-hold controller so that not to lose agility of the system in flight level changes, as suggested by Fig. 6.

Implementation of hard constraints on the control variable incremental variation $U$ is a must since violation of such limits means actuator saturation which is not acceptable in control. For the lateral as well as longitudinal controllers, $\sin \phi$ and $\sin \theta$ as the manipulated variables should not deviate much from zero so as to maintain validity of linearizations and the model reduction technique used. This requirement has been met by implementation of hard constraints on them to stay within -2 to +2 degrees range or -0.03 to +0.03 rad as shown in Fig. 3. For the altitude-hold controller this has been implemented as $-12 < Lift < +4$ so as not to violate the $0.06 < PWM < 0.1$ range of DC motors' PWM signal. This is suggested by Fig. 5. Eventually, the offset-free tracking capability of the autopilot control system along a square trajectory for the unmanned quad-rotor helicopter is illustrated in Fig. 7.

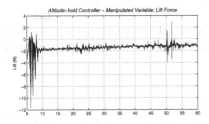
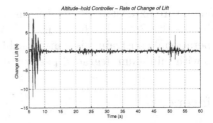

**Fig. 5.** Constraints on the Amplitude of the Control Variable - Altitude-hold Controller

**Fig. 6.** Constraints on the Control Variable Incremental Variation - Altitude-hold Controller

Due to the constrained optimal control framework developed, as presented in Fig. 8, all the four PWM signals have stayed within their acceptable rages throughout the flight test, leaving the 0.095 to 1 margin for robustness against probable disturbances prevalent in the experimental environment.

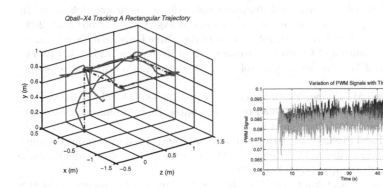

**Fig. 7.** Autonomous Flight: The Quad-rotor Helicopter 3D Tracking Performance

**Fig. 8.** Illustration of Four PWM Signals Staying within the Operational Rang: 0.06 - 0.1

## 5    Conclusion and Future Work

In this work, by deployment of a fast QP solver known as Hildreths Quadratic Programing Procedure, as well as adaptation of an Integral-Action-Embedded MPC controller, it has been tried to address the main two drawbacks of MPC known as on availability of hight computational power as well as a precise mathematical model of the control plant for the sake of offset-free tacking. Basically this control structure is a centralized design. In contrast to the decentralized design, it does not simply adds control inputs from MPC and Integral algorithms but instead, the integral action is incorporated in the formulation. This way, the steady state error can be eliminated and the control structure is capable of constraint handling since the integrator dynamics is included in the QP formulation.

The future extension of this work is suggested to be deployment of the Constrained MPC Controller for Fault Tolerant Control studies where consideration of operational constraints is indispensable to fulfil a mission under faulty conditions with minimum degraded performance.

# References

1. Erginer, B., Altug, E.: Modeling and PD Control of a Quadrotor VTOL Vehicle. In: IEEE Intelligent Vehicles Symposium, pp. 894–899 (2007)
2. Oner, K., Cetinsoy, E., Unel, M., Aksit, M., Kandemir, I., Gulez, K.: Dynamic Model and Control of a New Quadrotor UAV with Tilt-wing Mechanism. In: World Academy of Science, Engineering and Technology (2008)
3. Efe, M.O.: Robust Low Altitude Behavior Control of a Quadrotor Rotorcraft through Sliding Modes. In: Mediterranean Conf. on Control and Automation (2007)
4. Bouadi, H., Bouchoucha, M., Tadjine, M.: Sliding Mode Control Based on Backstepping Approach for an UAV Type Quadrotor. In: World Academy of Science, Engineering and Technology (2007)
5. Madani, T., Benallegue, A.: Backstepping Control for a Quadrotor Helicopter. In: International Conference on Intelligent Robots and Systems, pp. 3255–3260 (2006)
6. Lee, J.H.: Model Predictive Control: Review of the Three Decades of Development. International Journal of Control, Automation, and Systems 9(3), 415–424 (2011)
7. Maciejowski, J.M.: Predictive Control with Constraints. Prentice-Hall (October 2000)
8. Abdolhosseini, M., Zhang, Y., Rabbath, C.A.: An Efficient Model Predictive Control Scheme for an Unmanned Quad-rotor Helicopter. In: International Conference on Unmanned Aircraft Systems (2012)
9. Liu, Y.C.: Model Predictive Control with Integral Control and Constraint Handling for Mechatronic Systems. In: International Conference on Modelling, Identification and Control, Taiwan, pp. 424–429 (2010)
10. Lai, L.C., Yang, C.C., Wu, C.J.: Time-Optimal Control of a Hovering Quad-Rotor Helicopter. Journal of Intelligent and Robotic Systems, 115–135 (2006)
11. Quansers Rapid Control prototyping (QuaRC), http://www.quanser.com/quarc
12. Zhang, Y.M., Jiang, J.: Integrated Design of Reconfigurable Fault-Tolerant Control Systems. AIAA Journal of Guidance, Control, and Dynamics, 133–136 (2001)
13. Wang, L.: Model Predictive Control System Design and Implementation Using MATLAB. Springer, London (2009)
14. Fletcher, R.: Practical Methods of Optimization, 2nd edn. John Wiley & Sons (1987)
15. Dimitrov, D., Wieber, P.B., Stasse, O., Ferreau, H.J., Diedam, H.: An Optimized Linear Model Predictive Control Solver, pp. 309–318. Springer (2010)

# Parallel Tracking and Mapping with Multiple Cameras on an Unmanned Aerial Vehicle

Adam Harmat, Inna Sharf, and Michael Trentini

**Abstract.** This paper presents the development and testing of a new multi-camera system designed for tracking and mapping aboard a small unmanned aerial vehicle. In order to be resistant to failure from loss of tracking, the large field of view cameras are positioned in such a way as to cover a large portion of the vehicle's surroundings. The proposed algorithm is tested indoors, and it is found that the system achieves good performance. More importantly, it is shown that the system is resistant to failure by comparing it to a system with fewer cameras that loses tracking during certain portions of the test.

**Keywords:** Multiple camera, tracking, mapping, omnidirectional vision, SLAM.

## 1 Introduction

Small Unmanned Aerial Vehicles (UAVs) have become popular in the last few years as they promise to replace conventional aircraft in many inspection, surveillance, and videography tasks. In order to be useful, they need to exhibit some degree of autonomy, such as self-stabilization, localization, and planning. The higher the degree of autonomy required, the more sensors the aircraft needs to carry in order to satisfy its mission. However, small UAVs have a very limited payload, and hence the sensors suite needs to be chosen carefully to save weight.

Visual cameras have emerged as a popular sensor choice due to the fact that they are extremely lightweight, consume little power and collect a large amount of data in each image. A serious drawback, however, is that the captured images need significant post-processing in order to extract useful information about the state of the vehicle. In most approaches, features in an image need to be tracked over time, and the more features that can be tracked the greater the accuracy achieved by the system [1]. To this end, cameras with large fields of view (FOV) are becoming popular since the probability of finding good features to track increases with the amount of scene visible in an image.

In this paper, we introduce a visual tracking and mapping system for a small UAV that aims to achieve robustness by tracking an extremely large number of points through two means: using multiple cameras configured in an arbitrary arrangement, and fitting those cameras with ultra-wide angle fisheye lens with FOV greater than 180 degrees. Using the existing implementation of Parallel Tracking and Mapping (PTAM) [2], a highly successful monocular visual SLAM system, we describe the steps required to implement the aforementioned modifications. Finally, an experimental flight is shown which demonstrates the system's

C.-Y. Su, S. Rakheja, H. Liu (Eds.): ICIRA 2012, Part I, LNAI 7506, pp. 421–432, 2012.

resistance against failure due to image feature starvation, a common problem for visual systems.

## 2    Related Work

### 2.1    UAVs and Vision

To give a full overview of the differnet ways vision sensors have been integrated with UAVs would be prohibitive, hence here we focus on some key areas of UAV autonomy. Some of the earliest work in this field was at Carnegie Mellon University with their Autonomous Helicopter Project [3]. They investigated a host of problems, such as stability control, takeoff, landing and mapping, all based on vision fused with other sensors. More recently, several projects have taken a minimalist approach towards using vision onboard helicopters, such as [4] which uses a single camera as the only exteroceptive sensor to build a map and localize itself while flying. Finally, UAVs have recently succeeded in flying indoors where position estimates from GPS are not available [5]. Virtually all of the work in the literature uses either a monocular or stereo camera setup for vision sensing. We have found one paper where more than two cameras with non-overlapping views are used for the position estimate of a small aerial vehicle [6], however, there are strong assumptions made about the arrangement of the cameras.

### 2.2    Omnidirectional Cameras

The two principal ways of capturing images with large FOVs are with catadioptric cameras and fisheye lenses. Catadioptric camera systems combine a camera, a refractive element (a lens), and a reflective element (a mirror) to enable the capture of large FOV images. Fisheye lenses are simply lenses with a very wide FOV, and use purely refractive elements to achieve this. A thorough examination of both catadioptric and fisheye cameras is presented in [7], which also deals with camera calibration and introduces the Taylor camera model, which we use in the present work.

Omnidirectional cameras have been used in several areas of robotics, such as in controlling aerial vehicles through the calculation of vanishing points in [8] and tracking the horizon in [9]. In [10], a stereo catadioptric camera is developed and tested on a ground robot, while in [11] depth measurements are made using stereo fisheye cameras. Finally, [1] compares the performance of monocular SLAM with a standard camera to a catadioptric camera, and concludes that the latter outperforms the former.

### 2.3    Multiple Camera Rigs

In almost all work on camera-equipped vehicles, the cameras are positioned so they view the same scene, allowing the application of textbook multi-view geometry methods for calibrating the relative poses of the cameras. The problem of using, and thus calibrating, multiple cameras in arbitrary arrangements has received much less focus. There are two calibration methods that appear in the literature for multiple camera rigs with non-overalpping views: the frame-to-frame estimation method and the monocular SLAM based method.

Examples of the frame-to-frame method include a multiple camera rig constructed to form a single spherical camera for UAV motion estimation in [6], and the approach of [12]. In all cases, frame-to-frame rotation and position is estimated for all the cameras, and the relative transforms between them are solved with a linear equation. The monocular SLAM based method is described in [13], and involves three phases: independent tracking of the cameras, map alignment, and nonlinear refinement. One of the cameras in the system is designated as a reference camera, and the poses of the other cameras are solved relative to that camera. We used an approach very similar to this during the calibration of our experimental setup.

## 3 Approach

### 3.1 Parallel Tracking and Mapping

Parallel Tracking and Mapping was developed to track a single camera in a relatively confined area for the purposes of augmented reality. It uses a keyframe-based approach to visual SLAM rather than the filter-based approaches that were popular before its introduction. Keyframe-based algorithms have been proven to significantly outperform filter-based approaches in almost all cases [14]. This is because tracking a large number of image points between fewer frames in the keyframe approach yeilds more information about the state of the camera and the world than tracking a small number of image points between more frames in the filter approach. Being the first succesful keyframe-based visual SLAM approach, and having released the source code online, PTAM has become very popular both as a complete solution and as a starting point for the development of other SLAM algorithms.

The workflow of PTAM is as briefly described here. When a new camera image is received, the current estimate of the pose of the camera is updated from a simple motion model. Next, some of the potentially visible map points are projected into the image, and correspondences are searched for at four different image scales. Once all correspondences have been made, a refined camera pose is calculated by reducing the correspondence errors through nonlinear minimization. Finally, if a new keyframe is requested by the map maker, the tracker creates it from the current data and hands it off.

When the mapper receives a new keyframe, it first searches for any map points that the tracker did not have time to find. Next, it finds the keyframe nearest the newly added one, and new map points are created through triangulation. The new keyframe and its nearest neighbors, as well as the map points visible from them, are optimized through bundle adjustment [15]. Lastly, if the mapper has time, it performs various duties like global bundle adjustment and making new measurements.

Our modifications to PTAM include changing the camera model to one supporting ultra-wide FOV lenses, and adding the capability to track and map with multiple cameras configured in arbitrary poses. The only requirement is that the cameras are rigidly connected and that the transform relating their poses is available, such as from a calibration method discussed in section 2.3. In addition, cameras that function as a stereo pair should be synchronized if it is necessary to generate a correctly scaled map. We call the modified algorithm MC-PTAM for Multi Camera Parallel Tracking and Mapping. The next three subsections discuss the modifications in detail.

## 3.2   Modifications: Camera Model

Part of the reason for PTAM's popularity is due to its very well-designed front end, which consists of everything the tracker does (motion model, feature warping, feature matching, etc.). Unlike many other visual SLAM systems, PTAM's front-end does not require the camera images to be de-warped and normalized prior to processing, using instead a built-in camera projection model. This not only avoids a costly dense remapping of every camera image, but also allows the use of non-standard camera models. For example, cameras with FOV greater than 180 degrees cannot be represented by the standard pinhole model used by most visual algorithms, ands thus the images cannot be de-warped onto a sensor plane.

Since we wish to use cameras with ultra-wide FOV lenses exceeding 180 degrees for maximum scene coverage per camera, we integrated the Taylor lens model of [7] with the PTAM system. In the standard pinhole model (Fig. 1a), light rays are represented as lines that pass through a center of projection and intersect with the sensor plane. Correcting for lens radial distortion is handled by remapping the sensor plane to an image plane. In contrast, the Taylor lens model uses a spherical mapping where light rays are represented as half lines emenating from the sphere's center (Fig. 1b). The unit vector representing the half line is then mapped through functions $g$ and $h$ directly to an image plane.

There were two major modifications required to PTAM once the Taylor camera model was integrated. It is necessary to calculate the Jacobians of image points with respect to the map point it represents, as well as the camera pose, in order to perform optimizations in both tracking and mapping. With a pinhole camera model, these Jacobians are calculated on the sensor plane in Euclidean coordinates, but with a spherical camera the Jacobians need to be calculated on the surface of the unit sphere using spherical coordinates [1].

The second modification was to the epipolar searching algorithm necessary to find new point correspondances and thus triangulte new map points. With the pinhole model, epipolar lines project as lines to the sensor plane, but with the spherical model they project as arcs of great circles onto the unit sphere [16]. When searching for matches along the epipolar lines, points need to be rejected based not on Euclidean distance from a line in a plane, but rather based on angular distance away from a great circle arc on the unit sphere.

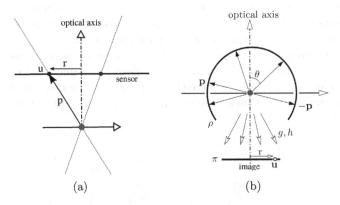

**Fig. 1.** Projections in two camera models. a) A pinhole camera treats light rays as lines passing though the focal point. b) A spherical camera treats light rays as half lines passing through the sphere center [17].

### 3.3  Modifications: Tracking

All of the tracking steps described in section 3.1 are applied directly to each camera in MC-PTAM, except for the final step of pose alignment. Point projection, feature warping and feature matching are performed on multiple images independetly from one another, after which the pose of the whole system is optimized by using measurements from all of the cameras and minimizing the reprojection error:

$$T_c = \underset{T_c}{\mathrm{argmin}} \sum_{i=1}^{M} \sum_{j \in S_i} F\left(\frac{|e_{ij}|}{\sigma_{ij}}\right) \tag{1}$$

where $T_c$ is the camera pose, $M$ is the number of cameras used in the pose optimization, $S_i$ is the set of succesfully found map points in the $i^{th}$ image, $e_{ij}$ is the error of the $j^{th}$ point in the $i^{th}$ image, and $\sigma_{ij}$ is the standard deviation of the error derived from the image scale at which the point was found. The function $F(...)$ is a robust objective function that reduces the effect of outliers by downweighting them. In both PTAM and MC-PTAM, the Tukey biweight is used for this, and the minimization of 1 is performed using weighted least squares.

### 3.4  Modifications: Mapping

Two major changes are required to the map building component of PTAM: bookkeeping to handle the additional cameras and their associated measurements, and a modification of the bundle adjustment algorithm so that multiple measurements per map point are possible. When the tracker wants to add a new keyframe, the multiple cameras together form a new entity called a multi-keyframe, which has a reference pose, a list of cameras, and a list of measurements these cameras have made. All operations that were performed on keyframes are now performed on multi-keyframes instead.

In traditional monocular bundle adjustment, the set of camera poses and map point positions form a simple graph with no more than one edge between vertices and no loops. The vertices are either camera poses or map point positions, and an edge represents a measurement made by one camera of one map point (Fig. 2a).

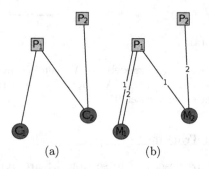

(a)                    (b)

**Fig. 2.** Bundle adjustment as a graph of (C)ameras, (M)ulti-keyframes, and (P)oints showing a) monocular bundle adjustment, and b) bundle adjustment with multiple cameras. The number of an edge indicates which camera of the multi-keyframe made the measurement.

The optimal solution to this graph is expressed by the equation

$$x = \operatorname*{argmin}_{x} \sum_{(i,j) \in C} e_{ij}^T \Sigma_{ij}^{-1} e_{ij} \qquad (2)$$

where $x$ is a vector of all vertices in the graph, $e_{ij}$ is the error of the measurement represented by the edge connecting vertices $i$ and $j$, and $\Sigma_{ij}^{-1}$ is the information matrix of that measurement. The solution to 2 is typically found using the sparse Levenberg-Marquardt algorithm, which (at each iteration) solves the equation

$$J\delta = \epsilon \qquad (3)$$

for $\delta$. $J$ is the Jacobian matrix of measurements with respect to the graph vertices, $\epsilon$ is a vector of all errors $e_{ij}$, and $\delta$ is the increment that is applied to the vector $x$ in order to step towards the minimum error solution. Details of the algorithm can be found in [18]. The Jacobian has a well defined block structure, and for the graph of Fig. 2a, it is structured as in Fig. 3a. This structure needs to be modified when extending the problem to perform bundle adjustment in MC-PTAM.

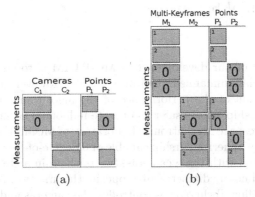

**Fig. 3.** Structure of the Jacobian matrix $J$ for the case of a) monocular bundle adjustment, and b) bundle adjustment with multiple cameras. Blocks of zeros due to the structure of the graph are indicated. The left superscripts in the blocks of b) indicate which camera in the multi-keyframe a measurement came from.

When multiple rigidly connected cameras observe a map point, there are two ways of constructing the bundle adjustment graph. The first is to combine the errors observed by each camera into one edge. For example, a measurement where two cameras observe a point could be written as $(x, y, u, v)$, which is simply a concatenation of the pixel coordinates of the point in the two cameras. However, because points are not always measured by all cameras, the dimensions of the edges in the graph would differ.

Another approach is to make the bundle adjustment graph a multigraph, allowing multiple edges to connect any two vertices. With this approach, the graph vertices are the map point positions and the poses of the multi-keyframes. Measurements are simply the pixel coordinates of image features, and when more than one camera within a multi-keyframe observes the same point, multiple edges are inserted into the graph (Fig. 2b). Note that edges must also carry information about which camera in the multi-keyframe the measurement came from in order to allow projection errors to be computed. The advantage of this approach is that it allows the straightforward reweighting of edges based on a robust objective function, whereas with the first approach individual components of an error vector would need to be weighted differently. For this reason, we use a multigraph approach in MC-PTAM.

The Jacobian of the multigraph of Fig. 2a is shown in Fig. 3b, which is similar to the Jacobian developed in [19]. Note how points that are observed in multiple cameras at once have multiple block entries under the same multi-keyframe. In the sparse Levenberg-Marquardt algorithm, the Jacobian is multiplied by its inverse and thus the multiple blocks are summed, leading to a structure identical to regular bundle adjustment which is then solved as before.

# 4   Experimental Setup

## 4.1   Aircraft

The ultimate goal of our development of MC-PTAM is to enable autonomous behaviours in a small unmanned quadrotor vehicle. However, in order carry out the initial evaluation of the performance of the algorithm presented here, we chose to use an airship that is safer to operate indoors. The satellite emulation testbed at the Aerospace Mechatronics Laboratory of McGill University includes a neutrally buoyant spherical airship capable of 6 degree-of-freedom control. The airship was outfitted with three cameras, two of them in a stereo pair with the third one mounted nearly diametrically opposite the first two. A small computer board from Ascending Technologies controlled the cameras and transmitted the images over a wireless connection. Due to the weight of the stereo cameras and the computer board, the airship was unbalanced and both cameras in the stereo pair were viewing primarily the ground. Providing ground truth data in the experiment was a Vicon optical motion capture system, which tracked the airship's reference frame.

## 4.2   Calibration

Calibrating the relative poses of the three cameras was made challenging by the fact that the third camera's FOV does not overlap with the FOV of either of the cameras in the stereo pair, and therefore standard pattern-based calibration methods could not be employed. We employed a method similar to [13], where multiple cameras perform visual SLAM independently and then the results are merged and optimized to obtain the relative poses between cameras. The main difference in our approach is that we use a known calibration pattern to initialize the location of each independently tracked camera, and the points of the calibration pattern are held fixed during global optimization. This ensures that, unlike [13], we are able to correctly estimate the scale of the translation vector between cameras.

## 4.3   Flight

The airship was flown in a simple trajectory with roughtly three phases:

1. A lateral translation and rotation about an axis perpendicular to the ground.
2. A descent which brought the stereo cameras close to the ground.
3. An ascent and a return towards the starting position.

The purpose of the descent was to make the stereo cameras lose sight of trackable features in order to demonstrate the resiliance of the system to such failures since the third camera is able to continue tracking.

## 5   Experimental Results

### 5.1   Trajectory Alignment

In order to compare the performance of MC-PTAM to the ground truth data provided by the motion capture system, it is necessary to know the transform relating the origin of the motion capture world to the origin of the MC-PTAM world, as well as the pose of the camera frame relative to the airship. Both of these transforms can be found by aligning the time-stamped trajectories generated by the two systems, which is accomplished by minimizing the sum of squared errors between corresponding poses. At any time in the trajectory, the pose of the reference camera frame calculated by MC-PTAM relative to that of the motion capture system is shown in Fig. 4 and is given by

$$T_{va}T_{ac} = T_{vw}T_{wc} \tag{4}$$

where $T_{va}$ is the pose of the airship in the motion capture world frame, $T_{ac}$ is the pose of the camera system in the airship frame, $T_{vw}$ is the pose of the MC-PTAM world in the motion capture world, and $T_{wc}$ is the pose of the camera frame in the MC-PTAM world. The transforms are represented by 4x4 matrices which are members of the Lie group SE(3), the set of all rigid body transformations in three dimensions.

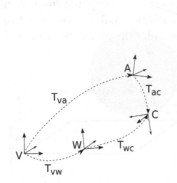

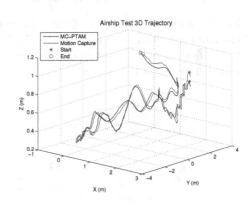

**Fig. 4.** The coordinate frames and transforms of the test system

**Fig. 5.** The trajectories from MC-PTAM with 3 cameras and motion capture

Equation 4 is satisfied by definition when all the transforms are perfectly known. However, both the motion capture system and MC-PTAM introduce errors into their pose estimates, so the relationship between poses becomes

$$T_e = T_{va}^{-1}T_{vw}T_{wc}T_{ac}^{-1} \tag{5}$$

where $T_e$ is the error. Optimal trajectory alignment is obtained by minimizing the error transforms of all $N$ corresponding poses, given by

$$T_{vw}, T_{ac} = \operatorname*{argmin}_{T_{vw}, T_{ac}} \sum_{i=1}^{N} ||\boldsymbol{r}_{e,i}|| \qquad (6)$$

where $\boldsymbol{r}_{e,i}$ is the six dimensional minimal parameterization of $T_e$ for the $i^{th}$ set of frames. Equation 6 can be solved using Levenberg-Marquardt nonlinear minimization.

The above method relies on knowing the correspondances between the poses generated by the motion capture system and MC-PTAM, which can be accomplished by matching timestamps. However, when the processes are running on physically separate hardware with no time synchronization, it is impossible to ensure correctly matching timestamps are generated. Therefore, it is necessary to account for a possible time offset between the trajectories in the error minimization algorithm. We handle this by including a time offset variable which is held fixed during nonlinear optimization. Once optimization reaches a minimum, the time offset variable is updated, and nonlinear optimization is attempted again. The selection of time offset is performed in a gradient-descent fashion until convergence.

## 5.2   Ground Truth Comparison

Fig. 5 shows the trajectory of the reference camera frame, computed from both the motion capture system and MC-PTAM after alighment calculation. The two trajectories appear to correspond well, as can be seen by the plot of position and rotation errors in Fig. 6a.

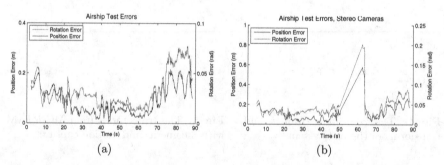

**Fig. 6.** The position and rotation errors of MC-PTAM with a) 3 cameras and b) 2 cameras with motion capture as ground truth

Oddly, both position and rotation errors are lowest near the halfway point of the trajectory, where the airship approached the ground in order to make the stereo pair lose tracking capability. The reason for this is that both the overhead lighting and the motion capture system lighting created reflections on the ground of our lab, causing false features to be tracked and added to the map by the stereo cameras when the airship was at a higher elevation. The behaviour of PTAM (and thus MC-PTAM) is such that features which are poorly tracked after being added to the map are eventually deleted. Therefore, the false features did not permanently corrupt the map but did make tracking poorer when they were visible.

### 5.3   Failure Resistance

To show how having an extremely wide field of view afforded by multiple cameras facing in arbitrary directions improves tracking performance, we processed the captured image sequence of the airship test using only the two cameras in a stereo configuration. As the airship descended towards the ground in the second phase of its motion, these cameras get very close to a mostly featureless floor. Without the information provided from the third camera, the system loses tracking capability, as shown in Fig. 6b between 50 and 60 seconds. At about 62 seconds, the cameras see enough reliable features to recover from failure and tracking continues normally.

## 6   Conclusions

We have presented a system for tracking and mapping using any number of ultra-wide FOV cameras arranged in arbitrary poses. To do this we have shown the integration of the Taylor camera model into the popular PTAM system, as well as the modifications necessary to accomodate multiple cameras for pose optimization in the tracking phase and for bundle adjustment in the mapping phase. Real-world testing of the algorithm onboard a spherical airship indicates it has good performance, and is shown to be resistant to failure due to feature starvation, a problem faced by many visual SLAM systems.

Future tests will explore the effects of different camera placements, flight on different types of aircraft, and flight outdoors. Also, the effect of additional cameras on processing speed needs to be investigated. It is clear that processing more images at once will increase the computational time, but a possibly more important consideration is the bandwidth available to transfer the images. In the present algorithm, all cameras are triggered synchronously, but this presents a data transfer bottleneck as the number of cameras increase. However, as mentioned in section 3.1, this is not necessary for all cameras, and the performance of the system under asynchronous triggering will be investigated.

**Acknowledgment.** This work was supported by Defence Research and Development Canada.

# References

1. Rituerto, A., Puig, L., Guerrero, J.J.: Comparison of omnidirectional and convential monocular systems for visual slam. In: OMNIVIS 2010 Workshop on Omnidirectional Vision, Camera Networks, and Non-classical Cameras, Zaragoza, Spain (2010)
2. Klein, G., Murray, D.: Parallel tracking and mapping for small ar workspaces. In: Int. Symp. Mixed and Augmented Reality, pp. 1–10 (2007)
3. Amidi, O., Kanade, T., Miller, R.: Vision-based autonomous helicopter research at Carnegie Mellon Robotics Institute 1991-1997 (1998)
4. Blosch, M., Weiss, S., Scaramuzza, D., Siegwart, R.: Vision based mav navigation in unknown and unstructured environments. In: IEEE International Conference on Robotics and Automation, Anchorage, AK, pp. 21–28 (2010)
5. Achtelik, M., Bachrach, A., He, R., Prentice, S., Roy, N.: Stereo vision and laser odometry for autonomous helicopters in gps-denied indoor environments. In: SPIE, Orlando, FL, vol. 7332, pp. 733219-10 (2009)
6. Kim, J.-S., Hwangbo, M., Kanade, T.: Motion estimation using multiple non-overlapping cameras for small unmanned aerial vehicles. In: IEEE Int. Conf. Robotics and Automation, Pasadena, CA, USA, May 19-23, pp. 3076–3081 (2008)
7. Scaramuzza, D.: Omnidirectional vision: From calibration to robot motion estimation. Ph.D. dissertation, ETH Zurich (2008)
8. Tarhan, M., Altug, E.: Control of a quadrotor air vehicle by vanishing points in catadioptric images. In: International Symposium on Optomechatronic Technologies, Istanbul, Turkey (2009)
9. Demonceaux, C., Vasseur, P., Regard, C.: Omnidirectional vision on uav for attitude computation. In: IEEE International Conference on Robotics and Automation, Orlando, FL, pp. 2842–2847 (2006)
10. Kim, J., Yoon, K.-J., Kim, J.-S., Kweon, I.: Visual slam by single-camera catadioptric stereo. In: SICE-ICASE Int. Joint Conference, October 18-21, pp. 2005–2009 (2006)
11. Nishimoto, T., Yamaguchi, J.: Three-dimensional measurement using fisheye stereo vision. In: SICE Annual Conference, Japan, vol. 7, pp. 61–66 (2007)
12. Esquivel, S., Woelk, F., Koch, R.: Calibration of a Multi-camera Rig from Non-overlapping Views. In: Hamprecht, F.A., Schnörr, C., Jähne, B. (eds.) DAGM 2007. LNCS, vol. 4713, pp. 82–91. Springer, Heidelberg (2007)
13. Carrera, G., Angeli, A., Davison, A.J.: Slam-based automatic extrinsic calibration of a multi-camera rig. In: Int. Conf. Robotics and Automation, pp. 2652–2659 (2011)
14. Strasdat, H., Montiel, J.M.M., Davison, A.J.: Real-time monocular slam: Why filter? In: IEEE Int. Conf. on Robotics and Automation (2010)
15. Triggs, B., McLauchlan, P.F., Hartley, R.I., Fitzgibbon, A.W.: Bundle adjustment - a modern synthesis. In: International Workshop on Vision Algorithms, London, UK, pp. 298–372 (2000)
16. Geyer, C., Daniilidis, K.: Catadioptric projective geometry. Journal of Computer Vision 49, 223–243 (2001)
17. Micusik, B.: Two-view geometry of omnidirectional cameras. Ph.D. dissertation, Czech Technical University (2004)
18. Hartley, R., Zisserman, A.: Multiple View Geometry in Computer Vision. Cambridge University Press (2003)
19. Kurz, C., Thormählen, T., Seidel, H.-P.: Bundle adjustment for stereoscopic 3d. In: 5th Int. Conf. on Computer Vision (2011)

# Rotorcraft UAV Actuator Failure Detection Based on a New Adaptive Set-Membership Filter

Chong Wu[1,2], Dalei Song[1], Juntong Qi[1], and Jianda Han[1]

[1] State Key Laboratory of Robotics, Shenyang Institute and Automation, Chinese Academy of Sciences, Shenyang 110016, China
[2] The Graduate School of the Chinese Academy of Sciences, Beijing 100080, China
{wuchong,daleisong,qijt,jdhan}@sia.cn

**Abstract.** Actuator failure detection method based on a new Adaptive Extended Set-Membership Filter (AESMF) is proposed for Rotorcraft Unmanned Aerial Vehicle (RUAV). The AEMSF proposed in this paper is based on MIT method to optimize the set boundaries of process noises which may be incorrect in modeling or time-variant in operation; estimation stability and boundaries accuracy can be improved compared to the conventional ESMF. Actuator Healthy Coefficients (AHCs) is introduced into the dynamics of RUAV to denote the actuator failure model. Based on AESMF, online estimation of the AHCs can be obtained along with the flight state. With the estimated AHCs, actuator failure can be detected as soon as possible which provide valuable information for fault tolerant control. Efficiency and improvement of this method compared with other online parameters estimation methods is demonstrated by simulation using ServoHeli-20 model.

**Keywords:** RUAV, Actuator Failure Detection, AESMF, AHCs.

## 1 Introduction

Rotorcraft Unmanned Aerial Vehicles (RUAV), with the advantage of vertical takeoff and landing, hovering, lateral free moving, can be used in many scenarios where the fix wing unmanned aircrafts are difficult to finish the tasks such as longtime surveillance in a fix point, low altitude flight in urban city for anti-terrorism mission. To finish the predefined mission, automatic control systems of the vehicles are becoming more and more complex and the control algorithms become more and more sophisticated. Therefore, fault tolerance flight which can be achieved not only by improving the individual reliabilities of the functional units but also by an efficient fault detection, isolation and accommodation (FDIA) concept has attracted many researches around the world.

Fault is the malfunction of an actual system either in the sensors or actuators or the components of the system. Analytical methods for fault detection and tolerance control are believed more prospective and favorable compared to the physical redundancy [1]. In this paper, we will mainly focus on the actuator failure detection. Generally we can classify the actuator failure into hard failure and soft failure: hard

C.-Y. Su, S. Rakheja, H. Liu (Eds.): ICIRA 2012, Part I, LNAI 7506, pp. 433–442, 2012.

failure in the sense that the actuator sticks at a certain value regardless of the command; soft failure in the sense that an actuator's performance degrades in quality but is not completely useless.

Fault diagnosis approaches include parameter estimation techniques [2], expert system applications [3], kalman filter based algorithms [4] and wavelets transformation based algorithms [5]. In [4], based on the MIT rule, an adaptive algorithm is developed to update the covariance of process noise by minimizing the cost function. The updated covariance is then fed back into the normal UKF. Such an adaptive mechanism intends to release the dependence of UKF on a prior knowledge of the noise environment and improve the convergence speed and estimation accuracy of normal UKF. In [5], a wavelet transform algorithm is proposed to detect the sensor failure in each sensor acquisition channel. Generally, these algorithms are mainly based on the Bayes estimation theory which gives the detection result in a probability distribution form and the guaranteed detection result is impossible to obtain. Besides that, most of these algorithms make the assumption that the noise is in a pre-known distribution which is not exactly in many application.

The set-membership filter (SMF), which just makes the unknown but bounded (UBB) noise assumption and describes the true state in a compact feasible set, provides an attractive alternative for fault detection because the bound of prediction state can be attained by using this guaranteed estimation method and the noise assumption is more realistic in real application. SMF was firstly introduced by Scheweppe [7], he proposed the idea of describing the true state in an ellipsoidal set in the state space and gave the fundamental ellipsoidal set sum and intersection operation principle. Even though there exist many other ways to describe the uncertain set such as ellipsoid, orthotope and paralleltope, the ellipsoid is most widely used because of its less demand of information for representing the feasible set, more insightful for analogizing the covariance, invariance with respect to linear transformations in the sense that an ellipsoid remains an ellipsoid after a linear transformation, convenience of optimization, etc [10]. As to the nonlinear system case, since SMF is based on the linear system model, it can't be used directly. An extended version of set-membership filter (ESMF) was proposed by Scholte and Campbell in [9] [10] to implement SMF in nonlinear system. They linearized the nonlinear system equation around the current prediction state and incorporated the linearization error into the system and measurement noise through the interval analysis method. Besides that, an adaptive strategy for the ESMF coefficients' selection was proposed by Zhou [11] to optimize the compact feasible set and make a balance between the computation complexity and estimation accuracy. However, these algorithms all with the assumption that the system noised bound to be correct, pre-known and unchanged, such assumption won't be satisfied exactly in many applications.

In this paper, a novel adaptive ESMF algorithm is proposed for actuator failure estimation of RUAV. In order to do this, the AHCs are introduced to describe the actuators' failures, and the AESMF is used to estimate both the states and the AHCs in real time. Simulations with the Shenyang Institute of Automation RUAV test-bed SIA-Heli-20 model have been conducted. At last, comparisons with the normal ESMF and MIT-based adaptive ESMF are discussed.

## 2    Standard Extended Set-Membership Filter

Since ellipsoid set has many advantages over other set description, ellipsoid set is selected as the presentation of the system state feasible set [8].

$$E(\hat{x},P)=\left\{x\in\mathbb{R}^{n}\mid(x-\hat{x})^{T}P^{-1}(x-\hat{x})\leq1\right\} \tag{1}$$

Where $\hat{x}$ is the center of the ellipsoid, and $P$ is a positive definite envelope matrix defines the ellipsoid characteristics.

A discrete nonlinear system is written as follow,

$$x_{k+1}=f(x_{k})+w_{k} \tag{2}$$

$$y_{k+1}=h(x_{k+1})+v_{k+1} \tag{3}$$

Where $x_{k}\in\mathbb{R}^{n}$ and $y_{k+1}\in\mathbb{R}^{m}$ are respectively the state and measurement variables, $w_{k}\in\mathbb{R}^{n}$ and $v_{k+1}\in\mathbb{R}^{m}$ are respectively process and measurement noise with $w_{k}\in E(0_{n\times1},Q_{k})$ and $v_{k+1}\in E(0_{m\times1},R_{k+1})$, $Q_{k}$ and $R_{k+1}$ are both positive definite symmetric matrix.

To incorporated the nonlinear system equation into the SMF algorithm, the nonlinear equations are linearized around current state $x_{k}$ and $\hat{x}_{k+1,k}$ respectively [9],

$$x_{k+1}=f(x)\big|_{x=x_{k}}+\frac{\partial f(x)}{\partial x}\bigg|_{x=x_{k}}(x-x_{k})+O(f)+w_{k} \tag{4}$$

$$y_{k+1}=h(x)\big|_{x=\hat{x}_{k+1k}}+\frac{\partial h(x)}{\partial x}\bigg|_{x=\hat{x}_{k+1k}}(x-\hat{x}_{k+1k})+O(h)+v_{k+1} \tag{5}$$

$O(f)$ and $O(h)$ represents the respective remaining high order linearization term of $f$ and $h$. With the pre-calculated ellipsoidal bound of $\hat{x}_{k}$, $\hat{x}_{k+1k}$, we get the interval of $X_{k}$ and $X_{k+1k}$ respectively [9] as:

$$X_{k}^{i}\in\left[\hat{x}_{k}^{i}-\sqrt{P_{k}^{i,i}},\hat{x}_{k}^{i}+\sqrt{P_{k}^{i,i}}\right] \tag{6}$$

$$X_{k+1k}^{i}\in\left[\hat{x}_{k+1k}^{i}-\sqrt{P_{k+1k}^{i,i}},\hat{x}_{k+1k}^{i}+\sqrt{P_{k+1k}^{i,i}}\right] \tag{7}$$

Through the interval analysis, we can get the interval $O(f)\in X_{f}$ and $O(h)\in X_{h}$. The calculated $X_{f}$ and $X_{h}$ is in rectangle form and then will be bounded in ellipsoid form through the equation.

$$O(f) \in \bar{Q} \quad \left[\bar{Q}\right]_{O(f)}^{i,i} = 2\left(X_f^i\right)^2, \left[\bar{Q}\right]_{O(f)}^{i,j} = 0 \text{ if } i \neq j$$

$$O(h) \in \bar{R} \quad \left[\bar{R}\right]_{O(h)}^{i,i} = 2\left(X_h^i\right)^2, \left[\bar{R}\right]_{O(h)}^{i,j} = 0 \text{ if } i \neq j$$

Then we can incorporate the linearization error into the noise by recalculate the new noise ellipsoid as the intersection of linearization error ellipsoid with the system noise ellipsoid: $\hat{R} = R \cap \bar{R}$, $\hat{Q} = Q \cap \bar{Q}$. With the adjusted noise ellipsoid, standard SMF can be implemented to the linearized nonlinear equation.

Define $A_k = \left.\dfrac{\partial f(x)}{\partial x}\right|_{x=x_k}$, $C_k = \left.\dfrac{\partial h(x)}{\partial x}\right|_{x=\hat{x}_{k+1|k}}$, the standard ESMF [11] is given as

follow. In the equation, the coefficient $\beta_k$ is adaptively selected based on the least trace principle, and the coefficient $\rho_k$ is adaptively selected based on the principle of least $\delta_{k+1}$ up-bound [11].

**Prediction Step**

$$\hat{x}_{k+1,k} = f(\hat{x}_k)$$

$$P_{k+1|k} = A_k \frac{P_k}{1-\beta_k} A_k^T + \frac{\hat{Q}_k}{\beta_k} \tag{8}$$

$$\beta_k = \frac{\sqrt{Tr(\hat{Q}_k)}}{\sqrt{Tr(\hat{Q}_k)} + \sqrt{Tr(A_k P_k A_k^T)}}$$

**Measurement Update Step**

$$W_k = C_{k+1} \frac{P_{k+1,k}}{1-\rho_k} C_{k+1}^T + \frac{\hat{R}_{k+1}}{\rho_k}$$

$$K_{k+1} = \frac{P_{k+1,k}}{1-\rho_k} C_{k+1}^T W_k^{-1}$$

$$\hat{x}_{k+1} = \hat{x}_{k+1,k} + K_{k+1}\left[y_{k+1} - h\left(\hat{x}_{k+1,k}\right)\right]$$

$$\bar{P}_{k+1} = \frac{P_{k+1,k}}{1-\rho_k} - \frac{P_{k+1,k}}{1-\rho_k} C_{k+1}^T W_k^{-1} C_{k+1} \frac{P_{k+1,k}}{1-\rho_k} \tag{9}$$

$$\delta_{k+1} = 1 - \left[y_{k+1} - h\left(\hat{x}_{k+1,k}\right)\right]^T W_k^{-1}\left[y_{k+1} - h\left(\hat{x}_{k+1,k}\right)\right]$$

$$P_{k+1} = \delta_{k+1}\bar{P}_{k+1}$$

$$\rho_k = \frac{\sqrt{\max(eig(\hat{R}_{k+1}))}}{\sqrt{\max(eig(C_{k+1}P_{k+1,k}C_{k+1}^T))} + \sqrt{\max(eig(\hat{R}_{k+1}))}}$$

## 3    MIT Rule Based Adaptive Extended Set-Membership Filter

In the aforementioned standard ESMF algorithm, proper selection of the initial parameter and the noise bound is critical for guarantying the performance of the algorithm, the AESMF algorithm suffers from the mismatch of the process boundaries in practical usage. In this section, we will try to adaptively update the process noise $Q_k$ online to ensure $\delta_k > 0$.

To simplify the problem, we assume $Q_k = diag\{q_k^1, q_k^2, ..., q_k^n\}$ and $q_k^i$ is irrelevant with each other.

Define the optimization function as follow which can make a balance between the algorithm's stability and the least output noise bound:

$$J_k(Q_k) = (1 - \delta_k) \bullet tr\{P_{k+1}\} \tag{10}$$

$$Q_k = \arg \min_{Q_k} J_k(Q_k) \tag{11}$$

Since $Q_k$ is assumed in diagonal form and each parameter is irrelevant with each other, then we can simplify the derivation as follow to derive the optimal $Q_k$:

$$\frac{\partial J_k(Q_k)}{\partial q_k^i} = tr\left\{\frac{\partial(1 - \delta_k)\delta_k \overline{P}_{k+1}}{\partial q_k^i}\right\} = 0 \tag{12}$$

Here MIT rule is selected as the updating rule of $Q_k$

$$\hat{q}_{k+1}^i = \hat{q}_k^i - \Delta T \bullet \eta_k \frac{\partial J_k}{\partial q_k^i}|_{q_k^i = \hat{q}_k^i} \tag{13}$$

$\eta_k$ is the adaptive updating rate which control the convergence rate of the variables and satisfying: $\eta_k \geq 0, \sum_k \eta_k = \infty, \sum_k \eta_k^2 < \infty$. Then we have the updating rule as follow, the convergence of this MIT rule based AESMF is discussed in another paper to be published [13] and is beyond the scope of this paper.

$$\hat{q}_{k+1}^i = \hat{q}_k^i - \Delta T \bullet \eta_k \bullet tr\left\{(1 - 2\delta_k)\frac{\partial \delta_k}{\partial q_k^i}\overline{P}_{k+1} + (1 - \delta_k)\delta_k \frac{\partial \overline{P}_{k+1}}{\partial q_k^i}\right\} \tag{14}$$

$(if \ |(1 - \delta_k) \bullet tr\{P_{k+1}\}| < \mu, else \ \hat{q}_{k+1}^i = \hat{q}_k^i)$

Where $\eta_k$ is the parameter for converge rate selected by hand satisfing $\eta_k \geq 0, \ \sum_k \eta_k = \infty \sum, \ \eta_k^2 < \infty$. $\frac{\partial \delta_k}{\partial q_k^i}$ and $\frac{\partial \overline{P}_{k+1}}{\partial q_k^i}$ is derived as follow (details of the derivation can be found in [13], only the result is given because of the scope limitation).

$$\frac{\partial \overline{P}_{k+1}}{\partial q_k^i} = \frac{1}{\beta_k \beta_{Q_k}(1-\rho_k)} \{ diag\{\underbrace{0,...,0}_{i-1},1,\underbrace{0,...,0}_{n-i}\} - diag\{\underbrace{0,...,0}_{i-1},1,\underbrace{0,...,0}_{n-i}\}$$

$$H_{k+1}^{\mathrm{T}} W_k^{-1} H_{k+1} \frac{P_{k+1,k}}{1-\rho_k} - \frac{P_{k+1,k}}{1-\rho_k} H_{k+1}^{\mathrm{T}} W_k^{-1} H_{k+1} diag\{\underbrace{0,...,0}_{i-1},1,\underbrace{0,...,0}_{n-i}\} \qquad (15)$$

$$H_{k+1}^{\mathrm{T}} W_k^{-1} H_{k+1} \frac{P_{k+1,k}}{1-\rho_k} - \frac{P_{k+1,k}}{1-\rho_k} H_{k+1}^{\mathrm{T}} W_k^{-1} H_{k+1} diag\{\underbrace{0,...,0}_{i-1},1,\underbrace{0,...,0}_{n-i}\} \}$$

$$\frac{\partial \delta_k}{\partial q_k^i} = -\frac{1}{\beta_k \beta_{Q_k}(1-\rho_k)} \left[ y_{k+1} - h\left(\hat{x}_{k+1,k}\right) \right]^{\mathrm{T}} W_k^{-1} H_{k+1} diag\{\underbrace{0,...,0}_{i-1},1,\underbrace{0,...,0}_{n-i}\}$$

$$H_{k+1}^{\mathrm{T}} W_k^{-1} \left[ y_{k+1} - h\left(\hat{x}_{k+1,k}\right) \right]^{\mathrm{T}} \qquad (16)$$

# 4    Set-Membership Filter Actuator Failure Detection Model

In the hovering mode, a simplified helicopter model can be used as follow [12] with the coordinates defined in Figure. 1.

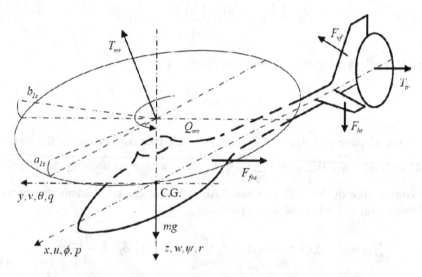

**Fig. 1.** Corrdinates in helicopter

$$\ddot{p} = \begin{bmatrix} 0 & 0 & g \end{bmatrix}^T - \frac{1}{m} R(\phi \quad \theta \quad \psi) \begin{bmatrix} 0 & 0 & T_m \end{bmatrix}^T$$

$$\dot{R} = R\hat{\omega} \qquad (17)$$

$$\dot{\omega} = I_b^{-1}\left(M_c - \omega \times I_b \omega\right)$$

$$M_c = \begin{bmatrix} L^s & M^s & N^s \end{bmatrix}$$

$$
\begin{aligned}
L^s &= S_{L1}b_{1s} + S_{L2}Q_M^S, M^s = S_{M1}a_{1s} + S_{M2}T_M^S + S_{M3}Q_T^S, \\
N^s &= S_{N1}Q_M^S + S_{N2}T_T^S, T_M^S = S_{T_M1}\theta_M + S_{T_M2}, \\
T_T^S &= S_{T_T1}\theta_T + S_{T_T2}, Q_M^S = S_{Q_M1}\theta_M + S_{Q_M2}, Q_T^S = S_{Q_T1}\theta_T + S_{Q_T2}
\end{aligned}
\tag{18}
$$

$U = \begin{bmatrix} \theta_M & \theta_T & b_{1s} & a_{1s} \end{bmatrix}$ is the main rotor torque, tail rotor torque, longitudinal and lateral flapping angle respectively.

Actuator failure model with AHCs is as follow [4]:

$$
\begin{aligned}
U_{out} &= \Gamma_f U_{in} + \Delta_f \\
\Gamma_f &= diag(\tau_1, \tau_2 \cdots \tau_r) \\
\Delta_f &= diag(\sigma_1, \sigma_2 \cdots \sigma_r)
\end{aligned}
\tag{19}
$$

To estimate the AHCs in real time, AHCs are extended into the state vectors as:

$$\bar{x}_k = \begin{bmatrix} P_x, P_y, P_z, v_x, v_y, v_z, \phi, \theta, \psi, p, q, r, \tau_1, \tau_2 \cdots \tau_{rf}, \sigma_1, \sigma_2 \cdots \sigma_r \end{bmatrix} \tag{20}$$

Estimation can be done recursively by introducing AESMF into the extended dynamic model:

$$
\begin{cases}
\bar{x}_k = \bar{f}\left(\bar{x}_{k-1}, U_k\right) + \bar{w}_k \\
y_k = h\left(\bar{x}_k\right) + \bar{v}_k
\end{cases}
\tag{21}
$$

## 5    Simulation

ServoHeli-20 mathematical model was used as the simulation dynamic model parameters. The simulation structure is as follow:

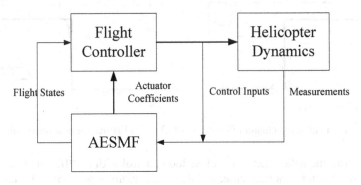

**Fig. 2.** Simulation Structure

The simulation coefficients of helicopter dynamics are listed in Table 1.

**Table 1.** Simulation Coefficients of Helicopter Dynamics

| Coefficient | Value | Coefficient | Value | Coefficient | Value |
|-------------|-------|-------------|-------|-------------|-------|
| $S_{L1}$ | 65.0398 | $S_{L2}$ | -0.062 | $S_{M1}$ | 65.0398 |
| $S_{M2}$ | -0.01 | $S_{M3}$ | -1.0 | $S_{Tmr1}$ | 1777 |
| $S_{Tmr2}$ | 39.8 | $S_{N1}$ | -1.0 | $S_{N2}$ | 0.8980 |
| $S_{Ttr1}$ | 106.2 | $S_{Ttr2}$ | 6.9 | $S_{Qmr1}$ | 95.6 |
| $S_{Qmr2}$ | -1.8 | $S_{Qtr1}$ | -3.9 | $h_{tr}$ | 0.062m |
| $h_{mr}$ | 0.2340m | $l_{tr}$ | 0.898m | $y_{mr}$ | 0m |
| $l_{mr}$ | 0.01m | $M$ | 9.502kg | | |

For simplification, only lateral actuator's coefficients are simulated in this paper, and the state is selected as:

$$\overline{x}_k = \left[ P_x, P_y, P_z, v_x, v_y, v_z, \phi, \theta, \psi, p, q, r, \tau_{lat}, \sigma_{lat} \right]$$

The initial states value and ellipsoidal envelop matrix are as follow:

$$\overline{x}_0 = [0,0,0,0,0,0,0,0,0,0,0,0,1,0]$$

$$Q_0 = diag\{0.01, 0.01...0.01\} \; R_0 = diag\{0.01, 0.01...0.01\}$$

In Fig. 3(a), an abrupt change of actuator's proportional effectiveness is designed in 1032. In Fig. 3(b), an abrupt change of actuator's failure bias is designed in 1000. As the coefficients change abruptly, the normal system model's ellipsoidal envelop is not accurate and the normal ESMF track the changed coefficients slowly, but the AESMF can quickly adjust the ellipsoidal envelop and convergent to the current coefficients in an much more short time.

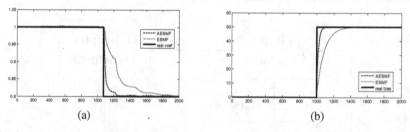

(a)                                        (b)

**Fig. 3.** (a) Estimation of actuator effectiveness factor, (b) Estimation of actuator failure bias

In Fig. 4(a), the helicopter is in a close loop control with an PID controller. Before 118000, the actuator is normal case, and then the actuator's proportional effectiveness is abruptly changed to 0.5. An impulse expectation of lateral velocity is excited by the man controller, the performances in different actuator's proportional effectiveness is shown in Fig. 5. As we can see, since the actuator's proportional effectiveness is change to 0.5, the precalibrated PID controller can't stablize the helicopter anymore. In Fig. 4(b), an AESMF is introduced to estimate the actuator coefficients online and the estimated actuator coefficients is introduced into the controller to compensate for the actuator failure, the same simulation is conducted as Fig. 4(a), and we can find that the controller can get an almost the same performance in normal and abnormal condition with the online actuator failure detection and compensation.

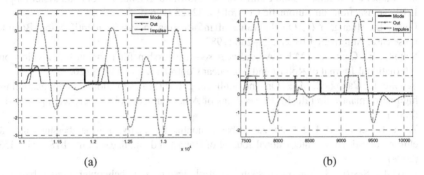

(a)                                      (b)

**Fig. 4.** (a) Comparison of Helicopter performance in normal and abnormal condition, (b)Comparison of Helicopter performance in normal and abnormal condition with actuator failure compensation

## 6    Conclusion and Future Research

A new Adaptive Extended Set-Membership Filter based on MIT method is introduced into Rotorcraft Unmanned Aerial Vehicle Actuator Healthy Coefficients online estimation. In simulation, with the estimated AHCs, actuator failure can be detected effectively and compensate in flight controller to gurantee the performance even in actuator failure condition.

**Acknowledgments.** This work is supported by National Key Technology R&D Program (2011BAD20B07); National High Technology Research and Development Program (863 Program) under Grant: 2012AA041501; National High Technology Research and Development Program (863 Program) under Grant: 2011AA040202.

## References

1. Frank, P.M.: Fault diagnosis in dynamic systems using analytical and knowledge-based redundancy: A survey and some new results. Automatica 26, 459–474 (1990)
2. Isermann, R.: Fault diagnosis of machines via parameter estimation and knowledge processing–Tutorial paper. Automatica 29, 815–835 (1993)

3. Visinsky, M., et al.: Expert system framework for fault detection and fault tolerance in robotics. Computers & Electrical Engineering 20, 421–435 (1994)
4. Qi, J., et al.: Rotorcraft UAV actuator failure estimation with KF-based adaptive UKF algorithm. In: American Control Conference, pp. 1618–1623 (2008)
5. Qi, J., Han, J.: Application of wavelets transform to fault detection in rotorcraft UAV sensor failure. Journal of Bionic Engineering 4(4), 265–270 (2007)
6. Roumeliotis, S.I., et al.: Sensor fault detection and identification in a mobile robot. In: Proceedings of the IEEE/RSJ International Conference on Intelligent Robots and Systems, vol. 3, pp. 1383–1388 (1998)
7. Schweppe, F.: Recursive state estimation: unknown but bounded errors and system inputs. IEEE Transactions on Automatic Control 13, 22–28 (1968)
8. Fogel, E., Huang, Y.F.: On the value of information in system identification–Bounded noise case. Automatica 18(2), 229–238 (1982)
9. Scholte, E., Campbell, M.E.: A nonlinear set-membership filter for on-line applications. International Journal of Robust and Nonlinear Control 13, 1337–1358 (2003)
10. Scholte, E., Campbell, M.E.: On-line nonlinear guaranteed estimation with application to a high performance aircraft. In: Proceedings of American Control Conference, pp. 184–190 (2002)
11. Zhou, B., et al.: A UD factorization-based nonlinear adaptive set-membership filter for ellipsoidal estimation. International Journal of Robust and Nonlinear Control 18, 1513–1531 (2008)
12. Koo, T., Sastry, S.: Output tracking control design of a helicopter model based on approximated linearization. In: Proceedings of the 37th IEEE conference on Decision & Control, Tampa, Florida, USA, pp. 3625–3640 (December 1998)
13. Song, D., Wu, C., Qi, J., Han, J.: A MIT-based nonlinear adaptive set-membership filter for ellipsoidal estimation. Acta Automatica Sinica (to be published)

# Robust Attitude Control Design for Spacecraft under Assigned Velocity and Control Constraints

Qinglei Hu[1], Bo Li[1], and Youmin M. Zhang[2]

[1] Department of Control Science and Engineering,
Harbin Institute of Technology, Harbin, 150001, China
[2] Department of Mechanical and Industrial Engineering,
Concordia University, Montreal, Quebec H3G 2W1, Canada

**Abstract.** A novel feedback controller under the constraints of assigned velocity and actuator control is investigated for attitude stabilization of a rigid spacecraft. More specifically, a robust nonlinear controller is firstly developed by explicitly taking into account the constraints on individual angular velocity components in the presence of external disturbances, and the associated stability proof is constructed and accomplished by the development of a novel Lyapunov function. Considering further actuator misalignments as well as the torque magnitude deviation, a modified robust least squares based control allocation is employed, in which the focus of the control allocation is to find the optimal control vector of actuators by minimizing the worst-case residual error using programming algorithms, under the condition of the uncertainties mentioned and control constraints such as actuator saturation. Finally, numerical simulation results for a rigid spacecraft model show good performance which validates the effectiveness and feasibility of the proposed scheme.

**Keywords:** spacecraft, assigned angular velocity, actuator uncertainties, actuator constraints, control allocation.

## 1 Introduction

Attitude control plays an important role in achieving spacecraft operational services, such as remote sensing, communication, International Space Station (ISS) supplying and repairing. Some of these orbiting operations require to achieving the maneuvers under the physical constraint that the angular velocity sensor measurement is limited. In addition, the actuator uncertainties due to misalignment during installation and magnitude deviation increase further the complexity of the attitude control system.

Recently, many studies related to attitude control law design have been extensively studied in literature based on several inspired approaches, such as optimal control [1], nonlinear feedback control [2,3], adaptive control [4], and robust control or their integrated applications [5,6]. More specifically, for some practical applications, the constraints on rigid body angular velocity components might be required. In Ref. [7], a nonlinear feedback control logic which accommodates the actuator and sensor saturation limits is introduced, but the uncertainties and external disturbances are not

C.-Y. Su, S. Rakheja, H. Liu (Eds.): ICIRA 2012, Part I, LNAI 7506, pp. 443–452, 2012.

involved. Accordingly, the angular velocity constraints problem was also taken into account in Refs. [8-10] with various method; especially, Hu [9] utilized the log-term in the Lyapunov function to analyze and prove the system stabilization by dealing with the velocity constraints effectively, which is motivated by the Lyapunov function introduced in Ref. [10].

However, these above-mentioned studies have been derived under the implicit assumption that the actuators are able to provide any requested joint torque, but this assumption is rarely satisfied in practice because of misalignment of the actuators during installation, and magnitude deviation due to aging and wearing out of the mechanical and electrical parts, etc. To solve this problem, the adaptive control combined with other effective methods have been adopted to handle the actuator misalignments and magnitude deviation [11,12], but it is hard directly to apply these method to orbiting spacecraft control system design in practice. To solve this problem effectively, here we develop a new control allocation strategy for explicitly considering these constraints.

Control allocation is able to deal with distributing the desired control demand derived from the virtual controller design to the individual actuators while accounting for their constraints [13]. The general approaches of control allocation have been deeply investigated with several methods proposed, such as: daisy chaining [14], linear or nonlinear programming based on optimization algorithms [15], direct allocation [16], dynamic control allocation [17], etc. Most previous works study linear control allocation by programming algorithms, which can be iteratively conducted to minimize the error between the commands produced by virtual control law and the moments produced by practical actuator combinations. Recently, a robust least-squares based control allocation [18] is applied in flight control system with an uncertain control effectiveness matrix is investigated, which is inspired by the Refs. [19,20], in which the robust least-squares problems are considered with the coefficient matrices are unknown but bounded, however the actuator magnitude deviation or loss of effectiveness are not considered.

In this work, an attempt is made to provide a simple and robust nonlinear feedback control strategy incorporating with a modified robust least squares control allocation for spacecraft attitude stabilization system. For the first case, it can achieve the desired rotation maneuvers under assigned angular velocity and be robust to the external disturbances by involving a nonlinear term. For the second case, it can deal with the problem of distributing the total former command into the individual actuator properly by involving a control allocator, under the condition of the uncertainties included in the actuator configuration matrix, magnitude deviation and control constraints like saturation.

# 2     Spacecraft Modeling and Problem Formulation

## 2.1     Spacecraft Attitude Dynamics

Consider a rigid space system described by the following attitude kinematics and dynamics equations [21]:

$$\begin{bmatrix} \dot{q}_0 \\ \dot{q} \end{bmatrix} = \frac{1}{2} \begin{bmatrix} -q^T \\ q_0 I + q^\times \end{bmatrix} \omega \qquad (1)$$

$$J\dot{\omega} = -\omega \times J\omega + u(t) + d(t) \qquad (2)$$

where $q_0$ and $q = \begin{bmatrix} q_1 & q_2 & q_3 \end{bmatrix}^T$ are the scalar and vector components of the unit quaternion, satisfying the constraint $q^T q + q_0^2 = 1$; $\omega$ is the angular velocity of a body-fixed reference frame with respective to an inertial reference frame expressed in the body-fixed reference frame; and $q^\times$ denotes a skew-symmetric matrix, that is,

$$q^\times = \begin{bmatrix} 0 & -q_3 & q_2 \\ q_3 & 0 & -q_1 \\ -q_2 & q_1 & 0 \end{bmatrix} \qquad (3)$$

$J$ is the total inertia matrix of the spacecraft, $u(t)$ denotes the combined control torque produced by the actuators, and $d(t)$ denotes the external disturbance torque, which is assumed to be unknown but bounded, i.e., $\|d(t)\| \leq \bar{d}$ for a constant $\bar{d}$.

Note that, for some specific applications the constraints on rigid body angular velocity might be required, the assigned velocity constraint states that

$$|\omega_1| < k_1, \quad |\omega_2| < k_2, \quad |\omega_3| < k_3 \qquad (4)$$

for some constants $k_i$ ($i = 1, 2, 3$).

In addition, for physical limitations on the actuator, we assume that actuator output torques have the same constraint value $(\underline{\tau}, \bar{\tau})$, i.e.

$$\tau(t) \in \Omega := \{ \tau \in R^m \mid \underline{\tau} \leq \tau_i \leq \bar{\tau}, i = 1, 2, \ldots, m \} \qquad (5)$$

## 2.2 Control Objective

Considering the spacecraft attitude system given by Eqs. (1) and (2) under the constraints from Eq. (4), design a control law such that, for all physically realizable initial conditions, the states of the closed-loop system can be stabilized, which can be expressed as: $\lim_{t \to \infty} q = \lim_{t \to \infty} \omega = 0$.

# 3    Nonlinear Control Law Design for Spacecraft under Velocity Constraint

In this section, we aim to design a feedback control law for the system described by Eqs. (1) and (2) to regulate the rigid spacecraft attitude control under the velocity constraint given in Eq. (4). For this purpose, let us consider following candidate Lyapunov function

$$V = k_p \left[ (1 - q_0)^2 + q^T q \right] + \frac{1}{2} \log \left[ \frac{\prod\limits_{i=1}^{3} k_i^2}{\prod\limits_{i=1}^{3} (k_i^2 - \omega_i^2)} \right] \tag{6}$$

Differentiating this Lyapunov function with respect to time and using Eq. (1) yields

$$\dot{V} = k_p q^T \omega + \omega^T diag \left( \frac{1}{k_1^2 - \omega_1^2}, \frac{1}{k_2^2 - \omega_2^2}, \frac{1}{k_3^2 - \omega_3^2} \right) \dot{\omega} \tag{7}$$

Then, let $\Xi = diag \left( \dfrac{1}{k_1^2 - \omega_1^2}, \dfrac{1}{k_2^2 - \omega_2^2}, \dfrac{1}{k_3^2 - \omega_3^2} \right)$, above expression leads to

$$\dot{V} = k_p q^T \omega + \omega^T \Xi J^{-1} \left[ -\omega \times J\omega + u + d \right] \tag{8}$$

To this end, the control law is selected as

$$u = \omega \times J\omega - J\Xi^{-1} \left( k_p q + k_d \omega \right) - \beta \, \mathrm{sgn}(\omega) \tag{9}$$

with $\beta > \bar{d}$ ; then Eq. (8) can be reduced to

$$\dot{V} \le -\omega^T k_d \omega - \left\| \Xi J^{-1} \right\| \| \omega \| \left( \beta - \bar{d} \right) \le -\omega^T k_d \omega \tag{10}$$

Since $\dot{V} \le 0$ and $V > 0$, this implies that $\omega$ and $q$ are bounded, and then $V$ is bounded; then using Barbalat's lemma, one has $\omega \to 0$ as $t \to \infty$ ; then further using LaSalle's invariance principle leads to $q \to 0$ as $t \to \infty$ .

# 4    Control Allocation Design under Actuator Uncertainties

## 4.1    Model of a Rigid Spacecraft under Actuator Uncertainties

A common configuration with four reaction wheels, in which three reaction wheels' rotation axes are orthogonal to the spacecraft ontology shaft and the forth one is installed with the equiangular direction with the ontology three axis. Then the spacecraft dynamics in Eq. (2) can be written as

$$J\dot{\omega} = -\omega \times J\omega + D\tau(t) + d(t) \tag{11}$$

where $D$ is the reaction wheel configuration matrix.

Referring to Fig. 1, it is assumed that the reaction wheel mounted on X axis is tilted over nominal direction with constant angles, $\Delta\alpha_1$ and $\Delta\beta_1$; also for other reaction wheels mounted left are assumed to be tilted over nominal direction with $\Delta\alpha_2$, $\Delta\beta_2$, $\Delta\alpha_3$, $\Delta\beta_3$, $\Delta\alpha_4$ and $\Delta\beta_4$ respectively. To this end, the real reaction wheel torque with misalignment is expressed as

$$u = \tau_1 \begin{bmatrix} \cos\Delta\alpha_1 \\ \sin\Delta\alpha_1\cos\Delta\beta_1 \\ \sin\Delta\alpha_1\sin\Delta\beta_1 \end{bmatrix} + \tau_2 \begin{bmatrix} \sin\Delta\alpha_2\cos\Delta\beta_2 \\ \cos\Delta\alpha_2 \\ \sin\Delta\alpha_2\sin\Delta\beta_2 \end{bmatrix} + \tau_3 \begin{bmatrix} \sin\Delta\alpha_3\cos\Delta\beta_3 \\ \sin\Delta\alpha_3\sin\Delta\beta_3 \\ \cos\Delta\alpha_3 \end{bmatrix}$$
$$+ \tau_4 \begin{bmatrix} \cos(\alpha_4+\Delta\alpha_4)\cos(\beta_4+\Delta\beta_4) \\ \cos(\alpha_4+\Delta\alpha_4)\sin(\beta_4+\Delta\beta_4) \\ \sin(\alpha_4+\Delta\alpha_4) \end{bmatrix} \tag{12}$$

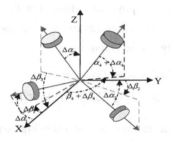

**Fig. 1.** Four reaction wheels with misalignments

Generally, the misalignment angles $(\Delta\alpha_i, \Delta\beta_i)$ are very small in practice, and the following relationships are adopted to approximate Eq. (5):

$$\cos\Delta\alpha_i \approx \cos\Delta\beta_i \approx 1, \sin\Delta\alpha_i \approx \Delta\alpha_i, \sin\Delta\beta_i \approx \Delta\beta_i \tag{13}$$

Then the configuration matrix can be represented as

$$D = D_0 + \Delta D \tag{14}$$

$$D_0 = \begin{bmatrix} 1 & 0 & 0 & \cos\alpha_4\cos\beta_4 \\ 0 & 1 & 0 & \cos\alpha_4\sin\beta_4 \\ 0 & 0 & 1 & \sin\alpha_4 \end{bmatrix} \tag{15}$$

$$\Delta D = \begin{bmatrix} 0 & \Delta\alpha_2\cos\Delta\beta_2 & \Delta\alpha_3\cos\Delta\beta_3 & -\Delta\alpha_4\sin\alpha_4\cos\beta_4-\Delta\beta_4\cos\alpha_4\sin\beta_4 \\ \Delta\alpha_1\cos\Delta\beta_1 & 0 & \Delta\alpha_3\sin\Delta\beta_3 & -\Delta\alpha_4\sin\alpha_4\sin\beta_4+\Delta\beta_4\cos\alpha_4\cos\beta_4 \\ \Delta\alpha_1\sin\Delta\beta_1 & \Delta\alpha_2\sin\Delta\beta_2 & 0 & \Delta\alpha_4\cos\alpha_4 \end{bmatrix} \tag{16}$$

where $D_0$ denotes the nominal value, and $\Delta D$ denotes the uncertainty; and in addition, the magnitude deviation of the actuator is considered, which is defined as

$\Delta\tau(t) = \lambda \cdot \tau(t)$ by introducing a small random variable $\lambda$. Accordingly, the space-craft dynamics under this uncertain configuration matrix can be rewritten as

$$J\dot{\omega} = -\omega \times J\omega + (D_0 + \Delta D)(\tau(t) + \Delta\tau(t)) + d(t) \tag{17}$$

## 4.2    A Novel Robust Least-Squares Control Allocation Scheme

From the principle of control allocation, an equivalent representation of the Eq. (11) can be written as

$$\begin{cases} J\dot{\omega} = -\omega \times J\omega + B_u u(t) + d(t) \\ B_u u(t) = B_\tau \tau(t) \end{cases} \tag{18}$$

where $u(t)$ is the virtual control input, $B_u$ the virtual input matrix, and $B_\tau$ is used to describe distribution of the physical actuators with $B_\tau = D + \Delta D$. With such a choice, the virtual input $u(t)$ represents exactly the total torques produced by the actuators, and the following can be given

$$\begin{cases} J\dot{\omega} = -\omega \times J\omega + u(t) + d(t) \\ u(t) = (D_0 + \Delta D)(\tau(t) + \Delta\tau(t)) \end{cases} \tag{19}$$

To solve this control allocation problem, the following assumptions are obeyed.

**Assumption 1:** $\Delta D$ is an unknown matrix but satisfying $\|\Delta D\|_\infty \le \varsigma_1$;

**Assumption 2:** $\Delta u$ is an unknown matrix but satisfying $\|\Delta u\|_\infty \le \varsigma_2$;

Note that if there are no actuator uncertainties $\Delta D$ or $\Delta\tau$, this kind of control allocation, like the pseudo-inverse control allocation, can be easily realized by

$$\tau(t) = D^\dagger u(t) \tag{20}$$

where $D^\dagger = D^T(DD^T)^{-1}$. However, when considering this kind of uncertainties, the problem becomes more challenge. Fortunately, inspired by the robust least-squares control allocation (RLSCA) scheme proposed in Refs. [23-25] with uncertain control distribution matrix $\Delta D$ and magnitude deviation $\Delta\tau$, the optimal control vector $\tau$ can be found by minimizing the worst-case residual.

Then the optimal actuator control vector $\tau_{RLSCA}$ can be described by

$$\tau_{RLSCA} = \arg \min_{\underline{\tau} \le \tau \le \bar{\tau}} \max_{\|\Delta D\| \le \varsigma_1} \|(D_0 + \Delta D)(\tau + \Delta\tau) - u\| \tag{21}$$

By defining term $(D_0 + \Delta D)\Delta\tau$ as $-\Delta u$, Eq.(21) can then be rewritten as

$$\tau_{RLSCA} = \arg \min_{\underline{\tau} \le \tau \le \bar{\tau}} \max_{\substack{\|\Delta D\| \le \varsigma_1 \\ \|\Delta u\| \le \varsigma_2}} \|(D_0 + \Delta D)\tau - (u + \Delta u)\|$$

Then, for a variable $\tau$, the worst-case residual is

$$\gamma(\tau) = \max_{\|\Delta D\|_\infty \le \varsigma_1, \|\Delta u\|_\infty \le \varsigma_2} \left\| (D_0 + \Delta D)\tau - (u + \Delta u) \right\| \tag{22}$$

Using the triangle inequality ,

$$\gamma(\tau) \le \|D_0\tau - u\| + \max_{\|\Delta D\|_\infty \le \varsigma_1, \|\Delta u\|_\infty \le \varsigma_2} (\|\Delta D\tau\| + \| \Delta u \|) \tag{23}$$

Assume that

$$\Delta = [\Delta D; \Delta u] = \varepsilon [\frac{\varsigma_1}{\|\tau\|} \tau^T ; \varsigma_2] \tag{24}$$

where $\varepsilon = \begin{cases} \dfrac{D_0\tau - u}{\|D_0\tau - u\|}, & \text{if } D_0\tau \ne u \\ \text{any unit norm vector,} & \text{otherwise} \end{cases}$.

Then, in the direction of $\varepsilon$, the worst-case residual is

$$\gamma(\tau) = \|D_0\tau - u\| + \varsigma(\|\tau\| + 1) \tag{25}$$

where $\varsigma = \max\{\varsigma_1, \varsigma_2\}$ is defined.

The worst-case residual in Eq. (25) satisfies the following constraints

$$\|D_0\tau - u\| + \varsigma(\|\tau\| + 1) \le \kappa \tag{26}$$

where $\kappa$ is the upper bound of the residual to be minimized.

Thus, the RLSCA problem can be written as a second-order cone programming (SOCP) problem

$$\min_{\tau, \mu, \kappa} \quad \kappa$$

$$\text{subject to}: \|D_0\tau - u\| \le \kappa - \mu, \quad \varsigma(\|\tau\| + 1) \le \mu \tag{27}$$

$$\tau \le \overline{\tau}, \quad -\tau \le -\underline{\tau}$$

To this end, the following statements can be concluded:

**Theorem 2:** The optimal solution $\tau_{RLSCA}$ to the RLSCA problem is given by

$$\tau_{RLSCA} = \begin{cases} \left(\eta I + D_0^T D_0\right)^{-1} D_0^T u, & \text{if } \eta \triangleq \dfrac{(\kappa - \mu)\mu}{\mu_1^2 + \mu_2^2 + s} > 0 \\ D_0^\dagger u & \text{else} \end{cases} \tag{28}$$

where $\eta > 0$, $s = \underline{\tau}^2 + \overline{\tau}^2$, $\mu_1 = \mu/(\varsigma - 1)$, $\mu_2 = \mu/(\|\tau\| + 1)$, $\kappa$ and $\mu$ are the optimal solution to the above problem.

Proof is omitted here due to consideration of space limitation.

## 5     Simulation and Comparison Results

To verify the effectiveness and performance of the proposed scheme, numerical simulations have been carried out with the parameters are provided in Table.1, and the external disturbances are assumed to be

$$d(t) = 0.2 \times 10^{-3} * \begin{bmatrix} 3\cos(10\omega_d t) + 4\sin(3\omega_d t) - 10 \\ -1.5\sin(2\omega_d t) + 3\cos(5\omega_d t) + 15 \\ 3\sin(10\omega_d t) - 8\sin(4\omega_d t) + 10 \end{bmatrix} \qquad (29)$$

**Table 1.** Simulation parameters and initial conditions

| | |
|---|---|
| Model parameters | $J =$[20 0 0.9; 0 17 0; 0.9 0 15], initial angular velocity $\omega_0 =$[0; 0; 0], initial quaternion $Q_0 =$[ 0.9; -0.3; 0.26; 0.18] |
| | $\alpha_4 =$35.26, $\beta_4 =$45, $\Delta\alpha_i =$[0.2; 0.1; 0.2; 0.1], $\Delta\beta_i =$[0.1; 0.2; 0.1; 0.2] |
| FCUVC | $k_1 = k_2 = k_3 = 0.06$, $k_p = 6.2$, $k_d = 7.6$, $\beta = 0.06$, $\rho = 0.036$, $\omega_d = 1$ |
| RLSCA | $\varsigma_1 = \varsigma_2 = 0.8$, $\bar{\tau} = 0.15$, $\underline{\tau} = -0.15$ |

In simulations, the proposed feedback controller under velocity constraints (FCUVC) incorporated with the proposed robust least squares control allocator (RLSCA) is noted as FCUVC+RLSCA. All the computations and plots are performed using the MATLAB/Simulink software package.

In this case, firstly, to show the effect of the proposed FCUVC incorporated with RLSCA, simulations have been carried out under the given initial condition. The time histories of quaternion, velocity and torques are shown in Figs. 2-4 with external disturbances and uncertainties included in actuator misalignments and magnitude deviation. It is demonstrated that an acceptable and feasible orientation response is achieved, and the spacecraft states reaches the demanded position with a settling time less than 40 sec. Moreover, there are a few oscillations in the time responses of attitude and velocity, but the time responses settle within 40 sec even if the external disturbances and actuator uncertainties are considered simultaneously, and the angular velocity components in the three axes are bounded in the assigned set specification obviously which is defined as Eq. (4) with the assumption of $k_1 = k_2 = k_3 = 0.06$. This illustrates that the designed controller is capable of rejecting the disturbances and actuator uncertainties while maintaining the rotational capability of the spacecraft, with high accuracy smaller than 0.0003 and 0.0005 (rad/sec) for quaternion and velocity, respectively. In addition, from Figs. 4, it can be easily seen that the output torque of each reaction wheel is within the saturation limitation 0.15 Nm because the RLSCA explicitly considers the control saturation constraints, and it is satisfied with the practical engineering applications due to the actuators constraints.

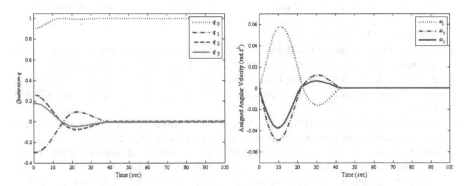

Fig. 2. The time responses of quaternion    Fig. 3. The time responses of the velocity

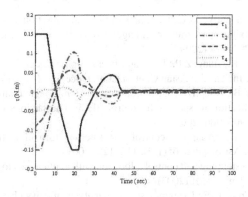

Fig. 4. The time responses of actuator torques $\tau$

## 6    Conclusion

In this paper, the proposed nonlinear feedback control scheme is involved to design the virtual feedback control to achieve attitude stabilization under undesired disturbances and assigned angular velocity constraints, and then the robust least squares based control allocation scheme is involved separately to suitably distribute the total virtual control command into the active actuators, considering actuator uncertainties and saturation. Numerical implementation of the novel control strategy was also presented to confirm the advantages and improvements over existing controllers especially the control allocation method to distribute the virtual control command into individual actuator in the present of actuator uncertainty.

## References

1. Sharma, R., Tewari, A.: Optimal nonlinear tracking of spacecraft attitude maneuvers. IEEE Transactions on Control Systems Technology 12(5), 677–682 (2004)
2. Xing, G.Q., Parvez, S.A.: Nonlinear attitude state tracking control for spacecraft. Journal of Guidance, Control, and Dynamics 24(3), 624–626 (2001)

3. Ross, I.M., Sekhavat, P., Fleming, A., et al.: Optimal feedback control: foundations, examples, and experimental results for a new approach. Journal of Guidance, Control, and Dynamics 31(2), 307–321 (2008)

4. Junkins, J.L., Akella, M.R., Robinett, R.D.: Nonlinear adaptive control of spacecraft maneuvers. Journal of Guidance, Control, and Dynamics 20(6), 1104–1110 (1997)

5. Boskovic, J.D., Li, S.M., Mehra, R.K.: Robust tracking control design for spacecraft under control input saturation. Journal of Guidance, Control, and Dynamics 27(4), 627–633 (2004)

6. Hu, Q.L., Ma, G., Xie, L.: Robust and adaptive variable structure output feedback control of uncertain systems with input nonlinearity. Automatica 44(2), 552–559 (2008)

7. Wie, B., Bailey, D., Heiberg, C.: Rapid multitarget acquisition and pointing control of agile spacecraft. Journal of Guidance, Control, and Dynamics 25(1), 96–104 (2002)

8. Singla, P., Singh, T.: An adaptive attitude control formulation under angular velocity constraints. In: AIAA Guidance, Navigation, and Control Conference and Exhibt, vol. 21, pp. 67–79 (2008)

9. Hu, Q.L.: Robust adaptive backstepping attitude and vibration control with L-2 gain performance for flexible spacecraft under angular velocity constraint. Journal of Sound and Vibration 327(3), 285–298 (2009)

10. Ngo, K.B., Mahony, R., Jiang, Z.P.: Integrator backstepping design for motion systems with velocity constraint. In: The 5th Asian Control Conference, pp. 141–146 (2004)

11. Yoon, H., Agrawal, B.: Adaptive control of uncertain Hamiltonian multi-input multi-output systems: with application to spacecraft control. IEEE Transactions on Control Systems Technology 17(4), 900–906 (2009)

12. Lim, H.C., Bang, H.: Adaptive control for satellite formation flying under thrust misalignment. Acta Astronautica 65(1-2), 112–122 (2009)

13. Härkegård, O.: Backstepping and control allocation with applications to flight control., PhD Thesis, Linköpings Universitet (2003)

14. Buffington, J.M., Enns, D.F.: Lyapunov stability analysis of daisy chain control allocation. Journal of Guidance, Control, and Dynamics 19(6), 1226–1230 (1996)

15. Durham, W.: Constrained control allocation. Journal of Guidance, Control, and Dynamics 16(4), 717–725 (1993)

16. Durham, W.: Constrained control allocation: three moment problem. Journal of Guidance, Control and Dynamics 17(2), 330–337 (1994)

17. Harkegard, O.: Dynamic control allocation using constrained quadratic programming. Journal of Guidance Control and Dynamics 27(6), 1028–1034 (2004)

18. Cui, L., Yang, Y.: Disturbance rejection and robust least-squares control allocation in flight control system. Journal of Guidance, Control, and Dynamics 34(6), 1632–1643 (2011)

19. El, G.L., Lebret, H.: Robust solutions to least-squares problems with uncertain data. SIAM Journal on Matrix Analysis and Applications 18, 1035–1064 (1997)

20. Ghaoui, L.E., Oustry, F., Lebret, H.: Robust solutions to uncertain semi-definite programs. SIAM Journal on Optimization 9(1), 33–52 (1998)

21. Sidi, M.J.: Spacecraft dynamics and control. Cambridge University Press (1997)

# Fault-Tolerant Control of a Class of Switched Nonlinear Systems with Application to Flight Control

Ying Jin[1,2], Jun Fu[3], Youmin M. Zhang[2,*], and Yuanwei Jing[1]

[1] College of Information Science & Engineering,
Northeastern University, Shenyang, Liaoning, 110189, China
[2] Department of Mechanical and Industrial Engineering,
Concordia University, Montreal, Quebec H3G 1M8, Canada
ymzhang@encs.concordia.ca
[3] Department of Mechanical Engineering, Massachusetts
Institute of Technology (MIT), Cambridge, MA, 02139, USA

**Abstract.** This paper considers robust fault-tolerant control problem of a class of uncertain switched nonlinear systems. A new state feedback fault-tolerant control method is proposed for global stabilization of the nonlinear switched systems against actuator faults and structure uncertainties. Compared with the existing results on fault-tolerant control of switched systems, this paper mainly features: 1) the proposed controller can stabilize a class of nonlinear systems with actuator faults and its nominal systems (i.e., without actuator faults) without necessarily changing any structures and/or parameters of the proposed controllers; 2) the proposed method treats all actuators in a unified way without necessarily classifying all actuators into faulty actuators and healthy ones; 3) the proposed method is independent on arbitrary switching polices. Simulation studies on a numerical example and on the longitudinal dynamics of an F-18 aircraft operating on different heights show the effectiveness of the proposed method.

**Keywords:** Fault-tolerant control, switched systems, flight control.

## 1    Introduction

Switched systems are a special class of hybrid dynamic systems. It consists of a limited number of subsystems, one of which is activated for a specific time interval under a switching law to achieve a certain target [1]. As high performance requirements of control systems for handling nonlinearities, uncertainties and operating condition variations and also fault-induced dynamic changes, much attention has been paid on switched systems and available results on switched systems have been applied widely and practically [2-6, 20, 26, 27]. However, most of the existing results are presented on theoretical research of switched linear systems and their applications [2, 4, 6]. Since the nature of hybrid dynamic systems is inherently

---

* Corresponding author.

C.-Y. Su, S. Rakheja, H. Liu (Eds.): ICIRA 2012, Part I, LNAI 7506, pp. 453–462, 2012.
© Springer-Verlag Berlin Heidelberg 2012

nonlinear, studies of switched nonlinear systems have become one of the key topics in the control community.

Undoubtedly, stability is the first requirement for a system to work normally, thus stability of switched systems is the first and important task in research interests on switched systems. Due to the complexity of switched nonlinear systems, the available results on stability of switched nonlinear systems are limited, see [3, 7-13] and the references therein. Thus, switched nonlinear systems with special structures are explored for stability-related problems [3, 10, 11, 12, 13]. Namely, Reference [10] considered a class of cascaded nonlinear systems by switching gains of controllers of the linear subsystems to achieve invariant control and semi-globally asymptotic stability. The result in [10] was extended to a multiple-input case in [11]. Reference [3] studied quadratic stability of a class of switched nonlinear systems without control input. Reference [12] considered adaptive neural control for a class of switched nonlinear systems in a strict lower triangular form. Reference [13] concerned global stabilization for a class of switched nonlinear feedforward systems. As shown by these results, stability of switched nonlinear systems with special structures is still an important research area.

On the other hand, maintenances or repairs in the highly automated industrial systems cannot be always achieved immediately. For preserving safety and reliability of the systems, the possibility of occurrence and presence of uncertain faults must be taken into account during the system analysis and control design to avoid life-threatening prices and heavy economic costs caused by faults [6, 14, 15, 21, 22, 28], which makes fault-tolerant control attract more and more attention [16-20]. Reference [16] considered decentralized fault-tolerant control for a class of interconnected nonlinear systems consisting of finite subsystems to achieve desired tracking objectives and guarantee stability of the closed-loop systems. However, [16] only considered bounded fault functions which satisfy matching conditions and bounded interconnected uncertain structures, but the authors did not explicitly consider faults of the actuators which transmit control signal into the plant. References [17-19] designed fault-tolerant controllers for the nonlinear systems with actuator faults to guarantee reliable stability of the systems. Their common feature is that actuators are decomposed into two parts, one of which is susceptible to faults, the other of which is robust to faults, to compensate for actuator faults effectively. However, in order to implement the control design, the two-part decomposition has to be known in advance. It may be in general difficult to obtain in practice.

From the above analysis on switched systems and fault-tolerant control, fault-tolerant control of switched nonlinear systems is one of promising research interests due to the fact that many practical systems can be cast into hybrid dynamic systems. Compared with available results on switched systems and traditional fault-tolerant control, there are very few results on fault-tolerant control of switched nonlinear system [6, 23, 24]. Reference [6] gave a sufficient condition on robust fault-tolerant control of a class of nonlinear switched systems by decomposing actuators into two parts, the same as the way in [17], i.e., one of which is robust to actuator faults, and the other is susceptible to actuator faults. Thus, the method in [6] has the above-mentioned disadvantages with such a fault model. In addition, structural uncertainties of input matrices were not considered for this class of nonlinear switched systems in [6]. In [23], by uniting safe-parking and reconfiguration-based approaches for a class of switched nonlinear systems, the authors proposed two switching strategies to realize fault-tolerant controls against actuator faults. But when actuator faults occur, the two methods both need to determine reparation time for faulty actuators, which is not easy to acquire in many real-world scenarios. Reference [24] considered observer-based fault-tolerant control of a class of switched nonlinear system with external disturbances. From a system structure point of view, the nonlinear item in this paper is connected to the system in a parallel way, which can be directly compensated for by control signals. However, it is worth noting that fault-tolerant control for nonlinear cascaded systems is much more complicated, where the nonlinear term, as a nonlinear subsystem, is cascaded to other subsystems.

This paper considers the problem of robust fault-tolerant control of a class of nonlinear switched cascaded systems with structural uncertainties existing in both system matrices and input matrices, and proposes a fault-tolerant control method for this class of switched systems by using common Lyapunov function techniques. A numerical example and the longitudinal dynamics of an F-18 aircraft are given to verify the effectiveness of the proposed method.

## 2 Problem Description

Consider a class of uncertain switched nonlinear systems described by:

$$\dot{z} = g_i(z, x),$$
$$\dot{x} = (A_i + \Delta A_i)x + (B_i + \Delta B_i)u_i, \tag{1}$$

where $x \in R^r$ and $z \in R^{n-r}$ are system states, $u_i \in R^{q_i}$ is control input, $i(t): [0, +\infty) \to M = \{1, 2, \cdots, m\}$ is a switching signal, $g_i(z, x)$ is a known nonlinear function, $A_i$ and $B_i$ are known constant matrices, and $\Delta A_i$ and $\Delta B_i$ are matrix functions representing structural uncertainties.

We now make following assumptions for system (1):

**Assumption 1:** Assume that $(A_i, B_i)$ is controllable and $A_i$ is stabilizable, and that all the states are available for feedback.

**Assumption 2:** Assume that $\Delta A_i$ and $\Delta B_i$ are the structural uncertainties with bounded norms, i.e.,

$$\|\Delta A_i\| \le \delta, \text{ and } \|\Delta B_i\| \le \theta. \tag{2}$$

**Assumption 3:** Assume that $g_i(z, x)$ satisfies global Lipschitz condition, i.e., there exists constant $L_i > 0$ such that

$$\|g_i(z, x_1) - g_i(z, x_2)\| \le L_i \|x_1 - x_2\|, \quad \forall z, x_1, x_2.$$

**Assumption 4:** There exists a smooth positive-definite function $W(z)$ with $W(0) = 0$, and constants $\beta_i > 0, \gamma > 0$, and $i \in M$ such that

$$\frac{dW(z)}{dz} g_i(z, 0) \le -\beta_i \|z\|^2, \tag{3}$$

$$\left\|\frac{dW(z)}{dz}\right\| \leq \gamma \|z\|. \tag{4}$$

Then, we design state feedback controllers as follows:

$$u_i = K_i x \tag{5}$$

where $K_i \in R^{q_i \times r}$ are constant matrices.

Given whether a fault occurs on each actuator or not, a matrix $L_s{}^i$ is introduced to represent fault situation of the actuators of the $i^{th}$ subsystem as follows:

$$L_s^i = diag\,(l_1^i, l_2^i, \cdots, l_q^i) \tag{6}$$

where if $l_j^i = 1$ actuator $j$ is normal and if $l_j^i = 0$ actuator $j$ is faulty, $(j \in 1,2,\cdots,q)$, and $L_s^i \neq 0$.

Therefore, the closed-loop switched nonlinear systems involving uncertain structures and actuator faults are given as follows:

$$\begin{aligned} \dot{z} &= g_i(z,x), \\ \dot{x} &= [(A_i + \Delta A_i) + (B_i + \Delta B_i)L_s^i K_i]x. \end{aligned} \tag{7}$$

Then the control objective is to design feedback gain matrices $K_i$ $(i \in M)$ such that switched nonlinear system (7) under arbitrary switching policies are globally asymptotically stable for all uncertain matrices $\Delta A_i, \Delta B_i$ and the actuator faults.

# 3     Controller Design of Switched Systems

This section will present the main results on the robust fault-tolerant control of the nonlinear switched cascaded systems (1) and stability analysis of the closed-loop systems (7). Before presenting the main theorem, we need the following lemma.

**Lemma 1 [22]:** For $\forall x, y \in R^r$ and constant $\varepsilon > 0$ and symmetric positive matrix $\Pi$, the inequalities as follows hold:

$$x^T y + y^T x \leq \frac{x^T \Pi x}{\varepsilon} + \varepsilon y^T \Pi^{-1} y \leq \frac{x^T \Pi x}{\varepsilon} + \varepsilon \frac{y^T y}{\lambda_{\min}(\Pi)} \tag{8}$$

**Theorem 1:** Suppose that Assumptions 1-4 are satisfied. If there exist $\varepsilon > 0$ and symmetric positive matrices $H_i, U_i$ and $Q_i$, such that the following Riccati equations

$$A_i^T P + P A_i + P\left[\frac{1}{\varepsilon}H_i + \varepsilon \theta^2 I_r + B_i\left(\frac{1}{\varepsilon}U_i + \frac{\varepsilon}{\lambda_{\min}(U_i)}I_{q_i} + \frac{1}{\varepsilon}I_{q_i}\right)B_i^T\right]P \tag{9}$$

$$+ \frac{\varepsilon}{\lambda_{\min}(H_i)}\delta^2 I_r = -Q_i, \quad i \in M$$

have a symmetric positive definite solution $P$. Then, under arbitrary switching rules the closed-loop systems (7) are globally asymptotically stable with $K_i = -B_i^T P$, i.e., $u_i = K_i x = -B_i^T P x$ are fault-tolerant feedback controllers which stabilize switched systems (1) globally and asymptotically.

**Proof:** Consider the function below as a common Lyapunov candidate function:

$$V(x, z) = \mu x^T P x + W(z), \tag{10}$$

where $\mu > 0$ is a constant to be determined. Along the trajectory of systems (7), the time derivate of $V(x, z)$ is

$$\dot{V} = \mu x^T \left( A_i^T P + P A_i + \Delta A_i^T P + P \Delta A_i - 2 P B_i L_s^i B_i^T P \right.$$
$$\left. - P B L_s^i \Delta B_i^T P - P \Delta B_i L_s^i B_i^T P \right) x + \frac{dW(z)}{dz} g_i(z, x) \tag{11}$$

According to Lemma 1, for the constant $\varepsilon > 0$ and symmetric positive definite matrices $H_i$ and $U_i$, also noting that Assumption 2 and (9)-(11), one easily has

$$\dot{V} \le \mu x^T \left\{ A_i^T P + P A_i + P \left[ \frac{1}{\varepsilon} H_i + \varepsilon \theta L_r + B_i \left( \frac{1}{\varepsilon} U_i + \frac{\varepsilon}{\lambda_{min}(U_i)} I_{q_i} + \frac{1}{\varepsilon} I_{q_i} \right) B_i^T \right] P \right.$$
$$\left. + \frac{\varepsilon}{\lambda_{min}(H_i)} \delta^2 I_r \right\} x + \frac{dW(z)}{dz} g_i(z, x)$$

and thus,

$$\dot{V} \le \mu x^T \left\{ A_i^T P + P A_i + P \left[ \frac{1}{\varepsilon} H_i + \varepsilon \theta L_r + B_i \left( \frac{1}{\varepsilon} U_i + \frac{\varepsilon}{\lambda_{min}(U_i)} I_{q_i} + \frac{1}{\varepsilon} I_{q_i} \right) B_i^T \right] P \right.$$
$$\left. + \frac{\varepsilon}{\lambda_{min}(H_i)} \delta^2 I_r \right\} x + \frac{dW(z)}{dz} g_i(z, 0) + \frac{dW(z)}{dz} [g_i(z, x) - g_i(z, 0)]$$
$$= -\mu x^T Q_i x + \frac{dW(z)}{dz} g_i(z, 0) + \frac{dW(z)}{dz} (g_i(z, x) - g_i(z, 0))$$

According to the global Lipschitz condition in Assumption 3, and (3) and (4), then one has

$$\dot{V} \le -\mu \lambda_{min}(Q_i) x^T x - \beta_i \|z\|^2 + \gamma L_i \|z\| \|x\|$$
$$= -\mu \lambda_{min}(Q_i) \|x\|^2 - \beta_i \left( \|z\| - \frac{\gamma L_i}{2 \beta_i} \|x\| \right)^2 + \frac{\gamma^2 L_i^2}{4 \beta_i} \|x\|^2$$
$$= -\left[ \mu \lambda_{min}(Q_i) - \frac{\gamma^2 L_i^2}{4 \beta_i} \right] \|x\|^2 - \beta_i \left( \|z\| - \frac{\gamma L_i}{2 \beta_i} \|x\| \right)^2$$

Thus, if one chooses

$$\mu > \frac{\gamma^2 L_i^2}{4\lambda_{\min}(Q_i)\beta_i} > 0,$$

(1) and (5) are globally asymptotically stable under arbitrary switching policies to all uncertain structural uncertainties and the actuator faults. The proof is thus completed.

**Remark 1:** Pre- and post-multiplying both sides of matrix inequalities (9) by $\Gamma = P^{-1}$, applying Schur Complement Lemma, and letting $\sigma$ be a sufficiently small constant, inequality (9) can be transformed into the following LMIs $(i \in M)$:

$$\begin{bmatrix} \Gamma A_i^T + A_i\Gamma + \Lambda_i & \Gamma & \Gamma \\ * & -[\dfrac{\varepsilon_i}{\lambda_{\min}(H_i)}\cdot\delta^2 - \sigma]^{-1}I_r & 0 \\ * & * & -Q_i^{-1} \end{bmatrix} < 0$$

where

$$\Lambda_i = \frac{1}{\varepsilon}H_i + \varepsilon\theta^2 I_r + B_i\left[\frac{1}{\varepsilon}U_i + \frac{\varepsilon}{\lambda_{\min}(U_i)}I_{q_i} + \frac{1}{\varepsilon}I_{q_i}\right]B_i^T.$$

# 4     Simulation Studies

In this section, two examples are studied to show the effectiveness of the proposed method. One is a numerical example; the other is the longitudinal dynamics of an F-18 aircraft taken from [29] to show potential applications of the proposed method.

## 4.1     A Numerical Example

Consider the following uncertain nonlinear switched systems

$$\dot{z} = g_i(z, x),$$
$$\dot{x} = (A_i + \Delta A_i)x + (B_i + \Delta B_i)u_i,$$

(12)

where $i = 1, 2,$ and the matrices and parameters are listed below:

$$A_1 = \begin{bmatrix} -4 & -2 & 0 \\ 0 & -4 & 0 \\ -0.4 & 1 & -4 \end{bmatrix}, \quad B_1 = \begin{bmatrix} 1 & 0 \\ 0.5 & 0.5 \\ -0.5 & 1 \end{bmatrix}, \quad U_1 = \begin{bmatrix} 1 & 0 \\ 0 & 1 \end{bmatrix}, \quad L_s^1 = \begin{bmatrix} 0 & 0 \\ 0 & 1 \end{bmatrix},$$

$$A_2 = \begin{bmatrix} -2 & -2 & 0 \\ 0 & -2.5 & 0 \\ -0.4 & 1 & -2 \end{bmatrix}, \quad B_2 = \begin{bmatrix} 1 & 0 \\ 0.6 & 0.5 \\ -0.6 & 0.9 \end{bmatrix}, \quad U_2 = \begin{bmatrix} 2 & 0 \\ 0 & 2 \end{bmatrix}, \quad L_s^2 = \begin{bmatrix} 1 & 0 \\ 0 & 0 \end{bmatrix},$$

$$Q_1 = \begin{bmatrix} 0.7244 & 0.4067 & 0.1153 \\ 0.4067 & 0.6398 & -0.3002 \\ -.1153 & -0.3002 & 0.6398 \end{bmatrix}, \quad Q_2 = \begin{bmatrix} 0.8244 & 0.4067 & 0.1153 \\ 0.4067 & 0.6398 & -0.3002 \\ 0.1153 & -0.3002 & 0.7363 \end{bmatrix},$$

$$H_1 = \begin{bmatrix} 0.1 & 0.002 & 0 \\ 0.002 & 0.1 & 0 \\ 0 & 0 & 0.1 \end{bmatrix}, \ H_2 = \begin{bmatrix} 0.2 & 0.002 & 0 \\ 0.002 & 0.2 & 0 \\ 0 & 0 & 0.2 \end{bmatrix},$$

$\varepsilon_2 = 1.5, \delta_2 = 0.1, \theta_2 = 0.2, \varepsilon_1 = 1.2, \ \theta_1 = 0.2, \delta_1 = 0.1, g_1(z,x) = -z^3 + x_1 \sin(z)$, and $g_2(z,x) = -z^3 + x_1 \cos(z)$.

Solving Riccati equation (9) with the parameters given above gives a positive definite matrix solution as shown below:

$$P = \begin{bmatrix} 0.5019 & -0.0995 & -0.1530 \\ -0.0995 & 0.5229 & -0.0121 \\ -0.1530 & -0.0121 & 0.5120 \end{bmatrix}$$

Then, according to $u_i = K_i x = -B_i^T P x$ $(i = 1,2)$ the controller can be designed. Let initial conditions be $x(0) = [-3,3,-2]^T$ and $z(0) = 2$. As Fig. 1 shows, the state feedback control law guarantees that systems (12) under arbitrary switching rules are still asymptotically stable when the second actuator of the first subsystem and the first actuator of the second subsystem have faults, as indicated by $L_s^1$ and $L_s^2$. Fig. 1 is the time history of the states, where the stars represent switching points. Fig. 2 represents switching sequences of controller gains. From the figures, the effectiveness of the proposed control method is shown by this numerical example.

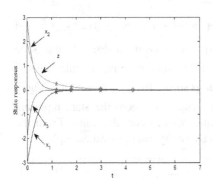

**Fig. 1.** System state responses

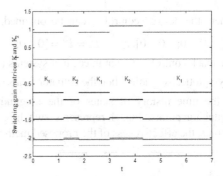

**Fig. 2.** Switching sequences of gain matrices

### 4.2   Longitudinal Dynamics of an F-18 Aircraft

Due to the fact that an F-18 aircraft needs to operate at all possible altitudes and that stability has to be persevered for all the possible operation points in the presence of actuator faults, thus it is necessary to design a control system to stabilize the longitudinal dynamics independent from altitudes, i.e., under arbitrary switching policies.

Now we apply the proposed method to the following longitudinal dynamics of the F-18 aircraft operating on three different heights, which are given in [29].

$$\dot{z} = g_i(z, x),$$
$$\dot{x} = (A_i + \Delta A_i)x + (B_i + \Delta B_i)u_i, \tag{16}$$

where $x = [\alpha \quad q]$ represent angle of attack and pitch rate, $\dot{x} = [\dot{\alpha} \quad \dot{q}]$ represent changing rate of angle of attack and pitch acceleration, $u_i = [\delta_i^E \quad \delta_i^{PTV}]$ represent symmetric elevator position and symmetric pitch thrust velocity nozzle position on the $i$-th operation point,

$$A_1 = A_{long}^{m3h26} = \begin{bmatrix} -0.2296 & 0.9931 \\ 0.02436 & -2.046 \end{bmatrix}, \quad A_2 = A_{long}^{m5h40} = \begin{bmatrix} -0.2423 & 0.9964 \\ -2.342 & -0.1737 \end{bmatrix},$$

$$A_3 = A_{long}^{m7h14} = \begin{bmatrix} -1.175 & 0.9871 \\ -8.458 & -0.8776 \end{bmatrix}, \quad B_1 = B_{long}^{m3h26} = \begin{bmatrix} -0.0434 & 0.01145 \\ -1.73 & -0.517 \end{bmatrix},$$

$$B_2 = B_{long}^{m5h40} = \begin{bmatrix} -0.0416 & 0.01141 \\ -2.595 & -0.8161 \end{bmatrix}, \quad B_3 = B_{long}^{m7h14} = \begin{bmatrix} -0.194 & -0.03593 \\ -19.29 & -3.803 \end{bmatrix},$$

therein the nomenclature, e.g., $A_{long}^{m3h26}$ is the longitudinal state matrix at velocity of Mach 3 and height of 26k feet [29], $z = 0$, $g_1 = g_2 = g_3 = 0$, and $\Delta A_1, \Delta A_2, \Delta B_1$ and $\Delta B_2$ are zero matrices. We can easily verify the Assumptions 1-4. With the LMI solver, a common solution $P$ can be obtained as:

$$P = \begin{bmatrix} 34.8327 & -12.1261 \\ -12.1261 & 20.0152 \end{bmatrix},$$

Then, the desired controller can be obtained. Let initial values be $x(0) = [-3,3]^T$ and $L_s^1 = [1 \quad 0; \quad 0 \quad 0]$, and $L_s^2 = L_s^3 = [0 \quad 0; \quad 0 \quad 1]$. As shown in Fig. 4, the state feedback control law guarantees that systems (16) under arbitrary switching rules are still asymptotically stable when the actuator faults occur as shown by $L_s^1$, $L_s^2$ and $L_s^3$. Fig. 3 is the time history of states of the longitudinal dynamics, where the stars represent switching points. Fig. 4 represents switching sequences of controller gains. From the figures, the effectiveness of the proposed method is shown by this practical example.

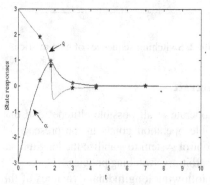

**Fig. 3.** System state responses

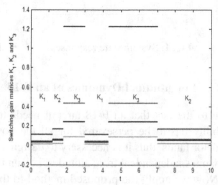

**Fig. 4.** Switching sequences of gain matrices

# 5    Conclusion

This paper studies robust fault-tolerant control of a class of uncertain switched nonlinear systems. By designing feedback control law and using common Lyapunov function technique, a sufficient condition is given on globally asymptotical stabilization of the switched nonlinear systems against actuator faults under arbitrarily switching signals. This method can also be easily applied to robust fault-tolerant control problems of uncertain switched systems with sensor faults, or with both sensor and actuator faults. The simulation results on a numerical example and the longitudinal dynamics of the F-18 aircraft operating on different altitudes show the effectiveness of the proposed method.

**Acknowledgments.** The research work in this paper is partially supported by the Natural Sciences and Engineering Research Council of Canada (NSERC), the National Natural Science Foundation of China (61004009), the Fundamental Research Funds for the Central Universities (N100708001, N100408004) and the Specialized Research Fund for the Doctoral Program of Higher Education of China under Grant 20100042120033, and by SRF for Returned Overseas Chinese Scholars of State Education Ministry.

# References

1. Zhao, J., Hill, D.J.: Dissipativity theory for switched systems. IEEE Trans. Automatic. Control 36(11), 1228–1240 (2008)
2. Liberzon, D.: Switching in Systems and Control. Springer, New York (2003)
3. Zhao, J., Dimirovsk, G.M.: Quadratic stability of a class of switched nonlinear systems. IEEE Trans. Automatic Control 49, 574–578 (2004)
4. Sun, Z.D., Ge, S.S.: Switched Linear Systems-Control and Design. Springer, New York (2004)
5. Xie, G.M., Wang, L.: Controllability and stabilizability of switched linear systems. Systems & Control Letters 48, 135–155 (2003)
6. Jin, G., Wang, R., Zhao, J.: Roust fault-tolerant control for a class of switched nonlinear systems in lower triangular form. Asian Journal of Control 9(1), 68–72 (2007)
7. De Persis, C., De Santis, R., Morse, A.S.: Switched nonlinear systems with state-dependent dwell-time. Systems & Control Letters 50, 291–302 (2003)
8. Hu, B., Xu, X.P., Michel, A.N., Antsaklis, P.J.: Stability analysis for a class of nonlinear switched systems. In: Proceedings of the 38th IEEE Conference on Decision and Control, Phoenix, USA, pp. 4374–4379 (December 1999)
9. El-Farra, N.H., Mhaskar, P., Christofides, P.D.: Output feedback control of switched nonlinear systems using multiple Lyapunov functions. Systems & Control Letters 54(12), 1163–1182 (2005)
10. Mareczek, J., Buss, M., Spong, M.W.: Invariance control for a class of cascade nonlinear systems. IEEE Trans. Automatic Control 47, 636–640 (2000)
11. Cronin, B., Spong, M.W.: Switching control for multi-input cascade nonlinear systems. In: Proceedings of the 42nd IEEE Conference on Decision and Control, pp. 4277–4282 (2003)
12. Han, T.T., Ge, S.S., Lee, T.H.: Adaptive neural control for a class of switched nonlinear systems. Systems & Control Letters 58, 109–118 (2009)

13. Long, L.J., Zhao, J.: Global stabilization for a class of switched nonlinear feedforward systems. Systems & Control Letters 60, 734–738 (2011)
14. Zhang, Y.M., Jiang, J.: Fault tolerant control system design with explicit consideration of performance degradation. IEEE Trans. Aerospace & Electronics Systems 39(3), 838–848 (2003)
15. Xiao, B., Hu, Q., Zhang, Y.M.: Adaptive sliding mode fault tolerant attitude tracking control for flexible spacecraft under actuator saturation. IEEE Transactions on Control Systems Technology (October 25, 2011)
16. Panagi, P., Polycarpou, M.M.: Decentralized fault tolerant control of a class of interconnected nonlinear systems. IEEE Trans. Automatic Control 56, 178–184 (2011)
17. Veillette, J.R.: Reliable linear-quadratic state-feedback control. Automatica 31, 137–143 (1995)
18. Wang, Z.D., Huang, B., Unbehauen, H.: Robust reliable control for a class of uncertain nonlinear state-delayed systems. Automatica 35, 955–963 (1999)
19. Liang, Y.W., Liaw, D.C., Lee, T.C.: Reliable control of nonlinear systems. IEEE Trans. Automat. Control 45, 706–710 (2000)
20. Zhang, Y.M., Jiang, J.: Bibliographical review on reconfigurable fault-tolerant control systems. Annual Reviews in Control 32, 229–252 (2008)
21. Yurtseven, E., Heemels, W.P.M.H., Camlibel, M.K.: Disturbance decoupling of switched linear systems. Systems & Control Letters 61, 69–78 (2012)
22. Han, Q.L., Yu, J.S.: A new feedback design method for uncertain continuous-time systems possessing integrity. Acta Automatica Sinica 24, 768–775 (1998)
23. Du, M., Mhaskar, P.: Uniting safe-parking and reconfiguration-based approaches for fault-tolerant control of switched nonlinear systems. In: 2010 American Control Conference, pp. 2829–2834 (2010)
24. Yang, H., Jiang, B., Cocquempot, V.: A fault tolerant control framework for periodic switched non-linear systems. International Journal of Control 82, 117–129 (2009)
25. Mahapatra, S., Zefran, M.: Stable haptic interaction with switched virtual environments. In: The 2003 IEEE International Conference on Robotics & Automation, pp. 1241–1246 (September 2003)
26. Yang, G.H., Che, W.W.: Non-fragile H-infinity filter design for linear continuous-time systems. Automatica 44(11), 2849–2856 (2008)
27. Fu, J., Jin, Y., Zhao, J.: Nonlinear control of power converters: a new adaptive backstepping approach. Asian Journal of Control 11(6), 653–656 (2009)
28. Dai, S.-L., Fu, J., Zhao, J.: Robust reliable tracking control for a class of uncertain systems and its application to flight control. Acta Automatica Sinica 32(5), 738–745 (2006)
29. Jafarov, E., Tasaltin, R.: Robust sliding-mode control for the uncertain MIMO aircraft model F-18. IEEE Transactions on Aerospace and Electronic Systems 36(4), 1127–1141 (2000)

# Leak Detection in Water Distribution Networks with Optimal Linear Regression Models

Myrna V. Casillas[1], Luis E. Garza-Castañón[1],
Vicenç Puig[2], and Adriana Vargas-Martínez[1]

[1] Tecnológico de Monterrey, Campus Monterrey
64849 Monterrey, México
[2] Universidad Politécnica de Cataluña,
Barcelona, España
{mv.casillas.phd.mty,legarza,adriana.vargas.mtz}@itesm.mx,
vicenc.puig@upc.edu

**Abstract.** This paper proposes a methodology for leak detection and isolation in Water Distribution Systems (WDS). Our work is based on the construction of regression models with optimal parameters which describe the behavior of the network in a normal scenario (no leaks) and comparing these models against predicted output for actual data obtained from pressure measurements along a time horizon. The proposed detection method takes into account possible presence of noise in the demand (assumed known) and/or in the measurements obtained from sensors located in the nodes of the network. A typical water network testbed is employed to validate the proposed methodology. Epanet® software was used to perform the simulations of leak scenarios in order to validate the effectiveness of the proposed approach. Encouraging results are obtained in scenarios with noise and different demand patterns.

**Keywords:** Leak detection, isolation, regression models, sensitivity.

## 1   Introduction

Water Distribution Systems (WDS) are used in everyday life, whether being employed for domestic or for industrial use. They are usually large scale systems which demand the design of better leak detection and isolation methods to prevent water waste. Leaks in WDS can cause significant economic losses giving as a consequence an extra cost to the final user. In summary, in a world struggling with satisfying water demands, leaks cannot be tolerated.

Several works have been published on leak detection for WDS. Model based leak detection and isolation techniques, based on pressure measurements and sensitivity analysis have been studied [1], however the parameter estimation of non-linear models of water networks is not an easy task. Recently the efforts to achieve leak detection in water networks have been approached with the use of binary codification of residuals to compose the fault signature and corresponding binary detection tests to detect the leak. However it has been shown that such approach produces a loss of

C.-Y. Su, S. Rakheja, H. Liu (Eds.): ICIRA 2012, Part I, LNAI 7506, pp. 463–472, 2012.
© Springer-Verlag Berlin Heidelberg 2012

information which diminishes performance [2]. Alternatively, it is possible to use a relationship between the residuals and faults, such as the sensitivity, in order to improve the results [3]. In [4], a method to locate leaks with Support Vector Machines (SVM) classifiers is presented. This research presents a way to analyze data obtained by a set of pressure control sensors in order to locate and compute the leak size. A method to detect and locate leaks based on the transitory inverse analysis is presented in [5]. Gertler proposes in [6] a leakage localization method based on pressure measurements and the application of principal component analysis to the fault diagnosis in WDS. Closer to our work, a method using pressure measurement and the sensitivity residuals is presented [7]. This methodology is based on a model free of leaks, obtained offline, and then computed residuals are analyzed on line against a proposed threshold. If any inconsistency is found, an analysis to detect leaks begins using an established mapping.

Linear Parameter Varying (LPV) models proposed in [8] have been used recently within the FDI research community for application to non linear systems. However, even with the use of LPV models, modeling errors are inevitable in complex engineering systems. In [9], a leak detection and isolation methodology in pressurized water pipe networks is proposed based on computing residuals and is applied to a small case study in order to discuss the effectiveness of the approach. In [10], the same case study was tested in presence of a leak but adding to the leak detection method the use of zonotopes.

The contribution of this paper is to present a new detection and isolation method for WDS based on regression models which describe system dynamics, and taking advantage of the analysis of a time horizon as proposed in [11]. The methodology is based on the comparison of two situations. First, the network behavior using the pressure measurements and the parametric model in leak absence. Second, the predicted model obtained from the pressure measurements of the last 24 hours. Then, the biggest discrepancy along the time horizon between the predicted model and the expected pressure indicates the existence and location of a leak.

This paper is organized as follows. Section 2 describes the proposed methodology. In particular, we explain our modeling and the leak detection technique. Section 3 presents the description and application of the proposed analysis and the design of experiments for the considered network. Section 4 collects the most important results. Finally, in section 5, the principal conclusions are presented.

## 2 Methodology

### 2.1 Modeling

We are proposing a new method for leak detection where we know analytically the behavior of the network using the pressure measurements. This methodology requires the knowledge of the pressure for each node based on the known demands:

$$P = \begin{bmatrix} p_{1,1} & \cdots & p_{1,m} \\ \vdots & \ddots & \vdots \\ p_{n,1} & \cdots & p_{n,m} \end{bmatrix}, \tag{1}$$

where:

       $P$ is the matrix of normal demand state pressures,

       $p_{i,k}$ represents the normal demand pressure of node $i$ at time $k$,

       $n$ is the number of nodes,

       $m$ is the number of samples according to the time horizon.

Then, we obtain the connections that will explain how a node is interconnected with each of its neighbor nodes. First, we initialize the junction matrix as an identity matrix of size $n \times n$, then, we apply on the matrix the equation (2):

$$\phi_{ij} = \begin{cases} 1 & \text{if node } i \text{ is next to node } j \\ 0 & \text{otherwise} \end{cases}, \tag{2}$$

Once we know the junction matrix, it is necessary to propose adequate equations to compute a model for each node. Based on the concept of *sensitivity*, we know that in the ideal case, for a time sample $k$ the pressure of every node is given by:

$$P_k = SD_k \quad for \ k = 1,2,\dots,m \tag{3}$$

being $S$ the sensitivity matrix and $D_k$ the vector of normal demands for every node at time $k$.

    Then, we built the following structure for node pressure measurement on a given time, based on the idea proposed in [9]:

$$\begin{aligned} p_1 &= s_{11}d_1 + s_{12}d_2 + \cdots + s_{1n}d_n + \delta_1 \\ p_2 &= s_{21}d_1 + s_{22}d_2 + \cdots + s_{2n}d_n + \delta_2 \\ &\;\;\vdots \qquad\quad \vdots \qquad\qquad\quad \vdots \\ p_n &= s_{n1}d_1 + s_{n2}d_2 + \cdots + s_{nn}d_n + \delta_n \end{aligned}, \tag{4}$$

where:

    $s_{ij}$ is the sensitivity which affects the node $i$ according to a demand change in node $j$,

    $\delta_i$ is the free factor that explains the behavior of the pressure measured on each node,

    $d_i$ is the demand of node $i$ at a given time,

    $p_i$ is the pressure of node $i$ at a given time.

Each value of the sensitivity will be given by an equation depending on the number of connections that has the respective node, as we can see in equation (5):

$$s_{ij} = \alpha_i d_1(\phi_{ij}) + \beta_i d_2(\phi_{ij}) + \cdots + \gamma_i d_n(\phi_{ij}) \tag{5}$$

According to the previous equation, if $\phi_{ij}$ is zero in the junction matrix, the demand $j$ will not be considered in the computation of the actual sensitivity. Once we have constructed $n$ sensitivities for each node, by combining them with equation (4) we obtain the pressures in function of the parameters $\alpha, \beta, \gamma$, etc. Then, we are able to create the function necessary to obtain each parameter thanks to the following optimization method:

$$P_i = \theta_i * x_i \quad for \ i = 1,2,...,n, \tag{6}$$

where:
$\theta_i$ is the matrix with the corresponding demands along the time horizon,
$x_i$ is the vector of parameters to compute.
Then, the minimization function is:

$$\min(\psi = (P_i - \theta_i * x_i)^2). \tag{7}$$

Using the least squares method to solve equation 7 we have computed the parameters necessary to describe the behavior of the network and we have an adequate model for each node.

## 2.2    Detection and Isolation

In order to achieve the leak detection, we need the pressure measurements of the actual behavior of the network given by equation (8).

$$P_{meas} = \begin{bmatrix} p_{meas_{1,1}} & \cdots & p_{meas_{1,m}} \\ \vdots & \ddots & \vdots \\ p_{meas_{n,1}} & \cdots & p_{meas_{n,m}} \end{bmatrix}, \tag{8}$$

where $P_{meas}$ represents the actual pressure measurements matrix for which we need to inquire the possible existence of a leak.

Now, we have to find the minimum leak detectable in the network. This value will allow us to discriminate if there is a leak or if it is just noise present in the system. Since in the case of noise present in the demand we will be able to detect only a leak with magnitude bigger than the noise, we will assume that in our network, the probable noise along the time horizon is around 4% of the expected demand. Also, we will use this value to assume noise in each node, meaning that we will have a new demand given by:

$$D_{nss_i} = D + nss_i \quad for \ i = 1,2,...,n. \tag{9}$$

Where $nss_i$ is a vector containing the supposed noise along the time horizon that is affecting the node $i$. Then, using this new matrix of demands, we will be able to detect any continuous leak with a magnitude bigger than the supposed noise. Moreover we have to build a new $\theta$ for each node and for each supposed place of the leak in the network because each node has a different demand behavior. Then, we will have as many new $\theta$ vectors as nodes for each supposed demand, and the error in the analytical model is given by:

$$\varepsilon_i = \sum_{j=1}^{m}(P_{meas_{ij}} - \theta_{nss_{ij}} * x_i) \quad for \; i = 1,2,\dots,n.$$  (10)

Taking into account that the leak will be continuous, we assume such leak value in each of the nodes, and compute the error in the model according to the actual measured pressure. Then we look for the highest negative error and we compare this error with a threshold previously computed. Then we can say that the error found has to be lower than the threshold according to the equation (11).

$$leak_{node_i} = \begin{cases} 1 & if \; \varepsilon_i = \min(\varepsilon) \; and \; \varepsilon_i < th \\ 0 & otherwise \end{cases}.$$  (11)

Where $leak_{node_i}$ represents the index of the node in presence of a leak and $th$ is the adequate threshold necessary for the detection.

The above means that we are detecting a leak as a function of the change in the pressure of the nodes, since we know that a leak represents a drop in pressure and this is why we are looking for the highest negative value of the error found. If the difference is positive or the absolute error is lower than the threshold, it means that we are detecting noise.

## 3    Analysis and Experiments

The proposed methodology was applied to the Quebra Network obtained from Epanet® [12]. This network is shown in figure 1 and has 54 nodes and the shown demand pattern. Following the methodology previously described, we obtained an adequate model for each node of the network. Also, it is important to mention that depending on the number of neighbor nodes, the number of necessary parameters for the model will be given by:

$$\rho_i = n(\lambda_i + 1) + 1, \quad i = 1\dots n,$$  (12)

where:
$\rho_i$ is the number of parameters in node $i$,
$\lambda_i + 1$ is the number of neighbor nodes plus the demand of the node.

### 3.1    Example of Application

Consider the Quebra network and a single and continuous leak of magnitude 0.2 liters per second along a time horizon of 24 hours, affecting the node 4. According to equation (12), the model of node 4 will have 217 parameters, since this node has 3 neighbor nodes, plus its own demand and the free parameter.

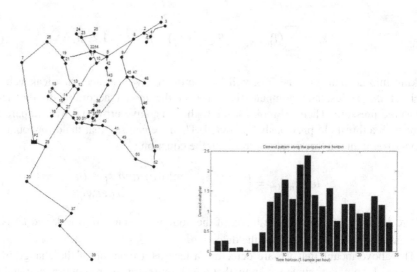

**Fig. 1.** Quebra network structure and assumed demand pattern

In figure 2 we can see the pressure measured along the 24 hours, the model obtained with our method and the model in presence of the mentioned leak, compared with the behavior in the 3 cases with a node without leak (in this example we are comparing with node 50). As it can be observed, the leak causes the pressure measured to deviate from its model. This feature indicates a significative pressure drop occasioned by a leak in the node.

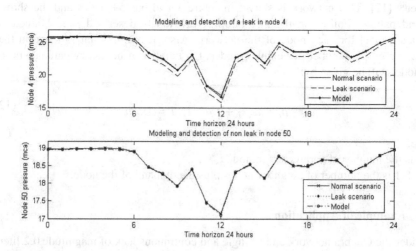

**Fig. 2.** Application of the method in the Quebra network. In case of leak in node 4, a deviation appears in the model for this node whereas it does not appear in node 50.

Regarding the noise magnitude that can be present in the network, we assume that the maximum noise for each node is 0.02 liters per second which means that the method will be able to detect every leak with a magnitude higher than this value. Experimentally we found that the highest negative difference that may come from such a noise is $-9 \times 10^{-3}$. This leads to equation (13):

$$leak_{node_i} = \begin{cases} 1 & if \; \varepsilon_i = min(\varepsilon) \; and \; \varepsilon_i < -9 \times 10^{-3} \\ 0 & otherwise \end{cases}. \qquad (13)$$

As we can see, the application of the proposed methodology achieves the leak detection based on the difference between the model of the network and its behavior when a leak is present.

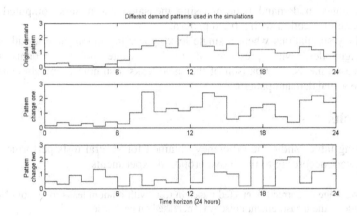

**Fig. 3.** Different demand patterns used to test the feasibility of the method

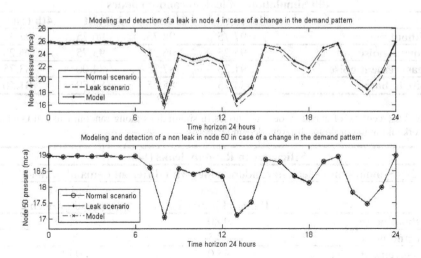

**Fig. 4.** Leak detection taking into account a new demand pattern

Another important point that has to be considered is when changes occur in the demand pattern. To address this issue we proposed other scenarios with a demand pattern that is now obtained randomly (see figure 3) and results under leak and no-leak scenarios are shown in figure 4.

### 3.2   Design of Experiments

In order to test the feasibility of the method, we design a variety of scenarios for which we try to detect a leak in the network:

1. Diversity of leak magnitudes varying from the minor leak detectable of 0.021 to 0.315 liters per second (considering as noise in the network any value equal or minor to 0.02 liters per second).
2. Presence of noise in demands and/or noise in measurements around 4% of the expected value.
3. Changes in demand patterns using the same parameters computed in the modeling section with a fixed pattern.
4. Many simulations where a single leak appear in random nodes, with random magnitudes, with presence of random white noise in demands and measurements. Comparison of the same leaks assuming a probable change in the actual demand pattern.

## 4     Results

The following tables show the efficiency obtained for several tests performed in the Quebra network according to the above proposed experiments.

**Table 1.** Percentage of correctly detected nodes in tests with random leaks in Quebra Network. The magnitude of the measurement noise was increased on each test.

| Efficiency in Random leaks (%) | | | |
|---|---|---|---|
| 400 Simulations of leak in random nodes | | | |
| | 1st test | 2nd test | 3th test | 4th test |
|---|---|---|---|---|
| **Without noise** | 97.75 | 98.75 | 96.75 | 97.50 |
| **Demand noise** | 95.25 | 96.25 | 95.75 | 96.25 |
| **Measurement noise** | 91.25 | 87.75 | 84.00 | 83.75 |
| **Noise in both** | 84.75 | 85.25 | 84.50 | 81.50 |

**Table 2.** Percentage of correctly detected nodes in simulations along random leaks in Quebra Network taking into account different demand patterns.

| Efficiency in Random leaks (%) | |
|---|---|
| 200 Simulations of leak in random nodes with different demand pattern | |
| | 1st test Demand pattern 1 | 2nd test Demand pattern 2 |
|---|---|---|
| **Without noise** | 99.0 | 94.5 |
| **Demand noise** | 98.5 | 96.0 |
| **Measurement noise** | 95.0 | 93.5 |
| **Noise in both** | 93.0 | 94.0 |

**Table 3.** Efficiency in percentage of leak detection in every node changing the leak magnitude and the demand pattern in scenarios with and without noise

| Efficiency testing leak magnitude increasing (%) | | | | | |
| Original pattern | | | Changed Pattern | | |
| Leak Magnitude | Without noise | Moderate noise* | Worst case of noise** | Without noise | Moderate noise* | Worst case of noise** |
|---|---|---|---|---|---|---|
| 0.021 | 94.444 | 87.037 | 81.481 | 92.593 | 44.444 | 14.815 |
| 0.042 | 94.444 | 92.592 | 81.481 | 96.296 | 70.370 | 51.852 |
| 0.063 | 94.444 | 88.888 | 74.074 | 96.296 | 75.925 | 61.111 |
| 0.084 | 96.296 | 90.740 | 83.333 | 98.148 | 92.592 | 64.815 |
| 0.105 | 96.296 | 96.296 | 83.333 | 98.148 | 98.148 | 66.667 |
| 0.126 | 96.296 | 92.592 | 83.333 | 98.148 | 98.148 | 74.074 |
| 0.147 | 96.296 | 94.444 | 85.185 | 100.00 | 98.148 | 77.778 |
| 0.168 | 96.296 | 90.740 | 81.481 | 100.00 | 98.148 | 79.630 |
| 0.189 | 96.296 | 96.296 | 87.037 | 100.00 | 98.148 | 85.185 |
| 0.210 | 96.296 | 90.740 | 83.333 | 100.00 | 98.148 | 88.889 |
| 0.231 | 96.296 | 94.444 | 81.481 | 100.00 | 98.148 | 87.037 |
| 0.252 | 96.296 | 92.592 | 83.333 | 100.00 | 98.148 | 92.593 |
| 0.273 | 96.296 | 94.444 | 77.777 | 100.00 | 98.148 | 90.741 |
| 0.294 | 96.296 | 94.444 | 87.037 | 100.00 | 98.148 | 90.741 |
| 0.315 | 96.296 | 96.296 | 81.481 | 98.148 | 98.148 | 90.741 |

*Considered between 2 and 4% of the expected value
**Considered between 4 and 6% of the expected value

## 5   Conclusions

In this paper, a leak detection and localization method based on the error between models of the network in normal and leakage affected scenarios has been proposed. The leak localization methodology was described by means of linear regression models. The highest negative error in the predicted model indicates an important and continuous pressure drop. Promising results have been obtained from simulations representing a large number of scenarios. In particular, our method finds adequate parameters for describing the network behavior even in case of demand pattern changes and it provides reliable results in case of single leaks. Besides, the methodology has the particularity that it can discriminate between a real leak and a moderate quantity of noise. As future work, the proposed methodology will be applied to a real network with hundreds or thousands of nodes and taking into account as few pressure sensors as possible.

# References

1. Perez, R., Puig, V., Pascual, J.: Leakage detection using pressure sensitivity analysis. In: Computing and Control in the Water Industry Conference, Sheffield, UK (2009)
2. Puig, V., Schmid, F., Quevedo, J., Pulido, B.: A new fault diagnosis algorithm that improves the integration of fault detection and isolation. In: Proceedings of the 44th IEEE Conference on Decision and Control, and the European Control Conference, Seville, Spain (2005)
3. Meseguer, J., Puig, V., Escobet, T.: Observer gain effect in linear interval observer-based fault detection. In: Proceedings Sixth IFAC Symposium on Fault Detection, Supervision and Safety of Technical Processes, Beijing, PR China (2006)
4. Mashford, J., De Silva, D., Marney, D., Burn, S.: An approach to leak detection in pipe networks using analysis of monitored pressure values by support vector machine. In: Third International Conference on Network and System Security, pp. 534–539 (2009)
5. Covas, D., Ramos, H.: Hydraulic Transients used for Leak Detection in Water Distribution Systems. In: 4th International Conference on Water Pipeline Systems, BHR Group, pp. 227–241 (2001)
6. Gertler, J., Romera, J., Puig, V., Quevedo, J.: Leak detection and isolation in water distribution networks using principal components analysis and structured residuals. In: 2010 Conference on Control and Fault Tolerant Systems. Final program and book of abtracts, pp. 191–196. IEEE Press. Institute of Electrical and Electronics Engineers (2010)
7. Pérez, R., Puig, V., Pascual, J., Quevedo, J., Landeros, E., Peralta, A.: Leakage Isolation using Pressure Sensitivity Analysis in Water Distribution Networks: Application to the Barcelona case study. In: 12th IFAC Symposium on Large-Scale Systems: Theory and Applications, pp. 1–6 (2010)
8. Bamieh, B., Giarré, L.: Identification of linear parameter varying models. International Journal of Robust and Nonlinear Control, 841–853 (2002)
9. Vento, J., VicençPuig: Leak Detection and Isolation in Water Pipe Networks using Interval LPV Models.Reporte Técnico UPC (2012)
10. Blesa, J., Puig, V., Saludes, J., Vento, J.: Leak Detection, Isolation and Estimation in Pressurized Water Pipe Networks Using LPV Models and Zonotopes. In: IFAC Symposium in Nonlinear Control Systems, vol. 1, pp. 36–41 (2010)
11. Casillas, M., Garza, L., Puig, V.: Extended-Horizon Analysis of Pressure Sensitivities for Leak Detection in Water Distribution Networks. In: 8th IFAC Symposium on Fault Detection, Supervision and Safety of Technical Processes, SafeProcess, pp. 1–6 (accepted for publication, 2012)
12. Epanet®, http://www.arnalich.com/w/epanet/descargascasosok.html

# Experimental Test of an Interacting Multiple Model Filtering Algorithm for Actuator Fault Detection and Diagnosis of an Unmanned Quadrotor Helicopter

Mohammad Hadi Amoozgar, Abbas Chamseddine, and Youmin M. Zhang*

Department of Mechanical and Industrial Engineering, Concordia University,
1455 Maisonneuve Blvd. West, Montreal, Quebec, Canada H3G 1M8

**Abstract.** This paper addresses the problem of Faut Detection and Diagnosis (FDD) of quadrotor helicopter system in the presence of actuator faults. To this end an Interacting Multiple Model (IMM) Filtering Algorithm is used to simultaneously estimate and isolate possible faults in each actuator. The faults are modelled as changes in control effectiveness of rotors. Two fault scenarios are investigated: the loss of control effectiveness in all actuators and the loss of control effectiveness in one single actuator. The developed FDD algorithm is evaluated through experimental application to an unmanned quadrotor helicopter testbed available at the Department of Mechanical and Industrial Engineering of Concordia University, called *Qball-X4*. The obtained results show the effectiveness of the proposed FDD method.

**Keywords:** Helicopter, Interacting Multiple Model, Faut Detection and Diagnosis, Actuator Fault.

## 1 Introduction

Quadrotor helicopter is a relatively simple, affordable and easy to fly system. It has been widely used by control and automation society to develop, implement and test different technologies. These include control, fault diagnosis, fault tolerant control, multi-agent based technologies in formation flight, cooperative control, distributed control, surveillance and search missions, mobile wireless networks and communications [1]. Some theoretical works consider the problems of control [2], formation flight [3] and fault diagnosis [4] of the quadrotor Unmanned Aerial Vehicle (UAV). However, few research laboratories are carrying out advanced theoretical and experimental works on the system. A team of researchers

---

* This work is supported by the Natural Sciences and Engineering Research Council of Canada (NSERC) Postdoctoral Fellowship (PDF) program to the second author and the NSERC Strategic Project Grant and Discovery Project Grant led by the third author. Support from Quanser Inc. and colleagues from Quanser Inc. for the development of the Qball-X4 UAV test-bed is also highly appreciated.

C.-Y. Su, S. Rakheja, H. Liu (Eds.): ICIRA 2012, Part I, LNAI 7506, pp. 473–482, 2012.
© Springer-Verlag Berlin Heidelberg 2012

is also currently working at the Department of Mechanical and Industrial Engineering of Concordia university to develop, implement and test approaches in Fault Detection and Diagnosis (FDD), Fault-Tolerant Control (FTC) and cooperative control with experimental application to the quadrotor helicopter. For more information on the research activities carried out, interested readers are referred to the Networked Autonomous Vehicles (NAV) laboratory [5].

Over the last two decades, reliability, maintainability and survivability of UAVs, have drawn significant attention into FDD problem. Accurate information about the time, location and severity of the fault help designers to reconfigure the control structure and will help them to avoid system shut down, break down or even material or human damages in the event of the fault. One of the key challenges in this area is to design an FDD scheme which is highly sensitive to faults and less sensitive to external disturbances. In some research works on FTC, it has been assumed that perfect information of the fault is available [6] while such assumption may not be realistic in real world applications. Indeed, to design a fault-tolerant reconfigurable controller, the FDD scheme should provide detailed information of the post-fault system as accurate as possible [7]. Relatively small number of researches addressed the problem of fault detection of helicopter [8]. Heredia *et al.* [9] used a simple observer to detect and diagnose the fault in helicopter's actuator.

In this paper, the Interacting Multiple Model Filtering Algorithm (IMM) based FDD [10] is applied to the Q-ball x4 . The IMM-based FDD scheme has the advantage of not only detecting faults but also providing the information on location and magnitude of the fault. For partial faults, the magnitude can be determined by the probabilistically weighted sum of the fault magnitudes of the corresponding partial fault model. In addition, FDD is integrated with state estimation. A complete survey on fault-tolerant control can be found in [11]. The proposed method in this paper is quite generic and can be readily extended and applied to other types of rotary-wing vehicles.

The remaining of this paper is organized as follows. Section 2 describes the quadrotor dynamics. Section 3 describes the FDD method. Finally in Section 4 experimental results are presented followed by conclusions.

## 2   Description and Dynamics of the Quadrotor UAV System

The quadrotor UAV available at the NAV Lab is the Qball-X4 testbed (Figure 1) which was developed by Quanser Inc. partially under the financial support of NSERC (Natural Sciences and Engineering Research Council of Canada) in association with an NSERC Strategic Project Grant led by Concordia University since 2007. The quadrotor UAV is enclosed within a protective carbon fiber round cage (therefore a name of Qball-X4) to ensure safe operation. It uses four 10-inch propellers and standard RC motors and speed controllers. It is equipped with the Quanser Embedded Control Module (QECM), which is comprised of a Quanser HiQ aero data acquisition card and a QuaRC-powered Gumstix embedded computer. The Quanser HiQ provides high-resolution accelerometer, gyroscope, and magnetometer IMU sensors as well as servo outputs to drive four motors. The on-board Gumstix computer runs QuaRC (Quanser's real-time control software), which allows to rapidly develop and deploy controllers designed in MATLAB/Simulink environment to control the Qball-X4 in real-time. The controllers run on-board the vehicle itself and runtime sensors measurement, data logging and parameter tuning are supported between the host ground computer and the target vehicle. A commonly employed quadrotor UAV model [12] is:

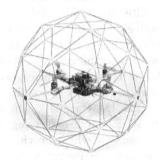

**Fig. 1.** The Quanser Qball-X4 quadrotor UAV

$$
\begin{aligned}
m\ddot{x} &= u_z \left( cos\phi sin\theta cos\psi + sin\phi sin\psi \right); & J_1\ddot{\theta} &= u_\theta \\
m\ddot{y} &= u_z \left( cos\phi sin\theta\ sin\psi - sin\phi cos\psi \right); & J_2\ddot{\phi} &= u_\phi \\
m\ddot{z} &= u_z \left( cos\phi cos\theta \right) - mg; & J_3\ddot{\psi} &= u_\psi
\end{aligned}
\tag{1}
$$

where $x$, $y$ and $z$ are the coordinates of the quadrotor UAV center of mass in the earth-frame. $m$ is the mass and $J_i$ $(i = 1, 2, 3)$ are the moments of inertia along $y$, $x$ and $z$ directions respectively. $u_z$ is the total lift generated by the four propellers and applied to the quadrotor UAV in the $z$-direction (body-fixed frame). $u_\theta$, $u_\phi$ and $u_\psi$ are respectively the applied torques in $\theta$, $\phi$ and $\psi$ directions which are the pitch, roll and yaw Euler angles respectively. A simplified linear model can be obtained by assuming hovering conditions ($u_z \approx mg$ in the $x$ and $y$ directions) with no yawing ($\psi = 0$) and small roll and pitch angles:

$$
\begin{aligned}
\ddot{x} &= \theta g; & J_1\ddot{\theta} &= u_\theta \\
\ddot{y} &= -\phi g; & J_2\ddot{\phi} &= u_\phi \\
\ddot{z} &= u_z/m - g; & J_3\ddot{\psi} &= u_\psi
\end{aligned}
\tag{2}
$$

The relation between the lift/torques and the thrusts $T_i$ is:

$$
\begin{aligned}
u_z &= T_1 + T_2 + T_3 + T_4 & u_\theta &= L(T_1 - T_2) \\
u_\phi &= L(T_3 - T_4) & u_\psi &= K_\psi T_1 + K_\psi T_2 - K_\psi T_3 - K_\psi T_4
\end{aligned}
\tag{3}
$$

where $L$ is the distance from the center of mass to each motor and $K_\psi$ is a constant.

## 3 Interacting Multiple Model for FDD

The Interacting Multiple Model (IMM) method is one of the most efficient approaches for FDD applications, which was first published in [10]. The IMM runs a bank of filters in parallel, each based on model matching to a particular mode (healthy or faulty) of the system and by switching from one model to the other in a probabilistic manner. Each filter interacts with each other in a highly cost-effective fashion and thus leads to significantly improved performance. The initial estimate at the start of each cycle for each filter is a mixture of all most recent estimates from each filter. It is this mixing and interacting that offers advantages in IMM to effectively consider the small changes induced by fault quickly, which is mostly failed to be recognized by conventional multiple model approaches. Such a significant feature makes IMM approach much more suitable for FDD or manoeuvring target tracking applications. A summary of the IMM method is provided below and for a complete description of IMM the interested readers are referred to [10]. The IMM algorithm in each step (cycle) consists of four steps which are interacting/mixing, filtering, mode probability update and final combination of the models which provides the combined state estimate and its associated covariance matrix. In addition, for the above-mentioned four steps, fault isolation can also be performed based on the probability function. All the five steps are shown in Fig. 2 for the quad-rotor application. The

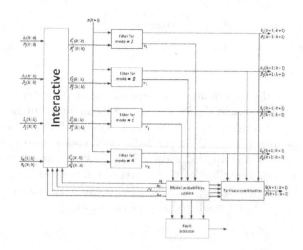

**Fig. 2.** Block diagram of IMM-based FDD

IMM-based FDD scheme assumes that the actual system at any time can be modelled sufficiently by a stochastic hybrid system given in (4).

$$x(k+1) = F(k, m(k+1))x(k) + G(k, m(k+1))u(k)$$
$$+ T(k, m(k+1))\varepsilon(k, m(k+1))$$

$$z(k) = H(k, m(k))x(k) + D(k, m(k))u(k) + \eta(k, m(k))$$

(4)

with the system mode sequence assumed to be a first-order Markov chain with following transition probabilities:

$$P\{m_j(k+1)|m_i(k)\} = \pi_{ij}(k) \qquad \forall m_i, m_j \in S \tag{5}$$

and

$$\sum_j \pi_{ij}(k) = 1 \qquad i = 1, \ldots, s \tag{6}$$

here $x \in R^{n_x}$ is the base state vector, $z \in R^{n_z}$ is the measurement vector, $u \in R^{n_u}$ is control input vector, $\varepsilon \in R^{n_n}$ and $\eta \in R^{n_z}$ are mutually independent discrete-time process and measurement noises with mean $\bar{\varepsilon}$ and $\bar{\eta}$, covariance $Q(k)$ and $R(k)$; $P\{.\}$ denotes probability; $m(k)$ is the discrete-valued modal state at time $k$, which denotes the mode in effect during the sampling period ending at $t_k$; $\pi_{ij}$ is the transition probability from mode $m_i$ to mode $m_j$; the event that $m_j$ is in effect at time $k$ is denoted as $m_j(k) \triangleq \{m(k) = m_j\}$. $S = \{m_1, m_2, \ldots, m_s\}$ is the set of all possible system modes; the initial state is assumed to have mean $\hat{x}_0$ and covariance $P_0$ and be independent of $\varepsilon$ and $\eta$ . The mathematical description of IMM-based FDD scheme is given in the following equations. As mentioned earlier, we will divide the IMM procedure for FDD into 4 different steps. The first involves interacting/mixing of the estimates for the four different models considered. The predicted mode probability and mixing probability at one cycle is given in Eq. (7).

$$\mu_j(k+1|k) \triangleq P\{m_j(k+1)|z^k\} = \sum_{i=1}^{s} \pi_{ij}\mu_j(k)$$

$$\mu_{i|j}(k) \triangleq P\{m_j(k)|m_j(k+1), z^k\} = \frac{\pi_{ij}\mu_i(k)}{\mu_j(k+1|k)} \qquad i,j = 1, \ldots, s \tag{7}$$

Based on the mixing probability and mode probability, the mixed initial state and covariance estimates to be used for next time-step of filter update are given in Eq. (8).

$$\hat{x}_j^0 \triangleq E\left[x(k)|m_j(k+1), z^k\right] = \sum_{i=1}^{s} \hat{x}_i(k|k)\mu_{i|j}(k) \qquad j = 1, \ldots, s$$

$$P_j^0(k|k) \triangleq cov\left[\hat{x}_j^0|m_j(k+1), z^k\right] \tag{8}$$
$$= \sum_{i=1}^{s}\left[P_i(k|k)\left[\hat{x}_j^0(k|k) - \hat{x}_j(k|k)\right]\left[\hat{x}_j^0(k|k) - \hat{x}_j(k|k)\right]^T\right]\mu_{i|j}(k)$$
$$j = 1, \ldots, s$$

The next step involves the filtering calculation for each healthy and faulty mode, respectively. The predicted state for each model and its associated covariance matrix is given in Eq. (9).

$$\hat{x}_i(k+1|k) \triangleq E\left[x(k+1)|m_j(k+1), z^k\right]$$
$$= F_j(k)\hat{x}_j^0 + G_j(k)u(k) + T_j(k)\bar{\varepsilon}_j(k)$$

$$\tag{9}$$

$$P_i(k+1|k) \triangleq cov\left[\hat{x}_j(k+1|k)|m_j(k+1), z^k\right]$$
$$= F_j(k)P_j^0(k|k)F_j(k)^T + T_j(k)Q_j(k)T_j(k)^T \qquad j = 1, \ldots, s$$

The measurement residual covariance is computed using Eq. (10).

$$
\begin{aligned}
v_j(k+1) &\triangleq z(k+1) - E\left[z(k+1)|m_j(k+1), z^k\right] \\
&= z(k+1) - H_j(k+1)\hat{x}_i(k+1|k) - D_j(k+1)u(k) - \bar{\eta}(k+1) \quad (10) \\
&\hspace{6cm} j = 1,\ldots,s
\end{aligned}
$$

and the residual covariance and filter gain are obtained as Eq. (11).

$$
\begin{aligned}
S_j(k+1) &\triangleq cov\left[v_j(k+1|k)|m_j(k+1), z^k\right] \\
&= H_j(k+1)P_j(k+1|k)H_j(k+1)^T + R_j(k+1)
\end{aligned} \quad (11)
$$

$$
K_j(k+1) = P_j(k+1|k)H_j(k+1)^T S_j(k+1)^{-1} \quad j = 1,\ldots,s
$$

Using the above residuals, the updated state for each mode (healthy or faulty) is given in Eq. (12).

$$
\begin{aligned}
\hat{x}_j(k+1|k+1) &\triangleq E\left[x(k+1)|m_j(k+1), z^{k+1}\right] \\
&= \hat{x}_i(k+1|k) + K_j(k+1)v_j(k+1)
\end{aligned}
$$

$$
\begin{aligned}
P_j(k+1|k+1) &\triangleq cov\left[\hat{x}_j(k+1|k+1)|m_j(k+1), z^k\right] \\
&= P_j(k+1|k) - K_j(k+1)S_j(k+1)K_j(k+1)^T \quad j = 1,\ldots,s
\end{aligned}
$$
$$(12)$$

The equations (9) to (12) form the model conditional filtering for each mode. The third step involves the mode probability update for FDD decision making. The likelihood function at each step is given in Eq. (13).

$$
\begin{aligned}
L_j(k+1|k+1) &\triangleq N\left[v_j(k+1), 0, S_j(k+1)\right] \\
&= \frac{1}{\sqrt{|(2\pi)S_j(k+1)|}}e^{\left[-\frac{1}{2}v_j(k+1)^T S_j(k+1)^{-1}v_j(k+1)\right]} \quad j = 1,\ldots,s
\end{aligned}
$$
$$(13)$$

The mode probability is obtained as Eq. (14).

$$
\mu_j(k+1) \triangleq P\{m_j(k+1)|z^k\} = \frac{\mu_j(k+1|k)L_j(k+1)}{\sum\limits_{i=1}^{N}\mu_i(k+1|k)L_i(k+1)} \quad j = 1,\ldots,s \quad (14)
$$

The fault decision logic is obtained using the Eq. (15).

$$
\frac{\mu_p(k+1)}{max(\mu_i(k+1))}
\begin{cases}
\geq \mu_T' = H_j : fault \ j \ occurred \\
\qquad\qquad i = 1,\ldots,p-1, p+1,\ldots,s \\
< \mu_T' = H_1 : no \ fault
\end{cases} \quad (15)
$$

where $\mu_p(k+1)$ is:

$$
\mu_p(k+1) = max(\mu_i(k+1)) \quad i = 1,\ldots,s \quad (16)
$$

The following equations provide the combination of estimates of overall estimates and its covariance.

$$\hat{x}(k+1|k+1) \triangleq E\left[x(k+1)|z^{k+1}\right] = \sum_{j=1}^{s} \hat{x}_j(k+1|k+1)\mu_j(k+1)$$

$$\begin{aligned}
P(k+1|k+1) \triangleq\ & E\left[[x(k+1) - \hat{x}(k+1|k+1)]\right. \\
& \left. [x(k+1) - \hat{x}(k+1|k+1)]^T|z^{k+1}\right] \\
=\ & \sum_{j=1}^{s} [P_j(k+1|k+1) + [\hat{x}(k+1|k+1) - \hat{x}_j(k+1|k+1)] \\
& [\hat{x}(k+1|k+1) - \hat{x}_j(k+1|k+1)]^T\Big] \mu_j(k+1)
\end{aligned}$$

$$(17)$$

This summarizes the complete cycle of the IMM-based FDD scheme using Kalman filters as its mode matched filters. Equation (15) not only provides fault detection but also provides isolation, magnitude and fault occurrence time. Given a brief description of the IMM-based FDD method the next section attempts to implement the IMM algorithm for Fault Detection and Diagnosis of actuator faults in Q-ball X4.

## 4   Experimental Results

The IMM has been experimentally tested on the Qball-X4 testbed. The filter is built using Matlab/Simulink to be run off-board with a frequency of 200 $Hz$. In all experiments, the system is required to hover at an altitude of 1 $m$ and the faults are taking place at time instant $t = 15$ $s$. As mentioned before, to use IMM for the fault detection and diagnosis a linearized state space model is required. Sixteen different model have been used inside the FDD block. One represents healthy mode, and other fifteen models represent faulty modes. In real fly, due to actuator saturation, the Q-ball X4 can not tolerate more than 40 $\sim$ 45 percent loss of effectiveness in each actuator. In other words, if the fault goes beyond 40 $\sim$ 45 percent, Q-ball can not recover and will crash. Tacking this fact into consideration, faulty models are designed based on 40 percent loss of actuator's effectiveness. Table 1 shows description of models used as multiple models. For example Model 7 is used to show the case in which Actuator 1 and 3 perform normally, while Actuator 2 and 4 lose 40 percent of their effectiveness.

Table 1. Description of models used in IMM, H: Actuator is Healthy, F: Actuator is Faulty

| Rotor \ Model | 1 | 2 | 3 | 4 | 5 | 6 | 7 | 8 | 9 | 10 | 11 | 12 | 13 | 14 | 15 | 16 |
|---|---|---|---|---|---|---|---|---|---|---|---|---|---|---|---|---|
| Actuator 1 | H | F | H | H | H | F | H | F | H | H | F | H | F | F | F | F |
| Actuator 2 | H | H | F | H | H | H | F | F | F | H | H | F | H | F | F | F |
| Actuator 3 | H | H | H | F | H | F | H | H | F | F | H | F | F | H | F | F |
| Actuator 4 | H | H | H | H | F | H | F | H | H | F | F | F | F | F | H | F |

## 4.1    Single Fault Scenario: Control Effectiveness Loss in Third Motor

In the first scenario, a loss of control effectiveness of 40% is rendered in the third motor. As can be seen in Figure 3, this fault does not affect the system along the $x$-direction but it results in loss of altitude of 20 $cm$ and a deviation of 80 $cm$ from the desired position along the $y$-direction. Due to the presence of a controller, the system recovers and goes back to the desired hover position. Figure 4 shows the system's behavior in the 3D space upon fault injection.

The PWM inputs to the four motors are illustrated in Figure 5. It is clear that before fault (up to 15 seconds), all the four PWM inputs are almost the same. After fault injection in the third motor, the baseline controller reacts by automatically increasing the third PWM input to compensate the occurred fault. The mode probabilities of all sixteen models is given in Figure 6. The experimental application shows a fast and precise estimation of the fault amplitude despite model uncertainties using IMM. As it can be seen from figure 6 the probability of the first model (represents healthy model) is the highest (around 0.9). In the 15 second when the fault is occurred probability of the forth model (represents fault in third actuator) increases (around 1). Figure 7 also show the effective model over the time.

## 4.2    Simultaneous Faults Scenario: Control Effectiveness Loss in All Motors

In the second scenario, a loss of control effectiveness of 30% is rendered in all motors. Unlike the previous case, this fault does not affect the system position in the $x$ and $y$ directions but results in a larger loss in altitude due to the feature of the faults, where the system drops to 0.4 $m$ (see Figure 8). Figure 9 shows the system's behavior in the 3D space upon fault injection. The PWM inputs to the four motors are illustrated in Figure 10. Up to 15 seconds and before fault injection, all the four PWM inputs are almost the same. After fault injection, the baseline controller automatically increases the PWM inputs to compensate the occurred faults. The mode probabilities of all sixteen models is given in Figure 11. As it can be seen from figure 11 the probability of the first model (represents healthy model) is the highest (around 0.9). In the 15 second when the fault is occurred probability of probability of the first model decreases (around 0.3) and the probability of the sixteenth model(represents fault in all actuator) increases (around 0.7). Figure 12 also show the effective model over the time.

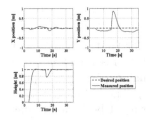 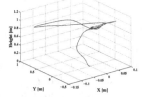 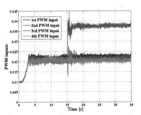

**Fig. 3.** System position with fault in the third motor

**Fig. 4.** System position in the 3D space with fault in the third motor

**Fig. 5.** PWM inputs with fault in the third motor

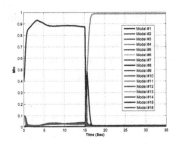 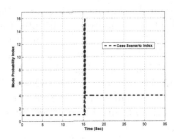

**Fig. 6.** Mode probabilities for single fault in the third motor

**Fig. 7.** Effective model index for single fault in the third motor

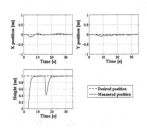 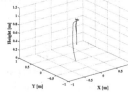 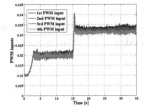

**Fig. 8.** System position with faults in all motors

**Fig. 9.** System position in the 3D space with faults in all motors

**Fig. 10.** PWM inputs with faults in all motors

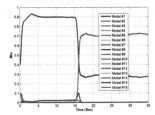 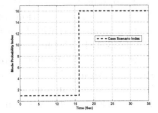

**Fig. 11.** Mode probabilities for faults in all motors

**Fig. 12.** Effective model index for faults in all motors

# 5   Conclusions

In this study an *Interacting Multiple Model* is proposed for Faut Detection and Diagnosis (FDD) of the quadrotor helicopter testbed in the presence of actuator faults. The developed FDD algorithm is evaluated through experimental application to a quadrotor helicopter testbed called *Qball-X4*. The obtained results showed the effectiveness of the proposed method in terms of both rapid fault detection and correct isolation of faults.

# References

[1] Amoozgar, M.H., Chamseddine, A., Zhang, Y.M.: Fault-tolerant fuzzy gain scheduled PID for a quadrotor helicopter testbed in the presence of actuator faults. In: IFAC Conference on Advances in PID Control, Brescia, Italy (March 2012)
[2] Dierks, T., Jagannathan, S.: Neural network output feedback control of a quadrotor UAV. In: Proceedings of the 47th IEEE Conference on Decision and Control, Cancun, Mexico, December 9-11, pp. 3633–3639 (2008)
[3] Dierks, T., Jagannathan, S.: Neural network control of quadrotor UAV formations. In: American Control Conference, St. Louis, Missouri, USA, June 10-12, pp. 2990–2996 (2009)
[4] Rafaralahy, H., Richard, E., Boutayeb, M., Zasadzinski, M.: Simultaneous observer based sensor diagnosis and speed estimation of unmanned aerial vehicle. In: Proceedings of the 47th IEEE Conference on Decision and Control, Cancun, Mexico, pp. 2938–2943 (December 2008)
[5] NAV, http://users.encs.concordia.ca/~ymzhang/UAVs.htm (cited February 29, 2012)
[6] Sharifi, F., Mirzaei, M., Gordon, B.W., Zhang, Y.M.: Fault-tolerant control of a quadrotor UAV using sliding mode control. In: Conference on Control and Fault-Tolerant Systems, Nice, France, October 6-8, pp. 239–244 (2009)
[7] Zhang, Y.M., Jiang, J.: Active fault-tolerant control system against partial actuator failures. IEE Proceedings on Control Theory and Applications 149(1), 95–104 (2002)
[8] Montes de Oca, S., Puig, V., Theilliol, D., Tornil-Sin, S.: Fault-tolerant control design using LPV admissible model matching: Application to a two-degree of freedom helicopter. In: 17th Mediterranean Conference on Control and Automation, Thessaloniki, Greece, June 24-26, pp. 522–527 (2009)
[9] Heredia, G., Ollero, A., Bejar, M., Mahtani, R.: Sensor and actuator fault detection in small autonomous helicopter. Mechatronics 18(2), 90–99 (2008)
[10] Zhang, Y.M., Li, X.R.: Detection and diagnosis of sensor and actuator failures using IMM estimator. IEEE Transactions of Aerospace and Electronics Systems 34(4), 1293–1313 (1998)
[11] Zhang, Y.M., Jiang, J.: Bibliographical review on reconfigurable fault tolerant control systems. Annual Reviews in Control 32(2), 229–252 (2008)
[12] Xu, R., Ozguner, U.: Sliding mode control of a quadrotor helicopter. In: Proceedings of the 45th IEEE Conference on Decision and Control, San Diego, California, USA, pp. 4957–4962 (December 2006)

# Reliability Analysis of Fault Tolerant Wind Energy Conversion System with Doubly Fed Induction Generator

Philippe Weber[1,2], Florent Becker[1,2,3,4], Antoine Mathias,
Didier Theilliol[1,2], and Youmin M. Zhang[5]

[1] Université de Lorraine, CRAN, UMR 7039, Vandoeuvre, F-54506, France
[2] CNRS, CRAN, UMR 7039, Vandoeuvre, F-54506, France
[3] Université de Lorraine, LIEN, Vandoeuvre, F-54506, France
[4] Université de Lorraine, GREEN, EA 4366, Vandoeuvre, F-54506, France
[5] Concordia University, Montreal, Quebec H3G 1M8, Canada
{philippe.weber,florent.becker,
didier.theilliol}@univ-lorraine.fr,
ymzhang@encs.concordia.ca

**Abstract.** This paper deals with the design of a reliable fault tolerant converter topology for grid connected Wind Energy Conversion System (WECS) with Double Fed Induction Generator (DFIG) based on functional redundancy. The main contribution of the developed topology consists to achieve a reconfiguration mechanism based on the functional compensation principle in the presence of components failures. Various reliability analyses based on Markov chain model are developed to determine the effectiveness of this fault tolerant control topology against failures. Application results are presented on a WECS simulator.

**Keywords:** Wind energy conversion system, fault tolerant system, reliability analysis, Markov chain model.

## 1 Introduction

Wind power capacity has experienced tremendous growth in the past decade, thanks to the wind power's environmental benefits, the technological advances, and the government incentives. The poor accessibility to the systems of wind energy generation (such as offshore) justifies the implementation of an autonomous control system able to ensure the functioning especially during times of excessive consumption and thus improves the quality and the reliability of the services. In this paper, the conversion system of the energy produced and the reliability of the energy delivered by wind turbines are studied. Energy conversion is a power electronics device capable to deliver alternative voltages and currents. The reactive power compensation and active filtering are the most concerned.

Moreover, control systems or more conventional controllers are designed for systems without failure. To overcome these limitations, complex modern systems use

C.-Y. Su, S. Rakheja, H. Liu (Eds.): ICIRA 2012, Part I, LNAI 7506, pp. 483–492, 2012.

sophisticated controllers that are developed with accommodation capacities and fault tolerance to meet the requirements of reliability and performance. Fault tolerant control (FTC) system can maintain system performance closely to the desirable one and preserves stability conditions, not only in fault-free case but also in the presence of component failure, or at least ensures degraded performance, which can be accepted as a trade-off. FTC has been motivated by different goals for different applications; it could improve reliability and safety in industrial processes and safety-critical applications such as flight control and nuclear power plant operation [1]. Various studies on FTC are based on hardware redundancy or analytical reconfiguration. The hardware redundancy technique consists of switching from the failed part(s) of the process to another for achieving the same task. An application to WECS is proposed in [1]. The functional redundancy is an alternative to solve the FTC problem for avoiding the disadvantages of the hardware redundancy such as high cost, increase of energy consumption, added weight and space etc.

Let us define the control problem by the triplet $< \gamma_g, C, U >$, [2], where:

- $\gamma_g$     Global objectives
- $C$     A set of constraints given by the structure of system $S_m$, and the parameters of closed-loop system $\theta$
- $U$     A set of control laws

The FTC problem is then defined by $< \gamma_g, C, U >$, which has a solution that could achieve $\gamma_g^{nom}$ by changing the structure, parameters and/or control law of the post-failure system. The failure occurrence leads to a modification of the system structure $C$, to which the objectives may or may not be satisfied. Switching on hardware components modifies C. Moreover, after the failure occurrence, the controller $U$ may be changed or adapted by software switching.

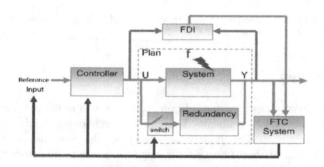

**Fig. 1.** A general FTC system architecture

Fig.1 presents the general architecture of an FTC system with ability of disconnection or replacement of some faulty sub-parts of the system.

In this paper, a fault tolerant WECS with Double-Fed Induction Generator (DFIG) is studied. The WECS normal control is not the goal of this paper and therefore it is not detailed in the paper. Interested readers are referred to [3], [4], [5] for the detailed control strategies of system normal operation or performance. Nevertheless, the present paper proposes a reliability analysis studied in the framework of fault tolerant system with the general architecture as presented in Fig. 1. The system includes functional redundancy together with a fault-tolerant topology with imperfect switching.

The paper is organized as follows: Section 2 is devoted to the description for the fault tolerant WECS topology. Section 3 deals with the reliability computation methods of analytical reconfiguration or cold standby with imperfect switching. A simulation example is considered in Section 4 to compute the reliability and to compare to the initial system reliability. Finally, concluding remarks are given in Section 5.

## 2   Fault Tolerant WECS Topologies

### 2.1   Conventional WECS Based on a Six-Leg Converter

The wind turbine feeds a DFIG through a multiplier. The DFIG produces a part of the power directly to the network through the stator [6]. The rotor through the converters gives the second part of power. The advantage of such a topology is demonstrated by the fact that converters are calibrated for only a part of the nominal power of the machine. Therefore this topology is much cheaper than a standard machine where the converters are directly connected to the network. The failure mode behavior of static converters and the fault tolerant control of voltage source inverter systems have been covered in [7], [8], [9].

As illustrated in Fig. 2, two converters are defined for a nominal converter topology for WECS with DFIG: the Rotor Side Converter (RSC) and the Grid Side Converter (GSC):

- The control of the RSC will allow us to control: the electromagnetic torque; the stator reactive power of the DFIG.
- The control of the GSC will allow us to control: the DC bus voltage; Reactive power exchanged with the network.

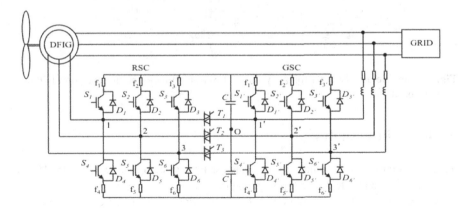

**Fig. 2.** FT converter topology for WECS with DFIG

## 2.2     WECS Six-Leg Fault Tolerant Converter

Fig. 2 shows the six-leg topology of the fault tolerant system. It is based on two 3-leg converters ($S_1,..., S_6, S_{1'},..., S_{6'}$), two capacitors $C$ and three triacs ($T_1, ..., T_3$). Without failure in this nominal structure $M_{nom}$, all the switches ($T_1, ..., T_3$) are open. The switch allows the reconfiguration of the WECS after the detection of the failure without component ($S_i$) redundancy. A specific controller is used to take advantage of the functional redundancy after isolation of the leg in failure.

The capacitors were used in order to measure the voltages points O, necessary for the failure detection. In the presence of a failure on the first or the second converter, the wind conversion chain is reconfigured thanks to the switches ($T_1, ..., T_3$). Fig. 2 presents the system before the reconfiguration in the normal operating condition. When a failure occurs on the component $S_6$, thanks to the triacs $T_3$ the FTC system isolates the third leg of the first converter. It is a hardware reconfiguration Fig. 3 [10]. The component $S_6$ is out of order then the structure $M_3$ represents the new configuration of the WECS, which allows smooth operation and continuity of service. The component $T_3$ supports the RCS and GSC part, a specific controller is used, consequently it is more reliable than in conventional case. This strategy can be used in the case of one failure of one of the components ($S_1,..., S_6, S_{1'},..., S_{6'}$), leading to three structures $M_1, M_2, M_3$ by the control of one switch of ($T_1,..., T_3$). The diagnosis and FTC system and the 4 specific controllers adapted to the fourth structures $M_{nom}, M_1, M_2, M_3$ are software devices supported by FPGA [4], [5].

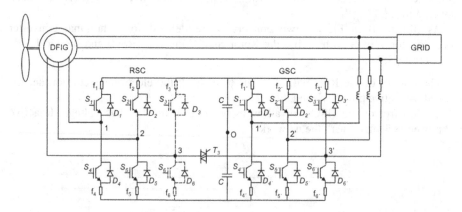

**Fig. 3.** Fault tolerant converter topology for WECS with DFIG in the presence of a failure on the component $S_6$

## 3     Reliability Analysis

This part focuses on the reliability analysis for FTC system that switch from $M_{nom}$ to $M_1, M_2,$ or $M_3$ (6 legs to 5 legs topologies) [1].

Representing system failure in a probabilistic way is attractive because it naturally accounts the uncertainty. Process behaviour is considered as a random variable that takes its value from a finite state space corresponding to the possible process states.

Then a discrete time stochastic process models the deteriorations. In the case of finite or countable state space, Markov processes are represented by a graph called Markov Chain (MC) [11]. Markov chain models are used to estimate the system reliability under the assumption that sub-systems are defined through two states: intact (available) or failed (unavailable) [2], [11], [12].

Markov chain models a sequence of random variables $\{X_k,\ k=0,1,2,...\}$ for which the Markov property is held. Let $\{\eta_1,...,\eta_M\}$ be a finite set of the possible mutually exclusive states of each $X_k$. The probability distribution over these states is represented by the vector $p(X_k)$:

$$p(X_k) = \left[ p(X_k = \eta_1),...,p(X_k = \eta_m),...,p(X_k = \eta_M) \right] \ with: \sum_{m=1}^{M} p(X_k = \eta_m) = \tag{1}$$

In this paper, failure rates are assumed constants. The transition probabilities, based on homogenous Markov chains, are time invariant and depend only on the system states as follows:

$$p_{ij} = p(X_{k+1} = \eta_i | X_k = \eta_j) = p(X_{k+2} = \eta_i | X_{k+1} = \eta_j) \tag{2}$$

In a homogeneous discrete-time Markov chain, the transition matrix $\mathbf{P}_{MC}$ between the states is defined from failure rate parameters. For instance, let us consider the passive redundancy system described in Fig.4a). The associated MC, composed of three states $\{1, 2, 3\}$ is presented in Fig.4b).

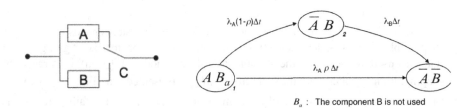

a) Reliability bloc diagram        b) Markov chain modeling

**Fig. 4.** Passive redundant system and imperfect switching

With a transition matrix $\mathbf{P}_{MC}$ defined as follows:

$$\mathbf{P}_{MC} = \begin{bmatrix} 1-(p_{12}+p_{13}) & p_{12} & p_{13} \\ 0 & 1-p_{23} & p_{23} \\ 0 & 0 & 1 \end{bmatrix} \tag{3}$$

where:

- $p_{12} \cong \lambda_A \cdot (1-\rho) \cdot \Delta t$: $\lambda_A$ is a constant failure rate of the component $A$; $\rho$ is the commutation failure probability and $\Delta t$ is the time interval. The probability $p_{12}$ can be interpreted as the probability that the component $A$ fails after the time $\Delta t$ and the commutation on the component $B$ is successful.
- $p_{13} \cong \lambda_A \cdot \rho \cdot \Delta t$ is the probability that the component $A$ fails after the time $\Delta t$ and the commutation on the component $B$ is not successful.
- $p_{23} \cong \lambda_B \Delta t$: $\lambda_B$ is a constant failure rate of the component $B$. The probability $p_{23}$ is the probability that the component $B$ fails after the time $\Delta t$.

Given an initial distribution over states $p(X_0)$, the probability distribution over states after $k$ stage $p(X_k)$ is obtained from the Chapman-Kolmogorov equation:

$$p(X_k) = p(X_0) \prod_{i=0}^{K} \mathbf{P}_{MC} \tag{4}$$

Assuming that $i \in \{0,...,l\}$ represents the functioning states, system reliability is defined as:

$$R_S(k) = \sum_{i \in \{0...l\}} p(X_k = s_i) \tag{5}$$

the Mean Time To Failure (MTTF) is computed by:

$$MTTF = \int_0^\infty R_S(t) dt \tag{6}$$

The use of classic Markov chain to model deterioration in systems needs to enumerate all possible states that lead sometimes to a huge transition matrix. Aggregation of states is used to decrease the complexity of the model. Fig. 5a) illustrates this simplification applied to the structure $M_{nom}$ presented in Fig. 2, with the parameters: $\lambda_{Si}$ the failure rate of the component $S_i$ and $\lambda_{Cdc/2}$ the failure rate of the component $C$.

## 4    Reliability Analysis: WECS Six-Leg Fault Tolerant Converter

The classical converter topology of the WECS is modelled as Markov chain model in Fig. 5b), and the fault tolerant system with functional redundancy is modelled as Markov chain in Fig. 5c) (for simplicity $\Delta t$ is considered equal to $1$ $hour$). Concerning the topology with fault tolerant control system, the Markov chain shown in Fig. 5c) takes into account the tension variations in the converter due to the switch to a specific controller when the structure $M_1$, $M_2$, or $M_3$ are activated after the failure occurrence.

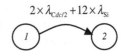

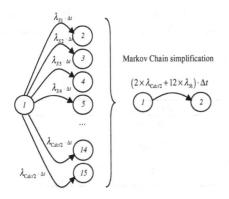

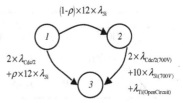

b) System with the nominal topology without redundancy

c) WECS topology with 6-leg fault tolerant functional redundancy and imperfect switching

a) Simplification of the WECS nominal topology without redundancy

**Fig. 5.** Markov chains

The following table presents the value of the failure rate according to the voltage and the MTTF in the classical topology.

**Table 1.** Failure rates and MTTF of the elementary components

|  | Failure rates ($h^{-1}$) | MTTF (h) |
|---|---|---|
| $\lambda_{Si}$ | $2.32 \; 10^{-6}$ | 431 868 |
| $\lambda_{Cdc/2}$ | $6.72 \; 10^{-6}$ | 148 920 |

According to [9], for the nominal structure $M_{nom}$, the voltage level in one leg is limited to a maximum value:

$$V_{dc} \geq \max(u_1, u_2) \times 2 \times \sqrt{3} \tag{7}$$

After reconfiguration, the system operates with only 5 legs, the voltage in one leg is:

$$V_{dc} \geq (u_1 + u_2) \times 2 \times \sqrt{3} \tag{8}$$

where $u_1$ is the input voltage (grid) and $u_2$ is the output voltage (load). The standard voltage in 1 leg is fixed to 350V before the reconfiguration. After the reconfiguration, the voltage at the terminals of a leg is approximately 700V. The voltage level at the terminal on an IGBT (thyristor) has a significant impact on the reliability of the component. Due to the fact that the reconfiguration mechanism increases the voltage, consequently the temperature increases and affects the failure rate of the components the same effect is considered on the failure rates of the capacitors when the voltage increases:

$$\lambda_{Si}(350V) < \lambda_{Si}(700V) \qquad\qquad \lambda_{Cdc/2}(350V) < \lambda_{Cdc/2}(700V) \tag{9}$$

For components affected by various voltage levels, the Table 2 presents the value of the failure rate according to the voltage and the MTTF. The Table 3 presents the switched failure probability $\rho$ of triacs $T_i$.

**Table 2.** Failure rates and MTTF of the components after reconfiguration

|  | Failure rates ($h^{-1}$) | MTTF (h) |
|---|---|---|
| $\lambda_{Si}$(700V) | 2.04 $10^{-5}$ | 49 056 |
| $\lambda_{Cdc/2}$(700V) | 1.38 $10^{-5}$ | 72 708 |
| $\lambda_{Ti}$(OpenCircuit) | 1.43 $10^{-6}$ | 700 800 |

**Table 3.** Switched failure probability of the triacs

|  | Failure rates (/solicitation) |
|---|---|
| $\rho$ | 12.5 $10^{-5}$ |

The reliability of the systems is shown in Fig. 6a). With reconfiguration, the reliability is greater than the initial topology. Other scalar criteria such as MTTF could be evaluated to compare the topologies. The MTTF is computed and equal to 24213 h for the classical topology without FTC system, and 26856 h for the WECS six-leg topology with FTC system. The analysis of the MTTF confirms the previous performance. The mean time before the failure of the system after a reconfiguration is equal to the mean time to transit from the state $\eta_2$ to the state $\eta_3$ (as shown in Fig. 7). This time is given by the equation:

$$\frac{1}{2\times\lambda_{Cdc/2}(700V)+10\times\lambda_{Si}(700V)+\lambda_{Ti}(OpenCircuit)}=4295h$$

Therefore, when a failure on the component $S_i$ occurred, the FTC system generates an alarm and switches to the appropriated structure $M_1$, $M_2$, or $M_3$. The mean time before a novel failure is 4295 h, this value corresponds to the time available for the preparation of the maintenance intervention to repair system. Unfortunately this time is available only if the system is in the state $\eta_2$. The Markov model allows computing the probability distribution over the system states. Therefore it is interesting to compute the probability that the system used a reconfiguration by the FTC system. In order to calculate this probability, the Markov chain model is modified as presented in Fig. 7.

The state $\eta_4$ represents the failure of the system after a reconfiguration. Based on this new Markov chain model, the computation leads to a probability close to 0.68 thus, for 68% of the failure in the system, the FTC system produces an alarm and the maintenance have a mean time of 4295 h for the operations before the critical failure.

As illustrated in Fig. 6b), the state $\eta_3$ represents the critical failure of the switch or the capacitors with the probability close to 32% of the FTC system to be not able to operate.

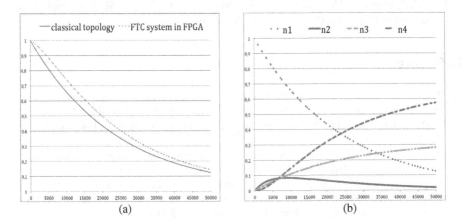

(a)                                                                                  (b)

**Fig. 6.** Reliability (time in hours)

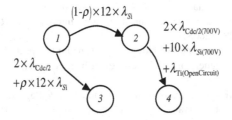

**Fig. 7.** Markov chain of a 6-leg fault tolerant converter topology

## 5   Conclusion

This paper deals with the design of a reliable fault tolerant converter topology for grid connected Wind Energy Conversion System (WECS) with Double Fed Induction Generator (DFIG) based on functional redundancy. The topology can achieve continuous operation even if a complete loss of one of the converter, providing the global objective for maintaining nominal feeding of electric power to the grid. When a failure is detected, 68% of the system is reconfigured in a new topology using functional redundancy. The switch removes the faulty leg and a reconfiguration of the order has been implemented in the FPGA.

The main contribution of the developed topology consists to achieve a reconfiguration mechanism based on the functional compensation principle in the presence of components failures. This method involves changing tensions, which have an impact on the reliability of the system. Also, for this topology, the reliability is more important than a classical system without FTC system. The reliability analysis provides to design the best topology under all components fault/failures. Such FTC design in tandem with reliability analysis allows preparing the maintenance intervention without stopping the WECS.

**Acknowledgements.** This work was supported by the ECO SUR project from Lorraine region CPER MISN 2007-2013 SSS – France.

# References

1. Weber, P., Poure, P., Theilliol, D., Saadate, S.: Design of hardware fault tolerant control architecture for wind energy conversion system with DFIG based on reliability analysis. In: IEEE International Symposium on Industrial Electronics, Cambridge, UK, June 30-July 2 (2008)
2. Staroswiecki, M., Hoblos, G., Aitouche, A.: Sensor network design for fault tolerant estimation. Int. J. Adapt. Control and Signal Process. 18, 55–72 (2004)
3. Boyette, A., Poure, P., Saadate, S.: Direct and indirect control of a doubly fed induction generator wind turbine including a storage unit. In: 32th Annual Conference of the IEEE Industrial Electronics Society, Paris, France (November 2006)
4. Karimi, S., Poure, P., Saadate, S.: FPGA-based fully digital fast power switch fault detection and compensation for three-phase shunt active filters. Electric Power Systems Research 78(11), 1933–1940 (2008)
5. Karimi, S., Poure, P., Saadate, S.: FPGA in the loop prototyping methodology for fully digital power electronics systems control design. International Review of Electrical Engineering 3, 281–289 (2008)
6. Gaillard, A., Poure, P., Saadate, S.: Novel control method of grid connected converter of doubly fed induction generator to achieve disturbances rejection. IEEE Wind Energy (October 2009)
7. Kastha, D., Bose, B.K.: Investigation of fault modes of voltage-fed inverter system for induction motor drive. IEEE Transactions on Industry Applications 30, 1028–1038 (1994)
8. Thybo, C.: Fault-tolerant control of induction motor drive applications. In: Proceedings of the American Control Conference, June 25-27, vol. 4, pp. 2621–2622 (2001)
9. Jacobina, C.B., Lúcio de Araujo Ribeiro, R., Lima, A.M.N., Cabral da Silva, E.R.: Fault-tolerant reversible AC motor drive system. Transactions on Industry Applications 39(4), 1077–1084 (2003)
10. Wu, N.E.: Reliability of fault tolerant control systems. In: IEEE Conference on Decision and Control, Part I, Orlando, Florida, USA (2001)
11. Shahbazi, M., Poure, P., Saadate, S., Reza Zolghadri, M.: Five-leg converter topology for wind energy conversion system with doubly fed induction generator. Renewable Energy 36, 3187–3194 (2011)
12. Bobbio, A.: Dependability analysis of fault-tolerant systems: a literature survey. Microprocessing and Microprogramming 29, 1–13 (1990)

# Distribution Rates Analysis
## of Symplectic Geometry Spectrum
## for Surface EMG Signals on Healthy Hand Muscles

Lei Min[1], Meng Guang[1], Gu Yudong[2], and Zhang Kaili[2]

[1] Institute of Vibration, Shock and Noise,
State Key Laboratory of Mechanical System and Vibration,
Shanghai Jiao Tong University, Shanghai 200240, P.R. China
[2] Hua Shan Hospital, Fudan University, Shanghai 200040, P.R. China
leimin@sjtu.edu.cn

**Abstract.** The assessment of muscle function has been an intractable issue in several fields of biomechanics, sports medicine and rehabilitation medicine. The surface EMG signals are often used to evaluate the muscle function. However, even for the muscles of the healthy hands, some characteristics of the surface EMG signals are also usually obviously different, such as the values of amplitude, mean spectral frequency, etc. It is difficult to use these values as the reference standards to assess the corresponding muscles. For this, this paper applies a kind of the nonlinear values----the distribution rates of the symplectic geometry spectrum (SGS) method to analyze the surface EMG signals. By comparing the distribution rates of SGS between the original surface EMG signals and their surrogate data, the results show that the surface EMG signals are not from a random process but a nonlinear deterministic process. And the distribution rate value can be taken as a reference standard to analyze the surface EMG signals.

**Keywords:** Surface EMG, Symplectic geometry spectrum, Nonlinear time series analysis, Surrogate data.

## 1    Introduction

The dynamical behaviour of a muscle system is very complex. As for a state variable of the muscle system, the surface EMG (SEMG) signal contains the electrical properties of muscle contraction. These properties can reflect the function of the muscle system. At present, the study of the surface EMG signal has been widely concerned for the assessment of muscle function in several fields of biomechanics, sports, rehabilitation and geriatric medicine because of its convenience and noninvasiveness[1]. Many researchers have used the linear analysis methods to study the SEMG, such as mean, standard deviation, mean spectral frequency (MNF) and median spectral frequency (MDF)[2]. However, the SEMG signal is a nonstationary signal for sustaining muscle contractions. It is difficult to use these linear methods to assess the muscle system. For this, some authors have applied various nonlinear

C.-Y. Su, S. Rakheja, H. Liu (Eds.): ICIRA 2012, Part I, LNAI 7506, pp. 493–498, 2012.

techniques to study the characteristics of SEMG during isotonic contraction, isokinetic contraction, and isometric contraction. Yang et al. have calculated some nonlinear indexes of SEMG of 20000 points in the muscle contracted state and relaxed state, including complexity, correlation time, correlation dimension, Lyapunov exponent and entropy[3]. Gupta et al. have applied 10000 point SEMG data to compute its fractal dimension[4]. Lei et al. have improved the surrogate data method to detect the nonlinearity of SEMG in limb different movement states[5]. This paper proposes to apply the symplectic geometry spectrum (SGS) method[6,7] and the surrogate data method to analyze the SEMG signals in sustaining muscle contraction.

The remainder of this paper is organized as follows. The algorithm of distribution rates analysis is given based on symplectic geometry in Section 2. Section 3 analyzes the SGS distribution rates of SEMG in sustained muscle contractions. Section 4 contains our conclusions.

## 2     Methodology

### 2.1     Symplectic Geometry Spectrum of Time Series

For the measured time series $x$, $x$ can be built into a matrix $X$ according to Takens' embedding theorem. The data length is $n$ points. That is,

$$X = \begin{bmatrix} \overline{X}_1^T \\ \overline{X}_2^T \\ \vdots \\ \overline{X}_m^T \end{bmatrix} = \begin{bmatrix} x_1 & x_2 & \cdots & x_d \\ x_2 & x_3 & \cdots & x_{d+1} \\ \vdots & \vdots & \cdots & \vdots \\ x_m & x_{m+1} & \cdots & x_n \end{bmatrix} \tag{1}$$

where $d$ is embedding dimension. $m = n - d + 1$ is the number of dots in $d$-dimension vector $\overline{X}_i^T$, ($i = 1, ..., m$), that denotes a dot in the phase space. For the above matrix $X$, the $d{\times}d$ square matrix $A$ is given by $A = X^T X$.

A Hamilton matrix $M$ in the symplectic space can be built by using the matrix $A$. That is:

$$M = \begin{pmatrix} A & 0 \\ 0 & -A^T \end{pmatrix} \tag{2}$$

The $2d$ eigenvalues of $M$ are calculated by using the symplectic $QR$ decomposition in terms of the Ref.[6]. The symplectic geometry spectrum $\sigma_i$ of $A$ is made by the $d$ eigenvalues of $M$ in descending order, that is:

$$\sigma_1 = \left| \lambda_{\max}(B) \right|, \ldots, \sigma_d = \left| \lambda_{\min}(B) \right|, \ i = 1, \cdots, d \tag{3}$$

Then, the symplectic geometry spectrum $\sigma_x$ of the time series $x$ is equal to $\sigma_i$ and has the following feature, i.e.

$$\sigma_1 > \sigma_2 > \cdots > \sigma_k \gg \sigma_{k+1} \geq \cdots \geq \sigma_d \tag{4}$$

These spectrum values $\sigma_x$ reflect the energy distribution of the signal $x$ in the corresponding direction projections that represent the modes of the original system with symplectic orthonormal bases. It is well known that a chaotic process can have finite number of modes for description whereas a stochastic process needs the infinitely large number of modes. That is, for the chaotic process, the energy distribution is different in the different bases (see Eq.(4)). The values of $\sigma_i$, $i = k+1$, ..., $d$, are called as the noise floor that reflect the noise level in the data. For the stochastic process, there are $\sigma_1 = \sigma_2 = \cdots = \sigma_d$ [6]. This shows that the energy distribution of the stochastic time series is the same in each orthonormal base.

## 2.2    Distribution Rates of Symplectic Geometry Spectrum

Here, we use the distribution rates $D$ of symplectic geometry spectrum $\sigma_x$ to illuminate the total energy distribution of the signal $x$. The distribution rates $D$ of symplectic geometry spectrum $\sigma_x$ can be computed:

$$D(i) = \log(\sigma_i / \sum_{i=1}^{d} \sigma_i) \tag{5}$$

The $D(d)$ can be described as the noise level in the data. The $D(d)$ of the chaotic time series is different from that of the stochastic data. This paper uses this value to study the surface EMG signals when $d=19$.

# 3     Analysis of Surface EMG Signals

For the muscles of the two hands of a healthy subject, the surface EMG signals are often obviously different during trying the best of muscle contraction. In order to explore the consistency of healthy left and right hand muscles, this paper applies the left and right abductor digiti minimi muscles of a healthy woman subject to analyze the surface EMG signals with the sampling frequency $25k$Hz. The testing time is twenty seconds. The analysis window length is 4096 points. The Figure 1 gives the surface EMG signals of the left and right hand muscles and their mean values, standard deviation values, mean frequency (MNF) values, etc. From the Figure 1, we can see that although the left and right hand muscles are both healthy, the amplitude values of the surface EMG signals of the left abductor digiti minimi muscle are smaller than those of the right one (see Figure 1a and 1b). Meanwhile, some linear properties of the left abductor digiti minimi muscle are also obviously different from those of the right one, for example, the standard deviation, the mean of the absolute values, the standard deviation of the absolute values and the MNF values except the mean values are almost equal to zero (see Figure 1c, 1d, 1e and 1f). It is hard to effectively evaluate the muscle function by the mean values of the orignal surface EMG data. These results show that from the view of the linear analysis, the left abductor digiti minimi muscle is not equivalent to the right one. It is difficult to use these values of a healthy muscle as the reference standards to evaluate the other corresponding pathologic muscle. Figure 2 gives the $D(d)$ values of the surface EMG signals by using symplectic geometry spectrum from the view of nonlinear analysis. All the $D(d)$ values are almost all around -18 (see Figure 2). The results show that the left and right abductor digiti minimi muscles have the same muscle function.

Furthermore, in order to test the nonlinearity of the surface EMG signal, 39 sets of surrogate data based on the SEMG signals are generated by the Fourier transform technique in the literature [5] (see Figure 2). The $D(d)$ values of these surrogate data vary in the wider range. Meanwhile, these values are obviously distinguished from those of the original surface EMG data. The results imply that SEMG is not from a random process but a nonlinear deterministic process.

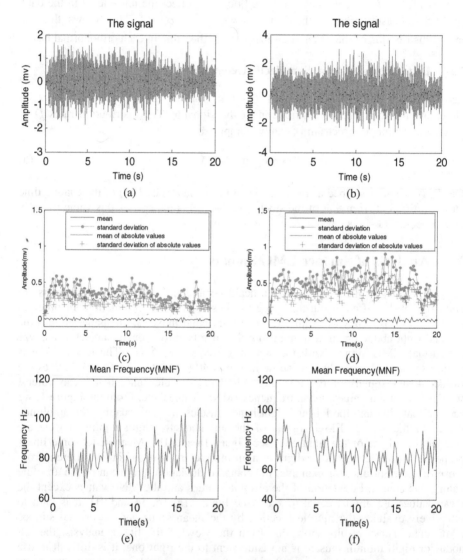

**Fig. 1.** The analysis of the SEMG signals during trying the best of muscle contraction for the left (*left figure*) and right (*right figure*) abductor digiti minimi muscles: (a) and (b) the raw time series; (c) and (d) the mean, standard deviation, mean of absolute values, standard deviation of absolute values; (e) and (f) the MNF values

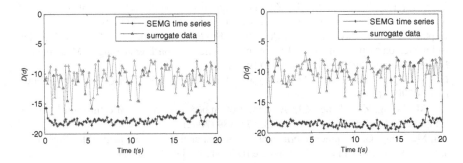

**Fig. 2.** For the left (*left figure*) and right (*right figure*) abductor digiti minimi muscles: (a) and (b) the distribution rate $D(d)$ values of the surface EMG signals

# 4     Conclusions

This paper applies the distribution rates of the symplectic geometry spectrum (SGS) to analyze the surface EMG signals of the left and right abductor digiti minimi muscles during trying the best of muscle contraction. The $D(d)$ values of the SEMG signals are obviously different from those of their surrogate data. The results show that the surface EMG signals could be nonlinear. Meanwhile, the $D(d)$ values of the SEMG signals vary in the small range during muscle contraction. The $D(d)$ values of the left abductor digiti minimi muscle are almost the same as those of the right one. The results indicate that the two muscles should be equivalent from the view of nonlinear analysis. The abductor digiti minimi muscles have the same nonlinear characteristics for a healthy subject. To sum up, the method of this paper provides a new idea for the assessment of muscle function.

**Acknowledgements.** This work is supported by the National Natural Science Foundation of China (No. 10872125), Science Fund for Creative Research Groups of the National Natural Science Foundation of China(No. 50821003), State Key Lab of Mechanical System and Vibration and Project supported by the Research Fund of State Key Lab of MSV, China (Grant No. MSV-MS-2010-08), the Ministry of Science and Technology of China (grant Nos. 2009CB824900, 2009CB824904) , Key Laboratory of Hand Reconstruction, Ministry of Health, Shanghai, People's Republic of China, Shanghai Key Laboratory of Peripheral Nerve and Microsurgery, Shanghai, People's Republic of China.

# References

1. Al-Mulla, M.R., Sepulveda, F., Colley, M.: I A review of non-invasive techniques to detect and predict localized muscle fatigue. Sensor 11, 3545–3594 (2011)
2. Georgakis, A., Stergioulas, L.K., Giakas, G.: Fatigue Analysis of the Surface EMG Signal in Isometric Constant Force Contractions Using the Averaged Instantaneous Frequency. IEEE Trans. on Biomed. Eng. 50(2), 262–265 (2003)

3. Yang, Z., Liu, B., Peng, J., Ma, Z.: The Preliminary Nonlinear Dynamical Analysis of Surface Electromyogram. Space Med. & Med. Eng. 12(3), 185–187 (1999)
4. Gupta, V., Suryanarayanan, S., Reddy, N.P.: Fractal dimension of surface EMG during isokinetic contractions. In: 17th IEEE Annual Conference on Engineering in Medicine and Biology Society, vol. 2, pp. 1331–1332 (1995)
5. Lei, M., Wang, Z.Z., Feng, Z.J.: Detecting nonlinearity of action surface EMG signal. Phys. Lett. A 290(5-6), 297–303 (2001)
6. Lei, M., Wang, Z.Z., Feng, Z.J.: A method of embedding dimension estimation based on symplectic geometry. Phys. Lett. A 303, 179–189 (2002)
7. Lei, M., Meng, G.: Symplectic principal component analysis: a new method for time series analysis. Math. Prob. in Eng. 2011, article ID 793429, 14 pages (2011)

# Mutual Information Analysis with Ordinal Pattern for EMG Based Hand Motion Recognition

Gaoxiang Ouyang, Zhaojie Ju, and Honghai Liu[*]

Intelligent Systems & Biomedical Robotics Group, School of Creative Technologies,
University of Portsmouth, England, PO1 2DJ, UK
{Gaoxiang.ouyang,Zhaojie.ju,Honghai.liu}@port.ac.uk

**Abstract.** It is challenging to understand the inter-muscular interactions from electromyogram (EMG) signals in the research of human movements. Based on ordinal pattern analysis, this paper proposes a mutual information (MI) measure to describe correlations of EMG recordings during hand open and hand close states. Linear discriminant analysis (LDA) is utilized to evaluate the performance of the MI measure for identifying different hand states from various subjects. Experimental results show that the MI measure is effective to extract correlations among EMG recordings, with which the different human hand open and close states have been successfully distinguished, and thus the MI measure is able to reveal the characteristics of intermuscular interactions from EMG signals.

**Keywords:** Mutual information, EMG, Ordinal pattern analysis, Hand movement.

## 1    Introduction

The electromyogram (EMG) signal is a measure of the summed activity of a number of motor unit action potentials (MUAP) lying in the vicinity of the recording electrode [1]. The composition of a EMG signal from MUAPs results in a nonlinear and stochastic signal because of the different firing rates and the large number of motor units that contribute [2]. Thus, the surface EMG (sEMG) signals are complex data that needs to be condensed with useful information [3]. Moreover, the intermuscular interaction plays an important role in the human movements. The interaction between muscles also determines the overall muscular pattern during human movement [4]. Several interactions have already been assessed by means of different linear techniques such as: cross-spectrum between EMG signals [5], magnitude squared coherence [6] and cross-correlation [7]. Although these techniques provide interesting information about intermuscular interactions, they do not evaluate nonlinear interactions.

Mutual information (MI) is the amount of information one random variable contains about another [8]. Therefore, MI of two time series can be considered as an alternative to the well-known correlation analysis. The key issue in MI analysis is how to estimate the probability distribution of the given time series. Various methods

---

[*] Corresponding author.

C.-Y. Su, S. Rakheja, H. Liu (Eds.): ICIRA 2012, Part I, LNAI 7506, pp. 499–506, 2012.

have been proposed to estimate the probability distribution ranging from traditional histogram method to nonlinear phase space methods [8]. Most of these methods involve the quantification of certain aspects of nearest neighbors in phase space and, as a result, are computationally expensive. To circumvent this difficulty, Bandt and Pompe suggest that the ordinal pattern should come naturally from the time series, without further model assumptions, and therefore computationally fast [9,10]. Motivated by the merits of ordinal pattern analysis, we propose a MI measure based on ordinal pattern analysis to explore whether the MI can be effectively used to represent the intermuscular interactions during hand open and hand close states.

## 2     Methods

### 2.1     EMG Data

Eight (2 female, 6 male) healthy right-handed subjects volunteered for this study. Their ages range from 23 to 40 and average is 32.5 years; body height average is 175.5 cm; body mass average is 70 kg. All participants gave informed consent prior to the experiments according to the University of Portsmouth CCI Faculty Ethics Committee. The experiment consisted of both freely hand open and hand close. Each type of states was repeated 10 times for each subject. Every motion lasted about 2 seconds. The four sEMG electrodes were applied to the subject's right forearm muscles, i.e. flexor carpi ulnaris (FCU), flexor carpi radialis (FCR), flexor pollicis longus (FPL) and flexor digitorum profundus (FDP). The EMG data were recorded using DataLINK system from Biometrics LTD with a gel-skin contact area of about 4 $cm^2$ for each bipolar electrode and a centre to centre recording distance of 20 mm. The sampling frequency of DataLINK system in our experiment was set to be 1000Hz and sEMG signals were amplified 1000 times and bandwidth is 15 to 460 Hz using a EMG amplifier (SX230FW sEMG Amplifier, Biometrics LTD). To investigate the synchronization between all pairs of EMG data, EMG signals were selected and dissected from hand open (dataset I) and hand close (dataset II). In this study, 80 4-channel 1-sec EMG epochs were selected for each dataset.

### 2.2     Mutual Information Based on Ordinal Pattern Analysis

In this study, a novel mutual information (MI) measure, which is based on ordinal pattern analysis, is proposed to analyse EMG data. As a continuously varying signal, EMG's amplitude and frequency change over time. It's composed of ascending and descending patterns. The statistical analysis of these two simple patterns may indicate the change of muscle activities. In order to obtain more complicated patterns, it is important to set up more complicated ordinal patterns. Here, these different patterns are referred to as the ordinal pattern. The EMG signals consist of a sequence of order patterns. Based on the probability distribution of these ordinal patterns, the MI between EMGs from different muscles can be estimated. The algorithm of MI based on the ordinal pattern analysis is described as follows:

(1)  Given a time series of length $L$, $\{x_1, x_2, \cdots, x_L\}$, a vector can be generated using an embedding procedure: $S_t = [x_t, x_{t+1}, \cdots, x_{t+m-1}]$ where $m$ is the pattern dimension.

(2)  This vector $S_t$ can be rearranged in an ascending order, $[x_{t+j_1} \leq x_{t+j_2} \cdots \leq x_{t+j_m}]$. For $m$ different numbers, there will be $m! = (1 \times 2 \times \cdots \times m)$ possible ordinal patterns $\pi_i$. For example, for $m = 3$, there are six order patterns between $x_t, x_{t+1}$ and $x_{t+2}$.

(3)  Then we can count the occurrences of the ordinal pattern $\pi_i$, which is denoted as $C(\pi_i)$, and the relative frequency is calculated by $p(\pi_i) = C(\pi_i)/(L-m+1)$, $i = 1, 2, \cdots m!$.

(4)  Suppose two EMG signals $X = \{x_t\}$ and $Y = \{y_t\}$ are recorded from two different muscle areas, respectively. The joint probability of the occurrence of each ordinal pattern in the EMG signals, $p(x, y)$, can also be calculated.

(5)  Once we obtain the probability distribution functions of two EMG series $X$ and $Y$, MI can be obtained by the following equation:

$$MI(X;Y) = \sum_{x \in X} \sum_{y \in Y} p(x, y) \log p(x, y) - \sum_{x \in X} p(x) \log p(x) - \sum_{y \in Y} p(y) \log p(y)$$
$$= H(X) + H(Y) - H(X, Y) \tag{1}$$

MI is a measure derived from Shannon's information theory to estimate the information gained from observations of the effect of one random event on another [8]. Therefore, MI measure is proposed to estimate synchronization between all pairs of EMG signals during hand open and hand close states.

## 2.3    Linear Discriminant Analysis

The performance of the MI measures to discriminate between groups also is evaluated by means of a linear discriminant analysis (LDA). The basic idea of LDA is to project high-dimensional data onto a low-dimensional space such that the data are reshaped to maximize the class separability [11]. Consider a classification problem with $K$ classes ( $K \geq 2$ ). Suppose the training data contain $M$ observations $(x_i, y_i)$, $i = 1, 2, \cdots, M$, with $x_i \in R^p$ and $y_i \in \{1, 2, \cdots, K\}$. Fisher's approach is to find the linear combination $c'x$, which maximizes the ratio of $c'Bc/c'Wc$ where $B$ and $W$ denote the $p \times p$ between-group and within-group covariance matrices, respectively. $B$ and $W$ are defined by:

$$B = \sum_{k=1}^{K} \frac{n_k}{N} (\mu^{(k)} - \mu)(\mu^{(k)} - \mu)^T \tag{2}$$

and

$$W = \sum_{k=1}^{K} \frac{n_k}{N} \hat{\Sigma}_k \qquad (3)$$

where $\mu^{(k)}$ and $\hat{\Sigma}_k$, $k = 1, 2, \cdots, K$, are the sample means and covariance matrices of each class (with $n_k$ samples) and $\mu$ is the total sample mean vector. The maximization problem in this method has been shown to be equivalent to solve the Eigenproblem: $(W^{-1}B - \lambda I)c = 0$. Thus, if $W$ is a non-singular matrix, Fisher's criterion is maximized when the projection matrix $c$ is composed of the Eigenvectors of $W^{-1}B$ with at most $K$-1 corresponding non-zero Eigenvalues [9]. In this study, LDA is used to evaluate the performance of the MI measures to discriminate between different groups.

## 3    Results

### 3.1    MI Measure of EMG Data

Fig. 1 shows the ordinal pattern analysis of EMG recordings from muscles FCU and FCL during hand open and hand close, respectively. Ordinal pattern analysis depends on the selection of pattern dimension m. When m is too small (less than 3), the scheme will not work well since there are only a few distinct states for EMG recordings. Often, for a long EMG recording, a large value of m is preferable. However, in order to allow every possible joint ordinal pattern of dimension m to occur in EMG recordings of length L, the condition must hold. For this reason, pattern dimension m=4 is selected in this study. As shown in Fig. 1, the joint probability distributions and their corresponding marginal probability distributions of EMG recordings have changed dramatically between hand open and close states.

The MI measure based on ordinal pattern analysis is applied to analyze the synchronization between all 160 1-sec four-channel EMG epochs (80 from each dataset I and II). As the EMG recordings are collected from four muscles, i.e., FCU, FCR, FPL and FDP, there are six MI values among each four-channel EMG epochs. For the hand open state, the MI values for EMG epochs are averaged at 0.159±0.066 for FCU-FCR pair, 0.112±0.007 for FCU-FPL pair, 0.130±0.024 for FCU-FDP pair, 0.112±0.010 for FCR-FPL pair, 0.126±0.016 for FCR-FDP pair and 0.111±0.007 for FPL-FDP pair, respectively. For the hand close state, the MI values for EMG epochs are averaged at 0.272±0.100 for FCU-FCR pair, 0.126±0.020 for FCU-FPL pair, 0.182±0.108 for FCU-FDP pair, 0.134±0.029 for FCR-FPL pair, 0.162±0.029 for FCR-FDP pair and 0.128±0.033 for FPL-FDP pair, respectively. Next, in order to investigate whether their distributions over the two states are significantly different, the one-way ANOVA with Scheffe's post-hoc test is used for MI values on each EMG-EMG pair. The population distribution of the MI of each EMG-EMG pair is shown in Fig. 2 as boxplot. It can be seen that, on all six EMG-EMG pairs, the MI values in hand close state are significantly higher than ones in hand open state (*P*<0.05).

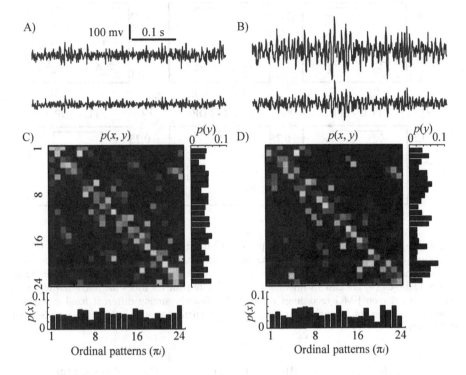

**Fig. 1.** The probability distribution of ordinal patterns in EMG recordings. The examples of EMG epochs from the muscles FCU and FCR during hand open (A) and hand close (B) states. The joint probability distribution $p(x,y)$ of ordinal patterns (pattern dimension is 4) of EMG from the muscles FCU and FCR and their corresponding marginal probability distributions $p(x)$ and $p(y)$ during hand open (C) and hand close (D) states.

In order to compare the extraction information of EMG between MI based on ordinal pattern analysis and traditional histogram methods, the traditional histogram MI (hMI) measure is also used to analyse the EMG data. The similar results of synchronization between EMG epochs can be obtained from hMI measure, i.e., the hMI values in hand close state are higher than ones in hand open state. Next, in order to investigate whether their distributions over the two states are significantly different, the one-way ANOVA with Scheffe's *post-hoc* test is used for hMI values on each EMG-EMG pair. The population distribution of the hMI of each EMG-EMG pair is shown in Fig. 3 as *boxplot*. It can be seen that, on all six EMG-EMG pairs, the hMI values in hand close state are significantly higher than ones in hand open state (*P*<0.05).

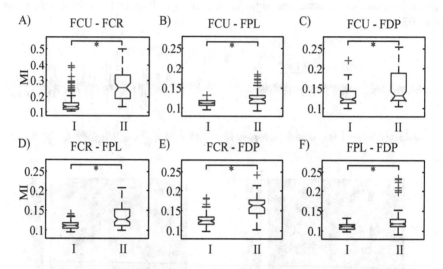

**Fig. 2.** *Boxplots* for the MI between all pairs of EMG signals, grouped by hand open (I) and hand close (II) state. Each box presents the interquartile range that contains 50% of values with a line at the median. The whiskers show overall data range, excluding outlines and extreme values. Outlines (+) are cases with values that are more than 1.5 times the interquartile range. MI values between EMG recordings differed significantly among different hand movement states (indicated as star on graphs) as determined by statistical analyses (Scheffe's *post-hoc* test *P*<0.05 (*)).

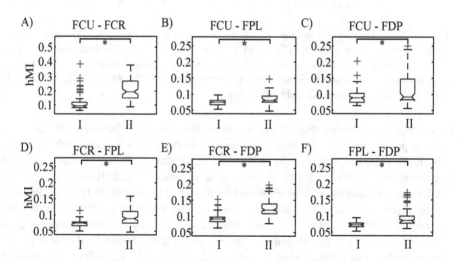

**Fig. 3.** *Boxplots* for the traditional histogram MI (hMI) between all pairs of EMG signals, grouped by hand open (I) and hand close (II) state

## 3.2   Classification

The performance of the MI measure to discriminate two groups is also evaluated using a LDA algorithm. The calculated MI measure is used as input data with 6 features (dimension of the extracted feature vectors) in the LDA classifier. These features are projected down to a two-dimensional space as shown in Fig. 4. It can be seen that the data separate into well-defined clusters, correctly classifying 159 of 160 subjects using the MI measure, giving approximately 99.4% separability. In order to compare the performance of MI measure based on ordinal pattern analysis and traditional histogram methods, the calculated hMI values are used as input data with 6 features (dimension of the extracted feature vectors) in the LDA classifier. In the same way, these features are projected onto a two-dimensional space, which is shown in Fig. 5. It is found that here is an overlap between the the hand open and close state. A classification accuracy of 92.5% is achieved based on hMI measures.

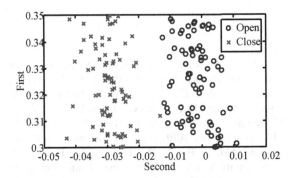

**Fig. 4.** Linear discriminant analysis of two groups: the hand open (o) and close (x) states. The six-dimensional feature vectors (MI values) are projected down to two dimensions.

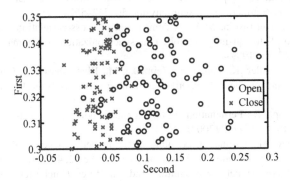

**Fig. 5.** Linear discriminant analysis of two groups: the hand open (o) and close (x) states. The six-dimensional feature vectors (MI values) are projected down to two dimensions.

## 4    Conclusion

In this study, a novel MI measure based on ordinal pattern analysis is proposed to estimate intermuscular interactions from EMG signals. The experimental study on the efficacy of the proposed MI measure as a tool to identify correlation between EMG signals has been presented. The results show that there is an increasing of MI between EMG from hand open state to hand close state. Meanwhile, LDA is applied to evaluate the performance of the MI measures to identify the hand open/close states. The test results show that a classification accuracy of 99.4% is achieved for MI measure based on ordinal pattern analysis, while the classification accuracy is 92.5% for the traditional hMI measure. These results suggest that the proposed MI measure has potential in identifying the EMG signals from different hand movements.

**Acknowledgments.** This work was supported by the Leverhulme Visiting Fellowship.

## References

1. McGill, K.C., Marateb, H.R.: Rigorous a Posteriori Assessment of Accuracy in EMG Decomposition. IEEE Trans. Neural. Syst. Rehabil. Eng. 19, 54–63 (2011)
2. Farfan, F.D., Politti, J.C., Felice, C.J.: Evaluation of EMG processing techniques using Information Theory. BioMedical Engineering OnLine 9, 72 (2010)
3. Artemiadis, P.K., Kyriakopoulos, K.J.: An EMG-based robot control scheme robust to time-varying EMG signal features. IEEE Trans. Inf. Technol. Biomed. 14, 582–588 (2010)
4. Alonso, J.F., Mananas, M.A., Hoyer, D., Topor, Z.L., Bruce, E.N.: Evaluation of respiratory muscles activity by means of cross mutual information function at different levels of ventilatory effort. IEEE Trans. Biomed. Eng. 54, 1573–1582 (2007)
5. Mananas, M.A., Fiz, J.A., Morera, J., Caminal, P.: Analyzing dynamic EMG and VMG signals of respiratory muscles. IEEE Eng. Med. Biol. Mag. 20, 125–132 (2001)
6. Bruce, E.N., Akerson, L.M.: High-frequency oscillations in human electromyograms during voluntary contractions. J. Neurophysiol. 56, 542–553 (1986)
7. Semmler, J.G., Nordstrom, M.A.: A comparison of cross-correlation and surface EMG techniques used to quantify motor unit synchronization in humans. J. Neurosci. Methods 90, 47–55 (1999)
8. Hlavackova-Schindler, K., Palus, M., Vejmelka, M., Bhattacharya, J.: Causality detection based on information-theoretic approaches in time series analysis. Physics Reports 441, 1–46 (2007)
9. Bandt, C., Pompe, B.: Permutation entropy: a natural complexity measure for time series. Phys. Rev. Lett. 88, 174102 (2002)
10. Li, X., Ouyang, G.: Estimating coupling direction between neuronal populations with permutation conditional mutual information. Neuroimage 52, 497–507 (2010)
11. Webb, A.R.: Statistical pattern recognition, 2nd edn. Wiley, Chichester (2006)

# Design of an Anthropomorphic Prosthetic Hand towards Neural Interface Control

Shunchong Li, Xinjun Sheng, Jianrong Zhang, and Xiangyang Zhu

State Key Laboratory of Mechanical System and Vibration,
School of Mechanical Engineering, Shanghai Jiao Tong University,
Shanghai 200240, P.R. China
evenfour@sjtu.edu.cn

**Abstract.** This paper presents the design of an anthropomorphic artificial hand called SJT-3 towards neural-controlled prosthetic applications, focusing on mechanism and local control. The hand has 5 fingers, 15 joints and 6 intrinsic motors, and is similar to a human hand in appearance, size and weight. The hand can achieve various basic grasps and common gestures, required in daily life. It is connected with a 3-DOF artificial forearm. A local controller integrated in the prosthesis based on master-slave structure is adopted in order to keep the dexterity under the limited inputs of current neural interface. The prototype has been developed, and evaluated with a surface EMG interface.

**Keywords:** anthropomorphic hand, artificial hand, neural interface.

## 1 Introduction

Upper limb prosthesis is one of the significant application fields of humanoid robotics research. Modern prostheses could be controlled via biological signals that rely on advanced neural interface technologies. These prostheses are more powerful than cosmetic hands and body-powered prostheses, and can be controlled in an intuitive way. They assist people who lose a hand from amputation to restore part of the hand's original functionality. Some commercial prostheses, such as Otto Bock's prostheses[1] and i-Limb from Touch Bionics[2], have been available and widely used.

However, these commercial prostheses are still unable to fit the requirements due to simple structure and control strategy. For example, Otto Bock's Sensor-Hand, which is the most well-known and worldwide implanted prosthetic hand, provides just one DOF like a gripper. Although a recent version prosthesis of Otto Bock called Michelangelo Hand and the i-Limb are multi-fingered and possess more DOFs, they are not multifunctional indeed, because a small number of electrodes are adopted to acquire surface EMG signals, and control strategies are too simple to drive all independent actuators.

Meanwhile, many experimental EMG prostheses have been developed, such as Revolutionizing Prosthetics[3], MANUS-HAND[4] and CyberHand[5]. These

C.-Y. Su, S. Rakheja, H. Liu (Eds.): ICIRA 2012, Part I, LNAI 7506, pp. 507–517, 2012.
© Springer-Verlag Berlin Heidelberg 2012

advanced prostheses have got a lot of breakthroughs in mechatronics design and biological signal processing, but there is still a long way from practical stage.

There are two challenges towards the development of an advanced prosthesis. One is that the current biological signal processing can only provide limited information implicating motion intention of human. The other one is certainly that of building a multifunctional, dexterous, and anthropomorphic prosthetic hand for the neural interface.

In this paper, design of an anthropomorphic prosthesis, named SJT-3, is described. The prosthetic hand imitates a real human hand, comprises a thumb and four fingers with 15 joints and is actuated by six independent intrinsic actuators. In addition, a 3-DOF forearm, which can achieve motions like human wrist and forearm, has been accomplished as well. A control system is also integrated into the palm for coordinating joints movements. A surface EMG interface, which has been achieved in our previous work, is used to control the SJT-3.

## 2    Objectives

The anthropomorphic artificial hand is a part of neural interface based prosthesis system, the block diagram of which is shown in Fig.1. This system allows users to control the prosthesis via biological signals such as EMG or EEG signal that implicates the motion intention of users, and to get sensory feedback via electrical or mechanical stimulation.

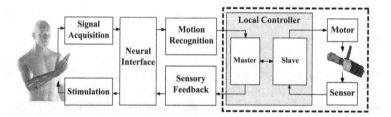

**Fig. 1.** Block diagram of neural interface prosthetic system

Some previous works have been done on motion recognition via EMG signal[6], and we have developed an artificial hand called SJT-2 exploited this biological interface. Several preliminary experiments have been carried out on this platform[7]. Nevertheless, the performances of the SJT-2 is not satisfactory due to low grasp force, lack of dexterity, size and weight, hence a new generation of artificial hand comes up on the agenda for further studies. We focus on design of the artificial hand, both the mechanism and the local controller included, which is highlighted in Fig.1.

Investigations indicate that lack of sufficient functionality, poor cosmetic appearance and low controllability are main reasons why amputees abandon using their prostheses[5].

Current commercial prosthetic hands are structurally simple, consequently they are reliable but the functionalities available are limited and far from requirements. In order to increase the user acceptances, more basic functionalities are expected as follows:

- Power grasp
- Precision grasp
- Lateral pinch
- Expressive gesture

Cosmetic appearance is another factor that affects the acceptance. From the view of biomimetics, both size and proportion of the hand segments should be similar to natural hand, possessing five fingers and a human-like palm.

Furthermore, several other factors should be taken into account as follows:

- Weight: no more than 500 g (including intrinsic actuators and local controller)
- Power consumption: work for a whole day without battery recharge
- Modular design: easy for manufacture and maintenance
- Reliability and durability

Despite of progress on biological signal processing technologies over past years, neural interface is still a bottleneck for prosthetic applications. Limited motion intention information can be obtained, especially non-invasive interface, which is more acceptable than invasive methods. The performance of neural interface is hardly to improve significantly in the foreseeable future, that means human can not control all the joints of the artificial hand directly. Therefore, a hierarchical local control structure is ought to be adopted to overcome the limitation. The low-level control is responsible for detailed control of the joints movements, and the high-level control is responsible for obtaining the motion intention and coding it to the motion pattern according to the protocol between the two levels.

# 3   Mechanical Design

## 3.1   Kinematic Arrangement of Joints

First of all, a suitable kinematic model should be found in order to imitate a natural hand. Then rational simplification of this model is used to balance the complexity and realism in terms of functionality requirements and constraints of human hand movements.

It is commonly regarded that human hand can be described as a kinematic model with 15 joints and as many as 21 DOFs[8]. Each finger, except the thumb, possesses three joints referred to from the root as metacarpophalangeal (MCP) joint, proximal interphalangeal (PIP) joint and distal interphalangeal (DIP) joint. There are 2 DOFs for MCP joint, and 1 DOF for PIP and DIP joints. The thumb is more flexible and complex than the other fingers. It can be modeled by a 5-DOF kinematic chain with 2 DOFs for trapeziometacarpal (TM) and MCP joints and 1 DOF for interphalangeal (IP) joint, and plays an crucial role in grasp.

Human hand motion is highly articulate, but fortunately it is also highly constrained. Based on this point, kinematical structure can be simplified.

For the four fingers, since human has limited ability to control all joints independently, they can be made with coupled joints for flexion/extension. To reduce the complexity, abd/adduction motion is not considered for the moment; For the thumb, it is hard to reproduce all DOFs in a limited space. Conclusions drawn from the biomechanical analysis suggest that two independent DOF to be the minimum necessary to achieve multiple grasping tasks, by replicating the mobility of the TM and MCP joint in abd/adduction and flexion/extension axes[9].

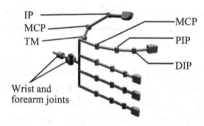

**Fig. 2.** Kinematic configuration of joints in the SJT-3

In addition, a 3-DOF wrist and forearm is also taken into account. Consequently, the kinematical arrangement of joints in the SJT-3 is shown in Fig.2.

## 3.2   Intrinsic Actuators

A part of the muscles acting on the hand is located on the forearm, which are called extrinsic muscles, driving fingers through tendons. Inspired by this, actuator units are put into the forearm and drive fingers via wires in many robotic hands[10][11]. It effectively reduces the weight of the end effector, and solves the problem how to increasing grasp force with the lack of high power density actuators. But this approach is not suitable for prosthesis because there is no enough space for actuator units integrated in a forearm socket.

In order to fit the prosthesis for different amputation levels of upper limb, all the actuator units and their electronic components ought to be built in the prosthetic hand. This also embodies modular design. The prosthetic hand can be considered as an independent part, and be easy to connect with a robotic arm or a forearm socket.

### 3.3   The Fingers

The fingers of most commercial products like Otto Bock's SensorHand are fixed shape, and they can only bend around the MCP joint. Consequently, the contact areas between object and the hand are small results in a instable grasp. Moreover, it does not look like a human finger movement from a cosmetic point of view.

In the SJT-3, three joints of the finger are coupled (Fig.3(a)). The relationship between the flexion angles of the joints refers to a study of human finger motion[12]. Table 1 shows main parameters of the finger.

**Table 1.** Parameters of the finger

| Phalange length (mm) | | | Joint movement range (°) | | |
|---|---|---|---|---|---|
| Proximal | Middle | Distal | MCP | PIP | DIP |
| 45 | 30 | 26 | 0~85 | 0~105 | 0~75 |

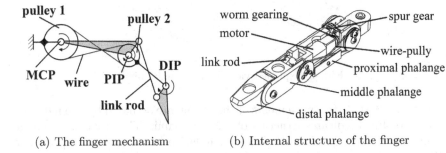

(a) The finger mechanism          (b) Internal structure of the finger

**Fig. 3.** Design of the finger

Fig.3(b) shows the structure of a finger. In the prototype, all the fingers are the same for easy fabrication and maintenance. A small DC motor with gearbox is placed into the proximal phalange. A worm gearing plus spur gear mechanism is incorporated in the MCP joint as a transmission and drives this joint.

The reason why we adopt a worm gearing is that it will be considerably smaller in volume than one made from bevel or crown gear, and gets a higher reduction ratio. Moreover, self-locking characteristics of the worm gearing ensures that the drive system of the finger is passively stationary, and allows prosthetic hand grasping object without additional power consumption.

We adopt a wire-pulley mechanism at the side of the proximal phalange, since the actuator unit nearly fill this phalange. Two pulleys are fixed respectively in the finger root and the middle phalange, and connected by a figure-8 nylon wire. And the middle phalange and the distal phalange are connected by a link rod.

The flexion angle of the finger is measured by a magnetic sensor embedded in the MCP joint. The torque of finger is measured indirectly by armature current of motor, and the fingertip force is measured by a force sensitive resistors (FSR) sensor.

## 3.4   The Thumb

The thumb is crucial to make various grasping patterns possible, increasing the prosthesis dexterity. But most commercial products lack flexible thumb. In Otto Bock's SensorHand, the thumb is fixed. And i-Limb Hand just processes a passive TM joint for abd/adduction. In some experimental prosthetic hand, the thumb is driven by one actuator for movements in two planes using novel mechanism[4]. They can achieve both flexion and opposition movement, but the mechanism is much complex and the functionality is slightly limited.

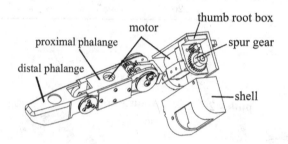

**Fig. 4.** Exploded view of the thumb unit

In the SJT-3, these two movements of the thumb are actuated by two independent motors. Fig.4 indicates structure of the thumb unit. The proximal phalange and the distal phalange of the thumb are similar to the other four fingers. The MCP joint is driven by a motor embedded in the proximal phalange, and is coupled with IP joint via wire-pulley to achieve flexion/extension movement. The TM joint is driven by another motor via a pair of spur gears housed in the root of thumb for abd/adduction movement.

## 3.5   Wrist and Forearm

A three-DOF forearm has also been designed in order to connect the hand and perform the flexion/extension, the abd/adduction, and the pronation/supination like a human wrist and forearm.

It consists of a proximal forearm and a distal forearm supported by a pair of bearings to allow rotation of the distal forearm relative to the proximal forearm. A motor is housed in the proximal forearm to actuate the distal forearm by spur gears to perform pronation/supination (Fig.5(a)).

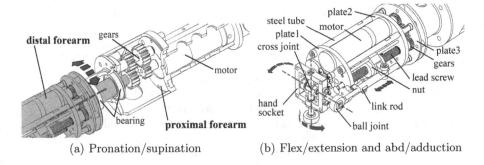

(a) Pronation/supination         (b) Flex/extension and abd/adduction

**Fig. 5.** Structure of the forearm

Flexion/extension and abd/adduction of wrist is achieved with a 2-DOF universal cross joint, which is located at the end of the distal forearm (Fig.5(b)). The artificial hand is able to be connected with the wrist by the socket. It's actuated by two motors via lead screw nut plus link rod transmission housed in the distal forearm. A ball joint is adopted at the end of the link rod due to coupling of the wrist movement. A space frame structure is adopted for the wrist actuation units, consisting of three plates which are connected by steel tubes. The space frame is compact, solid, lightweight, and easy for maintenance.

## 4   Finalized Prototype

### 4.1   Prosthesis Prototype

A prototype of the SJT-3 described above has been accomplished. It is installed on a humanoid model for experiments as shown in Fig.6. The size, weight and appearance of the SJT-3 is approximate to a natural hand. The main structure frames are made from aluminium alloy. Round holes are used for weight reduction. The weight of the hand is less than 490 g. And the finger unit weighs 66 g. The details are shown in Table 2.

**Fig. 6.** Overall profile of the prototype

**Table 2.** Main parameters of the prosthesis prototype

| Feature | Value |
| --- | --- |
| DOFs | 15 (hand) + 3 (forearm) |
| Number of actuators | 6 (hand) + 3 (forearm) |
| Weight | 490 g (the hand including electric circuit boards) |
| | 900 g (the wrist and forearm) |
| Dimension | 195 mm (length from fingertip of the middle finger to the wrist root) |
| | 85 mm (width of the palm) |
| | 32 mm (thickness of the palm) |

### 4.2 Control System

Since limited motion information can be obtained through neural interface, a hierarchical control architecture is adopted to overcome it. A local controller integrated in the prosthesis is designed to share responsibility for neural interface.

On the other hand, as an open system, this hierarchical architecture is indispensable. In the SJT-2, hand control was mixed in a main controller, and this led to a poor portability of system.

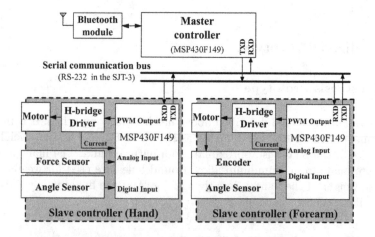

**Fig. 7.** Prosthesis control architecture

The architecture of the local controller is depicted in Fig.7. It also adopts modular design, forms itself into a single-master and multiple-slave structure that can entitle prosthesis control system better flexibility and expansibility. The master and the slaves are connected through a serial communication bus (RS232 bus currently in the SJT-3) which allows bi-directional communication between them. The master is in charge of communication with a high-level controller via bluetooth to obtain recognized motion pattern and coordinating all slaves.

At present, two slaves are used to control the hand and the forearm respectively, and they are in charge of motor control and sensor feedback. The slave drives DC motors by PWM outputs through H-bridge drivers, and collects the position, fingertip force and motor current from the sensors distributed in the prosthesis.

## 5  Experimental Evaluation

### 5.1  Prototype Performance

A series of objects with different shape and size, such as cylindrical tin, stopwatch, wallet and so on, were used to evaluate the grasping capability, and common gestures can be achieved as well. The movements of the wrist and forearm is shown in Fig.8. It is capable of ±30° flexion/extension and abd/adduction, and 360° rotation.

(a) Grasping different objects

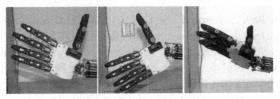

(b) Wrist and forearm movements

**Fig. 8.** Postures of the SJT-3 prototype

Two different rechargeable Li-ion batteries, one for the motors (11.1V 2.8Ah) and one for the controller (7.4V 0.75Ah) are used to supply power. In general conditions, it can continuously work at least 8 hours before recharge.

### 5.2  EMG Control of SJT-3

As a prosthetic hand for neural interface, SJT-3 was also connected to an EMG-based motion recognition system, which had been achieved in our previous work[6].

Eight channels of surface EMG signal are collected from subject's forearm using a self-designed wireless EMG collection instrument. It looks like a cuff of blood pressure meter that consists of electrodes, two-step amplifiers, a microcontroller and a bluetooth module. EMG signals are digitalized by microcontroller and transmitted to a PC through bluetooth for motion recognition (see Fig.9).

**Fig. 9.** Using EMG signals to control the prosthetic hand

Time domain statistic (TDS) method is employed for feature extraction, and a two-layer neural network is adopted as a classifier. For training classifier, the subject is required to perform 30 trials following the screen instructions. After the training session, the subject uses his surface EMG signals to control the prosthesis. Once the motion pattern is identified, the prosthesis controller will coordinate the joints to achieve hand or wrist movements following the subject's intention.

# 6    Conclusion and Further Work

In this paper we have presented the design of an anthropomorphic prosthesis based on a neural interface experimental platform. The artificial hand has a total of 15 joints actuated by 6 independent intrinsic motors, and is connected with a 3-DOF wrist and forearm for experiments. Both basic functionalities and biomimetic factors are taken into account. The prosthesis can accomplish a series of functionalities that include various grasping, common gestures and wrist movements. It processes a human-like appearance, and the size and the weight are close to those of the natural hand. A modularized control system is designed to embed into the prosthesis for low-level control, which is expected to overcome the limitation of the neural interface nowadays.

Further work will address the improvements of grasping performance, sensory system and low-level control strategy. More analysis will be performed in order to find optimized parameters of the mechanism. Passive compliant joints will be used in the fingers to obtain adaption in grasp with different shape objects. More different types of sensors will be embedded in the prosthesis to provide information to low-level control system and biofeedback to users. Further clinical experiments on the disabilities will be performed on this platform.

**Acknowledgments.** This work is supported by the National Basic Research Program (973 Program) of China (Grant No. 2011CB013305), the Science and Technology Commission of Shanghai Municipality (Grant No. 11JC1406000), and the State Key Laboratory of Mechanical System and Vibration (Grant No. MSVZD201204).

# References

1. Ottobock: myoelectric arm prostheses,
   `http://www.ottobock.com/cps/rde/xchg/ob_com_en/hs.xsl/384.html`
2. TouchBionics: active prostheses,
   `http://www.touchbionics.com/products/active-prostheses/`
3. Adee, S.: The revolution will be prosthetized. IEEE Spectrum 46(1), 44–48 (2009)
4. Pons, J., Rocon, E., Ceres, R., Reynaerts, D., Saro, B., Levin, S., Van Moorleghem, W.: The manus-hand dextrous robotics upper limb prosthesis: mechanical and manipulation aspects. Autonomous Robots 16(2), 143–163 (2004)
5. Carrozza, M., Cappiello, G., Micera, S., Edin, B., Beccai, L., Cipriani, C.: Design of a cybernetic hand for perception and action. Biological Cybernetics 95(6), 629–644 (2006)
6. Hu, P., Li, S., Chen, X., Zhang, D., Zhu, X.: A Continuous Control Scheme for Multifunctional Robotic Arm with Surface EMG Signal. In: Liu, H., Ding, H., Xiong, Z., Zhu, X. (eds.) ICIRA 2010, Part I. LNCS, vol. 6424, pp. 81–91. Springer, Heidelberg (2010)
7. Zhang, D., Chen, X., Li, S., Hu, P., Zhu, X.: Emg controlled multifunctional prosthetic hand: Preliminary clinical study and experimental demonstration. In: 2011 IEEE International Conference on Robotics and Automation (ICRA), pp. 4670–4675. IEEE (2011)
8. Wu, Y., Huang, T.: Hand modeling, analysis and recognition. IEEE Signal Processing Magazine 18(3), 51–60 (2001)
9. Light, C., Chappell, P.: Development of a lightweight and adaptable multiple-axis hand prosthesis. Medical Engineering & Physics 22(10), 679–684 (2000)
10. Fite, K., Withrow, T., Wait, K., Goldfarb, M.: A gas-actuated anthropomorphic transhumeral prosthesis. In: 2007 IEEE International Conference on Robotics and Automation, pp. 3748–3754. IEEE (2007)
11. Tuffield, P., Elias, H.: The shadow robot mimics human actions. Industrial Robot: An International Journal 30(1), 56–60 (2003)
12. Becker, J., Thakor, N.: A study of the range of motion of human fingers with application to anthropomorphic designs. IEEE Transactions on Biomedical Engineering 35(2), 110–117 (1988)

# Adaptive Pattern Recognition of Myoelectric Signal towards Practical Multifunctional Prosthesis Control

Jiayuan He, Dingguo Zhang, and Xiangyang Zhu

State Key Laboratory of Mechanical System and Vibration,
Shanghai Jiao Tong University, Shanghai 200240, China
hejiayuan@sjtu.edu.cn

**Abstract.** Towards the real-world application of multifunctional prostheses based on electromyography (EMG) signal, an unsupervised adaptive myoelectric control approach was presented in order to improve the long-time classification performance of EMG pattern recognition. The widely-used linear discriminant analysis (LDA) was improved to three new different classifiers separately termed as linear discriminant analysis with single pattern updating (SPLDA), linear discriminant analysis with multiple patterns updating (MPLDA), and linear discriminant analysis with selected data updating (SDLDA). The experimental result showed that the three new classifiers significantly outperformed the original version. MPLDA and SDLDA provided two different methods to decrease the influence of misclassification and got lower classification error rates than SPLDA. Strategies to decrease the influence of misclassification are the key to the application of unsupervised myoelectric control in the future.

**Keywords:** EMG, prosthesis, pattern recognition, adaptation, LDA.

## 1 Introduction

Surface electromyography (EMG) signal, which is noninvasive and contains rich information associated with the muscle electrical activities, is considered to be an important input for the control of electrically powered prostheses [1]. To increase the number of functions of prostheses, much attention has been drawn to a pattern recognition based approach to the myoelectric control in last two decades and some promising results have been achieved [2-4].

By learning the nature of muscle contraction patterns for the intended movements of a specific user, pattern recognition can provide the advantage of recognizing the subtleties of the user's muscular activity at a particular instance in time. However, it does not accommodate changes in the EMG patterns over time and the good performance cannot maintain for a long time because of the EMG variations, due to electrodes condition, muscle fatigue, sweating and so on [5]. This problem has become an obstacle for the commercialization of advanced myoelectric controlled prostheses developed in laboratory environment.

The conventional pattern recognition method is accomplished in two parts, training and testing. The parameters acquired at the training contain limited information, and

C.-Y. Su, S. Rakheja, H. Liu (Eds.): ICIRA 2012, Part I, LNAI 7506, pp. 518–525, 2012.

they cannot be representative to the data of the whole temporal span in application period including testing step. It is the main cause to the above remarked problem. Therefore, how to make the parameters more representative to the EMG signal is the key to improve the long-time performance.

In this paper, we exploited EMG information in the testing part, and an unsupervised adaptive myoelectric control approach was presented to improve the long-time classification performance of EMG pattern recognition. As the Linear Discriminant Analysis (LDA) is a computationally efficient algorithm with similar performance to more complex algorithms [4], it was improved with this approach and the new classifier, linear discriminant analysis with single pattern updating (SPLDA), was constructed. The experimental results showed a significant improvement in long time performance, compared with the original version. However, the existence of misclassification would bring adverse effect on the classifier and lead to a bad result. To reduce its influence, two different methods were proposed, which were separately from the aspects of data selection and multiple patterns updating. The corresponding classifiers were called linear discriminant analysis with multiple patterns updating (MPLDA), and linear discriminant analysis with selected data updating (SDLDA). The performance of MPLDA and SDLDA would compare with SPLDA, and they could be used in the control of multifunctional prostheses.

## 2    Methods

### 2.1    Overview

The traditional myoelectric control based on pattern recognition generally contains segmentation, feature extraction, and classification [6]. The decision streams are finally generated for the motion controller. Unlike the traditional method, a feedback to the classifier is added in the unsupervised adaptive myoelectric control and it is illustrated in Figure. 1. Samples tagged with the results of the classifier were used to retrain the classifier to make it adaptive to the changes of EMG signal over time.

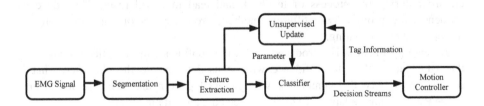

**Fig. 1.** Block diagram of the unsupervised adaptive myoelectric control scheme

## 2.2     Linear Discriminant Analysis (LDA)

A widely-used classification algorithm in EMG research is the LDA. A linear classifier, in general, tries to establish a hyperplane separating the signal space into individual subspaces for all classes [7]. It can be found in literature [8] that the formulae of LDA based on a multivariate normal distribution to each group, with a pooled estimate of covariance.

## 2.3     Adaptive Linear Discriminant Analysis

The main parameters of the LDA classifier are the mean vector of each class and the pooled covariance matrix. Suppose that there are N patterns used for training the classifier, and the new-coming testing EMG feature patterns are acquired as $x_{N+1}$, $x_{N+2}$, $x_{N+3}$, cet. Let the pattern $x_{N+1}$ be $z$ and labeled as class $k$ by the original classifier. The updated mean vector $\tilde{\mu}_k$ for class $k$ is

$$\tilde{\mu}_k = \frac{n_k * \mu_k + z}{n_k + 1},\tag{1}$$

where $n_k$ is the number of future patterns for class $k$, and $\mu_k$ is the original mean vector.

The pooled covariance matrix $\tilde{\Sigma}_W$ is updated by

$$\tilde{\Sigma}_W = \frac{N}{N+1}\Sigma_w + \frac{1}{N+1} * \frac{n_k}{n_k + 1}(z - \mu_k)(z - \mu_k)^T,\tag{2}$$

where $\Sigma_w$ is the original pooled covariance matrix.

## 2.4     Decrease of Influence of Misclassification

There are different strategies to update the classifier. The most common one is to recalculate the parameters when one single pattern is generated, and we call it adaptive LDA with single pattern updating (SPLDA). However, it is known that the classification error is inevitable and patterns with wrong tags may damage the classifier during the process of feedback and lead to a bad result. To reduce its influence, we propose two different methods from aspects of data selection and multiple patterns updating.

An entropy function is introduced to test the confidence of classification and only the data that is of high confidence will be used to update the classifier. That is intended to reduce the number of wrong-tagged pattern and decrease its adverse influence. We call it adaptive LDA with selected data updating (SDLDA).

The entropy function used for data selection in SDLDA is [9]

$$E(n) = -\sum_{k=1}^{K} p_k(n)ln\,(p_k(n)),\tag{3}$$

where $K$ is the number of classes to be considered and $p_k(n)$ is the probability of class $k$ in future pattern n defined as follows,

$$p_k(n) = \frac{1/d_k(n)}{\sum_{k=1}^{C} 1/d_k(n)}, \qquad (4)$$

$$d_k(n) = (z - \mu_k)^T \Sigma_w (z - \mu_k), \qquad (5)$$

Another way is to use more than one pattern to update the classifier. In SPLDA, if one pattern is attached with a wrong label, its influence will be immediately reflected on the next pattern's calculation. It may lead to accumulative error and impair the classifier. However, if we decrease the frequency of updating and update the classifier after more than one pattern is calculated. Then the right-tagged pattern will weaken the influence of the wrong-tagged and reduce the accumulative error of the classifier. In this way, the influence of misclassification is reduced. It is called adaptive LDA with multiple patterns updating (MPLDA).

Therefore, three adaptive LDA classifiers were developed, which were separately called SPLDA, SDLDA, and MPLDA. MPLDA and SDLDA are better than SPLDA theoretically.

## 2.5    EMG Data Acquisition

The data were collected from three able-bodied subjects with four bipolar electrodes placed on palmaris longus, flexor carpi ulnaris, flexor digitorum supercifialis, and extensor digitorum. The motion classes were consisted of wrist flexion/extension, forearm pronation/supination, hand open/close, radial flexion, ulnar flexion and resting (no motion). Motions are shown in Figure. 2. Signals were pre-amplified and filtered using a commercial myoelectric system (Delsys Inc., Trigno$^{TM}$ Wireless System, 20-450 Hz band pass filter) and recorded at a sampling rate of 2 kHz. Four time-domain EMG features (mean absolute value, waveform length, zero crossings, and slope changes) [3] extracted from 200 ms windows of filtered EMG from each channel resulted in a 16-element feature vector. The feature vector was calculated at 25 ms intervals (175 ms of overlapping data per window).

A single experimental trial is defined as follows. Subjects perform each of the nine contraction classes for 5 seconds with a 5-second rest between contractions. For each hour, five consecutive trials were performed and the whole temporal span of the experiment for each subject was 7 hours (40 trials of data were collected). The first five trials were assigned as a training set and the next thirty-five trials as a testing set.

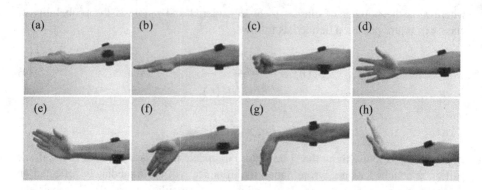

**Fig. 2.** Photo of different types of motions. (a) Forearm pronation. (b) Forearm supination. (c) Hand close. (d) Hand open. (e) Radial flexion. (f) Ulnar flexion. (g) Wrist flexion. (h) Wrist extension.

## 3    Results and Discussion

To compare the performance of different types of classifiers, the classification error rate was used as a measure, which was defined as

$$\frac{\text{Number of incorrectly classified samples}}{\text{Total number of testing samples}} \times 100 \ (\%).$$

The average classification error rate of different classifiers for each subject is listed in Table. 1, and the best performance for each subject is highlighted in bold.

**Table 1.** Average classification error rate of different classifiers

|         | Error Rate (%) | | | |
|---------|------|-------|-------|-------|
| Subject | LDA | SPLDA | MPLDA | SDLDA |
| S1 | 11.01 | 5.49 | 3.24 | **2.68** |
| S2 | 20.15 | 11.55 | **8.44** | 8.81 |
| S3 | 29.93 | 22.52 | 19.67 | **19.58** |
| mean | 20.36 | 13.19 | 10.45 | 10.36 |

From this table, it can be seen that the performance of each subject was different for a certain classify. The average classification error rate across subjects of LDA is 20.36%, whereas SPLDA, MPLDA and SDLDA are 13.19%, 10.45%, 10.36%, respectively. It can be concluded that SPLDA, MPLDA and SDLDA significantly outperform LDA. In addition, the performance of SPLDA is approximately the same as MPLDA, which is superior to LDA.

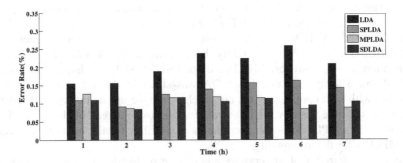

**Fig. 3.** Classification error rate of different classifiers. Result is averaged across all subjects.

The error rate of different classifiers over time is shown in Figure. 3. A one-way Analysis of Variance (ANOVA) was applied to analyze the classifier factor. By analyzing the performance of LDA and SPLDA, it is showed that pattern updating significantly decreases the error rate ($p < 0.01$). Meanwhile, by analyzing the results of SPLDA, MPLDA and SPLDA, SDLDA, it can be concluded that decrease of influence of misclassification has the same effect ($p < 0.05$) as pattern updating.

To determine the quality of EMG signal, the concept of minimum error was introduced [5]. It was defined as the classification error rate which was used for assessing the performance of a classifier trained and tested by the same data set. Of the three subjects, the quality of signal of subject 1 was the best and subject 3 was the worst. The classification error rate over time for S1 and S3 was shown in Figure. 4.

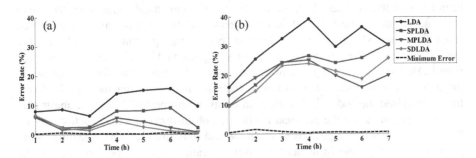

**Fig. 4.** Classification error rate over time. (a) Subject 1, which has the best performance. (b) Subject 3, which has the worst performance.

It can be seen that the classification error of LDA increased over time, which was caused by the variations of EMG signal. For the signal with low minimum error, the performance of SPLDA was similar to MPLDA and SDLDA. However, it was quite different from the signal of high minimum error. The different performance of SPLDA was caused by the feedback of wrong tagged samples. With the signal of high quality, the classification error was low and most of samples were right tagged. So the classifier can adapt to the changes of signal and produce better results. On the contrary, with the signal of low quality, the classification error was high and most of samples were wrong tagged. The classifier may be impaired and the results were bad. So it was necessary to decrease the influence of misclassification.

MPLDA and SDLDA provided two ways to reduce the influence of misclassification. SDLDA was slightly better than MPLDA from the aspect of classification error. However, MPLDA outperformed SDLDA during hour 5-7 in Figure. 4 (b). The update rate of SDLDA was slow for the low-quality signal, of which data with high confidence was not much, while the update rate of MPLDA was constant. As the time went by, SDLDA could not follow the trend of changes of EMG signal as well as MPLDA. So we recommended SDLDA for the high-quality signal, while MPLDA for the low-quality.

It can be inferred that supervised adaptive myoelectric control approach can achieve better results than unsupervised. However, it will increase the burden of users of prostheses and is impractical in the real world. So towards the application of prostheses in the real world, unsupervised adaptive myoelectric approach is the mainstream. SDLDA and MPLDA present two different ways to degrade the influence of misclassification. However, both of them have a coeffiecent to adjust and may not be easy enough to be applied in the real world. So further study should be done to develop a new method that is convenient and easy to use in the unsupervised myoelectric control.

# 4    Conclusions

The long-time performance of EMG pattern recognition is an important issue in the research of EMG controlled prostheses. Various supervised adaptation methods have been reported to overcome this problem. However, in practical application, the actual intention of the subject is not always known to the system, and unsupervised adaptation methods are needed. In this paper, the preliminary study of the unsupervised adaptive myoelectric control was presented. A new classifier derived from LDA was constructed and achieved a better performance than the original one in the following experiment. This confirms the effectiveness of our method. Different from supervised method, misclassification exists in unsupervised method, and it may cause big problems for the practical application of unsupervised myoelectric control. So two different strategies, data selection and multiple patterns updating, were proposed to reduce the influence of misclassification, and the performance of the classifiers was improved further. Towards the real-world application, our future work will focus on the method to eliminate the misclassification influence and improve the online performance of the long-time adaptive myoelectric control.

**Acknowledgments.** This work was supported by the National Basic Research Program (973 Program) of China (Grant No. 2011CB013305), the Science and Technology Commission of Shanghai Municipality (Grant No. 11JC1406000), and the State Key Laboratory of Mechanical System and Vibration (Grant No. MSVZD201204).

# References

1. Parker, P., Englehart, K., Hudgins, B.: Myoelectric signal processing for control of powered limb prostheses. Journal of Electromyography and Kinesiology 16, 541–548 (2006)
2. Hudgins, B., Parker, P., Scott, R.N.: A new strategy for multifunction myoelectric control. IEEE Transactions on Biomedical Engineering 40, 82–94 (1993)
3. Englehart, K., Hudgins, B.: A robust, real-time control scheme for multifunction myoelectric control. IEEE Transactions on Biomedical Engineering 50, 848–854 (2003)
4. Hargrove, L.J., Scheme, E.J., Englehart, K.B., Hudgins, B.S.: Multiple binary classifications via linear discriminant analysis for improved controllability of a powered prosthesis. IEEE Transactions on Neural Systems and Rehabilitation Engineering 18, 49–57 (2010)
5. Sensinger, J.W., Lock, B.A., Kuiken, T.A.: Adaptive pattern recognition of myoelectric signals: exploration of conceptual framework and practical algorithms. IEEE Transactions on Neural Systems and Rehabilitation Engineering 17, 270–278 (2009)
6. Zecca, M., Micera, S., Carrozza, M., Dario, P.: Control of multifunctional prosthetic hands by processing the electromyographic signal. Critical Reviews in Biomedical Engineering 30, 459 (2002)
7. Blumberg, J., Rickert, J., Waldert, S., Schulze-Bonhage, A., Aertsen, A., Mehring, C.: Adaptive classification for brain computer interfaces. In: Proc. 29th Ann. Int. Conf. of the IEEE EMBS, pp. 2536–2539 (2007)
8. Duda, R., Hart, P., Stork, D.: Pattern Classification. Wiley, New York (2001)
9. Fukuda, O., Tsuji, T., Kaneko, M., Otsuka, A.: A human-assisting manipulator teleoperated by EMG signals and arm motions. IEEE Transactions on Robotics and Automation 19, 210–222 (2003)

# SSVEP Based Brain-Computer Interface Controlled Functional Electrical Stimulation System for Knee Joint Movement

Lin Yao, Dingguo Zhang[*], and Xiangyang Zhu

State Key Laboratory of Mechanical System and Vibration
Shanghai Jiao Tong University
Shanghai, China, 200240
dgzhang@sjtu.edu.cn

**Abstract.** Knee joint movement control plays an important part in the rehabilitation of lower limb locomotion. In this work, a functional electrical stimulation (FES) training system utilizing steady-state visual evoked potential (SSVEP) based brain-computer interface (BCI) was designed to realize the functional control of knee movement, including selection of multiple patterns: left or right knee joint for stimulation, start or stop of knee movement, acceleration or deceleration of knee movement. In order to investigate the problem of FES artifact on EEG signals, two classifiers were trained under normal condition (electrical artifact free) and artifact condition (initiatively adding FES artifact) respectively. The classifiers were used in pre-stimulation and on-stimulation separately after training. During the experiment, the subject was required to realize the predefined experiment paradigm, during which both the knee joint angle and real-time SSVEP selection were recorded to evaluate the coordination of BCI and FES integration. The experiment result showed the necessity and effectiveness of the proposed real-time classifier strategy, and knee joint movement control was successfully realized by subject's intention.

**Keywords:** SSVEP, BCI, FES, EEG, Knee Movement.

## 1 Introduction

Functional electrical stimulation (FES) is a well-known technology in rehabilitation engineering, which activates muscles to contract by stimulation of the motor neurons with low-level electrical current, so as to restore or recover patient's impaired motor function, which gives hope to people who lose their body control ability [1]. The applied low-level electrical current acts as action potential from central nervous system, which drives muscles to contract. Traditionally, this electrical current is mainly controlled in a passive way, i.e. the subject's intention is not fully expressed and the whole process is pre-fixed. If the subject's mind is actively participating in the rehabilitation process, much like a natural mind-body control way, the subject's needs in rehabilitation could be flexibly met by herself or himself. With benefits of Brain-computer interface (BCI) technology, the subject's mind control could be now

---

[*] Corresponding author.

C.-Y. Su, S. Rakheja, H. Liu (Eds.): ICIRA 2012, Part I, LNAI 7506, pp. 526–535, 2012.
© Springer-Verlag Berlin Heidelberg 2012

possible [2]. BCI is a non-muscular control technology with potential to restore or augment lost motor behaviors for people with severe motor injury, and also enables them to communicate with outside world in a way that is very different from traditional ways such as voice based communication. As BCI directly translates human thought to command, it would be adopted as a substitution of conventional neuromuscular pathways to offer patients who lost motor ability with a new communication and control channel. Electroencephalogram (EEG) is a noninvasive method to record weak electrical signals produced by a large amount of brain neurons activity, and is favored in BCI society [3].

Limited work has been done in the integration of BCI and FES, most of which are mainly concentrated in the upper limb rehabilitation. In 2003, Pfurtscheller et al. did a groundbreaking experiment [4], helping patients with upper limb hemiplegia to conduct hand grasping by triggering FES system through motor imagery based BCI. Similarly, using motor imagery based BCI, other research teams developed BCI-FES systems for rehabilitation on stroke patients, which showed the feasibility for stroke patients to accomplish the BCI triggered FES rehabilitation training [5, 6]. Differently, Bentley et al. proposed a P300 based BCI [7] and Gollee et al. proposed an SSVEP based BCI [8] for FES application, respectively. But lower extremity rehabilitation received less attention [9]. As BCI development has mainly focused on individuals with severe paralysis, such as locked-in syndrome or high cervical SCI, those people would mostly benefit from BCI technology to communicate with a computer device or upper extremity control for basic functions such grasping, rotation of wrist. Meanwhile, wheeled chair would be a robust and effective way for substitution of lower extremity paralysis. Besides, the electrical artifact is obvious especially when the electrical stimulation is applied to the leg which needs a stronger electrical current to contract, and the severely contaminated EEG signal may not be as a reliable control source.

Lower extremity locomotion is very important in daily life. Leg movement training is necessary when the subject is injured or temporally lost the control ability. Knee joint movement is a part of locomotion, and it is a benchmark task in FES field [10, 11]. Here, we developed an SSVEP based BCI in controlling of the knee movement via FES, such that the start or stop of the knee moment and acceleration or deceleration of knee movement could freely be controlled by himself or herself.

## 2    System Overview

The schematic diagram of the knee movement training system is shown in Fig. 1. There are three flickering lights of separate frequencies which are mapped to different action command. The subject selectively stares at one of the flickering lights, and simultaneously the EEG signals are acquired from the scalp. After on-line processing of the acquired EEG signals, including feature extraction and pattern recognition, the intention about which light is being focused on could be detected. Then the user's intention is sent to FES system through BCI-FES interface, which triggers FES to produce the corresponding leg muscular activation.

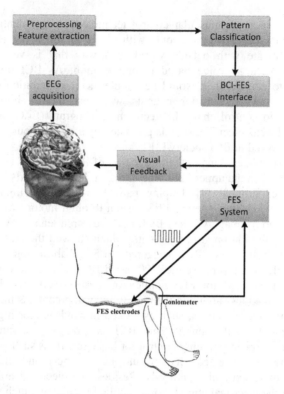

**Fig. 1.** Schematic diagram of the knee movement training system

## 3    Methodology

When the human focuses on instantaneous visual stimulus of constant time interval, steady state visual evoked potential (SSVEP) will occur in primary visual cortex of the brain [12]. By measuring the electrical activity on the scalp, the EEG signal shows that the corresponding stimulus frequency and its harmonic components stick out in frequency domain as shown in Fig. 2.

When we use SSVEP-BCI to control FES device, the problem comes from the artifact of the electrical stimulation of FES device. From the time domain as shown is Fig. 3(a),(b), that the EEG signal is highly contaminated by electrical artifact. The artifact may be disasters for raw EEG signal processing as even the experienced researcher couldn't find any useful information from the EEG map. So artifact avoidance or removal should be carried out to see the masked essential insight of the cerebral electrical activity. Our main purpose is to on-line detect which flickering light the subject is staring at, so existence of the distinguishable feature space becomes essential to our on-line experiment implementation when the electrical artifact is produced. As shown in Fig. 3(c),(d), the SSVEP characteristic still exists when the electrical stimulation is carried on. Two classifiers will be trained under two

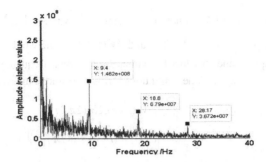

**Fig. 2.** EEG spectrum from occipital region CB2 channel. when the subject is focusing on the visual flickering light of frequency 9.37Hz. The fundamental frequency and its first and second harmonic component stick out from the spectrum map.

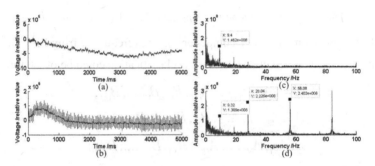

**Fig. 3.** (a) Time serials of EEG channel CB2 at artifact free condition. (b) Time serials of EEG channel CB2 when electrical stimulation is powered on. The EEG signal is severely contaminated by electrical noise, and the useful cerebral electrical activity seems to be submerged in electrical artifact from FES. (c) EEG spectrum from occipital region CB2 channel at artifact free condition. (d) EEG spectrum from occipital region CB2 channel under FES stimulation (28Hz electrical stimulation), while the subject is still focusing on the visual stimulation flickering light. Although the electrical artifact power is strong such as 28Hz fundamental stimulation frequency and first and second harmonic component, the electrical activity of SSVEP still exist.

different conditions. Classifier 1 is trained under electrical artifact free condition for the purpose of subject's selection in pre-stimulation. Classifier 2 will be trained under electrical stimulation condition for the purpose of subject's selection in on-stimulation. Both of the classifiers use the same feature extraction and classification strategy, but they are trained under different situations, and will be used in pre-stimulation and on-stimulation respectively.

### 3.1    Feature Extraction and Classification

Based on previous work [13], visual stimulation frequencies and its first harmonic wave components should be extracted as the features for pattern recognition. And an LDA classifier is adopted for real-time classification of EEG signal. For convenience, we only give a brief introduction to the pattern recognition algorithm.

Suppose $S_i(t)$ is the EEG signal from channel $i$ with $i = 1...N$, and $f_j$ is the $j$ th stimulus frequency with $j = 1...M$, and $W(t-c)$ is the window function with the center at $c$. We apply inner product to extract the specified frequency as projecting the signal to sine and cosine space. The continuous forms of feature extractions are given as

$$A_{ij}(c) = sqrt(\left|\langle S_i(t)W(t-c), \cos(2\pi f_j t)\rangle\right|^2 \tag{1}$$
$$+\left|\langle S_i(t)W(t-c), \sin(2\pi f_j t)\rangle\right|^2)$$

$$B_{ij}(c) = sqrt(\left|\langle S_i(t)W(t-c), \cos(2\pi \cdot 2 f_j t)\rangle\right|^2 \tag{2}$$
$$+\left|\langle S_i(t)W(t-c), \sin(2\pi \cdot 2 f_j t)\rangle\right|^2)$$

where $A_{ij}(c)$ is the $j$ th frequency component from EEG channel $i$ at time point $c$; $B_{ij}(c)$ is the harmonic wave component of $j$ th frequency from EEG channel $i$ at time point $c$. So the feature vector for the classification could be of the form

$$F = (A_{11}, A_{12}, ..., A_{1M}, B_{11}, B_{12}, ..., B_{1M},$$
$$A_{21}, A_{22}, ..., A_{2M}, B_{21}, B_{22}, ..., B_{2M}, \tag{3}$$
$$..., A_{N1}, A_{N2}, ..., A_{NM}, B_{N1}, B_{N2}, ..., B_{NM})^T$$

Regarding $i$ th and $j$ th categories classification problem for example, suppose $F^i$ and $F^j$ be $i$ th and $j$ th training feature sets, the average features of the two sets are

$$\mu_i = E(F^i) \tag{4}$$

$$\mu_j = E(F^j) \tag{5}$$

$E$ denotes the expectation operator, and the within class covariance is defined as

$$S_w^{ij} = E\left[(F^i - \mu_i)(F^i - \mu_i)^T\right]$$
$$+ E\left[(F^j - \mu_j)(F^j - \mu_j)^T\right] \tag{6}$$

The discriminant plane can be expressed in the linear formulation as

$$y = w^T x + b \tag{7}$$

where

$$w = S_w^{ij-1}(\mu_1 - \mu_1)$$

$$b = -w^T \frac{\mu_1 + \mu_1}{2}$$

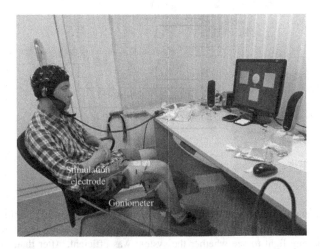

**Fig. 4.** Experiment Setup. The surface stimulation electrode is attached to rectus femoris, and the goniometer is to measure the knee joint angle.

# 4    Experimental Work

There were two healthy subjects participated in the experiment, with age 24 and 25 years old, both male. They were all informed the whole experiment process. The study was approved by the Institutional Review Board of Shanghai Jiao Tong University.

## 4.1    Experiment Setup

The stimulator (Compex Motion II, Switzerland) with four channels was adopted, which stimulated muscles via surface electrodes. EEG signals were recorded using a SynAmps system (Neuroscan, U.S.A.) in a shielded room which could reduce interference from the noise and electromagnetic in open environment. And knee joint angle was measured via Goniometer (Biometrics, UK).

Two channels of FES device were chosen to stimulate rectus femoris and hamstring respectively. Stimulation for rectus femoris was set to bipolar current impulse with pulse width of 200us, pulse frequency of 28Hz, and current intensity 25~35 mA accordingly. While stimulation for hamstring had the same setting, except the current intensity was much smaller 10-15mA. One goniometer sensor was attached to the knee joint, and data was acquired for off-line analysis. The surface electrodes of FES and goniometer sensor were shown in Fig. 4.

Eight channels in EEG cap located on occipital region were used to collect brain potential signals, which were PO3, POz, PO4, O1, Oz, O2, CB1, CB2 according to international 10/20 system. The reference electrode was located between Cz and CPz, and ground electrode was located on forehead. An analog bandwidth filter with 0.5~30Hz and a notch filter with 50Hz to diminish power line interference were applied to the original signals, which are sampled at 1000Hz.

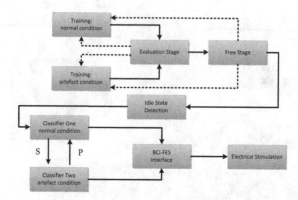

**Fig. 5.** Experimental paradigm. The subject was trained under normal condition and artifact condition respectively, and evaluated correspondingly. In the Free Stage, the subject randomly chose any flickering light to see whether the system was efficient. After that, the system ran into Idle State Detection stage. When the subject was about to use the system, the system jumped to normal condition. After "S" was chosen, predefined stimulation of FES began and classifier 2 started to work. Classifier 2's output was used to control the speed of knee movement. If subject chosen "P", i.e. the subject wanted to stop the stimulation, the system jumped to normal condition again.

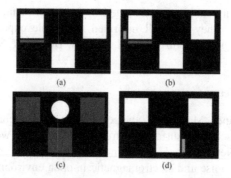

**Fig. 6.** The user interface of visual stimulation. (a) the subject focus his or her attention to the flickering light indicated by the red horizontal bar for the purpose of training of the classifier. (b) the subject also focus his or her attention to the flickering light indicated by the red horizontal bar, meanwhile the growing energy bar indicates which light the subject is looking at via the classification algorithm. (c) the interface via which the subject enters into the system by focusing on the circular flickering light. (d) the FES control interface, the subject chooses different electrical stimulation mode by focusing on the mode represented flickering light, and also the energy bar indicating which light the subject is focusing on.

## 4.2    Experiment Paradigm

The whole experiment process was shown in Fig. 5. The subject was required to achieve the following tasks. First of all, there was a flickering circle of 8.33Hz which was used for the detection of idle state. The subject should focus his or her attention to that flickering light, waiting for the start of whole system. Then three flickering squares appeared, with frequency of 12.5Hz, 8.33Hz, 6.82Hz from left to right as shown in Fig. 6, and each was mapped to command of choosing left leg stimulation, start of stimulation, right leg stimulation respectively. After choosing of the middle flickering light, the electrical stimulation was applied to the chosen leg. When the electrical stimulation began, the electrical artifact severely affected the original EEG signals, so another classifier was applied to this on-stimulation stage which was called classification under artifact condition. The visual stimuli were the same, but each was mapped to different function: acceleration, stop and deceleration of knee movement respectively from left to right. Finally before the subject's stimulation task, both the classifier 1 and classifier 2 and parameters in idle state detection algorithm were trained to achieve a good performance.

In order to quantitatively evaluate the subject's performance, the following fixed task as shown in Fig. 7 was required to achieve. Then the whole performance could be evaluated.

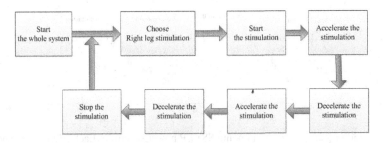

**Fig. 7.** Evaluation task which the subject is required to achieve

## 5    Results and Discussion

In the online experiment, the window size for feature extraction and classification was 1s, and the moving step size was 0.1s. The following Table 1 showed the classification accuracy of the two classifiers in pre-stimulatin (Artifact free to Artifact free) and on-stimulation (Artifact to Artifact) condition respectively, which was done via 10 fold cross validation. The two classifiers performed quite well when the classified data was in the same condition. Interestingly, the classifier 2 in artifact condition outperformed the classifier 1 in artifact free condition, which might be explained that certain amount of electrical stimulation would help the subject concentrate his or her attention in focusing on the flickering light during the training. Furthermore, the artifact data and artifact free data were used as training and testing set separately. And it turned out that there was performance reduction when just one classifier was trained to classify data which wasn't in the same situation as with training condition. It could be seen that two classifiers in different condition strategy was necessary, as it could achieve a higher performance than the single classifier.

The relationship between knee movement and SSVEP was shown as in Fig. 9. It could be seen that the subject succeed in achieving the predefined training process, from start of stimulation to acceleration, deceleration, acceleration, deceleration, and stop of stimulation. And the delay of stimulation pattern exchange is about 2s.

**Table 1.** Classification accuracy comparison in different situations. Artifact free to Artifact free means the classifier is trained under artifact free dataset to classify artifact free data, so does Artifact to Artifact. ArtifactFree to Artifact means using Artifact Free data as a training set while Artifact data as a testing set for the classifier, so does the Artifact to ArtifactFree.

| Subject | Session No. | Artifact free to Artifact free | Artifact to Artifact | Artifact free to Artifact | Artifact to Artifact free |
|---------|-------------|--------------------------------|----------------------|---------------------------|---------------------------|
| S1 | I | 94.68% | 95.68% | 91.08% | 87.93% |
| | II | 89.37% | 96.40% | 90.99% | 84.32% |
| S2 | I | 91.71% | 92.43% | 82.97% | 80.36% |
| | II | 93.87% | 94.95% | 89.91% | 87.84% |

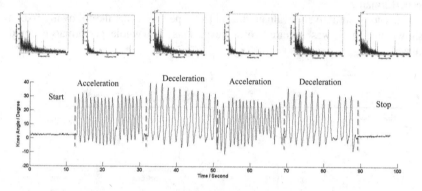

**Fig. 8.** Knee joint angle and corresponding SSVEP power spectrum. Each EEG power spectrum is mapped to different pattern, controlling knee joint movement.

## 6    Conclusion and Future Work

In this work, two classifiers were used in the knee joint movement training system. One is for pre-stimulation subject's intention recognition, while the other is for on-stimulation. The experiment result showed the reliable performance of the two classifiers strategy in the on-line subject's intention detection. Meanwhile the FES and BCI system coordinates well as measure by the knee joint angles and BCI output. So the designed knee joint movement training system works and could provide the subject with intention control of his or her knee joint movement.

Knee joint movement is only a part of lower limb locomotion, some work still needs to be done to fully realize the locomotion of patients, such as ankle joint and hip joint which should be coordinated with knee joint movement. Now the experiment are mainly carried out and tested on healthy subjects to evaluate the performance of the whole system setup. The next-stage work will transform to patients who have partly or entirely lost their knee joint movement control, and more reliable and easy-to-use training system will be designed.

**Acknowledgement.** This work is supported by the National Natural Science Foundation of China (Grant No.51075265), the National Basic Research Program (973 Program) of China (Grant No.2011CB013305), and the State Key Laboratory of Mechanical System and Vibration (Grant No. MSVMS201112).

# References

1. Lynch, C.L., Popovic, M.R.: Functional electrical stimulation. IEEE Control Systems Magazine 28, 40–50 (2008)
2. Wolpaw, J.R., Birbaumer, N., McFarland, D.J., Pfurtscheller, G., Vaughan, T.M.: Brain-computer interfaces for communication and control. Clinical Neurophysiology 113, 767–791 (2002)
3. Blankertz, B., Muller, K.R., Curio, G., Vaughan, T.M., Schalk, G., Wolpaw, J.R., Schlogl, A., Neuper, C., Pfurtscheller, G., Hinterberger, T.: The BCI competition 2003: progress and perspectives in detection and discrimination of EEG single trials. IEEE Transactions on Biomedical Engineering 51, 1044–1051 (2004)
4. Pfurtscheller, G.: 'Thought'-control of functional electrical stimulation to restore hand grasp in a patient with tetraplegia. Neuroscience Letters 351, 33–36 (2003)
5. Meng, F., Tong, K., Chan, S., Wong, W., Lui, K., Tang, K., Gao, X., Gao, S.: BCI-FES training system design and implementation for rehabilitation of stroke patients. In: IEEE International Joint Conference on Neural Networks, pp. 4103–4106 (2008)
6. Tan, H., Kong, K., Shee, C., Wang, C., Guan, C., Ang, W.: Post-acute stroke patients use brain-computer interface to activate electrical stimulation. In: Annual International Conference of the IEEE EMBC, pp. 4234–4237 (2010)
7. Bentley, A.S.J., Andrew, C.M., John, L.R.: An offline auditory P300 brain-computer interface using principal and independent component analysis techniques for functional electrical stimulation application. In: Annual International Conference of the IEEE EMBC, pp. 4660–4663 (2008)
8. Gollee, H., Volosyak, I., McLachlan, A.J., Hunt, K.J., Graser, A.: An SSVEP-Based Brain–Computer Interface for the Control of Functional Electrical Stimulation. IEEE Transactions on Biomedical Engineering 57, 1847–1855 (2010)
9. Do, A.H., Wang, P.T., King, C.E., Abiri, A., Nenadic, Z.: Brain-Computer Interface Controlled Functional Electrical Stimulation System for Ankle Movement. Journal of Neuroengineering and Rehabilitation 8, 49 (2011)
10. Chang, G.C., Lub, J.J., Liao, G.D., Lai, J.S., Cheng, C.K., Kuo, B.L., Kuo, T.S.: A neuro-control system for the knee joint position control with quadriceps stimulation. IEEE Transactions on Rehabilitation Engineering 5, 2–11 (1997)
11. Ferrarin, M., Palazzo, F., Riener, R., Quintern, J.: Model-based control of FES-induced single joint movements. IEEE Transactions on Neural Systems and Rehabilitation Engineering 9, 245–257 (2001)
12. Wang, Y., Gao, X., Hong, B., Jia, C., Gao, S.: Brain-computer interfaces based on visual evoked potentials. IEEE Engineering in Medicine and Biology Magazine 27, 64–71 (2008)
13. Yao, L., Zhang, D., Huang, G., Zhu, X.: Using SSVEP based brain-computer interface to control functional electrical stimulation training system. In: 2011 IEEE 5th International Conference on Cybernetics and Intelligent Systems (CIS), pp. 323–328 (2011)

# A Feedforward Compensation Method
# for Control of Join Equilibrium Position

Xiao-Gang Duan[*], Yi Zhang, Hua Deng, and Hou-Zhong Yang

State Key Laboratory of High Performance Complex Manufacturing,
Central South University, Changsha 410083, China
xgduan@csu.edu.cn

**Abstract.** In this paper, a feedforward compensation method is proposed to control a joint equilibrium position. Human hand is dexterous due to the voluntary and reflex. Voluntary and reflex have different control period. The former is relatively slow, and the latter is relatively fast. Thus, a feedforward compensation is used to imitate the voluntary control, and a fuzzy logic controller (FLC) is used to imitate the reflex control. The proposed control method is applied to control a joint. The simulation results demonstrate the effectiveness of the proposed control method.

**Keywords:** Bionic, feedforward compensation, fuzzy logic controller.

# 1 Introduction

Bionic hands are widely used in situations where humans cannot use their own hands directly [1], such as prosthetic hand for upper limb amputee, robot hands, and industrial hands, etc.. Thus, many bionic hands have been developed. A key function of the bionic hand is to grip and to imitate the movement of the human hand. In precise manipulations, bionic hands with high efficiency and dexterity are required. In order to achieve a stable grasping, joint control usually plays an important role in controlling bionic hands. Good joint control can greatly improve the motion performance of bionic hand, and can ensure satisfying the stability criterions [2].

There are some approaches in joint feedback control, such as proportional derivative (PD) feedback, adaptive output regulation, artificial neural network (ANN), etc. [3]. The common feature of these control approaches is that sampling period is often fixed. They may not directly achieve good performance in the bionic hand joint.

The human neural system that control posture and movement is a complex, nonlinear system [4]. It presents adaptive behavior and can easily accommodate disturbances in both environment and task specifications. It is known that human movement controlled by voluntary and reflex. Someone who has a with abnormal muscle tone including spasticity, dystonia or Parkinson's disease, can not maintain posture very well. Literatures show that the voluntary response is relatively slower than that the reflex [5].

Motivated by previous discussion, a feedforward compensation method is proposed to control a joint equilibrium position. A PD controller is used to imitate voluntary in

---

[*] Corresponding author.

C.-Y. Su, S. Rakheja, H. Liu (Eds.): ICIRA 2012, Part I, LNAI 7506, pp. 536–544, 2012.
© Springer-Verlag Berlin Heidelberg 2012

the feedforward control loop. A fuzzy logic controller (FLC) is used to imitate reflex in the feedback control loop. The sampling period of the PD controller is slower than that of FLC controller. The proposed control method is applied to control a joint. The simulation results demonstrate the effectiveness of the proposed control method.

## 2  Joint Dynamics

A dynamic joint of human is complex. It may be separated into two components: intrinsic dynamics, encompassing the mechanical properties of the joint, active muscle, and passive visco-elastic tissues; and reflex dynamics, arising from changes in muscle activation due to the stretch reflex [6]. A joint dynamic property is approximated by the following equation

$$I(t)\frac{d^2\theta}{dt^2} + B(t)\frac{d\theta}{dt} = U \tag{1}$$

where $I(t)$ and $B(t)$ denote the moment of inertia and the coefficient of viscosity, respectively; $\theta$ is the joint angle; $U$ is the drive torque.

## 3  Control of Human Motions

The posture and movement of human is regulated by the proprioceptive reflexes and voluntary [7]. Someone who has a with abnormal muscle tone including spasticity, dystonia or Parkinson's disease, can not maintain posture very well. In reflex, a stimulus causes a single synapse response, as shown dashed frame in Fig. 1. The center of this reflex is the spinal cord, where a fast feedback is produced. The response time of reflex is about 35 milliseconds after a stimulus is perceived by sensing elements. Meanwhile, the stimulus is transferred to brain through neural system. The brain processes the stimulus signal, make decision, adjust the reflex response and produce a voluntary movement, as shown in Fig.1. The feedback of the voluntary movement is a slow and response time is about 140 milliseconds [5].

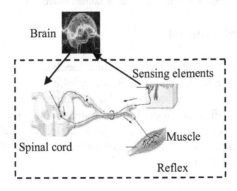

**Fig. 1.** Basic scheme of voluntary and reflex movement

A healthy person can execute very complex and smooth motion by combining the voluntary and reflex response. The never control system has a hierarchical structure that provides the flexibility necessary for achieving the desired adaptation and robust stability [7], [8], as shown in Fig. 2. At the bottom, the local feedback loops for basic reflex actions in the spinal cord. At the high level, the brain produces command and modulates the local feedback loops with renshaw cell.

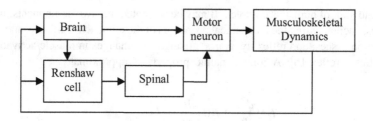

**Fig. 2.** A frame of human movement

The control system of human neuron is simply described in Fig. 3, where it includes a voluntary controller, a reflex controller and a coordination controller. The voluntary controller executes the decision from brain. Human brain has prediction function. The reflex controller generates torque to reduce disturbances. The coordination controller is used to combine the voluntary and reflex controller.

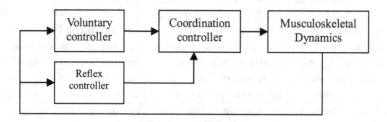

**Fig. 3.** Control scheme of human movement

## 4    Feedforward Control

It is still unclear how the voluntary and reflex feedbacks are coordinated. But, a common view is that the human movement is controlled by the reflex and voluntary simultaneously. Thus, a feed-forward compensation control method is proposed in Fig. 4, where a PD and a FLC are used imitate human voluntary and reflex control, respectively; $r(t)$ is reference, $\theta(t)$ is the joint angle; $w_V$ and $w_R$ are weight of the PD controller and the FLC, respectively; $e = r - \theta$ denotes error. The comprehensive control action is

$$U = w_V u_{PD} + w_R u_f \tag{2}$$

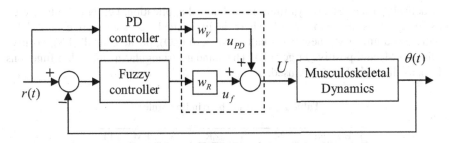

**Fig. 4.** Feedforward control structure

## 4.1 PD Controller

The classical PD controller is described by the following time model [9]

$$u_{PD} = K_P(e + T_d \dot{e})$$ (3)

where $u_{PD}$ is the control signal acting on the error signal $e$, $K_P$ is the proportional gain, $T_d$ is derivative time constant.

## 4.2 Fuzzy Logic Controller

The detail design of the FLC was discussed in [10] and [11]. Here, only the structure of the FLC is shown in Fig. 5. Generally, for a FLC, the fuzzy rule adopts "If $E$ is $A_i$ and $R$ is $B_j$ then $\tilde{u}$ is $G_{i+j}$," where $E$, $R$ and $A_i$, $B_j$ $(i, j = -N, \cdots, -1, 0, 1, \cdots, N)$ denote input variables and input fuzzy sets, respectively; $\tilde{u}$ and $G_{i+j}$ denotes the control action and output fuzzy set, respectively; $N$ denotes the number of input fuzzy sets.

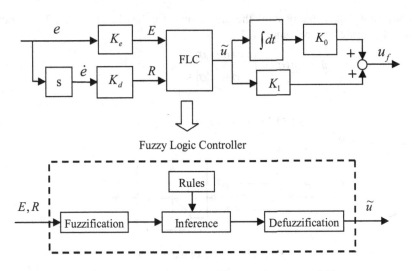

**Fig. 5.** Membership functions of input and output variable

Practically, rules are always finite in real-world application, i.e., N is finite. Here, we select N=3, as shown in Table 1, where the linguistic labels are negative large (NL), negative medium (NM), negative small (NS), zero (ZO), positive small (PS), positive medium (PM) and positive large (PL). The standard triangular membership functions (MFs), as shown in Fig. 6, are used.

**Table 1.** Fuzzy rule base in finite rules

| R/E | NL | NM | NS | ZR | PS | PM | PL |
|-----|----|----|----|----|----|----|----|
| PL | ZR | PS | PM | PL | PL | PL | PL |
| PM | NS | ZR | PS | PM | PL | PL | PL |
| PS | NM | NS | ZR | PS | PM | PL | PL |
| ZR | NL | NM | NS | ZR | PS | PM | PL |
| NS | NL | NL | NM | NS | ZR | PS | PM |
| NM | NL | NL | NL | NM | NS | ZR | PS |
| NL | NL | NL | NL | NL | NM | NS | ZR |

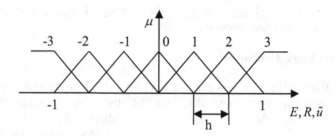

**Fig. 6.** Membership functions of input and output variable

Thus, finite rules clearly show the saturation effect, as shown in Fig. 7. The output model of the rule base becomes [12]

$$\tilde{u} = sat(\sigma) = \begin{cases} \text{sgn}(\sigma) & |\sigma| > 1 \\ g(\sigma) & |\sigma| \le 1 \end{cases} \tag{4}$$

with

$$g(\sigma) = \sigma + (1-\gamma)(kh-\sigma) \tag{5}$$

where $\sigma = E + R$.

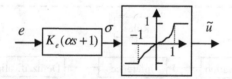

**Fig. 7.** Saturation of the rule base

Thus, the mathematical model of the fuzzy PID controller can be easily derived as from Fig. 5

$$u_f = K_0 \int \tilde{u} dt + K_1 \tilde{u} = K_0 \int sat(\sigma) dt + K_1 sat(\sigma) \qquad (6)$$

where $\tilde{u}$ is given in (4).

## 5    Simulations

The proposed feedforward compensation method was used to control the joint dynamics described in (1). The weights $w_V$ and $w_R$ are set as 1 for simplicity. The sampling period of the feedforward loop and the feedback loop are selected as 0.05 seconds and 0.01 seconds, respectively. The coefficient of viscosity, $B(t)$, is given as follows

$$B(t) = a[b + c \times rand(t)] \qquad (7)$$

where $rand(t)$ is a random function; $a$, $b$ and $c$ are positive constant.

### 5.1    Step Response

Let $a = 0.12$, $b = c = 5$. The parameters of the PD controller are chosen as $K_P = 0.2$, $T_D = 0.5$. The parameters of the FLC are selected as $K_3 = 0.3$, $K_d = 0.1$, $K_0 = 0.6$ and $K_1 = 1$. The control performance is shown in Fig. 8.

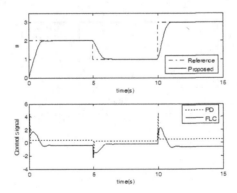

**Fig. 8.** Step response of the proposed control method

A same sampling period of the feedforward loop and the feedback loop is used. The simulation results are shown in Fig. 9. When both of the PD and the FLC adopt a sampling time, i.e. 0.01s, there is not obvious difference between Fig.8 and Fig. 9(a). However, there exits large impulse signal in the latter. When both of them adopt 0.05s, the control performance of the latter is poor, as shown in Fig. 9(b).

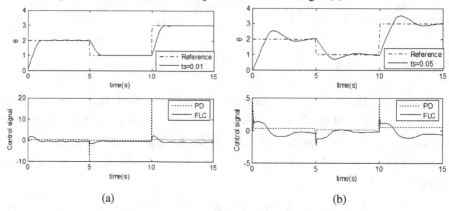

(a)                                        (b)

**Fig. 9.** Step response under different sampling period, 0.01s and 0.05s (a) ts=0.01s, (b) ts=0.05s

## 5.2    Sine Response

Let Let $a = 0.03$, $b = 5$, $c = 2$, $r(t) = \sin(0.5\pi t)$ and the parameter of the FLC $K_0 = 0.4$. The other parameters are invariant. The sine response is shown in Fig. 10, where the sinusoid curve controlled by the proposed control method can track the reference well.

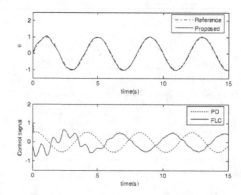

**Fig. 10.** Tracking sinusoid performance of the proposed control method

In order to compare the control performance, a same sampling period of the feedforward loop and the feedback loop is used. The simulation results are shown in Fig. 11. When both of the PD and the FLC adopt a sampling time, i.e. 0.01s and 0.05s, the control performance is poor, as shown in Fig. 10(a) and Fig. 109(b), respectively.

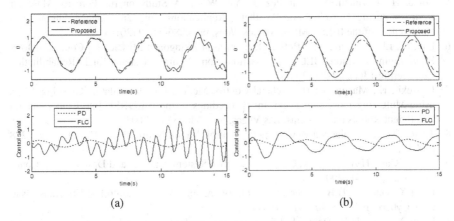

(a)                                    (b)

**Fig. 11.** Sine response under different sampling period, a) ts=0/01s, b) ts=0.05s

## 6    Conclusion

A feedforward compensation control method is proposed to control a joint dynamics. A PD controller is used to imitate voluntary control in human, which can compensate the change of set-point. A FLC is used to imitate reflex in human, which can suppress disturbance, such as unmodeled dynamics. The PD controller is a relatively slow control loop, and the FLC is a relatively fast control loop. The proposed control method is applied to control a joint. The simulation results demonstrate the effectiveness of the proposed control method.

**Acknowledgments.** The work described in this paper was partially supported by the grants from National Basic Research Program 973 of China (Grant Nos. 2011CB013302), a Postdoctoral Foundation of Central South University, China.

## References

1. Bauer, C., Milighetti, G., Yan, W., Mikut, R.: Human-like Reflexes for Robotic Manipulation using Leaky Integrate-and-Fire Neurons. In: The IEEE/RSL International Conference on Iintellgient Robots and Systems, Taipei, pp. 2572–2577 (2010)
2. Xing, D., Su, J., Liu, Y., Zhong, J.: Robust Approach for Humanoid Joint Control based on a Disturbance Observer. IET Control Theory and Applications 5(14), 1630–1636 (2011)

3. Nataraj, R., Audu, M.L., Kirsch, R.F., Triolo, R.J.: Comprehensive Joint Feedback Control for Standing by Functional Neuromuscular Stimulation—A Simulation Study. IEEE Transactions on Neural Systems and Rehabilitation Engineering 18(6), 646–657 (2010)
4. He, J.P., Maltenfort, M.G., Wang, Q.J., Hamm, T.M.: Learing from Biological Systems: Modeling Neural Control. IEEE Control Systems Magazine, 55–69 (2001)
5. Soma, H., Horiuchi, Y., González, J., Yu, W.W.: A Study on the Forearm Muscular Reflexes during Grasping For Prosthetic Applications. In: 32nd Annual International Conferences of the IEEE EMBS, Buenos Aires, pp. 4886–4889 (2010)
6. Lan, N., Li, Y., Yang, F.S.: Reflex Regulation of Antagonist Muscles for Control of Joint Equilibrium Position. IEEE Transactions on Neural Systems and Rehabilitation Engineering 13(1), 60–71 (2005)
7. Imazeki., K., Maeno, T.: Hierarchical Control Method for Manipulating/Grasping Tasks using Multi-fingered Robot Hand. In: Proceedings of tne IEEE/RSL Intl. Conference on Iintellgient Robots and Systems, Las Vegas, pp. 3686–3691 (2003)
8. Tresch, M.C.: A balanced view of motor control. Nature Neuroscience 10(10), 1227–1228 (2007)
9. Li, Y., Kiam, H.A., Gregory, C.Y.: PID Control System Analysis and Design. IEEE Contr. Syst. Mag., 32–41 (2006)
10. Li, H.X., Gatland, H.B., Green, A.W.: Fuzzy variable structure control. IEEE Trans. Syst. man, Cybern. B 27(2), 306–312 (1997)
11. Duan, X.G., Li, H.X., Deng, H.: Effective tuning method for fuzzy PID with internal model control. Ind. Eng. Chem. Res. 47(21), 8317–8323 (2008)
12. Duan, X.G., Li, H.X., Deng, H.: Robustness of fuzzy PID controller due to its inherent saturation. Journal of Process Control 22(2), 470–476 (2012)

# A New 4M Model-Based Human-Machine Interface for Lower Extremity Exoskeleton Robot

Zhao Guo[1,2], Yuanjie Fan[1], Jianjun Zhang[1], Haoyong Yu[2], and Yuehong Yin[1]

[1] State Key Laboratory of Mechanism System and Vibration, Institute of Robotics,
Shanghai Jiao Tong University, 200240, Shanghai, China
[2] Department of Bioengineering, National University of Singapore, 117576, Singapore
{guozhao,fantian,zhangjianjun,yhyin}@sjtu.edu.cn,
bieyhy@nus.edu.sg

**Abstract.** This paper presents a Human-Machine Interface (HMI) for controlling lower limb exoskeleton robot intelligently with the joint torque estimated by a new biomechanical model of skeletal muscle. Based on the Microscopic working Mechanism of Molecular Motor (4M) in sacromere, this 4M model is established to reveal the relation between the characteristics of sEMG signal and active contraction force of muscle fiber. We discuss the interaction mechanism between human body and exoskeleton via analyzing the dynamics of exoskeleton robot and knee joint respectively. The knee joint torque that generated by skeletal muscle can be predicted accurately with the 4M model via measuring the sEMG signals on muscle surface. An active strategy for controlling exoskeleton robot has been proposed to train the lower limb on human intention. Experimental results show that the operator can exercise harmoniously with the exoskeleton, which prove the validity of this theoretical biomechanical model.

**Keywords:** Exoskeleton, skeletal muscle, biomechanical model, human-machine interface (HMI), sEMG, active control, 4M model.

## 1 Introduction

Lower extremity exoskeleton robot is a wearable mechanism to assist human walking, rehabilitation training. Nowadays, many exoskeleton systems (BLEEX [1], HAL[2], LOPES[3], ALEX[4], LOKOMAT[5], TUPLEE[6], et al) have been developed by researchers around the world to help human walking effectively. However, little exoskeleton system has successfully been applied in clinic. A good human-machine interface (HMI) is needed in the intelligent control of exoskeleton. HMI is the "link" between the exoskeleton robot and human body including many sensors to obtain the state of human motion in real-time. Therefore, HMI is the essential part in the realization of intelligent control of exoskeleton.

sEMG signal is usually used as means of information transportation to recognize the patterns in control of upper limb prostheses with a HMI. Due to the simple motion mode of lower limb (mainly extension/flexion), it is not effective to control the exoskeleton via identifying the motion mode. Because sEMG signals are essentially made up of superimposed motor unit action potentials on the muscle cell surface,

C.-Y. Su, S. Rakheja, H. Liu (Eds.): ICIRA 2012, Part I, LNAI 7506, pp. 545–554, 2012.

which can be used to describe the activation of muscle contraction. Many researchers have utilized sEMG signals to control exoskeleton. In [6] TUPLEE is developed and driven by a biomechanical model that evaluates the EMG signals to obtain the desired action. In [7] a neural network is built to predict the joint torque for an ankle exoskeleton. In [8, 9] EMG signals have been evaluated with a Hill-type muscle model to estimate the elbow joint moment. This information is useful for controlling the exoskeleton, while a biomechanical muscle model is needed to calculate muscle force and joint torque. Ordinary, there are two typical muscle models to describe the mechanical characteristics of skeletal muscle. The first one is the Hill-type model, which derived from muscle experiments in *vitro* and mainly describes the macroscopic properties. However, Hill's model is not accurate to calculate muscle force in *vivo* during human movement. Another is the Huxley-type model used to describe the microscopic properties, but it also has some shortages [10]. Skeletal muscle contraction is generated by the collective cooperation of myosin motors on thin filament and controlled by the central nervous system via action potential. A new biomechanical model of skeletal muscle is required to reflect the microscopic working mechanism of molecular motor and the relationship between the character frequency of sEMG and the active contraction force. With this model, the joint torque can be estimated accurately with the surface sEMG signals. Therefore, we can control the exoskeleton with the estimated information based on sEMG signals.

This paper presents a HMI based on a new biomechanical model of skeletal muscle according to the microscopic working mechanism of molecular motor in sarcomere. The relationship between the characteristics of sEMG signal and muscle active force is established. We analyze the interaction mechanism and model the dynamics of exoskeleton robot and human knee joint respectively. The joint torque is estimated with forward dynamics of human body based on the 4M model of skeletal muscle. At last, an active control strategy is formulated to control the exoskeleton. Experimental research is carried out to validate the theoretical model.

## 2    A New Biomechanical Model of Skeletal Muscle

According to the structure of sarcomeres arranged in series and in parallel, we deduce a new biomechanical model of skeletal muscle for calculating active contraction force based on the Microscopic working Mechanism of Myosin Motors in a sarcomere (abbreviated to 4M model) [11,12]:

$$F_a^m = \frac{A\alpha\beta n_0 k_c}{s} \int_0^L x\rho(x,t)dx. \tag{1}$$

Where $k_c$ is the elasticity coefficient of myosin head, $n_0$ is the total number of myosin motors in a thick filament. $A$ is the cross-sectional area of all muscle fiber, $s$ is the area of a thick filament and six thin filaments. $A/s$ means the number of thick filament in the skeletal muscle. $\alpha$ is the overlap degree between thin and thick filaments. $\beta$ is the activation degree of muscle, which is the function of $[Ca^{2+}]$ in sarcoplasmic depending on the stimulation frequency of action potential. $\rho(x,t)$ is the probability density that myosin motor at position $x$ at time $t$. $L$ is the distance between two binding sites on a thin filament.

If the ATP concentration is saturated and skeletal muscle is not in fatigue, active contraction force mainly depends on the frequency characteristics of action potential, we define the isometric force of skeletal muscle in maximal activation degree as $F_{ma}$. Active force model in different activation degree can be simplified as follows.

$$F_a^m = \beta \cdot \alpha \cdot F_{ma} . \tag{2}$$

Normally a skeletal muscle consists of multiple muscle fibers, when the stimulation frequency of single muscle fiber reaches its maximum, human body can still recruit other types of muscle fibers to generate greater force. We define the activation degree of a macroscopic skeletal muscle as

$$\beta = \mu f(\omega) . \tag{3}$$

Where $f(\omega)$ represents the activation degree of single muscle fiber decided by the stimulation frequency of action potential [14,15]. $\mu$ means the ratio of recruited muscle fibers in a skeletal muscle.

Because sEMG signal is the formation of the superimposed action potential on the surface of muscle fibers. The frequency of action potential can be characterized by the sEMG signal. We carry out real-time Fourier transform within each sampling period of sEMG signal. The characteristic frequency is defined as

$$\omega = (\sum_{i=1}^{N} C_i n_i) / (\sum_{i=1}^{N} C_i) . \tag{4}$$

Where $C_i$ denotes the amplitudes of the points on the half Fourier spectrum on each sampling period, $n_i$ is the position of the point, and $N$ denotes total number of sampling points. Characteristic Frequency reflects the activation of muscle fibers, determined by the frequency of action potentials.

Because the RMS value of sEMG signal can be used to represent the number of recruited muscle fibers. When the RMS increases, the human body will recruit more activated muscle fibers to get force. If muscle reaches the maximum voluntary contraction (MVC), muscle will produce the maximum force. We define the RMS value of sEMG signal as

$$a_{rms} = \sqrt{\frac{1}{N} \sum_{i=1}^{N} v_i^2} . \tag{5}$$

Where $v_i$ is the voltage value of the $i$-th sampling point. The maximum value of RMS is represented as $a_{MVC}$. We define the ratio of recruited muscle fibers $\mu = a_{rms}/a_{mvc}$. Therefore an activation degree of a skeletal muscle can be used to calculate active contraction force by measuring the sEMG signal.

On the other hand, muscle can be passive stretched by external load in extension state, which is mainly determined by the titin protein. Because of the nonlinear visco-elastic character, muscle passive force includes the damping force and elastic force.

$$F_p^m = k_m \Delta l^m - \gamma v . \tag{6}$$

Where $k_m$ is the stiffness of titin protein, $\gamma$ is the drag coefficient, $v$ is muscle contraction speed.

The contraction force is composed of active force $F_a{}^m$ and passive force $F_p{}^m$.

$$F_m = F_a^m + F_p^m . \tag{7}$$

Because muscle connects to bone via tendon, muscle force along the tendon direction is $F_{mt}=F_m \cos \psi$, The length of muscle and tendon is given by.

$$l^{mt} = l^m + l^t \cos \psi . \tag{8}$$

Where $\psi$ is the pennation angle between tendon and muscle fiber, $l^m$, $l^t$ is the length of muscle and tendon respectively.

# 3     Human-Machine Interaction Mechanism

## 3.1     Human-Machine Interface

A Lower Extremity Exoskeleton Robot (LEER) is developed by our group for gait training and joint rehabilitation in fig.1. [16]. The exoskeleton includes hip and knee joint, a body weight system, a mobile platform and other protective equipments. Operator can adjust the height and width of the two legs of exoskeleton to meet the user's different requirement.

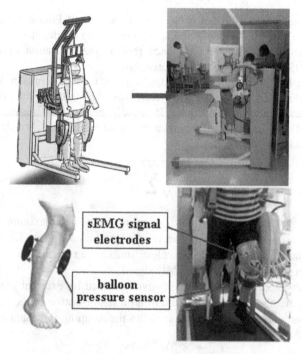

**Fig. 1.** Exoskeleton robot and HMI

An interface between the user and exoskeleton is designed to control exoskeleton. We utilize the sEMG signal and contact force as the control information. The interface hardware mainly consists of sEMG signal electrodes, pressure sensor, data acquisition card and DSP processor. Here a balloon as the pressure sensor connecting with gas tubes is bound to the human leg, and both of the balloon and the human leg are bound to exoskeleton, this pressure sensor is used to measure the interaction force between the human body and exoskeleton. sEMG electrodes are located at the middle surface of muscle to monitor its stimulation level.

During the training process, the interaction force can come from human body or exoskeleton. Exoskeleton provides force to assist human joint movement and partially compensates human body for the insufficient muscle force to complete the desired action. On the other hand, if the exoskeleton is fixed, human body also can take force on exoskeleton, the interaction force produced by muscle contraction can be measured with the pressure sensor. And the parameters of our 4M model can be quantified with the data measured by pressure sensor. Meanwhile, sEMG signal of each contraction muscle can be collected with electrodes to represent the activation degree. That means we can calculate the muscle contraction force with sEMG signal and estimate the joint torque via modeling the dynamics of human body.

### 3.2   Dynamical Analysis of Exoskeleton

Exoskeleton has 4 degrees of freedom. A simplified system is shown in figure 2. In the right leg, $a_{1r}$ is the length of exoskeleton thigh, $l_{1r}$ is the distance between the center of thigh gravity and hip joint. $l_{2r}$ is the distance from the calf gravity center to knee joint, $\theta_{1r}$, $\theta_{2r}$ is the hip and knee joint angle respectively, $T_{1r}$, $T_{2r}$ is the required hip and knee torque, $F_{e1r}$, $F_{e2r}$ is the interaction force on exoskeleton thigh and calf, $m_{1r}$, $m_{2r}$ is the quality of thigh and calf. The critical size of exoskeleton is designed as follows: $a_{1r}$= 0.422m, $l_{1r}$= 0.26687m, $l_{2r}$= 0.055785m, $m_{1r}$=4.3kg, $m_{2r}$=0.51kg.

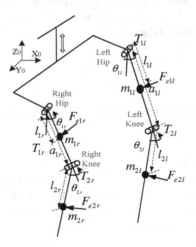

**Fig. 2.** A simplified model of exoskeleton robot, and right is abbreviated as 'r', Left is abbreviated as 'l'

Given the rotational speed of hip and knee joint, the required torque can be calculated by Lagrangian method.

$$\begin{cases} T_{ir} = \dfrac{d}{dt}\dfrac{\partial L_r}{\partial \dot{\theta}_{ir}} - \dfrac{\partial L_r}{\partial \dot{\theta}_{ir}} \\ T_{il} = \dfrac{d}{dt}\dfrac{\partial L_l}{\partial \dot{\theta}_{il}} - \dfrac{\partial L_l}{\partial \dot{\theta}_{il}} \end{cases} \quad i = 1, 2. \tag{9}$$

Considering the interaction force on exoskeleton, the active torque of each joint is given by these equations.

$$\begin{cases} T_{air} = T_{ir} + F_{eir} \times r_{eir} \\ T_{ail} = T_{il} + F_{eil} \times r_{eil} \end{cases} \quad i = 1, 2. \tag{10}$$

### 3.3     Dynamical Analysis of Human Knee Joint

#### 3.3.1     Forward Dynamics

Human knee joint is one of the biggest joints in human body. The flexion of knee is controlled by Biceps Femoris (BF), Semitendinosus (ST), semimembranosus (SM), and the extension of knee is controlled by Rectus Femoris (RF),Vastus Intermedius (VI), Vastus Lateralus (VL), Vastus Medialus (VM). They are mutually antagonistic muscles. We analyze the forward dynamics of knee joint based on the opensim2.2 software provided by Stanford University [17], the parameters of each muscle (such as PCSA, starting point, muscle and tendon length et al) are given on this software.

Different from the Hill-type model, we use our own 4M model to analyze the forward dynamics of knee joint. The sEMG signals are used to represent the activation of skeletal muscle. With this biomechanical model, the active contraction force will be calculated. The active joint torque can be obtained based on the forward dynamics using the anatomical data.

$$T = \sum_{i=1}^{8} F_i^{mt} r_i \tag{11}$$

Where $F_i^{mt}$ is the contraction force of the $i$th muscle, $r_i$ is the moment arm of this muscle.

#### 3.3.2     Inverse Dynamics

On the other hand, we can measure the knee angle and interaction force between the human leg and exoskeleton with sensors. The angular velocity and angular acceleration of knee joint can be calculated with the angle data. The torque of knee joint can be calculated by inverse dynamical equation.

$$T' = J_\omega \dot{\omega}_k + G \times r_g + F \times r_f \tag{12}$$

Where $J_{\omega}$ is the moment inertia, $\dot{\omega}_k$ is angular acceleration of knee, $G$ is the gravity of calf. $F$ is interaction force, $r_g$, $r_f$ is the moment arm.

Theoretically, the torque calculated by inverse dynamical method is equal to the active torque of muscle contraction.

$$T - T' = 0 \qquad (13)$$

Due to the individual difference, the anatomical data of each person is not the same. We need to quantify the parameters of the muscle model. An optimization method can be used, and the mechanical index (such as total energy consumption, etc.) is limited in the minimum domain, here we use the square of torque error as the objective function, a least square method is used to calibrate the model's parameters.

$$\min : (\sum_{i=1}^{8} F_i^{mt} r_i - T')^2 \qquad (14)$$

## 4    Active Control Strategy

The active control strategy is shown in Fig. 3.

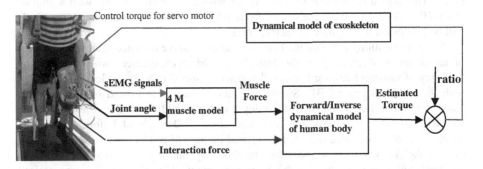

**Fig. 3.** Active control strategy

The purpose of this strategy is to control the exoskeleton robot with HMI intelligently. Operator can walk on the help of exoskeleton robot. Based on the dynamical analysis of human body, collecting the EMG signals of skeletal muscle (BF, RF muscles in the thigh), the actual torque of human joint is estimated with the 4M muscle model, which can be used as the required torque to understand the human motion intention. HMI utilizes this information to control the exoskeleton. Then exoskeleton provides force to assist the user. Therefore, human motion is fulfilled on the help of exoskeleton based on the 4M muscle model.

The detail control process is described as follow: Firstly, the interaction force measured by pressure sensor in real-time is used to quantity the 4M muscle model. The parameters are calibrated based on the least square method with equation (14). Secondly, active force is calculated with the collecting sEMG signals of muscles and the joint angle of lower limb with the quantitative muscle model. And the predicted knee torque on the forward dynamical model is multiplied by the support ratio giving the target torque for the torque control loop. This loop is realized in the exoskeleton control system driven by a 200W panasonic MSMD ac servo motor. The exoskeleton actuator consists of a ball screw creating a maximum force of 4341N and torque of 269Nm in the exoskeleton knee joint. According to the inverse dynamical model of exoskeleton, the estimated toque will be inputted into the servo motor driver to control the exoskeleton and help human joint training intelligently. The whole controller works as a torque amplifier without position control.

## 5    Experiments and Discussion

This active training has been done on a tester. The subject is a 30-year-old healthy male, human leg is fixed on the exoskeleton. sEMG signals under different contraction condition of RF and BF muscles are obtained with the sEMG electrodes. This two sEMG signals are processed to control the exoskeleton flexion/extension. The interaction force is measured by the pressure sensor. The sampling rates of EMG signals and balloon tension signal are both 2000 Hz, so one datum is recorded every 400 sampling interval, the data recording period is $\Delta T = 0.2$ s. sEMG signals during every $\Delta T$ are dealt with Fourier transform and the characteristic frequency is extracted in real time. Because the sEMG signal on the skin is weak and from the uV to the mV range. This signal is amplified 6826.7 times with an amplifier circuit with a gain of 2048*10/3 V/V and a band pass filter from 10Hz to 500Hz. Recorded sEMG signals will be processed to calculate the active force.

During the training process, the operator wants to move his knee joint with the help of exoskeleton. According to the tester's first-hand experience, when he has the tendency of moving backward, exoskeleton will respond quickly to flex the lower leg with the sEMG signal of BF. Similarly, when he wants to extend his leg upward, exoskeleton also can assist the human leg moving quickly with the sEMG signal of RF. Because sEMG signals are generated about 200ms ahead before the muscle contraction, this estimated muscle force based on the 4M model can be used to control the exoskeleton as soon as possible. In this way, human body does not need to consume too much energy for the joint movement. This interaction force mainly comes from the exoskeleton robot and can reduce the energy consumption of muscle contraction. As shown in Fig.4. The sEMG signals of RF and BF, predicted force and the measured interaction force between the exoskeleton and human body are recorded respectively during the extension and flexion process. Because the BF and RF muscles are a pair of antagonistic muscles, sEMG signals of the two muscles are shown alternately, thus we can use the sEMG signals to describe the muscle activation degree and calculate the required torque of joint movement. Compared with the estimated muscle force, the interaction force can follow the predicted control signal of servo motor very well. These two signals have the same trend, indicating that human motion is mainly supported by the exoskeleton. Meanwhile, it is shown that the voltage signal predicted by the muscle model in the extension process is larger than the signal of flexion process. Because human need to overcome the gravity of leg during the extension process, the interaction force provided by exoskeleton is smaller than the force in the flexion process. This experiment proves the effectiveness of this active control strategy with our proposed 4M muscle model.

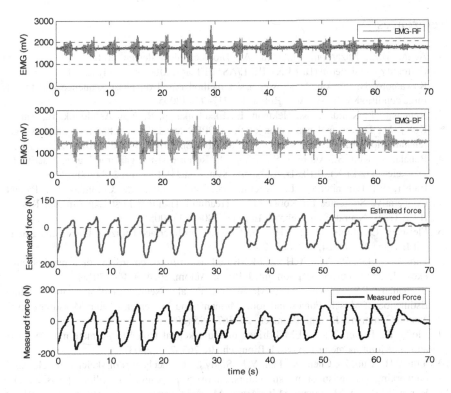

**Fig. 4.** Experimental Results

## 6    Conclusion

We design a HMI based on a new 4M model of skeletal muscle according to the microscopic working mechanism of molecular motors in a sarcomere. The relationship between sEMG signal and active force of muscle contraction is established from the point of view of frequency analysis. The human-machine interaction mechanism is analyzed via modeling the dynamics of exoskeleton and the human knee joint respectively. Knee joint torque is predicted by the forward dynamical model based on the 4M muscle model with the collected sEMG signals to understanding the motion intention of human. Estimated force is used to control the exoskeleton successfully. These results prove the effectiveness of the HMI based on our 4M muscle model.

**Acknowledgment.** This work was supported by the National Natural Science Foundation of China (61075101,60643002), the National Basic Research Program of China (2011CB013203),the Science and Technology Intercrossing and the Medical and Technology Intercrossing Research Foundation of Shanghai Jiao Tong University (LG2011ZD$_1$06,YG2010ZD$_1$01).

# References

1. Adam, B.Z., Kazerooni, H., Chu, A.: Biomechanical design of the Berkeley Lower Extremity Exoskeleton (BLEEX). IEEE/ASME Trans. Mechatron. 11, 128–138 (2006)
2. Kawamoto, H., Sankai, Y.: Power assist method based on phase sequence and muscle force condition for HAL. Adv. Robot. 19, 717–734 (2005)
3. Veneman, J., Kruidhof, R., Hekman, E., Ekkelenkamp, R., Van Asseldonk, E., van der Kooij, H.: Design and evaluation of the LOPES exoskeleton robot for interactive gait rehabilitation. IEEE Trans. Neural. Syst. Rehabil. Eng. 15, 379–386 (2007)
4. Banala, S., Kim, S., Agrawal, S., Scholz, J.: Robot assisted gait training with active leg exoskeleton (ALEX). IEEE Trans. Neural Syst. Rehabil. Eng. 17, 2–8 (2009)
5. Riener, R., Lunenburger, L., Jezernik, S., Anderschitz, M., Colombo, G.: Patient-Cooperative Strategies for Robot-Aided Treadmill Training: First Experimental Results. IEEE Trans. Neural. Syst. Rehabil. Eng. 13, 380–394 (2005)
6. Fleischer, C., Hommel, G.: A Human–Exoskeleton Interface Utilizing Electromyography. IEEE Trans. Robot. 24, 872–882 (2008)
7. Fan, Y.J., Guo, Z., Yin, Y.H.: sEMG-Based neuro-fuzzy controller for a parallel ankle exoskeleton with proprioception. Int. J. Robot. Autom. 26, 450–460 (2011)
8. Buchanan, T.S., Lloyd, D.G., Manal, K., et al.: Neuromusculoskeletal Modeling: Estimation of Muscle Forces and Joint Moments and Movements From Measurements of Neural Command. J. Appl. Biomech. 20, 367–395 (2004)
9. Lloyd, D., Besier, T.: An EMG-driven musculoskeletal model to estimate muscle forces and knee joint moments in vivo. J. Biomech. 36, 765–776 (2003)
10. Yin, Y.H., Guo, Z., Chen, X., Fan, Y.J.: Study on biomechanics of skeletal muscle based on working mechanism of myosin motors: An overview. Chin. Sci. Bull. (in press, 2012)
11. Rosen, J., Brand, M., Fuchs, M.B., Arcan, M.: A Myosignal-Based Powered Exoskeleton System. IEEE Trans. Syst., Man, Cybern. 31, 210–222 (2001)
12. Guo, Z., Yin, Y.H.: Coupling mechanism of multi-force interactions in the myosin molecular motor. Chin. Sci. Bull. 55, 3538–3544 (2010)
13. Yin, Y.H., Guo, Z.: Collective mechanism of molecular motors and a dynamic mechanical model for sarcomere. Sci. China-Technol. Sci. 54, 2130–2137 (2011)
14. Guo, Z., Yin, Y.H.: A dynamic model of skeletal muscle based on collective behavior of myosin motors—Biomechanics of skeletal muscle based on working mechanism of myosin motors (I). Sci. China-Technol. Sci. 55, 1589–1595 (2012)
15. Yin, Y.H., Chen, X.: Bioelectrochemical control mechanism with variable-frequency regulation for skeletal muscle contraction-Biomechanics of skeletal muscle based on the working mechanism of myosin motors (II). Sci. China-Technol. Sci. 55, 2115–2125 (2012)
16. Yin, Y.H., Fan, Y.J., Xu, L.D.: EMG & EPP-Integrated Human-machine Interface between the Paralyzed and Rehabilitation Exoskeleton. IEEE T. Inf. Technol. B. 3, 542–549 (2012)
17. https://simtk.org/home/opensim
18. Zhang, J.J., Yin, Y.H.: SMA-based bionic integration design of self-sensor–actuator-structure for artificial skeletal muscle. Sens. Actuators A: Phys. 181, 94–102 (2012)

# Design and Performance Evaluation
# of a Rotary Series Elastic Actuator

Mitchell Donald and Qingguo Li

Bio-Mechatronics and Robotics Laboratory
Department of Mechanical and Materials Engineering, Queen's University
K7L 3N6, Kingston ON, Canada

**Abstract.** The purpose of rotary series elastic actuators (RSEAs) is to reduce the interface stiffness between an actuator and the user, while achieving torque control, less inadvertent damage, high shock tolerance, and energy storage. In this paper we developed a RSEA test platform and control system for identifying the factors that affect performance. The effectiveness of a RSEA is studied by a sequence of experiments where a series of torque profiles are supplied to a handle, which the user holds while providing rotation about the elbow joint. By comparing desired torque outputs with those found via the spring deflection and those measured by an in-system load cell, the performance of the system is analyzed. The results indicated that the system is mostly limited by the torsion spring, its attachment, and the nonlinearities associated with it. The spring itself has a large impact on the torque/frequency bandwidth of the RSEA.

**Keywords:** rotary series elastic actuator, torque control, torsion spring.

## 1    Introduction

In robotics, safety is crucially important when human-robot interaction is present. This is important because no matter how robust a system is, there is always a chance of unpredictable or undesired behaviour. Current, hydraulic, pneumatic, and electromagnetic actuators with position control are often used in robotics, but are not inherently safe [1]. Small errors in position control may cause catastrophic consequences in the aforementioned systems, thus series elastic actuators (SEAs) are introduced to offer a more complaint and safer robotic system. The added elasticity component offers many advantages including shock tolerance, stable accurate force control, lower reflected inertia, less damage prone, and ability to store elastic energy [2]. The demand for safer and more compliant systems in the area of human-robot interaction further excites the development of various types of SEAs. Example applications range from orthotics and prosthetics [3], exoskeletons [4], robotics [5] to power augmentation devices [6].

Series elastic actuators can be categorized as linear or rotary SEA depending on the movement the actuator intends to perform. A rotary series elastic actuator (RSEA)

C.-Y. Su, S. Rakheja, H. Liu (Eds.): ICIRA 2012, Part I, LNAI 7506, pp. 555–564, 2012.

consists of a rotary actuator in series of a torsion spring to provide torque to the user. Linear SEAs may be bulkier and more complicated, with a smaller range of motion but offer more symmetrical spring/torque characteristics. A generic schematic of an RSEA is shown in Fig. 1. Recently, RSEAs have been developed for walking assistance [7], robotic arms [8], walking rehabilitation [9], and simulating aquatic exercises [10]. The success of the RSEA depends in large part on the spring dynamics and the effectiveness of the chosen control scheme.   System modeling and the selection of an appropriate control system is a complex process due to the nonlinear friction forces, spring model uncertainty, and vibration [11]. Vibration is caused by the PID gains, as well as the current and gain settings of the servo amplifier. Vibration and precision form a design trade-off. When vibration is increased the torque error is minimized, but noise and discomfort to the user increase [11]. Although RSEAs are currently used in various applications there is a need for a flexible RSEA test platform for understanding the fundamental behaviour of a RSEA system. The main objective of this paper is to develop a RSEA platform and evaluate its performance. The system is designed in such a way that all components can be easily adjusted, and the control system can be easily manipulated, which allows for a wide variety of experiments. It could be used for identifying potential problems of RSEAs and evaluating different control schemes. The developed RSEA prototype can be potentially used for arm or leg rehabilitation.   A closely related design with linear springs was developed [7], with the difference being that in our system a load cell is incorporated to directly measure the interaction torque. Our design enables a direct evaluation of the performance of a RSEA for torque generation, an important aspect in understanding system performance. Almost all of the previous work estimated the output torque from the spring deflection and assumed that to be the same as the torque actually applied to the user. In practice, the measured spring deflection from encoders is most likely different from actual spring deflection, which causes inaccuracy in the torque calculation. With the embedded load cell, we are able to evaluate the validity of torque prediction from spring deflection and analyze system performance. The linearity of the torsion spring was also examined via experiments with varying desired torque profiles. In another experiment the system was set to provide zero torque; this is important to test tracking ability and eliminate model resistance.

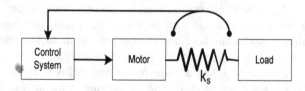

**Fig. 1.** RSEA schematic

This paper is organized as follows. In Section 2 the system design is explained. In Section 3.1 the experimental procedure is explained in a general sense to set up the specific experimental results that follow in Section 3.2. This is followed by a discussion in Section 4 and a conclusion in Section 5.

## 2    System Design

### 2.1    Mechanical System of the RSEA

The RSEA was designed as a prototype for experimental research, and is not meant to be installed as part of an exoskeleton, orthotic, or other device. Thus, components were chosen based on functionality and reliability, without significant size and weight limitations. The system is shown in Fig. 2 and Fig. 3, and as a schematic in Fig. 4.

In this paper, a PID control system is implemented, with position feedback from two encoders. The encoders used have a resolution of 1000 counts per 360°. A torsion spring (spring constant of 0.03883 Nm/deg) and Maxon DC motor (150 W, 15 Nm, 74:1 gear ratio) were selected to ensure the required torques can be supplied without sacrificing response time. The load cell (1% accuracy, ATI Industries) is installed in series with the spring, located on the handle (i.e. user) side of the device. It measures the actual torque the user feels. This allows for the comparison of actual torque and the torque provided by the angle difference as

$$\tau = k_{spring} * (\theta_{motor} - \theta_{human})$$ (1)

The load cell measurement is not used for control feedback, but merely for performance evaluation of the RSEA in torque production. Most RSEA systems assume the torque in Equation 1 to be accurate and do not compare this to the actual torque felt by the user.

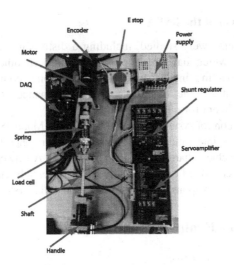

**Fig. 2.** RSEA experimental setup

**Fig. 3.** Load cell and spring setup

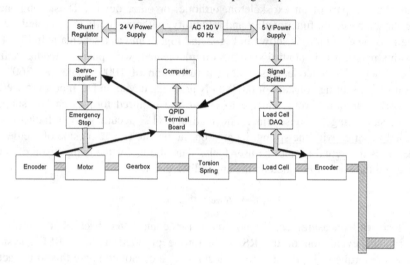

**Fig. 4.** Overall structure of the RSEA, with communication paths illustrated

## 2.2 Control System of the RSEA

Various control systems were studied, including a disturbance observer (DOB) and feed-forward filters, which have been previously used in other SEA designs [9]. However, due to modeling inconsistency these additional control schemes have a minimal improvement on the overall system performance, so PID control was determined to be sufficient for our RESA platform.

For the RSEA, the control system was constructed using Matlab/Simulink (Mathworks, Natick, MA), with C++ integration and additional Quanser supported software and data acquisition system to achieve hardware-in-loop simulation. A PID controller was chosen, and the parameters were found experimentally by incrementally changing the values to minimize the torque error, response time, and oscillation of the system.

## 3 Performance Evaluation and Results

### 3.1 Experimental Procedure

Three experiments were conducted following a similar procedure. A desired torque input is specified in the control system and is converted to an angle difference, based upon the spring constant. This angle difference, measured by two encoders, determines the PWM control sent by the servo amplifier to the motor for position control. Torque measured by the load cell is compared with the torque calculated from the angle difference. During each experiment, angles, and torque data are recorded for data analysis.

## 3.2    Performance of Position Tracking

Position tracking ability is a measure of how accurately the motor can dynamically provide a zero angle difference across the spring. Any tracking error will directly result a non-zero torque.

The gain and current limits of the servoamplifier were adjusted such that higher frequencies can be tracked effectively with the downside being added noise at low frequencies. This vibration is negligible and does not affect the user due to the chosen gains and current limits, although the vibration is easily picked up by the torque transducer. A plot of the desired angle of the handle and the angle of the motor are shown in Fig. 5 (a), it indicated that the motor was able to track accurately of the input angle in both directions under different frequency and amplitude. The bland-Altman plot (Fig. 5(b)) demonstrated that the angle difference is less than 1 degree (equivalent to 0.04Nm) for 95% of time. The RMSE of the angle tracking is 0.5 deg.

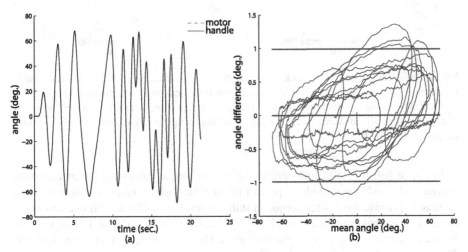

**Fig. 5.** Performance of RSEA in angle tracking. (a) angle of the motor and angle of the handle. (b) Bland-Altman plot of angles.

## 3.3    Performance of Static Torque Generation

Even if angle tracking is accurate, torque output may still be inaccurate due to slack and undesired geometrical changes in the spring as well as the uncertainty in the specified spring constant. A traditional torsion spring is not designed for applications such as this with rapid repeated motion in both directions. The mechanical design and assembly tolerance will also result discrepancies in calculated torque from spring and the actual torque. Thus, it is important to analyze the validity of torque calculation using the manufacturer's spring constant in both directions. This was done by providing a linearly increasing desired torque as control input, which results in an increasing angle difference due to the fixed spring constant. The handle was held still during this experiment.

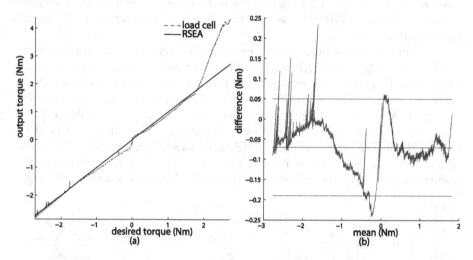

**Fig. 6.** RSEA torque generation under static conditions. (a). the torque output calculated based on spring deflection and measured with load cell when the desired torque changes from -2.5 Nm to 3 Nm. The spring is in compression when torque is positive and in extension when the torque is negative. (b). Bland-Altman plot for the calculated torque from spring and the measured torque from load cell.

In Fig. 6 (a), the solid line depicts the output torque calculated based on spring Equation (1), and it is provides a perfect linear relationship, indicating the motor can accurately provide the desired torque in static experiments. The dashed line shows the actual torque measured with the load cell, and the load cell can be assumed to measure the exact output torque the user feels. The load cell has an uncertainty of 1%. The error in the extension region between -1 and 0 Nm is significant, with a maximum error over 0.2Nm. This is much bigger than 0.04N, the predicted torque uncertainty from the angle tracking error. A sharp change of the error in actual torque output near 0° was also noticed. When the torque reaches 1.8Nm, the spring can no longer be assumed linear (i.e. non-linear spring rate) in the compression direction. The Bland-Altman plot (Fig. 6(b)) indicated that the mean error between the torque generated by the RSEA and the torque measure by the load cell is -0.07Nm. The difference will lie in the interval of [-0.19 0.05] with 95% possibility. This experiment indicated that the RSEA functions poorly in the extension region between

-1 and 0 Nm. The dead-zone behavior in torque production is mostly due to the tolerance in the installation of the torsion spring. Outside that region, RSEA can be controlled to the desired torque with an error less than 0.1 Nm.

### 3.4    Dynamic Torque Assistance

In the following experiments the desired torque output is dependent upon the real-time position and velocity of the handle. This task is motivated for upper or lower limb rehabilitation applications where the RSEA either assist or resist the limb motion based on the limb configuration. Based on the user's motion, the control system should   respond with an appropriate torque. The task is illustrated in Fig. 7 (a), where the limb is attached to the handle and is asked to move up and down in the positive and negative direction. Any time when the limb is under a upswing, an assistant torque will be supplied by the RSEA, regardless the direction of motion. To achieve this task, the control system divides the cyclic motion into four regions (Fig. 7 (b)) based on whether handle position and velocity are greater than or less than zero. To avoid undesired movement or vibration, buffer regions were established at $0 \pm 3°$, and $0 \pm 30°/s$. In these regions the actuator is set to track the handle, rather than provide an assistive torque.   The RSEA provides positive torque in the region R1, and negative assistive torque in the region R3. In the regions R2 and R4, no active assistive torque is provided. Here we focus on   an "assist" system, but any combination and magnitude of assist and resist are possible with this system depending on the application or experiment.

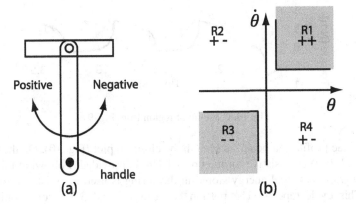

**Fig. 7.** Dynamic Torque Assistance Task. (a). A limb is attached to the handle and is asked to move up and down in the positive and negative direction. (b). Four regions of the limb motion based on the angle and angular velocity of the limb. Assistive torque is provided in the shaded regions during the limb upswing to compensate the effect of gravity.

Fig. 8 shows the encoder angle on either side of the spring versus time, for a 10 second interval. Since assistance is provided, the actuator side (black) is always leading. The assistive torque provided is also shown in Fig. 9. Fig. 10 provides a close-up view of a portion of this plot for further explanation.

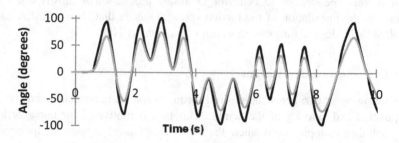

**Fig. 8.** Plot of angle vs. time for user-controlled if-statement

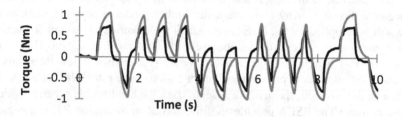

**Fig. 9.** Calculated torque from RSEA and actual torque from load cell. The black line is the actual torque output and the grey is from the angle difference.

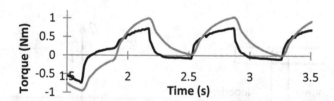

**Fig. 10.** Close-up of region from Fig. 9

The torque profile can better be seen in the close-up plot (Fig. 10). On the upswing portion (1.7-2.2s) an assistive torque up to 1 Nm is provided. Following this, on the downswing, the potential energy stored in the spring is used to assist, but to a lesser extent. This cycle repeats. The portion between 1.7 and 3.5 seconds only shows positive angles. Torque is negative for negative angles, which is also assistive. It can be seen from Fig. 10, that the torque profile is not sinusoidal even the spring angle difference is. Future work may be done to determine the effect on the user's motion. This also reflects the compromise when selecting an appropriate spring constant. If the spring is stiffer, the system has a more accurate and fast response, but the advantages attributed the elastic element will lessen. If the spring is less stiff, the system will have better human-compatible movements, but fail at high frequencies.

# 4    Discussion

Torsion springs present a delicate compromise in that the more rigid the system, the faster the response can be. This means for a high spring constant, there is a smaller angle change required to achieve the same torque as in a less stiff spring. For a given application, the advantages of added elasticity must be compared to the decreased ability for fast responses. Power consumption (and thus motor selection), although not studied here, will also be affected by the chosen spring constant.

Traditional torsion springs have a few disadvantages due to nonlinearity, especially with small angle differences. The springs also contribute to difficulty in the design process as they change diameter and length upon angle changes. To avoid this torsion springs may be designed to be symmetrical and planar. NASA and GM have developed planar torsion springs for a humanoid robot, now in operation at the International Space Station [12]. It may also be possible to further increase the bandwidth by avoiding torsion springs altogether. One alternative is to use linear springs and convert the linear motion to rotary motion (if needed). Several linear springs may also be arranged in a circular pattern via connecting pins in order to replicate a torsion spring [7]. This method would ensure the system is linear and symmetrical regardless of the direction of rotation. However, this method vastly limits the angle difference that can be achieved and increases the bulkiness of the system.

The torque measured by the load cell is generally less than the desired torque, due to undesired changes in spring geometry, and other movement (or lack thereof) between components of the physical design. Thus, the system may have a multiplier constant that recognizes and accounts for the average percent difference between the two torque measurements. A smaller modified spring constant could be determined through calibration with the load cell, which may then be removed from the RSEA.

# 5    Conclusions

In this paper, an easy-to-use test platform and control system for a RSEA has been developed with a load cell to measure real-time output torque. Real-time control was implemented using Matlab and Quanser. The behaviour of the spring and torque generation of the system were quantified, and an illustration of torque assistance control method is also provided to demonstrate the   usefulness of this RSEA system.

It was found that the RSEA can accurately follow desired angle differences with minimal error and little vibration within the relevant human bandwidth; The spring acts as both the torque sensor and source, thus system performance relies heavily upon the spring and its installation. The drawback is with torsion spring reliability, as the spring rate is not linear, and the relatively unknown properties of the energy return of the spring creates a larger gap between actual and desired torque, especially in the small torque region. To eliminate these problems, the spring can be more accurately modeled to include nonlinearities. Furthermore, the spring can be placed before the gear train in order to decrease the needed spring size and stiffness [6]. Linear series elastic actuators are a viable alternative to eliminate the disadvantages associated with torsion springs. Alternatively, a calibration of the RSEA system can be performed to find the actual spring constant in the system.

# References

1. Zinn, M., Roth, B., Khatib, O., Salisbury, J.K.: A New Actuation Approach for Human Friendly Robot Design. The International Journal of Robotics Research 23, 379–398 (2004)
2. Pratt, G.A., Williamson, M.M.: Series elastic actuators. In: IEEE International Conference on Intelligent Robots and Systems, vol. 1, pp. 399–406 (1995)
3. Sulzer, J.M., Peshkin, M.A., Patton, J.L.: MAMONET: An Exotendon-Driven Rotary Series Elastic Actuator for Exerting Joint Torque. In: The 9th International Conference on Rehabilitation Robotics, pp. 103–108 (2005)
4. Kong, K., Tomizuka, M.: Flexible Control of Exoskeletons Inspired by Fictitous Gain in Human Model. IEEE/ASME Transactions on Mechatronics 14, 1179–1184 (2009)
5. Pratt, J.E., Krupp, B.T.: Series Elastic Actuators for legged robots. In: Proceedings of SPIE - the International Society for Optical Engineering, vol. 5422, pp. 135–144 (2004)
6. Kong, K., Bae, J., Tomizuka, M.: A Compact Rotary Series Elastic Actuator for Human Assistive Devices. IEEE/ASME Transactions on Mechatronics 17, 288–297 (2012)
7. Rinderknecht, M.D., Delaloye, F.A., Crespi, A., Ronsse, R., Ijspeert, A.J.: Assistance using adaptive oscillators: Robustness to errors in the identification of the limb parameters. In: Conference on Rehabilitation Robotics (ICORR), pp. 1–6 (2011)
8. Pratt, J., Krupp, B., Morse, C.: Series elastic actuators for high fidelity force control. Industrial Robot: An International Journal 29, 234–241 (2002)
9. Kong, K., Tomizuka, M.: Flexible Joint Actuator for Patient's Rehabilitation Device. In: The 16th IEEE International Conference on Robot & Human Interactive Communication, pp. 1179–1184 (2007)
10. Kong, K., Moon, H., Hwang, B., Jeon, D., Tomizuka, M.: Impedance Compensation of SUBAR for Back-Drivable Force-Mode Actuation. In: Proceedings of IEEE Transactions on Robotics, vol. 25, pp. 512–521 (2009)
11. Bae, J., Kong, K., Tomizuka, M.: Gait Phase-Based Smoothed Sliding Mode Control for a Rotary Series Elastic Actuator Installed on Knee Joint. In: Proceedings of American Control Conference, pp. 6030–6035 (2010)
12. Diftler, M.A., Mehling, J.S., Abdallah, M.E., Radford, N.A., Bridgwater, L.B., Sanders, A.M., Askew, R.S., Linn, D.M., Yamokoski, J.D., Permenter, F.A., Hargrave, B.K., Piatt, R., Savely, R.T., Ambrose, R.O.: Robonaut 2 - The first humanoid robot in space. In: IEEE International Conference on Robotics and Automation (ICRA), pp. 2178–2183 (2011)

# Realistic Dynamic Posture Prediction of Humanoid Robot: Manual Lifting Task Simulation

Ali Leylavi Shoushtari[1,2] and Parvin Abedi[2]

[1] Department of Mechatronics, South Tehran Branch,
Islamic Azad University, Tehran, Iran
[2] Department of Computer Engineering, Shoushtar Branch,
Islamic Azad University, Shoushtar, Iran
st_a_leilavi@azad.ac.ir, pr.abedi@iau-shoushtar.ac.ir

**Abstract.** A well known question mooted in biomechanics is how the central nerves system manages the body posture during various tasks. A 5DOF biomechatronical model of human body subjected to simulate the manual lifting task of humanoid robot. Simulation process is based on optimization approach named predictive dynamics using inverse dynamics. An objective function in term of ankle torques during lifting time, subjected to be minimized. It assumed that CNS considered this function to perform lifting motion balanced. In the other optimization-based simulations, balancing motion was guaranteed by a nonlinear inequality constraint which restricts the total moment arm of the links to an upper and lower boundary. In this method there is no need to use this constraint. Result shows that the motion is performed balanced. According to the comparison the results with the experimental data, the body posture of humanoid robots, predicted as similar as actual human posture.

**Keywords:** Human body simulation, Biomechatronical model of human body, Lifting motion modeling, ankle torques.

## 1 Introduction

Multibody dynamics of human body, subjected to an extensive area of researches such as robotics, biomechatronics, biomedical engineering etc, Because it can provide an approach to find some variables that are not possible to measure like: torques and internal forces of joints and stress exerted to joint's soft tissues. These mechanical parameters are so important to understand joint disease initiation and progression, like osteoarthritis [1], [2]. In addition to pathological aspects, simulation purposes are one of the major causes of human body modeling.

In order to know how the body postures varies during different movements to construct motion animation of human body, a model of whole human body dynamics applied to movement simulation process. Simulation and analysis of human movements commonly used for athletics in order to improve performance of the motion and so prevent injuries in cause of incorrect movements [3]. Some abnormalities accrued in

C.-Y. Su, S. Rakheja, H. Liu (Eds.): ICIRA 2012, Part I, LNAI 7506, pp. 565–578, 2012.
© Springer-Verlag Berlin Heidelberg 2012

parts of musculoskeletal system resulted in inaccurately function to muscle activation and control [4]-[6].

Therefore it is so important to know that how the central nervous system (CNS) controls the body posture varies during different tasks.

Biomechatronical model with large number of degree of freedom needed to done the human motion simulation more exactly and accurately. The multiplicity of joint space variables (DOFs) causes model maneuverable but creates redundancy problem. We face with the redundancy problem when the number of DOFs is more than needed to perform a task. This problem is also mooted in the robotic researches in kinematics, dynamics and control aspects [7]-[10]. Human body models usually contained large number of DOFs. For applying these models to motion simulation, optimization-based approaches are good methods to overcome with the redundancy problem. Some of these techniques are applied to robotic manipulator models with redundant DOFs [9] and [11]-[13]. Optimization-based solutions are suitable ways to solve problem with large number of variables, because this method uses a few amount of data as inputs to result a large number of variables as output set. The input contains two set of constraints impose to motion simulation process: 1. Constraints obtained from motion dynamics and 2. Variety limitation of variables to be optimized. The second type used as inequality constraints and the first one contain some algebraic and differential equations.

CNS manages the task with the balanced movements. Walking, running, sitting and lifting are good examples of tasks related to daily living activities performed completely balanced involuntarily. CNS uses an unknown algorithm to manage tasks unconsciously. Optimization-based simulation methods have performance analogous with CNS function caused balanced movements. These approaches used objective function description subjected to minimizing which is duality of CNS algorithm manner. On the other hand to simulate a movement as like as shape that biological system does, it assumed that optimization approach minimized the objective function considered that CNS try to minimize it too. Description of stability can be found in medicine and engineering as different meanings but these meanings follows joint goal. In optimization approach motion stability caused by constraints which restrict total moment arm of body segments (TMA) in each configuration, between horizontal position of heel and toe (base of support) [14],[15]. In fact this constraint prevent of figurate postures will caused to falling to forward and backward. In this research we use an optimization-based algorithm named predictive dynamics [16]. With objective function consist of ankle torque summation during lifting time. In this novel inverse dynamics, joints torque limitation and joint ranges of motion are used as constraints to shape the motion as lifting movement. In this algorithm by and large two kinds of constraints are used. 1. The constraints which shape the simulated motion as lifting movement consist of two type constraints. 1-1. Kinematical constraints which formed motion like ones which determine initial and final position of box, body collision avoidance and constraints which guarantee moving up motion of box. These kinds named "*kinematical governing constraints*". 1-2. Inverse dynamics of system is a differential equation implemented as equality constraint to govern the dynamics of motion to simulation process, named "*dynamic governing constrain*". 2. The 2nd type named "*bounder constraint*" which limits the range of variation of variables to be optimized. This classification illustrated in figure1.

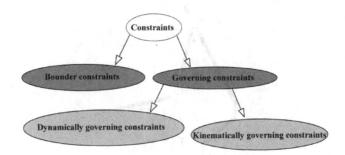

**Fig. 1.** Constraints classification

Ankle torque amplitude considered as stability index and the optimization algorithm tries to minimize integral of ankle torque squares during lifting time. A five DOF biomechatronical model of whole human body represented in part 2 obtained from kinematical modeling based on D-H method [17], [18]. Based on Lagrangian method dynamics of motion be formulated and results equation of motion named inverse dynamics. In part 3 simulation process is described and parts 4 and 5 present simulation results and conclusion respectively.

## 2    Modeling

A planar model with 5DOF in sagittal plane utilized to represent coordination system of human body (Fig. 2). All the limbs as shank, thigh, spine, arm and forearm subjected to modeling and considered as rigid bars with mass points at center of mass of each link which named: $l_1, l_2, l_3, l_4, l_5$ respectively. For human major joints as ankle, knee, hip, shoulder and elbow had considered joint angles in modeling to figurate human body posture and represented by the names: $q_1, q_2, q_3, q_4, q_5$ respectively.

The box assumed jointed to human body at the wrist with a horizontal orientation. Biomechatronical models of human body with coordination systems illustrated by fig. 2. Human body dynamics commonly model as open kinematics chain like robot manipulators as mentioned before [19], [20]. So the method used to modeling the dynamics of motion of this kinematical chain is like ones used for robotic manipulators. In this approach it's needed to calculate systems' kinetic and potential energies, and finally by minimizing the integral of system's lagrangian, the equations which govern the dynamics of motion will be obtained.

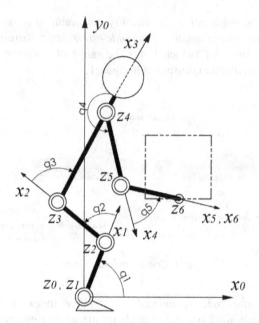

**Fig. 2.** 5DOF model of human body with coordination systems attached to each link

The kinetic energy of the model presented before define as bellow equation:

$$K = \frac{1}{2}\dot{q}^T D(q)\dot{q} \tag{1}$$

$$D(q) = \sum_{i=1}^{5}(m_i J_{vc_i}{}^T J_{vc_i} + J_{\omega_i}{}^T R_i^0 I_i R_i^0) \tag{2}$$

In equation (2) $\dot{q}$ is $5 \times 1$ vector of angular velocities of joints, and $\dot{q}^T$ is transpose matrix of $\dot{q}$, $D(q)$ is $5 \times 5$ matrix related to mass and inertial properties of the model [24]. $J_{vc_i}$, $J_{\omega_i}$ are $3 \times 5$ Jacobin matrix which translate linear and angular velocities of COM of i'th link to universal coordinate system respectively. $R_i^0$ is rotational transformation matrix which interpret the orientation of i'th links from its coordinate to ground coordinate. $m_i$ is mass of i'th link. By considering $g$ as gravitational force vector, and $r_{c_i}$ as height of i'th link's COM from ankle position, System's potential energy describes as bellow:

$$V = \sum_{i=1}^{5}(m_i g^T r_{c_i}) \tag{3}$$

A function of systems' energy which called Lagrangian calculated as bellow:

$$L = K - V = \frac{1}{2}\dot{q}^T D(q)\dot{q} - \sum_{i=1}^{5}(m_i g^T r_{c_i}) \tag{4}$$

A functional in term of systems' energy $S$ defines as integral of system's lagrangian during lifting time interval$[0 \ T]$, as bellow equation:

$$S = \int_{t=0}^{T} L(q, \dot{q}, t)dt \tag{5}$$

$$\frac{d}{dt}\left(\frac{\partial L}{\partial \dot{q}}\right) - \frac{\partial L}{\partial q} = \Gamma \tag{6}$$

Based on Hamiltonian principle extremizing integral $S$ resulted in motion equation. Euler-Lagrange formulation (6) subjected to extremizing $S$[24]. In (6)$\Gamma$ is generalized joints torque vector inserted. Finally general form of motion equations will be obtains as(7) [24].

$$D(q)\ddot{q} + C(q, \dot{q})\dot{q} + V(q) = \Gamma \tag{7}$$

In (7)$C(q, \dot{q})$ is a term related to centrifugal and coriolis forces and $V(q)$ is gravitational forces vector, this term calculates as bellow:

$$C(q, \dot{q}) = \dot{D}(q) - \frac{1}{2}\dot{q}^T\left(\frac{\partial D(q)}{\partial q}\right) \tag{8}$$

$$V(q) = \left(\frac{\partial V}{\partial q}\right)^T \tag{9}$$

Generalized joint torque represented in (7) divided in two parts: 1. torques resulted in muscle forces and 2. Torques due to the box load exerted on wrist. These kinds obtain as (10):

$$\Gamma = \tau_{muscle} - \tau_{box} \ ; \ \tau_{box} = J^T(m_{box}g^T) \tag{10}$$

In (12) $J^T$ is transpose of Jacobean matrix which project box load to joints $m_{box}$ is box mass and $g^T$ is transpose of gravity force vector.

## 3     Simulation Process

In this paper lifting movement simulation considered as optimization problem which CNS do either. In this problem an objective function subjected to be optimized with some constraints which limit the motions boundary to a feasible range to construct motion naturally. In other words it's being assumed that CNS try to minimize a particular function value to perform each task, and musculoskeletal system impose some constraints to the motion too. Predictive dynamics is a novel used to motion simulation [16], [23]; it implements inverse dynamics as a major constraint to modeling the dynamics of the motion in the simulation process. The joints torques and angles are the optimization process variables, so by using this method we can obtain joint angles and torques as output according to task constraints used as inputs. Simulation elements are described in bellow sections.

## A. Objective function

Considering the lifting task as a simple inverted pendulum motion, can represents an insight to motion stability analysis. In other hand If lifting motion modeled as a inverted pendulum (fig. 3) [21] we can claim that magnitude of pendulum joints torque has relation to amount of deviation from stability position ($\theta = 0°$) directly. Therefore we can use of a particular function which constructed in term of ankle torque as motion stability index. We propose this function as integral of ankle torque squares in each time sequence (11).

$$F(q, \tau, t) = \int_{t=0}^{T} \tau_{ankle}^2 \, dt \qquad (11)$$

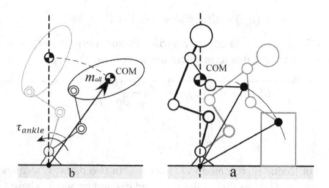

**Fig. 3.** a) 5DOF model of human body for lifting motion task, b) Inverted pendulum equivalent model for lifting task.

## B. Constrants

The constraints used in this research are: joints torques and angles limitations, initial and final position of box, elevating constraint, inverse dynamics, and body collision avoidance constraint used for prevent of collision box with body. Vertical position of wrist (12) is a function of joint angles $q(t)$ calculated from forward kinematics (22):

$$Y_{wrist}(t) = y(q(t)) \qquad (12)$$

In each time sequence $Y_{wrist}(t)$ should be higher than previous sequence:

$$Y_{wrist}(i) > Y_{wrist}(i-1) \qquad (13)$$

So the elevating constraint defined by:

$$y(q(t-1)) - y(q(t)) < 0 \qquad (14)$$

In fact elevating constraint guaranteed moving up motion of box during time sequences. The equality constraints which impose initial and final position of box to optimization process are defined by (15).

$$\begin{cases} x(q(0)) - x_{initial} = 0 \\ y(q(0)) - y_{initial} = 0 \\ x(q(T)) - x_{final} = 0 \\ y(q(T)) - y_{final} = 0 \end{cases} \tag{15}$$

Which $X_{wrist}(t)$ and $Y_{wrist}(t)$ are respectively horizontal and vertical position of wrist considered fixed to box. According to fourfold constraints set (15) wrist should be placed at initial position $x_{initial}$ ,$y_{initial}$ and final position $x_{final}$ , $y_{final}$ of box at $t = 0$ and $t = T$ respectively. Inverse dynamics constraint express as bellow:

$$\tau - \tau_{invd} = 0 \; ; \; \tau_{invd} = f(q,t) \tag{16}$$

In equation (16) $\tau$ is joints torque vector should be predicted, and $\tau_{invd}$ is joints torque vector obtained from inverse dynamics. Body collision avoidance implemented in this simulation is a systematic method to check the penetration value of the box into the body in each iteration of optimization process to determine horizontal position of the box to collision avoidance adaptively. This process described as bellow briefly:

The collision avoidance considered in optimization process as a constraint to prevent penetration of box with the body. It's inequality constraint and defined as a term of sufficient horizontal distance $dx$ which wrist should move to prevent collision box with the body.

$$X_{bounndary} - X_{wrist_d} < 0 \tag{17}$$

$$X_{bounndary} = X_{wrist_{pr}} + d_x \tag{18}$$

Distance which wrist should move to arrive to horizontal boundary position $X_{bounndary}$ represent by $d_x$, and boundary position is a horizontal position of wrist which box edge touch the body. $X_{wrist_d}$ is desire horizontal position of wrist which should be greater than $X_{bounndary}$. $X_{wrist_{pr}}$ is horizontal position of wrist obtained from optimization algorithm in current iteration.

According to Figure 5 penetration value of the box in the body $d$ would be obtained through equation (19), $X_{body}$ and $X_{edge}$ obtain from body line and box line respectively.

$$d = X_{body} - X_{edge} \tag{19}$$

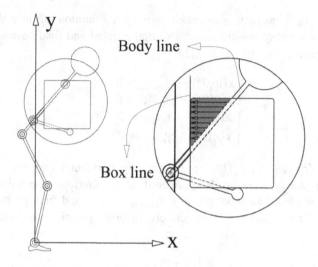

**Fig. 4.** Collision box with body, box line, body line and penetration area

Maximum penetration value determine the horizontal distance which wrist should move to arrive to boundary position, $d$ is penetration index so $d_x$ is maximum value of $d$.

$$d_x = MAX(d) \tag{20}$$

## 4     Results

The optimization process designed for 10 evenly distributed time sequences. By considering 5 angles of joints and 5 joint's torques for each time segment, we have

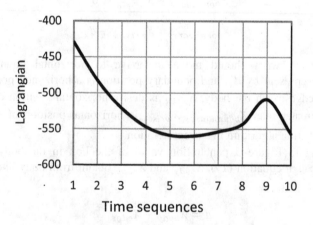

**Fig. 5.** Lagrangian values during time sequences

100 variables subjected to be optimized. Inertial properties considered as data used previously [22]. The experimental data used in [23] implemented to validate the simulation process. Lifting task parameters presented in table I.

Lagrangian value calculated from (4) plotted for time sequences and illustrate in figure6. It shows that lagrangian value is always minus, so according to (4) it have been concluded that the motion is so slowly or in other words it's static motion approximately. Respect to this statement, a statically index presented to evaluate the motion stability during all the time sequences.

Total moment arm (TMA) of all the links are calculated as (21) it's calculated from the moments respect to all of the links weight for each configuration related to time sequence.

$$TMA(t) = \frac{1}{m_{all}} \sum_{i=1}^{N} m_i x_i(t) \tag{21}$$

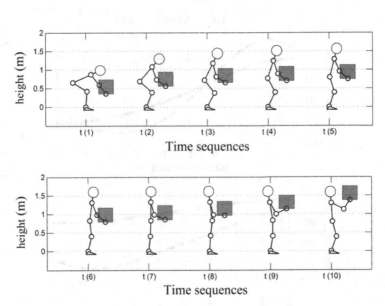

**Fig. 6.** Body postures of humanoid robot, during lifting task. The horizontal axis is time in term of second, by scaling 0.12.

$m_{all}$ is total weight of body and $x_i(t)$ is horizontal position of $i'th$ links at time $t$, and $N$ is number of links. Optimized joint angles show that how the body posture varies during lifting task, it illustrated in figure 6.

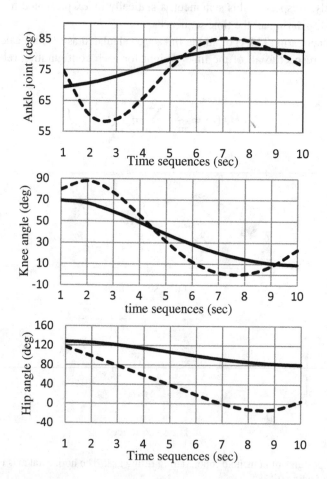

**Fig. 7.** Joints angles profiles resulted in optimization process in comparison with experimental results. The solid line is experimental and the dashed line is predicted profile. The vertical axis is joint angle and is in term of degree. The horizontal axis is time in term of second, by scaling 0.12.

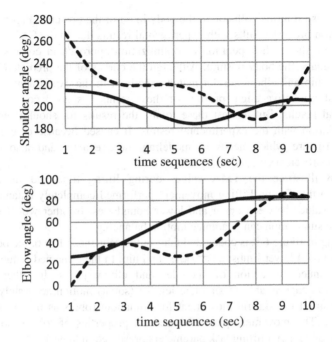

**Fig. 7.** (*continued*)

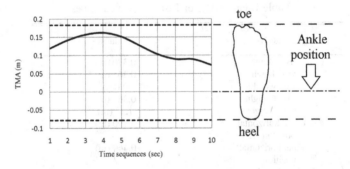

**Fig. 8.** TMA values during lifting time. To prevent falling forward or backward, TMA values should be restricted between base of support (distance between heel and toe).

## 5    Conclusion

Simulation process implemented 5DOF biomechatronical model of human body to simulate lifting motion by using predictive dynamics approach. The constraints which applied to this process, limit motion space to a feasible region that human limbs move through it. Major constraint named inverse dynamics, implement the dynamics of the motion in simulation process and finally the optimized postures shaped by objective function minimization. Figure 6 Shows that posture variation does in a natural shape. The box motion is extremely uprising, and it situate at initial and final position exactly and also it hasn't collision to the body in all of the postures. Figure 7 compare the simulation process results with experimental results due to the CNS, on the other hand figure 7 shows the operation of optimization approach in contrast with CNS action to manage the body posture. Although the curves of the predicted profiles for ankle, knee, hip and elbow are not match exactly with the experimental results, but the trend of predictive angle profiles of these joints has good compatibility with experimental results. But against these joints, the results for shoulder joint haven't good correlation with the experimental results. It caused because of complexity of shoulder structure which needs to modeling more exactly and also considering suitable and sufficient constraints.

Figure 8 illustrate the TMA values during lifting time and its boundaries. According to this figure, Lifting movement performed completely balanced because TMA have values between upper and lower boundaries. In other words minimizing ankle torque summation can guarantee motion balancing.

According to figure 6 it is concluded that: in the sequences 1 to 6, the box lifted by action of joints of lower limbs: ankle, knee and hip. In the remained sequences lifting motion continued by action of shoulder and elbow joints. In other hand this simulation approach is able to simulate leg lift (squat) motion accurately. It can be used to construct the skillful movement for humanoid robots as like as motion that human does. The movement planned based on properties of robot's bodies which presented in table 2 and lifting task parameters presented in table 1.

**Table 1.** Parameters of Task and related values

| Parameters | Values |
|------------|--------|
| Box depth | 0.370 (m) |
| Box height | 0.365 (m) |
| Box weight | 9 (kg) |
| Initial height | 0.365 (m) |
| Final height | 1.37 (m) |
| Initial horizontal position | 0.490 (m) |
| Final horizontal position | 0.460 (m) |
| Lifting time duration | 1.2 (s) |

Units are used in table; s = second, m = meter, kg = kilogram.

# References

1. Andriacchi, T.P., Mundermann, A., Smith, R.L., Alexander, E.J., Dyrby, C.O., Koo, S.: A framework for the in vivo pathomechanics of osteoarthritis at the knee. Ann. Biomed. Eng. 32(3), 447–457 (2004)
2. Miyazakai, T., Wada, M., Kawahara, H., Sato, M., Baba, H., Shimada, S.: Dynamic load at baseline can predict radiographic disease progression in medial compartment knee osteoarthritis. Ann. Rheum. Dis. 61(7), 617–622 (2002)

3. Demircan, E., Khatib, O., Wheeler, J., Delp, S.: Reconstruction and EMG-Informed Control, Simulation and Analysis of Human Movement for Athletics: Performance Improvement and Injury Prevention. In: Proc. IEEE International Conf. on Engineering in Medicine and Biology Society, Minneapolis, MN, pp. 6534–6537 (2009)
4. Li, G., Kaufman, K.R., Chao, E.Y., Rubash, H.E.: Prediction of antagonistic muscle forces using inverse dynamic optimization during flexion/extension of the knee. Journal of Biomech. Eng. 121(3), 316–322 (1999)
5. Zeinali-Davarani, S., Hemami, H., Barin, K., Shirazi-Adl, A., Parnianpour, M.: Dynamic stability of spine using stability-based optimization and spindle reflex. Proc. IEEE Transaction on Neural System Rehabilitation Enginering 16(1), 106–118 (2008)
6. Nussbaum, M.A., Chaffin, D.B.: Lumbar muscle force estimation using a subject-invariant 5-parameter EMG-based model. Journal of Biomechanics 31(7), 667–672 (1998)
7. Wang, J., Li, Y., Zhao, Z.: Inverse Kinematics and Control of a 7-DOF Redundant Manipulator Based on the Closed-Loop Algorithm. International Journal of Advanced Robotic System 7(4), 1–12 (2010)
8. Park, K.C., Chang, P.H., Lee, S.: Analysis and control of redundant manipulator dynamics based on an extended operational space. Robotica 19(6), 649–662 (2001)
9. Schafer, B., Krenn, R., Rebele, B.: On inverse kinematics and kinetics of redundant space manipulator simulation. Journal of Computational and Applied Mechanics 4(1), 53–70 (2003)
10. Peters, J., Mistry, M., Udwadia, F., Nakanishi, J., Schaal, S.: A unifying framework for robot control with redundant DOFs. Autonomous Robots 24(1), 1–12 (2007)
11. Oh, Y., Chung, W., Youm, Y., Suh, I.H.: A Passive-based motion control of redundant manipulators using weighted decomposition of joint space. In: Proc. IEEE International Conference on Robotic and Automation, Monterey, CA, pp. 125–131 (1997)
12. Zhang, Y., Zhu, H., Tan, Z., Cai, B., Yang, Z.: Self-motion planning of redundant robot manipulators based on quadratic program and shown via PA10 example. In: Proc. IEEE 2nd International Symposium on Systems and Control in Aerospace and Astronautics, Shenzhen, pp. 1–6 (2008)
13. Wang, J., Li, Y., Zhao, X.: Inverse Kinematics and Control of a 7-DOF Redundant Manipulator Based on the Closed-Loop Algorithm. International Journal of Advanced Robotic Systems 7(4), 1–10 (2010)
14. Sitoh, M.K., Chen, J.G., Long, K., Jung, H.S.: A graphical computer system for modeling the manual lifting task via biomechanical and psychophysical-biomechanical optimization approaches. Computers in Industry 21(2), 149–165 (1993)
15. Chang, V.C., Brown, D.R., Bloswick, D.S., Hsiang, S.M.: Biomechanical Simulation of manual lifting using time space. Journal of Biomechanics 34(4), 527–532 (2001)
16. Xiang, Y., Arora, J.S., Rahmatalla, S., Abdel-Malek, K.: Optimization-based dynamic human walking prediction: one step formulation. International Journal for Numerical Methods in Engineering 79(6), 667–695 (2009)
17. Denavit, J., Hartenberg, R.S.: A kinematic notation for lower-pair mechanisms based on matrices. Transaction of ASME Journal of Applied Mechanics 23, 215–221 (1955)
18. Siciliano, B., Khatib, O.: Springer handbook of robotics. Springer (2008)
19. Khatib, O., Demircan, E., De Sapio, V., Sentic, L., Besier, T., Delp, S.: Robotic-based Syntesis of human motion. Journal of Physiology-ParisI (3-5), 211–219 (2009)
20. Khatib, O., Warren, J., De Sapio, V., Sentic, L.: Human-like motion from physiologically-based potential energy. On Advances in Robot Kinematics, 149–163 (2004)

21. Arisumi, H., Chardonnet, J.R., Kheddar, A., Yokoi, K.: Dynamic Lifting Motion of Humanoid Robots. In: IEEE International Conference on Robotics and Automation, Rome, Italy (2007)
22. Blajer, W., Dziewiecki, K., Mazur, Z.: Multibody modeling of human body for the inverse dynamics analysis of sagittal plane movements. Multibody Systems Dynamics 18(2), 217–232 (2007)
23. Xiang, Y., Arora, J.S., Rahmatalla, S., Marler, T., Bhatt, R., Abdel-Malek, K.: Human lifting simulation using a multi-objective optimization approach. Multibody Dynamics 23(4), 431–451 (2010)
24. Spong, M.W., Vidyasagar, M.: Robot Dynamics and Control, ch. 5. John Wiley and Sons, Inc. (1989)

# Appendix

Body segments parameters of biomechatronical model presented in figure 1 is as follow:

**Table 2.** Parameters of Body

| segments | Inertia (N.m^2) | COM (m) | Mass (kg) | Length (m) |
|----------|-----------------|---------|-----------|------------|
| $l_1$ | 0.183 | 0.147 | 9.68 | 0.50 |
| $l_2$ | 0.505 | 0.209 | 33.48 | 0.46 |
| $l_3$ | 0.325 | 0.360 | 41.65 | 0.66 |
| $l_4$ | 0.070 | 0.144 | 6.36 | 0.32 |
| $l_5$ | 0.035 | 0.130 | 4.80 | 0.30 |

Transformer matrixes used to calculate forward kinematics are as bellow matrixes:

$$ {}^0_6T = {}^0_1T \cdot {}^1_2T \cdot {}^2_3T \cdot {}^3_4T \cdot {}^4_5T \cdot {}^5_6T \tag{22} $$

$$ {}^0_1T = \begin{bmatrix} C\theta_1 & -S\theta_1 & 0 & 0 \\ S\theta_1 & C\theta_1 & 0 & 0 \\ 0 & 0 & 1 & 0 \\ 0 & 0 & 0 & 1 \end{bmatrix} \quad {}^1_2T = \begin{bmatrix} C\theta_2 & -S\theta_2 & 0 & l_1 \\ S\theta_2 & C\theta_2 & 0 & 0 \\ 0 & 0 & 1 & 0 \\ 0 & 0 & 0 & 1 \end{bmatrix} $$

$$ {}^2_3T = \begin{bmatrix} C\theta_2 & -S\theta_2 & 0 & l_2 \\ -S\theta_2 & -C\theta_2 & 0 & 0 \\ 0 & 0 & -1 & 0 \\ 0 & 0 & 0 & 1 \end{bmatrix} \quad {}^3_4T = \begin{bmatrix} C\theta_4 & -S\theta_4 & 0 & l_3 \\ -S\theta_4 & -C\theta_4 & 0 & 0 \\ 0 & 0 & -1 & 0 \\ 0 & 0 & 0 & 1 \end{bmatrix} $$

$$ {}^4_5T = \begin{bmatrix} C\theta_5 & -S\theta_5 & 0 & l_4 \\ S\theta_5 & C\theta_5 & 0 & 0 \\ 0 & 0 & 1 & 0 \\ 0 & 0 & 0 & 1 \end{bmatrix} \quad {}^5_6T = \begin{bmatrix} 1 & 0 & 0 & l_5 \\ 0 & 1 & 0 & 0 \\ 0 & 0 & 1 & 0 \\ 0 & 0 & 0 & 1 \end{bmatrix} $$

# Human Brain Control of Electric Wheelchair
# with Eye-Blink Electrooculogram Signal

Bo Ning, Ming-jie Li, Tong Liu, Hui-min Shen[*], Liang Hu, and Xin Fu

The State Key Lab of Fluid Power Transmission and Control,
Zhejiang University, Hangzhou 310027, China
shen_huimin@163.com

**Abstract.** In this paper, a human brain-based control method of electric wheelchair is presented for individuals with motor disabilities. In this method, intended eye-blink electrooculogram (EOG) signal measured by a single dry electrode is utilized as communication channel for random direction control of wheelchair. Here, a close-loop wheelchair control system with human-machine interface (HMI) based on this method is introduced, and the feedback is realized by human vision. To validate feasibility of this brain-controlled electric wheelchair system with eye-blink EOG signal, user is required to operate wheelchair with the proposed control system to move along three kinds of designated routes. The results show good performance of this brain-controlled wheelchair system with eye-blink EOG signal. Application of the proposed hand-free control system is expected to help people with motor disabilities live an improved lifestyle with more autonomy.

**Keywords:** Brain control, human-machine interface (HMI), wheelchair control, eye-blink electrooculogram (EOG), dry electrode, visual feedback.

## 1 Introduction

Motor disabled people lose normal muscular control functions due to brainstem stroke, brain or spinal cord injury, or some other diseases. For those who are severely affected, they even lost all voluntary muscle control functions, and become totally locked-in to their bodies. Great social effort and cost have been paid on maintaining their normal lives, which are partly or completely depended on nursing staffs. To provide them with a more independent lifestyle, numerous communication methods based on human-machine interface (HMI) using biological signals from users' body are developed for increasing their life qualities, such as electromyogram (EMG) [1], electrooculogram (EOG) [2] and electroencephalogram (EEG) [3] signals.

In HMI technology with brain signals, namely brain-machine interface (BMI), there are invasive BMI with electrocorticogram (ECoG) signals [4] and non-invasive BMI using EEG signals [5]. In invasive BMI technology, intracortical recordings with good spatial-temporal resolution acquired from electrodes implanted into cortical

---

[*] Corresponding author.

C.-Y. Su, S. Rakheja, H. Liu (Eds.): ICIRA 2012, Part I, LNAI 7506, pp. 579–588, 2012.
© Springer-Verlag Berlin Heidelberg 2012

tissue are used for control, but since surgery is required, risk of infection or tissue damage may be brought in [6]. As to non-invasive BMI technology, EEG signals are measured by scores of scalp electrodes prepared with electrolytic gel to acquire enough signal with better quality, but when quantities of experiments are needed, the preparation procedure can be tedious and time consuming [6]. Besides, BMI technologies using EMG and EOG signals, which are always subtracted as interferences in BMI technology [6, 7], also make great appeal to researchers, taking advantages of requiring fewer electrodes and less complex signal process. However, EMG signal cannot be detected in people with severe motor dysfunction, such as locked-in syndrome, in which eye is one of few organs can be controlled by individual. Various HMI technologies with EOG signal are developed, e.g. in [8-10] HMI technology with EOG signals generated by eye movement, which are used to generate decisions from users, is proposed; and in [11] eye-blink EOG signals divided into different control signals according to blink times is presented.

In this paper, we present a brain-controlled wheelchair system with control command derived from conscious eye-blink EOG signals for people with severe motor disabilities. The eye-blink EOG signal is measured by a single dry electrode without complex preparation, providing great convenience and practice for application in those people who require HMI-based motor assistive system. The controlled electric wheelchair can be operated in random direction, rather than in predefined directions or locations [12], where estimation of the destination in advance is required.

The paper is organized as follows:

— Firstly, this brain-controlled wheelchair system with eye-blink signal will be presented in detail, including measurement headset for eye-blink EOG signal acquisition, a dedicated GUI on the basis of PC for information exchange between user and target wheelchair, and an electric wheelchair for control;
— Successively, to evaluate feasibility of the proposed brain-controlled electric wheelchair system in practical application, some experiments are performed, in which user is required to operate the wheelchair to move along three kinds of routes, including straight line, s-route and z-route, and the results show that the movements of controlled wheelchair match well with designated routes.

## 2     System and Method

### 2.1     System and Set-Up

From the functional block diagram shown in Fig.1 (a), we can see that this brain-controlled electric wheelchair system consists of three parts: headset for raw brain signal measurement by a single dry electrode embedded in, and eye-blink signal extraction from raw EOG signal; PC, as carrier of control algorithm and GUI; electric wheelchair to be controlled. In the control procedure, magnitude of user's eye-blink signal, which can change according to blink intensity controlled by human brain, is utilized as feature signal for device command derivation. Thus, commands with different levels of eye-blink signals consciously can be issued for wheelchair control, taking advantages of rapid reactivity and flexibility in control procedure. Magnitude of eye-blink signal and system status are displayed on the GUI during operation to get user informed and realize the information exchange between user's intention and wheelchair control by translating eye-blink signal into device control signals. The target wheelchair performance, including location and direction, along with GUI status, can be known with user's visual feedbacks, and user can make correct choices and proper adjustments accordingly.

Set-up of this system is illustrated in Fig.1 (b). The dry electrode embedded in the headset for measurement is placed on user's forehead above the left eyebrow, and an electrode for reference is attached to the left earlobe. Information transmission between headset and PC is accomplished via radiofrequency communication. To translate digital signal sent from PC into analog signal for electric wheelchair control, an NI USB-6216 data acquisition card (DAC) is used as device command generator. The target wheelchair, driven by two DC motors, is controlled to accomplish a series of motions in accordance to user's intentions, including forward/backward movement, clockwise/counter-clockwise rotation and emergency stop.

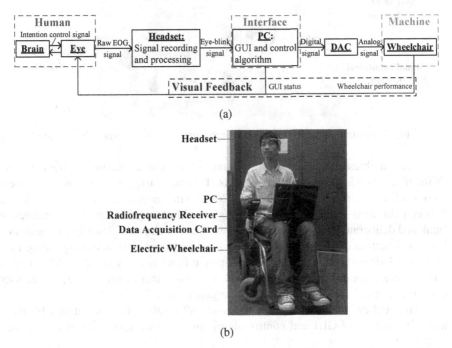

(a)

(b)

**Fig. 1.** (a) Functional block diagram illustrating the presented brain-controlled wheelchair system with eye-blink signal; (b) System set-up

This brain-controlled electric wheelchair makes it possible for people with severe motor disabilities to move according to their intentions without any manual operation in a flexible and convenient way.

## 2.2    GUI of the Brain-Controlled Wheelchair System

As shown in Fig.2, a PC-based GUI embedded with control algorithm is provided, displaying user's eye-blink EOG signal conditions and operation status simultaneously for visualization of information exchange and motion control.  As the bridge connecting user with target wheelchair, the GUI translates eye-blink EOG signals into digital signals with the help of embedded control algorithm through the platform of Labview, then digital signals are translated into device-recognizable analog signals by DAC.

Based on the functions to be performed, including system running condition, signal condition and motion status, the GUI is divided into three regions: system status region, signal condition region illustrating magnitude of eye-blink EOG signal and the threshold for control commands extraction, and motion status region showing direction to be chosen (forward, backward, clockwise and counter-clockwise), and indicating action/stop motion status, as indicated in Fig.2.

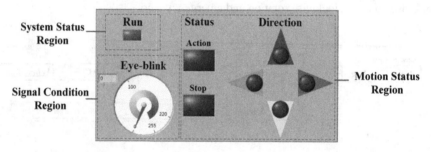

**Fig. 2.** Illustration of GUI developed for this brain-controlled wheelchair system

Based on threshold principle, two kinds of control commands extracted from different eye-blink EOG signals are utilized, namely trigger command and severe command, depended on user's intention. Considering the variance of eye-blink levels between different users, samples of users' eye-blink signals, involving instinctive blink and deliberate blink, are needed and analyzed in advance. The trigger command, acted as selection command, is generated when the magnitude of corresponding eye-blink EOG signal is between that of instinctive blink and severe blink deliberately; and the severe command, whose magnitude is close to that of strongest eye-blink user can give, is used for reselection and emergency stop, for instance giving a wrong command and encountering a pedestrian, and will result in the current step breakout and initialization of GUI and control algorithm to ensure user's security in sudden conditions.

When moving towards a destination, user can choose random movement directions and run/stop status, and make proper adjustments at any time. To ensure the safety and reliability, in the operation user is not allowed to change the moving direction of the wheelchair before it is stopped.

Operation procedure of the electric wheelchair using proposed GUI is illustrated as following:

*Signal detection:* After system initialization and startup, EOG signals are checked firstly and displayed in real time until eye-blink signal in trigger command level appears, and the control process goes into direction selection.

*Direction selection:* As shown in Fig.2, there are four movement directions for selection, including forward/backward movement, clockwise/counter-clockwise rotation. Each direction is candidate for chosen only when corresponding indicator is lightening, and to provide more automation in the operation procedure each indicator is lightening automatically in clockwise order one at a time with one-second interval.

*Adjustment in movement:* During movement of the controlled wheelchair, eye-blink EOG signals are checked continuously until signal in trigger level or severe level is detected to stop the motion, and then the process jumps to the step of direction selection again.

Considering the reaction time before sending out corresponding control signal, a simple training is needed for pre-judgment and being familiar with this wheelchair control system.

# 3    Experiments and Results

## 3.1    Brain-Controlled Wheelchair Moving along Designated Routes

To validate flexibility and convenience of this control system, a subject was enrolled in some designed experiments to operate the wheelchair with the proposed eye-based control system to move along three different designated routes. The three routes are designated with various types of movements and rotations to get the system fully tested. As illustrated in schematic diagrams below, right-rear wheel of wheelchair is taken as tracking point for experimental path track description. The experimental tracks recorded by videos (marked by yellow lines) are compared with designated routes (marked by red lines) for validation.

*Case I: Moving along a straight line*
The subject was asked to control the wheelchair to move along a straight line, during which he is required to move forward to the end of the line firstly, and then turn half circle and move forward towards the start point, as illustrated in Fig.3 (a). This experiment tests performance of the system concerning mobility, stability and rapid reactivity in straight motions. The pratical movement in this experiment is shown in Fig.3 (b).

*Case II: Moving along an s-route*
As shown in Fig.4 (a), in this experiment the subject is required to control the wheelchair to move along an s-route.  During the motion process, the subject operates the electric wheelchair to move forward and make quarter turn rotations in clockwise or counter-clockwise direction in sequence, which tested performance of the system in terms of rapid reactivity regarding rotating and short-distant operations. Fig.4 (b) illustrates the practical movement in the experiment.

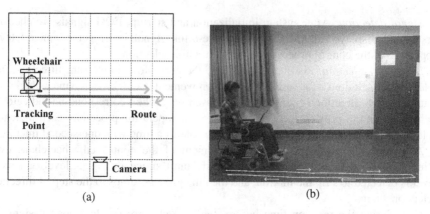

**Fig. 3.** (a) Schematic of straight reciprocating movement; (b) Experimental movement

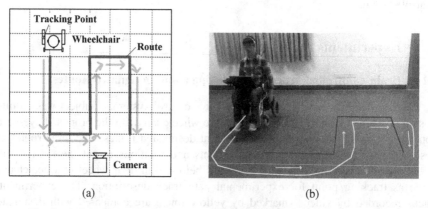

**Fig. 4.** (a) Schematic of movement along s-route; (b) Experimental movement

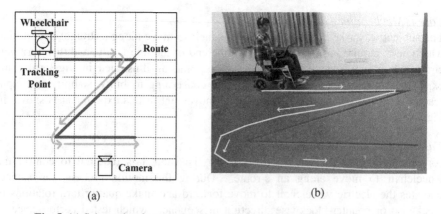

**Fig. 5.** (a) Schematic of movement along z-route; (b) Experimental movement

*Case III: Moving along a z-route*
As illustrated in Fig.5 (a), the third experiment requiring moving along a z-route was proposed to testify accuracy and flexibility of the system. In the experiment, the subject was asked to move along the given route by performing motions as moving forward, rotating at irregular angles. Fig.5 (b) shows the practical movement in the experiment.

## 3.2    Results and Discussion

*Case I:*
Practical motion route of the wheelchair presented by track of right-rear wheel of wheelchair in the first experiment is highlighted in Fig.3 (b). This control system shows an excellent performance in straight motions including moving forward, rapid suspension and half circle rotation, and the practical movement matched well with the designated one. As shown in Fig. 6 and Table 1, the subject finished the mission in 24s without mistake, and 6 selection commands are involved. However, compared with waiting time marked by grey blocks in Fig. 6, the actual time that the wheelchair was on function marked by other color blocks is 13s during the total 24s, accounting for only about half of the entire experimental time. This is caused by the fact that when in the process of direction selection, the subject had to wait for the indicator in the motion status region cycling until the direction wanted was ready for selection.

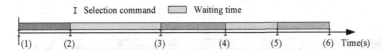

**Fig. 6.** Illustration of control procedure in straight route experiment on timeline

**Table 1.** Time spent on movement in straight route experiment

| Movement | Selection Command | Time (s) |
|---|---|---|
| Forward | (1) (2) | [0,4] |
| Half Circle Rotation | (3) (4) | [11,16] |
| Forward | (5) (6) | [20,24] |
| Total | 6 | 13 |

*Case II:*
From the practical motion route highlighted in Fig.4 (b), we can see that the performance of the system maintains well both in continuous movement of short distance and quarter turn rotation. And the deviation from designated route dues to that the controlled wheelchair is operated with certain speed which results in inertia, and couldn't be stopped immediately once the command was issued. As a consequence, a simple adaptive training is needed for user before operation to get familiar with the proposed brain-controlled wheelchair system. It can be seen from Fig.7 and Table 2 that the subject finished the experiment in 75s during which a few mistakes are made and 18 selection commands are involved, and excluding the

waiting time marked by grey blocks wasted in direction selection process, the actual time spent on wheelchair function marked by other color blocks is 24s, accounting for one-third of the total time.

**Fig. 7.** Illustration of control procedure in s-route experiment on timeline

**Table 2.** Time spent on movement in s-route experiment

| Movement | Selection Command | Time (s) |
|---|---|---|
| Forward | (1) (2) | [0,3] |
| Quarter Turn Rotation | (3) (4) | [12,16] |
| Forward | (5) (6) | [23,25] |
| Quarter Turn Rotation | (7) (8) | [29,33] |
| Forward | (9) (10) | [40,41] |
| Quarter Turn Rotation | (11) (12) | [48,52] |
| Forward | (13) (14) | [56,58] |
| Quarter Turn Rotation | (15) (16) | [68,69] |
| Forward | (17) (18) | [72,75] |
| Total | 18 | 24 |

*Case III:*

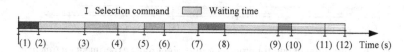

**Fig. 8.** Illustration of control procedure in z-route experiment on timeline

**Table 3.** Time spent on movement in z-route experiment

| Movement | Selection Command | Time (s) |
|---|---|---|
| Forward | (1) (2) | [0,3] |
| Rotation I | (3) (4) | [10,15] |
| Forward | (5) (6) | [19,22] |
| Rotation II | (7) (8) | [27,31] |
| Forward | (9) (10) | [40,46] |
| Total | 10 | 21 |

The practical route of the third experiment is highlighted in Fig.5 (b). The illustration makes it clear that in addition to aforementioned motion types, rotating at non-right angles can also be accurately realized by the control system in accordance to use's intention. And similar with case II, with more adaptive trainings provided, user can promote the performance of more accurate and rapid control of the wheelchair. From Fig.8 and Table 3, it is shown that the subject finished the experiment in 46s with 10 selection commands and spent 21s (marked by non-grey blocks) on direction selection and adjustments, accounting for half of the total time.

# 4    Conclusion

In this paper, a brain-controlled electric wheelchair system using conscious eye-blink EOG signals in different intensity levels for control commands extraction is presented. The proposed system, with a single dry electrode for signal recording, possesses great advantages of simplicity and efficiency. To validate pratical performance of this system, three experiments on wheelchair control along three different designated routes were conducted. The experiments testified good performance of the system to accomplish different types of motion with great stability, flexibility and rapid reactivity.

For further researches, mode for selection procedure with high-efficiency should be developed, and considering the different physical conditions of normal people and people with disabilities, application study on disabled individuals should be conducted.

This brain-controlled method with eye-blink EOG signals can also be applied in control of computer, prosthetic arm and household appliances. We hope that application of the proposed brain-controlled electric wheelchair system with eye-blink signals measured by a single dry electrode can bring much benefit to people with disabilities and live an improved life.

**Acknowledgments.** The authors are grateful to the financial support of the National Natural Science Foundation of China (No. 51105329), the National Basic Research Program (973) of China (No. 2011CB013300) and Postdoctoral Science Foundation of China (No. 20100481416).

# References

1. Reaz, M.B.I., Hussain, M.S., Mohd-Yasin, F.: Techniques of EMG Signal Analysis: Detection, Processing, Classification and Applications. Biol. Proced. Online 8(1), 11–35 (2006)
2. Deng, L.Y., Hsu, C.L., Lin, T.C., Tuan, J.S., Chang, S.M.: EOG-Based Human-Computer Interface System Development. Expert Syst. Appl. 37, 3337–3343 (2010)
3. Birbaumer, N., Cohen, L.G.: Brain-Computer Interfaces: Communication and Restoration of Movement in Paralysis. J. Physiol. 579(3), 621–636 (2007)
4. Leuthardt, E.C., Miller, K.J., Schalk, G., Rao, R.P.N., Ojemann, J.G.: Electrocorticography-Based Brain Computer Interface-the Seattle Experience. IEEE Trans. Neural Syst. Rehab. Eng. 14, 194–198 (2006)
5. Wolpaw, J.R., Birbaumer, N., McFarland, D.J., Pfurtscheller, G., Vaughan, T.M.: Brain-Computer Interfaces for Communication and Control. Clin. Neurophysiol. 113, 767–791 (2002)
6. Graimann, B., Allison, B., Pfurtscheller, G.: Brain-Computer Interfaces: Revolutionizing Human-Computer Interaction. Springer, Heidelberg (2010)
7. Fatourechi, M., Bashashati, A., Ward, R.K., Birch, G.E.: EMG and EOG Artifacts in Brain Computer Interface Systems: a Survey. Clin. Neurophysiol. 118(3), 480–494 (2007)

8. Barea, R., Boquete, L., Mazo, M., Lopez, E.: System for Assisted Mobility Using Eye Movements Based on Electrooculography. IEEE Trans. Neural Syst. Rehab. Eng. 10(4), 209–218 (2002)

9. Gu, J.J., Meng, M., Cook, A., Faulkner, M.G.: A Study of Natural Eye Movement Detection and Ocular Implant Movement Control Using Processed EOG Signals. In: Proceedings 2001 ICRA. IEEE International Conference on Robotics and Automation, pp. 1555–1560 (2001)

10. Barea, R., Boquete, L., Mazo, M., Lopez, E.: Wheelchair Guidance Strategies Using EOG. J. Intell. Robot. Syst. 34, 279–299 (2002)

11. Duguleana, M., Mogan, G.: Using Eye Blinking for EOG-Based Robot Control. In: Camarinha-Matos, L.M., Pereira, P., Ribeiro, L. (eds.) DoCEIS 2010. IFIP AICT, vol. 314, pp. 343–350. Springer, Heidelberg (2010)

12. Lin, J.S., Chen, K.C., Yang, A.W.C.: EEG and Eye-Blinking Signals through a Brain-Computer Interface Based Control for Electric Wheelchairs with Wireless Scheme. In: The 4th Int. Conf. on New Trends in Information Science and Service Science, Gyeongju, Korea, vol. II, pp. 731–734 (2010)

# Development of an Endoscopic Continuum Robot to Enable Transgastric Surgical Obesity Treatment

Kai Xu[1], Jiangran Zhao[1], and Albert J. Shih[2]

[1] University of Michigan - Shanghai Jiao Tong University Joint Institute,
Shanghai Jiao Tong University, Shanghai, 200240, China
{k.xu,zjr318}@sjtu.edu.cn
[2] Department of Mechanical Engineering, University of Michigan, Ann Arbor, MI, 48109
shiha@umich.edu

**Abstract.** This paper presents the development of an endoscopic continuum robot for surgical obesity treatment using a transgastric approach. This proposed transgastric gastroplasty approach performs suturing and resizing of a stomach from inside, aiming at further reducing postoperative complications by avoiding the use of skin incisions. The presented design can be inserted into the stomach in a folded configuration and can be unfolded into a working configuration to perform surgical interventions. It uses sutures fabricated from pre-curved super-elastic NiTi (Nickel-Titanium) alloy to facilitate the motion of tissue penetration. Role of the NiTi needle is demonstrated in in-vitro tissue penetrating experiments, while deployment of this endoscopic robot was verified on the prototype.

**Keywords:** continuum robots, surgical robots, endoscopic robots, NOTES, obesity treatment.

## 1 Introduction

Obesity has become a public health concern in the United states and Europe because of its fast prevalence in the past decades [1, 2]. It is widely accepted that morbid obesity is often associated with diabetes, dyslipidemia, cardiovascular diseases, etc. Although various methods could be used for obesity control (e.g., behavior therapy and pharmacologic intervention), surgery remains the most effective treatment of morbid obesity [3]. Current surgical interventions mainly include i) gastric restrictive methods (e.g. Vertical Banded Gastroplasty, VBG [4], Laparoscopic Adjustable Gastric Banding, LAGB [5], Laparoscopic Sleeve Gastrectomy, LSG [6]), ii) malabsorptive procedures (e.g. jejunoileal bypass [7], Laparoscopic Roux-en-Y Gastric Bypass, LRGB [8]), and iii) combination of the two methods (e.g. VBG-RGB procedures [9]).

Although the surgical treatment is quite effective, it is only considered for patients with morbid obesity (Body Mass Index, BMI over 40 kg/m$^2$), because of high postoperative complication rates and many premature deaths even when most procedures were performed laparoscopically [3]. If the postoperative complications

C.-Y. Su, S. Rakheja, H. Liu (Eds.): ICIRA 2012, Part I, LNAI 7506, pp. 589–600, 2012.

and premature deaths could be further reduced, surgical treatment for obesity might be applied to a greater population with mild obesity.

NOTES (Natural Orifice Translumenal Endoscopic Surgery) might be a way to further reduce postoperative complications. NOTES is a recent development after the minimally invasive laparoscopic procedures. It uses patient's natural orifices (e.g. vagina, esophagus and stomach, etc.) for surgical interventions [10, 11]. Recent clinical studies [12] and many animal studies [13] have shown NOTES effective in further diminishing postoperative complications. Encouraged by these results, a NOTES gastroplasty (it is transgastric in this case), which performs suturing and resizing of a stomach inside the stomach, could possibly greatly reduce the postoperative risks. Hence surgical treatment could be potentially offered to more patients with mild or moderate obesity.

An endoscopic continuum robot shown in Fig. 1 was designed and constructed to verify design concepts which could lead to the accomplishment of a NOTES gastroplasty.

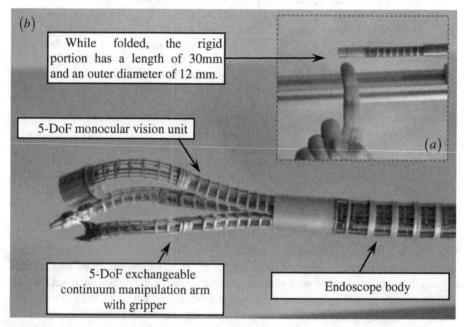

(b)

While folded, the rigid portion has a length of 30mm and an outer diameter of 12 mm.

5-DoF monocular vision unit

(a)

5-DoF exchangeable continuum manipulation arm with gripper

Endoscope body

**Fig. 1.** Design of an endoscopic continuum robot for transgastric gastroplasty: (a) the folded configuration and (b) the unfolded working configuration

In order to accomplish a transgastric gastroplasty, an endoscopic robotic device which could effectively perform suturing and knot tying in confined spaces will be needed. This robot could also be useful in other NOTES procedures to close incisions in walls of stomach or vagina. Previous studies showed that, if a traditional rigid circular suture is used, suturing (and knot tying) in confined spaces is still very difficult even when the task was assisted by robots [14-16] or it was manually performed using a specially designed endoscope [17]. The design shown in Fig. 1 was conceived to overcome these difficulties.

This design is inspired by the work done by Xu *et al* [18] where a robotic system is designed for SPA (Single Port Access) laparoscopic surgery. In the folded configuration, the current device would be easily swallowed by patients; after deployed into the stomach, the device can perform operational procedures in an unfolded configuration. The use of pre-curved NiTi needle is inspired by the work done by Webster *et al* [19, 20] and Dupont *et al* [21] where continuum robots made from pre-curved concentric NiTi tubes were studied for navigation and drug delivery.

Major contribution of this paper is the proposal of using continuum robots and pre-curved super-elastic suture to facilitate both suture penetration and knot tying. Minor contribution is the presentation of one possible design to realize this proposed concepts.

The paper is organized as the following. Section 2 presents design requirements and a new surgical concept on how a NOTES gastroplasty could be performed. System overview and detailed design descriptions are presented in Section 3. Prototype deployment are presented in Section 4 with conclusion and future work followed in Section 5.

## 2    Design Requirements and Surgical Concepts

A NOTES (transgastric) gastroplasty demands a endoscopic robotic device with the following capabilities:

1) The device should be foldable to facilitate its insertion into stomach through pharynx and esophagus. Gastroscopes from Olympus® have outer diameters from 11.3mm (GIF-1TQ160) to 12.6mm (GIF-XTQ160), while existing endoscopes for NOTES [17] usually have outer diameters from 14.3mm (Olympus "R" scope) to 18mm (USGI Transport scope). The presented design shall have a comparable or smaller diameter (currently 12mm).
2) The device can deploy itself into a working configuration for suturing, knot tying, ablation, etc.
3) Additional channels should be available for insufflation, manipulation tools for knot-tying, ablation, etc.
4) The device can be positioned and oriented to achieve suturing and knot tying within the entire stomach. This can be achieved by placing the device at the distal tip of an endoscope such as the ShapeLock® [22].
5) The device has a vision unit with integrated illumination.
6) The device is actuated by its actuation unit located outside patient's mouth.

Using such an endoscopic robotic device with these aforementioned capabilities, a transgastric gastroplasty can be achieved in many ways. One possibility is shown in Fig. 2. This endoscopic robotic device will firstly be inserted into the stomach. Medical balloons can be placed near pylorus so that the stomach can be sealed and inflated. After enough space is created, the device deploys itself into the working configuration to perform suturing. A lockable band could be attached to the inner wall of the stomach by multiple stitches. After the robotic device is retracted, the band can then be tightened and locked to create a small pouch to achieve the stomach resizing.

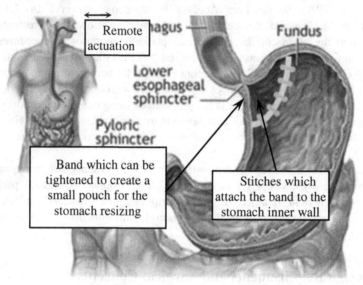

**Fig. 2.** Schematic drawing of a proposed new surgical concept for stomach resizing. The stomach diagram is from the University of Maryland Medical Center Encyclopedia.

## 3     System Overview and Design Description

The endoscopic stitching device in Fig. 1 was conceived to meet the requirements mentioned in Section 2. In the folded configuration, the device can be inserted into stomach through the esophagus. Its forward-looking vision unit could guide the surgeons through the insertion phase. In the stomach, the device first inflates the stomach to generate enough space for its unfolded working configuration. Suturing and knot-tying can then be performed. The deployment process is experimentally verified by the prototype shown in Fig. 10.

As shown in Fig. 1, the device consists of one 5-DoF (Degrees of Freedom) monocular vision unit and two 5-DoF snake-like exchangeable continuum manipulation arms with grippers. The continuum manipulator arm can be replaced by sensor modules (e.g. an ultrasound probe) or energy sources (e.g. a cautery).

Within the vision unit and the manipulation arms, there are continuum segments as shown in Fig. 3 and Fig. 4. A structural similarity shared by these continuum segments is that these continuum segments consist of a base disk, a end disk, several spacer disks and several backbones (made from super elastic nickel-titanium alloy). Backbones are attached to the end disks and can slide in holes of spacer disks and base disks. Synchronized pushing or pulling of these backbones deflect the segments into desired shapes. Actuation unit of these backbones will remain outside patient's month, as indicated in the inset of Fig. 2. Motion discrepancy caused by backlash or friction might be compensated as in [23]. Design considerations and solutions for critical components will be discussed as follows.

## 3.1   Vision Unit

CAD design of the 5-DoF monocular vision is shown in Fig. 3. Once inserted into stomach, the vision unit can be extended to provide space for the deployment of manipulation arms, as shown in Fig. 10.

As shown in Fig. 3, the vision unit consists of continuum segment I with three DoFs, segment II with two DoFs and the monocular camera head. Both segment I and segment II can bend sideward any direction, which is a 2-DoF bending motion. The additional DoF of the segment I is its variable length when extended from the endoscope.

CCD chip intended for the camera head is the chip CSH14V4R1 from NET Inc. with an outer diameter of 6.5mm. Since the diameter of the camera head is 12mm, only one CCD chip can be fitted in. If a smaller CCD chip can be used, the vision unit can be easily turned into a stereo vision. Camera field of view is also considered in the CAD model to make sure manipulation of the inserted arms will be seen.

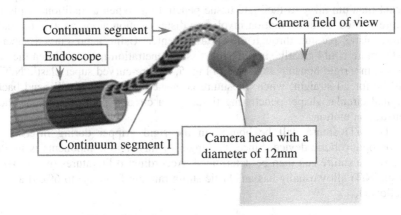

**Fig. 3.** The 5-DoF monocular vision unit

## 3.2   Continuum Manipulation Arms

CAD design of the 5-DoF exchangeable continuum manipulation arm is shown in Fig. 4. After insertion into one's stomach, the vision unit extends itself to provide space for the continuum manipulation arm to be deployed as shown in Fig. 10.

As shown in Fig. 4, the continuum manipulation arm consists of continuum segment I with three DoFs, segment II with two DoFs and a gripper integrated with a suture. Both segment I and segment II can bend sideward any direction, which is a 2-DoF bending motion. The additional DoF of the segment I is its variable length when extended from the endoscope.

Function of the suture will be detailed in the next session.

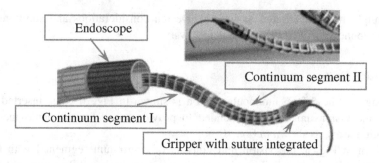

**Fig. 4.** The 5-DoF exchangeable continuum manipulation arm with a gripper attached and a NiTi suture embedded: the inset shows the prototype

Within all the segments, significantly redundant backbones are used in order to increase the stiffness of the continuum arms.

### 3.3    Super-Elastic Nickel-Titanium Suture

Key innovation introduced in this paper is to fabricate the suture using super-elastic nickel titanium alloy to facilitate tissue penetration. When a traditional rigid circular suture is used, suturing motion involves a distal rotation along an axis normal to the suture plane, passing through the suture's center. Using a pre-curved super-elastic NiTi suture could greatly simplify this tissue penetration motion. When the suture is housed in a rigid housing as shown in Fig. 5, the pre-curved super-elastic NiTi suture will be forced straight; when the suture is pushed outwards, it will bend back to its original circular shape, penetrating tissues in a circular path to facilitate the tissue penetration motion.

The NiTi suture will be housed in the rigid gripper during insertion of the endoscopic robotic device. Since the length of this rigid components is limited, the size of the suture can then be determined. According to literatures (e.g. [24]), super-elastic NiTi alloy usually has an elastic strain ranging from 4% to 6%. If a 4% strain is allowed,

$$\varepsilon_{strain} = r_{needle}/R_{suture} \leq 4\% \Rightarrow r_{needle} \leq 0.04 R_{suture} \tag{1}$$

Where $r_{needle}$ is the radius of the needle's round cross section and $R_{suture}$ is the radius of the suture.

If a $3\pi/4$ suture with a length of 20mm will be used,

$$3\pi R_{suture}/4 = 20mm \tag{2}$$

$$R_{suture} = 8.49mm \xrightarrow{r_{needle} \leq 0.04 R_{suture}} r_{needle} \leq 0.34mm \tag{3}$$

In the design and in the in-vitro tissue penetrating experiments, a NiTi tube with an outer diameter of 0.69mm is then used. Although this selection does not comply with Eq. (3) strictly, strain slightly over 4% usually still falls in the elastic region for super-elastic NiTi alloy.

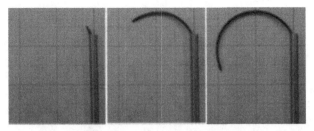

**Fig. 5.** A Ø0.69mm suture made from pre-curved NiTi alloy: it bends back to its original circular shape after released from a straight rigid housing. The suture's radius is about 9mm. Thinnest grids in the background are 1mm x 1mm.

The idea of using a NiTi suture to facilitate tissue penetration is also validated by an in-vitro experiment on a porcine model as shown in Fig. 6: (a) the suture housing approached the tissue and (b) then pushed against the tissue; (c) the NiTi suture was pushed out to start the penetration; (d) and the suture generated a circular cutting path; (e) it was shown this penetration could grip enough tissue; (f) the suture could be retracted back to the housing to carry out a second penetration.

Using a pre-curved super-elastic NiTi suture only simplifies the motion tissue penetration. To achieve a complete stitch, a suture thread should be guided through the tissue as well. The proposed idea is to insert a thread through channel in the NiTi suture which is made from a tube. As shown in Fig. 7, one end of the thread is hung outside the suture. During tissue penetration, the thread will be brought through the tissue by the non-cutting edge of the suture tip. After penetration, the thread will be picked up by the other manipulation arm, before the suture is retracted. After the suture is retracted, the thread is left through tissue and ready for knot tying.

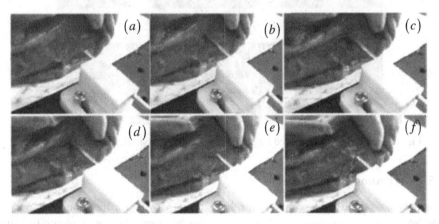

**Fig. 6.** In vitro tissue penetrating experiments: the Ø0.69mm NiTi suture penetrates and grips a porcine stomach wall

**Fig. 7.** The suture thread passes through the channel in the NiTi suture

### 3.4     Knot Tying Using the Manipulation Arms

Each continuum manipulation arm has five degrees of freedom while during knot tying, a point on a thread will need to follow a spatial curve which only requires three degrees of freedom. With proper dimension synthesis, knot tying could be realized.

Comparable results have been reported in [15] where continuum robots with similar structures realized knot tying, as shown in Fig. 8. These results combined with the results from Section 3.C proved that the proposed robotic device could realize endoscopic suturing hence potentially suitable for transgastric surgery of stomach resizing.

Workspace analysis and instantaneous kinematics of such a continuum manipulation arm are available in [15, 18].

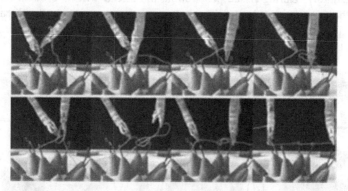

**Fig. 8.** Knot tying was achieved by continuum robots with similar structures as in [15]

### 3.5     Actuation Unit

The presented endoscopic continuum robots have 15 DoFs for the monocular vision unit and two manipulation arms. Each arm also has two addition elements to drive which are the NiTi suture and the gripper.

Due to the limits on the budget, the actuation unit was not motorized yet. All the actuation, including pushing and pulling of all the backbones, sutures and grippers, are all currently manual. Fig. 9 shows the endoscopic continuum robot assembled with the manual actuation unit.

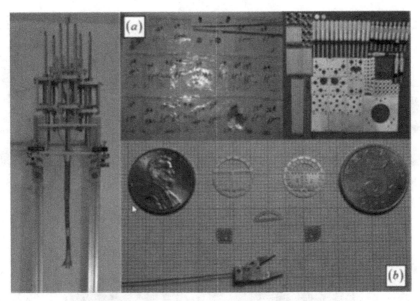

**Fig. 9.** The endoscopic continuum robot assembled with the manual actuation unit: (a) all the components of the endoscopic continuum robots and (b) a few components with respect to US and Chinese coins on a piece of graph paper

## 4     Experimental Validation of the Prototype

Motivation of this presented work is to valid a few design concepts: i) suture made from super-elastic NiTi alloy could facilitate the tissue penetration, ii) the current design can enter the stomach in a folded configuration and then be deployed into a working configuration. Other functionality, such as ability of tying a knot, has been proved by previously published results.

While the tissue penetration has been demonstrated in Fig. 6, the deployment of this endoscopic device is shown in Fig. 10: (a) after the endoscopic device is inserted into a stomach in a folded configuration, (b) the monocular vision unit starts extend itself, (c) after the vision unit is extended to the intended length, the vision unit starts to bend sideward and (d) reaches a desired pose; space is generated so that (e) continuum manipulation arms can be inserted; (f) the two manipulation arms can be inserted individually or together; (g) after the two arms are fully inserted, the arms can be actuated to (h) form various poses for surgical interventions. Since the actuation unit is not motorized, poses in Fig. 10 are all generated by manually actuating the backbones of the continuum segments. The exchangeable manipulation arm can also be replaced by sensor modules (e.g. an ultrasound probe) or energy sources (e.g. a cautery).

Preliminary tissue penetration experiments were also carried out on a porcine model using the current prototype, as shown in Fig. 11

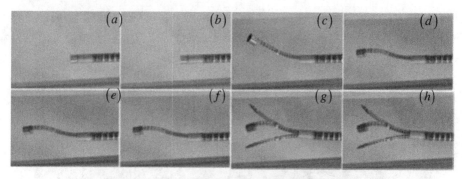

**Fig. 10.** Deployment of the endoscopic robotic device

**Fig. 11.** Preliminary tissue penetration experiments using the presented prototype

## 5     Conclusion and Future Work

This paper proposed a design of an endoscopic robotic device for transgastric surgical obesity treatment. This proposed transgastric gastroplasty using a NOTES approach performs suturing and resizing of a stomach from inside, aiming at further reducing postoperative complications hence making surgical obesity treatments available for a bigger population with mild obesity.

The prototype of this endoscopic continuum robot was constructed to verify the proposed ideas, which is a updated version of the design presented in [25]. Experiments showed that the current design can be inserted into the stomach in a folded configuration and can be unfolded into a working configuration to perform suturing and stitching. It uses pre-curved super-elastic NiTi alloy suture to facilitate the motion of tissue penetration. Suture thread can also be delivered through the hollow suture since the suture is made from a tube. Since knot tying had been realized by a laryngoscopic robot with similar structure as shown in Fig. 8, conclusion can be extended that the current design potentially has all the desired capabilities to perform a transgastric stomach resizing.

Future work regarding this design includes i) motorizing the actuation unit so that knot tying can be actually verified using the current prototype; ii) investigating control algorithm using inverse kinematics so that master controllers, such as the Phantom Omni® devices from the Sensable Inc., can be used to control this endoscopic robot.

**Acknowledgement.** This work was supported in part by the National Science Foundation of China Grant # 51005146 and in part by the University of Michigan - Shanghai Jiao Tong University Collaborative Research Fund.

# References

1. Ogden, C.L., Carroll, M.D., Curtin, L.R., McDowell, M.A., Tabak, C.J., Flegal, K.M.: Prevalence of Overweight and Obesity in the United States, 1999-2004. The Journal of the American Medical Association 295(13), 1549–1555 (2006)
2. Berghöfer, A., Pischon, T., Reinhold, T., Apovian, C.M., Sharma, A.M., Willich, S.N.: Obesity Prevalence from a European Perspective: a Systematic Review. BMC Public Health 8(200), 1–10 (2008)
3. Glenny, A.M., O'Meara, S., Melville, A., Sheldon, T.A., Wilson, C.: The Treatment and Prevention of Obesity: a Systematic Review of the Literature. International Journal of Obesity 21(9), 715–737 (1997)
4. Gomez, C.A.: Gastroplasty in the Surgical Treatment of Morbid Obesity. The American Journal of Clinical Nutrition 33(Suppl. 2), 406–415 (1980)
5. Belachew, M., Legrand, M., Vincent, V., Lismonde, M., Docte, N.L., Deschamps, V.: Laparoscopic Adjustable Gastric Banding. Would Journal of Surgery 22(9), 955–963 (1998)
6. Baltasar, A., Serra, C., Pérez, N., Bou, R., Bengochea, M., Ferri, L.: Laparoscopic Sleeve Gastrectomy: A Multi-purpose Bariatric Operation. Obesity Surgery 15(8), 1124–1128 (2006)
7. Deitel, M., Shahi, B., Anand, P.K., Deitel, F.H., Cardinell, D.L.: Long-term Outcome in a Series of Jejunoileal Bypass Patients. Obesity Surgery 3(3), 247–252 (1993)
8. Schauer, P.R., Ikramuddin, S., Gourash, W., Ramanathan, R., Luketich, J.: Outcomes After Laparoscopic Roux-en-Y Gastric Bypass for Morbid Obesity. Annals of Surgery 232(4), 515–529 (2000)
9. Capella, J.F., Capella, R.F.: An Assessment of Vertical Banded Gastroplasty-Roux-en-Y Gastric Bypass for the Treatment of Morbid Obesity. The American Journal of Surgery 183(2), 117–123 (2002)
10. Giday, S.A., Kantsevoy, S.V., Kalloo, A.N.: Principle and History of Natural Orifice Translumenal Endoscopic Surgery (NOTES). Minimally Invasive Therapy and Allied Technologies 15(6), 373–377 (2006)
11. McGee, M.F., Rosen, M.J., Marks, J., Onders, R.P., Chak, A., Faulx, A., Chen, V.K., Ponsky, J.: A Primer on Natural Orifice Transluminal Endoscopic Surgery: Building a New Paradigm. Surgical Innovation 13(2), 86–93 (2006)
12. Horgan, S., Cullen, J.P., Talamini, M.A., Mintz, Y., Ferreres, A., Jacobsen, G.R., Sandler, B., Bosia, J., Savides, T., Easter, D.W., Savu, M.K., Ramamoorthy, S.L., Whitcomb, E., Agarwal, S., Lukacz, E., Dominguez, G., Ferraina, P.: Natural Orifice Surgery: Initial Clinical Experience. Surgical Endoscopy 23(7), 1512–1518 (2009)

13. Flora, E.D., Wilson, T.G., Martin, I.J., O'Rourke, N.A., Maddern, G.J.: A Review of Natural Orifice Translumenal Endoscopic Surgery (NOTES) for Intra-abdominal Surgery: Experimental Models, Techniques, and Applicability to the Clinical Setting. Annals of Surgery 247(4), 583–602 (2008)

14. Kapoor, A., Simaan, N., Taylor, R.H.: Suturing in Confined Spaces: Constrained Motion Control of a Hybrid 8-DoF Robot. In: International Conference on Advanced Robotics (IACR), Seattle, USA, pp. 452–459 (2005)

15. Simaan, N., Xu, K., Kapoor, A., Wei, W., Kazanzides, P., Flint, P., Taylor, R.H.: Design and Integration of a Telerobotic System for Minimally Invasive Surgery of the Throat. International Journal of Robotics Research 28(9), 1134–1153 (2009)

16. Staub, C., Osa, T., Knoll, A., Bauernschmitt, R.: Automation of Tissue Piercing using Circular Needles and Vision Guidance for Computer Aided Laparoscopic Surgery. In: IEEE International Conference on Robotics and Automation (ICRA), Anchorage, Alaska, USA, pp. 4585–4590 (2010)

17. Bardaro, S.J., Swanstrom, L.: Development of Advanced Endoscopes for Natural Orifice Transluminal Endoscopic Surgery (NOTES). Minimally Invasive Therapy and Allied Technologies 15(6), 378–383 (2006)

18. Xu, K., Goldman, R.E., Ding, J., Allen, P.K., Fowler, D.L., Simaan, N.: System Design of an Insertable Robotic Effector Platform for Single Port Access (SPA) Surgery. In: IEEE/RSJ International Conference on Intelligent Robots and Systems (IROS), St. Louis, MO, USA, pp. 5546–5552 (2009)

19. Webster, R.J., Romano, J.M., Cowan, N.J.: Mechanics of Precurved-Tube Continuum Robots. IEEE Transactions on Robotics 25(1), 67–78 (2009)

20. Webster, R.J., Okamura, A.M., Cowan, N.J.: Toward Active Cannulas: Miniature Snake-Like Surgical Robots. In: IEEE International Conference on Intelligent Robots and Systems, Beijing, China, pp. 2857–2863 (2006)

21. Dupont, P.E., Lock, J., Itkowitz, B., Butler, E.: Design and Control of Concentric-Tube Robots. IEEE Transactions on Robotics 26(2), 209–225 (2010)

22. Swanstrom, L.L., Kozarek, R., Pasricha, P.J., Gross, S., Birkett, D., Park, P.-O., Saadat, V., Ewers, R., Swain, P.: Development of a New Access Device for Transgastric Surgery. Journal of Gastrointestinal Surgery 9(8), 1129–1137 (2006)

23. Xu, K., Simaan, N.: Actuation Compensation for Flexible Surgical Snake-like Robots with Redundant Remote Actuation. In: IEEE International Conference on Robotics and Automation (ICRA), Orlando, Florida, USA, pp. 4148–4154 (2006)

24. Nemat-Nassera, S., Guo, W.-G.: Superelastic and Cyclic Response of NiTi SMA at Various Strain Rates and Temperatures. Mechanics of Materials 38(5-6), 463–474 (2006)

25. Xu, K., Zhao, J., Geiger, J., Shih, A.J., Zheng, M.: Design of an Endoscopic Stitching Device for Surgical Obesity Treatment Using a N.O.T.E.S Approach. In: IEEE/RSJ International Conference on Intelligent Robots and Systems (IROS), San Francisco, CA, USA, pp. 961–966 (2011)

# Fuzzy Adaptive Backstepping Control of a Two Degree of Freedom Parallel Robot

Xiaoping Liu* and Angelo Liadis

Faculty of Engineering, Lakehead University,
955 Oliver Road, Thunder Bay, Ontario, P7B 5E1, Canada
xliu2@lakeheadu.ca

**Abstract.** This paper proposes three fuzzy adaptive controller design methods based on the backstepping design technique. In the first method, the original parameters in a fuzzy logic system are updated real-time, on the other hand, in the second and third methods, the square of the norm of the original parameters is used as an unknown parameter. The third method utilizes the fact that the norm of the fuzzy logic system is less than or equal to one and the resulting controller is independent of the fuzzy logic system. The three methods were tested on the two-degree-of-freedom robot which was custom-made. The test results show that all three methods work and the first method works better than the other two methods with and without loads because it involves no simplification during the design process even though it requires longer computation time.

**Keywords:** Adaptive control, fuzzy control, backstepping, parallel robots.

## 1   Introduction

Typically, links of serial robots are connected in series, thus forming open-chain mechanisms and all their joints are actuated. On the other hand, links of parallel robots are connected in a combination of both serial and parallel fashions, thus forming closed-chain mechanisms and not all their joints are actuated. The actuators of parallel robots are placed on the base or close to the base, which makes moving parts lighter. Parallel robots have high structural stiffness since the end effector is supported in several places at the same time. Even though parallel robots have some drawbacks such as limited workspace and loss of stiffness in singular positions completely, they have found their applications in industries, such as airplane, automobile simulators, fiber alignment, high speed/high-precision milling machines, and so on.

In general, modeling of parallel robots is more challenging than that of serial robots. Serial robots can be modeled using ordinary differential equations,

---

* Dr. Liu's research is supported by Natural Sciences and Engineering Research Council of Canada.

C.-Y. Su, S. Rakheja, H. Liu (Eds.): ICIRA 2012, Part I, LNAI 7506, pp. 601–610, 2012.

however, the model of parallel robots contains both algebraic equations and ordinary differential equations [1]. Therefore, analysis and control for parallel robots are more complex than serial robots. Like serial robots, parallel robots can be controlled by using model-based controllers, such as PID controllers [1], computed-torque controllers [2], impedance control [3], and adaptive control [4], [5], and non-model-based controllers, such as fuzzy logic controllers [6], neural network controllers [7].

Among the existing adaptive controller design techniques, adaptive backstepping is able to handle nonlinear systems in lower triangular form with known nonlinearities and unknown parameters [8], which has been well recognized as a big advancement compared with traditional design methods for systems with matching conditions. Over the last two decades, adaptive backstepping design technique has been used to design non-modeled-based controllers, such as neural network controllers and fuzzy logic controllers for nonlinear systems in lower triangular form with unknown nonlinearities due to the ability of neural network and fuzzy logic systems to approximate nonlinearities with reasonable accuracy. Lot of research has been done and many papers have been published on fuzzy adaptive backstepping and it is not wise to list all of them here. However the following papers are worth mentioning, which are relevant to this research. The backstepping was first time applied to design fuzzy adaptive controllers in [9]. The fuzzy adaptive backstepping controllers proposed in [9] and [10] contains too many parameters, which requires very long computation time and large memory space and hinders the on-line implementation. To overcome the drawbacks mentioned above, [11] proposed to use upper-bounds of unknown nonlinearities as unknown parameters so that the number of parameters to be learned on-line is reduced to twice the order of systems in consideration. Motivated by [11], the square of the norm of unknown parameters was used to reduce the number of adaptive parameters in [12] and the fuzzy adaptive controllers proposed in [13] are independent of fuzzy approximators since the fact that the norm of the known function in the fuzzy approximator is always less than one was used. The design idea, similar to [11], was used to design fuzzy logic controllers for multi-input multi-output nonlinear systems in lower triangular forms [14], which have the same number of unknown parameters as used in [11].

The aim of this paper is to investigate the effectiveness of the fuzzy adaptive backstepping design technique on a two degree of freedom parallel robot. Three fuzzy adaptive controllers will be designed by combining fuzzy logic approximators and backstepping. The first controller will be designed based on the method used in [10], the second controller by using the idea in [12], and the third with the design approach in [13]. The first fuzzy adaptive controller has many parameters to be updated on-line, on the other hand, the second and third have only two parameters which have to be learned on-line. The difference between the second and third controllers is that the third controller does not depend on the fuzzy logic approximators, so it requires least computation time among three controllers. The three fuzzy adaptive controllers have been tested on the custom-built parallel robot.

The rest of the paper is organized as follows. In Section 2, the dynamic model of the two degree of freedom parallel robot under study is presented. In Section 3, three fuzzy adaptive controllers are designed by using backstepping technique. In Section 4, the experimental results for the controllers are presented. Finally conclusions are drawn in Section 5.

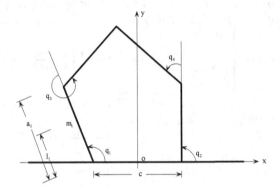

**Fig. 1.** The Two-Degree-of-Freedom Parallel Robot

## 2   Dynamic Equations

The two degree of freedom parallel robot is shown in Fig. 1. The differential equation described in [1] defines the dynamic model of the parallel robot as

$$D'(q')\ddot{q}' + C'(q',\dot{q}')\dot{q}' + G'(q') = u',$$
$$\phi(q') = 0.$$

with $q' = \begin{bmatrix} q_1 & q_2 & q_3 & q_4 \end{bmatrix}^T$ and $u' = \begin{bmatrix} u_1 & u_2 & 0 & 0 \end{bmatrix}^T$ where $q_i$ is the joint angle of joint $i$, $u_1$ and $u_2$ are the torque applied at joints 1 and 2, respectively. $D'(q') =$
$$\begin{bmatrix} d_{11} & 0 & d_{13} & 0 \\ 0 & d_{22} & 0 & d_{24} \\ d_{31} & 0 & d_{33} & 0 \\ 0 & d_{42} & 0 & d_{44} \end{bmatrix}, \quad C'(q',\dot{q}') = \begin{bmatrix} c_{11} & 0 & c_{13} & 0 \\ 0 & c_{22} & 0 & c_{24} \\ c_{31} & 0 & 0 & 0 \\ 0 & c_{42} & 0 & 0 \end{bmatrix}, \quad G'(q') = \begin{bmatrix} g_1 & g_2 & g_3 & g_4 \end{bmatrix}^T,$$
$\phi(q') = \begin{bmatrix} \phi_1 & \phi_2 \end{bmatrix}^T$ with $d_{11} = m_1 l_1^2 + m_3(a_1^2 + l_3^2 + 2a_1 l_3 \cos q_3) + I_1 + I_3$, $d_{22} = m_2 l_2^2 + m_4(a_2^2 + l_4^2 + 2a_2 l_4 \cos q_4) + I_2 + I_4$, $d_{13} = m_3(l_3^2 + a_1 l_3 \cos q_3) + I_3$, $d_{24} = m_4(l_4^2 + a_2 l_4 \cos q_4) + I_4$, $d_{31} = d_{13}$, $d_{42} = d_{24}$, $d_{33} = m_3 l_3^2 + I_3$, $d_{44} = m_4 l_4^2 + I_4$, $c_{11} = -m_3 a_1 l_3 \sin q_3 \dot{q}_3$, $c_{22} = -m_4 a_2 l_4 \sin q_4 \dot{q}_4$, $c_{13} = -m_3 a_1 l_3 \sin q_3 (\dot{q}_1 + \dot{q}_3)$, $c_{24} = -m_4 a_2 l_4 \sin q_4 (\dot{q}_2 + \dot{q}_4)$, $c_{31} = m_3 a_1 l_3 \sin q_3 \dot{q}_1$, $c_{42} = m_4 a_2 l_4 \sin q_4 \dot{q}_2$, $g_1 = g((m_1 l_1 + m_3 a_1) \cos q_1 + m_3 l_3 \cos(q_1 + q_3))$, $g_2 = g((m_2 l_2 + m_4 a_2) \cos q_2 + m_4 l_4 \cos(q_2 + q_4))$, $g_3 = g(m_3 l_3 \cos(q_1 + q_3))$, $g_4 = g(m_4 l_4 \cos(q_2 + q_4))$, $\phi_1 = a_1 \cos q_1 + a_3 \cos(q_1 + q_3) - c - a_2 \cos q_2 - a_4 \cos(q_2 + q_4)$, $\phi_2 = a_1 \sin q_1 + a_3 \sin(q_1 + q_3) - a_2 \sin q_2 - a_4 \sin(q_2 + q_4)$.

The equations of motion of the parallel robot expressed in terms of the independent generalized coordinates are defined as [1]

$$D(q)\ddot{q} + C(q,\dot{q})\dot{q} + G(q) = u \tag{1}$$

where $q = \begin{bmatrix} q_1 & q_2 \end{bmatrix}^T$, $u = \begin{bmatrix} u_1 & u_2 \end{bmatrix}^T$, $D(q') = \rho^T(q')D'(q')\rho(q')$, $C(q',\dot{q}') = \rho^T(q')C'(q',\dot{q}')\rho(q') + \rho^T(q')D'(q')\dot{\rho}(q',\dot{q}')$, $G(q') = \rho^T(q')G'(q')$, $\rho(q') = \begin{bmatrix} 1 & 0 \\ 0 & 1 \\ \rho_{31} & \rho_{32} \\ \rho_{41} & \rho_{42} \end{bmatrix}$, $\dot{\rho}(q',\dot{q}') = \begin{bmatrix} 0 & 0 \\ 0 & 0 \\ \dot{\rho}_{31} & \dot{\rho}_{32} \\ \dot{\rho}_{41} & \dot{\rho}_{42} \end{bmatrix}$ with $q_3 = \tan^{-1}\left[\frac{\tilde{\mu}+a_4\sin(q_2+q_4)}{\tilde{\lambda}+a_4\cos(q_2+q_4)}\right] - q_1$, $q_4 = \tan^{-1}(\tilde{b}/\tilde{a}) - q_2 - \pi - \tan^{-1}(\sqrt{\tilde{a}^2 + \tilde{b}^2 - \tilde{c}^2}/\tilde{c})$, $\tilde{\lambda} = a_2\cos q_2 - a_1\cos q_1 + c$, $\tilde{\mu} = a_2\sin q_2 - a_1\sin q_1$, $\tilde{a} = 2a_4\tilde{\lambda}$, $\tilde{b} = 2a_4\tilde{\mu}$, $\tilde{c} = a_3^2 - a_4^2 - \tilde{\lambda}^2 - \tilde{\mu}^2$. $\rho_{31} = -\frac{a_1\sin(q_1-q_2-q_4)+a_3y}{a_3y}$, $\rho_{32} = -\frac{a_2\sin q_4}{a_3y}$, $\rho_{42} = -\frac{a_2\sin(q_1-q_2+q_3)+a_4y}{a_4y}$, $\rho_{41} = \frac{a_1\sin q_3}{a_4y}$, $y = \sin(q_1 - q_2 + q_3 - q_4)$.

It should be noted that $D(q')$ is positive definite and $\dot{D}(q') - 2C(q',\dot{q}')$ is skew symmetric [1].

## 3    Fuzzy Adaptive Backstepping Controller Design

A fuzzy logic system, composed of a rule base, a fuzzifer, a fuzzy inference engine, and a defuzzifier, is used to approximate the unknown nonlinear terms in the controller design process. The rule base for a fuzzy logic system is composed of the following $N$ fuzzy rules

$$R_i : IF \ x_1 \ is \ F_1^i, \cdots, \ x_n \ is \ F_n^i, \ THEN \ y \ is \ B^i$$

where $i = 1, 2, \cdots, N$, $x = [x_1, x_2, \cdots, x_n]^T$ is the input and $y$ is the output, $F_j^i$ and $B^i$ are fuzzy sets. Let $\mu_{F_j^i}(x_j)$ be the membership of $F_j^i$ and $\Phi_i$ be the point at which $\mu_{B^i}(y)$ reaches its maximum. When a singleton fuzzifier, center-average defuzzifier, and product inference are used, the fuzzy logic system can be expressed as $y(x) = \theta^T S(x)$ where $S(x) = [\xi_1(x), \xi_2(x), \cdots, \xi_N(x)]^T$ and $\theta = [\Phi_1, \Phi_2, \cdots, \Phi_N]^T$ with

$$\xi_i(x) = \frac{\prod_{j=1}^n \mu_{F_j^i}(x_j)}{\sum_{i=1}^N [\prod_{j=1}^n \mu_{F_j^i}(x_j)]}$$

It has been proved in [15] and [16] that if Gaussian functions are used as membership functions, any continuous function $f(x)$ can be approximated by a fuzzy logic system $\theta^T S(x)$ with error $\delta$ arbitrarily small, that is,

$$f(x) = \theta^T S(x) + \delta \tag{2}$$

The main objective of this paper is to design adaptive controllers to control the parallel robot so that its end effector follows a circle. To this end, it is appropriate to set the error and change in error as: $x_1 = q_{1d} - q_1$, $x_2 = q_{2d} - q_2$, $x_3 = \dot{q}_{1d} - \dot{q}_1$ and $x_4 = \dot{q}_{2d} - \dot{q}_2$, where $q_{1d}$ and $q_{2d}$ are the desired angles, $q_1$ and $q_2$ are the actual angles, $\dot{q}_{1d}$ and $\dot{q}_{2d}$ are the desired angular velocities, $\dot{q}_1$ and $\dot{q}_2$ are the actual angular velocities, $\ddot{q}_{1d}$ and $\ddot{q}_{2d}$ are the desired angular accelerations. The following system is in lower triangular form, which can be produced by differentiating $x_1$, $x_2$, $x_3$ and $x_4$.

$$\dot{x}_1 = x_3$$

$$\dot{x}_2 = x_4$$

$$\begin{bmatrix} \dot{x}_3 \\ \dot{x}_4 \end{bmatrix} = D^{-1}(q') \left( -u + C(q', \dot{q}') \begin{bmatrix} \dot{q}_1 \\ \dot{q}_2 \end{bmatrix} + g(q') \right) + \begin{bmatrix} \ddot{q}_{1d} \\ \ddot{q}_{2d} \end{bmatrix} \tag{3}$$

Define a Lyapunov function as $V_1 = 0.5x_1^2 + 0.5x_2^2$. The derivative of $V_1$ is

$$\dot{V}_1 = x_1 x_3 + x_2 x_4 = -c_1 x_1^2 - c_2 x_2^2 + x_1 z_1 + x_2 z_2 \tag{4}$$

with $\alpha_1 = -c_1 x_1$ and $\alpha_2 = -c_2 x_2$, where $c_1$ and $c_2$ are positive constants and

$$z_1 = x_3 - \alpha_1 \, , \, z_2 = x_4 - \alpha_2 \tag{5}$$

Now define a Lyapunov function candidate as $W = V_1 + 0.5 \begin{bmatrix} z_1 & z_2 \end{bmatrix} D(q') \begin{bmatrix} z_1 \\ z_2 \end{bmatrix}$.
The time derivative of $W$ becomes

$$\dot{W} = \dot{V}_1 + \begin{bmatrix} z_1 & z_2 \end{bmatrix} D(q') \begin{bmatrix} \dot{z}_1 \\ \dot{z}_2 \end{bmatrix} + 0.5 \begin{bmatrix} z_1 & z_2 \end{bmatrix} \dot{D}(q') \begin{bmatrix} z_1 \\ z_2 \end{bmatrix} \tag{6}$$

Note that $\dot{D}(q') - 2C(q', \dot{q}')$ is skew symmetric [1], which implies that

$$0.5 \begin{bmatrix} z_1 & z_2 \end{bmatrix} \dot{D}(q') \begin{bmatrix} z_1 \\ z_2 \end{bmatrix} = 0.5 \begin{bmatrix} z_1 & z_2 \end{bmatrix} C(q', \dot{q}') \begin{bmatrix} z_1 \\ z_2 \end{bmatrix} \tag{7}$$

Substituting equations (3) and (7) into (6) yields

$$\dot{W} = \dot{V}_1 + z_1 (f_1 - u_1) + z_2 (f_2 - u_2)$$

where $f_1$ and $f_2$ are defined as

$$\begin{bmatrix} f_1 \\ f_2 \end{bmatrix} = D(q') \begin{bmatrix} (\ddot{q}_{1d} - \dot{\alpha}_1) \\ (\ddot{q}_{2d} - \dot{\alpha}_2) \end{bmatrix} + C(q', \dot{q}') \begin{bmatrix} (\dot{q}_{1d} - \alpha_1) \\ (\dot{q}_{2d} - \alpha_2) \end{bmatrix} + g(q') \tag{8}$$

The subsequent procedure consists of estimating $f_i$ with the fuzzy system approximator defined in (2), namely

$$f_i = \kappa_i^T S_i + \delta_i, \ i = 1, 2. \tag{9}$$

With $z_i \delta_i \leq 0.5 z_i^2 + 0.5 \delta_i^2$, substituting (9) into (8) gives

$$\dot{W} = \dot{V}_1 + z_1 \left( \kappa_1^T S_1 + \delta_1 - u_1 \right) + z_2 \left( \kappa_2^T S_2 + \delta_2 - u_2 \right)$$
$$\leq \dot{V}_1 + z_1 \left( \kappa_1^T S_1 + 0.5 z_1 - u_1 \right) + z_2 \left( \kappa_2^T S_2 + 0.5 z_2 - u_2 \right)$$
$$+ 0.5 \left( \delta_1^2 + \delta_2^2 \right) \tag{10}$$

Now it is ready to design fuzzy adaptive controllers for both $u_1$ and $u_2$. In the following, three design methods are provided.

## 3.1   Method 1

Define a Lyapunov function candidate as

$$V_2 = W + 0.5(\kappa_1 - \hat{\kappa}_1)^T \Gamma_1 (\kappa_1 - \hat{\kappa}_1) + 0.5(\kappa_2 - \hat{\kappa}_2)^T \Gamma_2 (\kappa_2 - \hat{\kappa}_2) \qquad (11)$$

where $\hat{\kappa}_1$ and $\hat{\kappa}_2$ are the estimations of $\kappa_1$ and $\kappa_2$, respectively and $\Gamma_1$ and $\Gamma_2$ are positive definite matrices.

Differentiating $V_2$ with respect to time produces:

$$\dot{V}_2 = \dot{W} - (\kappa_1 - \hat{\kappa}_1)^T \Gamma_1 \dot{\hat{\kappa}}_1 - (\kappa_2 - \hat{\kappa}_2)^T \Gamma_2 \dot{\hat{\kappa}}_2 \qquad (12)$$

By substituting equation (10) into equation (12), it is possible to achieve:

$$\dot{V}_2 \leq \dot{V}_1 + \begin{bmatrix} z_1 & z_2 \end{bmatrix} \begin{bmatrix} \hat{\kappa}_1^T S_1 + 0.5 z_1 - u_1 \\ \hat{\kappa}_2^T S_2 + 0.5 z_2 - u_2 \end{bmatrix} + 0.5\delta_1^2 + 0.5\delta_2^2$$
$$- (\kappa_1 - \hat{\kappa}_1)^T (\Gamma_1 \dot{\hat{\kappa}}_1 - z_1 S_1) - (\kappa_2 - \hat{\kappa}_2)^T (\Gamma_2 \dot{\hat{\kappa}}_2 - z_2 S_2) \qquad (13)$$

The controller can now be defined as:

$$u_1 = c_3 z_1 + x_1 + \hat{\kappa}_1^T S_1 \ , \ u_2 = c_4 z_2 + x_2 + \hat{\kappa}_2^T S_2 \qquad (14)$$

and the adaptive law as

$$\dot{\hat{\kappa}}_1 = \Gamma_1^{-1} z_1 S_1 - \sigma_1 \hat{\kappa}_1 \ , \ \dot{\hat{\kappa}}_2 = \Gamma_2^{-1} z_2 S_2 - \sigma_2 \hat{\kappa}_2 \qquad (15)$$

where $c_3 > 0.5$ and $c_4 > 0.5$ represent positive constant gains.

Substituting equations (14) and (15) into (13) produces

$$\dot{V}_2 \leq -c_1 x_1^2 - c_2 x_2^2 - (c_3 - 0.5) z_1^2 - (c_4 - 0.5) z_2^2 + 0.5\delta_1^2 + 0.5\delta_2^2 \qquad (16)$$

## 3.2   Method 2

Note that $\kappa_i$ can be rewritten as $\kappa_i = \|\kappa_i\| \frac{\kappa_i}{\|\kappa_i\|} = \|\kappa_i\| \kappa_i^*$ with $\kappa_i^* = \frac{\kappa_i}{\|\kappa_i\|}$. It can be shown that $\kappa_i^{*T} \kappa_i^* = 1$. Therefore, applying Young's inequality gives

$$z_i \kappa_i^T S_i \leq \frac{z_i^2 \|\kappa_i\|^2 S_i^T S_i}{2 b_i^2} + \frac{b_i^2}{2} \kappa_i^{*T} \kappa_i^* = \frac{1}{2 b_i^2} z_i^2 \|\kappa_i\|^2 S_i^T S_i + \frac{b_i^2}{2} \qquad (17)$$

where $b_i$ is a positive constant. Set $\theta_i = \|\kappa_i\|^2$ and define a Lyapunov function candidate as

$$V_2 = W + 0.5 \Gamma_1 (\theta_1 - \hat{\theta}_1)^2 + 0.5 \Gamma_2 (\theta_2 - \hat{\theta}_2)^2 \qquad (18)$$

where $\hat{\theta}_1$ and $\hat{\theta}_2$ are the estimations of $\theta_1$ and $\theta_2$, respectively and $\Gamma_1$ and $\Gamma_2$ are positive constants.

Differentiating $V_2$ with respect to time produces:

$$\dot{V}_2 \leq \dot{W} - \Gamma_1 (\theta_1 - \hat{\theta}_1) \dot{\hat{\theta}}_1 - \Gamma_2 (\theta_2 - \hat{\theta}_2) \dot{\hat{\theta}}_2 \qquad (19)$$

By substituting equations (10) into equation (19), the following can be obtained.

$$\dot{V}_2 \le \dot{V}_1 + \begin{bmatrix} z_1 & z_2 \end{bmatrix} \begin{bmatrix} \frac{1}{2b_1^2} z_1 \theta_1 S_1^T S_1 + 0.5 z_1 - u_1 \\ \frac{1}{2b_2^2} z_2 \theta_2 S_2^T S_2 + 0.5 z_2 - u_2 \end{bmatrix} + 0.5(b_1^2 + b_2^2 + \delta_1^2 + \delta_2^2)$$

$$- \Gamma_1(\theta_1 - \hat{\theta}_1)\dot{\hat{\theta}}_1 - \Gamma_2(\theta_2 - \hat{\theta}_2)\dot{\hat{\theta}}_2$$

$$\le \dot{V}_1 + \begin{bmatrix} z_1 & z_2 \end{bmatrix} \begin{bmatrix} \frac{1}{2b_1^2} z_1 \hat{\theta}_1 S_1^T S_1 + 0.5 z_1 - u_1 \\ \frac{1}{2b_2^2} z_2 \hat{\theta}_2 S_2^T S_2 + 0.5 z_2 - u_2 \end{bmatrix} + 0.5(b_1^2 + b_2^2 + \delta_1^2 + \delta_2^2)$$

$$- (\theta_1 - \hat{\theta}_1)(\Gamma_1 \dot{\hat{\theta}}_1 - \frac{1}{2b_1^2} z_1^2 S_1^T S_1) - (\theta_2 - \hat{\theta}_2)(\Gamma_2 \dot{\hat{\theta}}_2 - \frac{1}{2b_2^2} z_2^2 S_2^T S_2) \quad (20)$$

The controller can now be defined as:

$$u_1 = (c_3 + \frac{1}{2b_1^2} \hat{\theta}_1 S_1^T S_1) z_1 + x_1 \; , \; u_2 = (c_4 + \frac{1}{2b_2^2} \hat{\theta}_2 S_2^T S_2) z_2 + x_2 \quad (21)$$

and the adaptive law as

$$\dot{\hat{\kappa}}_1 = \Gamma_1^{-1} \frac{1}{2b_1^2} z_1^2 S_1^T S_1 - \sigma_1 \hat{\kappa}_1 \; , \; \dot{\hat{\kappa}}_2 = \Gamma_2^{-1} \frac{1}{2b_2^2} z_2^2 S_2^T S_2 - \sigma_2 \hat{\kappa}_2 \quad (22)$$

where $c_3 > 0.5$ and $c_4 > 0.5$ represent positive constant gains.

Therefore by substituting equation (21) and (22) into equation (20), the final result will be

$$\dot{V}_2 \le -c_1 x_1^2 - c_2 x_2^2 - (c_3 - 0.5) z_1^2 - (c_4 - 0.5) z_2^2 + 0.5(b_1^2 + b_2^2 + \delta_1^2 + \delta_2^2) \quad (23)$$

## 3.3  Method 3

It follows from Young's inequality and $\|S_i\| \le 1$ that

$$z_i \kappa_i^T S_i \le \frac{1}{2b_i^2} z_i^2 \|\kappa_i\|^2 + 0.5 b_i^2 \|S_i\|^2 \le \frac{1}{2b_i^2} z_i^2 \theta_i + 0.5 b_i^2 \quad (24)$$

where $b_i$ is a positive constant and $\theta_i = \|\kappa_i\|^2$. Define a Lyapunov function candidate as

$$V_2 = W + 0.5\Gamma_1(\theta_1 - \hat{\theta}_1)^2 + 0.5\Gamma_2(\theta_2 - \hat{\theta}_2)^2 \quad (25)$$

where $\hat{\theta}_1$ and $\hat{\theta}_2$ are the estimations of $\theta_1$ and $\theta_2$, respectively and $\Gamma_1$ and $\Gamma_2$ are positive constants.

Differentiating $V_2$ with respect to time, it follows from (10) that

$$\dot{V}_2 \le \dot{V}_1 + \begin{bmatrix} z_1 & z_2 \end{bmatrix} \begin{bmatrix} \frac{1}{2b_1^2} z_1 \theta_1 + 0.5 z_1 - u_1 \\ \frac{1}{2b_2^2} z_2 \theta_2 + 0.5 z_2 - u_2 \end{bmatrix} + 0.5(b_1^2 + b_2^2 + \delta_1^2 + \delta_2^2)$$

$$- \dot{\hat{\theta}}_1^T \Gamma_1 \left( \theta_1 - \hat{\theta}_1 \right) - \dot{\hat{\theta}}_2^T \Gamma_2 \left( \theta_2 - \hat{\theta}_2 \right)$$

$$\le \dot{V}_1 + \begin{bmatrix} z_1 & z_2 \end{bmatrix} \begin{bmatrix} \frac{1}{2b_1^2} z_1 \hat{\theta}_1 + 0.5 z_1 - u_1 \\ \frac{1}{2b_2^2} z_2 \hat{\theta}_2 + 0.5 z_2 - u_2 \end{bmatrix} + 0.5(b_1^2 + b_2^2 + \delta_1^2 + \delta_2^2)$$

$$+ \left( \frac{1}{2b_1^2} z_1^2 - \dot{\hat{\theta}}_1^T \Gamma_1 \right) \left( \theta_1 - \hat{\theta}_1 \right) + \left( \frac{1}{2b_2^2} z_2^2 - \dot{\hat{\theta}}_2^T \Gamma_2 \right) \left( \theta_2 - \hat{\theta}_2 \right) \quad (26)$$

The controller can now be defined as:

$$u_1 = (c_3 + \frac{1}{2b_1^2}\hat{\theta}_1)z_1 + x_1 \ , \ u_2 = (c_4 + \frac{1}{2b_2^2}\hat{\theta}_2)z_2 + x_2 \tag{27}$$

and the adaptive law as

$$\dot{\hat{\kappa}}_1 = \Gamma_1^{-1}\frac{1}{2b_1^2}z_1^2 - \sigma_1\hat{\kappa}_1 \ , \ \dot{\hat{\kappa}}_2 = \Gamma_2^{-1}\frac{1}{2b_2^2}z_2^2 - \sigma_2\hat{\kappa}_2 \tag{28}$$

where $c_3 > 0.5$ and $c_4 > 0.5$ represent positive constant gains.

Therefore by substituting equation (27) and (28) into equation (26), it is obtained that

$$\dot{V}_2 \le -c_1 x_1^2 - c_2 x_2^2 - (c_3 - 0.5)z_1^2 - (c_4 - 0.5)z_2^2 + 0.5(b_1^2 + b_2^2 + \delta_1^2 + \delta_2^2)(29)$$

In summary, it can be proved that $x_1, x_2, z_1, z_2, \kappa_1 - \hat{\kappa}_1, \kappa_2 - \hat{\kappa}_2$ are bounded, so are $x_1, x_2, x_3, x_4$ by using (16), (23), and (29) with the assumption $0 \le \lambda_m I \le D(q') \le \lambda_M I$, which is a standard assumption for robot dynamics.

## 4　Experimental Results

A two-degree-of freedom parallel robot was made for testing the proposed fuzzy adaptive backstepping controllers. The parallel robot is composed of four links. Two links are driven by two DC motors mounted on the base while the other two are not actuated and tied to an end-effector. The two motors are controlled by a DSP circuit board through a motor driver board. The position feedback signals from the two actuated links are fed back to a DSP circuit board using potentiometers. The controllers are implemented on a PC computer through a RS232 serial port with a Baud rate of 115200. The feedback signals collected by the DSP board are sent to the PC computer through the RS232 serial port and filtered with a second-order Butterworth low-pass filter of 10 Hz cutoff frequency. The derivatives of the angle feedback are calculated using the numerical differentiation, together with a 15 Hz second-order Butterworth filter. Both filtered angle feedback signals and their derivatives are used to generate torques using the proposed algorithms. The torques are send back to the DSP board through the RS232 serial port after converted to duty-ratios. The DSP board outputs the duty-ratios to control the DC motors. The proposed controllers were tested with a sample time of 0.005s. The desired trajectory is a circle given by $x = 0.03\sin(\pi t)$ and $y = 0.15a_1 - 0.03\cos(\pi t)$ where $x$ and $y$ are the Cartesian coordinates of the end-effector, as shown in Figure 1. $a_i = 0.22688m$ and $l_i = 0.5a_i$, $i = 1, 2, 3, 4$. $m_1 = 0.14719$kg, $m_2 = 0.14392$kg, $m_1 = 0.12555$kg, $m_4 = 0.14413$kg. $I_1 = 0.06679$kg·m$^2$, $I_2 = 0.06531$kg·m$^2$, $I_1 = 0.056795$kg·m$^2$, $I_4 = 0.06540$kg·m$^2$

The test was run for 50 cycles and the test results on the root-mean-square tracking errors are plotted in Fig. 2. It can be observed from the figure that the method 1 performs better than the methods 2 and 3 with loads because both methods 2 and 3 are more conservative than the first method due to the simplifications involved in the methods 2 and 3. However, the computation time for method 3 is less then 0.02 ms, which is almost ten times shorter than the first two methods.

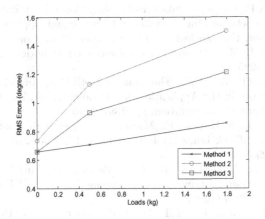

**Fig. 2.** Experimental Results

## 5   Conclusion

Three fuzzy adaptive backstepping controllers have been developed for tracking control of a two degree of freedom parallel robot using fuzzy logic theory and backstepping design technique. The proposed controllers are able to handle parameter uncertainties and guarantee that the tracking errors are bounded. The first fuzzy adaptive controller has many parameters to be updated on-line, which requires longest computation time, on the other hand, the second and third have only two parameters which have to be learned on-line. The difference between the second and third controllers is that the third controller does not depend on the fuzzy logic approximators, so it requires least computation time among three controllers. The experiments have been conducted to compare the three controllers. The test results have shown that all the controllers perform similarly when there was no additional payload. However, when an additional payload was added to the robot, the first controller was able to achieve the smaller tracking errors than the other controllers.

## References

1. Ghorbel, F., Chetelat, O., Gunawardana, R., Longchamp, R.: Modeling and Set Point Control of Closed-Chain Mechanisms: Theory and Experiment. IEEE Trans. on Control Systems Technology, 801–815 (2000)
2. Paccot, F., Andreff, N., Martinet, P., Khalil, W.: Vision-Based Computed Torque Control for Parallel Robots. In: IEEE Annual Conference on Industrial Electronics, pp. 3851–3856 (2006)

3. Fasse, E.D., Gosselin, C.M.: Spatio-Geometric Impedance Control of Gough–Stewart Platforms. IEEE Trans. on Robotics and Automation 15, 281–288 (1999)
4. Lin, H.M., McInroy, J.E.: Adaptive Sinusoidal Disturbance Cancellation for Precise Pointing of Stewart Platforms. IEEE Trans. on Control System Technology 11, 267–272 (2003)
5. Wang, L., Liu, X.P., Liu, K.F.: Adaptive Tracking Control of Parallel Robot: Back-stepping and PD Schemes. Int. J. of Control Theory and Applications 1 (2009)
6. Begon, P., Pierrot, F., Dauchez, P.: Fuzzy Sliding Mode Control of a Fast Parallel Robot. In: IEEE International Conference on Robotics and Automation, pp. 1178–1183 (1995)
7. Gao, G.Q., Yan, Q., Wu, Y.Z.: The Control Method of Adaptive Backstepping and Neural Network in the Application of a Parallel Robot. In: 6th International Conference on Natural Computation, pp. 1397–1400
8. Kanellakopoulos, I., Kokotovic, P., Morse, A.S.: Systematic Design of Adaptive Controllers for Feedback Linearizable Systems. IEEE Trans. on Automatic Control 36, 1241–1253 (1991)
9. Hsu, F.Y., Fu, L.C.: A Novel Adaptive Fuzzy Variable Structure Control for a Class of Nonlinear Uncertain Systems via Backstepping. In: 37th IEEE on Decision and Control, pp. 2228–2233 (1998)
10. Wang, W.Y., Chan, M.L., Lee, T.T., Liu, C.H.: Adaptive Fuzzy Control for Strict-Feedback Canonical Nonlinear Systems with H Tracking Performance. IEEE Trans. on Systems, Man, and Cybernetics - Par B: Cybernetics 30, 878–885 (2000)
11. Yang, Y.S., Feng, G., Ren, J.S.: A Combined Backstepping and Small-Gain Approach to Robust Adaptive Fuzzy Control for Strict-Feedback Nonlinear Systems. IEEE Trans. on Systems, Man, and Cybernetics - Part A: Systems and Humans 34 (2004)
12. Chen, B., Liu, X.P., Tong, S.C.: Adaptive Fuzzy Output Tracking Control of MIMO Nonlinear Uncertain Systems. IEEE Trans. on Fuzzy Systems 15, 287–300 (2007)
13. Chen, B., Liu, X.P., Liu, K.L., Lin, C.: Fuzzy-Approximation-Based Adaptive Control of Strict-Feedback Nonlinear Systems With Time Delays. IEEE Trans. on Fuzzy Systems 18, 883–892 (2010)
14. Liu, Y.J., Wang, W., Tong, S.C., Liu, Y.-S.: Robust Adaptive Tracking Control for Nonlinear Systems Based on Bounds of Fuzzy Approximation Parameters. IEEE Trans. on Systems, Man, and Cybernetics - Part A: Systems and Humans 40, 170–184 (2010)
15. Wang, L.X., Mendel, J.M.: Fuzzy Basis Functions, Universal Approximation and Orthogonal, Least Squares Learning. IEEE Trans. on Neural Networks 3, 807–814 (1992)
16. Wang, L.X.: Stable Adaptive Fuzzy Control of Nonlinear Systems. IEEE Trans. on Fuzzy Systems 1, 146–155 (1993)

# Non-smooth Observer for Mechanical Systems Based on Sandwich Model with Backlash

Zupeng Zhou[1], Yonghong Tan[2,*], Ruili Dong[2], and Hong He[2]

[1] School of Electronic Engineering, Xidian University,
Xi'an Shanxi 710071, China
[2] College of Information, Mechanical and Electrical Engineering,
Shanghai Normal University, Shanghai 200234, China
tany@shnu.edu.cn

**Abstract.** In this paper, a novel non-smooth observer is proposed to handle the state estimation of mechanical transmission systems described by sandwich model with backlash. Based on the characteristic of the system, a non-smooth state-space function is constructed in terms of the separation principle. Then, a non-smooth observer is developed based on the obtained non-smooth state-space model. The observer can switch among the different operating zones automatically in terms of the variation of operation conditions. Finally, the simulation results are presented.

**Keywords:** Non-smooth observer, backlash, sandwich model, state estimation, mechanical systems.

## 1 Introduction

It is known that backlash usually exists in mechanical transmission systems such as gearbox, hydraulic valves and ball-screw et al. For example, in a typical mechanical transmission system, the load is usually driven by a gearbox. Then, the gearbox is driven by a motor. In this system, the load and motor can be described by linear dynamic models, respectively. The gearbox, on the other hand, can be considered as a backlash. According to the physical architecture of the mentioned mechanical transmission system, we note that the backlash is embedded between two linear dynamic subsystems. Thus, this system can be described by a so-called sandwich system with backlash [1-3]. In practical engineering, the input and output of gearbox are considered as the internal variables, which are usually not measurable directly. Therefore, it is necessary to estimate the states of those internal variables for control strategy design or for fault diagnosis [4-5]. Therefore, construction of an observer for such systems in order to estimate the states accurately is one of the important issues.

Until today, there have been many literatures concerning the design of observers for nonlinear systems. For instance, in [6], an adaptive robust observer is constructed

---

* Corresponding author.

C.-Y. Su, S. Rakheja, H. Liu (Eds.): ICIRA 2012, Part I, LNAI 7506, pp. 611–621, 2012.
© Springer-Verlag Berlin Heidelberg 2012

for estimating the states of the nonlinear system with delay and uncertainty. In [7], by solving the matrix inequalities, the switch observer is developed to estimate the states of mechanical systems described Weiner model with hysteresis. [8] has constructed a high gain observer for the estimation of the states as well as dead zone simultaneously based on the Hammerstein model with dead zone. Moreover, [9] employed a two-layer neural network to construct the observer to estimate the states of a complex and nonlinear system. However, based on the authors' knowledge, almost few published papers have mentioned the construction of observers for sandwich systems with backlash. It is noted that the sandwich systems with backlash usually have the structure that the backlash in embedded between the input linear subsystem and the output linear subsystem. The interval variables i.e., the input and output of the backlash is usually un-measurable. Moreover, the embedded backlash is a non-smooth function with multi-valued mapping. Therefore, it is a much complicated system than traditional ones. Clearly, construction of a non-smooth observer for sandwich system with backlash to estimate its states is an important and meaningful work for the optimal control and fault diagnosis research of the mechanical systems involved with backlash.

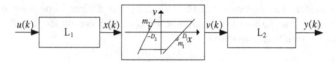

**Fig. 1.** The structure of the sandwich model with backlash

## 2    Sandwich Model with Backlash

The architecture of sandwich model with backlash is illustrated in Fig.1, where $u(k)$ and $y(k)$ are the measurable input and output of the system, respectively. $x(k)$ and $v(k)$ are the internal variables which cannot be measured directly. $L_1$ is the input linear subsystem and $L_2$ is the output linear subsystem. On the other hand, the characteristic of the backlash is embedded between the two linear blocks, where $D_1$ and $D_2$ are the width of backlash ($0 < D_1 < \infty$ and $0 < D_1 < \infty$), respectively. Moreover, the slopes of the linear zones of the backlash are defined as $m_1$ and $m_2$ ($0 < m_1 < \infty$ and $0 < m_2 < \infty$), individually.

For the convenience of constructing the observer, a state space model based on the model proposed in [2] is developed. In the state space model, the in linear subsystem $L_1$ can be described by

$$x_1(k+1) = A_{11}x_1(k) + B_{11}u(k) \tag{1}$$

$$y_1(k) = C_1x_1(k) \tag{2}$$

and the output linear subsystem $L_2$ can be described by:

$$x_2(k+1) = A_{22}x_2(k) + B_{22}v(k) \tag{3}$$

$$y_2(k) = C_2x_2(k) \tag{4}$$

where $x_i \in R^{n_i \times 1}$, $A_{ii} \in R^{n_i \times n_i}$, $B_{ii} \in R^{n_i \times 1}$, $y_i \in R^{1 \times 1}$, $C_i \in R^{1 \times n_i}$, $u \in R^{1 \times 1}$, $v \in R^{1 \times 1}$, $i = 1,2$. $x_{1i}$ and $x_{2i}$ represent the *ith* state variable of $L_1$ and $L_2$ respectively. $A_i \in R^{n_i \times n_i}$ is the state transition matrix, $B_i \in R^{n_i \times 1}$ is the input matrix, $y_i \in R^{1 \times 1}$ is the output variable, $n_i$ represents the dimension of the *ith* linear subsystem, $u \in R^{1 \times 1}$ is the input variable, $x \in R^{1 \times 1}$ and $v \in R^{1 \times 1}$ are the input and output variables of the backlash. Without loss of generality, in the state space function for $L_1$, set $x_{1n_1}(k) = x(k)$, and for $L_2$, set $x_{2n_2}(k) = y(k)$. Based on [2] and [10], the following backlash model can be obtained:

Define $m(k)$ and $v_1(k)$, respectively, as the imposed variables, i.e.,

$$m(k) = m_1 + (m_2 - m_1)g(k) \tag{5}$$

$$v_1(k) = m(k)(x(k) - D_1g_1(k) + D_2g_2(k)) \tag{6}$$

where, $\Delta x(k) = x(k) - x(k-1)$, and the switch functions are defined as :

$$g(k) = \begin{cases} 0, & \Delta x \geq 0 \\ 1, & \Delta x < 0 \end{cases}, \quad g_1(k) = \begin{cases} 1, & x(k) > \dfrac{v(k-1)}{m_1} + D_1 \,\&\, \Delta x(k) > 0 \\ 0, & \text{else} \end{cases},$$

and $g_2(k) = \begin{cases} 1, & x(k) < \dfrac{v(k-1)}{m_2} - D_2 \,\&\, \Delta x(k) < 0 \\ 0, & \text{else} \end{cases}$.

Considering the characteristics of input and output relationship of backlash yields:

$$\begin{aligned} v(k) &= v_1(k) + [v(k-1) - v_1(k)]g_3(k) \\ &= (1 - g_3(k))v_1(k) + g_3(k)v(k-1) \end{aligned} \tag{7}$$

where $g_3(k) = \begin{cases} 1, & g_1(k)+g_2(k)=0 \\ 0, & g_1(k)+g_2(k)=1 \end{cases}$ is the switch function utilized to separate

the linear zones from the memory zone. According to (7) , when $g_3(k)=0$, the system operates in linear zone and $\overset{\sqcup}{v}(k) = v_1(k)$ while $g_3(k)=1$, the system operates in the memory and $\overset{\sqcup}{v}(k) = v_1(k) - v_1(k) = 0$.

By rearranging the above-stated formulae, we obtain the state space description of the sandwich model with backlash, i.e.

$$\begin{bmatrix} \mathbf{x}_1(k+1) \\ \mathbf{x}_2(k+1) \end{bmatrix} = \begin{bmatrix} A_{11} & \mathbf{0} \\ A_{21i} & A_{22} \end{bmatrix} \begin{bmatrix} \mathbf{x}_1(k) \\ \mathbf{x}_2(k) \end{bmatrix} + \begin{bmatrix} B_{11} \\ \mathbf{0} \end{bmatrix} u(k) + \begin{bmatrix} \mathbf{0} \\ \theta_{22i} \end{bmatrix} \tag{8}$$

$$\mathbf{y}(k) = C\mathbf{x}(k)$$

The three operating zones are defined as :

$$i = \begin{cases} 1, & x_{1n_1}(k) > \dfrac{v(k-1)}{m_1} + D_1 \,\&\Delta x_{1n_1}(k) > 0 \\ 2, & \text{else} \\ 3, & x_{1n_1}(k) < \dfrac{v(k-1)}{m_2} - D_2 \,\&\Delta x_{1n_1}(k) < 0 \end{cases}$$

where, $A_{21i} = \begin{bmatrix} \beta_1 & \beta_{2i} \end{bmatrix}$, $\beta_1 = \mathbf{0} \in R^{n_2 \times (n_2-1)}$,

$$\beta_{2i} = \begin{cases} B_{22}m_1(k), & i=1 \\ \mathbf{0}, & i=2 \\ B_{22}m_2(k), & i=3 \end{cases}, \beta_{2i} \in R^{n_2 \times 1},$$

$$\theta_{22i} = \begin{cases} -B_{22}m_1(k)D_1, i=1 \\ B_{22}m(k)v(k-1), i=2, \quad \theta_{22i} \in R^{n_2 \times 1} \text{ .and} \\ B_{22}m_2(k)D_2, i=3 \end{cases}$$

$$C = [C_{11} \quad C_{22}],$$

where $C_{11} = [0,0,...,0] = \mathbf{0} \in R^{1 \times n_1}$, $C_{22} = [0,0,...,1] \in R^{1 \times n_2}$ and

$$\mathbf{x}(k) = \begin{bmatrix} x_1(k) \\ x_2(k) \end{bmatrix} \in R^{(n_1+n_2)\times 1} \ . \ \text{Set} \ \ A_i = \begin{bmatrix} A_{11} & 0 \\ A_{21i} & A_{22} \end{bmatrix}, \quad B = \begin{bmatrix} B_{11} \\ 0 \end{bmatrix},$$

$$\mathbf{\eta}_i = \begin{bmatrix} 0 \\ \theta_{22i} \end{bmatrix}, \quad (\, i = 1,2,3). \ \text{Then,} \ \ (8) \ \text{can be re-written as:}$$

$$\mathbf{x}(k+1) = A_i \mathbf{x}(k) + Bu(k) + \mathbf{\eta}_i, \ i=1,2,3 \tag{9}$$

where $A_i$ represents the transition matrix in different operating zones, $B$ is the input matrix, and $\mathbf{\eta}_i$ is the switch vector.

## 3    Nonsmooth Observer of Sandwich Systems with Backlash

Note that only the input $u(k)$ and output $y(k)$ of the system are measurable. Then, the sandwich system with backlash is only completely observable in the linear operating zone, i.e. as $j=1,3$, the rank of the observable matrix $N = \begin{bmatrix} C, CA_j, ..., CA_j^{n_1+n_2-1} \end{bmatrix}^T$ equals $n_1+n_2$. In the memory zone, the rank of the observable matrix would be $n_2$. Thus, only the output linear subsystem $L_2$ is completely observable but the input linear subsystem $L_1$ is not observable. Therefore, the whole system is not completely observable. As the observer design depends on both traditional method of feedback gain matrix design and the Lyapunov's method, it requires the system to be completely observable. In this case, the two methods mentioned-above will not be available to the sandwich system with backlash .

Based on (9), the Luenberger's observer is proposed for the sandwich system with backlash:

$$\hat{\mathbf{x}}(k+1) = A_j \hat{\mathbf{x}}(k) + Bu(k) + \hat{\mathbf{\eta}}_j + K(\mathbf{y}(k) - \hat{\mathbf{y}}(k)), \quad (j=1,2,3) \tag{10}$$

$$\hat{\mathbf{y}}(k) = C\hat{\mathbf{x}}(k)$$

where, $\hat{\mathbf{\eta}}_j = \begin{bmatrix} 0 \\ \hat{\theta}_{22j} \end{bmatrix}$, $\hat{\theta}_{22j} = \begin{cases} -B_{22}m_1(k)D_1, j=1 \\ B_{22}m(k)\hat{v}(k-1), j=2 \\ B_{22}m_2(k)D_2, j=3 \end{cases}$, and feedback gain matrix

$K = \begin{bmatrix} K_1 \\ K_2 \end{bmatrix}, K_1 \in R^{n_1\times 1}, K_2 \in R^{n_2\times 1}$ .

It is worth noticing that because only $u(k)$ and $y(k)$ of the sandwich system with backlash is measurable and the state variables $x_{1n_1}$, $\Delta x_{1n_1}$ and $v$ which determine the operating zone is not measurable. Thus, the observer can only be switched according to the estimates of $\hat{x}_{1n_1}$, $\Delta \hat{x}_{1n_1}$, and $\hat{v}$. However, the difference between the initial states values of the observer and the initial values of the real system, at the starting stage, may lead to a wrong estimation of the operating zone so as to result in large estimation error of the states. Thus, the following state difference based observer is constructed, i.e.

$$\mathbf{e}(k+1) = F_g \mathbf{e}(k) + \Delta A_{sg} \mathbf{x}(k) + \Delta \eta_{sg}, \tag{11}$$

where $F_g = (A_{g(k)} - KC)$, $\Delta A_{sg} = A_{s(k)} - A_{g(k)}$, and $\Delta \eta_{sg} = \eta_{s(k)} - \hat{\eta}_{g(k)}$, as well as $g(k) \in \{1,2,3\}$ and $s(k) \in \{1,2,3\}$ represent the number of operating zones of the observer and the number of operating zones of the system, respectively. For instance, if the observer works in zone 1 but the system operates 1n zone 2, then $g(k) = 1$ and $s(k) = 2$. (11) can be further represented by

$$\begin{bmatrix} \mathbf{e}_1(k+1) \\ \mathbf{e}_2(k+1) \end{bmatrix} = \begin{bmatrix} A_{11} & -K_1 C_{22} \\ & \\ A_{21g(k)} & A_{22} - K_2 C_{22} \end{bmatrix} \begin{bmatrix} \mathbf{e}_1(k) \\ \mathbf{e}_2(k) \end{bmatrix} + \begin{bmatrix} 0 & 0 \\ \Delta A_{21sg} & 0 \end{bmatrix} \begin{bmatrix} \mathbf{x}_1(k) \\ \mathbf{x}_2(k) \end{bmatrix}$$
$$+ \begin{bmatrix} 0 \\ \Delta \theta_{22sg} \end{bmatrix}$$

where $\Delta A_{21sg} = A_{21s(k)} - A_{21g(k)}$, $\Delta \theta_{22sg} = \theta_{22s(k)} - \hat{\theta}_{22g(k)}$, and $\mathbf{e}(k) = \mathbf{x}(k) - \hat{\mathbf{x}}(k)$, moreover, $\hat{\mathbf{x}}(k)$ is the estimate of the state, $\hat{\mathbf{y}}(k)$ is the estimate of the output, and $\mathbf{e}(k)$ is the state estimation error.

It can be proved that if sub-state $\mathbf{x}_1$ is bounded, i.e., $\forall k, \|\mathbf{x}_1(k)\|_m \leq x_b$ where $x_b \geq 0$ is the given constant, and the initial estimation error of the observer is also bounded, i.e. $\|\mathbf{e}_1(1)\|_m \leq e_b$, $e_b \geq 0$ is the given constant while all the eigenvalues of both $A_{11}$ and $(A_{22} - K_2 C_{22})$ are in the unit circle, the state estimation error of the observer will eventually converge to zero.

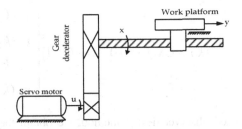

**Fig. 2.** The mechanical transmission system

# 4    Simulation

Suppose that a mechanical transmission system servomotor, gearbox, screw and work platform is shown in Fig. 2. In this system, the servomotor is used to drive a gearbox connected with a mechanical work platform through a screw. In this system, u is the servomotor rotational angle, x is the angle of the gearbox, and y is the displacement of the work platform. The work platform can be considered as smoothly linear dynamic subsystems. However, the gearbox and screw in this system is a typical backlash-like hysteresis due to the tear and wear of the gear teeth. It is assumed that this transmission system can be desceibed by the following state space sandwich model with backlash, i.e.

The servomotor is described by :

$$\begin{bmatrix} x_{11}(k+1) \\ x_{12}(k+1) \end{bmatrix} = \begin{bmatrix} 0.8 & 0 \\ 0.01 & 0.45 \end{bmatrix} \begin{bmatrix} x_{11}(k) \\ x_{12}(k) \end{bmatrix} + \begin{bmatrix} 0.004107 \\ 0 \end{bmatrix} u(k),$$

the gearbox is represented as :

$$v(k) = \begin{cases} x_{12}(k) - 0.04, & x_{12}(k) > v(k-1) + 0.04 \& \Delta x_{12}(k) > 0 \\ v(k-1), & \text{else} \\ x_{12}(k) + 0.04, & x_{12}(k) < v(k-1) - 0.04 \& \Delta x_{12}(k) < 0 \end{cases},$$

where, $m_1 = m_2 = 1, D_1 = D_2 = 0.04$; and the work platform is denoted as

$$\begin{bmatrix} x_{21}(k+1) \\ x_{22}(k+1) \end{bmatrix} = \begin{bmatrix} 0.8 & 0 \\ 0.2 & 0.9 \end{bmatrix} \begin{bmatrix} x_{21}(k) \\ x_{22}(k) \end{bmatrix} + \begin{bmatrix} 0.25 \\ 0 \end{bmatrix} v(k);$$

$$y(k) = C\mathbf{x}(k) = \begin{bmatrix} 0 & 0 & 0 & 1 \end{bmatrix} \begin{bmatrix} x_{11}(k) \\ x_{12}(k) \\ x_{21}(k) \\ x_{22}(k) \end{bmatrix}.$$

Based on the proposed observer design method, we obtain the following sandwich model in state space, i.e.

$$\mathbf{x}(k+1) = \begin{cases} A_1\mathbf{x}(k) + Bu(k) + \boldsymbol{\eta}_1(k), & x_{12}(k) > 0.01 \\ A_2\mathbf{x}(k) + Bu(k) + \boldsymbol{\eta}_2(k), & -0.01 \le x_{12}(k) \le 0.01 \; ; \\ A_3\mathbf{x}(k) + Bu(k) + \boldsymbol{\eta}_3(k), & x_{12}(k) < -0.01 \end{cases}$$

$$y(k) = C\mathbf{x}(k) = \begin{bmatrix} 0 & 0 & 0 & 1 \end{bmatrix}\mathbf{x}(k).$$

where, $\mathbf{x}(k) = \begin{bmatrix} x_{11} & x_{12} & x_{21} & x_{22} \end{bmatrix}^T$,

$$A_1 = A_3 = \begin{bmatrix} 0.8 & 0 & 0 & 0 \\ 0.01 & 0.45 & 0 & 0 \\ 0 & 0.25 & 0.8 & 0 \\ 0 & 0 & 0.2 & 0.9 \end{bmatrix}, A_2 = \begin{bmatrix} 0.8 & 0 & 0 & 0 \\ 0.01 & 0.45 & 0 & 0 \\ 0 & 0 & 0.8 & 0 \\ 0 & 0 & 0.2 & 0.9 \end{bmatrix}$$

$$B = \begin{bmatrix} 0.004107 \\ 0 \\ 0 \\ 0 \end{bmatrix} \quad \eta_1 = \begin{bmatrix} 0 \\ 0 \\ -0.01 \\ 0 \end{bmatrix}, \eta_2 = \begin{bmatrix} 0 \\ 0 \\ 0.25v(k-1) \\ 0 \end{bmatrix}, \eta_3 = \begin{bmatrix} 0 \\ 0 \\ 0.01 \\ 0 \end{bmatrix} \quad , \quad \text{and}$$

$C = \begin{bmatrix} 0 & 0 & 0 & 1 \end{bmatrix}$. Moreover, the decomposition of the corresponding transition, input and output matrixes are $A_{11} = \begin{bmatrix} 0.8 & 0 \\ 0.01 & 0.45 \end{bmatrix}, A_{22} = \begin{bmatrix} 0.8 & 0 \\ 0.2 & 0.9 \end{bmatrix},$

$B_{11} = \begin{bmatrix} 0.004107 \\ 0 \end{bmatrix}, C_{11} = \begin{bmatrix} 0 & 0 \end{bmatrix}$, and $C_{22} = \begin{bmatrix} 0 & 1 \end{bmatrix}$.

Note that the eigenvalues of $A_{11}$ are $\begin{bmatrix} 0.8 & 0.45 \end{bmatrix}$ which are in the unit circle and when we choose the feedback gain matrix as $K = \begin{bmatrix} 0 & 0 & 0.1 & 0.1 \end{bmatrix}^T$, then the eigenvalues of $(A_{22} - K_2C_{22})$ are [0.8000+0.1414i, 0.8000-0.1414i] which are also in the unit circle, therefore, the estimation error of the observer will convergence to zero eventually.

For comparison, the conventional observer is also used for state estimation of this system. In this case, the effect of the backlash is neglected in the observer design. Thus, the sandwich system will be considered as a linear system which composed of two linear subsystems with a proportion gain. The corresponding conventional observer is of the form:

$$\hat{\mathbf{x}}(k+1) = A\hat{\mathbf{x}}(k) + Bu(k) + K_l(y(k) - \hat{y}(k))$$

where the feedback gain matrix is chosen as $K_l = [0\,0\,0.1\,0.1]^T$.

Set the initial states of the observer as $\hat{\mathbf{x}}(0) = [5, 0.2, 0.5, 0.02]^T$ and the initial values of the real states as $\mathbf{x}(0) = [0,0,0,0]^T$.

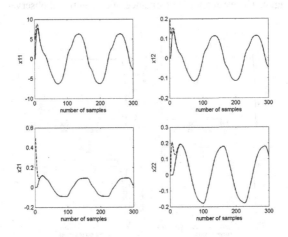

**Fig. 3.** The estimate performance of the non-smooth observer

Fig.3 shows the estimate results of the proposed non-smooth observer, in which the solid line and the dash line represent the real data and the estimated state values of the non-smooth observer, respectively. It is clearly showed that the non-smooth observer can track the real states of the sandwich system with backlash accurately.

On the other hand, Fig. 4 illustrates the estimate results of the conventional observer. In Fig.3, the solid line and the dash line represent the real data and the estimated states of the conventional observer, respectively. It is clearly showed that the conventional observer can not track the real states of the system accurately especially.

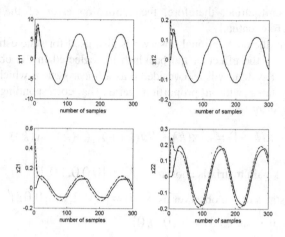

**Fig. 4.** The estimation performance of conventional observer

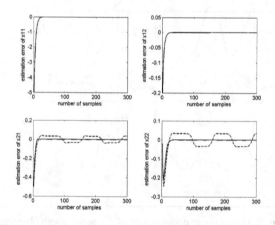

**Fig. 5.** Estimation error compassion of two kinds of observer

Moreover, Fig. 5 presents the comparison of estimate errors between the proposed method and the conventional approach. Obviously, the estimate errors of the conventional observer for the states $x_{21}$ and $x_{22}$ are much larger than the others due to the effect of backlash inherent in the gearbox embedded between the motor and work platform. Those results also show that the proposed non-smooth observer has achieved much better performance than the conventional one.

## 5    Conclusion

In this paper a non-smooth observer is proposed for the state estimation of mechanical systems described by sandwich models with backlash. A non-smooth state-space model is constructed with the switch functions to mimic the property of backlash. Then, the non-smooth observer is designed based on the obtained non-smooth state space model.

The simulation results show that the proposed non-smooth observer can track the states of the transmission system accurately. It is rather promising to be applied to engineering practice.

**Acknowledgment.** This work is partially supported by the Leading Academic Discipline Project of Shanghai Normal University (Grant Nos.:DZL811& DRL904), the Innovation Program of Shanghai Municipal Education Commission (Grant No. 11YZ92), the National Science Foundation of China (NSFC Grant Nos.:60971004 and 61171088), the Natural Science Foundation of Shanghai (Grant No.: 09ZR1423400) and the Science and Technology Commission of Shanghai Municipality (Grants No.: 09220503000 and 10JC1412200).

# References

1. Xie, Y., Tan, Y., Dong, R.: Identification of Sandwich Systems with Backlash With Hybrid Inputs. In: 8th IEEE International Conference on Control and Automation, pp. 1999–2004. IEEE Press, New York (2010)
2. Dong, R., Tan, Q., Tan, Y.: Recursive identification algorithm for dynamic systems with output backlash and its convergence. Int. J. of Applied Mathematics and Computer Science 19(4), 631–638 (2009)
3. Dong, R., Tan, Y., Chen, H.: Recursive identification for dynamic systems with backlash. Asian Journal of Control 12(1), 26–38 (2010)
4. Caccavale, F., Cilibrizzi, P., Pierri, F., Villani, L.: Actuator fault diagnosis for robot manipulators with uncertain model. Control Engineering Practice 17, 146–157 (2010)
5. Caccavale, F., Pierri, F., Villani, L.: Adaptive Observer for fault diagnosis in nonlinear discrete-time systems. ASME Journal of Dynamic System, Measurement, and Control 130, 1–9 (2008)
6. Wu, H.: Adaptive Robust State Observers for a Class of Uncertain Nonlinear Dynamical Systems With Delayed State Perturbations. IEEE Transactions on Automatic Control 54(6), 1407–1412 (2002)
7. Nouailletas, R., Koenig, D., Mendes, E.: LMI design of a switched observer with model uncertainty: Application to a hysteresis mechanical system. In: The 46th IEEE Conference on Decision and Control, pp. 6298–6303. IEEE Press, New York (2007)
8. Ibrir, S.: Simultaneous state and dead-zone parameter estimation using high-gain observers. In: 2009 IEEE International Conference on Systems, Man, and Cybernetics, pp. 311–316. IEEE Press, New York (2009)
9. Shaik, F.A., Purwar, S.: A nonlinear state observer design for 2 – DOF twin rotor system using neural networks. In: 2009 International Conference on Advances in Computing, Control, and Telecnmmunication Technologies, pp. 15–19. IEEE Press, New York (2009)

# Robust Proportional-Derivative Control
# of a Three-Axis Milling Machine Tool

F. Beltrán-Carbajal[1], E. Chavez-Conde[2], S. Villanueva[1], Z. Damián[1],
E. Montes[1], P. Puerta, R. Pérez, and G. Alvarez

[1] Universidad Autónoma Metropolitana, Unidad Azcapotzalco,
Av. San Pablo No. 180, Col. Reynosa Tamaulipas,
C.P. 02200 México, D.F., México
fbeltran@correo.azc.uam.mx
[2] Universidad del Papaloapan, Campus Loma Bonita,
Departamento de Mecatrónica,
Av. Ferrocarril s/n, CD. Universitaria,
C.P. 68400 Loma Bonita, Oaxaca, México

**Abstract.** A Proportional-Derivative (PD) control scheme based on on-line compensation of disturbance signals is proposed for robust and efficient tracking of desired motion trajectories in a three-axis milling machine tool. The friction and cutting forces are lumped into an unknown bounded time-varying disturbance input signal affecting the dynamics of the motion axes of the milling machine. An estimation method is applied for on-line estimation of the disturbance and velocity signals required to implement the motion controllers. Simulation results are provided to show the efficient and robust tracking performance of the proposed motion control scheme and the fast and effective estimation of the perturbation and velocity signals.

**Keywords:** Milling Machine, Motion Control, Perturbation Estimation.

## 1 Introduction

Robust and efficient control of automatic metal-cutting machine tools has become a very important and challenging research topic because of the modern manufacturing systems demand high levels of production and quality of manufactured products. Therefore, the motion control algorithms for these mechatronic machines must guarantee real-time, fast, and accurate tracking of the specified machining trajectories, minimizing the positioning and contouring errors. In addition, the designed controllers should be simple and low cost for their practical implementation. Thus, the reduction of the number of sensors is an important aspect that must be taken into account in the design process of any control scheme for automatic machining.

On the other hand, the machining process dynamics are very complex, involving nonlinear friction and cutting forces, structural nonlinearities, parametric uncertainty, undesirable vibrations, and other nonlinear effects (see [1-2] and references therein). Hence the motion control schemes should be robust with respect to those perturbation

C.-Y. Su, S. Rakheja, H. Liu (Eds.): ICIRA 2012, Part I, LNAI 7506, pp. 622–631, 2012.

dynamics and their design will be commonly based on simplified mathematical models. In fact, there exist several interesting developments of controllers for machine tools, which are based on Lyapunov methods, classical control, neural networks, adaptive force control, nonlinear observer-based control, variable-gain control, fuzzy logic control and $H_\infty$ control (see [3-8] and references therein).

In this paper a Proportional-Derivative (PD) control scheme with compensation of disturbance signals is proposed for robust and accurate tracking tasks of reference trajectories specified for the motion axes of a three-axis milling machine tool, using position output measurements only. Our control design methodology differs from others in that the control problem is seen as a bounded disturbance signal processing problem, which allows the design of quite simple and feasible robust control schemes to be implemented using commercial embedded control technologies. In the control design process, a simplified mathematical model of the motion axes subjected to unknown bounded disturbance signals is considered. These disturbance signals include the cutting and friction forces. A family of Taylor polynomials is proposed to locally model the disturbance signals. The extended disturbance-plant mathematical model is used to design a Luenberger high-gain dynamic observer to estimate the disturbance and velocity signals required for implementation of the controllers. This estimation scheme of disturbance signals and states is based on the design methodology of robust observers with respect to un-modeled perturbation input signals of polynomial type presented by Sira-Ramírez et al. in [9]. Simulation results are provided to show the robust and efficient performance of the proposed disturbance observer-control scheme.

## 2    Mathematical Model of the Milling Machine Axes

Consider the schematic diagram of a rigid motion axis of a milling machine shown in Fig. 1, where $x$ is the linear displacement of the cart, $\theta$ is the angular displacement of the power transmission screw, $m$ is the mass of the cart, $J$ is the mass moment of inertia of the ball screw, $c_b$ and $c_t$ are the equivalent viscous damping coefficients of the cart and screw bearings, respectively, and $\tau$ is the control input torque.

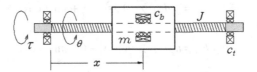

**Fig. 1.** Schematic diagram of a milling machine rigid axis

Then, the mathematical model that describes the dynamic behavior of the X, Y and Z motion axes of a three-axis milling machine is given by

$$m_{1e}\ddot{x}+c_{1e}\dot{x}+\mu_1 sign(\dot{x})=\frac{1}{a}\tau_x-F_{cx}$$

$$m_{2e}\ddot{y}+c_{2e}\dot{y}+\mu_2 sign(\dot{y})=\frac{1}{a}\tau_y-F_{cy} \qquad (1)$$

$$m_{3e}\ddot{z}+c_{3e}\dot{z}+\mu_3 sign(\dot{z})=\frac{1}{a}\tau_z-F_{cz}$$

where

$$m_{1e}=m_1+\frac{J_1}{a^2}, \; m_{2e}=m_2+\frac{J_2}{a^2}, \; m_{3e}=m_3+\frac{J_3}{a^2},$$

$$c_{1e}=c_{b1}+\frac{c_{t1}}{a^2}, \; c_{2e}=c_{b2}+\frac{c_{t2}}{a^2}, \; c_{3e}=c_{b3}+\frac{c_{t3}}{a^2}$$

In the above, "sign" denotes the *signum* function, $J_1$, $J_2$ and $J_3$ are the mass moments of inertia of each screw of the X, Y, and Z axes, respectively, $m_1$, $m_2$ and $m_3$ are the masses of each cart, which are displaced by the screws, $c_{bi}$ and $c_{ti}$, $i = 1, 2, 3$, are the equivalent viscous damping coefficients of the nut and guideways bearings, and of the support bearings of the screws of each axis, respectively. Here, $a = p/2\pi$ is the proportionality constant of the angular-linear displacement, $x = a\theta$, and $p$ is the pitch of the transmission screw, $\mu_1$, $\mu_2$ and $\mu_3$ are the Coulomb friction forces for each axis of the machine, $F_{cx}$, $F_{cy}$ and $F_{cz}$ are the cutting forces induced by the machining process in the X, Y and Z directions. In addition, $\tau_x$, $\tau_y$ and $\tau_z$ denote the control input torques applied to the X, Y and Z motion axes, respectively. In our study, it is assumed that the milling machine uses counterweights to properly compensate the gravity loads (see [10]). Note that the gravitational force in the Z direction can also be considered as a perturbation input term for purposes of control design.

In this study, the Kline's quasi-static model for prediction of the cutting forces for slotting and side milling operations described in [2] is used to evaluate the robustness of the proposed motion control scheme

$$v_m = \cos^{-1}\left(1-\frac{2b}{D}\right)$$

$$F_{cx} = u_s d_a f \sum_{i=1}^{n_t}(0.3\sin^2 v_i+\sin v_i \cos v_i)$$

$$F_{cy} = u_s d_a f \sum_{i=1}^{n_t}(\sin^2 v_i-0.3\sin v_i \cos v_i) \qquad (2)$$

$$F_{ti} = u_s d_a f \sin v_i$$

$$F_{cz} = 0.3 F_{ti} \tan \lambda$$

where $u_s$ is the power required to machine a unit volume of the work material, $d_a$ is the axial depth of cut, $f$ is the feed per tooth, $n_t$ is the number of teeth on the cutter in contact with the workpiece, $D$ is the diameter of the milling cutter, $\lambda$ is the angle of the cutting edges, $b$ is the radial depth of cut, $v_i$ is the tool rotation angle, $(v_0, v_m)$ is the angular range of a cutting edge cuts.

In this work, the cutting forces for a slotting operation on soft steel ($u_s$ = 0.5 kW/cm$^3$/min) resulting from applying the mechanistic model (2) will be considered as terms of the unknown disturbance signals affecting the dynamics of the machine motion axes. For this operation, a vertical cutter with two edges is employed, with $\lambda = 45°$, $D = 10$ mm, $d_a = 0.005$ m, $f = 0.001$ m and spindle speed $N = 1800$ rpm, $n_t = 1$ and $b = 10$ mm.

## 3    PD Control with Disturbance Compensation

In the design process of the motion controllers for the $X$, $Y$ and $Z$ axes, the following simplified mathematical model subjected to the disturbance signals $\xi_x$, $\xi_y$ and $\xi_z$ is considered

$$
\begin{aligned}
\ddot{x} &= b_x \tau_x + \xi_x(t) \\
\ddot{y} &= b_y \tau_y + \xi_y(t) \\
\ddot{z} &= b_z \tau_z + \xi_z(t)
\end{aligned}
\tag{3}
$$

where

$$
b_x = \frac{1}{am_{1e}}, \quad b_y = \frac{1}{am_{2e}}, \quad b_z = \frac{1}{am_{3e}}
$$

$$
\xi_x(t) = -\frac{c_{1e}}{m_{1e}}\dot{x} - \frac{\mu_1}{m_{1e}}sign(\dot{x}) - \frac{1}{m_{1e}}F_{cx}
$$

$$
\xi_y(t) = -\frac{c_{2e}}{m_{2e}}\dot{y} - \frac{\mu_2}{m_{2e}}sign(\dot{y}) - \frac{1}{m_{2e}}F_{cy}
$$

$$
\xi_z(t) = -\frac{c_{3e}}{m_{3e}}\dot{z} - \frac{\mu_3}{m_{3e}}sign(\dot{z}) - \frac{1}{m_{3e}}F_{cz}
$$

Assuming temporally perfect knowledge of those disturbance signals, we obtain from (3) the following PD controllers with compensation of the perturbation for tracking tasks of desired reference trajectories for motion of the axes of the milling machine:

$$
\tau_x = \frac{1}{b_x}\left[\ddot{x}^*(t) - \alpha_{1,x}(\dot{x} - \dot{x}^*(t)) - \alpha_{0,x}(x - x^*(t)) - \xi_x\right]
$$

$$
\tau_y = \frac{1}{b_y}\left[\ddot{y}^*(t) - \alpha_{1,y}(\dot{y} - \dot{y}^*(t)) - \alpha_{0,y}(y - y^*(t)) - \xi_y\right]
\tag{4}
$$

$$
\tau_z = \frac{1}{b_z}\left[\ddot{z}^*(t) - \alpha_{1,z}(\dot{z} - \dot{z}^*(t)) - \alpha_{0,z}(z - z^*(t)) - \xi_z\right]
$$

where $x^*(t)$, $y^*(t)$ and $z^*(t)$ are the desired reference trajectories for the displacements of the carts of the $X$, $Y$ and $X$ axes, respectively.

The use of the controllers (4) yield the following set of differential equations for the closed-loop dynamics of the tracking errors, $e_x = x - x^*(t)$, $e_y = y - y^*(t)$ and $e_z = z - z^*(t)$:

$$\ddot{e}_i + \alpha_{1,i}\dot{e}_i + \alpha_{0,i}e_i = 0, \quad i = x, y, z \tag{5}$$

The characteristic polynomials are then given by .

$$p_i(s) = s^2 + \alpha_{1,i}s + \alpha_{0,i}, \quad i = x, y, z \tag{6}$$

Therefore, selecting the design parameters $\alpha_{0,i}$, $\alpha_{0,i}$, $i = x$, $y$, $z$, so that the characteristic polynomials (6) are *Hurwitz* polynomials, the asymptotic tracking of the reference trajectories is guaranteed.

In this paper the following *Hurwitz* polynomials are proposed to get the gains of the controllers:

$$p_{d,i}(s) = s^2 + 2\zeta_{c,i}\omega_{c,i}s + \omega_{c,i}, \quad i = x, y, z \tag{7}$$

where $\omega_{c,i} > 0$ and $\zeta_{c,i} > 0$ are the natural frequencies, and viscous damping ratios, respectively, for the desired closed-loop dynamics of the tracking errors.

Since the controllers (4) require information of the disturbance signals $\xi_x$, $\xi_y$ and $\xi_z$, and the velocities of the carts of the milling machine, this paper propose the application of the design methodology of robust observers with respect to polynomial type perturbation input signals presented by Sira-Ramírez *et al.* in [9] for on-line estimation of the disturbance and velocity signals. The proposed disturbance observer is called a Generalized Proportional Integral (GPI) observer, because its design approach is the dual counterpart of the so-called GPI controllers.

## 4     Estimation of Disturbance Signals

In the design process of the observers, it is assumed that the perturbation input signals can be locally approximated by a family of Taylor polynomials of $(r-1)$th degree as

$$\xi_i(t) = \sum_{j=0}^{r-1} p_{i,j}t^j, \quad i = x, y, z \tag{8}$$

where all the coefficients $p_{j,i}$ are completely unknown.

An extended approximate state space model for the perturbed dynamics of the axes of the milling machine is then given by

$$\begin{aligned}
\dot{\eta}_{1,i} &= \eta_{2,i} \\
\dot{\eta}_{2,i} &= b_i\tau_i + \xi_{1,i} \\
\dot{\xi}_{1,i} &= \xi_{2,i} \\
\dot{\xi}_{2,i} &= \xi_{3,i} \\
&\vdots \\
\dot{\xi}_{r-1,i} &= \xi_{r,i} \\
\dot{\xi}_{r,i} &= 0
\end{aligned} \tag{9}$$

where $\eta_{1,i} = i$, $\eta_{2,i} = \dot{\eta}_{1,i}$, $\xi_{1,i} = \xi_i$, $\xi_{2,i} = \dot{\xi}_i$, $\xi_{3,i} = \ddot{\xi}_i$, ..., $\xi_{r,i} = \xi_i^{(r-1)}$, $i = x, y, z$.

Then the disturbance and velocity signals can be estimated by the following Luenberger state observers

$$\dot{\hat{\eta}}_{1,i} = \hat{\eta}_{2,i} + \beta_{r+1,i}(\eta_{1,i} - \hat{\eta}_{1,i})$$

$$\dot{\hat{\eta}}_{2,i} = b_i \tau_i + \hat{\xi}_{1,i} + \beta_{r,i}(\eta_{1,i} - \hat{\eta}_{1,i})$$

$$\dot{\hat{\xi}}_{1,i} = \hat{\xi}_{2,i} + \beta_{r-1,i}(\eta_{1,i} - \hat{\eta}_{1,i})$$

$$\dot{\hat{\xi}}_{2,i} = \hat{\xi}_{3,i} + \beta_{r-2,i}(\eta_{1,i} - \hat{\eta}_{1,i})$$

$$\vdots$$

$$\dot{\hat{\xi}}_{r-1,i} = \hat{\xi}_{r,i} + \beta_{1,i}(\eta_{1,i} - \hat{\eta}_{1,i})$$

$$\dot{\hat{\xi}}_{r,i} = \beta_{0,i}(\eta_{1,i} - \hat{\eta}_{1,i})$$

$$(10)$$

The dynamics of the estimation errors, $e_{1,i} = \eta_{1,i} - \hat{\eta}_{1,i}$, $e_{2,i} = \eta_{2,i} - \hat{\eta}_{2,i}$, $e_{pk,i} = \xi_{k,i} - \hat{\xi}_{k,i}$, $k = 1, 2, ..., r$, $i = x, y, z$, are then given by

$$\dot{e}_{1,i} = -\beta_{r+1,i}e_{1,i} + e_{2,i}$$

$$\dot{e}_{2,i} = -\beta_{r,i}e_{1,i} + e_{p1,i}$$

$$\dot{e}_{p1,i} = -\beta_{r-1,i}e_{1,i} + e_{p2,i}$$

$$\dot{e}_{p2,i} = -\beta_{r-2,i}e_{1,i} + e_{p3,i}$$

$$\vdots$$

$$\dot{e}_{p(r-1),i} = -\beta_{1,i}e_{1,i} + e_{p,r,i}$$

$$\dot{e}_{p,r,i} = -\beta_{0,i}e_{1,i}$$

$$(11)$$

From this expression, it is not difficult to see that the dynamics of the observation errors, $e_{1,i} = x, y, z$, satisfy the following set of differential equations

$$e_{1,i}^{(r+2)} + \beta_{r+1,i}e_{1,i}^{(r+1)} + \beta_{r,i}e_{1,i}^{(r)} + \beta_{r-1,i}e_{1,i}^{(r-1)} + ...$$
$$+ \beta_{2,i}\ddot{e}_{1,i} + \beta_{1,i}\dot{e}_{1,i} + \beta_{0,i}e_{1,i} = 0$$

$$(12)$$

which are completely independent of any coefficients $p_{i,j}$ of the Taylor polynomial expansions of the disturbance signals $\xi_{r,i}(t)$.

The design parameters of the observer (10) are chosen so that the characteristic polynomials of the dynamics of the observation errors are *Hurwitz* polynomials described by

$$p_{o,i}(s) = (s + p_{o,i})(s^2 + 2\zeta_{o,1}\omega_{o,i}s + \omega_{o,i}^2)^3$$

$$(13)$$

where $p_{o,i}$, $\zeta_{o,i}$, $\omega_{o,i} > 0$, $i = x, y, z$.

## 5    Simulation Results

Some numerical simulations were performed to verify the robustness of the proposed motion scheme and the fast estimation of the disturbance signals using the following parameters for the milling machine axes: $m_1 = m_2 = m_3 = 8$ Kg, $c_{t1} = c_{t2} = c_{t3} = 2.5$ Ns/m, $c_{b1} = c_{b2} = c_{b3} = 2.5$ Ns/m, $J_1 = J_2 = J_3 = 0.005$ N-m$^2$, $\mu_1 = \mu_2 = \mu_3 = 0.3$ N, $p_1 = p_2 = p_3 = 0.01$ m.

Fig. 3 shows the motion trajectory specified for the cutting operation in the x-y plane. The first desired movement is a straight line starting at the point 1 and ending at the point 2. Next, the cutter moves from point 2 toward point 3 in straight line as well. The axial depth of cut is a constant value of 5 mm, and the modulus of the $x$ path from point 2 to point 3 is 80 mm, which is the same for the modulus of the $y$ path from point 1 to point 2. This path of 80 mm of length is specified to be performed into a time of 26.667 s.

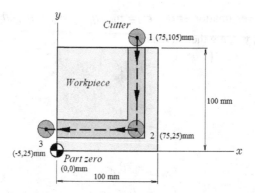

**Fig. 2.** Trajectory specified for the cutting operation

According to the parameters used in the quasi-static mathematical model (2) for prediction of the cutting forces (axial depth of cut of 5 mm, feed per cutter tooth of 0.05 mm, number of teeth on the cutter of 2, and spindle speed of 1800 revolutions per minute), one gets the feed rate of 3 mm/s and the time required to mill the path of 80 mm as 26.667 s.

The expressions of the straight line trajectories are described as follows. From point 1 to point 2:

$$x_d(t) = 0.075\,[m], \quad \dot{x}_d(t) = 0\,[m/s]$$

$$y_d(t) = \frac{y_f - y_i}{t_f - t_i}(t - t_i) + y_i\,[m], \quad \dot{y}_d(t) = \frac{y_f - y_i}{t_f - t_i}\,[m/s]$$

$$z_d(t) = -0.005\,[m], \quad \dot{z}_d(t) = 0\,[m/s]$$

with initial ($i$) and final ($f$) conditions:

$$t_i = 0 \ s, \quad t_f = 26.667 \ s, \quad x_i = x_f = -0.075 \ m, \quad y_i = -0.105 \ m,$$

$$y_f = -0.025 \ m, \quad z_i = z_f = -0.005 \ m$$

From point 2 to point 3:

$$x_d(t) = \frac{x_f - x_i}{t_f - t_i}(t - t_i) + x_i \ [m], \quad \dot{x}_d(t) = \frac{x_f - x_i}{t_f - t_i} \ [m/s]$$

$$y_d(t) = -0.025 \ [m], \quad \dot{y}_d(t) = 0 \ [m/s]$$

$$z_d(t) = -0.005 \ [m], \quad \dot{z}_d(t) = 0 \ [m/s]$$

with initial ($i$) and final ($f$) conditions:

$$t_i = 26.667 \ s, \quad t_f = 53.334 \ s, \quad x_i = -0.075 \ m, \quad x_f = 0.005 \ m,$$

$$y_i = y_f = -0.025 \ m, \quad z_i = z_f = -0.005 \ m$$

Figs. 3, 4 and 5 depict the robust and efficient tracking performance of the proposed control approach rejecting disturbances directly affecting the dynamics of the motion axes of the milling machine. In addition, one can observe the fast and effective estimation of the disturbance signals. The control gains were selected to get *Hurwitz* polynomials according to the equation (8), with $\omega_{c,i} = 12$ rad/s and $\zeta_{c,i} = 0.7071$, $i = x, y, z$. The gains of the disturbance observer were set to have $\omega_{o,i} = p_{o,i} = 700$ rad/s and $\zeta_{o,i} = 0.7071$.

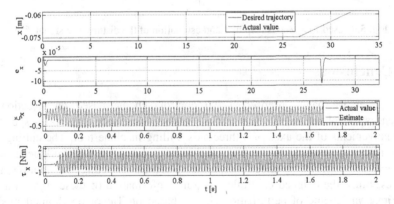

**Fig. 3.** Closed-loop x-axis response and estimation of the disturbance signal $\xi_x$

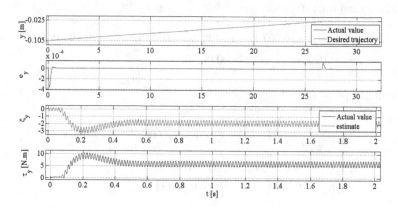

**Fig. 4.** Closed-loop y-axis response and estimation of the disturbance signal $\xi_y$

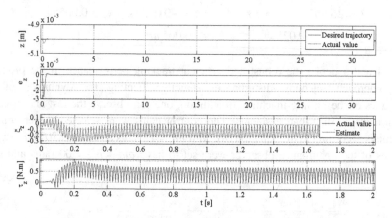

**Fig. 5.** Closed-loop z-axis response and estimation of the disturbance signal $\xi_z$

## 6     Conclusions

In this paper we have proposed a PD control scheme based on rejection of disturbances for robust and efficient tracking tasks of reference trajectories specified for the movements of the axes of a three-axis milling machine tool. The cutting and friction forces generated during the machining process of the workpiece were considered as unknown bounded perturbation signals affecting the motion axes dynamics. Since the deigned controllers requires information of these signals, a on-line estimation scheme of perturbation signals based on Taylor polynomial models has been applied. Simulations results show the robust and efficient performance of the proposed disturbance observer-control approach and the fast and effective estimation of the disturbances signals.

# References

1. Schmitz, T.L., Smith, K.S.: Machining Dynamics – Frequency Response to Improved Productivity. Springer, New York (2009)
2. Stephenson, D.A., Agapiou, J.S.: Metal Cutting Theory and Practice, 2nd edn. Taylor & Francis (2006)
3. Lee, J., Dixon, W.E., Ziegert, J.C.: Adaptive Nonlinear Contour Coupling Control. Int. J. Adv. Manuf. Technol (2011), doi:10.1007/s00170-011-3760-1
4. Fortgang, J., Singhose, W., Márquez, J., Perez, J.: Command Shaping Control for Micromilling Operations. International Journal of Control, Automation, and Systems 9(6), 1136–1145 (2011)
5. Byung-Sub, K., Seung-Kook, R., Jong-Kweon, P.: Development of a 3-axis Desktop Milling Machine and a CNC System Using Advanced Modern Control Algorithms. International Journal of Precision Engineering and Manufacturing 11(1), 39–47 (2010)
6. Yao, B., Al-Majed, M., Tomizuka, M.: High-Performance Robust Motion Control of Machine Tools: An Adaptive Robust Control Approach and Comparative Experiments. IEEE/ASME Transactions on Mechatronics 2(2), 63–76 (1997)
7. Zheng-Hong, T., Syh-Shiuh, Y., Pau-Lo, H.: The Integrated Linear and Nonlinear Motion Control Design for Precise CNC Machine Tools. In: 2004 IEEE International Conference on Control Applications, pp. 724–729. IEEE Press, Taipei (2004)
8. Zheng, J., Zhang, M., Meng, K.: Modeling and Design Servo System of CNC Machine Tools. In: 2006 IEEE International Conference on Mechatronics and Automation, pp. 1964–1969. IEEE Press, Luoyang (2006)
9. Sira-Ramirez, H., Feliu-Batlle, V., Beltran-Carbajal, F., Blanco-Ortega, A.: Sigma-Delta Modulation Sliding Mode Observers for Linear Systems Subject to Locally Unstable Inputs. In: 16th Mediterranean Conference on Control and Automation, pp. 344–349. IEEE Press, Ajaccio (2008)
10. Albano, L.D., Suh, N.P.: Engineering Design. In: Kreith, F. (ed.) Mechanical Engineering Handbook, pp. 11-1–11-109. CRC Press, Boca Raton (1999)

# A Novel Stabilization Scheme for Asymmetric Bilateral Teleoperation Systems with Time Varying Delays

Trent Hilliard and Ya-Jun Pan*

Department of Mechanical Engineering, Dalhousie University,
P.O. Box 15000, Halifax, NS, Canada B3H 4R2
Yajun.Pan@Dal.Ca

**Abstract.** This paper proposes a novel stabilization scheme to deal with time varying delays within a bilateral teleoperation system. The master and slave manipulators were modeled as linear single degree of freedom systems. The human user force was modeled based on the band limited availability of human motion, and the environmental force was modeled as a spring and damper combination based on the slave position. An impedance matching approach was applied to the master side dynamics, while a static error feedback gain was used to stabilize the slave side dynamics. A Lyapunov functional based on the error of the system is proposed with consideration for the maximum level of delay experienced within the system. From here, LMI approaches are used with Jensen's inequality to determine the static feedback control gain $K_c$. The cone complementarity algorithm is used to deal with non-linear terms within the LMI. Numerical simulations were conducted using Matlab and Simulink toolkits to demonstrate the stability and performance of the algorithms.

## 1 Introduction

Teleoperation schemes (where one manipulator controls the movement of another at a remote location with force feedback) are becoming a more common tool used in today's world. They allow remote access to a site that is unsafe for human occupation, but for which work needs to be done. While working with a remote robot, tactile response from the environment in terms of force feedback can greatly improve the user's performance over solely visual and audio cues [7]. Most current control algorithms strike a balance between stability (range of safe operation) and transparency (level of system precision) as typically one is reduced to help improve the other. The majority of research in the field is currently focused on advanced modeling of non-linear systems and subsequent controllers for these devices, and on systems in which the master and slave are identical. Unfortunately, many of the challenges requiring a teleoperation system do not allow for symmetric manipulators, typically due to size constraints

---

* Thanks to NSERC and CFI Canada for financially supporting this research work.

C.-Y. Su, S. Rakheja, H. Liu (Eds.): ICIRA 2012, Part I, LNAI 7506, pp. 632–642, 2012.

(e.g. a micro sized slave manipulator for precision work), or strength/weight consideration depending on the environment (such as deep sea pressures).

While accurate modeling of systems is one challenge, a second important challenge is in dealing with properties of network behavior such as time delay. With the expanding desire for use of teleoperation schemes and network control systems on less reliable networks (such as the internet), renewed focus has been placed on control schemes that can overcome the obstacles presented by lower Quality-of-Service (QoS) networks. While extensive work has been done for higher QoS of networks with algorithms such as $H_\infty$ [1], and passivity based methods [8], a more general overview of teleoperation can be found in [9]. The main factors to overcome on lower QoS networks are increased and variable time delay, along with issues of data dropout and/or packet loss depending on the particulars of the network. The reasons for exploring lower QoS networks involve cost, ease of implementation, wireless setup, existing infrastructure, etc.

In this paper the work focuses on a novel stabilization scheme with applications to asymmetrical teleoperation with time varying delays. Individual control schemes are derived for the master(impedance matching) and slave (constant feedback gain) systems, while a Lyapunov based stabilization criterion is used to prove the stability. The paper discusses the modeling choices for the systems in Section 2, the controller design methodology in Section 3.1, stability analysis in Section 3.2, simulation results in Section 4, and concluding remarks.

## 2    Problem Formulation

The goal of the work is to provide a high performance teleoperation system with strong levels of feedback and positional tracking on lower QoS networks such as the internet. The work focuses on an asymmetric teleoperation scenario as laid out in Fig. 1, which consists of a master and slave manipulator pair working together over a network with variable time delay such as the internet.

**Master Side General Dynamics.** Consider a single degree of freedom manipulator with linear properties and only have mass and damping, the general dynamic equation representing the system is:

$$m_m\ddot{x}_m + b_m\dot{x}_m = F_h + U_m \tag{1}$$

where $m_m$ represents the mass of the system, $b_m$ represents the damping, $x_m$ the position, $F_h$ the human input force and $U_m$ the control signal to the system. The system can be represented in the state-space form:

$$\dot{\mathbf{x}}_m = A_m\mathbf{x}_m + B_m(F_h + U_m)$$

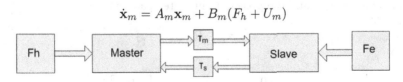

**Fig. 1.** Block Diagram of the Bilateral Teleoperation System

where:
$$A_m = \begin{bmatrix} 0 & 1 \\ 0 & -b_m/m_m \end{bmatrix}, \quad B_m = \begin{bmatrix} 0 \\ 1/m_m \end{bmatrix}.$$

For simplicity in controller design, an impedance matching approach is applied to master side (similar to work in [2]) such that the master manipulator will have the same impedance as the following system:

$$M\ddot{x}_m + B\dot{x}_m + Kx_m = F_h - F_e(t - \tau_s(t)) \tag{2}$$

where M, B and K represent the mass, damping and stiffness of the desired impedance system respectively. The desired impedance system can be represented in state space as:

$$\dot{\mathbf{x}}_m = A_M\mathbf{x}_m + B_M(F_h - F_e(t - \tau_s(t))) \tag{3}$$

where:
$$A_M = \begin{bmatrix} 0 & 1 \\ -K/M & -B/M \end{bmatrix}, \quad B_M = \begin{bmatrix} 0 \\ 1/M \end{bmatrix}.$$

An impedance matching approach is used as to allow for a constant system control gain $K_c$ to be design later on to only have an impact on the slave side dynamics. By allowing the user to control the master side impedance dynamics through the choice of B, K and M, the level of stability in the system can be tuned to match what is necessitated by the application. The master controller is designed as

$$U_m = (b_m - \frac{m_m}{M}B)\dot{x}_m + (\frac{m_m}{M} - 1)F_h - \frac{m_m}{M}(F_e(t - \tau_s(t)) + Kx_m) \tag{4}$$

which can realize the desired impedance model in Eq.(3).

**Slave Side General Dynamics.** Similar to the master dynamics, we consider the slave manipulator to be modeled as a single degree of freedom manipulator with only mass and damping properties. The dynamic equation governing the system is:

$$m_s\ddot{x}_s + b_s\dot{x}_s = U_s - F_e \tag{5}$$

where $m_s$ represents the mass of the system, $b_s$ represents the damping, $x_s$ the position, $F_e$ the environmental contact force and $U_s$ the control signal to the system. The system can be represented in state-space as:

$$\dot{\mathbf{x}}_s = A_s\mathbf{x}_s + B_s(U_s - F_e)$$

where:
$$A_s = \begin{bmatrix} 0 & 1 \\ 0 & -b_s/m_s \end{bmatrix}, \quad B_s = \begin{bmatrix} 0 \\ 1/m_s \end{bmatrix}$$

**Environmental Force.** For simulation work it is necessary to model the expected environmental forces that would act upon the slave manipulator in an experimental setting. For this work, the chosen scenario was when the slave manipulator is positioned against a non-rigid surface (such as foam), where motion into the foam would cause a reactionary force, and motion away from the foam would cause no environmental force (air drag is considered minimal at low speeds and thus neglected). The foam is modeled as a spring and damper system (Coefficients of $B_e$ and $K_e$) based on the position of the slave manipulator when $\mathbf{x}_s \geq 0$ , and 0 when $\mathbf{x}_s < 0$. The approach has been previously used in [5].

# 3   Static Feedback Controller Design

This section shows the main results of the work, namely the static feedback controller design for a system with variable time delay with a known upper bound. Using the previously defined system dynamics in Section 2, the following LMI problem can be used as a stabilization criterion.

## 3.1   Slave Side Controller Design

It is necessary to derive the error dynamics of the system in order to properly substitute into Lyapunov candidate derivative terms in (11) and design the system control $U_s$. For most teleoperation applications, it is desirable for the slave to track the position of the master in real time i.e. $e(t) = \mathbf{x}_s(t) - \mathbf{x}_m(t)$. Hence

$$\dot{e} = A_m e + (A_s - A_m)\mathbf{x}_s + B_m F_e(t - \tau_s(t)) - B_m F_h + B_s U_s - B_s F_e \quad (6)$$

where $\tau_s(t)$ represents the time delay in communication from the slave to the master, and $\tau_m(t)$ represents the delay from the master to the slave.

From (6), the term $(A_s - A_m)x_s$ needs to be eliminated using the slave side control law. The term $(A_s - A_m)$ can be represented as:

$$A_s - A_m = \begin{bmatrix} 0 & 0 \\ \delta_1 & \delta_2 \end{bmatrix}, \quad \delta_1 = K/M, \quad \delta_2 = B/M - b_s/m_s \quad (7)$$

where all the terms lie is the same channel the control input $U_s$, in the $\dot{x}_{2s}$ channel, which means that a portion of the $U_s$ can be used to eliminate it.

Now design a control signal of the form:

$$U_s = -m_s[\delta_1 x_{1s} + \delta_2 x_{2s}] + K_c(\mathbf{x}_s(t - \tau_m(t)) - \mathbf{x}_m(t - \tau_m(t)))$$
$$+ \alpha F_h(t - \tau_m(t)) - \beta F_e(t) + F_e(t) . \quad (8)$$

where the first term $(-m_s[\delta_1 x_{1s} + \delta_2 x_{2s}])$ of the control input $U_s$ is to deal with the asymmetry of the system as represented in (7). The second term $(K_c(\mathbf{x}_s(t - \tau_m(t)) - \mathbf{x}_m(t - \tau_1(t))))$ is the controller input on the delayed error, as the current value of position is not available to the slave side, but with an ability to record states and send time stamps, the delayed value of the slave states can be made available. The remaining terms $(\alpha F_h(t - \tau_m(t)) - \beta F_e(t - \tau_s(t)) + F_e(t))$ are used to provide a bound to the external disturbances $F_h$ and $F_e$.

Substituting (8) into (6) yields:

$$\dot{\mathbf{e}} = A_m \mathbf{e} + B_m F_e(t - \tau_s(t)) - \beta B_s F_e(t) + \alpha B_s F_h(t - \tau_m(t))$$
$$- B_m F_h(t) + B_s K_c \mathbf{e}(t - \tau_m(t))].$$

From the error dynamics we design an $\alpha = m_s/M$ values to combine the $\alpha B_s F_h(t - \tau_m(t)) - B_m F_h(t)$ terms from the error dynamics to a single difference term. Similarly we want to bound $B_m F_e(t - \tau_s(t)) - \beta B_s F_e(t)$ to a single difference term by selecting $\beta = m_s/M$. Then the error dynamics becomes:

$$\dot{\mathbf{e}} = A_m \mathbf{e} + B_s K_c \mathbf{e}(t - \tau(t)) + D \tag{9}$$

where $D = B_m[d_1 + d_2]$ with $d_1 = F_h(t - \tau_m(t)) - F_h(t)$ and $d_2 = F_e(t - \tau_s(t)) - F_e(t)$, and for simplicity, $\tau(t) = \tau_m(t)$.

## 3.2   Stability Analysis

**Theorem 1.** *For given constant $\tau_2$, if there exist matrices $X > 0$, $\hat{Q} > 0$, $\hat{R} > 0$ and $Y$ with appropriate dimensions, such that the following LMI*

$$\begin{bmatrix} -\hat{Q} - \hat{R} & 0 & 0 & 0 & \hat{R} & 0 & 0 \\ * & \hat{Q} + A_m X + X A_m^T - \hat{R} & I & 0 & \hat{R} + B_s Y & X A_m^T & \tau_2 X A_m^T \\ * & * & -\gamma_1 I & X & 0 & 0 & 0 \\ * & * & * & -I & 0 & 0 & 0 \\ * & * & * & * & -2\hat{R} & Y^T B_s^T & \tau_2 Y^T B_s^T \\ * & * & * & * & * & -\gamma_2 I & 0 \\ * & * & * & * & * & * & -X\hat{R}^{-1}X \end{bmatrix} < 0 \tag{10}$$

*holds, then systems (2) and (5) are asymptotically stable.*

*Proof.* Let us choose a Lyapunov Candidate of the following form similar as in [3]:

$$V = V_1 + V_2 + V_3 \tag{11}$$

$$V_1 = \mathbf{e}(t)^T P \mathbf{e}(t); \quad V_2 = \int_{t-\tau_2}^{t} \mathbf{e}^T(s) Q \mathbf{e}(s) ds$$

$$V_3 = \int_{-\tau_2}^{0} \int_{t+s}^{t} \dot{\mathbf{e}}^T(v) \tau_2 R \dot{\mathbf{e}}(v) dv ds$$

where $\tau_2$ is the maximum level of time delay of the time varying delay $\tau(t)$. It is also noted that $P, Q, R > 0$. The time derivatives of each function are:

$$\dot{V}_1 = \mathbf{e}(t)^T P \dot{\mathbf{e}}(t) + \dot{\mathbf{e}}(t)^T P \mathbf{e}(t)$$
$$\dot{V}_2 = \mathbf{e}^T(t) Q \mathbf{e}(t) - \mathbf{e}^T(t - \tau_2) Q \mathbf{e}(t - \tau_2)$$
$$\dot{V}_3 = (\dot{\mathbf{e}}^T(t) \tau_2^2 R \dot{\mathbf{e}}(t) - \int_{t-\tau_2}^{t} \dot{\mathbf{e}}^T(v) \tau_2 R \dot{\mathbf{e}}(v) dv)$$

We can then apply Jensen's Inequality ( [3] or [4]) for the following term:

$$-\int_{t-\tau_2}^{t} \dot{\mathbf{e}}^T(v)\tau_2 R_2 \dot{\mathbf{e}}(v)dv \leq \begin{bmatrix} \mathbf{e}(t) \\ \mathbf{e}(t-\tau(t)) \\ \mathbf{e}(t-\tau_2) \end{bmatrix}^T \begin{bmatrix} -R & R & 0 \\ * & -2R & R \\ * & * & -R \end{bmatrix} \begin{bmatrix} \mathbf{e}(t) \\ \mathbf{e}(t-\tau(t)) \\ \mathbf{e}(t-\tau_2) \end{bmatrix} \quad (12)$$

Then by substituting (9) into (11),

$$\dot{V} = \mathbf{e}^T(t)(Q + PA_m + A_m^T P + \gamma_1^{-1}PP)\mathbf{e}(t) + \mathbf{e}^T(t)PB_sK_c\mathbf{e}(t-\tau(t))$$
$$+\mathbf{e}(t-\tau(t))K_c^T B_s^T P\mathbf{e}(t) - \mathbf{e}^T(t-\tau_2)Q_2\mathbf{e}(t-\tau_2)$$
$$+\dot{\mathbf{e}}^T(t)(\tau_2^2 R)\dot{\mathbf{e}}(t) + \gamma_1 D^T D$$

Ignoring the $\dot{\mathbf{e}}^T(t)(\tau_2^2 R)\dot{\mathbf{e}}(t)$ temporarily and converting to an LMI form with the previous terms from (12):

$$\begin{bmatrix} \mathbf{e}(t) \\ \mathbf{e}(t-\tau(t)) \\ \mathbf{e}(t-\tau_2) \end{bmatrix}^T \begin{bmatrix} \Pi_1 & \Pi_2 & 0 \\ * & -2R & R \\ * & * & -Q-R \end{bmatrix} \begin{bmatrix} \mathbf{e}(t) \\ \mathbf{e}(t-\tau(t)) \\ \mathbf{e}(t-\tau_2) \end{bmatrix} + \gamma_1 D^T D$$

where:

$$\Pi_1 = Q + PA_m + A_m^T P + \gamma_1^{-1}PP - R; \Pi_2 = R + PB_sK_c$$

Let $\zeta(t) = \begin{bmatrix} \mathbf{e}(t) \\ \mathbf{e}(t-\tau(t)) \end{bmatrix}$. We can then rewrite the LMI of this portion as:

$$\begin{bmatrix} \mathbf{e}(t-\tau_2) \\ \zeta \end{bmatrix}^T \begin{bmatrix} -Q-R & \Pi_4 \\ * & \Pi_3 \end{bmatrix} \begin{bmatrix} \mathbf{e}(t-\tau_2) \\ \zeta \end{bmatrix} + \gamma_1 D^T D$$

where:

$$\Pi_3 = \begin{bmatrix} \Pi_1 & \Pi_2 \\ * & -2R \end{bmatrix}, \qquad \Pi_4 = \begin{bmatrix} 0 & R \end{bmatrix}.$$

The next term that needs to be examined is $\dot{\mathbf{e}}^T(t)(\tau_2^2 R)\dot{\mathbf{e}}(t)$, which can be represented as

$$\begin{bmatrix} \mathbf{e}(t) \\ \mathbf{e}(t-\tau(t)) \end{bmatrix}^T \begin{bmatrix} A_m & B_sK_c \end{bmatrix}^T (\tau_2 R\tau_2 + \gamma_2^{-1}I) \begin{bmatrix} A_m & (B_sK_c) \end{bmatrix} \begin{bmatrix} \mathbf{e}(t) \\ \mathbf{e}(t-\tau(t)) \end{bmatrix}$$
$$+D^T(\tau_2^2 R)D + \gamma_2 D^T(\tau_2^2 R^T R\tau_2^2) \quad (13) \cdot$$

Substituting (13) into the main LMI and applying the Schur Complement yields

$$\dot{V} \leq \begin{bmatrix} -Q-R & 0 & R & 0 & 0 \\ * & Q + PA_m + A_m^T P + \gamma_1^{-1}PP - R & R+B_sK_c & A_m^T & \tau_2 A_m^T \\ * & * & -2R & K_c^T B_s^T & \tau_2 K_c^T B_s^T \\ * & * & * & -\gamma_2 & 0 \\ * & * & * & * & -R^{-1} \end{bmatrix}$$
$$+ \gamma_1 D^T D + D^T(\tau_2^2 R)D + \gamma_2 D^T(\tau_2^2 R^T R\tau_2^2)D$$
$$\leq \Theta - \mathbf{e}^T\mathbf{e} + D^T(\gamma_1 I + \tau_2^2 R + \gamma_2 \tau_2^2 R^T R\tau_2^2)D$$

where

$$\Theta = \begin{bmatrix} -Q-R & 0 & & R & 0 & 0 \\ * & Q+PA_m+A_m^T P+\gamma_1^{-1}PP-R+I & R+B_sK_c & A_m^T & \tau_2 A_m^T \\ * & * & -2R & Y^T B_s^T & \tau_2 Y^T B_s^T \\ * & * & * & -\gamma_2 & 0 \\ * & * & * & * & -R^{-1} \end{bmatrix}$$

If $\Theta < 0$ holds, then

$$\dot{V} \le -\|e(t)\|^2 + \|D^T(\gamma_1 I + \tau_2^2 R + \gamma_2\tau_2^2 R^T R\tau_2^2)D\|$$

which shows that the error is bounded and the bound is determined by the magnitude of the terms $\gamma_1$ and $\gamma_2$, $\|D\|$, the eigenvalues of $R$, and the upper bound of the delay $\tau_2$.

The next step is to linearize the above system by pre and post multiply by $diag(P^{-1}, P^{-1}, P^{-1}, I, I)$ and then make the following substitutions, while applying the Schur complement to linearize the diagonal terms:

$$X = P^{-1}, \quad Y = KX, \quad \hat{Q} = XQX, \quad \hat{R} = XRX$$

Which results in the following LMI:

$$\begin{bmatrix} -\hat{Q}-\hat{R} & 0 & 0 & 0 & \hat{R} & 0 & 0 \\ * & \hat{Q}+A_mX+XA_m^T-\hat{R} & I & 0 & \hat{R}+B_sY & XA_m^T & \tau_2XA_m^T \\ * & * & -\gamma_1 I & X & 0 & 0 & 0 \\ * & * & * & -I & 0 & 0 & 0 \\ * & * & * & * & -2\hat{R} & Y^T B_s^T & \tau_2 Y^T B_s^T \\ * & * & * & * & * & -\gamma_2 I & 0 \\ * & * & * & * & * & * & -X\hat{R}^{-1}X \end{bmatrix} < 0 \quad (14)$$

This completes the proof. $\square$

We then need a method to deal with the non-linear term $X\hat{R}^{-1}X$ in (10). We can replace this with a new variable G, and apply additional constraints to LMI system to approximate:

$$\begin{bmatrix} -\hat{Q}-\hat{R} & 0 & 0 & 0 & \hat{R} & 0 & 0 \\ * & \hat{Q}+A_mX+XA_m^T-\hat{R} & I & 0 & \hat{R}+B_sY & XA_m^T & \tau_2XA_m^T \\ * & * & -\gamma_1 I & X & 0 & 0 & 0 \\ * & * & * & -I & 0 & 0 & 0 \\ * & * & * & * & -2\hat{R} & Y^T B_s^T & \tau_2 Y^T B_s^T \\ * & * & * & * & * & -\gamma_2 I & 0 \\ * & * & * & * & * & * & -G \end{bmatrix} \quad (15)$$

where $G = X\hat{R}^{-1}X$. If we define $J = G^{-1}$, $P = X^{-1}$ and $L = R^{-1}$ we can translate G into:

$$\begin{bmatrix} J & P \\ * & L \end{bmatrix} \ge 0 \quad (16)$$

To help enforce the inverse relationships between variables we have:

Minimize Trace$(XP + JG + RL)$

subject to $X > 0, P > 0, G > 0, J > 0, L > 0, R > 0$

$$\begin{bmatrix} X & I \\ * & P \end{bmatrix} > 0; \quad \begin{bmatrix} G & I \\ * & J \end{bmatrix} > 0; \quad \begin{bmatrix} R & I \\ * & L \end{bmatrix} > 0 \quad (17)$$

In order to solve the new problem we can apply the cone complementarity algorithm [3].

## 4    Simulation Results

Simulation results for the design control algorithm were carried out using Matlab and Simulink. Matlab was used for the LMI solving routines as listed in Section 3.2, while Simulink was used as the simulation once the control gain $K_c$ has been found using the LMI algorithm. A pair of reference inputs were generated with Simulink to test the control algorithm under varying conditions.

The following are a list of system parameters used for computing the LMI and running the simulation: $m_m = 3\text{kg}$, $b_m = 3\text{Ns/m}$, $m_s = 2\text{kg}$, $b_s = 2\text{Ns/m}$, $M = 1\text{kg}$, $B = 4\text{Ns/m}$, $K = 4\text{N/m}$, $B_e = 0.1\text{Ns/m}$, $K_e = 4\text{N}$, $\tau_2 = 0.08\text{s}$. Using these system parameters, the LMI code((15)(16) and (17)) was run to achieve the following LMI variables:

$$X = \begin{bmatrix} 0.2805 & -0.1585 \\ -0.1585 & 0.1427 \end{bmatrix}; Y = \begin{bmatrix} 0.7430 & -0.5967 \end{bmatrix} \hat{R} = \begin{bmatrix} 1.6293 & -1.0585 \\ -1.0585 & 0.7286 \end{bmatrix}$$

$$\hat{Q} = 1*10^{-3} \begin{bmatrix} 0.3238 & -0.1608 \\ -0.1608 & 0.0821 \end{bmatrix}, \quad \gamma_1 = 3; \quad \gamma_2 = 0.9$$

which leads to the static feedback control gain of $K_c = \begin{bmatrix} 0.7628 & -3.3276 \end{bmatrix}$.

**Modified Step Input.** The first input considered is a modified step input, as a human operator cannot physically apply a true step input as human motion is frequency limited [6]. To build the frequency limited source, a ramp function is used as in Fig. 2(a).

Fig. 2(b) and (c) display the positions of the master and slave manipulators along with the respective error. As expected the largest level of error occurs at the point where the ramp converts to a constant, which would be the instant that the disturbance effect D would be at a maximum value. Once reaching a level value and the disturbance term is 0, the systems reach an equilibrium value as expected from the LMI results. In terms of quantifying the performance, the maximum error was recorded as 0.0035m, with a total travel of 0.13m, which yields a percent error of approximately 2.7 %.

**Sinusoidal Input.** A second input considered was that of a sinusoidal input, due to its constantly changing slopes which would be constantly affecting the system through the disturbance term D. A sinusoid with a magnitude of 5 N and period of 12.5 seconds was used as the test scenario, and can be seen in Fig.3(a). Fig. 3(b) displays the control signals $U_s$ and $U_m$ generated by the control algorithm that allows for position tracking with force feedback.

Figs. 4(a) and (b) display the positions of the master and slave manipulators along with the respective error. The tracking performance can be quantified by noting a maximum position error of 0.03 m, compared to the maximum travel of 1.17m from the origin, yielding a percent error of 2 %.

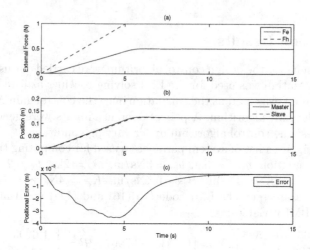

**Fig. 2.** Plots of (a) External Forces, (b) Position, and (c) Positional Error of an asymmetric bilateral teleoperation under a modified step input

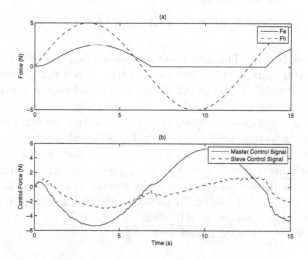

**Fig. 3.** Plots of (a) External Forces and (b) Control Forces of an asymmetric bilateral teleoperation under a sinusoidal input

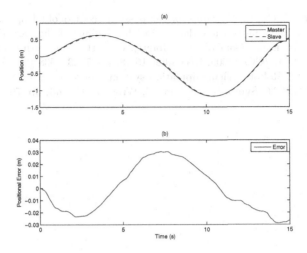

**Fig. 4.** Plots of (a) Position and (b) Positional Error of an asymmetric bilateral tele-operation under a sinusoidal input

## 5   Conclusions

This work has demonstrated the ability for tracking control of an asymmetrical teleoperation system subject to human input forces with corresponding contact forces on the slave side. Future work includes using a more robust Lyapunov candidate such that lower delay bounds can be considered, as well as the ability to deal with packet loss.

## References

1. Pan, Y., Canudas-de-Wit, C., Sename, O.: A New Predictive Approach for Bilateral Teleoperation With Applications to Drive-by-Wire Systems. IEEE Transactions on Robotics 22(6), 1146–1162 (2006)
2. Sha Sadeghi, M., Momeni, H.R., Amirifar, R.: $H_\infty$ and L1 control of a teleoperation system via LMIs. Applied Mathematics and Computation 206(2), 669–677 (2008)
3. Peng, C., Tian, Y.-C., Tad, M.O.: State feedback controller design of networked control systems with interval time-varying delay and nonlinearity. Int. J. Robust Nonlinear Control 18, 1285–1301 (2008)
4. Gu, K., Kharitonov, V.L., Chen, J.: Stability of Time-delay Systems. Birkhauser, Basel (2003)
5. Walker, K.: Stability and control of bilateral teleoperation over the internet with force feedback, Dalhousie University, Halifax NS Canada (2010)
6. Ang, W.T., Pradeep, P.K., Riviere, C.N.: Active tremor compensation in micro-surgery. In: Proceedings of the 26th Annual International Conference of the IEEE EMBS, San Fransico, CA, pp. 2738–2741 (September 2004)
7. de Barros, P.G., Lindeman, R.W., Ward, M.O.: Enhancing robot teleoperator situation awareness and performance using vibro-tactile and graphical feedback. In: 2011 IEEE Symposium on 3D User Interfaces, March 19-20, pp. 47–54 (2011)

8. Ye, Y., Pan, Y., Gupta, Y.: Time domain passivity control of teleoperation systems with random asymmetric time delays. In: Proceedings of the 48th IEEE Conference on Decision and Control, Held Jointly With the 2009 28th Chinese Control Conference, CDC/CCC 2009, December 15-18, pp. 7533–7538 (2009)
9. Melchiorri, C.: Robotic telemanipulation systems: an overview on control aspects. In: Proc. 7th IFAC Symp. Robot Control, Wroclaw, Poland, pp. 707–716 (2003)

# Adaptive Exponential Sliding Mode Control
# for Dynamic Tracking of a Nonholonomic Mobile Robot

Hasan Mehrjerdi[1], Youmin M. Zhang[1,*], and Maarouf Saad[2]

[1] Concordia University, Montreal, Canada
[2] École de Technologie Supérieure, Montréal, Canada
youmin.zhang@concordia.ca

**Abstract.** This paper presents an adaptive exponential sliding mode control as a solution to reduce chattering, uncertainties and disturbances for the trajectory tracking of a nonholonomic wheeled mobile robot. Compared to conventional sliding mode control, the exponential sliding mode control reduces chattering on input controls as well as delivering a high dynamic tracking performance in a steady-state mode. An adaptive control law is added to the developed exponential sliding mode control to overcome external disturbances and improve performance of the controller against uncertainties. The developed algorithm instructs the robot to keep moving on the desired trajectory while reducing tracking errors. The experimental testing results on a unicycle mobile robot are presented to demonstrate the performance of the adaptive exponential sliding mode controller against uncertainties and disturbances.

**Keywords:** Adaptive exponential sliding mode control, Chattering, Mobile robot, Trajectory tracking.

## 1    Introduction

Nonholonomics characteristic and nonlinearity modeling of mobile robots have attracted the attention of researchers over recent decades. Several different nonlinear control strategies have been proposed for the trajectory following of mobile robot. Sliding Mode Control (SMC) developed in the 1950's took the attention of the authors because it employs a nonlinear control strategy that uses a high speed switching control law with a discontinuous property [1]. SMC has previously been used for the control of mobile robots because of its simple structure, its fast response, good transient performance, as well as its robustness with regard to parameter variations. The most problematic issue in SMC applications is chattering, that is the high frequency finite amplitude control signal, which makes it difficult for use with real physical systems [2]. In order to attenuate and/or eliminate such a chattering problem in SMC systems in this application, the authors considered the following proposals. The use of a continuous smooth approximation [3], although these methods do decrease control chattering, they also unfortunately reduce the robustness and create an increase in the steady-state error.

---

* Corresponding author.

C.-Y. Su, S. Rakheja, H. Liu (Eds.): ICIRA 2012, Part I, LNAI 7506, pp. 643–652, 2012.
© Springer-Verlag Berlin Heidelberg 2012

The use of high-order sliding-mode approaches [4] was also considered. These approaches do have the advantages of a higher accuracy of motions, as well as chattering reduction and finite-time convergence for systems with relative degrees of two [5], [6]. Observer-based approaches are also effective in the presence of unmodeled dynamics [7]. However, all of these methodologies which are designed to mitigate chattering essentially involve low-pass filters and thus sacrifice steady-state errors.

Das and Kar [8] designed and implemented an adaptive fuzzy logic for wheeled mobile robots. Fukao et al [9] proposed the "backstepping method" for the dynamic model of a mobile robot and related to this work, Fierro and Lewis [10] developed an "adaptive backstepping method" with unknown parameters. Park et al [11] proposes an "adaptive neural sliding mode control method" for trajectory tracking of mobile robots with model uncertainties and external disturbances. They used self-recurrent wavelet neural networks for approximating arbitrary model uncertainties and external disturbances in the dynamics of a mobile robot. Corradin and Orland [12] proposed a "trajectory tracking problem" for a mobile considering the presence of uncertainties in the dynamical model. The proposed solution was based on a discrete sliding mode control, in order to ensure both robustness and the implement ability of the controller.

Having considered all above-mentioned works, the solution that was finally adopted in this paper to achieve an efficient and smooth robot movement builds upon the method presented by Fallah and Saad [13], in which the authors considered an exponential reaching law for multivariable systems. In this paper, we use the Adaptive Exponential Sliding Mode (AESM) method for the dynamic trajectory tracking of a mobile robot. Firstly, we perform a comparison of Exponential Sliding Mode (ESM) with Conventional Sliding Mode (CSM) to show its performance on chattering reduction and trajectory tracking for mobile robot. Then we adjoin an adaptive law on ESM to overcome external disturbances and improve performance of controller against uncertainties.

The paper is organized as follows: Section 2 presents the model description of a mobile robot. Section 3 describes adaptive exponential sliding mode control. Section 4 demonstrates the experimental results. Finally, we conclude the paper in Section 5.

# 2    Dynamics and Kinematics Modeling of the Mobile Robot

Fig. 1 shows the general model of the mobile robot which consists of two driving wheels mounted on the same axis at the front while the two back wheels can freely rotate.

In Fig. 1, $r$ is the radius of each driving wheel, $L$ is the distance between driving wheel and the axes of symmetry and $d$ is the distance between the geometric center of the robot and the center of mass ($C_0$). $q = [x, y, \psi]^T$ denotes the position and orientation vector of the robot, and $q_d = [x_d, y_d, \psi_d]^T$ represents desired trajectory.

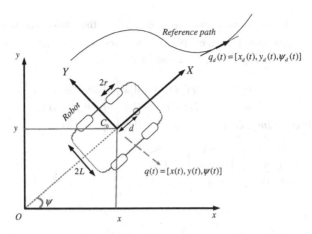

**Fig. 1.** Conceptual demonstration of a mobile robot for path following

Fig. 2 illustrates the block diagram which is proposed in this paper for using to track a trajectory for a mobile robot based on an Adaptive Exponential Sliding Mode (AESM) control strategy. There are two levels, lower or higher level respectively, of the controller. The lower level controller is designed and implemented to adjust the velocities of right and left wheels, whereas the higher level controller, which is an adaptive exponential sliding mode controller, is designed to follow a desired/targeted trajectory. Posture sensors are used to localize the robot, and a control algorithm uses this information to direct the robot along a desired trajectory. External disturbance is considered to add on torque control of motors to show performance of AESM comparing to ESM against disturbances.

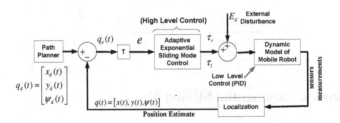

**Fig. 2.** Structure of the proposed two-level control of the mobile robot

For this mobile robot, the general dynamics equation is described by [9]:

$$M(q)\ddot{q} + C(q,\dot{q}) + G(q) = B(q)\tau + A^{T}(q)\lambda \tag{1}$$

where $\tau \in R^{r}$ is the input vector, $\lambda \in R^{m}$ is the vector of constraint forces, $M(q) \in R^{n \times n}$ is a symmetric and positive-definite inertia matrix, $C(q,\dot{q}) \in R^{n \times n}$ is the centripetal and coriolis matrix, $G(q) \in R^{n}$ is the gravitational vector, $B(q) \in R^{n \times r}$ is the input transformation matrix, and $A(q) \in R^{m \times n}$ is the matrix associated with the constraints. We consider that the robot is moving on flat terrain and therefore conclude that $G(q) = 0$. Equation (1) can be adapted as:

$$
\begin{bmatrix}
m & 0 & 2m_\omega d \sin \psi \\
0 & m & -2m_\omega d \cos \psi \\
2m_\omega d \sin \psi & -2m_\omega d \cos \psi & I
\end{bmatrix}
\begin{bmatrix} \ddot{x} \\ \ddot{y} \\ \ddot{\psi} \end{bmatrix}
+
\begin{bmatrix}
2m_\omega d \dot{\psi}^2 \cos \psi \\
2m_\omega d \dot{\psi}^2 \sin \psi \\
0
\end{bmatrix}
=
$$

$$
\frac{1}{r}
\begin{bmatrix}
\cos \psi & \cos \psi \\
\sin \psi & \sin \psi \\
L & -L
\end{bmatrix}
\begin{bmatrix} \tau_r \\ \tau_l \end{bmatrix}
+
\begin{bmatrix}
\sin \psi \\
-\cos \psi \\
d
\end{bmatrix} \lambda
\tag{2}
$$

and

$$
m = m_c + 2m_\omega , \quad I = I_c + 2m_\omega(d^2 + L^2) + 2I_m
\tag{3}
$$

where $m_c$ is the mass of the robot without the driving wheels, $m_\omega$ is the mass of each driving wheel plus the motor rotor, $I_c$ is the moment of inertia of the platform without the driving wheels, $I_\omega$ is the moment of inertia of each wheel including the motor rotor about the wheel axis and $I_m$ is the moment of inertia of each wheel and the motor rotor about a wheel diameter.

The kinematic constraints can be denoted as:

$$
A(q)\dot{q} = 0
\tag{4}
$$

where $A(q) = [\sin \psi \;\; -\cos \psi \;\; 0]$, then relation (4) can be rewritten as: $\dot{x}\sin \psi - \dot{y}\cos \psi = 0$. We can conclude that [9]:

$$
\dot{v} = \frac{(\tau_r + \tau_l)}{m \, r} , \quad \dot{\omega} = \frac{L(\tau_r - \tau_l)}{I \, r}
\tag{5}
$$

## 3    Adaptive Exponential Sliding Mode

In this section, we use the adaptive exponential sliding mode method for the dynamic trajectory tracking of a mobile robot. Multiplying equation (1) by $R^T(q)$ gives:

$$
R^T(q)M(q)\ddot{q} + R^T(q)C(q,\dot{q}) = R^T(q)B(q)\tau + R^T(q)A^T(q)\lambda
\tag{6}
$$

By combining (4) and (6) we get:

$$
\ddot{q} = -(R^T(q)M(q))^{-1}R^T(q)C(q,\dot{q}) + (R^T(q)M(q))^{-1}R^T(q)B(q)\tau
\tag{7}
$$

Equation (7) can be therefore rewritten as:

$$
\ddot{q} = F(q) + J(q)\tau \Rightarrow \tau = J(q)^{-1}(\ddot{q} - F(q))
\tag{8}
$$

where:

$$F(q) = -(R^T(q)M(q))^{-1}R^T(q)C(q,\dot{q})$$
$$J(q) = (R^T(q)M(q))^{-1}R^T(q)B(q)$$

$$(9)$$

Position, velocity and acceleration errors for trajectory following of mobile robot can be defined as:

$$\begin{cases} e = T(q - q_d) \\ \dot{e} = \dot{T}(q - q_d) + T(\dot{q} - \dot{q}_d) \\ \ddot{e} = \ddot{T}(q - q_d) + T(\ddot{q} - \ddot{q}_d) + 2\dot{T}(\dot{q} - \dot{q}_d) \end{cases}$$

$$(10)$$

where $T = \begin{bmatrix} \cos(\psi) & \sin(\psi) & 0 \\ -\sin(\psi) & \cos(\psi) & 0 \\ 0 & 0 & 1 \end{bmatrix}$.

The errors in position with respect to a frame attached to the robot are given by:

$$e = \begin{bmatrix} x_{err} \\ y_{err} \\ \psi_{err} \end{bmatrix} = \begin{bmatrix} \cos(\psi) & \sin(\psi) & 0 \\ -\sin(\psi) & \cos(\psi) & 0 \\ 0 & 0 & 1 \end{bmatrix} \begin{bmatrix} x - x_d \\ y - y_d \\ \psi - \psi_d \end{bmatrix}$$

$$(11)$$

The time derivative of the position errors take into account the constraint (4) which yields:

$$\dot{e} = \begin{cases} \dot{x}_{err} = v - v_d \cos(\psi_{err}) + y_{err}\omega \\ \dot{y}_{err} = v_d \sin(\psi_{err}) - x_{err}\omega \\ \dot{\psi}_{err} = \dot{\psi}_d - \dot{\psi} = \omega - \omega_d \end{cases}$$

$$(12)$$

The first step in the sliding mode control is to choose the switching function $S$ in terms of the tracking error. The general switching function for sliding mode control can be considered as:

$$S = (\frac{d}{dt} + \lambda)^{n-1}e$$

$$\text{if } n = 2 \Rightarrow S = \dot{e} + \lambda e$$

$$(13)$$

When the sliding surface is reached, the tracking error converges to zero as long as the error vector stays on the surface. The convergence rate is in direct relation with the value of $\lambda$.

If we consider Lyapunov function as:

$$V = \frac{1}{2}S^T S \Rightarrow \dot{V} = S^T\dot{S}$$

$$(14)$$

To make the system stable, we consider exponential sliding mode $\dot{S}$ as:

$$\dot{S} = -\frac{K}{Q(S)} sgn(S) = \ddot{e} + \lambda \dot{e} \tag{15}$$

where $Q(S) = \mu_o + (1 - \mu_o)e^{-\alpha|S|}$ and $\kappa = \begin{bmatrix} k_1 & 0 & 0 \\ 0 & k_2 & 0 \\ 0 & 0 & k_3 \end{bmatrix}$.

We can then easily conclude that $\dot{V} < 0, \forall k > 0$, which proves stability of the system because $Q(S)$ is always strictly positive.

Equation (15) can then be rewritten as:

$$\dot{S} = \ddot{e} + \lambda \dot{e} = -\frac{K}{\mu_o + (1 - \mu_o)e^{-\alpha|S|}} sgn(S) \tag{16}$$

where $\mu_o$ is a strictly positive offset less than $1 (0 < \mu_o < 1)$, and $\alpha$ is strictly positive.

By using equations (10) and (16), we get:

$$\ddot{T}(q - q_d) + T(\ddot{q} - \ddot{q}_d) + 2\dot{T}(\dot{q} - \dot{q}_d) + \lambda[\dot{T}(q - q_d) + T(\dot{q} - \dot{q}_d)] = -\frac{K}{Q(S)} sgn(S) \Rightarrow$$

$$\ddot{q} = \ddot{q}_d - T^{-1}\left[(\ddot{T} + \lambda \dot{T})(q - q_d) + (2\dot{T} + \lambda T)(\dot{q} - \dot{q}_d) + \frac{K}{Q(S)} sgn(S)\right] = \ddot{q}_d - T^{-1}\gamma \tag{17}$$

where $\gamma = \left[(\ddot{T} + \lambda \dot{T})(q - q_d) + (2\dot{T} + \lambda T)(\dot{q} - \dot{q}_d) + \frac{K}{Q(S)} sgn(S)\right]$

From equations (8) and (14) the control law can be found as:

$$\tau = J(q)^{-1}(\ddot{q}_d - T^{-1}\gamma - F(q)) \tag{18}$$

Generally, external disturbances on the system are unknown and parameter variations of the wheeled mobile robot are difficult to measure. Here we add adaptive law control on ESM to improve performance of the system against external disturbances and parameter variations.

The dynamic equation (8) in the presence of external disturbances can be rewritten as:

$$\ddot{q} = (\tilde{F}(q) + \Delta F(q)) + (\tilde{J}(q) + \Delta J(q))\tau + E_d =$$
$$(\tilde{F}(q) + \tilde{J}(q)\tau) + (\Delta F(q) + \Delta J(q)\tau) + E_d \tag{19}$$

where $E_d$ presents external disturbances on the torque and surface friction and $\Delta F(q), \Delta J(q)$ denote uncertainties on the system. We consider $\zeta = (\Delta F(q) + \Delta J(q)\tau) + E_d$.

The adaptive law is considered as:

$$\dot{\hat{\rho}} = \begin{bmatrix} k_1 \dfrac{s_1}{Q(s_1)} \operatorname{sgn}(s_1) & 0 & 0 \\[3mm] 0 & k_2 \dfrac{s_2}{Q(s_2)} \operatorname{sgn}(s_2) & 0 \\[3mm] 0 & 0 & k_3 \dfrac{s_3}{Q(s_3)} \operatorname{sgn}(s_3) \end{bmatrix}, \text{ then}$$

Equation (17) can be rewritten as:

$$\ddot{q} = \ddot{q}_d - T^{-1}\left[ (\ddot{T} + \lambda \dot{T})(q - q_d) + (2\dot{T} + \lambda T)(\dot{q} - \dot{q}_d) + \hat{\rho}\operatorname{sgn}(S) \right] = \ddot{q}_d - T^{-1}\hat{\gamma}$$

then we can obtain that:

$$\tau = \tilde{J}(q)^{-1}(\ddot{q}_d - T^{-1}\hat{\gamma} - \tilde{F}(q) - \zeta) \tag{20}$$

## 4    Experimental Results

The purpose of the experiments is to demonstrate the stability and the performance characteristics inferred from the theoretical development. Before presenting the experimental results, we briefly discuss here the experimental set up, communication and the design of the two-level controllers.

*A. Experimental set up*
Fig. 3 depicts the nonholonomic EtsRo mobile robot and structural design of the control and trajectory planning strategies for mobile robot to be used in the experimental tests. EtsRo is a unicycle type mobile robot with two actuated wheels, with the front wheels being equipped with two DC motors using $7.5\ volt$, $175\ rpm$ which are installed on the right and left front wheels. The incremental encoders are mounted on the motors counting with a resolution of $6000\ Pulses/Turn$. The wheels have a radius of $r = 4.5\ cm$, the length, width and height of EtsRo are 23, 20, and 11 $cm$ respectively. The total weight of the robot is around $2.3\ kg$. The maximum linear velocity is $1.12\ m/\sec$ and the maximum angular velocity is $5.74\ rad/s$. The experimental tests of our robot group are performed in a laboratory environment using a flat terrain with a work area of $4\times7$ meters. By using the following equation, we can obtain both the linear and angular velocities of robot:

$$v = \frac{v_R(t) + v_L(t)}{2}, \quad \omega = \frac{v_R(t) - v_L(t)}{L} \tag{21}$$

where $v_R(t)$ and $v_L(t)$ denote the right and left velocities and $L$ shows the distance between the two actuated wheels.

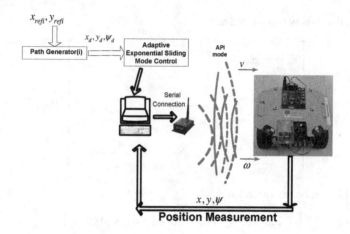

**Fig. 3.** EtsRo and control structural design

## B. Experimental tests and analyses

In this section, we discuss the results of the trajectory-following missions involving EtsRo mobile robot. Dynamics parameters for the EtsRo robot are given as following:

$$m_c = 2.3 \ kg \ , m_\omega = 0.28 \ kg \ , I_c = 0.01 kg \, / m^2 \ , I_\omega = 0.0056 \ kg \, / m^2$$
$$I_m = 0.0021 \ kg \, / m^2, r = 0.04 \, m \ , L = 0.1 m \ , d = 0.02$$

The experimental tests were performed on a sinusoid-shape trajectory.

In this scenario, at $40 \, ms$ the actual mass and inertia of Etsro have increased by 100% and at $120 \, ms$ an external disturbance is added on the torque of motors. These changes can be explained as:

$$\begin{cases} m : 2.3 \rightarrow 4.6 \ kg \\ I = 0.0196 \rightarrow .0392 \ \text{kg/m}^2 \end{cases} \quad t > 40 \, ms$$
$$E_d = 5\tau \qquad\qquad\qquad t > 120 ms$$

Initial position of the robot is $[x(t_0), y(t_0), \theta(t_0)]^T = [0,0,0]^T$. Figure 4 shows after $t > 120ms$, in the ESM method, robot starts to lose its trajectory while in AESM method, robot keeps following its desired trajectory. Linear and angular velocities of this test can be seen in Fig. 5 and Fig. 6. As can be seen in these figures, ESM and AESM are robust enough against changes related on uncertainties on mass and inertia. However, when there is a disturbance on torque after $t > 120ms$, ESM performance decreases significantly where AESM performance is still maintained. Fig. 7 shows trajectory errors on $x_{err}$. This figure confirms performance of AESM on trajectory tracking against disturbances on torque.

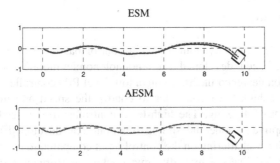

**Fig. 4.** Reference trajectories and real robot trajectories

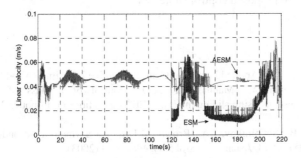

**Fig. 5.** Linear velocities of robot

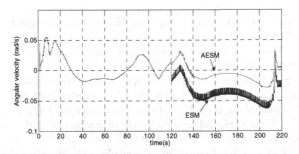

**Fig. 6.** Angular velocities of robot

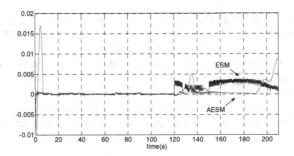

**Fig. 7.** Trajectory error $x_{err}$

# 5    Conclusion

In this paper, an efficient dynamic tracking control based on adaptive exponential sliding mode has been developed for a nonholonomic mobile robot. A two-level controller has been designed incorporating a low-level PID controller for the right and left motors, and a high-level controller to control the speed and movement of the robot for trajectory following. The high-level controller uses a feedback controller utilizing the adaptive exponential sliding function. The developed adaptive sliding mode control reduces chattering on the control input compared to conventional sliding mode control, and delivers a high dynamic tracking performance in a steady-state mode. The experimental results obtained using an EtsRo robot demonstrate the effectiveness of the proposed control strategies.

# References

[1] Slotine, J.J., Li, W.: Applied Nonlinear Control. Prentice-Hall, Englewood Cliffs (1991)
[2] Sankaranarayanan, V., Mahindrakar, A.D.: Control of a class of underactuated mechanical systems using sliding modes. IEEE Transactions on Robotics 25(2), 459–467 (2009)
[3] Shtessel, Y.B., Shkolnikov, I.A., Brown, M.D.J.: An asymptotic second-order smooth sliding mode control. Asian J. Control 5(4), 498–5043 (2003)
[4] Bartoliniand, G., Ferrara, A., Usani, E.: Second-order sliding-mode control of a mobile robot based on a harmonic potential field. IET Control Theory & Applications 2, 807–818 (2008)
[5] Bartolini, G., Ferrara, A., Pisano, A., Usai, E.: On the convergence systems. Int. J. Control 74, 718–731 (2001)
[6] Bartolini, G., Pisano, A., Usai, E.: Digital second order sliding mode control for uncertain nonlinear systems. Automatica 37(9), 1371–1377 (2001)
[7] Utkin, V.I.: Sliding Modes In Control And Optimization. Springer, Berlin (1992)
[8] Das, T., Kar, I.N.: Design and implementation of an adaptive fuzzy logic based controller of wheeled mobile robots. IEEE Trans. Control Syst. Technol. 14(3), 501–510 (2006)
[9] Fukao, T., Nakagawa, H., Adachi, N.: Adaptive tracking control of a nonholonomic mobile robot. IEEE Transactions on Robotics and Automation 16(5), 609–615 (2000)
[10] Fierro, R., Lewis, F.L.: Control of a nonholonomic mobile robot: backstepping kinematics into dynamics. In: Proc. 34th IEEE Conf. Decision Control, pp. 3805–3810 (1995)
[11] Park, B., Yoo, S.S., Park, J.B., Chou, Y.H.: Adaptive Neural Sliding Mode Control of Nonholonomic Wheeled Mobile Robots With Model Uncertainty. IEEE Transactions on Control Systems Technology 17(1), 207–214 (2009)
[12] Corradin, M.L., Orland, G.: Control of mobile robots with uncertainties in the dynamical model: a discrete time sliding mode approach with experimental results. Control Engineering Practice 10, 23–34 (2002)
[13] Fallah, C.: Etude de la commmande par mode de glissement sur les system mono et multi variables. Master Thesis, Quebec University (ETS), Montreal, Canada (2007)

# The Study of a Vision-Based Pedestrian Interception System

Wanfeng He, Yongchun Fang, and Xuebo Zhang

Institute of Robotics and Automatic Information Systems,
Nankai University, Tianjin 300071, China
{hewf,yfang,zhangxb}@robot.nankai.edu.cn

**Abstract.** This paper designs a vision-based pedestrian interception system with a mobile robot, which can be potentially utilized in such applications as service robots. Specifically, by employing the Histograms of Oriented Gradients(HOG), together with some Edge Detection (ED) method, we first propose a novel HOG-ED approach to detect a human being from the series of acquired images accurately, based on which the depth information is successfully extracted on the basis of some geometrical analysis. After that, a two-level vision-based control scheme integrating depth extraction is presented to drive a mobile robot to intercept the pedestrian. The accuracy of the proposed depth estimation method and the interception controller are validated through experimental results.

**Keywords:** target interception, human detection, depth estimation, robot control, service robot.

## 1 Introduction

Interception is an important task in a number of applications, ranging from active surveillance to automatic service. The development of effective methods for this task meets great challenges integrating human detection, filtering, control design and artificial intelligence strategy. Many different approaches have been proposed in the literature for the interception of a moving target, depending on the target motion characteristics as well as the robot kinematic model.

For an interception task, the motion of the dynamic target is usually unknown in advance, thus it is required to estimate its position/velocity on the basis of on-board sensors' measurements. In this sense, visual feedback [6] has proven to be an effective approach for interception tasks. Specifically, in position-based visual servoing, the target pose is estimated from visual data and geometric relationship. For instance, an omni-directional vision system is used in [1], [2], [3] to determine the robot pose from extracted features, so that some basic operations of a soccer robot can be implemented in terms of trajectory tracking and pose stabilization. In this context, Kalman filtering is often used to obtain a robust prediction of the target motion [3], [4], [5]. In image-based visual servoing, the spatial relationship between the target and the robot camera is directly estimated in the image plane. This approach, originally developed for robotic

C.-Y. Su, S. Rakheja, H. Liu (Eds.): ICIRA 2012, Part I, LNAI 7506, pp. 653–662, 2012.

manipulators equipped with an eye-in-hand system, has also been extended to nonholonomic mobile robots [7]. On the other hand, human-like strategies have been more and more often utilized in the interception problem with mobile robots. These works adopt some human-like behaviors, such as anthropomorphic driving, to accomplish interception tasks more wisely [8], [9]. Yet, these methods are usually empirical, and there is no theoretical guarantee for the performance of this kind of interception systems.

For some specific interception assignments, the target motion can be sometimes obtained as *a priori*. In this case, the task of intercepting the target can be equivalently turned into a robot trajectory planning/tracking problem, and various tracking controllers can then be employed to implement the task. For example, a robot navigation technique for intercepting a moving target from a specific angle is proposed in [10], [11]. This kind of techniques, when combined with tracking methods, can be further improved to achieve smooth interception trajectory with terminal velocity matching [6].

The interception approach employed in this paper makes use of visual information only and does not need long-term predictions of the target motion. It is particularly motivated by the potential applications in the general case when the target motion is unknown in advance. Further, a two-level vision-based control scheme integrating depth extraction is presented to drive a mobile robot to intercept the pedestrian. That is, on the lower level, the pan-tilt platform carrying an on-board camera is controlled so as to keep the target to the center of the image plane as close as possible. On the higher level, the relative position of the pedestrian is computed from the images and then employed in a feedback control law to enable the robot to intercept the pedestrian efficiently.

The rest of the paper is organized as follows. The problem statement is provided in section 2. The depth estimation of the moving target is presented in section 3. Then, the robot control law is discussed in section 4, together with the analysis on its performance. After that, some simulation and experiment results are included in section 5 to demonstrate the performance of the designed pedestrian interception system. Finally, the conclusion and future work are expressed in section 6.

## 2    Problem Development

As stated earlier, the robot will surveil the surrounding environment, and whenever the dynamic target appears, the robot, with the aid of the on-board PTZ-camera, starts to recognize the target and then intercepts it efficiently to provide some possible service. Based on this objective, the interception system is designed with the recognition/interception task achieved by the following steps. Firstly, after capturing an object, some computer vision algorithms will be employed to extract the features of the object, which will then be compared with those of the interested target to ensure correct target recognition. Meanwhile, the orientation of the camera is controlled to enable visual tracking for the target. Secondly, based on the height information of the target, some geometrical analysis is adopted to estimate the depth of the target. It should be noted that the first two steps are the research focuses of this paper. Thirdly, a vision-based control law proposed in [6], which integrates all of the above information, is employed to enable the robot to intercept the target efficiently.

# 3    Depth Estimation of the Moving Target

In this section, a vision-based depth estimation method is proposed, wherein the resulting depth of the target will be utilized in the subsequent interception control law.

## 3.1    HOG-ED Feature Based Human Detection

The accuracy of depth estimation is significant for a target interception task. To address this issue, we propose a HOG-ED (Histograms of Oriented Gradients and Edge Detection) human detection algorithm, which successfully integrates the HOG features [15] and edge features altogether to ensure the detection accuracy.

Human detection aims to calculate a closely-surrounding rectangle for the human body. To achieve this task, we propose a multi-feature fusion algorithm, which introduces edge features into the conventional HOG feature based detection procedure to successfully increase the accuracy. The procedure of the algorithm is described as follows:

1. A closely-surrounding rectangle for the human body is calculated based on the conventional HOG feature human detection procedure. After sufficient experiment testing, we know that due to the defects of the HOG detection procedure, the obtained area is always bigger than the actual human size, which will cause a serious problem for the subsequent depth estimation.
2. To attack the above problem, further processing is required to achieve a more accurate result, therefore, we introduce the edge detection algorithm to shrink the obtained rectangle to make a possibly perfect surrounding for the human. That is, since the human body in the detection area is the biggest HOG feature based occlusive region, we can then obtain the edge of the human body through edge detection method and filter out the noise to improve the accuracy of the detection results.

Further, the algorithm proposed in this paper aims to improve the accuracy on the size detection of targets, compared with other algorithms, such as [13] and [15]. It will be shown that the size detection accuracy is improved remarkably.

As supported by numerous experimental tests, the proposed method presents superior performance to yield a more accurate surrounding rectangle than that of the traditional HOG method. The result of one experiment test is shown in Fig. 1, where the three pictures represent the results of different steps of the human detection algorithm. That is, the left picture represents the human detection result by HOG method, the central one shows the human edge detection result, and the right one represents the human detection result by HOG-ED method. It can be seen that the black rectangle calculated through HOG-ED algorithm is more accurate than the blue one obtained through the traditional HOG method.

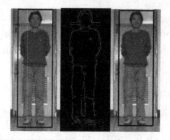

**Fig. 1.** HOG-ED based human detection. Left: human detection by HOG. Center: human edge detection. Right: human detection by HOG_ED.

## 3.2 Geometric Analysis-Based Depth Estimation

Based on the previous human detection results, some geometric analysis is utilized to compute the depth value. The geometric relationship among the target, the robot and the camera is shown in Fig. 2.

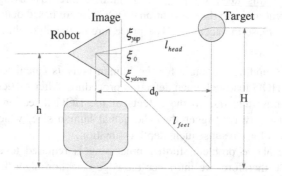

**Fig. 2.** The schematic diagram for depth estimation

Let $\xi_{yup}$ and $\xi_{ydown}$ denote the pixel coordinates of the human head and feet vertex, respectively, $\xi_0$ the camera optical center along the y axis. In Fig. 2, $h$ represents the constant distance between the optical axis and the horizontal floor, $H$ is the height of the pedestrian, $d_0$ is referred to as the initial depth from the robot to the human body. After some geometric analysis, it is pretty straightforward to obtain the following equations:

$$\begin{cases} \dfrac{\xi_{yup} - \xi_0}{f} = \tan \varphi_{up} = \dfrac{h}{d_0} \\[2mm] \dfrac{\xi_{ydown} - \xi_0}{f} = \tan \varphi_{down} = \dfrac{H - h}{d_0} \end{cases} \qquad (1)$$

where $f$ is the focal length, $\varphi_{up}$ and $\varphi_{down}$ are the intersection angles of $l_{head}$ and $l_{feet}$ with the optical axis respectively. It follows from (1) that the initial depth $d_0$ and the height $H$ can be obtained as:

$$
\begin{cases}
d_0 = \dfrac{hf}{\xi_{ydown} - \xi_0} \\
H = \dfrac{\xi_{yup} - \xi_0}{f} \cdot d_0 + h
\end{cases}
\tag{2}
$$

Since the pedestrian's height can be estimated through the previous image analysis, its depth can then be obtained through the geometric relationship shown in Fig. 2. That is, if we denote the PTZ-camera's pitch angle as $\phi(t)$, then the depth information can be calculated as:

$$
d = \frac{H - h}{\tan \phi}
\tag{3}
$$

For the previous depth information algorithm, numerous experiments have been implemented to test its performance. Tab. 1 shows the obtained depth estimation results for three different situations. As can be seen from these experimental results, the proposed depth estimation approach provides very accurate and stable results, with the estimation error around 2%.

**Table 1.** Experimental results of depth estimation algorithm

| Actual depth values (cm) | 492 | 502 | 512 |
|---|---|---|---|
| Estimated depth values (cm) | 490.46 | 499.18 | 508.33 |

## 4    Robot Control

The objective of this section is to employ a vision-based controller to enable a wheeled robot to achieve efficient interception with a dynamic target. In particular, we take the nonholonomic rolling constraint kinematic model as:

$$
\begin{cases}
\dot{x} = v \cos \theta \\
\dot{y} = v \sin \theta \\
\dot{\theta} = w
\end{cases}
\tag{4}
$$

where $\vec{P} = [x, y, \theta]^T$ is the robot pose expressed in the world frame, $v$ and $w$ are the robot linear and angular velocities.

Subsequently, the geometry relationship between the target and the robot, with reference to the problem statement part, is illustrated in Fig. 3.

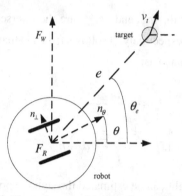

**Fig. 3.** Target interception with the mobile robot

In Fig. 3, $F_W$ and $F_R$ define the world and the robot frames, $e(t)$ denotes the distance error between the robot's current position and the target's position, and $n_\theta$ is the orientation of the robot's current pose, $\theta(t)$ represents the intersection angle of $n_\theta$ and the $X$ axis of $F_W$, $\theta_e(t)$ defines the intersection angle of $e(t)$ and the $X$ axis of $F_W$, $v_t$ is the velocity of the target in $F_R$.

The interception controller, derived from the Cartesian position regular of [14] by adding the angular velocity feedback term $|e|\sin\alpha$, which is the projection of $e(t)$ along the orthogonal direction, to the forward axis of the robot, can be expressed as:

$$\begin{cases} v = k_1 \, |e| \cos\alpha + v_t^T n_\theta \\ w = k_2\alpha + k_3 \, |e| \sin\alpha + \dot{\theta}_e \end{cases} \tag{5}$$

where the control gains $k_i > 0 (i = 1, 2, 3)$. With the feedback term, this controller results in a very effective interception of the target. Further, the global asymptotic stability of the position/orientation error can be guaranteed, as proven in [6].

Subsequently, the variables used in the controller are introduced to show how to calculate the controller. Above all, there is an offset between the image plane of the PTZ-camera and the geometric center of the robot, and we define it as $s$, which is a constant. Then based on the law of cosines, we can obtain $e(t)$ with the following equation:

$$|e| = \sqrt{d^2 + s^2 + 2ds\cos\gamma} \tag{6}$$

where $d(t)$ represents the time-varying depth signal of the moving target, which is obtained from the depth estimation algorithm described in Section 3.2, $\gamma(t)$ is an approximate representation of the horizontal rotation angle of the PTZ-camera.

The intersection angle $\alpha(t)$ of the orientation of the robot's current pose and the distance line $e(t)$ can be derived from the law of sines, and the equation is:

$$\alpha = \arcsin\frac{d\sin\gamma}{|e|} \tag{7}$$

Given the system sampling period $T$, the target's velocity can be calculated as follows [6]:

$$v_t^T n_\theta \approx v \cos \frac{wT}{2} + \frac{|e| \cos \alpha}{T} - \frac{|e| \cos(\alpha - wT)}{T} \tag{8}$$

Similarly, $\dot{\theta}_e$ can be obtained with the following equation:

$$\dot{\theta}_e = w + \frac{\Delta \alpha}{T} \tag{9}$$

where $\Delta \alpha$ is the increment of $\alpha(t)$ in a sampling period.

## 5    Simulation and Experiment Results

In this section simulations and experiments are carried out to verify the performance of the pedestrian interception system.

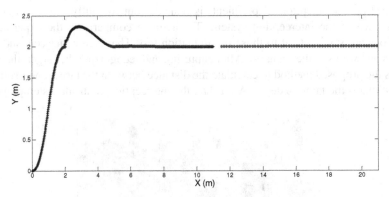

(a) The pedestrian walks in a straight trajectory (red curve)

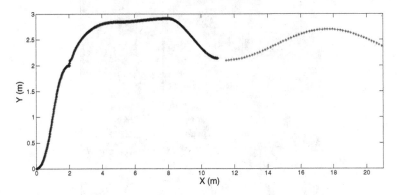

(b) The pedestrian walks in a sinusoidal trajectory (red curve)

**Fig. 4.** Interception trajectories for the mobile robot and the pedestrian

## 5.1     Simulation Results

In the simulation, the initial pose of the mobile robot is set as $p_R = [0,0,0]$, surveiling its surrounding environment. At this time, a pedestrian who will be served comes into the robot's vision, the robot automatically recognizes it and begins to intercept the target. When the distance between the target and the robot reaches to the desired value, the robot stops near the target to accomplish the given tasks.

The simulation results are presented in Fig. 4, which demonstrates the movement of the robot and the pedestrian, with the black and red curves representing the trajectory of the robot and the pedestrian, respectively. Further, in Fig. 4(a), the pedestrian walks in a straight line, and in Fig. 4(b), the pedestrian takes a sinusoidal trajectory. Please note that these two lines are very general and representative for human manner. It can be seen that the interception task is successfully accomplished and the robot stops near by the target when the distance comes to the desired value to avoid knocking down the pedestrian.

## 5.2     Experiment Results

A pedestrian interception experiment is carried out to fully demonstrate the performance of the interception system. To facilitate comparison, the experimental conditions are set identical to those of simulation test. That is, a pedestrian suddenly appears and walks in the scenario. After capturing and recognizing the target, the robot utilizes the proposed method to calculate the distance between the target and itself, and then estimates the target's depth. After that, the interception controller is employed to

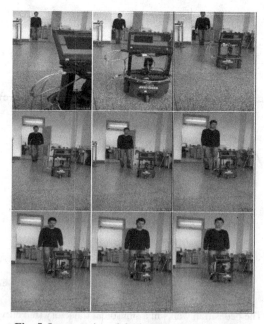

**Fig. 5.** Image series of the interception experiment

drive the robot to intercept the target. As shown in Fig. 5, the pedestrian walks through the door in a straight line, after capturing and recognizing the target, the robot is driven to intercept the pedestrian and stops in front of him successfully.

To gain more deep understanding of the proposed algorithm, the experimental results are compared with those of the previous simulation test. The comparison of the robot's velocity is recorded in Fig. 6, where the blue and red curves represent the simulation data and the experimental results from the encoder, respectively. As shown in the figure, the experimental results accord well with those of the simulation test, yet there is still some mismatch between these two curves, which mainly comes from the mechanical flaw of the system and the noise of the encoder measurement.

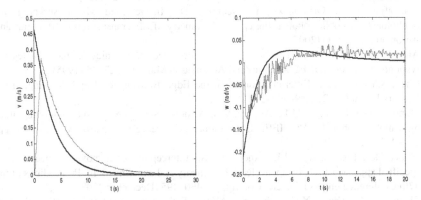

**Fig. 6.** A comparison of simulation and the experiment results. Left: the comparison of the robot's linear velocity. Right: the comparison of the robot's angular velocity.

## 6    Conclusion and Future Work

In this paper, we have presented a vision-based pedestrian interception system consisting of such components as human detection, depth estimation and interception controller. It has been validated through both simulation and experiment tests on a wheeled mobile robot, confirming its great applicability for service robots. The designed interception strategy can be extended to other complex platforms, such as an unmanned aerial vehicle, without much difficulty. Our future research will try to design a more efficient interception method suitable for a service robot, and we are also making an effort to predict the states of the moving target to further improve the performance of the interception controller, which enables the robot to intercept the target more accurately and more intelligently.

## References

1. Jolly, K.G., Sreerama Kumar, R., Vijayakumar, R.: Intelligent task planning and action selection of a mobile robot in a multi-agent system through a fuzzy neural network approach. Engineering Applications of Artificial Intelligence 23(6), 923–933 (2010)

2. Jolly, K.G., Sreerama Kumar, R., Vijayakumar, R.: An artificial nerral network based dynamic controller for a robot in a multi-agent system. Neurocomputing 73(1-3), 293–294 (2009)
3. Artus, G., Morin, P., Samson, C.: Tracking of an omnidirectional target with a nonholonomic mobile robot. In: Conference on Advanced Robotics, pp. 1468–1473 (2003)
4. Budiharto, W., Santoso, A., Purwanto, D., Jazidie, A.: A navigation system for service robot using stereo vision and Kalman Filtering. In: The 11th International Conference on Control, Automation and Systems, pp. 1771–1776 (2011)
5. Song, X.J., Seneviratne, L.D., Althoefer, K.: A Kalman filter-integrated optical flow method for velocity sensing of mobile robots. Transactions on Mechatronics, 551–563 (2011)
6. Freda, L., Oriolo, G.: Vision-based interception of a moving target with a nonholonomic mobile robot. Robotics and Autonomous Systems 55(6), 419–432 (2007)
7. Mariottini, G.L., Oriolo, G., Prattichizzo, D.: Image-based visual servoing for nonholonomic mobile robots using epipolar geometry. IEEE Transactions on Robotics and Automation, 87–100 (2007)
8. Aicardi, M., Casalino, G., Bicchi, A.: Closed loop steering of unicycle like vehicles via lyapunov techniques. IEEE Robotics and Automation Magazine, 27–35 (1995)
9. Chen, S.Y., Li, Y.F.: Determination of Stripe Edge Blurring for Depth Sensing. IEEE Sensors Journal 11(2), 389–390 (2011)
10. Manchester, I.R., Emily, M.L., Andrey, V.S.: Vision-based interception of a moving target by a mobile robot. In: 16th IEEE International Conference on Control Applications, pp. 397–402 (October 2007)
11. Manchester, I.R., Emily, M.L., Andrey, V.S.: Interception of a moving object with a specified approach angle by a wheeled robot: theory and experiment. In: Proceedings of the 47th Conference on Decision and Control, pp. 490–495 (December 2008)
12. Zhang, X.B., Fang, Y.C., Liu, X.: Motion-Estimation_Based Visual Servoing of Nonholonomic Mobile Robots. IEEE Transactions on Robotics, 1167–1175 (2011)
13. Wang, X.Y., Han, T.X., Yan, S.C.: An HOG-LOP Human Detector with Partial Occlusion Handing. In: IEEE 12th International Conference on Computer Vision, pp. 32–39 (2009)
14. De Luca, D., Oriolo, G.: Local incremental planning for nonholonomic mobile robots. In: IEEE International Conference on Robotics and Automation, pp. 104–110 (1994)
15. Dalal, N., Triggs, B.: Histograms of Oriented Gradients for Human Detection. In: IEEE Computer Society Conference on Computer Vision and Pattern Recognition, pp. 886–893 (2005)
16. Sabnis, A., Vachhani, L.: Single image based depth estimation for robotic applications. In: IEEE Conference on Recent Advances in Intelligent Computational Systems, pp. 102–106 (2011)

# Self-optimizing Handling System
# for Assembling Large Components

Markus Janssen[1] and Rainer Müller[2]

[1] Laboratory for Machine Tools and Production Engineering (WZL),
Chair of Production Metrology and Quality Management, RWTH Aachen University
Steinbachstraße 19, 52074 Aachen, Germany
m.janssen@wzl.rwth-aachen.de
[2] Zentrum für Mechatronik und Automatisierungstechnik (ZeMA) gGmbH,
Gewerbepark Eschberger Weg, 66121 Saarbrücken, Germany
rainer.mueller@mechatronikzentrum.de

**Abstract.** Efficiency in aircraft production can be increased by using reconfigurable handling systems for assembling large components. The development of such a handling system can be simplified by using existing control functions like trajectory generation and transformations, e.g. from a robot simulation tool. Also self-optimizing functions, like the integration of production metrology for error compensation, can be implemented through this approach. In order to use the simulation functions and data for online controlling of the real robots, a fast and reliable data transfer between the simulation tool and the real controllers is required. Reconfigurability is achieved by a consistent modular design, from a virtual model in a simulation tool to the mechatronic design of a real robot.

**Keywords:** robot control, self-optimizing assembly, integrative production.

## 1    Introduction

Many jobs in industrial countries are endangered to be outsourced to low-wage countries [1]. Especially producing enterprises are willing to shift capacity abroad [2]. In order to maintain jobs in high-wage European countries as a prerequisite for prosperity, producing companies have to ensure their global competiveness by efficient production systems. Whilst producers in emerging countries focus mainly on mass production with simple, robust and value stream oriented processes, companies in high-tech countries have to satisfy customer's specific desires and requirements by optimizing their processes with capital-intensive planning methods. To obtain a sustainable competition for production in high-tech countries, new solutions are required to increase product variability whilst producing at mass production costs. This can be achieved by more value-oriented process chains and a reduction of planning efforts [3].

One approach to reduce planning efforts are self-optimizing production systems, which allow an immediate adaptation of the value stream [4].

C.-Y. Su, S. Rakheja, H. Liu (Eds.): ICIRA 2012, Part I, LNAI 7506, pp. 663–672, 2012.

Self-optimizing production systems can increase planning efficiency by a recurring execution of the actions [5]

- continuous analysis of the current situation,
- determination of targets, and
- adaptation of the system's behavior to achieve these targets.

A need for self-optimization can occur in manufacturing as well as in assembly. One industrial application which is in focus of research is aircraft assembly. In this industry efficiency in assembly can be increased by replacing fixed jigs by more flexible, modular solutions.

## 2　Reconfigurable Production Systems for Aircraft Assembly

In aircraft production large components have to be assembled in small tolerances (relative to the dimensions of the product). In order to fulfill these requirements, fixed steel jigs are used which map the geometry of a component. For each component an individual jig has to be produced. As the jigs can be used for a product lifecycle of 10-15 years, the effort for designing and producing the jigs can be justified. But in the face of shorter lifecycles in aircraft production, new light-weight materials and the production of prototypes in small batches, more flexible production systems are desired.

One approach is to replace fixed jigs by flexible and programmable jigs, i.e. kinematic units or robots (Figure 1) [6]. Especially for the handling of large components, many robots are required to support the part at several points. For this task the capabilities of standard robots are usually too high as only a low payload and a reduced number of active joints are sufficient. By designing customized kinematic units, cost-efficient handling systems can be created [7].

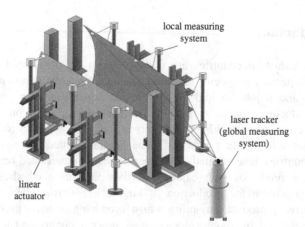

**Fig. 1.** Positioning system for the structural assembly of aircraft fuselage sections [6]

The idea is to develop a toolbox for the configuration of assembly systems for large components. Depending on the requirements of a specific assembly process, appropriate modules to comply with the workspace, accuracy, payload, degrees of freedom etc. can be selected. Special handling units as well as standard robots form this toolbox. Depending on the geometry of the component, the type of kinematic units/robots, their number and base position within an assembly platform and their grasp points at the object can be varied.

Besides the mechanical development of the kinematic units, the control system has to deal with different types of robots and changing configurations, too. As the mechanical design of special handling units causes huge engineering efforts, the development of the control system and the programming of the system should be as simple as possible. But path planning and programming of cooperating robots can be a complex and time-consuming task. In order not to stop a producing assembly station, this task is nowadays usually done in an offline simulation tool, where a virtual production cell is modeled and virtual robots are programmed. Before the programs can be transferred to the real robot controllers and used in a production cell, they have to be adapted in the real environment because of geometrical deviations and tolerances of the equipment. One present way to simplify programming is to derive the robot motions from the path of the handled component. The trajectory of each robot can be calculated from the grasp point at the object that has to be handled. The transformation of the objects' basis to each gripping point is considered constant during the motion and the resulting trajectory describes the movement of the tool center point (TCP) of each robot.

In order to simplify not only the programming of the handling units but also the development of the control system, it would be very helpful to use existing control functionalities from software applications, such as robot simulation tools. The idea is to use functions of path planning, trajectory generation and transformations in the simulation and to directly transfer the trajectories of each robot to its controller. That means that geometrical deviations of the real environment have to be modeled in the simulation very accurate, as adaptation of the trajectories is not possible. In order to provide interoperability between different robots, a standardized format of the data and a modular control system for coordination and synchronization is required.

The objective of this work is to

- implement a fast and reliable data transfer between a simulation tool and robot controllers. In order to use simulation data directly for robot control, inaccuracies of the real world have to be modeled in the virtual environment.
- define mechatronic handling modules that can be reconfigured easily and can be controlled by existing functions and online-data from a robot simulation tool.
- develop a modular control system for a reconfigurable handling system consisting of different robots/ kinematic units

The approach to achieve these objectives is described in the following chapters.

# 3    Integration of Simulation and Control

The development of a control system for specially designed handling units can be simplified by using existing control functionalities from a simulation tool. The simulation tool can be used to do the programming of different robots in only one programming language, to synchronize cooperating robots and to generate their trajectories.

The simulation tool is running on a PC, which has no real-time bus interface which is though essential for safety functions and a reliable transfer of the trajectories. Therefore, the data must first be transferred to a programmable logic controller (PLC), which can guarantee these requirements. This PLC will also be used as a central controller to coordinate cooperating robots. Also a fine interpolation of the motions can be done, before the data is distributed to several decentral robot controllers (RC) of the handling units. This leads to a control architecture with three types of controllers:

1. Simulation tool running on a PC
2. Coordinating central controller (PLC)
3. Decentral robot controllers (RC or PLC)

Starting point of implementing a new application is the path planning for the handling object. On the basis of the object trajectory a suitable system configuration, i.e. the type, number and base position of appropriate robots, can be determined. The resulting trajectories can be checked for collisions and reachability in the virtual environment. Monitoring and adaptation of the trajectories is done manually offline.

After a suitable movement has been determined, the motion data is exported from the simulation tool to a central control module, which has to coordinate the handling units. This approach replaces the efforts for adjusting the robot programs in the real environment and simplifies the commissioning of robot applications significantly, which is an important advantage, especially for frequently changing tasks. In order to achieve smooth robot motions, it is essential to generate accurate nominal values in a fast interpolation step. The motion of a robot can be described in robot's internal joint space or in 3-D Cartesian space [8]. The description in robot space has the advantage, that no further calculations for actuating the robot are required, as the values can be directly given to the drives. The description in Cartesian space has the advantage, that it is independent from the kinematic structure of the handling unit, which simplifies the adaptation of the assembly platform and the exchange of handling units. Therefore this approach is considered better for the depicted system, knowing that the inverse kinematic has to be implemented on the controller of each handling unit.

In the next step the motion data is distributed from the central control module to the kinematic modules via real time bus system. On each robot controller a simple program is running and awaiting instructions from the leading control module. This program can cope with all possible motions, instructions and signals that might occur, and thus does not need to be adapted when a task changes. Further functions are calculating the inverse kinematic and state control, e.g. of the gripper and the drives of a handling unit.

During handling, the motion of the handled object or the robot positions can be monitored by a measurement system. Thus, deviations between simulation and reality, which always exist, can be identified and compensated. Offsets between the nominal and the current position have to be fed back in order to correct the position of the object or a robot. When

- this analysis of the current position is done continuously,
- the new target position is calculated automatically and
- the compensation of deviations is done automatically,

we can speak of a self-optimizing system defined by [5]. Besides self-optimizing, the handling system should also be reconfigurable to meet industrial requirements. Therefore a modular design and a consistent definition of a mechatronic module are required.

## 4    Definition of Mechatronic Modules

In order to achieve easy reconfiguration, a consistent mechatronic modular design of the robots and kinematic units belonging to a toolbox has to be defined.
Mechatronics is an interdisciplinary field in which

- mechanical systems
- electronic systems and
- information technology

act together [9, 10]. In this context, standard industrial robots can be seen as mechatronic modules, as each robot has its mechanical structure, an electronic system for actuating the drives and information technology (software) running in a controller to generate trajectories, calculate transformations and communicate with its environment. As described before, in certain application the development of special kinematic units instead of using standard robots is cost-efficient. For easy reconfiguration, these kinematic units should also be defined as mechatronic modules. That means that a handling system, e.g. consisting of four kinematic units with three active joints each, should not be designed as one machine with 12 axes, but each handling unit should be defined as a mechatronic module with a mechanical system, electronic system and information technology. Of course, the modular design increases the number of mechanical, electronic and software interfaces in an assembly platform, but this has to be taken into account in order to simplify reconfiguration.

In contrast to the existing mechatronic definition of robots, this definition has to be extended when control functionalities and online-data from a simulation tool have to be integrated to a module. In order to use a robot within the control platform, also a virtual model must be part of the mechatronic module [11].

The virtual model is created in a simulation tool. As the model is a piece of software it can be assigned to the mechatronic element "information technology". On the other hand the virtual model consists of virtual mechanics, which can even have collisions etc. with other virtual mechanics, a virtual controller and virtual software. Therefore it can be seen as an additional virtual element of a mechatronic module (Figure 2).

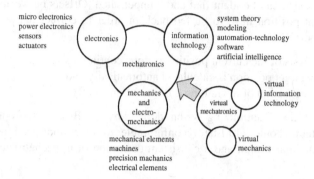

**Fig. 2.** Definition of mechatronic modules (based on [10])

Now the definition of a mechatronic module, which is part of a toolbox for the configuration of a handling system for large components, can be summarized. The mechanics comprise the mechanical and electrical elements of a serial or parallel kinematic structure with several links and joints. The electronics comprise the microelectronics, power electronics and servo drives (motor, encoder, ...) for the actuated joints of the mechanics. The information technology comprises the control hardware and software for real-time and safety requirements, especially pre-defined interfaces and protocols. The virtual mechatronics comprises a virtual robot model, which can be used in robot simulation tool, and functions, which are related to the simulation tool, e.g. trajectory generation. Interfaces to the user and for data exchange with other controllers have to be provided. The objective is to integrate all robots that fit to this definition, into the toolbox for the reconfigurable handling system.

For the handling of large components a large workspace as well as high precision is required. In the case of objects which have no intrinsic rigidity also the application of forces can be necessary to form the object into a specific shape. To fulfill these requirements, the path planning task can be divided into a three-level procedure (Figure 3). At first a global motion has to be planned to cover the workspace and to prepare the robot system for the next step, a regional motion to position the handled object. Finally a local motion may be necessary to compensate geometrical deviations e.g. by applying forces to the object. This layout leads to a handling system consisting of different types of robots for different movements, e.g. gantries for global, vertical articulated arms for regional and tools for local motions.

In order to provide reconfigurability, each module (for global, regional and local motions) has to meet the definition for a mechatronic module. For interoperability between different robots, a modular control system for coordination and synchronization has been developed for controlling the heterogeneous system [12]. The coordination of all mechatronic modules is done in a simulation tool, which guarantees a synchronous movement of the complete handling system.

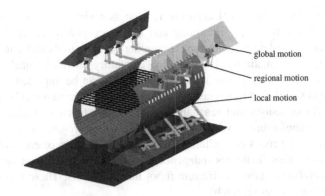

**Fig. 3.** Global, regional and local path planning for handling large components

A central control module enhances the flexibility and reconfigurability as no dependencies between decentral robots exist, which is a basic requirement for easy reconfiguration. Also the data management of central and decentral information has to be defined, in order to simplify and reduce modification after reconfiguration. Therefore all control data is distinguished in central data of the handling task, e.g. the path of the object and position of grasp point at the object, and decentral data of the kinematic module, i.e. its base position and kinematic parameters.

## 5    Implementation

A reconfigurable handling system consisting of special kinematic units and the depicted control system have been implemented in a demonstrator.

In order to allow easy reconfiguration by a worker without any mechanical support, the handling modules are designed light-weight and less massive than conventional industrial robots. Further reduction of weight is obtained by a simplified drive concept, as not all six joints of the kinematic modules are actuated by a servo drive but remain passive. Due to the low weight the assembly arms can be rearranged by a worker for each task, so that an automated handling system can be configured even for small series (Figure 4).

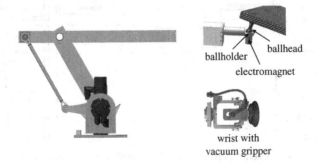

**Fig. 4.** Reconfigurable handling unit and grippers

A 3D robot simulation tool 'Easy-Rob' is used as a virtual environment for path planning, simulation-based programming and trajectory generation of the handling system [13]. The complete assembly cell, including fixtures, tools and standard robots as well as special kinematic units with up to 12 rotatory or translational axes can be modeled and visualized by geometric elements, which can be imported from a CAD tool. Within this simulation tool a task-specific robot configuration can be determined and checked for collisions and reachability. In contrast to conventional simulation tools of robot manufacturers, where an executable robot program is created offline and transferred to the robot controller, in this approach the data of each robot TCP is being transferred. This facilitates independency of any specific robot language and allows interoperability between different robot manufacturers. These capabilities are being validated in current research.

Another reason for selecting Easy-Rob is its open software interface, which is vital for the control concept described before. The simulation tool runs on a PC which is connected to the central control module via TCP/IP Ethernet for transferring the trajectories of the handling modules. The central control module as well as the decentral controllers of the handling units are supplied by 'B&R Automation' [14]. Each kinematic unit consists of its own control cabinet with standard components to provide basic robot capabilities for kinematic calculation. Coordination and synchronization is done by a superordinated controller in a separate control cabinet. The kinematic modules are connected to the central controller via real-time bus system (Figure 5).

The challenge of this control concept is to guarantee an efficient and safe communication between distributed control systems. Consistent motion data between the simulation tool and the robot controller is required to achieve smooth robot movements. One critical factor is the data transfers from the simulation tool via TCP/IP Ethernet to the central controller. First analysis show, that the central controller receives data in a cycle time of about 12 ms. In current examinations the signal flow, beginning at the trajectory generation in Easy-Rob and ending at the converter of each drive, is being analyzed in order to improve the performance of the control system.

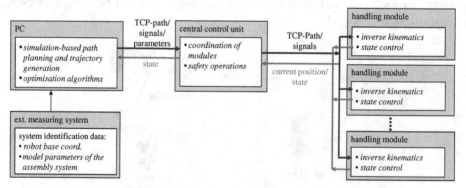

**Fig. 5.** Modular control architecture of a reconfigurable assembly platform

Further tasks in the field of communication are safety issues, as an error or emergency stop in one handling module has to be recognized by the central controller, which then has to stop the other robots quickly. In order to continue work after an emergency stop, the simulation systems has to be stopped and updated before new motion data is being transferred to the central controller.

An external measurement system (vision system, laser tracker or indoor GPS) is being integrated as an important element to implement self-optimization. After reconfiguration the base position of each handling unit is identified and fed to the simulation tool. This information is needed to generate accurate trajectories of each handling unit. During handling the measurement system provides data about the current position of the handled object and to implement self-optimization in the handling system. Therefore, this information is analyzed continuously in order to detect deviations, to calculate optimized target positions when needed and to feed the control system with data for compensation.

## 6    Conclusion

Reconfigurable, self-optimizing assembly systems can increase efficiency in aircraft production. Self-optimization is achieved by automated control functions which analyze the current state continuously, determine new targets and adapt the systems behavior automatically. The development of such a control system can be simplified by using existing control functions from a robot simulation tool.

Reconfigurability can be obtained by a modular design of an assembly system. Especially for assembling large components the development of customized modular handling units can be cost-efficient. In order to be able to use existing control functionalities from a robot simulation tool, the usual definition of mechatronic modules, consisting of mechanics, electronics and information technology, has to be expanded by a virtual model, which contains the control functionalities from the simulation tool.

The mechatronic handling units are integrated into a modular control architecture and coordinated by a central control module. The control concept in combination with simple kinematic units facilitates an easy reconfiguration of the handling system, so that it can be adapted to the requirements of different tasks and processes. Defining the handling object as the master of a motion makes it possible to compensate deviations of the workpiece directly by an inline measurement system. This approach replaces re-teaching of the robots to achieve high position accuracy and simplifies programming of the handling system.

The depicted research has been funded by the German Research Foundation DFG as part of the Cluster of Excellence "Integrative Production Technology for High-Wage Countries".

## References

1. Marschall, D., Clawson, L.: Outsourced – Sending Jobs Overseas: The Cost to America's Economy and Working Families, http://www.workingamerica.org/upload/ OutsourcingReport.pdf (March 02, 2012)

2. Alajääskö, P.: Plans for International Sourcing in Europe in 2007-2009. Eurostat – Statistics in focus – Industry, trade and services, 74(2009)
3. Brecher, C., Kozielski, S.: Vision of Integrative Production Technology, http://www.production-research.de/__C12577F20052BDC7.nsf/ html/de_d3c302e8c0563755c12577fb00353219.html (March 02, 2012)
4. Schmitt, R., et al.: Self-optimising Production Systems. Integrative Production Technology for High-Wage Countries, pp. 697–986. Springer (2012) ISBN: 978-3-642-21066-2
5. Adelt, P., Donath, J., Gausemeier, J., et al.: Selbstoptimierende Systeme des Maschinenbaus. In: Gausemeier, J., Rammig, F., Schäfer, W. (eds.) HNI-Verlagsschriftenreihe, vol. 234, Westfalia Druck GmbH, Paderborn (2009)
6. Wollnack, J., Stepanek, P.: Formkorrektur und Lageführung für eine flexible und automatisierte Großbauteilmontage. Wt Werkstattstechnik online 94(9), 414–421
7. Riedel, M., Nefzi, M., Corves, B.: Grasp Planning for a Reconfigurable Parallel Robot with an Underactuated Arm Structure. Mechanical Science 1, 33–42 (2010), doi:10.5194/ms-1-33-2010
8. Craig, J.J.: Introduction to Robotics – Mechanics and Control. Pearson (2005) ISBN 0-13-123629-6
9. VDI guideline 2206, Design methodology for mechatronic systems
10. Isermann, R.: Mechatronic systems: fundamentals. Springer, London (2005) ISBN 1-85233-930-6
11. Müller, R., Corves, B., Esser, M., Hüsing, M., Riedel, M., Janßen, M.: Modular Handling Platform For Easy Reconfiguration. In: 3rd CIRP Conference on Assembly Technologies and Systems CATS 2010, pp. 109–113 (2010) ISBN 978-82-519-2616-4
12. Müller, R., Esser, M., Janssen, M.: Integrative Path Planning and Motion Control for Handling Large Components. In: Jeschke, S., Liu, H., Schilberg, D. (eds.) ICIRA 2011, Part I. LNCS, vol. 7101, pp. 93–101. Springer, Heidelberg (2011)
13. Easy-Rob 3D Robot Simulation Tool, http://www.easy-rob.com
14. Bernecker + Rainer Industrie Elektronik Ges.m.b.H., http://www.br-automation.com

# Robot Assisted Manufacturing System
# for High Gloss Finishing of Steel Molds

André Driemeyer Wilbert[*], Barbara Behrens, Olaf Dambon,
and Fritz Klocke

Fraunhofer Institute for Production Technology IPT,
Steinbachstr. 17, Aachen 52074, Germany
andre.wilbert@ipt.fraunhofer.de

**Abstract.** For the manufacturing of molds and dies a considerable high amount of manufacturing costs and time are allocated into finishing procedures (grinding, lapping and polishing). As current automated finishing techniques are almost not applicable on parts with free form surfaces and function relevant edges, as commonly found in molds and dies, the finishing of these tools has to be done predominantly manually. This paper shows a robot assisted fine machining approach developed at Fraunhofer IPT, with which it was possible to grind, lap and polish free form surfaces. High gloss surface qualities with an Ra value of 15 nm and an Rt of 0,4 µm could be achieved.

**Keywords:** automation, process technology, finishing, grinding, lapping, polishing, industrial robotics, offline programming (OLP), CAM, force controlled process.

## 1    Introduction

In the last 20 years, automation and robotics have gotten continuously more importance for the manufacturing industry, as the customer demands for higher quality, faster delivery time and reduction of cost have grown steadily. A future winning margin in the global production sector, regardless the country, can be assured if existing technologies are enhanced with part automation and the use of robots.

The tooling industry in Europe represents an average annual turnover of 13 billion € and comprises more than 7.000 companies, 95% of them being SMEs/SMBs [1]. Due to the lack of available automated finishing technologies for free form surfaces, the finishing in the tooling industry is predominantly done manually. Manual finishing of injection and die casting molds is a time-consuming and cost-intensive process step, representing typically 12 up to 15 % of the manufacturing costs and 30 up to 50 % of the entire manufacturing time [2,6]. As a very demanding but monotone manual work, skilled craftsmen are a scarce resource and companies all over the world confront a large problem to recruit suitable employees for the manual finishing.

---

[*] Corresponding author

C.-Y. Su, S. Rakheja, H. Liu (Eds.): ICIRA 2012, Part I, LNAI 7506, pp. 673–685, 2012.
© Springer-Verlag Berlin Heidelberg 2012

In this paper a robot integrated finishing process, being currently developed at Fraunhofer Institute for Production Technology IPT in Germany, is presented. The essay focuses on the automated glossy finishing of two real free form milled workpieces, adopting abrasive tools to stepwise enhance the surface quality, driven by a pneumatic force controlled spindle to adjust the necessary surface pressure during the finishing process. Integrated to the spindle, two kinematic modules for rotational and translational movement have been developed and combined with an offline programmed six-axis robot in order to machine a large spectrum of free form geometries.

## 2    State of the Art

The so-called fine machining technologies include all manually applied processes such as grinding, lapping and polishing which are misleadingly simply referred to as "polishing" in industry. Scientific approaches to realize robot assisted finishing were started more than 30 years ago, since articulated robots gain more acceptance in industry. Despite of various published and partially promising results there is still no automated solution for the tooling industry commercially available [3-15].

It can be stated that apart from industrial solutions to automate the grinding process of welded joints on ship propellers, aircraft wings or bathroom fittings by belt grinding and/or wheel polishing from similar products, the analysis of the state-of-the-art showed that neither from scientific investigations nor from industrial developments a suitable approach can be derived to support the complex, multi-stage process of finishing of free-formed steel surfaces. Due to several technical reasons the existing finishing cells in the market are not capable to achieve the necessary surface finishing requirements (usually high gloss qualities of complex free-formed surfaces in cavities) from the tool and die making industry. This industry sector, as in many other ones, still has to be almost entirely manually conducted at the finishing stage.

Based on the understanding of Fraunhofer IPT, aiming a higher degree of a finishing automation process based on a robotic cell, the main following topics are necessary to be further developed and tested: robotic cell hardware equipment, robot programming and finishing process technology. The developed solutions should strongly regard the main requirements of the typical companies that offer manual finishing services, presenting an automated solution system with simplicity and robustness to handle the process and primarily low costs in the acquisition and maintenance.

## 3    Experimental Setup

### 3.1    Finishing Drive Systems

The overall objective of this research work is the development of an automated robot-assisted fine machining (grinding, lapping and polishing) by means of a force controlled finishing spindle and CAD/CAM-based process strategies in order to support the manual worker with a brush, glossy or mirror finish of free form steel molds and dies. Figure 1 depicts this concept, where the prototype of the modular force controlled tools are possibly mounted in a conventional electric spindle. Two modules are proposed to be integrated on a spindle, to allow the adoption of rotational and translational tools that provide singular different advantages, e.g. higher material removal rate, better accessibility in cavities or typical surface oriented structuring (brush finishing).

The adoption of such an approach is based fundamentally on the possibility to develop robust modules, capable to maintain the necessary forces and cutting velocities of the finishing process, without increasing additional costs in the installation in existing robot cells or even in NC-milling machines.

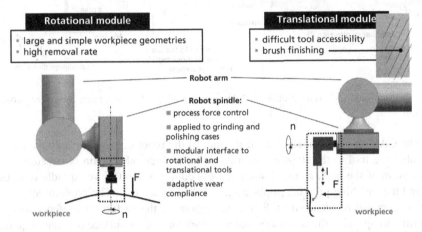

**Fig. 1.** Modular force controlled concept to rotational and translational finishing tools

As a principle of the force control during the finishing process, the pneumatic solution approach is adopted to regulate passively and actively the necessary pressure of the finishing tool against the worked surface. A prototype of a rotational finishing module (RMP-I), conceived to work orthogonally to the workpiece surface and with a compliance in the axial direction of the spindle was designed and fabricated (Figure 2 – left side). After some initial successful tests of the concept, another prototype, for translational movements (TMP-I) was designed with the similar application of pneumatic cylinders to apply the necessary force during the finishing procedures (Figure 2 – right side). The TMP-I converts mechanically the rotational movement from the conventional spindle in a stroke movement.

Both prototypes work essentially with the same system to regulate the process force during the finishing with a proportional electronic pressure regulator (SentronicD 609). The pressure regulator (added with filter for particles, oil etc.) can be set manually to a desired pressure from 0,5 up to 6 bar to work passively during the finishing process and guarantee a continuous pressure in the prototype modules (pm) during a complete operation (see figure Figure 2). The electronic regulator can additionally be actively controlled during the finishing operation in dependency of the position of the tool over a surface of the workpiece or of the operation time trough the programmed CAM-data.

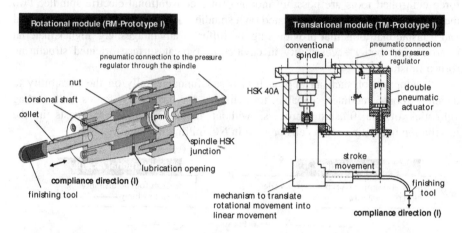

**Fig. 2.** Rotational and translational module concepts adopted with a pneumatic force control system

The CAM-data uploaded in the drive unit of the robot contain not only the path of the abrasive tool to the finishing operation, but include other main parameters set to each point of the path, as the desired process cutting velocity - vc (spindle rotation - n) and the finishing pressure applied against the surface (pf). The pressure applied in the process can be changed in distinctive regions of the surface or in dependency of the time to optimize the necessary material removal rate or surface roughness quality. This active control permits the addition of the following functionalities in the process:

- Finish distinct regions of a surface with individual selected finishing parameters, due to previously identified singular defects over the surface generated from milling operations.
- Finish distinct regions of a surface with more or less finishing pressure, due to deviance of contact area between abrasive tool and material surface.
- Finish distinct regions of a surface with variable finishing parameters, to achieve gradient of glossiness and generating desired structures.

The adopted pressure regulator with the rotational and translational modules was set during the proof of concept tests for the finishing process with forces in the compliance direction of the tools between 1 up to 20 N and with an approx. resolution of 0,5 N.

## 3.2    Finishing Tools for Rotational and Translational Movement

The selected tools to be applied in the automated finishing process with a robot are driven essentially by the rotational and translational modules. Rotational tools (Figure 3, left side) are recommended in cases where a high material rate is expected, however the accessibility of rotational tools in a mold cavity is limited. Therefore, translational tools (linear movement) are usually applied on the mold making industry.

### 3.3    Rotational Module – Axis-Symmetric Tools

In the finishing process with the rotational module, an axis-symmetric abrasive tool is mounted on a shaft of the rotational module which transmits the necessary torque from the spindle to rub the abrasive grains in the contact zone between tool and surface. The module permits an axial freedom of approx. 10 mm (l), allowing the shaft to slide and to apply a normal force from the abrasive tool against the mold surface. This feature permits the shaft to work similar as a piston of a pneumatic actuator and to transfer a necessary finishing pressure (pf) on the contact area between surface and tool from the pressure regulator system (pm), see Figure 3, left side. The rotation of the spindle (n) is simultaneously transmitted to the abrasive tool. The force applied to the process is directly dependent of the pressure set by the regulator and the area of contact between tool and surface (Ar). The pressure applied on the back side of the piston (pm) is conducted to the shaft/piston and subsequently to the finishing tool through a pneumatic canal crossing axially the spindle. The axial compliance of the shaft allows additionally the tool in case of wear or due to a deviance in the surface profile and robot path to be automatically compensated.

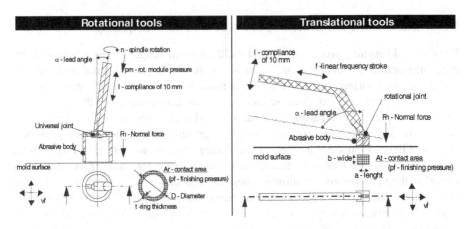

**Fig. 3.** Rotational and translational tools – basic tool and abrasive contact area geometry

Rotational tools with abrasion contact on the front side are set with an angle between the axial axes of the spindle and the surface orthogonal close to 90°. A smaller deviance on this angle has to be taken in consideration (α approx. ± 2°), due to the fact of the robot not to be a precise machine. Therefore the rotational finishing tool should admit a self adjustment of any uncorrected orthogonality. A simple solution for this requirement is the use of a universal joint, known as well as cardan joint, to adapt the deviance (see Figure 3, left side).

## 3.4    Translational Module – Cuboid Tools

Translational tools with an oscillation linear movement are commonly used in the finishing process of molds and dies of steel, especially in pieces deployed in the injection of plastic products, due to advantages of accessibility in frequent narrow slots and cavities. Another meaningful advantage in the utilization of translational tools is the possibility to provide a brush finishing texture to the surface. A brush finishing texture may assist to fill a mold with the melted plastic during the injection and subsequently facilitate the ejection of the molded part from the cavity.

The initial basic form for the translational tool body is a cuboid, although the form can be modified according to the geometry of the surface to be finished (Figure 3, right side). On the top of the tool exists an interface with a beam, which transmits the linear stroke frequency (ft) from the translational module to the abrasive body. The interface presents one rotational joint to permit possible deviances in the lead angle of the tool ($\alpha$). This degree of freedom is necessary as for the rotational module due to imprecision of the robot and eventually to increase the accessibility of the tool in constricted cavities. The force applied in the process (Fn), as the tools in the rotational model, are directly dependent of the pressure set in the pneumatic system and the contact between tool and finishing surface (At).

# 4    Proof of Concept and Results

## 4.1    Selection of Tools According to the Desired Surface Quality

The classical finishing procedure of steel molds is a multistage process where actually different machining procedures are taken in use. Regarding the material removal rate and the desired surface quality, machining procedures as grinding, honing, lapping and polishing are adopted. This sequence of fine machining procedures follow a tendency to present decreasing material removal capacities but to simultaneously increase reachable surface qualities from the grinding/honing up to the polishing process. Figure 4 presents a selected multistage process strategy that begins with grinding and honing stones to mainly eliminate surface structures generated by a typical milling process and to allow in subsequential stages the lapping and polishing process to progressively improve the roughness of the surface up to a glossy surface quality. This process strategy was selected from previous trials that provided the most consistent and reliable surface quality results.

The second chosen main step for both rotational and translational modules is the lapping process. Lapping is a finishing process defined as chipping material with loose grains distributed in a fluid or paste which are guided with a usually shape-transferring counterpart (lapping tool), featuring ideally undirected cutting paths of the individual grains. The main objective of the lapping process is to considerably improve the surface quality without changing its geometry.

Finally as last step the polishing process is applied to improve even further the surface quality of the mold using as for lapping loose grains in a fluid. The difference between both processes is practically the hardness of the counterpart tool. Lapping tools are generally harder than polishing tools and therefore press more intensively the lose abrasive grains against the surface. Polishing tools on the other hand, generate shallower cuts on the mold surface and subsequently lower roughness. During each finishing steps (grinding, honing, lapping and polishing), process parameters can be modified to obtain different cutting results.

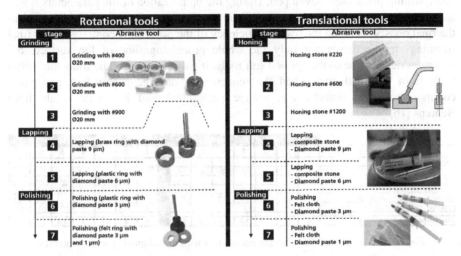

**Fig. 4.** Multistage process strategy for rotational and translational tools

The graphic on Figure 5 shows the average expected surface improvement after the conclusion of each finishing step for rotational and translational tools.

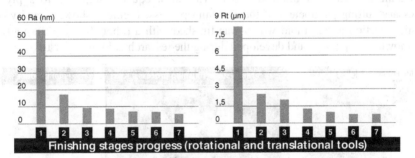

**Fig. 5.** Surface quality improvement following the adopted process strategy

Both rotational and translational tools, present a time efficiency to improve the milled surface up to a glossy surface between 10 up to 15 min/cm$^2$, being similar to results obtained in manual operations.

To achieve the desired surface qualities (Figure 5), additionally to the adopted tools to each stage of the finishing process, a range of parameters was optimized. Figure 6 presents the overview of the respective main optimized parameters, identified during the execution of the previous tests. Initial automated finishing process trials were conducted on planar milled surfaces of an usually adopted mold and die making industry steel grade - 1.2343 ESR. The experiments were enhanced with different finishing tools, free form surfaces and higher surface quality requirements until the finishing grade N1, following the standard DIN/ISO 1302. Due to this process advance, the involved parameters had to be adapted and new strategies and finishing paths were developed. During the optimization of the parameters it was established as a best practice rule, that the initial finishing steps should be longer than the final ones, enhancing the overall efficiency of the process. A contrary longer final finishing step increases not only the whole processing time of the surface, but generates defects due to the applied soft tools. It was observed in the trials that softer tools from the final stages had the tendency to damage the surface generating common polishing defects, e.g. orange peel, confirmed in former trials from Behrens [16].

| Finishing stage | Rotational tools | | | | | | | Translational tools | | | | | | |
|---|---|---|---|---|---|---|---|---|---|---|---|---|---|---|
| | 1 | 2 | 3 | 4 | 5 | 6 | 7 | 1 | 2 | 3 | 4 | 5 | 6 | 7 |
| Parameter | | | | | | | | | | | | | | |
| vc- cutting velocity (m/s) | 2 | 3 | 3 | 10 | 8 | 6 | 4 | - | - | - | - | - | - | - |
| f- linear frequency stroke (Hz) | - | - | - | - | - | - | - | 2000 | 2000 | 2000 | 2000 | 1500 | 1500 | 1000 |
| ls- stroke amplitude (mm) | - | - | - | - | - | - | - | 1,5 | 1,5 | 1,5 | 1,5 | 1,5 | 1,5 | 1,5 |
| pf- finishing pressure (N/cm^2) | 0,2 | 0,5 | 0,5 | 0,3 | 0,3 | 0,2 | 0,9 | 0,2 | 0,5 | 0,5 | 0,3 | 0,3 | 0,2 | 0,9 |
| vf- infeed velocity (mm/s) | 3 | 3 | 2 | 2 | 2 | 2 | 5 | 5 | 5 | 5 | 8 | 8 | 8 | 15 |
| Finishing efficiency (min/cm^2) | 3 | 2 | 1,5 | 1,5 | 1,5 | 1 | 0,5 | 4 | 3 | 2,5 | 2 | 1,5 | 1 | 0,5 |

**Fig. 6.** Furthermore adopted cutting parameters with the adopted process strategies

## 4.2    RMP-I Rotational Module Prototype I

The realization of the prototype was fundamental to assure the capabilities of the pneumatic system as solution and to provide an adequate equipment to apply the necessary cutting parameters of the finishing process. Figure 7 shows a cavity of a plastic injection airbag mold which was finished with a robot (IRB 4400), applying the knowledge acquired and developed during the research at Fraunhofer IPT.

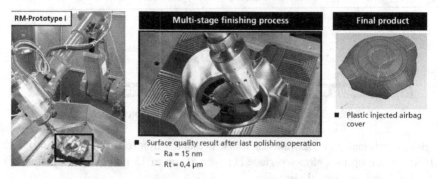

**Fig. 7.** Robot automated finished cavity of a plastic injection airbag mold

The airbag mold material of hardened steel 1.2343 ESR was previously fine milled until the desired geometry. The fine machining however generated severe waviness and pitch imperfections on the surface. Due to remaining 15 µm deep holes originated from the milling process, the subsequent automated finishing process had to be able to remove uniformly at least the correspondent 15 μm height of material to clear the optical defects on the surface and to keep a uniform concave surface geometry.

The initial milled surface presented a roughness of approximately Ra = 2,0 μm and Rt = 15 μm. After the multistage finishing process (Figure 7), a high gloss finished surface with the roughness values of Ra = 15 nm and Rt = 0,4 μm was achieved.

Important during the automated finishing process trial with the robot was the appliance and development of strategies and different movement paths to enhance the machined surface. According to the surface roughness, different rotational finishing tools were adopted and to each one appropriate process parameters were identified. The investigated tools differed in the type of machining technology (grinding, lapping and polishing tools) and in the specific characteristics, e.g. abrasive grain size, tool stiffness, contact geometry, etc. The tools applied from the first up to the 6th finishing stage had a diameter of 20 mm and a ring thickness of 2 mm. The last polishing stage was executed with rings of 20 mm diameter and 4 mm thickness.

Furthermore each investigated tool and corresponding processing step presented a tendency for an optimal process parameter combination, regarding basically to the abrasive cutting velocity (spindle rotation), the process in-feed (movement velocity of the robot), the process pressure (prototype force appliance) and the tool path strategy. Three basic tool path strategies were applied in the multi-stage finishing process according to the objectives of each finishing steps (Figure 8). The paths are named as parallel paths, spiral paths and "random" paths.

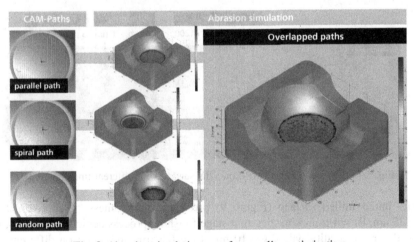

**Fig. 8.** Abrasion simulation – surface quality optimization

Parallel and spiral paths are directly derived from existing milling paths from conventional CAM software and are used primarily in the initial finishing steps to remove a high material volume of the surface through grinding and lapping. The new "random" paths are reserved to final finishing stages, due to its property to remove the material of a surface without leaving an optical pattern mark from the robot path.

Although this marks could be below the desired roughness of the surface, such marks are subjective not appraised by the human eye. The generation of the "random" path is actually not complete stochastic, but follows some rules as to the ones applied to solve the well known travelling salesman problem – TSP. The programming of the "random" path is generated using an algorithm written in MATLAB®.

A qualitative abrasion simulation tool is subsequently applied to foreseen the abrasion affect of the selected parameters, especially regarding the CAM-paths. The abrasion simulation tool was equally written in MATLAB® based on the Preston theory [17] and combined with the CAD data from the mold depicted as a point cloud and with the CAM path data. The simulation is based on a qualitative expected abrasion rate over the finished surface, through a theoretical contact area of the abrasive tool and workpiece.

### 4.3     TMP-I Translational Module Prototype I

First initial experiments were conducted over flat surfaces of hardened steel (1.2343 ESR, 54 HRC) to evaluate TM-Prototype I and positive results were achieved. The pneumatic system of TM-Prototype I was integrated to the robot controller and became off-line programmable. The proportional control used on the pneumatic system and its integration with the CAM data allowed the force controlled finishing process, to have a specified action force/pressure on each point of the programmed finishing path. As a result of this possibility, a variable adjustment during the process was given, according to the surface quality status.

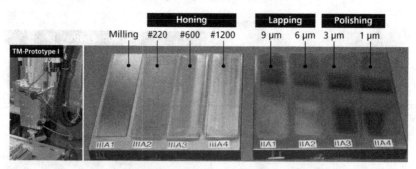

**Fig. 9.** Experiments of the TMP-I on a flat surface with different finishing tools

The initial milled surface (Figure 9) presented a roughness of approximately: Ra = 35 nm, Rt = 4 µm. After the multistage finishing process depict on Figure 4, the reached surface quality was Ra = 10 nm, Rt = 0,8 µm, measured on different and random spots over the surfaces.

After concluded the initial parameters set over the flat samples, the optimized parameter results were directly applied to finish a slight curved surface of a turbine blade (Figure 10) to develop the process on a real case. Both trials, over the flat and curved surfaces were conducted with cuboid tools with the same footprint dimensions of 6 x 8 mm (a and b, see Figure 3, right side). A light curvature was although preciously dressed in the finishing tools applied on the trials with the turbine blade, aimed to guarantee a best contact fit between abrasive body and part surface.

Before the trials it was important to set the overlapping strategy of different paths over a turbine surface and to optimize the required time to conclude a homogeneous finishing, avoiding the generation of spots on the surface with a non sufficient material removal (see Figure 10 deficient blue spot). Unfortunately, the exact material specification of the turbine can not be published on this paper, due to agreements with the provider of the blade, but a similar hardness of approximately 54 HRC was kept. After repeating the last finishing step with the 1 μm diamond paste, a surface quality of an average Ra of 30 nm and Rt of 0,4 μm was achieved.

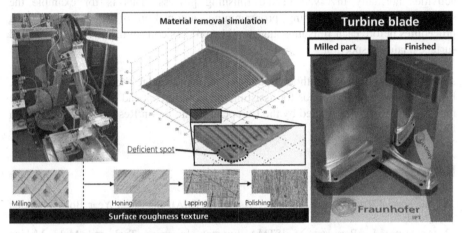

**Fig. 10.** Further preliminary study of the TMP-I on a light curved surface

## 5    Conclusion and Future Research

Although the design and machining processes in manufacturing of molds and dies have been developed in the past years, through remarkable improvement by new CAD/CAM software and NC machine tools, mostly finishing processes are still supported entirely by skilled workers.

In this paper, two concepts of force controlled tool driving systems, for rotational and translational tools were presented and their early trials of functionality proven. The positive results are not only depicted on the successful technical results of the surface quality reached by the tools in comparable consumed time to the manual efficiency, but the fact that the presented prototype systems are unparallel in the requirements of simplicity and cost, if compared with existing force controlled solutions in the market. Additionally to the module prototypes, the paper presented a developed strategy to finish free form surfaces with the rotational and translational tools. The developed strategies were proven to be adequate for further experiments, and optimization of the existing finishing steps to reduce the actual efficiency of 10 – 15 min/cm$^2$ down to 5min/cm$^2$ is believed to be possible.

The presented research showed as well the adoption a new "random" path strategy programmed with the assistance of the TSP theory to be applied on the last stages of the finishing process. This path strategy showed to be necessary to avoid the generation of patterns over the surface from the conventional CAM paths, generating a pattern over the surface that can not be perceived by the human eye.

The research in the near future to the automation of the finishing process at Fraunhofer IPT will focus, beside the optimization of the actual strategy with the robot, on the development of more robust driving tool modules and their directly integrability in NC machines. Other aspects that needs to be taken into account to the automation of the finishing process is the development of parallel or sequential activities normally involved in the finishing process. This is for example the simplification of the finishing programming, automation of necessary cleaning procedures before each finishing stage and the process control through the automated surface quality inspection.

**Acknowledgments.** The authors would like to acknowledge the contributions of M. Fink, T. Peters and H. Barrios for assisting the experiments and making available the results. This work was funded by the European Commission Research and Innovation DG (Project No. 246001).

# References

1. Int. Special Tooling and Machining Assoc. (ISTMA), Statistical Year Book – edition (2010)
2. Antonana, J. (President of ISTMA Europe): European Tool and Mold Making Tagungsband Werkzeugbau mit Zukunft, Aachen (2002)
3. Huissoon, J.P., Ismail, F., Jafari, A., Bedi, S.: Automated polishing of die steel surfaces. Advanced Manufacturing Technology 19, 285–290 (2002)
4. Sasaki, T., Miyoshi, T., Saito, K.: Knowledge acquisition and automation of polishing operation for injection mold. Int. Journal of the Japan Society 25, 193–199 (1991)
5. Zhao, J., Zhan, J., Jin, R., Tao, M.: An oblique ultrasonic polishing method by robot for free-form surfaces. Int. J. of Machine Tools & Manufacture 40, 795–808 (2000)
6. Takeuchi, Y., Ge, D., Asakawa, N.: Automated Polishing Process with a Human-like Dexterous Robot. In: Proceedings to the IEEE Conference, pp. 950–956 (1993)
7. Guvenc, L., Srinivasan, K.: Force controller design and evaluation for robot-assisted die and Mould polishing (1993)
8. Prabhakar, R. P., Biao.: Adaptive Control of Robotic Surface Finishing Processes. In: Proceedings of the American Control Conference, Arlington, pp. 630–635 (2001)
9. Cabaravdic, M., Kneupner, K., Kuhlenkoetter, K.: Methods for efficient optimization of robot supported grinding and polishing processes. In: 7. Int. Research Conference (2003)
10. Kuhlenkoetter, B., Zhang, X.: A Robot System for High Quality Belt Grinding and Polishing Processes, Cutting Edge Robotics, pp. 755–770 (2006)
11. Ryuh, B., Park, S., Pennock, G.R.: An automatic tool changer and integrated software for a robotic die polishing station. Mech. and Machine Theory 41, 415–432 (2006)
12. Márquez, J.J., Pérez, J.M., Ríos, J., Vizán, A.: Process modeling for robotic polishing. Journal of Materials Technology 159, 10 (2005)

13. Wu, X., Kita, Y., Ikoku, K.: New polishing technology of free form surface by GC. Journal of Materials Processing Technology, 81–84 (2007)
14. Brecher, C., Wenzel, C., Tuecks, R.: Development of a force controlled polishing tool. In: Proceedings of the 10th Euspen International Conference, Zurich, vol. I, pp. 438–442 (2008)
15. Klocke, F., Brecher, C., Zunke, R., Tücks, R., Zymla, C.: Hochglänzende Freiformflächen aus Stahlwerkzeugen. wt Werkstattstechnik online 6 (2010)
16. Behrens, B., Klocke, F., Dambon, O.: Analysis of Defect Mechanisms in Polishing of Tool Steels, Production Engineering, vol. 5(5), pp. 475–483. Springer (2010)
17. Klocke, F., König, W.: Fertigungsverfahren 2: Schleifen, Honen, Läppen: Schleifen, Honen, Lappen, vol. 4, p. 408. Springer, Heidelberg (2005)

# Measurement of the Cognitive Assembly Planning Impact

Christian Büscher[1], Eckart Hauck[2], Daniel Schilberg[1], and Sabina Jeschke[1]

[1] Institute of Information Management in Mechanical Engineering IMA, RWTH Aachen University, Dennewartstrasse 27, 52068 Aachen, Germany
[2] Institute for Management Cybernetics IfU e.V., Dennewartstrasse 27, 52068 Aachen, Germany
{christian.buescher,eckart.hauck,daniel.schilberg,
sabina.jeschke}@ima-zlw-ifu.rwth-aachen.com

**Abstract.** Within highly automated assembly systems, the planning effort forms a large part of production costs. Due to shortening product lifecycles, changing customer demands and therefore an increasing number of ramp-up processes these costs even rise. So assembly systems should reduce these efforts and simultaneously be flexible for quick adaption to changes in products and their variants. A cognitive interaction system in the field of assembly planning systems is developed within the Cluster of Excellence "Integrative production technology for high-wage countries" at RWTH Aachen University which integrates several cognitive capabilities according to human cognition. This approach combines the advantages of automation with the flexibility of humans. In this paper the main principles of the system's core component – the cognitive control unit – are presented to underline its advantages with respect to traditional assembly systems. Based on this, the actual innovation of this paper is the development of key performance indicators.

**Keywords:** Key performance indicators, Cognitive Control, Self-Optimization, Assembly Planning.

## 1    Introduction

In this paper, a set of key performance indicators (KPI) is discussed describing the impact of a cognitive interaction system of highly automated assembly systems. The basis is a cognitive interaction system which is designed within a project of the Cluster of Excellence "Integrative production technology for high-wage countries" at RWTH Aachen University with the objective to plan and control an assembly autonomously [1]. The overall objective of the Cluster of Excellence is to ensure the competitive situation of high-wage countries like Germany with respect to high-tech products, particularly in the field of mechanical and plant engineering. Yet these countries are facing increasingly strong competition by low-wage countries. The solution hypothesis derived in the mentioned Cluster of Excellence is seen in the resolution of the so-called Polylemma of Production [1]. The contribution of the project "Cognitive Planning and Control System for Production" is the development of a cognitive interaction system. Cognitive interaction systems in general are characterised by two facts. On the one hand, they comprise cognitive capabilities as

C.-Y. Su, S. Rakheja, H. Liu (Eds.): ICIRA 2012, Part I, LNAI 7506, pp. 686–695, 2012.

mentioned before and on the other hand, they feature an interaction between the technical system and human operators [2]. One of the major challenges of the Polylemma of Production is to increase the efficiency of planning and simultaneously utilise the value stream approach in the domain of assembly. The main results are the implementation of a cognitive control unit (CCU) as the key component of the cognitive interaction system and the construction of an assembly cell on the technical side to practically test the functionality of the CCU.

In this context, assembly tasks are a big challenge for planning systems, especially considering uncertain constraints, as implied in this approach. As a result, classic planning approaches have shown to be of little use due to the huge computational complexity. By calculating the complex planning problems prior to the actual assembly, this problem can be bypassed – but current and temporary changes cannot be taken into account. That is why in this project, a hybrid approach of pre- and re-planning of assembly tasks is followed. While the CCU plans and controls the whole assembly process, the operator only executes assembly steps, which cannot be fulfilled by the robots, and intervenes in case of emergency. In this way, the robot control, which is now based on human decision processes, will lead to a better understanding of the behaviour of the technical system.

The crucial point of the CCU is the reduction of planning costs compared to traditional automated assembly systems. This is reached by means of cognitive capabilities with simultaneously increasing the flexibility during the actual assembly process. To quantify this, a set of four KPIs is developed in this paper. These KPIs point out the influence of implementing a cognitive interaction system for assembly planning to the Polylemma of Production. The new KPIs therefore concentrate on the comparison of production systems with and without cognitive interaction systems while general performance measuring systems itself already exist [3], [4].

## 2     The Cognitive Control Unit

The main idea of the cognitive control unit is to autonomously plan and control the assembly of a product solely by its CAD description. Hence, it will be possible to decrease the planning effort in advance and to increase the flexibility of manufacturing and assembly systems [7]. Therefore several different approaches, which are suitable for the application on planning problems, are of great interest in the field of artificial intelligence. While generic planners like the ones by Hoffmann [8], Castellini [9] and Hoffmann & Brafman [10] are not able to compute any solution within an acceptable time in the field of assembly planning concerning geometrical analysis, other planners are especially designed for assembly planning, e.g. the widely used Archimedes System [11]. To find optimal plans, it uses AND/OR-graphs and an "assembly by disassembly" strategy. The approach of Thomas follows the same strategy, but uses only geometric information of the final product as input [12]. Nevertheless, both approaches are not adequate enough to deal with uncertainty. Another system developed by Zaeh & Wiesbeck [13] follows an approach which is similar to the CCU apart from the fact that it only plans and does not control the assembly. In this field, the CCU is a sophisticated system on the way to self-optimisation.

The CCU is able to take over tasks from an operator, for example repetitive, dangerous and not too complex operations, as it is capable to process procedural knowledge encoded in production rules and to control multiple robots. As knowledge-based behaviour as well as skill-based behaviour cannot be modelled and simulated by the CCU, it will cooperate with the operator on a rule-based level of cognitive control [6], [14]. The task of the CCU consists of the planning and the controlling of the assembly of a product that is described by its CAD data while the assembly actions are executed by the assembly robots. After receiving an accordant description entered by a human operator, the system plans and executes the assembly autonomously by means of a hybrid planner. With regard to the cooperation between the CCU and an operator it is crucial that the human operator understands the assembly plan developed by the CCU. Furthermore, a robot control which is based on human decision processes will lead to a better understanding regarding the behaviour of the technical system which is referred to as cognitive compatibility [2].

## 2.1    Hybrid Planner

The planning process of the CCU is separated into two assembly-parts to allow fast reaction times: the Offline Planner, executed prior to the assembly, and the Online Planner, executed in a loop during the assembly (Fig. 1). The Offline Planner allows computation times of up to several hours. Its task is to pre-calculate all feasible assembly sequences – from the single parts to the desired product. The output is a graph representing these sequences. This graph is transmitted to the Online Planner whose computation time must not exceed several seconds. Its task is to map repeatedly the current system state to a state contained in the graph during assembly. In a further step, the Online Planner extracts an assembly sequence that transforms the latest state into a goal state containing the finished product. Thus, the proposed procedure follows a hybrid approach [6].

A solution space for the assembly sequence planning problem is derived during the offline planning phase. As mentioned above, an "assembly by disassembly" strategy is applied to generate an assembly graph, which is first generated as an AND/OR-graph and which is then transformed into a state graph that can be efficiently interpreted during online planning [15]. Therefore, a description of the assembled product's geometry and its constituting parts, possibly enriched with additional mating directions or mating operation specifications, is used. The geometric data is read by the CCU from a CAD file. The main concept of this strategy is a recursive analysis of all possibilities of an assembly or subassembly [16]. Any assembly or subassembly is separated into two further subassemblies until only single parts remain. All related properties of the product's assembly are stored. Additionally, instances can be used to describe functional aspects. This will be relevant if additional data apart from the part geometries is taken into account by the assembly planner [12].

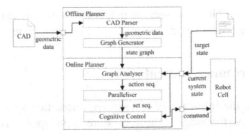

**Fig. 1.** Hybrid approach of the CCU

All data of the separation evaluators is stored in the state graph. The information contains static operation costs and mating operation descriptions for each assembly that might be active during assembly. All transition steps are represented by edges enhanced with the named costs. Each state contains the passive assembly, to which other parts may be added, starting with the empty one at the bottom up to the final product at the top.

The Online Planner derives the assembly plan during the assembly process. It uses the state graph provided by the Offline Planner as well as information about the current robot cell's situation. This approach is similar to the system developed by [13], in which assembly task instructions for a human operator are reactively generated.

The Graph Analyser receives the generated state graph from the offline planning phase and the actual world state describing the current situation of the assembly. Afterwards, the graph analyser maps this world state onto the matching state contained in the state graph. If this node and the "goal-node" are identical, the assembly has been completed and the process ends. Otherwise, the state graph is updated. Dynamic costs in terms of the availability of necessary parts are assigned to the state graphs edges – in addition to the costs, which already have been assigned to the edges during offline planning [6]. After this procedure, the optimal path to the goal-node is calculated using the A* search algorithm, which represents the optimal assembly plan for the given current situation [17]. This path is tested for parallelization and sent to the Cognitive Control component, which executes the assembly in a further step.

The Cognitive Control component receives the assembly sequence, triggers the accordant robot commands and communicates with the human operator so that the latter can operate e.g. in case of unforeseen changes. This component is based on Soar, a cognitive framework for decision finding that aims on modelling the human decision process [18]. Soar contains several production rules which are stored in the knowledge base. Furthermore, human assembly strategies are developed and implemented in the component to generate a higher degree of machine transparency and to enhance cognitive compatibility [14]. Thus, this component implements the cognitive capability of decision making so that the CCU in general is able to optimise its performance according to different delivered target states.

In this section, the background of the cognitive interaction system with regard to the planning algorithm and the possibilities of decision making within the technical system was described. The next section points out how this approach can help to improve the planning process by defining KPIs for cognitive interaction systems.

# 3    Key Performance Indicators

In order to measure the influence of a cognitive interaction system on the planning process, four key performance indicators were developed. As described in the previous sections, the reduction of planning efforts prior to the assembly is a main objective of cognitive interaction systems like the CCU. This approach enables a faster planning process for assembly and thereby comprises at best an increase of production volume during this phase. This has on the one hand a positive effect on the validity of the data generated and beyond that on the quality of the final production process. In addition, the increased flexibility allows not only a static assembly strategy like traditional automated systems, but the possibility to act adaptively within the framework of the generated plan. The four KPIs which show these advantages within the triple constraint (cost, time and quality) are:

- $K_{PE}$ – planning effort
- $K_{APV}$ – acceleration of production volume growth
- $K_{IPV}$ – increase of production volume
- $K_{PQ}$ – plan quality

The contribution to the the Polylemma of Production technology is determined by the comparison of the KPIs with and without the use of a cognitive interaction system to control an assembly of components of simple geometry like the scenario described in section 3.2 [5]. All KPIs are defined in a way that the larger the value, the more superior is the cognitive system compared to the traditional one. The turning point where both systems are equal is – depending on the context of the precise KPI – 0 or 1.

## 3.1    Planning Effort

The first KPI, the planning effort, refers to the phase of mounting and initial programming of the cognitive interaction system within an assembly system. The initial filing and maintenance of the knowledge base in a cognitive interaction system represents significantly more work compared to programming a traditional assembly system, for example by teaching the robot. This effort is too high for a production system that is designed only for one product since a traditional assembly system can be programmed very quickly for a specified manufacturing step and this programming has to be adjusted only marginally during production. However, if the assembly system needs to be able to assemble a wide range of products with small batches, a traditional assembly system has to be repeatedly reprogrammed and optimised. In contrast, an assembly system with a cognitive interaction system can be adapted with little effort on a new product.

The key performance indicator $K_{PE}$ is based on Schilberg [19] and is calculated from the sum over n different products to be assembled by the efforts of the programming of the system respectively the creation of the knowledge base and the optimisation of the assembly:

$$K_{PE} = 1 - \left( \frac{\sum_{i=1}^{n} PE_{i_{cognitive}}}{\sum_{i=1}^{n} PE_{i_{traditional}}} \right) \tag{1}$$

With     $K_{PE}$     : Key performance indicator of the planning effort

$PE_{i_{cognitive}}$     : Planning effort of an assembly system with a cognitive interaction system

$PE_{i_{traditional}}$     : Planning effort of a traditional assembly system.

The interval in which the KPI ranges is $[-\infty, +1]$. The extreme value $-\infty$ of the interval will be reached if the planning effort for $PE_{i_{traditional}}$ is arbitrarily small or if $PE_{i_{cognitive}}$ is an arbitrary large value. The other extreme value of 1 will be reached if $PE_{i_{cognitive}}$ is 0 [5].

By the automated assembly planning within the cognitive interaction system, this system only has to be reprogrammed if the assembly of the product to be manufactured contains steps that were not previously stored in the cognitive interaction system (for example if a new tool is available, which results in new possible operations). By the independent planning of the assembly process, under constraints which have passed by the operator to the cognitive interaction system, no new operation sequences have to be programmed. The adaptive adjustment of the assembly sequence can even ensure an assembly with a not previously known component supply which is impossible in a traditional assembly system. When a new sequence of steps is to be executed, the assembly system has to be reprogrammed and optimised, which represents a significant amount of work. This does not allow flexible responds of the assembly system to changes in product manufacturing or in the assembly sequence.

## 3.2   Acceleration of Production Volume Growth

The second KPI, acceleration of production volume growth, is determined by comparing the maximum increase in production volume per time unit at the site $t_i$.

Therefore, the KPI is calculated as:

$$K_{APV} = \left( \frac{\frac{\partial P_V}{\partial t} \big|_{cognitive}}{\frac{\partial P_V}{\partial t} \big|_{traditional}} \right) - 1 \tag{2}$$

With   $K_{APV}$                    : Key performance indicator for acceleration of production volume growth

$\frac{\partial P_V}{\partial t}|_{cognitive}$     : Slope at the inflection point of the production system with cognitive interaction systems

$\frac{\partial P_V}{\partial t}|_{traditional}$    : Slope at the inflection point of the traditional production system.

By forming the quotient, the KPI ranges in the interval $[-1, +\infty]$. A value of $-1$ means that the production volume growth of a production system with cognitive interaction systems is 0, so there is no production. The other extreme value means that the production volume growth with a cognitive interaction system is arbitrarily large respectively the production increase of a traditional production system is 0. This value is never reached because it would mean a discontinuity in the S-curve, which has to be differentiable by definition [5].

In case of a congruence of the inflection points of the ramp-up function $f(t)$ for both production systems, it is sufficient to determine the key performance indicator $K_{APV}$ if one production system dominates the other one. If the two inflection points do not match, it may happen that a production system, which has a steeper gradient but realises this at a significantly later time, possibly has a worse overall production volume.

### 3.3    Increase of Production Volume

In this case, a third KPI, namely the increase of total production volume during ramp-up, should be consulted. It is calculated by integrating over the starting function $f(t)$ in a given period. By the quotient, a direct comparison of production systems with and without cognitive interaction systems can be made.

Therefore, the KPI is calculated as:

$$K_{IPV} = \frac{\int_{t_0}^{t_{s_1}} f_{cognitive}(t)\,dt}{\int_{t_0}^{t_{s_2}} f_{traditional}(t)\,dt} \tag{3}$$

With    $K_{IPV}$    : Key performance indicator of the increase of production volume
        $t_0$    : Start of production
        $t_{s_i}$    : Time of series production with full capacity.

Under the condition that the integral of $f(t) > 0$, a cognitive system is superior to a traditional system if the KPI takes a value $> 1$. The key performance indicator $K_{APV}$ represents therefore the necessary condition for the superiority of a production system with cognitive interaction systems in the assembly, while the key performance indicator $K_{IPV}$ is the sufficient condition for a real improvement [5]. This consideration is only meaningful if both times to volume differ from each other marginally. Otherwise the "faster" production system would always be preferred since time is often the critical variable.

### 3.4    Plan Quality

The fourth KPI is the plan quality, which is borrowed from one criterion for evaluation of planners on the International Planning Competition (IPC) [20]. It is determined from the number of assembly steps required to manufacture a product. In a traditional system, the assembly sequence is either fully optimised and programmed in advance or a heuristic-based optimisation is used by the employee during programming. Depending on the complexity of the product to be assembled, the optimal assembly sequence may not be found in a reasonable time. In the context of this scenario and further scenarios which were analysed within the project, the CCU is able to generate the entire assembly graph in the Offline Planner. At this point no heuristics have to be used but such applications are possible. Thus, this KPI is defined with regard to more complex products where heuristics are relevant.

As described before, in a cognitive interaction system, it may also be necessary to resort to a heuristic to solve the planning problem in a reasonable time in a corresponding product complexity. This planning can be continued during the production, which means that the cognitive interaction system starts with an assembly sequence that was found using a heuristic. Then during the process the system is able to derive a better assembly sequence in parallel by using relaxing heuristics and by conducting a broader search within the AND/OR-graph. If the number of components is below a threshold, all possible decompositions of the AND/OR-graph can be saved and a guaranteed optimal solution of the planning problem can be found [5].

The plan quality of the traditional and the cognitive assembly system are identical in this case, provided that the same resources for computing capacity and time exist. However, the cognitive assembly system is able to perform a broader search during the actual assembly and thus to create the optimal assembly plan. In this example, this would mean a sum of costs of 40 instead of 50 although the first analysis step of the optimal solution is considerably larger than the one of the heuristic. The plan quality of a cognitive interaction system is thus at least as good as a traditional assembly system and is able to achieve a better plan quality which is expressed by a lower sum of costs in the assembly graph through an on-going continuation of the planning.

The KPI is calculated as:

$$K_{PQ} = \sum_{i=0}^{n} C_{i_{traditional}} - \sum_{i=0}^{m} C_{i_{cognitive}} \tag{4}$$

With    $K_{PQ}$        : Key performance indicator of the plan quality
       $n$          : number of assembly steps with traditional production system
       $m$          : number of assembly steps with cognitive interaction system
       $C_{i_{traditional}}$        : costs on optimal path with traditional production system
       $C_{i_{cognitive}}$        : costs on optimal path with cognitive interaction system.

Hence, $K_{PQ}$ is never less than zero. In addition, the cognitive interaction system has the ability to adjust the assembly sequence depending on the availability of the single components. The optimal assembly sequence that was found during this process has been created under the terms of a deterministic supply of components respectively the availability of all components and assemblies required. With regard to the possibility of dynamic allocation of the new edge costs within the assembly graph in case of storage of all possible decompositions, the cognitive assembly system is able to adapt the assembly sequence dynamically and to ensure the optimal plan quality in a dynamic environment at any time during assembly.

# 4     Conclusion

This paper proposes a set of KPIs which can determine the advantages of a cognitive interaction system in contrast to traditional automated systems to improve an assembly system. A precise cognitive interaction system in the domain of assembly planning systems is presented, which is the first self-optimising system in this domain. It comprises several cognitive capabilities implemented in the cognitive control unit (CCU) by a hybrid approach for assembly tasks, which enables robots to decide on their action during assembly autonomously.

To measure the systems' advantages involved, a set of key performance indicators is developed in this paper which can show the impact of this cognitive interaction system. These KPIs concentrate on the main improvements being achieved during assembly and its construction and sequence planning. The interaction of the four KPIs "planning effort", "acceleration of production volume growth", "increase of production volume" and "plan quality" evaluate the improvements in attaining the final production volume and in reducing the planning effort as well as the enhancement of the quality of the derived plan by means of the self-optimising capability of the CCU. These are developed in the context presented in this paper but designed to highlight the impact of cognitive interaction systems on production economics in general.

With respect to future research, there are plans to fill these KPIs with life, while in this paper the theoretical background for the next step has been set. Therefore, industrial applications are to be performed and analysed by comparing the assembly of a product with the use of the CCU on the one hand and with the traditional approach on the other hand. Therein, possible weaknesses can be detected and resolved. This practical testing may then be shifted to other cognitive interaction systems to demonstrate the transferability of the set of KPIs. The challenge of fundamental research like the technological innovations developed within this Cluster of Excellence often comprises the persuasion of industry of the high performance of such solutions and the implementation or the launch of a product out of this. However, companies need reliable predictions on the applicability and economic efficiency. At this, the developed KPIs can play a major role as they provide exactly this required evidence in the examined topic.

# References

1. Brecher, C., Klocke, F., Schmitt, R., Schuh, G.: Excellence in Production. Apprimus Verlag, Aachen (2007)
2. Mayer, M., Schlick, C., Ewert, D., Behnen, D., Kuz, S., Odenthal, B., Kausch, B.: Automation of robotic assembly processes on the basis of an architecture of human cognition. Production Engineering Research and Development 5(4), 423–431 (2011) ISSN 0944-6524

3. Pufall, A.A., Fransoo, J.C., de Kok, A.G.: What determines product ramp-up performance?: A review of characteristics based on a case study at Nokia Mobile Phones (BETA publicatie: working paper, No. 228). Technische Universiteit Eindhoven (2007)
4. Winkler, H., Heins, M., Nyhuis, P.: A controlling system based on cause-effect relationships for the ramp-up of production systems. Production Engineering – Research and Development 1(1), 103–111 (2007)
5. Hauck, E.: Ein kognitives Interaktionssystem zur Ansteuerung einer Montagezelle. VDI Reihe 10, Band 812. 1. Auflage. VDI-Verlag, Düsseldorf (2011)
6. Ewert, D., Thelen, S., Kunze, R., Mayer, M., Schilberg, D., Jeschke, S.: A Graph Based Hybrid Approach of Offline Pre-planning and Online Re-planning for Efficient Assembly under Realtime Constraints. In: Liu, H., Ding, H., Xiong, Z., Zhu, X. (eds.) ICIRA 2010, Part II. LNCS, vol. 6425, pp. 44–55. Springer, Heidelberg (2010)
7. Hauck, E., Gramatke, A., Henning, K.: A Software Architecture for Cognitive Technical Systems Suitable for an Assembly Task in a Production Environment. In: Automation Control – Theory and Practice, pp. 13–28. InTech (2009)
8. Hoffmann, J.: FF: the fast-forward planning system. The AI Magazine 22 (2001)
9. Castellini, C., Giunchiglia, E., Tacchella, A., Tacchella, O.: Improvements to satbased conformant planning. In: Proceedings of the 6th European Conference on Planning, ECP 2001 (2001)
10. Hoffmann, J., Brafman, R.: Contingent planning via heuristic forward search with implicit belief states. In: Proceedings of ICAPS 2005, pp. 71–80 (2005)
11. Kaufman, S.G., Wilson, R.H., Calton, R.E.J.T.L., Ames, A.L.: Automated planning and programming of assembly of fully 3d mechanisms. Technical Report SAND96-0433, Sandia National Laboratories (1996)
12. Thomas, U.: Automatisierte Programmierung von Robotern für Montageaufgaben. Fortschritte in der Robotik 13. Shaker Verlag, Aachen (2008)
13. Zaeh, M.F., Wiesbeck, M.: A Model for Adaptively Generating Assembly Instructions Using State-based Graph. In: Manufacturing Systems and Technologies for the New Frontier, pp. 195–198. Springer (2008)
14. Mayer, M., Odenthal, B., Faber, M., Kabuss, W., Kausch, B., Schlick, C.: Simulation of human cognition in self-optimizing assembly systems. In: Proceedings of the IEA 2009, 17th World Congress on Ergonomics (2009)
15. Homem de Mello, L.S., Sanderson, A.C.: Representations of mechanical assembly sequences. IEEE Transactions on Robotics and Automation 7(2), 211–227 (1991)
16. Chen, R.-S., Lu, K.-Y., Tai, P.-H.: Optimizing assembly planning through a three-stage integrated approach. International Journal of Production Economics 88(3), 243–256 (2004)
17. Hart, P.E., Nilsson, N.J., Raphael, B.: A formal basis for the heuristic determination of minimum cost paths. IEEE Transactions on Systems Science and Cybernetics 4(2), 100–107 (2007)
18. Langley, P., Laird, J.E., Rogers, S.: Cognitive architectures: Research issues and challenges. Journal of Cognitive Systems Research 10(2), 141–160 (2009)
19. Schilberg, D.: Architektur eines Datenintegrators zur durchgängigen Kopplung von verteilten numerischen Simulationen. Dissertation, RWTH Aachen (2010)
20. Gerevini, A.E., Haslum, P., Long, D., Saetti, A., Dimopoulos, Y.: Deterministic planning in the fifth international planning competition: PDDL3 and experimental evaluation of the planners. In: Artificial Intelligence, vol. 173, pp. 619–668. Elsevier Science Publishers Ltd. (2009)

# Selfoptimized Assembly Planning for a ROS Based Robot Cell

Daniel Ewert, Daniel Schilberg, and Sabina Jeschke

Institute of Information Management in Mechanical Engineering,
RWTH Aachen University, Germany
{daniel.ewert,daniel.schilberg,
sabina.jeschke}@ima.rwth-aachen.de

**Abstract.** In this paper, we present a hybrid approach to automatic assembly planning, where all computational intensive tasks are executed once prior to the actual assembly by an Offline Planner component. The result serves as basis of decision-making for the Online Planner component, which adapts planning to the actual situation and unforeseen events. Due to the separation into offline and online planner, this approach allows for detailed planning as well as fast computation during the assembly, therefore enabling appropriate assembly duration even in nondeterministic environments. We present simulation results of the planner and detail the resulting planner's behavior.

**Keywords:** assembly planning, cognitive production systems, ROS.

## 1 Introduction

### 1.1 Motivation

The industry of high-wage countries is confronted with the shifting of production to low-wage countries. To slow down this development, and to answer the trend towards shortening product life-cycles and changing customer demands regarding individualized and variant-rich products, new concepts for the production in high-wage countries have to be created. This challenge is addressed by the Cluster of Excellence "Integrative production technology for high-wage countries" at the RWTH Aachen University. It researches on sustainable technologies and strategies on the basis of the so-called polylemma of production [2]. This polylemma is spread between two dichotomies: First between scale (mass production with limited product range) and scope (small series production of a large variety of products), and second between value and planning orientation. The ICD D1.1 "Self-optimizing Production Systems" focusses on the reduction of the latter dichotomy. Its approach for the reduction of this polylemma is to automate the planning processes that precede the actual production. This results in a reduction of planning costs and ramp-up time and secondly it allows to switch between the production of different products or variants of a product , hence enabling more adaptive production strategies compared to current

C.-Y. Su, S. Rakheja, H. Liu (Eds.): ICIRA 2012, Part I, LNAI 7506, pp. 696–705, 2012.

production. Automatic replanning also allows to react to unforeseen changes within the production system, e.g. malfunction of machines, lack of materials or similar, and to adapt the production in time. In this paper we present the planning components of a cognitive control unit (CCU) which is capable to autonomously plan and execute a product assembly. We also describe how this planner can be integrated into the ROS framework, so that the planner can be easily interact with ROS supported robots.

## 1.2    Use Case Description

The CCU is developed along a use case scenario for an assembly task in a nondeterministic production environment [10]. This scenario is based on the robot cell depicted in Fig. 1.

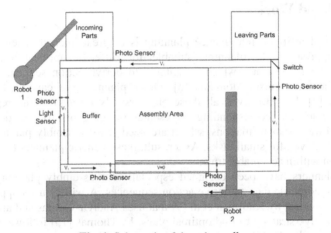

**Fig. 1.** Schematic of the robot cell

Of the two robots of the robot cell, only Robot2 is controlled by the CCU. Robot1 independently delivers parts in a random sequence to the circulating conveyor belt. The parts are then transported into the grasp range of Robot2 who then decides to pick them up, to immediately install them or to park them in a buffer area. The scenario also incorporates human-machine cooperation. In case of failure, or if the robot cannot execute a certain assembly action, the CCU is able to ask a human operator for assistance. To improve the cooperation between the operator and the machine, the operator must be able to understand the behavior and the intentions of the robot [11].

The only sources of information to guide the decision making of the CCU are a CAD description of the desired product, the number and types of single parts currently in the buffer and on the conveyor belt and the current state of the assembly within the Assembly Area. The planner is evaluated with different toy models (see Figure 2). The pyramid construct (a) serves as a benchmark for the computational complexity and is been used in different sizes (base areas of 2x2, 3x3, and 4x4 blocks). Construct b) and c) are used to demonstrate the planner's behavior.

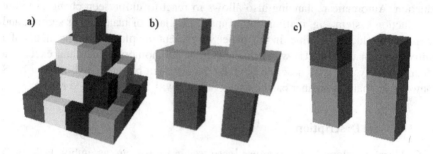

**Fig. 2.** Toy model products for planner evaluation

## 2    Related Work

In the field of artificial intelligence planning is of great interest. There exist many different approaches to planning suitable for different applications. Hoffmann developed the FF planner, which is suitable to derive action sequences for given problems in deterministic domains [6]. Other planners are capable to deal with uncertainty [7], [3]. However, all these planners rely on a symbolic representation based on logic. The corresponding representations of geometric relations between objects and their transformations, which are needed for assembly planning, become very complex even for small tasks. As a result, these generic planners fail to compute any solution within acceptable time.

Other planners have been designed especially for assembly planning and work directly on geometric data to derive action sequences. A widely used approach is the Archimedes system by Kaufman et al [9] that uses And/Or-Graphs and an "Assembly by Disassembly" strategy to find optimal plans. U. Thomas [15] follows this strategy, too, but where the Archimedes system relies on additional operator-provided data to find feasible subassemblies, Thomas uses only the geometric information about the final product as input. However, both approaches are not capable of dealing with uncertainty.

All of the mentioned works do not cover online adaption of assembly plans to react on changes in the environment. One exception is the system realized by Zaeh et al [16], which is used to guide workers through an assembly process. Dependent on the actions executed by the worker, the system adapts its internal planning and suggests new actions to be carried out by the worker. The CCU uses the same technique for plan adaption.

## 3    Autonomous Assembly Planning

### 3.1    Hybrid Assembly Planning

The overall task of the CCU is to assembly a desired construct in a nondeterministic environment: Parts are delivered to the robot cell in random sequence and the successful outcome of an invoked assembly action cannot be guaranteed. While assembly planning is already hard even for deterministic environments where all parts for the assembly are available or arrive in a given sequence [15], the situation becomes worse for this unpredictable situation. Our approach follows a hybrid strategy to allow for thorough but fast reasoning: All computational intensive tasks are executed once before the actual assembly. This is done by an Offline Planner component. Its results are handed to the Online Planner component, which adapts planning to the actual situation. Due to this separation, our approach (see Figure 3) allows for detailed planning as well as fast computation during the assembly. The Offline Planner contains a CAD Parser which derives the geometric properties. The currently supported format is STEP [1]. This data is then processed by the graph generator. The details of this process are explained in section 3.2. The Online Planner consists of the components Graph Analyzer, Parallelizer and Cognitive Control, which are detailed in section 3.3.

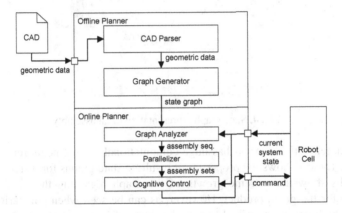

**Fig. 3.** System architecture of the hybrid planner

## 3.2    Offline: Graph Generation

The Offline Planner receives a CAD description of the desired final product. From this input it derives the relations between the single parts of the product via geometrical analysis as described in [4]. The results are stored in a connection graph. Assembly sequences are now derived using an assembly-by-disassembly strategy: Based on the connection graph, all feasible bipartite separations of the product are computed. The Separations can then be evaluated regarding certain criteria as stability, accordance to assembly strategies of human operators or similar. The result of this evaluation is stored as a score for each separation. This separation is recursively continued until only single parts remain. The separation steps are stored in an and/or graph [8], which is then converted into a state graph as displayed in Figure 4 using the method described in [4]. Nodes represent subassemblies of the assembly. Edges connecting two such nodes represent the corresponding assembly action which transforms one state into the other. Each action has associated costs, which depend on the type of action, duration, etc. Also, each edge optionally stores information about single additional parts that are needed for the related transformation.

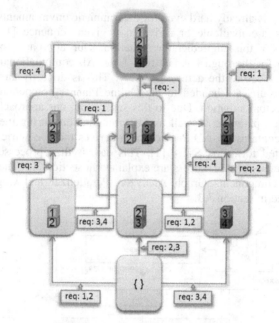

**Fig. 4.** State graph representation of an assembly

The graph generation process has huge computational requirements for time as well for space. Table 1 shows the properties of resulting state graphs for different products. The results show the extreme growth of the graph regarding the number of parts necessary for the given product. However, as can be seen when comparing the state graphs of both constructs with 14 parts, the shape of a product affects the graph, too: The more possible independent parts are from each other, the more different assembly sequences are feasible. Therefore the graph of the construct a) with 14 parts has almost twice the size of the state graph resulting from construct b).

**Table 1.** Properties of the State graph resulting from different products

| Product | #Parts | #Nodes of Graph | #Edges of Graph |
|---|---|---|---|
| construct a) (size 2x2) | 5 | 17 | 33 |
| construct c) | 6 | 16 | 24 |
| construct b) | 14 | 361 | 1330 |
| construct a) (size 3x3) | 14 | 690 | 2921 |
| construct a) (size 4x4) | 30 | 141,120 | 1,038,301 |

## 3.3    Online: Graph Analysis

The state graph generated by the Offline Planner is then used by the Online Planner to derive decisions which assembly actions are to be executed given the current situation. The Online Planner therefore executes the following process iteratively until the product is complete: The Graph Analyzer perceives the current situation of the assembly and identifies the corresponding node of the state graph. Using the A* algorithm [5] the Online Planner now derives the cheapest path connecting the node matching the actual state with a goal node, which presents one variant of the finished product. By doing so, it also actualizes the costs of the examined edges regarding the realizability of the related assembly action, which depends on the availability of the parts to be mounted. Unrealizable actions receive penalty costs which vary depending on how close in the future they would have to be executed. Therefore, the planning algorithm avoids currently unrealizable assemblies. Additionally, due to weaker penalties for more distanced edges, the algorithm prefers assembly sequences that rely on unavailable parts in the distant future to assemblies that immediately need those parts. This results in reduced waiting periods since missing parts have more time to be delivered until they are ultimately needed. The resulting path represents the at that time optimal assembly plan for the desired product. The Parallelizer component now identifies in parallel or arbitrary sequence executable plan steps and hands the result to the Cognitive Control for execution. Here the decision which action is actually to be executed is made. The process of parallelization is detailed in [4].

However, updating all edge cost reachable from the node representing the current state is a computational intensive task. To overcome this problem, the edge cost update can be combined with the A* algorithm, so that only edges which are traversed by A* are updated. This extremely reduces the computational time, since only a fraction of the graphs node is examined. So even for large graphs, the Online Planner is able to derive a decision in well under 100ms in worst case. Figure 5 shows the nodes reachable and examined by the Online Planner during the assembly of a 4x4 construct. Plateaus in the graph depict waiting phases where the assembly cannot continue because crucial parts are not delivered.

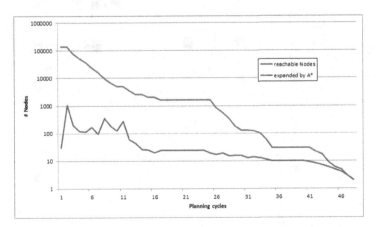

**Fig. 5.** Number of nodes reachable from the node representing the given situation and number of nodes that are examined by the A*-algorithm

## 3.4    Planner Behavior

Figure 6 shows the course of the assembly for the construct c). Newly arrived parts are shown in the third column. They can either be used for direct assembly (first column) or otherwise are stored in a buffer shown in column 2. The right column depicts the plan that is calculated based on the parts located. Here the number of a given block denotes the position where that block is to be placed. In step 0, no parts have been delivered. The planner therefore has no additional information and produces an arbitrary but feasible plan. In step 1 a new green block is delivered, which matches the first plan step. The related assembly action is therefore executed and the new block is directly put to the desired position. In step 2 a new red block is delivered. Given the current state of the assembly and the new red cube, the planner calculates an improved plan which allows to assemble this red block earlier than originally planned: Now it is more feasible to first mount two green blocks on top of each other (positions 1 and 3), because then the red block can be assembled, too (position 5). This plan step is executed in step 3 when a second green block becomes available. Now, in step 4, it is possible to mount a red block. From that step on only one feasible assembly sequence is possible, which is then executed.

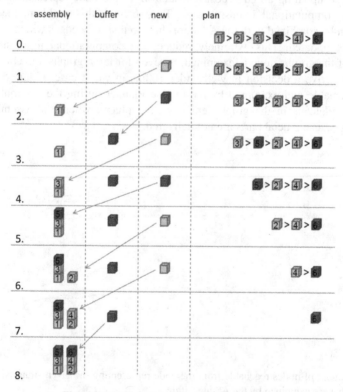

**Fig. 6.** Exemplary assembly of construct c)

The described behavior results in more rapid assemblies compared to simpler planning approaches: A purely reactive planner which would follow a bottom up strategy, would have placed the first two green blocks next to each other (positions 1 and 2). Thus, in step 5 no assembly action would have been possible and the assembly would have to stop until a further green cube would be delivered.

## 4     Implementation of Planner and Robot Controller

ROS [12] has established itself as the currently most used robot framework among mobile robot development. A similar trend can be expected for industrial robots [17]. Therefore, an ROS based implementation promises portability and extended reusability for future developments. ROS mainly supports C++ and Python as programming languages. However an interface to Java based applications has been provided with rosjava [18]. The planner itself is written in Java and relies on this interface. It is implemented as one ROS node which communicates with the reminding robot cell via two topics as depicted in Fig. 7. The planner listens for the topic assembly_state, which contains information about the components which have currently been assembled or are freely available. As soon as new information is published, the planner computes the corresponding assembly sequence and publishes it as topic assembly_plan. Both assembly_state and assembly_plan rely on lists of Components which hold the relevant data. Each component possesses an unique ID to identify it and contains data about its type and its pose. Within the assembly_state, the pose stores the actual location of the Component. When used in the context of assembly_plan, the pose holds the information on where to mount the respective component. This double use of the pose attribute allows for slim data structures and

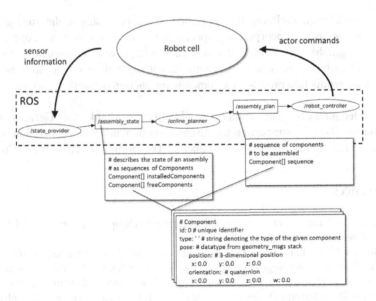

**Fig. 7.** ROS data structures for communication with the Online Planner

efficient data exchange. The nodes state_provider and robot_controller realize the interaction with the robot cell and can be exchanged with particular controllers for the given hardware.

# 5    Summary

In this paper we presented our hybrid approach for an assembly planner for nondeterministic domains. We described the workflow of the offline planner, which analyses CAD data describing the desired product. The outcome of the offline planner is a state graph which holds alle possible (and feasible) assembly sequences. This graph is generated by following an assembly by disassembly strategy: Recursively all possible separations of the final product are computed until only single parts remain. During the actual assembly, this state graph is updated to mirror the current situation of the assembly, specially the availability of newly delivered parts. Using the A* algorithm, the at that time optimal assembly sequence is derived and handed over to the cognitive control unit, which then decides which assembly step gets to be executed. This step is then executed and the outcome of that step is reported back to the planning system. This process is iterated until the product is completed. We expect the robot framework ROS to gain influence not only in the area of industrial research but also within industrial applications. Therefore we implemented our planner with ROS support to be able to integrate it with all robot controllers supporting ROS.

# 6    Outlook

Future work must optimize the described Planners. Using techniques of parallel programming and by incorporating specialized databases which can cope efficiently with large graphs, the planning duration can be improved. Subsequently, the planner will be extended to be able to deal with industrial applications as well as plan and control the production process of a complete production network.

**Acknowledgements.** The authors would like to thank the German Research Foundation DFG for supporting the research on human-robot cooperation within the Cluster of Excellence "Integrative Production Technology for High-Wage Countries".

# References

1. Anderl, R., Tripper, D.: STEP Standard for the Exchange of Product Model Data. B. G. Teubner, Stuttgart/Leipzig (2000)
2. Brecher, C., et al.: Excellence in Production. Apprimus Verlag, Aachen (2007)
3. Castellini, C., Giunchiglia, E., Tacchella, A., Tacchella, O.: Improvements to sat-based conformant planning. In: Proc. of 6th European Conference on Planning (2001)
4. Ewert, D., Schilberg, D., Jeschke, S.: Selfoptimization in adaptive assembly planning. In: Proceedings of the 26th International Conference on CAD/CAM, Robotics and Factories of the Future (2011)

5. Hart, P.E., Nilsson, N.J., Raphael, B.: A Formal Basis for the Heuristic Determination of Minimum Cost Paths. IEEE Transactions on Systems Science and Cybernetics SSC 4(2), 100–107 (1968)
6. Hoffmann, J.: FF: The Fast-Forward Planning System. The AI Magazine (2001)
7. Hoffmann, J., Brafman, R.: Contingent planning via heuristic forward search with implicit belief states. In: Proceedings of ICAPS 2005, pp. 71–80 (2005)
8. Homem de Mello, L.S., Sanderson, A.C.: And/Or Graph Representation of Assembly Plans. In: Proceedings of 1986 AAAI National Conference on Artificial Intelligence, pp. 1113–1119 (1986)
9. Kaufman, S.G., et al.: LDRD final report: Automated planning and programming of assembly of fully 3d mechanisms. Technical Report SAND96-0433, Sandia National Laboratories (1996)
10. Kempf, T., Herfs, W., Brecher, C.: Cognitive Control Technology for a Self-Optimizing Robot Based Assembly Cell. In: Proceedings of the ASME 2008 International Design Engineering Technical Conferences & Computers and Information in Engineering Conference, America Society of Mechanical Engineers, U.S (2008)
11. Mayer, M., et al.: Simulation of Human Cognition in Self-Optimizing Assembly Systems. In: Proceedings of 17th World Congress on Ergonomics IEA 2009, Beijing, China (2009)
12. Quigley, M., Gerkey, B., Conley, K., Faust, J., Foote, T., Leibs, J., Berger, E., Wheeler, R., Ng, A.: ROS: an open-source Robot Operating System. In: ICRA Workshop on Open Source Software (2009)
13. Röhrdanz, F., Mosemann, H., Wahl, F.M.: HighLAP: a high level system for generating, representing, and evaluating assembly sequences. In: 1996 IEEE International Joint Symposia on Intelligence and Systems, Seiten, pp. 134–141 (1996)
14. Tecnomatix (2011),
    http://www.plm.automation.siemens.com/en_us/products/tecnomatix/index.shtml
15. Thomas, U.: Automatisierte Programmierung von Robotern für Montage-aufgaben. Fortschritte in der Robotik, vol. 13. Shaker Verlag, Aachen (2009)
16. Zaeh, M., Wiesbeck, M.: A Model for Adaptively Generating Assembly Instructions Using State-based Graphs. In: Manufacturing Systems and Technologies for the New Frontier. Springer, London (2008)
17. http://code.google.com/p/swri-ros-pkg/wiki/MainPage
18. http://www.ros.org/wiki/rosjava

# Virtual Production Intelligence –
# A Contribution to the Digital Factory

Rudolf Reinhard, Christian Büscher, Tobias Meisen, Daniel Schilberg,
and Sabina Jeschke

Institute of Information Management in Mechanical Engineering (IMA)
RWTH Aachen University, IMA der RWTH Aachen, Dennewartstr. 27,
D-52068 Aachen, Germany
{rudolf.reinhard,christian.buescher,tobias.meisen,
daniel.schilberg,sabina.jeschke}@ima-zlw-ifu.rwth-aachen.de

**Abstract.** The usage of simulation applications for the planning and the designing of processes in many fields of production technology facilitated the formation of large data pools. With the help of these data pools, the simulated processes can be analyzed with regard to different objective criteria. The considered use cases have their origin in questions arising in various fields of production technology, e.g. manufacturing procedures to the logistics of production plants.

The deployed simulation applications commonly focus on the object of investigation. However, simulating and analyzing a process necessitates the usage of various applications, which requires the interchange of data between these applications. The problem of data interchange can be solved by using either a uniform data format or an integration system. Both of these approaches have in common that they store the data, which are interchanged between the deployed applications. The data's storage is necessary with regard to their analysis, which, in turn, is required to obtain an added value of the interchange of data between various applications that is e.g. the determining of optimization potentials. The examination of material flows within a production plant might serve as an example of analyzing gathered data from an appropriate simulated process to determine, for instance, bottle necks in these material flows.

The efforts undertaken to support such analysis tools for simulated processes within the field of production engineering are still at the initial stage. A new and contrasting way of implementing the analyses aforementioned consists in focusing on concepts and methods belonging to the subject area of Business Intelligence, which address the gathering of information taken from company processes in order to gain knowledge about these.

This paper focusses on the approach mentioned above. With the help of a concrete use case taken from the field of factory planning, requirements on a data-based support for the analysis of the considered planning process are formulated. In a further step, a design for the realization of these requirements is presented. Furthermore, expected challenges are pointed out and discussed.

**Keywords:** Application Integration, Data Analysis, Decision Support, Digital Factory.

C.-Y. Su, S. Rakheja, H. Liu (Eds.): ICIRA 2012, Part I, LNAI 7506, pp. 706–715, 2012.
© Springer-Verlag Berlin Heidelberg 2012

# 1    Introduction

Due to the global price competition, the increasing ranges of varieties and customer requirements as well as resulting shorter product lifecycles, production companies in high wage countries face a growing complexity within their production circumstances (Schuh et al. 2011 A). Methods and concepts which are used in order to overcome this complexity often fail to address the whole production process. Therefore, solutions are needed, which allow a holistic and integrated view of the relevant processes in order to achieve an increasing product quality, production efficiency and production performance (Brecher et al. 2011).

Within the last years, the usage of simulation applications in the field of production technology became a measure with a growing significance to overcome the complexity mentioned above. Because of the increasing computing performance concerning speed and storage, these simulation applications changed the way of carrying out planning and preparing activities within production. So, instead of engineering a concrete prototype at an early stage of product design, a digital model of this prototype is drafted containing a description of its essential characteristics. In a further step, this model is passed to a simulation application to predict the prototype's characteristics that may have changed after having passed the manufacturing step. The usage of these digital models is subsumed under the notion of virtual production, which "is the simulated networked planning and control of production processes with the aid of digital models. It serves to optimize production systems and allows a flexible adaptation of the process design prior to prototype realization." (VDI 2008), (VDI 2011)

Nowadays, various simulation applications exist within the field of virtual production, which allow for the simulated execution of manufacturing processes like heating and rolling. Herein, different file formats and file structures were independently developed to describe digital models. Through this, the simulation of single aspects of production can be examined more easily. Nevertheless, the integrative simulation of complex production processes cannot be executed without large costs and time efforts as the interoperability between heterogeneous simulation applications is commonly not given.

One approach to overcome this challenge is the creation of a new standardized file format, which supports the representation of all considered digital models. However, regarding the variety of possible processes, such an approach results in the creation of a complex, standardized file format. Its comprehension, maintenance and usage, again, require large costs and time efforts. Furthermore, necessary adaptations and extensions take a lot of time until their implementation is finished (Nagl et al. 2003), (Horstmann 2011).

Another approach considers the usage of concepts from data and application integration avoiding the definition of a uniform standard. Within this approach, the interoperability between the simulation applications is guaranteed by mapping the aspects of different data formats and structures onto a so called canonical data model (Steve 2008), (Schilberg 2010). Newer approaches extend these concepts with regard to semantic technologies by implementing intelligent behavior into such an integrative system. This approach is called Adaptive Application and Data Integration (Meisen et al. 2011), (Reinhard et al. 2012).

As a consequence, new possibilities concerning the simulation of whole production processes emerge, which allow the examination of different characteristics of the simulated process, e.g. material or machine behavior. With regard to the analysis of the integrated processes, new questions arise as methods for the analysis of the material or machine behavior mentioned above cannot be transferred to the analysis of the corresponding integrated process. A further challenge comes up as soon as suitable user interfaces are added, which are necessary for the handling of the integrated process and its traceability.

Similar questions emerge whilst the analysis of enterprise data. Applications giving answer to such questions are subsumed under the notion of Business Intelligence. These applications have in common that they identify, aggregate, extract and analyze data within enterprise applications (Byrne et al. 2008), (West 2011).

In this paper, an integrative concept is introduced that transfers the nature of these solutions to the field of application of production engineering. It contains the integration, the analysis and the visualization of data, which have been aggregated along simulated process chains within production engineering. In respect to the concept's application domain and its aim to contribute to the gaining of knowledge about the examined processes, it is called Virtual Production Intelligence. In order to illustrate this approach, in chapter 2, a use case scenario from factory planning is taken into consideration. In chapter 3, requirements are listed, which arise from the use case scenario described in chapter 2. The realization of these requirements makes it necessary to create new concepts, which are presented in chapter 4. Chapter 5 contains a description of expected challenges that come up while realizing the requirements defined in chapter 3. This paper concludes with a summary and an outlook on a further use case.

## 2   Use Case Factory Planning

The notion of virtual production comprises the planning of processes that are characteristic for factory planning. In this chapter, a scenario taken from the field of factory planning is introduced, which follows the concept of Condition Based Factory Planning (CBFP). This concept facilitates an efficient planning process without restricting its flexibility by making use of standardized planning modules (Schuh et al. 2011 B). With the help of this scenario, it is pointed out which data are aggregated and which questions are raised concerning the integration, analysis and visualization of data within the planning process of a factory aiming at the support of this planning process. In the following, after having illustrated the use case, the examination of the planning process aforementioned is subsumed under the notion of Virtual Production Intelligence.

The concept of CBFP is employed to analyze factory planning scenarios with the aim of facilitating the factory planning process by decomposing it into single modules (Schuh et al. 2011 B). These modules address various aspects within factory layouting like material flow or logistics. Because of the modular procedure, the characteristical non-linearity of planning processes can be mapped onto each process' modeling.

Within various workshops, requirements concerning the future factory are gathered in collaboration with the customer. For this purpose, table calculation and simulation applications are employed. Subsequent to these workshops, the gathered data are evaluated by one of the factory planners, who participated in the workshops, and suitable planning modules belonging to CBFP are identified. Thereby, different scenarios of the factory's workload are examined to guarantee the future factory's flexibility. Figure 1 illustrates this procedure focusing on the exemplary planning modules Product Planning, Process Planning, Capacity Planning, Planning of Floor Space Requirements, Logistics and Stock Design as well as Production Control.

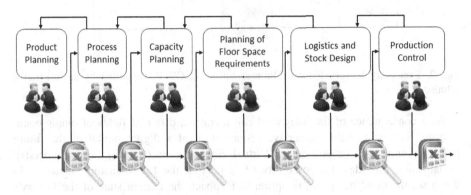

**Fig. 1.** Exemplary non-linear factory planning process following CBFP

Although the planning process is supported by the planning modules from CBFP, a significant disadvantage remains as the procedure is vulnerable concerning input errors committed by the user. Furthermore, the automated analysis of gathered data is complicated, due to the lack of a uniform data model.

The support of the planning process is based on a data model, which fulfills the planning modules' requirements. Thereby, the collection of data is performed by making use of familiar applications. Each analytical step, e.g. the calculation of different scenarios of the factory's workload, is computed on a dedicated server by the factory planer during the evaluation phase between two workshops. One advantage of this procedure is the coherent data handling during the entire planning process. Because of this coherent data handling, the design output can be made available for uninvolved and, in particular, new employees as well as for the executives after having finished a planning process. An interactive visualization allows for an explorative analysis of the simulation application's output. Such an integrative solution facilitates the location of possibilities for optimization within the examined processes. As an organizational consequence and a lasting effect, the experiences made during the implementation of optimization processes can be employed with regard to the composition of best practices for planning projects within the planning company. The implementation of the integrated solution is depicted in Figure 2.

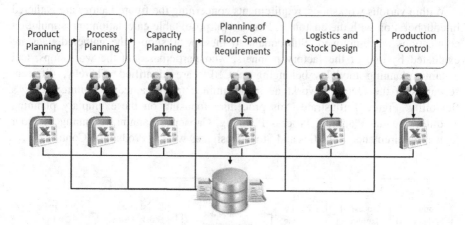

**Fig. 2.** Exemplary Factory Planning Process following CBFP, supported by an integrative solution

As a consequence of the integrated consideration, different fields of employment emerge, for instance the immersive visualization of a digital model of the future factory within a Cave Automatic Virtual Environment (CAVE). This immersive visualization provides the possibility of inspecting the future factory virtually. In doing so, the customer gets the option to feedback the current state of the factory's planning process, which in turn leads to an improved satisfaction regarding the planning's outcome. The creation of the interoperability between the involved applications, on the one hand, and the integrative data handling and analysis, on the other hand, results in the provision of such a solution without generating larger costs and time efforts.

Furthermore, the usage of this solution allows for the examination of different outcomes within a planning problem, e.g. the distribution of machines within a hall and the corresponding planning aspects like logistics or staff security, on a homogeneous data basis. Such a solution might also be adapted to the requirements of another field of application, like marketing, if the attention is directed to the presentation of the planned area rather than to the computing accuracy. Another field of application is the training effort for new employees. Its reduction is an important aim due to high wage costs. In this context, different views adapted to relevant questions of new employees can be used, which comprise the complete and detailed presentation of the current project as well as of past projects.

The scenario described above, which includes methods from factory planning, illustrates how the support of the planning process can be designed. In this scenario, the integration, the analysis and the visualization of data gathered during the planning process is realized. The following chapter comprises a description of requirements that need to be fulfilled when dealing with a system that provides the aforementioned support of the planning process.

# 3    Requirements on an Integrative Solution Based on an Analysis for Process Data

The virtual production aims at an entire mapping of the product as well as of the production within a model for experimental purposes. Thereby, the mapping should comprise the whole lifecycle of the product and of the production system (Bracht et al. 2011). Within an enterprise, the virtual production is established by employees, software tools such as Product-Lifecycle-Management applications (PLM applications) and organizational processes (Bracht et al. 2011).

The demanded possibilities for analysis serve the purpose of gaining knowledge by examining already completed planning processes. The term "intelligence" is commonly used to describe activities that are linked to those analyses. Software tools, which support the analysis and the interpretation of business data, are subsumed under the term "Business Intelligence".

As this term can be defined in different ways, at this point, the basic idea of "Business Intelligence" will be pointed out (Luhn 1958), (Kemper et al. 2006), (Hummeltenberg 2009). A common feature of the definitions referred to consists in the aggregation of relevant data from different data sources, which are applications within a company, into a central data storage. The transmission of data taken from the application data bases into this central data storage is realized by the well-known Extracting, Transforming and Loading process (ETL). Subsequently, the data are arranged in more dimensional data cubes following a logical order. In doing so, a company's IT is divided into two different categories:

- Operational: This category contains applications customized for e.g. the accounting department, the purchasing department or the production department of a company.
- Analytical: In this case, the category contains applications for the analysis of data arising from the applications mentioned in the operational category.

The fact that operational processes are not influenced by analytical processes can be regarded as an advantage of this division.

Requirements for a system that supports the described planning process in chapter 2, in particular the data and application integration, and which additionally follows the idea of Business Intelligence can be subsumed as below:

- Interoperability: Facilitating the interoperability between applications in use.
- Analytical abilities: Systematic analyses providing the recognition of potentials towards optimization and delivering fundamental facts for decision support.
- Alternative representation models: Taylor made visualization for the addressed target group, which provides appropriate analysis facilities based on a uniform data model.

In order to find a solution, which fulfills the requirements mentioned above, a concept formation is needed that addresses the field of application, that is, in this case, the virtual production already mentioned above, as well as the aim of gaining knowledge. This aim is also addressed by the term "Intelligence". The concept formation will take into account approaches, methods and concepts. These will contribute to the achievement of objectives concerning the gaining of knowledge with regard to the processes executed within the considered field of application, which is the virtual production. Therefore the concept formation results in the notion of Virtual Production Intelligence.

This notion will be described in the following chapter.

# 4     Objectives of the Virtual Production Intelligence

The Virtual Production Intelligence (VPI) is a holistic, integrated concept that is used for the collaborative planning of core processes in the fields of technology (material/machines), product, factory and production planning as well as for the monitoring and control of production and product development:

- Holistic: Addressing all of the product development's sub processes.
- Integrated: Supporting the usage and the combination of already existent approaches instead of creating new and further standards.
- Collaborative: Considering roles, which are part of the planning process, as well as their communication and delivery processes.

The VPI aims at contributing to the realization of the digital factory, which is defined as follows:

Digital factory is the generic term for a comprehensive network of digital models, methods and tools – including simulation and 3D visualization – integrated by a continuous data management system. Its aim is the holistic planning, evaluation and ongoing improvement of all the main structures, processes and resources of the real factory in conjunction with the product (VDI 2011).

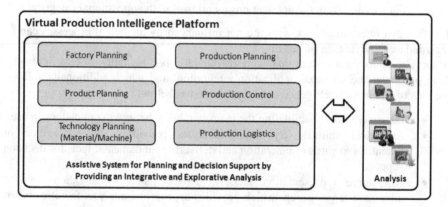

Fig. 3. - The concept of the Virtual Production Intelligence' Platform

The concept is evaluated by the technical implementation of a web-platform, which will serve as a support tool. This platform will serve for planning and support concerns by providing an integrated and explorative analysis in various fields of application. Figure 3 illustrates how the platform is used in these fields of application by various user groups. Within the figure, the use case "factory planning" is addressed as well other use cases, which will be described in future publications.

## 5    Challenges

The integrative approach of the VPI concept facilitates the use of various applications, which can, for example, be deployed whilst a planning process without requiring a uniform data format. At the beginning of the use case scenario already described above, different utilization rates of factory capacity are defined. As a consequence, further requirements arise, which concern, for example, the future factory's layout, logistics or stocks. Within the planning process of the factory, data are generated on a large extent. The use of these data depends on the future utilization rates of the factory capacity. In order to analyze the planned processes of the future factory, it is provided that these processes are evaluated beforehand. The planning of these processes will only create an additional value if the identified potentials for optimization are considered in the real process.

Comprehensively, the following questions have to be answered from a planner's point of view:

- Which of the data generated during the process planning are relevant?
- Which key performance indicators are needed with regard to the validation of the considered processes?
- How can the gained knowledge be fed back into the real process?

Regarding the field of information technology, the following questions arise:

- Which data model facilitates the data's analysis?
- Which data analysis methods known from Business Intelligence can serve as role models?
- How to validate the data model's and analysis' functionality appropriately?

Topics that were not considered above will be addressed by the following questions:

- Which simulation model for the considered process is preferred by the user?
- How can the process in consideration be decomposed?
- Which added value may the user expect?

In retrospect, these questions address technical, professional as well as organizational aspects.

## 6    Summary and Outlook

Within this paper, a concept named "Virtual Production Intelligence" (VPI) has been presented, which describes how the solutions developed within the field of "Business Intelligence" can be adapted properly to the one of virtual production. This concept, which is both holistic and integrated, is used for the collaborative planning, monitoring and control of core processes within production and product development in various fields of application.

Furthermore, the technical implementation of this concept was made a subject of discussion in terms of the Virtual Production Intelligence Platform (VPI-Platform). The platform's implementation is particularly based on concepts and methods established in the field of Cloud Computing. Challenges that might occur during the realization of the platform were taken into account with regard to technical, professional and organizational aspects.

A further scenario, which will point out the VPI's flexibility, will be taken from the field of laser cutting. Thereby, the focus will lie on the problem of analyzing a simulated cutting process in such a way that desired characteristics of the concrete cutting process can be realized. The configuration settings for the cutting machine resulting in the desired cutting quality are a part of the analysis outcome. An additional value for the real cutting process arises after feeding back the analysis outcomes into this process.

**Acknowledgement.** The authors would like to thank the German Research Foundation for the support of the depicted research within the Cluster of Excellence "Integrative Production Technology for High Wage Countries".

# References

[Bracht et al. 2011] Bracht, U., Geckler, D., Wenzel, S.: Digitale Fabrik. Springer, Heidelberg (2011)

[Brecher et al. 2011] Brecher, C.: Integrative Production Technology for High-Wage Countries. Springer (2011)

[Byrne et al. 2008] Byrne, B., Kling, J., McCarty, D., Sauter, G., Worcester, P.: The Value of Applying the Canonical Modeling Pattern in SOA. IBM (The information perspective of SOA design, 4) (2008)

[Horstmann 2011] Horstmann, C.: Integration und Flexibilitat der Organisation Durch Informationstechnologie, 1, pp. S.56–S.162. Gabler Verlag (2011)

[Hummeltenberg 2009] Hummeltenberg: 50 Jahre BI-Systeme (2009),
`http://www.uni-hamburg.de/fachbereiche-einrichtungen/fb03/`
`iwi-ii/Ausgewaehlte_Publikationen_/W.%20Hummeltenberg%20-`
`%2050%20Jahre%20Business%20Intelligence-Systeme.pdf` (accessed April 28, 2012)

[Kemper et al. 2006] Kemper, H., Henning, B.: Business Intelligence und Competitive Intelligence. IT-basierte Managementunterstützung und markt-/wettbewerbsorientierte Anwendungen. HMD Praxis der Wirtschaftsinformatik 43(247) (2006)

[Luhn 1958] Luhn, H.P.: A Business Intelligence System. IBM Journal, S. 314–S.319 (1958)

[Meisen et al. 2011] Meisen, T., Meisen, P., Schilberg, D., Jeschke, S.: Application Integration of Simulation Tools Considering Domain Specific Knowledge. In: Proceedings of the13th International Conference on Enterprise Information Systems (2011)

[Nagl et al. 2003] Nagl, M., Westfechtel, B.: Modelle, Werkzeuge und Infrastrukturen zur Unterstützung von Entwicklungsprozessen. In: Symposium (Forschungsbericht (DFG)). 1. Aufl., pp. S.331–S.332. Wiley-VCH (2003)

[Reinhard et al. 2012] Reinhard, R., Meisen, T., Beer, T., Schilberg, D., Jeschke, S.: A Framework Enabling Data Integration for Virtual Production. In: ElMaraghy, V. H.A. (hrsg.): Enabling Manufacturing Competitiveness and Economic Sustainability; Proceedings of the 4th International Conference on Changeable, Agile, Reconfigurable and Virtual Production (CARV 2011), Montreal, Canada, Berlin, Heidelberg, October 2-5, pp. S.275–S.280 (2011)

[Schilberg 2010] Schilberg, D.: Architektur eines Datenintegrators zur durchgängigen Kopplung von verteilten numerischen Simulationen. VDI-Verlag, Aachen (2010)

[Schuh et al. 2011 A] Schuh, G., Aghassi, S., Orilski, S., Schubert, J., Bambach, M., Freudenberg, R., et al.: Technology Roadmapping for the production in high-wage countries. Prod. Eng. Res. Devel. (Production Engineering) 5, S.463–473 (2011)

[Schuh et al. 2011 B] Schuh, G., Kampker, A., Wesch-Potente, C.: Condition based factory planning. Production Engineering 5, S.89–S.94 (2011)

[Steve 2008] Steve: Canonical Data Model. Information Management Magazine (August 01, 2008)

[VDI 2008] VDI Richtlinie 4499, Blatt 1, 2008: Digitale Fabrik – Grundlagen / Digital Factory – Fundamentals (2008)

[VDI 2011] VDI Richtlinie 4499, Blatt 2, 2011: Digitale Fabrik – Digitaler Fabrikbetrieb / Digital Factory – Digital Factory Operations (2011)

[West 2011] West, M.: Developing High Quality Data Models, 1st edn. Morgan Kaufmann, Burlington (2011)

# Author Index